CLASSICS OF PUBLIC ADMINISTRATION

CLASSICS OF PUBLIC ADMINISTRATION

Second Edition

Jay M. Shafritz
Graduate School of Public Affairs
University of Colorado at Denver

Albert C. Hyde
Department of Public Administration
San Francisco State University

The Dorsey Press
Chicago, Illinois 60604

ISBN 0-256-05532-7

Library of Congress Catalog Card No. 86–50818

Printed in the United States of America

1 2 3 4 5 6 7 8 9 0 K 3 2 1 0 9 8 7

Foreword

These are more than classics of public administration; they are required reading.

No biologist would dare venture into the field without an understanding of Charles Darwin's work *On the Origin of Species.* The biologist might not be familiar with Darwin's eight-year study on the evolution of barnacles, but he or she certainly would be expected, as a competent naturalist, to understand the elementary concepts upon which Darwin's general theory is based.

People who practice public administration have a similar obligation. Before venturing too far out into the field, they need to understand the enduring lessons that have been hauled, often with great difficulty, from the dizzy routine of government. They need to understand that the problems they face daily on the job have been thought about and researched ever since these classics first appeared.

Political interference in the job of the public administrator is as big an issue today as when Frank Goodnow wrote about it in 1900. Politicians still try to place loyalists in administrative positions where they can control agency policy; career executives still have to wrestle with the potential conflict between the wishes of politicians and professional standards of good administration.

Bureau chiefs still struggle to deliver their programs in the face of budget cuts. Ever since V. O. Key published his classic article on the budgetary process in 1940, practitioners have labored to predict how much money the lawmakers will appropriate and scholars have sought to construct theories that will help them do so.

At the turn of the century, an associate of Frederick Taylor promised that the railroads could save "a million dollars a day" by adopting Taylor's management methods. We have learned a lot about management improvement since then. When industrialist J. Peter Grace laid the same claim on the federal government 80 years later in 1984, the reward had grown to $390 million per day.

Practitioners still have to worry about whether the management reforms being pushed on them are long on promise and short on performance. Scholars still struggle with this problem, trying to discover ways to empirically verify the promise and in the process construct a "science" of public administration. Robert Dahl called for all that in 1947 and he was not the first.

One of the leading areas of research in modern public administration centers on the quest to understand why government employees bother to follow the wishes of their superiors. Mary Parker Follett gave one of the first really sound answers to this question in 1926 when she wrote her timeless article on "The Giving of Orders."

Lessons like these endure; knowledge like this accumulates. As a field of inquiry, public administration has a "half-life" approaching 20 years, meaning that half of the most significant works in the field were produced more than 20 years ago. Half of the works included in this new edition of the *Classics* were written prior to 1957. A practitioner committed only to the reading of "modern" works—ones published by the current generation—would miss half of the most important lessons in the field.

Jay Shafritz and Albert Hyde perform a great service by bringing both sets of lessons together. By combining old and new classics in one accessible volume, they make the lessons available to people who would otherwise go without them. As an idealist, I wish that every person with managerial responsibilities in government would go to the library, find the classics of public administration, and read them. As a realist, I know that practitioners do not have the time. So Shafritz and Hyde have done the work for them. This book ought to be on the shelf of anyone who expects to practice public administration; it is an indispensable reference guide.

This is the second edition of *Classics of Public Administration*, the first having been issued in 1978. Since classics are classics, it would seem only natural for the tens of thousands of readers who purchased the first edition to ask why they need to buy the second, or for that matter, to ask why Shafritz and Hyde felt obliged to prepare it.

The answer, in general, is that Shafritz and Hyde were given the opportunity to produce a larger book. This edition is larger in a number of respects, not just in the addition of three "new" classics from the 1980s. Shafritz and Hyde have expanded the whole book, adding two new pieces to the "early voices," four new pieces to the section "between the wars," and seven new pieces to the sections on the postwar period. They have tripled the size of the essays introducing each epoch and, as a bonus, added an elaborate six phase chronology of public administration.

The chronology, which outlines 200 years in the study and practice of public administration, will prove valuable to administrators and scholars alike. It will allow practitioners to look beyond the 49 selections contained in the book and identify other studies that have contributed to our understanding of public administration. It will give scholars a reference guide that will help them quickly explain the history and evolution of this practical field.

To construct a successful field of study or practice, people in public administration need to be very conscious of the foundation upon which they build. Any field which fails to do this condemns itself to a process of rediscovering old principles and repeating old mistakes. To move beyond the lessons that can be gained through common sense and a little experience, a field needs to rise above its foundation. By revealing the foundation and that which has been built upon it, this book elevates the field. Its success in doing this, since the publication of the first edition, has made it something of a classic in its own right.

Howard E. McCurdy
The American University

Preface

Be assured—the editors are not so bold as to assert that these are "the" classics of public administration. The field is so diverse that there can be no such list. However, we do contend that it is possible to make a list of many of the discipline's most significant writers and provide representative samples of their work. That is what we have attempted here. It is readily admitted that writers of equal stature have not found their way into this collection and that equally important works of some of the authors included here are missing. Considerations of space and balance necessarily prevailed.

The primary characteristic of a classic in any field is its enduring value. We have classic automobiles, classic works of literature, classic techniques for dealing with legal, medical, or military problems, and so on. Classics emerge and endure through the years because of their continuing ability to be useful. *The Three Musketeers* is as good an adventure story today as it was in 1844 when Alexandre Dumas wrote it. But how many other nineteenth-century novels can you name? Few have general utility for a twentieth-century audience. It has been no different with the professional literature of public administration. The intent of this collection is to make readily available some of the worthwhile material from the past that will be equally valuable for tomorrow.

Our criteria for including a selection were threefold. First, the selection had to be relevant to a main theme of public administration. It had to be a basic statement consistently echoed or attacked in subsequent years. It also had to be of continuing relevance today. This leads to our second criterion—significance. The selection had to be generally recognized as a significant contribution to the realm and discipline of public administration. An "unrecognized classic" seems to us to be a contradiction. As a rule of thumb, we asked ourselves, "should the serious student of public administration be expected to be able to identify this author and his or her basic themes?" If the answer was yes, then it was so because such a contribution has long been recognized by the discipline as an important theme by a significant writer. While one might criticize a particular piece's exclusion, one would find it difficult to honestly criticize us for our inclusions. This book brings together the most widely quoted and reprinted practitioners and academics in public administration. The final criterion for inclusion was readability.

We sought selections that would be read and appreciated by people with or without a substantial background in public administration.

The selections are arranged in chronological order over a 96-year period—from Woodrow Wilson in 1887 to Deil S. Wright in 1983. When read in this order, the collection will give the reader a sense of the continuity within the discipline's thinking. In this manner, how the various writers' themes are representative of a particular decade and build on each other becomes clearer. Obviously, many authors can and have spanned the decades with their contributions to the literature of the discipline. Nevertheless, the selections reprinted here should be viewed and discussed in their historical context. The tremendously wide use of the previous edition in schools of public administration since 1978 has given us a strong impetus to revise the original collection in several significant ways that we hope will render an even more useful volume.

This important second edition has given us the opportunity to: (1) include more (now 49 in number) selections; (2) expand on our chapter introductions; and (3) provide a unique chronology of the development of public administration from 1776 to 1985, which is divided to fit the time frames of each of the six chapters. This chronology is hardly exhaustive. (That would be a major book in itself!) But it does cover many of the landmark events in the evolution of the practice of public administration as well as important intellectual events in the development of the academic discipline of public administration. We feel that it should prove useful for framing the historical context of our *Classics of Public Administration.*

The following individuals were variously helpful in the preparation of this second edition and have earned our thanks: Sharon Winkle of the Englewood, Colorado, Public Library; Samuel Overman, J. Steven Ott, Marshall Kaplan, Mark Emmert, and Robert Gage of the University of Colorado at Denver; David H. Rosenbloom of Syracuse University; James Schloetter and Ray Pomerleau of San Francisco State University; Paul Flynn of Standard & Poor's; and G. Ronald Gilbert of Florida International University.

We also wish to acknowledge the helpful insight of many past users and experienced instructors, including: Carl Bellone, California State University, Hayward; Donna Cofer, Southwest Missouri State University; Richard Chakerian, Florida State University; Susan Cox, California State University–Long Beach; James Glass, North Texas State University; Andrew McNitt, Eastern Illinois University; Robert Miewald, University of Nebraska, Lincoln; and Philip Russo, Miami University.

Jay M. Shafritz

Albert C. Hyde

Chronological Contents

Topical Contents

I THE DISCIPLINE OF PUBLIC ADMINISTRATION

II THE POLITICAL CONTEXT OF PUBLIC ADMINISTRATION

III BUREAUCRACY

IV ORGANIZATION THEORY

V HUMAN RESOURCES MANAGEMENT

VI THE BUDGETARY PROCESS

VII PUBLIC MANAGEMENT

VIII PUBLIC POLICY AND ANALYSIS

IX PROGRAM EVALUATION

X INTERGOVERNMENTAL RELATIONS

XI PUBLIC SERVICE ETHICS

List of Figures and Tables

CHAPTER I

Early Voices

Writings on public administration go back to biblical time and before. The ancient Egyptians and Babylonians left considerable advice on the techniques of management and administration. So did the ancients of China, Greece, and Rome.[1] Modern management techniques can be traced from Alexander the Great's use of staff[2] to the assembly line methods of the arsenal of Venice[3]; from the theorizing of Niccolo Machiavelli on the nature of leadership[4] to Adam Smith's advocacy of the division of labor[5]; and from Robert Owen's assertion that "vital machines" (employees) should be given as much attention as "inanimate machines"[6] to Charles Babbage's contention that there existed "basic principles of management."[7] It is possible to find most of the modern concepts of management and leadership stated by one or another of the writers of the classical, medieval, and premodern world. Our concern is not with this prehistory of modern management, however, but with the academic discipline and occupational speciality that is American public administration.

While Alexander Hamilton,[8] Thomas Jefferson,[9] Andrew Jackson[10] and other notables of the first century of the republic have dealt with the problem of running the administrative affairs of the state, it was not until 1887 that we find a serious claim made that public administration should be a self-conscious, professional field. Accordingly, the first selection is Woodrow Wilson's famous 1887 essay, "The Study of Administration." While it attracted slight notice at the time, it has become customary to trace the origins of the academic discipline of public administration to it.

While Woodrow Wilson (1856–1924) would later be president, first of the American Political Science Association, then of Princeton University, and later of the United States; in the mid-1880s he was a struggling young instructor at the Bryn Mawr College for Women. During this time he worked on several textbooks now long forgotten; wrote fiction under a pen name (but it was all rejected); and wrote a political essay that remains his most enduring contribution as a political scientist. On November 11, 1886, Wilson wrote to the editor of the *Political Science Quarterly* to whom he had submitted his article. Wilson asserted that he had very modest aims for his work, which he thought of as "a semi-popular introduction" to administrative studies. He even said that he thought his work might be "too slight."[11] Ironically, nearly one hundred years later, the American Society for Public Administration would launch a Centennial's Agenda Project to identify the critical issues for the field and cite the publication of Wilson's essay as "generally regarded as the beginning of public administration as a specific field of study."[12]

In "The Study of Administration" Wilson attempted nothing less than to refocus political science. Rather than be concerned with the great maxims of lasting political truth, he argued that political science should concentrate on how governments are administered. This was necessary because, in his words, "It is getting harder to *run* a constitution than to frame one."

Wilson wanted the study of public administration to focus not only on personnel problems, as many other reformers of the time had advocated, but also on organization and management in general. The reform movement of the time, which had recently secured the passage of the first lasting federal civil service reform legislation, the Pendleton Act of 1883, had a reform agenda that both started and ended with merit appointments. Wilson sought to move the concerns of public administration a step further by investigating the "organization and methods of our government offices" with a view toward determining "first, what government can properly and successfully do, and secondly, how it can do these proper things with the utmost possible efficiency and at the least possible cost either of money or energy." Wilson was concerned with organizational efficiency and economy; that is, productivity in its most simplistic formulation. What could be more current?

In his essay, Wilson is also credited with positing the existence of a major distinction between politics and administration. This was a common and necessary political tactic of the reform movement because arguments that public appointments should be based on fitness and merit, rather than partisanship, necessarily had to assert that "politics" was out of place in public service. In establishing what became known as the politics-administration dichotomy, Wilson was really referring to "partisan" politics. While this subtlety was lost on many, Wilson's main themes—that public administration should be premised on a science of management and separate from traditional politics—fell on fertile intellectual ground. The ideas of this then obscure professor eventually became the dogma of the discipline and remained so until after World War II. While no longer dogma, they are still highly influential and absolutely essential to an understanding of the evolution of public administration.[13]

A more carefully argued examination of the politics-administration dichotomy was offered by Frank J. Goodnow (1859–1939) in his book, *Politics and Administration,* published in 1900. Goodnow, one of the founders and first president (in 1903) of the American Political Science Association, was one of the most significant voices and writers of the progressive reform movement.[14] To Goodnow, modern administration presented a number of dilemmas involving political and administrative functions that had now supplanted the traditional concern with the separation of powers among the various branches of government. Politics and administration could be distinguished, he argued, as "the expression of the will of the state and the execution of that will." We have reprinted here Goodnow's classic analysis of the distinction between politics and administration. Note how even Goodnow had to admit that when the function of political decision making and administration were legally separated, there developed a "tendency for the necessary control to develop extra-legally through the political party system."

At about the same time Woodrow Wilson was calling for a science of management, Frederick W. Taylor (1856–1915) was independently conducting some of his first experiments in a Philadelphia steel plant. Taylor, generally considered the "father of scientific management," pioneered the development of time and motion studies. Today, scientific management is frequently referred to as pseudoscientific management because of its conceptualization of people as merely extensions of machines—as human interchangeable parts of a large impersonal production machine. Premised upon the notion that there was "one best way" of accomplishing any given task, scientific management sought to increase output by discovering the fastest, most efficient, and least fatiguing production methods. The job of the scientific manager, once the one best way was found, was to impose this procedure upon all the workforce. Classical organization theory would evolve from this notion. If there was one best way to accomplish any given production task, then correspondingly, there must also be one best way to accomplish a task of social organization. Such principles of social organization were assumed to exist and to be waiting to be discovered by diligent scientific observation and analysis.

Strangely enough, while Taylor's 1911 book, *Principles of Scientific Management,*[15] is the work for which he is best known, the credit for coining the term *scientific management* belongs not to Taylor but to an associate of his, Louis D. Brandeis (1856–1941). Brandeis, who would later be a Supreme Court justice, needed a catchy phrase to describe the new style management techniques of Taylor and his disciples when he was to present arguments before the Interstate Commerce Commission that railroad rate increases should be denied. Brandeis dramatically argued that the railroads could save "a million dollars a day" by applying scientific management methods. The highly publicized hearings beginning in 1910 caused a considerable sensation and vastly expanded Taylor's reputation. Ironically, Taylor was initially opposed to the phrase, thinking that it sounded too academic. But he quickly learned to embrace it. So did the rest of the country. In the first half of this century scientific management was gospel and Frederick W. Taylor was its prophet.[16]

Taylor's greatest public sector popularity came in 1912 after he presented his ideas to a Special Committee of the House of Representatives to Investigate the Taylor and Other Systems of Shop Management. A portion of that testimony is reprinted here. Taylor's comprehensive statement of scientific management principles was focused on what he called the duties of management. These duties included (1) replacing traditional rule-of-thumb methods of work accomplishment with systematic, more scientific methods of measuring and managing individual work elements; (2) studying scientifically the selection and sequential development of workers to ensure optimal placement of workers into work roles; (3) obtaining the cooperation of workers to insure full application of scientific principles; and (4) establishing logical divisions within work roles and responsibilities between workers and management. What seems so obvious today was revolutionary in 1912.

Perhaps the most significant other early scholar of public administration along with Frank Goodnow (remember that Woodrow Wilson abandoned scholarship for politics) was William F. Willoughby (1867–1960). He was a member of the Taft Commission of 1912, which issued the first call for a national executive budgeting system, and later director of the Institute for Governmental Research, which would become part of the Brookings Institution. He also had a key role in writing the Budget and Accounting Act of 1921, which would finally accomplish the objectives of the Taft Commission by establishing an executive budget system at the national level along with the Budget Office and the General Accounting Office.

Willoughby wrote widely on the myriad issues of public administration. He believed that public administration had universal aspects that were applicable to all branches of government.[17] His early public administration text[18] was really the first of a trilogy covering all three branches of government.[19] But it is his early work on budgetary reform that is of special interest. Writing in 1918, he outlined developments that were leading to the creation of modern budget systems in state governments. In an excerpt from *The Movement Towards Budgetary Reform in the States*, Willoughby argues that budget reform would involve three major threads: (1) how budgets would advance and provide for popular control; (2) how budgets would enhance legislative and executive cooperation; and (3) how budgets would ensure administrative and management efficiency. Rather prophetic when you consider that taxpayer's revolts, "Proposition 13" movements, and other forms of expenditure and revenue limitation laws (thread 1: popular control); continued infighting between the executive and legislative branches over budgetary control, deficits, and balanced budgets (thread 2: executive-legislative cooperation); and the effectiveness or lack of it in overburdened budgeting systems in maintaining managerial practices (thread 3: management effectiveness) are everyday headlines.

These early voices—Wilson, Goodnow, Taylor, and Willoughby—all had profound influences on the development of public administration. To begin with, they identified many of the critical themes that would be permanent parts of the field of study that is modern public administration. But to an even greater extent, they were prophetic voices—writing at a time when government employment and expenditures were still at very minor levels. At the turn of the century in 1900, federal, state, and local governments included slightly more than a million employees combined. Total government outlays were under one and a half billion dollars. By the 1920s, government employment would triple and expenditures would be at just under nine billion.[20] Modern public administration would be founded on a scope that was without precedent in the United States' brief experience. In short, public administration was to be a field of study, not about a function or an enterprise, but rather an entire major sector of what would grow to be the largest and most influential economy the world has ever seen.

NOTES

1. For histories of ancient public administration, see: William C. Beyer, "The Civil Service of the Ancient World," *Public Administration Review* 19 (Spring 1959); Michael T. Dalby and Michael S.

Werthman, eds., *Bureaucracy in Historical Perspective* (Glenview, Ill.: Scott, Foresman, 1972); E. N. Gladden, *A History of Public Administration: Volume I. From the Earliest Times to the Eleventh Century* (London: Frank Cass, 1972).

2. William W. Tarn, *Alexander the Great* (Boston: Beacon Press, 1956); Donald W. Engels, *Alexander the Great and the Logistics of the Macedonian Army* (Berkeley: University of California Press, 1978).
3. Frederic Chapin Lane, *Venetian Ships and Shipbuilders of the Renaissance* (Baltimore: The Johns Hopkins Press, 1934).
4. See Machiavelli's *The Discourses* (1513) and *The Prince* (1532). For a modern appreciation, see: Antony Jay, *Management and Machiavelli: An Inquiry into the Politics of Corporate Life* (New York: Holt, Rinehart & Winston, 1967).
5. See Smith's *The Wealth of Nations* (1776), Chapter 1.
6. Robert Owen (1771–1858) was a Welsh industrialist, social reformer and utopian socialist who was one of the first writers to consider the importance of the human factor in industry. His model factory communities, New Lanark in Scotland and New Harmony in Indiana, were among the first to take a modern approach to personnel management. For biographies, see: J. F. C. Harrison, *Quest for the New Moral World: Robert Owen and the Owenites in Britain and America* (New York: Charles Scribner's Sons, 1969); Sidney Pollard, ed., *Robert Owen, Prophet of the Poor* (Lewisburg, Pa.: Bucknell University Press, 1971).
7. Charles Babbage (1792–1871) is the English inventor best known as the "father" of the modern computer; but he also built upon the assembly line concepts of Adam Smith and anticipated the scientific management techniques of Frederick W. Taylor. See his *On the Economy of Machinery and Manufactures* (London: Charles Knight, 1832).
8. See Lynton K. Caldwell, "Alexander Hamilton: Advocate of Executive Leadership," *Public Administration Review* 4, No. 2 (1944); Lynton K. Caldwell, *The Administrative Theories of Hamilton and Jefferson* (Chicago: University of Chicago Press, 1944); Leonard D. White, *The Federalists: A Study in Administrative History* (New York: Macmillan, 1948).
9. See Lynton K. Caldwell, "Thomas Jefferson and Public Administration," *Public Administration Review* 3, No. 3 (1943); Leonard D. White, *The Jeffersonians: A Study in Administrative History, 1801–1829* (New York: Macmillan, 1951).
10. See Albert Somit, "Andrew Jackson as Administrator," *Public Administration Review* 8 (Summer 1948); Leonard D. White, *The Jacksonians: A Study in Administrative History, 1829–1861* (New York: Macmillan, 1954).
11. Wilson's letter was reprinted in the *Political Science Quarterly* in December 1941.
12. James Carroll and Alfred Zuck, *"The Study of Administration" Revisited: Report on the Centennial Agendas Project* (Washington, D.C.: American Society for Public Administration, 1985).
13. For accounts of the influence of Wilson's essay, see: Louis Brownlow, "Woodrow Wilson and Public Administration," *Public Administration Review* 16 (Spring 1956); Richard J. Stillman II, "Woodrow Wilson and the Study of Administration: A New Look at an Old Essay," *American Political Science Review* 67 (June 1973); Jack Rabin and James S. Bowman, eds., *Politics and Administration: Woodrow Wilson and American Public Administration* (New York: Marcel Dekker, 1984).
14. For appreciations, see: Charles G. Haines and Marshall E. Dimock, eds., *Essays on the Law and Practice of Governmental Administration: A Volume in Honor of Frank J. Goodnow* (Baltimore: The Johns Hopkins Press, 1935); Lurton W. Blassingame, "Frank J. Goodnow: Progressive Urban Reformer," *North Dakota Quarterly* (Summer 1972).
15. (New York: Harper & Bros., 1911). Taylor's other major book is *Shop Management* (New York: Harper & Bros., 1903).
16. For biographies, see: Frank Barkley Copley, *Frederick W. Taylor: Father of Scientific Management* (New York: Harper & Bros., 1923); Subhir Kakar, *Frederick Taylor: A Study in Personality and Innovation* (Cambridge, Mass.: MIT Press, 1970).
17. Marshall Dimock, "W. F. Willoughby and the Administrative Universal," *Public Administrative Review* 35 (September-October 1975).
18. William F. Willoughby, *Principles of Public Administration* (Baltimore: The Johns Hopkins Press, 1927).

19. The other two were: *Principles of Judicial Administration* (Washington, D.C.: Brookings Institution, 1929); *Principles of Legislative Organization and Administration* (Washington, D.C.: Brookings Institution, 1936).

20. Solomon Fabricant, *The Trend of Government Activity in the United States Since 1900* (New York: National Bureau of Economic Research, 1952), pp. 11–24.

A CHRONOLOGY OF PUBLIC ADMINISTRATION: 1776–1917

1776 Declaration of Independence

Adam Smith in *The Wealth of Nations* advocates the ability-to-pay principle of taxation and discusses the optimal organization of a pin factory—the most famous and influential statement on the economic rationale of the factory system and the division of labor.

1787 Northwest Ordinance provides for (1) future states to enter the union and (2) federal aid to local public schools.

Constitutional convention convenes in Philadelphia.

1789 U.S. Constitution is adopted.

Congress establishes the first federal administrative agencies (the Departments of State, War, Treasury, and the Office of Attorney General).

The Federal Judiciary Act creates the Supreme Court; it is organized in 1790 with John Jay as the first chief justice.

New York City becomes the first capital of the United States.

1790 First national census sets population at four million; Philadelphia is the largest city with forty-two thousand people.

U.S. capital moved from New York to Philadelphia.

1791 Ratification of the Bill of Rights (the first ten amendments) to the Constitution is completed.

Congress passes the first internal revenue law, a tax on distilled spirits.

Alexander Hamilton's *Report on Manufactures* advocates government intervention in the economy.

1800 U.S. capital is moved from Philadelphia to Washington, D.C.

1803 The Supreme Court first asserts the right of judicial review in the case of *Marbury* v. *Madison.*

1806 In the case of *Commonwealth* v. *Pullis,* unions are judged to be criminal conspiracies at the Philadelphia trial of striking cordwainers (shoemakers).

1813 Robert Owen in his "Address to the Superintendants of Manufactories" puts forth the revolutionary idea that managers should pay as much attention to their "vital machines" (employees) as to their "inanimate machines."

1814 A president of the United States (James Madison) for the last time took to the field as commander-in-chief of the armed forces at the Battle of Bladenburg (Maryland); the British soundly defeated the Americans and then marched on to burn the White House.

1819 The Supreme Court case of *McCulloch* v. *Maryland* establishes the doctrine of implied constitutional powers and the immunity of the federal government from state taxation.

1823 Jeremy Bentham philosophizes that the role of government is to strive to do the greatest good for the greatest numbers.

1829 President Andrew Jackson in his first annual message to Congress provides justification for the spoils system that followed when he asserts that "the duties of public officers are, or at least admit of being made, so plain and simple that men of intelligence may readily qualify themselves for their performance. . . ."

1832 Senator William L. Marcy gives title to the spoils system when he asserts in a Senate debate that politicians "see nothing wrong in the rule, that to the victor belongs the spoils of the enemy."

1833 Charles Babbage's "analytical engine" is the first mechanical device to contain the basic elements of the modern computer.

1836 Alexis de Tocqueville publishes *Democracy in America,* his classic study of American political institutions and political culture.

1840 President Martin Van Buren establishes the ten-hour day for most federal employees.

1842 In *Commonwealth* v. *Hunt* the Supreme Judicial Court of Massachusetts issues the first ruling establishing the legality of the right of workers to strike for higher wages.

1844 The New York City Police Department is established by the Municipal Police Act; the mayor is empowered to select two hundred officers to patrol the streets twenty-four hours a day.

1849 The U.S. Department of the Interior is created.

1851 Massachusetts enacts the first law permitting towns to use tax revenues to support free libraries.

1862 The Morill Land Grant Act endows state colleges of agriculture and industry.

1863 First military draft enacted during the Civil War; but one could avoid conscription by paying for a substitute.

1865 New York City established the first fire department with full-time paid firefighters.

The Thirteenth Amendment abolishing slavery is ratified.

1868 Judge John F. Dillon first puts forth his rule that local governments may exercise only those powers unambiguously granted to them by their states.

The Fourteenth Amendment providing that no state shall "deprive any person of life, liberty, or property without due process of law" is ratified.

President Andrew Johnson is impeached by the House of Representatives; he is tried and acquitted by the Senate.

Congress mandates an eight-hour day for federally employed laborers and mechanics.

1871 A rider to an unrelated appropriations bill allows President U. S. Grant to create the short lived (1872–1873) first federal Civil Service Commission.

The exposure of corruption by New York's Tammany Hall would eventually send William "Boss" Tweed to prison.

1881 President James Garfield is assassinated by a deranged office seeker.

1883 The Pendleton Act creates the United States Civil Service Commission.

1885 Captain Henry Metcalfe, the manager of an army arsenal, published *The Cost of Manufactures and the Administration of Workshops, Public and Private,* which asserts that there is a "science of administration" that is based upon principles discoverable by diligent observation.

1886 Henry R. Towne's paper "The Engineer as an Economist," read to the American Society of Mechanical Engineers, encourages the scientific management movement.

American Federation of Labor is formed with Samuel Gompers as its president.

1887 Congress creates the Interstate Commerce Commission, the first federal regulatory commission.

Woodrow Wilson's "The Study of Administration" is published in the *Political Science Quarterly.*

1888 Lord James Bryce's analysis of the American political system, *The American Commonwealth,* finds the government of American cities to be a "conspicuous failure."

1894 National Municipal League founded to fight local government corruption.

The Dockery Act creates (1) the first federal fiscal accounting practices and (2) the Office of the Comptroller of the Treasury.

1899 National Municipal League issues the first Model City Charter.

Hollerith cards, punched cards used by computers, were first developed by Herman Hollerith for the U.S. Bureau of the Census.

1900 Frank J. Goodnow's *Politics and Administration* provides the first definition of the politics-administration dichotomy.

1901 Galveston, Texas, devastated by a hurricane in the previous year, is the first city to install the commission form of government.

1902 Vilfredo Pareto becomes the "father" of the concept of "social systems"; his societal notions would later be applied by Elton Mayo and the human relationists in an organizational context.

Oregon becomes the first state to adopt the initiative and referendum.

1903 Frederick W. Taylor publishes *Shop Management.*

Congress provides for a General Staff for the U.S. Army.

The American Political Science Association is founded.

U.S. Department of Commerce and Labor is established.

The Boston Police are the first to use an automobile, a Stanley Steamer, for regular patrol.

1904 Lincoln Steffens' muckraking *Shame of the Cities* finds Philadelphia to be "corrupt and contented," arouses sentiment for municipal reform.

Frank B. and Lillian M. Gilbreth marry; they then proceed to produce many of the pioneering works on motion study, scientific management, applied psychology, and twelve children.

Ukiah, California, establishes the first chief executive officer post to manage municipal affairs.

1905 New York City starts the first police motorcycle patrol.

1906 Bureau of Municipal Research was founded in New York City to further the management movement in government.

Pure Food and Drug Act is passed.

1908 Staunton, Virginia, appoints the first city manager (unless you want to consider Ukiah's chief executive officer to be the first city manager).

Arthur F. Bentley's *The Process of Government* argues that political analysis has to shift its focus from the forms of government to the actions of individuals in the context of groups.

1910 Louis D. Brandeis, an associate of Frederick W. Taylor (and later a Supreme Court justice) coins and popularizes the term *scientific management* in his Eastern Rate Case testimony before the Interstate Commerce Commission by arguing that railroad rate increases should be denied because the railroads could save "a million dollars a day" by applying scientific management methods.

Ohio is the first state to empower its governor to prepare and submit a budget to the legislature.

Los Angeles hires the first policewoman, Mrs. Alice Stebbins Wells, a former social worker.

1911 Frederick W. Taylor publishes *The Principles of Scientific Management.*

1912 The Commission on Economy and Efficiency, the Taft Commission, headed by President William Howard Taft, calls for a national executive budget.

The first position classification program is adopted at the municipal level in the city of Chicago.

Sumter, South Carolina, is first to install council-manager form of city government.

Lloyd-LaFollette Act guarantees the right of federal civilian employees to petition Congress, either individually or through their organizations, and provides the first statutory procedural safeguards for federal employees facing removal.

Congress approves eight-hour day for all federal employees.

1913 Hugo Munsterberg's *Psychology and Industrial Efficiency* calls for the application of psychology to industry.

The Sixteenth Amendment to the U.S. Constitution creates the first permanent federal income tax.

The Federal Reserve Act creates a central bank responsible for national monetary policy.

The U.S. Department of Commerce and Labor is divided into two separate cabinet departments.

1914 City Manager's Association formed (in 1924 it changed its name to the International City Manager's Association; in 1969 "Manager's" was changed to "Management").

The University of Michigan creates the first master's program in municipal administration.

Dayton, Ohio, is the first major city to have a city manager.

Robert Michels in his analysis of the workings of political parties and labor unions, *Political Parties,* formulates his iron law of oligarchy: "who says organization, says oligarchy."

1916 In France Henri Fayol publishes his *General and Industrial Management,* the first complete theory of management.

Institute for Government Research established in Washington, D.C., by Robert Brookings (in 1927 it became the Brookings Institution with William F. Willoughby as its first director).

1917 Robert M. Yerkes, president of the American Psychological Association, creates the first modern personnel research unit in the federal government by developing mental ability tests for the U.S. Army.

1
The Study of Administration

Woodrow Wilson

I suppose that no practical science is ever studied where there is no need to know it. The very fact, therefore, that the eminently practical science of administration is finding its way into college courses in this country would prove that this country needs to know more about administration, were such proof of the fact required to make out a case. It need not be said, however, that we do not look into college programmes for proof of this fact. It is a thing almost taken for granted among us, that the present movement called civil service reform must, after the accomplishment of its first purpose, expand into efforts to improve, not the *personnel* only, but also the organization and methods of our government offices: because it is plain that their organization and methods need improvement only less than their *personnel.* It is the object of administrative study to discover, first, what government can properly and successfully do, and, secondly, how it can do these proper things with the utmost possible efficiency and at the least possible cost either of money or of energy. On both these points there is obviously much need of light among us; and only careful study can supply that light.

Before entering on that study, however, it is needful:

I. To take some account of what others have done in the same line; that is to say, of the history of the study.

II. To ascertain just what is its subject matter.

III. To determine just what are the best methods by which to develop it, and the most clarifying political conceptions to carry with us into it.

Unless, we know and settle these things, we shall set out without chart or compass.

Source: Political Science Quarterly, 2 (June 1887).

I

The science of administration is the latest fruit of that study of the science of politics which was begun some twenty-two hundred years ago. It is a birth of our own century, almost of our own generation.

Why was it so late in coming? Why did it wait till this too busy century of ours to demand attention for itself? Administration is the most obvious part of government; it is government in action; it is the executive, the operative, the most visible side of government, and is of course as old as government itself. It is government in action, and one might very naturally expect to find that government in action had arrested the attention and provoked the scrutiny of writers of politics very early in the history of systematic thought.

But such was not the case. No one wrote systematically of administration as a branch of the science of government until the present century had passed its first youth and had begun to put forth its characteristic flower of systematic knowledge. Up to our own day all the political writers whom we now read had thought, argued, dogmatized only about the *constitution* of government; about the nature of the state, the essence and seat of sovereignty, popular power and kingly prerogative; about the greatest meanings lying at the heart of government, and the high ends set before the purpose of government by man's nature and man's aims. The central field of controversy was that great field of theory in which monarchy rode tilt against democracy, in which oligarchy would have built for itself strongholds of privilege, and in which tyranny sought opportunity to make good its claim to receive submission from all competitors. Amidst this high warfare of principles, administration could command no pause for its own consideration. The question was always: Who shall make law, and what shall that law be? The other question, how law should be administered with enlightenment, with equity, with speed, and without friction, was put aside as "practical detail" which clerks could arrange after doctors had agreed upon principles.

That political philosophy took this direction was of course no accident, no chance preference or perverse whim of political philosophers. The philosophy of any time is, as Hegel says, "nothing but the spirit of that time expressed in abstract thought"; and political philosophy, like philosophy of every other kind, has only held up the mirror to contemporary affairs. The trouble in early times was almost altogether about the constitution of government; and consequently that was what engrossed men's thoughts. There was little or no trouble about administration—at least little that was heeded by administrators. The functions of government were simple, because life itself was simple. Government went about imperatively and compelled men, without thought of consulting their wishes. There was no complex system of public revenues and public debts to puzzle financiers; there were, consequently, no financiers to be puzzled. No one who possessed power was long at a loss how to use it. The great and only question was: Who shall possess it? Populations were of manageable numbers; property was of simple sorts. There were plenty of farms, but no stocks and bonds: more cattle than vested interests.

I have said that all this was true of "early times"; but it was substantially true also of comparatively late times. One does not have to look back of the last century for the beginnings of the present complexities of trade and perplexities of commercial speculation, nor for the portentous birth of national debts. Good

Queen Bess, doubtless, thought that the monopolies of the sixteenth century were hard enough to handle without burning her hands; but they are not remembered in the presence of the giant monopolies of the nineteenth century. When Blackstone lamented that corporations had no bodies to be kicked and no souls to be damned, he was anticipating the proper time for such regrets by full a century. The perennial discords between master and workmen which now so often disturb industrial society began before the Black Death and the Statute of Laborers; but never before our own day did they assume such ominous proportions as they wear now. In brief, if difficulties of governmental action are to be seen gathering in other centuries, they are to be seen culminating in our own.

This is the reason why administrative tasks have nowadays to be so studiously and systematically adjusted to carefully tested standards of policy, the reason why we are having now what we never had before, a science of administration. The weightier debates of constitutional principle are even yet by no means concluded; but they are no longer of more immediate practical moment than questions of administration. It is getting to be harder to *run* a constitution than to frame one.

Here is Mr. Bagehot's graphic, whimsical way of depicting the difference between the old and the new in administration:

> In early times, when a despot wishes to govern a distant province, he sends down a satrap on a grand horse, and other people on little horses; and very little is heard of the satrap again unless he send back some of the little people to tell what he has been doing. No great labour of superintendence is possible. Common rumour and casual report are the sources of intelligence. If it seems certain that the province is in a bad state, satrap No. 1 is recalled, and satrap No. 2 sent out in his stead. In civilized countries the process is different. You erect a bureau in the province you want to govern; you make it write letters and copy letters; it sends home eight reports *per diem* to the head bureau in St. Petersburg. Nobody does a sum in the province without some one doing the same sum in the capital, to "check" him, and see that he does it correctly. The consequence of this is, to throw on the heads of departments an amount of reading and labour which can only be accomplished by the greatest natural aptitude, the most efficient training, the most firm and regular industry.[1]

There is scarcely a single duty of government which was once simple which is not now complex; government once had but a few masters; it now has scores of masters. Majorities formerly only underwent government; they now conduct government. Where government once might follow the whims of a court, it must now follow the views of a nation.

And those views are steadily widening to new conceptions of state duty; so that at the same time that the functions of government are every day becoming more complex and difficult, they are also vastly multiplying in number. Administration is everywhere putting its hands to new undertakings. The utility, cheapness, and success of the government's postal service, for instance, point towards the early establishment of governmental control of the telegraph system. Or, even if our government is not to follow the lead of the governments of Europe in buying or building both telegraph and railroad lines, no one can doubt that in some way it must make itself master of masterful corporations. The creation of national commissioners of railroads, in addition to the older state commissions, involves a very important and delicate extension of administrative functions. Whatever hold of authority state or federal governments are to take upon corporations, there must follow cares and responsibilities which will require not a little wisdom, knowledge, and experience. Such things must be studied in order to be well done. And these, as I have said, are only a few of the doors which are being opened to offices of government. The idea of the state and the consequent ideal of its duty are undergoing noteworthy change; and "the idea of the state is the conscience of administration." Seeing every day new things which the state ought to do, the next thing is to see clearly how it ought to do them.

This is why there should be a science of administration which shall seek to straighten the paths of government, to make its business less unbusinesslike, to strengthen and purify its organization, and to crown its dutifulness. This is one reason why there is such a science.

But where has this science grown up? Surely not on this side the sea. Not much impartial scientific method is to be discerned in our administrative practices. The poisonous atmosphere of city government, the crooked secrets of state administration, the confusion, sinecurism, and corruption ever and again discovered in the bureaux at Washington forbid us to believe that any clear conceptions of what constitutes good administration are as yet very widely current in the United States. No; American writers have hitherto taken no very important part in the advancement of this science. It has found its doctors in Europe. It is not of our making; it is a foreign science, speaking very little of the language of English or American principle. It employs only foreign tongues; it utters none but what are to our minds alien ideas. Its aims, its examples, its conditions, are almost exclusively grounded in the histories of foreign races, in the precedents of foreign systems, in the lessons of foreign revolutions. It has been developed by French and German professors, and is consequently in all parts adapted to the needs of a compact state, and made to fit highly centralized forms of government; whereas, to answer our purposes, it must be adapted, not to a simple and compact, but to a complex and multiform state, and made to fit highly decentralized forms of government. If we would employ it, we must Americanize it, and that not formally, in language merely, but radically, in thought, principle, and aim as well. It must learn our constitutions by heart; must get the bureaucratic fever out of its veins; must inhale much free American air.

If an explanation be sought why a science manifestly so susceptible of being made useful to all governments alike should have received attention first in Europe, where government has long been a monopoly, rather than in England or the United States, where government has long been a common franchise, the reason will doubtless be found to be twofold: first, that in Europe, just because government was independent of popular assent, there was more governing to be done; and, second, that the desire to keep government a monopoly made the monopolists interested in discovering the least irritating means of governing. They were, besides, few enough to adopt means promptly.

It will be instructive to look into this matter a little more closely. In speaking of European governments I do not, of course, include England. She has not refused to change with the times. She has simply tempered the severity of the transition from a polity of aristocratic privilege to a system of democratic power by slow measures of constitutional reform which, without preventing revolution, has confined it to paths of peace. But the countries of the continent for a long time desperately struggled against all change, and would have diverted revolution by softening the asperities of absolute government. They sought so to perfect their machinery as to destroy all wearing friction, so to sweeten their methods with consideration for the interests of the governed as to placate all hindering hatred, and so assiduously and opportunely to offer their aid to all classes of undertakings as to render themselves indispensable to the industrious. They did at last give the people constitutions and the franchise; but even after that they obtained leave to continue despotic by becoming paternal. They made themselves too efficient to be dispensed with, too smoothly operative to be noticed, too enlightened to be inconsiderately questioned, too benevolent to be suspected, too powerful to be coped with. All this has required study; and they have closely studied it.

On this side the sea we, the while, had known no great difficulties of government. With a new country, in which there was room and remunerative employment for everybody, with liberal principles of government and unlimited skill in practical politics, we were long exempted from the need of being anxiously careful about plans and methods of administration. We have naturally been slow to see the use or significance of those many volumes of learned research and painstaking examination into the ways and means of conducting government which the presses of Europe have been sending to our libraries. Like a lusty child, government with us has expanded in nature and grown great in stature, but has also become awkward in movement. The vigor and increase of its life has been altogether out of proportion to its skill in living. It has gained strength, but it has not acquired deportment. Great, therefore, as has been our advantage over the countries of Europe in point of ease and health of constitutional development, now that the time for more careful administrative adjustments and larger administrative knowledge has come to us, we are at a signal disadvantage as compared with the transatlantic nations; and this for reasons which I shall try to make clear.

Judging by the constitutional histories of the chief nations of the modern world, there may be said to be three periods of growth through which government has passed in all the most highly developed of existing systems, and through which it promises to pass in all the rest. The first of these periods is that of absolute rulers, and of an administrative system adapted to absolute rule; the second is that in which constitutions are framed to do away with absolute rulers and substitute popular control, and in which administration is neglected for these higher concerns; and the third is that in which the sovereign people undertake to develop administration under this new constitution which has brought them into power.

Those governments are now in the lead in administrative practice which had rulers still absolute but also enlightened when those modern days of political illumination came in which it was made evident to all but the blind that governors are properly only the servants of the governed. In such governments administration has been organized to subserve the general weal with the simplicity and effectiveness vouchsafed only to the undertakings of a single will.

Such was the case in Prussia, for instance, where administration has been most studied and most nearly perfected. Frederic the Great, stern and masterful as was his rule, still sincerely professed to regard himself as only the chief servant of the state, to consider his great office a public trust; and it was he who, building upon the foundations laid by his father, began to organize the public service of Prussia as in very earnest a service of the public. His no less absolute successor, Frederic William III, under the inspiration of Stein again, in his turn, advanced the work still further, planning many of the broader structural features which give firmness and form to Prussian administration to-day. Almost the whole of the admirable system has been developed by kingly initiative.

Of similar origin was the practice, if not the plan, of modern French administration, with its symmetrical divisions of territory and its orderly gradations of office. The days of the Revolution—of the Constituent Assembly—were days of constitution-*writing,* but they can hardly be called days of constitution-*making.* The Revolution heralded a period of constitutional development—the entrance of France upon the second of those periods which I have enumerated—but it did not itself inaugurate such a period. It interrupted and unsettled absolutism, but did not destroy it. Napoleon succeeded the monarchs of France, to exercise a power as unrestricted as they had ever possessed.

The recasting of French administration by Napoleon is, therefore, my second example of the perfecting of civil machinery by the single will of an absolute ruler before the dawn of a constitutional era. No corporate, popular will could ever have effected arrangements such as those which Napoleon commanded. Arrangements so simple at the expense of local prejudice, so logical in their influence to popular choice, might be decreed by a Constitutional Assembly, but could be established only by the unlimited authority of a despot. The system of the year VIII was ruthlessly thorough and heartlessly perfect. It was, besides, in large part, a return to the despotism that had been overthrown.

Among those nations, on the other hand, which entered upon a season of constitution-making and popular reform before administration had received the impress of liberal principle, administrative improvement has been tardy and half-done. Once a nation has embarked in the business of manufacturing constitutions, it finds it exceedingly difficult to close out that business and open for the public a bureau of skilled, economical administration. There seems to be no end to the tinkering of constitutions. Your ordinary constitution will last you hardly ten years without repairs or additions; and the time for administrative detail comes late.

Here, of course, our examples are England and our own country. In the days of the Angevin kings, before constitutional life had taken root in the Great Charter, legal and administrative reforms began to proceed with sense and vigor under the impulse of Henry II's shrewd, busy, pushing, indomitable spirit and purpose; and kingly initiative seemed destined in England, as elsewhere, to shape governmental growth at its will. But impulsive, errant Richard and weak, despicable John were not the men to carry out such schemes as their father's. Administrative development gave place in their reigns to constitutional struggles; and Parliament became king before any English monarch had had the practical genius or the enlightened conscience to devise just and lasting forms for the civil service of the state.

The English race, consequently, has long and successfully studied the art of curbing executive power to the constant neglect of the art of perfecting executive methods. It has exercised itself much more in controlling than in energizing government. It has been more concerned to render government just and moderate than to make it facile, well-ordered, and effective. English and

American political history has been a history, not of administrative development, but of legislative oversight—not of progress in governmental organization, but of advance in law-making and political criticism. Consequently, we have reached a time when administrative study and creation are imperatively necessary to the well-being of our governments saddled with the habits of a long period of constitution-making. That period has practically closed, so far as the establishment of essential principles is concerned, but we cannot shake off its atmosphere. We go on criticizing when we ought to be creating. We have reached the third of the periods I have mentioned—the period, namely, when the people have to develop administration in accordance with the constitutions they won for themselves in a previous period of struggle with absolute power; but we are not prepared for the tasks of the new period.

Such an explanation seems to afford the only escape from blank astonishment at the fact that, in spite of our vast advantages in point of political liberty, and above all in point of practical political skill and sagacity, so many nations are ahead of us in administrative organization and administrative skill. Why, for instance, have we but just begun purifying a civil service which was rotten full fifty years ago? To say that slavery diverted us is but to repeat what I have said—that flaws in our constitution delayed us.

Of course all reasonable preference would declare for this English and American course of politics rather than for that of any European country. We should not like to have had Prussia's history for the sake of having Prussia's administrative skill; and Prussia's particular system of administration would quite suffocate us. It is better to be untrained and free than to be servile and systematic. Still there is no denying that it would be better yet to be both free in spirit and proficient in practice. It is this even more reasonable preference which impels us to discover what there may be to hinder or delay us in naturalizing this much-to-be-desired science of administration.

What, then, is there to prevent?

Well, principally, popular sovereignty. It is harder for democracy to organize administration than for monarchy. The very completeness of our most cherished political successes in the past embarrasses us. We have enthroned public opinion; and it is forbidden us to hope during its reign for any quick schooling of the sovereign in executive expertness or in the conditions of perfect functional balance in government. The very fact that we have realized popular rule in its fulness has made the task of *organizing* that rule just so much the more difficult. In order to make any advance at all we must instruct and persuade a multitudinous monarch called public opinion—a much less feasible undertaking than to influence a single monarch called a king. An individual sovereign will adopt a simple plan and carry it out directly: he will have but one opinion, and he will embody that one opinion in one command. But this other sovereign, the people, will have a score of differing opinions. They can agree upon nothing simple: advance must be made through compromise, by a compounding of differences, by a trimming of plans and a suppression of too straightforward principles. There will be a succession of resolves running through a course of years, a dropping fire of commands running through a whole gamut of modifications.

In government, as in virtue, the hardest of hard things is to make progress. Formerly the reason for this was that the single person who was sovereign was generally either selfish, ignorant, timid or a fool—albeit there was now and again one who was wise. Nowadays the reason is that the many, the people, who are sovereign have no single ear which one can approach, and are selfish, ignorant, timid, stubborn, or foolish with the selfishnesses, the ignorances, the stubbornnesses, the timidities, or the follies of several thousand persons—albeit there are hundreds who are wise. Once the advantage of the reformer was that the sovereign's mind had a definite locality, that it was contained in one man's head, and that consequently it could be gotten at; though it was his disadvantage that that mind learned only reluctantly or only in small quantities, or was under the influence of some one who let it learn only the wrong things. Now, on the contrary, the reformer is bewildered by the fact that the sovereign's mind has no definite locality, but is contained in a voting majority of several million heads; and embarrassed by the fact that the mind of this sovereign also is under the influence of favorites, who are none the less favorites in a good old-fashioned sense of the word because they are not persons but preconceived opinions; *i.e.*, prejudices which are not to be reasoned with because they are not the children of reason.

Wherever regard for public opinion is a first principle of government, practical reform must be slow and all reform must be full of compromises. For wherever public opinion exists it must rule. This is now an axiom half the world over, and will presently come to be believed even in Russia. Whoever would effect a change in a modern constitutional government must first educate his fellow-citizens to want *some* change. That done, he must persuade them to want the particular change he wants. He must first make public opinion willing to listen and then see to it that it listen to the right things. He must stir it up to search for an opinion, and then manage to put the right opinion in its way.

The first step is not less difficult than the second. With opinions, possession is more than nine points of the law. It is next to impossible to dislodge them. Institutions which one generation regards as only a makeshift approximation to the realization of a principle, the next generation honors as the nearest possible approximation to that principle, and the next worships as the principle itself. It takes scarcely three generations for the apotheosis. The grandson accepts his grandfather's hesitating experiment as an integral part of the fixed constitution of nature.

Even if we had clear insight into all the political past, and could form out of perfectly instructed heads a few steady, infallible, placidly wise maxims of government into which all sound political doctrine would be ultimately resolvable, *would the country act on them?* That is the question. The bulk of mankind is rigidly unphilosophical, and nowadays the bulk of mankind votes. A truth must become not only plain but also commonplace before it will be seen by the people who go to their work very early in the morning; and not to act upon it must involve great and pinching inconveniences before these same people will make up their minds to act upon it.

And where is this unphilosophical bulk of mankind more multifarious in its composition than in the United States? To know the public mind of this country, one must know the mind, not of Americans of the older stocks only, but also of Irishmen, of Germans, of negroes. In order to get a footing for new doctrine, one must influence minds cast in every mould of race, minds inheriting every bias of environment, warped by the histories of a score of different nations, warmed or chilled, closed or expanded by almost every climate of the globe.

So much, then, for the history of the study of administration, and the peculiarly difficult conditions under which, entering upon it when we do, we must undertake it. What, now, is the subject-matter of this study, and what are its characteristic objects?

II

The field of administration is a field of business. It is removed from the hurry and strife of politics; it at most points stands apart even from the debatable ground of constitutional study. It is a part of political life only as the methods of the counting-house are a part of the life of society; only as machinery is part of the manufactured product. But it is, at the same time, raised very far above the dull level of mere technical detail by the fact that through its greater principles it is directly connected with the lasting maxims of political wisdom, the permanent truths of political progress.

The object of administrative study is to rescue executive methods from the confusion and costliness of empirical experiment and set them upon foundations laid deep in stable principle.

It is for this reason that we must regard civil-service reform in its present stages as but a prelude to a fuller administrative reform. We are now rectifying methods of appointment; we must go on to adjust executive functions more fitly and to prescribe better methods of executive organization and action. Civil-service reform is thus but a moral preparation for what is to follow. It is clearing the moral atmosphere of official life by establishing the sanctity of public office as a public trust, and, by making the service unpartisan, it is opening the way for making it businesslike. By sweetening its motives it is rendering it capable of improving its methods of work.

Let me expand a little what I have said of the province of administration. Most important to be observed is the truth already so much and so fortunately insisted upon by our civil-service reformers; namely, that administration lies outside the proper sphere of *politics*. Administrative questions are not political questions. Although politics sets the tasks for administration, it should not be suffered to manipulate its offices.

This is distinction of high authority; eminent German writers insist upon it as of course. Biuntschli, for instance, bids us separate administration alike from politics and from law.[2] Politics, he says, is state activity "in things great and universal," while "administration, on the other hand," is "the activity of the state in individual and small things. Politics is thus the special province of the statesman, administration of the technical official." "Policy does nothing without the aid of administration"; but administration is not therefore politics. But we do not require German authority for this position; this discrimination between administration and politics is now, happily, too obvious to need further discussion.

There is another distinction which must be worked into all our conclusions, which, though but another side of that between administration and politics, is not quite so easy to keep sight of: I mean the distinction between *constitutional* and administrative questions, between those governmental adjustments which are essential to constitutional principle and those which are merely instrumental to the possibly changing purposes of a wisely adapting convenience.

One cannot easily make clear to every one just where administration resides in the various departments of any practicable government without entering upon particulars so numerous as to confuse and distinctions so minute as to distract. No lines of demarcation, setting apart administrative from non-administrative functions, can be run between this and that department of government without being run up hill and down dale, over dizzy heights of distinction and through dense jungles of statutory enactment, hither and thither around "ifs" and "buts," "whens" and "howevers" until they become altogether lost to the common eye not accustomed to this sort of surveying, and consequently not acquainted with the use of the theodolite of logical discernment. A great deal of administration goes about *incognito* to most of the world, being confounded now with political "management," and again with constitutional principle.

Perhaps this ease of confusion may explain such utterances as that of Niebuhr's: "Liberty," he says, "depends incomparably more upon administration than upon constitution." At first sight this appears to be largely true. Apparently facility in the actual exercise of liberty does depend more upon administrative arrangements than upon constitutional guarantees; although constitutional guarantees alone secure the existence of liberty. But—upon second thought—is even so much as this true? Liberty no more consists in easy functional movement than intelligence consists in the ease and vigor with which the limbs of a strong man move. The principles that rule within the man, or the constitution, are the vital springs of liberty or servitude. Because dependence and subjection are without chains, are lightened by every easy-working device of considerate, paternal government, they are not thereby transformed into liberty. Liberty cannot live apart from constitutional principle; and no administration, however perfect and liberal its methods, can give men more than a poor counterfeit of liberty if it rest upon illiberal principles of government.

A clear view of the difference between the province of constitutional law and the province of administrative function ought to leave no room for misconception; and it is possible to name some roughly definite criteria upon which such a view can be built. Public administration is detailed and systematic execution of public law. Every particular application of general law is an act of administration. The assessment and raising of taxes, for instance, the hanging of a criminal, the transportation and delivery of the mails, the equipment and recruiting of the army, and navy, etc., are all obviously acts of administration; but the general laws which direct these things to be done are as obviously outside of and above administration. The broad plans of governmental action are not administrative; the detailed execution of such plans is administrative. Constitutions, therefore, properly concern themselves only with those instrumentalities of government which are to control general law. Our federal constitution observes this principle in saying nothing of even the greatest of the purely executive offices, and speaking only of that President of the Union who was to share the legislative and policy-making functions of government, only of those judges of highest jurisdiction who were to interpret and guard its principles, and not of those who were merely to give utterance to them.

This is not quite the distinction between Will and answering Deed, because the administrator should have and does have a will of his own in the choice of means for accomplishing his work. He is not and ought not to be a mere passive instrument. The distinction is between general plans and special means.

There is, indeed, one point at which administrative studies trench on constitutional ground—or at least upon what seems constitutional ground. The study of administration, philosophically viewed, is closely connected with the study of the proper distribution of constitutional authority. To be efficient it must discover the simplest arrangements by which responsibility can be unmistakably fixed upon officials; the best way of dividing authority without hampering it, and responsibility without obscuring it. And this question of the distribution of authority, when taken into the sphere of the higher, the originating functions of government, is obviously a central constitutional question. If administrative study can discover the best principles upon which to base such distribution, it will have done constitutional study an invaluable service. Montesquieu did not, I am convinced, say the last word on this head.

To discover the best principle for the distribution of authority is of greater importance, possibly, under a democratic system, where officials serve many masters, than under others where they serve but a few. All sovereigns are suspicious of their servants, and the sovereign people is no exception to the rule; but how is its suspicion to be allayed by *knowledge?* If that suspicion could be clarified into wise vigilance, it would be altogether salutary; if that vigilance could be aided by the unmistakable placing of responsibility, it would be altogether beneficient. Suspicion in itself is never healthful either in the private or in the public mind. *Trust is strength* in all relations of life; and, as it is the office of the constitutional reformer to create conditions of trustfulness, so it is the office of the administrative organizer to fit administration with conditions of clear-cut responsibility which shall insure trustworthiness.

And let me say that large powers and unhampered discretion seem to me the indispensable conditions of responsibility. Public attention must be easily directed, in each case of good or bad administration, to just the man deserving of praise or blame. There is no danger in power, if only it be not irresponsible. If it be divided, dealt out in shares to many, it is obscured; and if it be obscured, it is made irresponsible. But if it be centred in heads of the service and in heads of branches of the service, it is easily watched and brought to book. If to keep his office a man must achieve open and honest success, and if at the same time he feels himself intrusted with large freedom of discretion, the greater his power the less likely is he to abuse it, the more is he nerved and sobered and elevated by it. The less his power, the more safely obscure and unnoticed does he feel his position to be, and the more readily does he relapse into remissness.

Just here we manifestly emerge upon the field of that still larger question—the proper relations between public opinion and administration.

To whom is official trustworthiness to be disclosed, and by whom is it to be rewarded? Is the official to look to the public for his meed of praise and his push of promotion, or only to his superior in office? Are the people to be called in to settle administrative discipline as they are called in to settle constitutional principles? These questions evidently find their root in what is undoubtedly the fundamental problem of this whole study. That problem is: What part shall public opinion take in the conduct of administration?

The right answer seems to be, that public opinion shall play the part of authoritative critic.

But the *method* by which its authority shall be made to tell? Our peculiar

American difficulty in organizing administration is not the danger of losing liberty, but the danger of not being able or willing to separate its essentials from its accidents. Our success is made doubtful by that besetting error of ours, the error of trying to do too much by vote. Self-government does not consist in having a hand in everything, any more than housekeeping consists necessarily in cooking dinner with one's own hands. The cook must be trusted with a large discretion as to the management of the fires and the ovens.

In those countries in which public opinion has yet to be instructed in its privileges, yet to be accustomed to having its own way, this question as to the province of public opinion is much more readily soluble than in this country, where public opinion is wide awake and quite intent upon having its own way anyhow. It is pathetic to see a whole book written by a German professor of political science for the purpose of saying to his countrymen, "Please try to have an opinion about national affairs"; but a public which is so modest may at least be expected to be very docile and acquiescent in learning what things it has *not* a right to think and speak about imperatively. It may be sluggish, but it will not be meddlesome. It will submit to be instructed before it tries to instruct. Its political education will come before its political activity. In trying to instruct our own public opinion, we are dealing with a pupil apt to think itself quite sufficiently instructed beforehand.

The problem is to make public opinion efficient without suffering it to be meddlesome. Directly exercised, in the oversight of the daily details and in the choice of the daily means of government, public criticism is of course a clumsy nuisance, a rustic handling delicate machinery. But as superintending the greater forces of formative policy alike in politics and administration, public criticism is altogether safe and beneficent, altogether indispensable. Let administrative study find the best means for giving public criticism this control and for shutting it out from all other interference.

But is the whole duty of administrative study done when it has taught the people what sort of administration to desire and demand, and how to get what they demand? Ought it not to go on to drill candidates for the public service?

There is an admirable movement towards universal political education now afoot in this country. The time will soon come when no college of respectability can afford to do without a well-filled chair of political science. But the education thus imparted will go but a certain length. It will multiply the number of intelligent critics of government, but it will create no competent body of administrators. It will prepare the way for the development of a sure-footed understanding of the general principles of government, but it will not necessarily foster skill in conducting government. It is an education which will equip legislators, perhaps, but not executive officials. If we are to improve public opinion, which is the motive power of government, we must prepare better officials as the *apparatus* of government. If we are to put in new boilers and to mend the fires which drive our governmental machinery, we must not leave the old wheels and joints and valves and bands to creak and buzz and clatter on as best they may at bidding of the new force. We must put in new running parts wherever there is the least lack of strength or adjustment. It will be necessary to organize democracy by sending up to the competitive examinations for the civil service men definitely prepared for standing liberal tests as to technical knowledge. A technically schooled civil service will presently have become indispensable.

I know that a corps of civil servants prepared by a special schooling and drilled, after appointment, into a perfected organization, with appropriate hierarchy and characteristic discipline, seems to a great many very thoughtful persons to contain elements which might combine to make an offensive official class—a distinct, semi-corporate body with sympathies divorced from those of a progressive, free-spirited people, and with hearts narrowed to the meanness of a bigoted officialism. Certainly such a class would be altogether hateful and harmful in the United States. Any measures calculated to produce it would for us be measures of reaction and of folly.

But to fear the creation of a domineering, illiberal officialism as a result of the studies I am here proposing is to miss altogether the principle upon which I wish most to insist. That principle is, that administration in the United States must be at all points sensitive to public opinion. A body of thoroughly trained officials serving during good behavior we must have in any case: that is a plain business necessity. But the apprehension that such a body will be anything un-American clears away the moment it is asked, What is to constitute good behavior? For that question obviously carries its own answer on its face. Steady, hearty allegiance to the policy of the government they serve will constitute good behavior. That *policy* will have no taint of officialism about it. It will not be the creation of permanent officials, but of statesmen whose responsibility to public opinion will be direct and inevitable. Bureaucracy can exist only where the whole service of the state is removed from the common political life of the people, its chiefs as well as its rank and file. Its motives, its objects, its policy, its standards, must be bureaucratic. It would be difficult to point out any examples of impudent exclusiveness and arbitrariness on the part of officials doing service under a chief of department who really served the people, as all our chiefs of departments must be made to do. It would be easy, on the other hand, to adduce other instances like that of the influence of Stein in Prussia, where the leadership of one statesman imbued with true public spirit transformed arrogant and perfunctory bureaux into public-spirited instruments of just government.

The ideal for us is a civil service cultured and self-sufficient enough to act with sense and vigor, and yet so intimately connected with the popular thought, by means of elections and constant public counsel, as to find arbitrariness or class spirit quite out of the question.

III

Having thus viewed in some sort the subject-matter and the objects of this study of administration, what are we to conclude as to the methods best suited to it—the points of view most advantageous for it?

Government is so near us, so much a thing of our daily familiar handling, that we can with difficulty see the need of any philosophical study of it, or the exact point of such study, should it be undertaken. We have been on our feet too long to study now the art of walking. We are a practical people, made so apt, so adept in self-government by centuries of experimental drill that we are scarcely any longer capable of perceiving the awkwardness of the particular system we may be using, just because it is so easy for us to use any system. We do not study the art of governing: we govern. But mere unschooled genius for affairs will not save us from sad blunders in administration. Though democrats by long inheritance and repeated choice, we are still rather crude democrats. Old as democracy is, its organization on a basis of modern ideas and conditions is still an unaccomplished work. The democratic state has yet to be equipped for carrying those enormous burdens of administration which the needs of this industrial and trading age are so fast accumulating. Without comparative studies in government we cannot rid ourselves of the misconception that administration stands upon an essentially different basis in a democratic state from that on which it stands in a non-democratic state.

After such study we could grant democracy the sufficient honor of ultimately determining by debate all essential questions affecting the public weal, of basing all structures of policy upon the major will; but we would have found but one rule of good administration for all governments alike. So far as administrative functions are concerned, all governments have a strong structural likeness; more than that, if they are to be uniformly useful and efficient, they *must* have a strong structural likeness. A free man has the same bodily organs, the same executive parts, as the slave, however different may be his motives, his services, his energies. Monarchies and democracies, radically different as they are in other respects, have in reality much the same business to look to.

It is abundantly safe nowadays to insist upon this actual likeness of all governments, because these are days when abuses of power are easily exposed and arrested, in countries like our own, by a bold, alert, inquisitive, detective public thought and a sturdy popular self-dependence such as never existed before. We are slow to appreciate this; but it is easy to appreciate it. Try to imagine personal government in the United States. It is like trying to imagine a national worship of Zeus. Our imaginations are too modern for the feat.

But, besides being safe, it is necessary to see that for all governments alike the legitimate ends of administration are the same, in order not to be frightened at the idea of looking into foreign systems of administration for instruction and suggestion; in order to get rid of the apprehension that we might perchance blindly borrow something incompatible with our principles. That man is blindly astray who denounces attempts to transplant foreign systems into this country. It is impossible: they simply would not grow here. But why should we not use such parts of foreign contrivances as we want, if they be in any way serviceable? We are in no danger of using them in a foreign way. We borrowed rice, but we do not eat it with chopsticks. We borrowed our whole political language from England, but we leave the words "king" and "lords" out of it. What did we ever originate, except the action of the federal government upon individuals and some of the functions of the federal supreme court?

We can borrow the science of administration with safety and profit if only we read all fundamental differences of condition into its essential tenets. We have only to filter it through our constitutions, only to put it over a slow fire of criticism and distil away its foreign gases.

I know that there is a sneaking fear in some conscientiously patriotic minds that studies of European systems might signalize some foreign methods as better than some American methods; and the fear is easily to be understood. But it would scarcely be avowed in just any company.

It is the more necessary to insist upon thus putting away all prejudices against looking anywhere in the world but at home for suggestions in this study, because nowhere else in the whole field of politics, it would seem, can we make use of the historical, comparative method more safely than in this province of administration. Perhaps the more novel the forms we study the better. We shall the sooner learn the peculiarities of our own methods. We can never learn either our own weaknesses or our own virtues by comparing ourselves with ourselves. We are too used to the appearance and procedure of our own system to see its true significance. Perhaps even the English system is too much like our own to be used to the most profit in illustration. It is best on the whole to get entirely away from our own atmosphere and to be most careful in examining such systems as those of France and Germany. Seeing our own institutions through such *media,* we see ourselves as foreigners might see us were they to look at us without preconceptions. Of ourselves, so long as we know only ourselves, we know nothing.

Let it be noted that it is the distinction, already drawn, between administration and politics which makes the comparative method so safe in the field of administration. When we study the administrative systems of France and Germany, knowing that we are not in search of *political* principles, we need not care a peppercorn for the constitutional or political reasons which Frenchmen or Germans give for their practices when explaining them to us. If I see a murderous fellow sharpening a knife cleverly, I can borrow his way of sharpening the knife without borrowing his probable intention to commit murder with it; and so, if I see a monarchist dyed in the wool managing a public bureau well, I can learn his business methods without changing one of my republican spots. He may serve his king; I will continue to serve the people; but I should like to serve my sovereign as well as he serves his. By keeping this distinction in view—that is, by studying administration as a means of putting our own politics into convenient practice, as a means of making what is democratically politic towards all administratively possible towards each—we are on perfectly safe ground, and can learn without error what foreign systems have to teach us. We thus devise an adjusting weight for our comparative method of study. We can thus scrutinize the anatomy of foreign governments without fear of getting any of their diseases into our veins; dissect alien systems without apprehension of blood-poisoning.

Our own politics must be the touchstone for all theories. The principles on which to base a science of administration for America must be principles which have democratic policy very much at heart. And, to suit American habit, all general theories must, as theories, keep modestly in the background, not in open argument only, but even in our own minds—lest opinions satisfactory only to the standards of the library should be dogmatically used, as if they must be quite as satisfactory to the standards of practical politics as well. Doctrinaire devices must be postponed to tested practices. Arrangements not only sanctioned by conclusive experience elsewhere but also congenial to American habit must be preferred without hesitation to theoretical perfection. In a word, steady, practical statesmanship must come first, closet doctrine second. The cosmopolitan what-to-do must always be commanded by the American how-to-do-it.

Our duty is to supply the best possible life to a *federal* organization, to systems within systems; to make town, city, county, state, and federal governments live with a like strength and an equally assured healthfulness, keeping each unquestionably its own master and yet making all interdependent and cooperative, combining independence with mutual helpfulness. The task is great and important enough to attract the best minds.

This interlacing of local self-government with federal self-government is quite a modern conception. It is not like the arrangements of imperial federation in Germany. There local government is not yet, fully, local *self*-government. The bureaucrat is everywhere busy. His efficiency springs out of *esprit de corps,* out of care to make ingratiating obeisance to the authority of a superior, or, at best, out of the soil of a sensitive conscience. He serves, not the public, but an irresponsible minister. The question for us is, how shall our series of governments within governments be so administered that it shall always be to the interest of the public officer to serve, not his superior alone but the community also, with the best efforts of his talents and the soberest service of his conscience? How shall such service be made to his commonest interest by contributing abundantly to his sustenance, to his dearest interest by furthering his ambition, and to his highest interest by advancing his honor and establishing his character? And how shall this be done alike for the local part and for the national whole?

If we solve this problem we shall again pilot the world. There is a tendency—is there not?—a tendency as yet dim, but already steadily impulsive and clearly destined to prevail, towards, first the confederation of parts of empires like the British, and finally of great states themselves. Instead of centralization of power, there is to be wide union with tolerated divisions of prerogative. This is a tendency towards the American type—of governments joined with governments for the pursuit of common purposes, in honorary equality and honorable subordination. Like principles of civil liberty are everywhere fostering like methods of government; and if comparative studies of the ways and means of government should enable us to offer suggestions which will practicably combine openness and vigor in the administration of such governments with ready docility to all serious, well-sustained public criticism, they will have approved themselves worthy to be ranked among the highest and most fruitful of the great departments of political study. That they will issue in such suggestions I confidently hope.

NOTES

1. Essay on Sir William Pitt.
2. Politik, S. 467.

2
Politics and Administration

Frank J. Goodnow

If we analyze the organization of any concrete government, we shall find that there are three kinds of authorities which are engaged in the execution of the state will. These are, in the first place, the authorities which apply the law in concrete cases where controversies arise owing to the failure of private individuals or public authorities to observe the rights of others. Such authorities are known as judicial authorities. They are, in the second place, the authorities which have the general supervision of the execution of the state will, and which are commonly referred to as executive authorities. They are, finally, the authorities which are attending to the scientific, technical, and, so to speak, commercial activities of the government, and which are in all countries, where such activities have attained prominence, known as administrative authorities.

As government becomes more complex these three authorities, all of which are engaged in the execution of the will of the state, tend to become more and more differentiated. The first to become so differentiated are the judicial authorities. Not only is this differentiation of the judicial authorities first in point of time, it is also the clearest. Indeed, it is so clear in some instances as to lead many students, as has been pointed out, to mark off the activity of the judicial authorities as a separate power or function of government.

Enough has been said, it is believed, to show that there are two distinct functions of government, and that their differentiation results in a differentiation, though less complete, of the organs of government provided by the formal governmental system. These two functions of government may for purposes of convenience be designated respectively as Politics and Administration. Politics has to do with policies or expressions of the state will. Administration has to do with the execution of these policies.

It is of course true that the meaning which is here given to the word "politics" is not the meaning which has been attributed to that word by most political writers. At the same time it is submitted that the sense in which politics is here used is the sense in which it is used by most people in ordinary affairs. Thus the Century Dictionary defines "politics": "In the narrower and more usual sense, the act or vocation of guiding or influencing the policy of a government through the organization of a party among its citizens—including, therefore, not only the ethics of government, but more especially, and often to the exclusion of ethical principles, the art of influencing public opinion, attracting and marshalling voters, and obtaining and distributing public patronage, so far as the possession of offices may depend upon the political opinions or political services of individuals."

Source: Frank J. Goodnow, *Politics and Administration: A Study in Government* (New York: Russell & Russell, 1900), pp. 17–26.

An explanation of the word "administration" is not perhaps so necessary, since in scientific parlance it has not as yet acquired so fixed a meaning as has "politics." Block, in his *Dictionnaire de l'administration française,* defines "administration" as: "L'ensemble des services publiques destinés à concourir à l'exécution de la pensée du gouvernement et à l'application des lois d'intérêt general." The Century Dictionary speaks of it as: "The duty or duties of the administrator; specifically, the executive functions of government, consisting in the exercise of all the powers and duties of government, both general and local, which are neither legislative nor judicial."

These definitions, it will be noticed, both lay stress upon the fact that politics has to do with the guiding or influencing of governmental policy, while administration has to do with the execution of that policy. It is these two functions which it is here desired to differentiate, and for which the words "politics" and "administration" have been chosen.

The use of the word "administration" in this connection is unfortunately somewhat misleading, for the word when accompanied by the definite article is also used to indicate a series of governmental authorities. "The administration" means popularly the most important executive or administrative authorities. "Administration," therefore, when used as indicative of function, is apt to promote the idea that this function of government is to be found exclusively in the work of what are commonly referred to as executive or administrative authorities. These in their turn are apt to be regarded as confined to the discharge of the function of administration. Such, however, is rarely the case in any political system, and is particularly not the case in the American governmental system. The American legislature discharges very frequently the function of administration through its power of passing special acts. The American executive has an important influence on the discharge of the function of politics through the exercise of its veto power.

Further, in the United States, the words "administration" and "administrative," as indicative of governmental function, are commonly used by the courts in a very loose way. The attempt was made at the time of the formation of our governmental system, as has been pointed out, to incorporate into it the principle of the separation of powers. What had been a somewhat nebulous theory of political science thus became a rigid legal doctrine. What had been a somewhat attractive political theory in its nebulous form became at once an unworkable and unapplicable rule of law.

To avoid the inconvenience resulting from the attempt made to apply it logically to our governmental system, the judges of the United States have been accustomed to call "administrative" any power which was not in their eyes exclusively and unqualifiedly legislative, executive, or judicial, and to permit such a power to be exercised by any authority.[1]

While this habit on the part of the judges makes the selection of the word "administration" somewhat unfortunate; at the same time it is indicative of the fact to which attention has been more than once directed, that although the differentiation of two functions of government is clear, the assignment of such functions to separate authorities is impossible.

Finally, the different position assigned in different states to the organ to which most of the work of executing the will of the state has been intrusted, has resulted in quite different conceptions in different states of what has been usually called administration. For administration has been conceived of as the function of the executing, that is, the executive authority. Recently, however, writers on administration have seen that, from the point of view both of theoretical speculation and of practical expediency, administration should not be regarded as merely a function of the executive authority, that is, the authority in the government which by the positive law is the executing authority. It has been seen that administration is, on the contrary, the function of executing the will of the state. It may be in some respects greater, and in others less in extent than the function of the executing authority as determined by the positive law.

There are, then, in all governmental systems two primary or ultimate functions of government, viz. the expression of the will of the state and the execution of that will. There are also in all states separate organs, each of which is mainly busied with the discharge of one of these functions. These functions are, respectively, Politics and Administration.

THE FUNCTION OF POLITICS

The function of politics, it has been shown, consists in the expression of the will of the state. Its discharge may not, however, be intrusted exclusively to any authority or any set of authorities in the government. Nor on the other hand may any authority or set of authorities be confined exclusively to its discharge. The principle of the separation of powers in its extreme form cannot, therefore, be made the basis of any concrete political organization. For this principle demands that there shall be separate authorities of the government, each of which shall be confined to the discharge of one of the functions of government which are differentiated. Actual political necessity however requires that there shall be harmony between the expression and execution of the state will.

Lack of harmony between the law and its execution results in political paralysis. A rule of conduct, *i.e.*, an expression of the state will, practically amounts to nothing if it is not executed. It is a mere *brutum fulmen*. On the other hand the execution of a rule of conduct which is not the expression of the state will is really an exercise by the executing authority of the right to express the state will.

Now in order that this harmony between the expression and the execution of the state will may be obtained, the independence either of the body which expresses the state will or of the body which executes it must be sacrificed. Either the executing authority must be subordinated to the expressing authority, or the expressing authority must be subjected to the control of the executing authority. Only in this way will there be harmony in the government. Only in this way can the expression of the real state will become an actual rule of conduct generally observed.

Finally, popular government requires that it is the executing authority which shall be subordinated to the expressing authority, since the latter in the nature of things can be made much more representative of the people than can the executing authority.

In other words, practical political necessity makes impossible the consideration of the function of politics apart from that of administration. Politics must have a certain control over administration, using the words in the broad senses heretofore attributed to them. That some such relation must exist between the two ultimate functions of government is seen when we examine the political development of any state.

If, in the hope of preventing politics from influencing administration in its details, the attempt is made to provide for the legal separation of the bodies in the government mainly charged with these two functions respectively, the tendency is for the necessary control to develop extra-legally. This is the case in the American political system.

The American political system is largely based on the fundamental principle of the separation of governmental powers. It has been impossible for the necessary control of politics over administration to develop within the formal governmental system on account of the independent position assigned by the constitutional law to executive and administrative officers. The control has therefore developed in the party system. The American political party busies itself as much with the election of administrative and executive officers as it does with the election of bodies recognized as distinctly political in character, as having to do with the expression of the state will. The party system thus secures that harmony between the functions of politics and administration which must exist if government is to be carried on successfully.[2]

On the other hand, if no attempt is made in the governmental system to provide for the separation of politics and administration, and if the governmental institutions are not put into comparatively unyielding and inflexible form through the adoption of a written constitution, the control and superintendence of the function of administration tends to be assumed by the governmental body which discharges the political function.

NOTES

1. Bondy, "Separation of Governmental Powers," *Columbia College Series in History, Economics, and Public Law* 5, p. 202 *et seq.*
2. Mr. H. J. Ford in his book entitled *The Rise and Growth of American Politics*, a most valuable and interesting work, is the first writer to call attention to the fact that this most important duty has been assumed by the political party in the American system of government.

---

3 Scientific Management

Frederick W. Taylor

What I want to try to prove to you and make clear to you is that the principles of scientific management when properly applied, and when a sufficient amount of time has been given to make them really effective, must in all cases produce far larger and better results, both for the employer and the employees, than can possibly be obtained under even this very rare type of management which I have been outlining, namely, the management of "initiative and incentive," in which those on the management's side deliberately give a very large incentive to their workmen, and in return the workmen respond by working to the very best of their ability at all times in the interest of their employers.

Source: Testimony Before the U.S. House of Representatives, January 25, 1912.

I want to show you that scientific management is even far better than this rare type of management.

The first great advantage which scientific management has over the management of initiative and incentive is that under scientific management the initiative of the workmen—that is, their hard work, their good will, their ingenuity—is obtained practically with absolute regularity, while under even the best of the older type of management this initiative is only obtained spasmodically and somewhat irregularly. This obtaining, however, of the initiative of the workmen is the lesser of the two great causes which make scientific management better for both sides than the older type of management. By far the greater gain under scientific management comes from the new, the very great, and the extraordinary burdens and duties which are voluntarily assumed by those on the management's side.

These new burdens and new duties are so unusual and so great that they are to the men used to managing under the old school almost inconceivable. These duties and burdens voluntarily assumed under scientific management, by those on the management's side, have been divided and classified into four different groups and these four types of new duties assumed by the management have (rightly or wrongly) been called the "principles of scientific management."

The first of these four groups of duties taken over by the management is the deliberate gathering in on the part of those on the management's side of all of the great mass of traditional knowledge, which in the past has been in the heads of the workmen, and in the physical skill and knack of the workman, which he has acquired through years of experience. The duty of gathering in of all this great mass of traditional knowledge and then recording it, tabulating it, and, in many cases, finally reducing it to laws, rules, and even to mathematical formulae, is voluntarily assumed by the scientific managers. And later, when these laws, rules, and formulae are applied to the everyday work of all the workmen of the establishment, through the intimate and hearty cooperation of those on the management's side, they invariably result, first, in producing a very much larger output per man, as well as an output of a better and higher quality; and, second, in enabling the company to pay much higher wages to their workmen; and, third, in giving to the company a larger profit. The first of these principles, then, may be called the development of a science to replace the old rule-of-thumb knowledge of the workmen; that is, the knowledge which the workmen had, and which was, in many cases, quite as exact as that which is finally obtained by the management, but which the workmen nevertheless in nine hundred and ninety-nine cases out of a thousand kept in their heads, and of which there was no permanent or complete record.

A very serious objection has been made to the use of the word "science" in this connection. I am much amused to find that this objection comes chiefly from the professors of this country. They resent the use of the word science for anything quite so trivial as the ordinary, every-day affairs of life. I think the proper answer to this criticism is to quote the definition recently given by a professor who is, perhaps, as generally recognized as a thorough scientist as any man in the country—President McLaurin, of the Institute of Technology, of Boston. He recently defined the word science as "classified or organized knowledge of any kind." And surely the gathering in of knowledge which, as previously stated, has existed, but which was in an unclassified condition in the minds of workmen, and then the reducing of this knowledge to laws and rules and formulae, certainly represents the organization and classification of knowledge, even though it may not meet with the approval of some people to have it called science.

The second group of duties which are voluntarily assumed by those on the management's side, under scientific management, is the scientific selection and then the progressive development of the workmen. It becomes the duty of those on the management's side to deliberately study the character, the nature, and the performance of each workman with a view to finding out his limitations on the one hand, but even more important, his possibilities for development on the other hand; and then, as deliberately and as systematically to train and help and teach this workman, giving him, wherever it is possible, those opportunities for advancement which will finally enable him to do the highest and most interesting and most profitable class of work for which his natural abilities fit him, and which are open to him in the particular company in which he is employed. This scientific selection of the workman and his development is not a single act; it goes on from year to year and is the subject of continual study on the part of the management.

The third of the principles of scientific management is the bringing of the science and the scientifically selected and trained workmen together. I say "bringing together" advisedly, because you may develop all the science that you please, and you may scientifically select and train workmen just as much as you please, but unless some man or some men bring the science and the workmen together all your labor will be lost. We are all of us so constituted that about three-fourths of the time we will work according to whatever method suits us best; that is, we will practice the science or we will not practice it; we will do our work in accordance with the laws of the science or in our own old way, just as we see fit unless some one is there to see that we do it in accordance with the principles of the science. Therefore I use advisedly the words "bringing the science and the workman together." It is unfortunate, however, that this word "bringing" has rather a disagreeable sound, a rather forceful sound; and, in a way, when it is first heard it puts one out of touch with what we have come to look upon as the modern tendency. The time for using the word "bringing" with a sense of forcing, in relation to most matters, has gone by; but I think that I may soften this word down in its use in this particular case by saying that nine-tenths of the trouble with those of us who have been engaged in helping people to change from the older type of management to the new management—that is, to scientific management—that nine-tenths of our trouble has been to "bring" those on the management's side to do their fair share of the work and only one-tenth of our trouble has come on the workman's side. Invariably we find very great opposition on the part of those on the management's side to do their new duties and comparatively little opposition on the part of the workmen to cooperate in doing their new duties. So that the word "bringing" applies much more forcefully to those on the management's side than to those on the workman's side.

The fourth of the principles of scientific management is perhaps the most difficult of all of the four principles of scientific management for the average man to understand. It consists of an almost equal division of the actual work of the establishment between the workmen, on the one hand, and the management, on the other hand. That is, the work which under the old type of management practically all was done by the workman, under the new is divided into two great divisions, and one of these divisions is deliberately handed over to those on the management's side. This new division of work, this new share of the work assumed by those on the management's side, is so great that you will, I think, be able to understand it better in a numerical way when I tell you that in a machine shop, which, for instance, is doing an intricate business—I do not refer to a manufacturing company, but, rather, to an engineering company; that is, a machine shop which builds a variety of machines and is not engaged in manufacturing them, but, rather, in constructing them—will have one man on the management's side to every three workmen; that is, this immense share of the work—one-third—has been deliberately taken out of the workman's hands and handed over to those on the management's side. And it is due to this actual sharing of the work between the two sides more than to any other one element that there has never (until this last summer) been a single strike under scientific management. In a machine shop, again, under this new type of management there is hardly a single act or piece of work done by any workman in the shop which is not preceded and followed by some act on the part of one of the men in the management. All day long every workman's acts are dovetailed in between corresponding acts of the management. First, the workman does something, and then a man on the management's side does something; then the man on the management's side does something, and then the workman does something; and under this intimate, close, personal cooperation between the two sides it becomes practically impossible to have a serious quarrel.

Of course I do not wish to be understood that there are never any quarrels under scientific management. There are some, but they are the very great exception, not the rule. And it is perfectly evident that while the workmen are learning to work under this new system, and while the management is learning to work under this new system, while they are both learning, each side to cooperate in this intimate way with the other, there is plenty of chance for disagreement and for quarrels and misunderstandings, but after both sides realize that it is utterly impossible to turn out the work of the establishment at the proper rate of speed and have it correct without this intimate, personal cooperation, when both sides realize that it is utterly impossible for either one to be successful without the intimate, brotherly cooperation of the other, the friction, the disagreements, and quarrels are reduced to a minimum. So, I think that scientific management can be justly and truthfully characterized as management in which harmony is the rule rather than discord.

There is one illustration of the application of the principles of scientific management with which all of us are familiar and with which most of us have been familiar since we were small boys, and I think this instance represents one of the best illustrations of the application of the principles of scientific management. I refer to the management of a first-class American baseball team. In such a team you will find almost all of the elements of scientific management.

You will see that the science of doing every little act that is done by every player on the baseball field has been developed. Every single element of the game of baseball has been the subject of the most intimate, the closest study of many men, and, finally, the best way of doing each act that takes place on the baseball field has been fairly well agreed upon and established as a standard throughout the country. The players have not only been told the best way of making each important motion or play, but they have been taught, coached, and trained to it through months of drilling. And I think that every man who has watched first-class play, or who knows anything of the management of the modern baseball team, realizes fully the utter impossibility of winning with the best team of individual players that was ever gotten together unless every man on the team obeys the signals or orders of the coach and obeys them at once when the coach gives those orders; that is, without the intimate cooperation between all members of the team and the management, which is characteristic of scientific management.

4
The Movement for Budgetary Reform in the States

William F. Willoughby

INTRODUCTION: ORIGIN OF MOVEMENT

Of few movements for political reform is it feasible to determine precisely the causes to which it owes its rise or to fix exactly the date of its origin. If one seeks for an explanation of the modern movement, now under full way, for the adoption by the several governing bodies of the United States of a budget as the central and controlling feature of their systems of financial administration, it must be found in a number of more or less distinct movements which have each found in this device an important means for achieving or promoting the object sought.

The Budget as an Instrument of Democracy. Among these first place must be given to that effort continuously being put forth to devise means by which popular government, in the sense that the affairs of government shall be conducted in conformity with the popular will, may become a reality in fact as in name. It is hardly necessary to point out that the popular will cannot be intelligently formulated nor expressed unless the public has adequate means for knowing currently how governmental affairs have been conducted in the past, what are present conditions and what program for work in the future is under consideration. Of all means devised for meeting this requirement no single one approaches in completeness and effectiveness a budget if properly prepared. It at once serves to make known past operations, present conditions and future proposals, definitely locates responsibility and furnishes the means for control. Professor A. R. Hatton is thus justified when he says:

> Above and beyond its relation to economy and efficiency in public affairs it (the budget) may be made one of the most potent instruments of democracy. Given

Source: William F. Willoughby, *The Movement for Budgetary Reform in the States* (New York: D. Appleton and Company for the Institute for Government Research, 1918), pp. 1–8.

at least manhood suffrage, any government so organized as to produce and carry out a scientific budget system will be susceptible of extensive and intelligent popular control. On the contrary those governments, whatever their other virtues, which fail to provide adequate budget methods will neither reach the maximum of efficiency nor prove to be altogether responsible to the people.

A new spirit in American politics is manifesting itself in the powerful movement for the reform of governmental organization and procedure in the interest of popular control and efficiency. There are naturally many features in the program for the accomplishment of this twofold object. No single change would add so largely to both democracy and efficiency as the introduction of proper budget methods.[1]

The Budget as an Instrument for Correlating Legislative and Executive Action. Closely associated with this demand that more effective means be provided by which the popular will and the principle of popular control may be made effective is the feeling that the present working conditions of our legislative bodies and particularly their relations to the executive branch of government are far from satisfactory. The conviction has been growing that a mistake has been made in seeking to make of our legislatures boards of directors to concern themselves with the details of the activities, organization and methods of business of administrative services; that the true function of the legislature should be that of acting as an organ of public opinion in the larger sense and as the medium through which those concerned with the actual administration of affairs should be supervised, controlled, and held to a rigid accountability for the manner in which they discharge their duties.

This has led inevitably to the position that upon the executive should be placed the responsibility for the formulation of work programs and the decision, in the first instance at least, of the means to be employed in the putting of these programs into execution. This would appear to carry with it a great strengthening of the executive at the expense of the legislative branch of government. So it does in one sense. It is a canon of administrative science, however, that when discretionary powers and authority are increased a corresponding increase should be made in the means of controlling and supervising the manner in which these augmented powers are exercised. If legislatures are to surrender to the executive increased powers in respect to the conduct of administrative affairs, they must strengthen the means by which they may assure themselves that these powers are properly exercised. There are two methods by which superior direction, supervision and control may be exerted, by specification in advance, or, by the establishment of a proper accounting and reporting system, by establishing means through which full information may be currently available regarding the manner in which delegated authority is being exercised. Legislatures are being asked to give up the first method of control. If they do so, it is imperative that the conditions stated in the second alternative should be met.

It is at this point that the demand for the adoption of a budget finds its place as an integral part of the movement for the improvement of the working relations between the two branches of government. In the budget is to be found far the most effective means that has yet been devised whereby larger responsibility for the formulation and execution of financial and work programs may be conferred upon the executive and yet the latter be held to a more rigid accountability for the manner in which this responsibility is discharged. In a very true sense, therefore, the movement for the adoption of budgetary systems by our governing bodies is an integral and essential part of the whole greater movement for the accomplishment of governmental reforms generally.

The Budget as an Instrument for Securing Administrative Efficiency and Economy. Still another movement which has logically resulted in the demand for budgetary reforms is that for placing the purely technical methods of governmental organization and administration upon a more efficient and economical basis. The question has been raised as to whether there are any inherent reasons why government officers should not be held to the same standards of efficiency and honesty as are demanded in the business world. The demand that they should be has become more insistent as the tasks imposed upon governments have become more numerous and complex and, in many cases, more nearly similar to the character of the tasks which private corporations are called upon to perform. In the business world it is recognized that no undertaking of magnitude, certainly none performed under a corporate form of organization, can be efficiently administered which does not have a system of accounts and reports that will permit the directing body, the board of directors, and the stockholders, to secure a clear picture of past operations, present conditions and future programs of activities. In all proposals looking to the reform of methods of business of governmental bodies, chief attention has consequently been placed upon the demand for the improvement of the methods by which their financial affairs are conducted. It is inconsistent to the last degree that governments should insist that corporations controlled by them should have systems of accounting and reporting corresponding to the most approved principles of modern accountancy while not providing for equally efficient systems for the management of their own financial affairs. The demand for improved methods of public administration has thus inevitably centered primarily upon the demand for improved methods of financial administration and, in order that this may be secured, upon the specific demand for the adoption of a budgetary system as the central feature of such improved system.

Use of Budget First Demanded as a Feature of Municipal Reform. Turning now to a history of the movement itself, the point of departure must be found in the great movement which has been so much in evidence during the present generation, for the improvement of methods of municipal administration. After repeated disappointments persons interested in municipal reform came to an appreciation that permanent reform was not to be accomplished by the putting in the field of citizens' tickets and the ousting of officials who subordinated the public good to private gain. More and more it was borne in upon them that if lasting improvements were to be effected, the system of municipal government itself and methods of administration had to be changed, that there must be established principles of administration and means of direction, supervision and control that would automatically, as it were, result in better administration or at least make it possible for all interested parties to determine, without the necessity for special investigations, whether affairs were being efficiently and economically administered or the reverse. It was found, in a word, that the problem had to be attacked from the technical as well as the moral standpoint.

This change in the method of approach found expression not only in the altered character of the work attempted by such organizations as the National Municipal League, but in the appreciation that a thorough study of the technical problems of municipal administration with a view to the formulation of concrete measures of reform could only be successfully undertaken by permanent organization specially established and with a technically competent staff to undertake this work. Appreciation of this led to the creation by public spirited individuals of the large number of bureaus of municipal research which have contributed so powerfully during recent years to the improvement of methods of municipal administration in the United States. This is not the place to attempt any general characterization of the work of these bodies. It is only necessary for us to say that these bureaus have almost without exception concentrated a large part of their attention upon problems of financial administration and that all, likewise without exception, have bent their energies towards the securing by the cities with whose operations they concerned themselves of a budgetary system. This action was in large measure predicated upon the proposition that a municipality partakes in large measure of the characteristics of an ordinary business corporation and should be operated as such. This has meant that there should be employed by it the methods and agencies which have been found indispensable to the efficient operation of large business corporations. This view accepted, the demand at once arose that the expenditures of the city should be brought into direct relation to its possible or actual revenues and be based upon estimates and recommendations emanating from the spending departments. The advantage was at once seen of having the estimates and recommendations thus made by the several administrative services submitted to some central executive organ vested with authority to revise and reduce them when necessary and to bring them into due relation and proportion to one another. This was seen to be essential since spending departments are concerned primarily each in its own activities and are, therefore, interested in getting the largest possible allotment of funds from the general treasury. If the latter is to be protected and the relative as well as the absolute utility of different classes of work is to be determined some organ must exist within the administration which is not itself a spending department but has the special function of balancing demands of spending departments and of protecting the general treasury from the demands being made upon it beyond its resources.

This fundamental feature was appreciated by municipal reformers prior to the establishment of bureaus of municipal research. Thus the National Municipal League as early as 1899 included in its draft of a model municipal corporation act a section providing that:

> It shall be the duty of the Mayor from time to time to make such recommendations to the Council as he may deem to be for the welfare of the city and on the ——— day of ——— in each year to submit to the Council the annual budget of current expenses of the city, any item in which may be reduced or omitted by the Council; but the Council shall not increase any item in nor the total of said budget.

The course of budgetary reform in municipalities was also materially promoted by the Bureau of the Census through the continuous pressure which it exerted upon municipalities to improve their methods of accounting and reporting and especially through the standard classification of municipal expenditures which it worked out in connection with experts representing the accounting profession and the National Municipal League. In later years the development of the commission and city manager types of municipal government, and the policy adopted by a number of the leading cities in their recent charter revisions to provide for boards of estimates among whose functions the most important duty was that of passing upon and revising estimates as originally framed by the spending departments, have likewise contributed powerfully to the promotion of budgetary reform. These all represent the definite adoption of the most fundamental principle of a budget that there should be a central budget framing organ to stand between the estimating departments and the fund-granting authority. In few, if any, cases, however, has the principle been adopted of vesting final authority in respect to the framing of a budget in the chief executive officer.

After all is said, however, to the bureaus of municipal research and allied organizations established by boards of trade and other citizen agencies belongs the chief credit for the persistent demand that a budget be made the foundation stone of the system of financial administration of all municipalities. Not only have they urged this without ceasing but they have done a large amount of work in the way of working out and installing systems of financial administration in various cities resting on this basis.

Movement for Budgetary Reform Carried Over to the States. It was inevitable that the movement for budgetary reform in municipalities, once fairly under way, should be carried over to efforts looking to the improvement of state governments. Every reason dictating the necessity for this reform in the case of municipalities existed with increased force in the case of these governments. Here the conditions to be met, however, were much more difficult than those obtaining in the case of municipal governments. Broadly speaking, the administrative branch of municipal governments corresponds to the integrated type of organization, with the mayor at the head as administrator in chief. It has been pointed out in our consideration of the nature and functions of a budget[2] how essential is this form of organization to the proper operation of a budgetary system. It is unfortunate, both from the standpoint of budgetary reform and that of good administration generally, that this condition obtains in but few, if any, of the states. As is well known, in most if not all of the states the administrative branch consists of a large number of practically independent services. Only in small degree has the governor any positive powers of direction or any adequate power to control. The line of authority runs direct in each case to the legislature; and the authority of this body is often limited by the fact that the heads of these services owe their election to office, not to it, but to the people. It results from this that in the case of most, if not all, of the states the problem of the introduction of a thoroughly efficient budgetary system involves that of fundamentally recasting their systems of government.

NOTES

1. Foreword to Public Budgets, Annals of the American Academy of Political and Social Science, November, 1915.
2. The Problem of a National Budget, p. 1–29.

CHAPTER II

Between the World Wars

After World War I, public administration changed inexorably. At the conclusion of all previous wars, American government had returned to basic minimal levels, but this time the scope and influence of government in American life would not diminish. The United States was changing from a rural agricultural society to an urban industrial nation. This required a considerable response from public administration because so many new functions and programs would be established. Paved highways would see a tenfold increase in the 1920s. Cities would install traffic management systems and states would impose driving tests. As the population became increasingly urban, vastly expanded programs would be needed in public parks and recreation, public works, public health, and public safety. Public administration as an activity was booming all during the 1920s.[1] The federal government's response to the Great Depression of the 1930s would make it all the more pervasive as part of American life.

Public administration theorists, such as Dwight Waldo,[2] Vincent Ostrom,[3] Nicholas Henry,[4] and Howard McCurdy,[5] would describe the pattern of development within public administration between the world wars as a "period of orthodoxy." The tenets of this orthodox ideology held that "true democracy and true efficiency are synonymous, or at least reconcilable,"[6] that the work of government could be neatly divided into decision making and execution, and that administration was a science with discoverable principles. The initial imprint of the scientific management movement, the progressive reform political movement, and the politics-administration dichotomy became central foci for public administration both as a profession and a field of study.

A critical linkage for the study of administration was its concern, indeed almost obsession, with organization and control. By definition, control was to be built into organizational structure and design to assure both accountability and efficiency. In fact, early management theorists assumed that organization and control were virtually synonymous. Remember that traditional administrative notions were based on historical models provided by the military and the Roman Catholic Church, which viewed organizational conflict as deviancy to be severely punished. When government units were small, less significant, and relatively provincial, the management of their organizations was less consequential. However, as the size, scope, and level of effort increased, pressures for better organization and control mounted. Under the influence of the scientific management movement, public administration became increasingly concerned with understanding bureaucratic forms of organization. The division of labor; span of control; organizational hierarchy and chain of command; reporting systems; departmentalization; and the development of standard operating rules, policies, and procedures became critical concerns to scholars and practitioners in the field.

Bureaucracy emerged as a dominant feature of the contemporary world. Virtually everywhere one looked in both developed and developing nations, economic, social, and political life were extensively and ever increasingly influenced by bureaucratic organizations. *Bureaucracy,* while it is often used as a general invective to refer to any organization that is perceived to be inefficient, is more properly used to refer to a specific set of structural arrangements. It may also be used to refer to specific kinds of behavior—patterns of which are not restricted to formal bureaucracies. It is widely assumed that the structural characteristics of organizations correctly defined as "bureaucratic" influence the behavior of individuals—whether clients or bureaucrats—who interact with them.

Contemporary thinking along these lines begins with the work of the brilliant German sociologist Max Weber (1864–1920). His analysis of bureaucracy, first published in 1922 after his death, is still the most influential statement—the point of departure for all further analyses—on the subject. Drawing on studies of ancient bureaucracies in Egypt, Rome, China, and the Byzantine Empire, as well as on the more modern ones emerging in Europe during the nineteenth and early part of the twentieth centuries, Weber used an "ideal-type" approach to extrapolate from the real world the central core of features characteristic of the most fully developed bureaucratic form of organization. Weber's "Characteristics of Bureaucracy," reprinted here, is neither a description of reality nor a statement of normative preference. It is merely an identification of the major variables or features that characterize bureaucracies. The fact that such features might not be fully present in a given organization does not necessarily imply that the organization is nonbureaucratic. It may be an immature rather than a fully developed bureaucracy.

Weber's work on bureaucracy was not translated into English and made generally available until 1946. Still his influence was phenomenal. Usually credited with being the "father" of modern sociology, Weber's work emphasized a new methodological rigor that could advance the study of organizations. Weber, himself, played a crucial role in helping to write a constitution for the Weimar Republic in Germany just before his death in 1920. The experience of the ill-fated Weimar republic, certainly not attributable in any way to Weber, added perhaps another point of support to Woodrow Wilson's contention that it is harder to run a constitution than to frame one. Yet the clarity and descriptive quality of Weber's analysis of bureaucratic organizations provided both orthodox theorists and critics with a reference point from which to evaluate both the good and bad effects of bureaucratic structures.

While Woodrow Wilson provided the rationale for public administration to be an academic discipline and professional speciality, it remained for Leonard D. White (1891–1958) to most clearly articulate its preliminary objectives. While a United States Civil Service Commissioner from 1934 to 1937, White spent most of his career at the University of Chicago.[7] In the preface to his pioneering 1926 book, *Introduction to the Study of Public Administration,* the first text in the field, he noted four critical assumptions that formed the basis for the study of public administration: (1) administration is a unitary process that can be studied uniformly, at the federal, state, and local levels; (2) the basis for study is management, not law; (3) administration is still art, but the ideal of transformance to science is both feasible and worthwhile; and (4) the recognition that administration "has become, and will continue to be the heart of the problem of modern government."[8] We have reprinted the preface and first chapter from White's 1926 book, which through four decades and four editions would be the most influential of public administration texts.[9]

White's text was remarkable for its restraint in not taking a prescriptive cookbook approach to public administration. He recognized that public administration was above all a field of study that had to stay close to reality—the reality of its largely untrained practitioner base that still professed great belief in the art of administration. Even more interesting, his work avoided the potential pitfall of the politics-administration dichotomy. Defining public administration as emphasizing the managerial phase, he left unanswered "the question to what extent the administration itself participates in formulating the purposes of the state and avoids any controversy as to the precise nature of administrative action."[10]

Between the world wars, while management in both the public and private sectors was establishing itself as an identifiable discipline, the influence of scientific management or "Taylorism" was pervasive. The methodology used to divine the one best way to accomplish physical tasks was increasingly applied to the problem of social organization. Luther Gulick's (1892–)[11] "Notes on the Theory of Organization" is generally acknowledged to be the definitive statement on the "principles" approach to managing organizations. In 1937, he and Lyndall Urwick (1891–1983) edited a collection—*Papers on the Science of Administration.* Overall, the *Papers* were a statement of the state of the art of organization theory. It was here that Gulick introduced his famous mnemonic, POSDCORB, which stands for the seven major functions of management—planning, organizing, staffing, directing, coordinating, reporting, and budgeting.

Gulick helped shape a critical distinction in orthodox public administration: the study of management and administration was to be focused on the role of upper level management. Its organizational outlook took the point of view of the top. But this narrow focus was to be increasingly challenged. Even as Gulick wrote, his scientific approach to management was being confronted by the more humanistic focus that would ultimately supplant it. Although this was not immediately apparent, the theoreticians of the human-relations and behavioral-science approaches to management were very much contemporaries of Gulick; they were simply prophets before their time.

Mary Parker Follett (1868–1933)[12] was a major voice for what today would be called participatory management. She wrote about the advantages of exercising "power with" as opposed to "power over." Her "law of the situation" was contingency management in its humble origins. Reprinted here is her discussion, "The Giving of Orders," which draws attention to the problems caused when superior/subordinate roles inhibit the productivity of the organization.

It was during the late 1920s and early 1930s that the Hawthorne experiments were undertaken at the Hawthorne Works of the Western Electric Company near Chicago. This study, the most famous management study every reported, was conducted by Elton Mayo (1880–1949)[13] and his associates from the Harvard Business School. The decade-long series of experiments started out as traditional scientific management examinations of the relationship between work environment and productivity. But the experimenters, because they were initially unable to explain the results of their findings, literally stumbled upon a finding that today seems obvious—that factories and other work situations are, first of all, social situations. The workers, as Mary Parker Follett had suggested a decade earlier, were more responsive to peer pressure than to management controls. The Hawthorne studies are generally considered to be the genesis of the human-relation school of management thought.[14]

Chester I. Barnard (1886–1961) followed Follett's major themes with a far more comprehensive theory in *The Functions of the Executive.*[15] Barnard, a Bell System executive who was closely associated with the Harvard Business School and those faculty who were involved with the Hawthorne studies,[16] saw organizations as cooperative systems where the function of the executive was to maintain the dynamic equilibrium between the needs of the organization and the needs of its employees. In order to do this, management had to be aware of the interdependent nature of the formal and informal organizations. Barnard's chapter on the significance and role of informal organizations, "Informal Organizations and Their Relations to Formal Organizations," reprinted here, provided the theoretical foundations for a whole generation of empirical research. Time seems to have made Barnard's book only more significant and popular. Recently, it was even being offered as a selection by the Fortune Book Club.

Although the real battle between the human-relations approach and traditional mechanistic scientific management on the appropriateness of organizational structure would not be joined until the post–World War II period, there was great activity on the organizational front, especially reorganization. Reorganization is a recurring theme in the practice and literature of public administration. In recent years scholars such as Seidman,[17] Mosher,[18] and Szanton[19] would produce significant works arguing the merits, objectives, and results of reorganization efforts. But by far the classic example of reorganization, the one that to this day is still the most significant, is the reorganization recommended by the President's Committee on Administrative Management. This 1936–1937 committee was popularly known as the Brownlow Committee after its chairman Louis Brownlow (1879–1963),[20] a major figure in the development of city management as a profession. The other members of the committee were Charles Merriam (1874–1953) of the University of Chicago and Luther Gulick of Columbia University and the Institute of Public Administration in New York City.

Government grew rapidly during the New Deal period. Because there was little time, or, it was largely believed, inclination for planning, there existed many poorly conceived and poorly implemented organizational designs that were neither economical nor effective. These poor designs were often a reflection of the considerable political conflict between the executive and legislative branches. Both the presidency under Roosevelt and the Congress had deliberately contributed to this problem by establishing programs in new organizations or agencies only with regard to political objectives—as opposed to taking managerial considerations into account. This persistent struggle over organizational control would be addressed by the Brownlow Committee—which would provide the first formal assessment of government organization from a managerial perspective.[21]

The Brownlow Committee submitted its report to the president in January 1937. The proposals of the Committee were simple enough. Essentially they combined to say that "the president needs help"; that he needs men around him with a "passion for anonymity." This particular passion seems to have faded in recent years along with the public's belief that a modern president writes his own speeches.

Overall the committee recommended a major reorganization of the executive branch. Most of the Brownlow Committee's introduction to its Report and its section on "The White House Staff" are reprinted here. The president agreed, and appropriate legislation was submitted to Congress in 1938. But Congress, in the wake of the president's efforts to "pack" the Supreme Court and fearful of too much power in the presidency, killed the bill. The president resubmitted a considerably modified reorganization bill the following year, and the Congress passed the Reorganization Act of 1939. This law created the Executive Office of the President, brought into it the Bureau of the Budget (later to be the Office of Management and Budget) from the Department of Treasury, and authorized the president to prepare future reorganization plans subject to a congressional veto.[22]

The Brownlow report, the Executive Office of the President, and many of the other recommendations of the Brownlow Committee that would eventually become law[23] have been sanctified by time. Yet the Brownlow Committee's major proposals aroused considerable controversy at the time. Modern scholars now recognize that there were different schools of thought regarding the development of public administration. The executive administration school, espoused by Frank J. Goodnow, viewed the roles and functions of government almost exclusively as opportunities for executive actions. In contrast, the legislative-administrative school, as espoused by William F. Willoughby, viewed the relationship and especially the accountability of administration to the legislative branch as a central focus. This latter school believed that there was a considerable distinction between what was meant by "executive" and "administrative" and that the constitution gave administrative power mainly to the Congress.

While the Congress was considering the Brownlow Committee's various proposals, the forces opposed to an increase in the administrative powers of the president at the expense of the Congress marshalled their arguments. One of the most eloquent was Lewis Meriam's (1883–1972)[24] general analysis of the problem of reorganization, *Reorganization of the National Government: What Does It Involve?*, published in 1939 through the Brookings Institution. Just as the Committee's report argues for increased presidential power, Meriam was cautioning against it. Reprinted here is Meriam's first chapter on the "Concepts of Reorganization." Forty years later the only surviving member of the Brownlow Committee would concede a point to Meriam. In considering Nixon's abuses of the enhanced powers of the presidency that he helped to create, Luther Gulick wrote that "we all assumed in the 1930s that all management, especially public management, flowed in a broad, strong stream of value-filled ethical performance. Were we blind or only naive until Nixon came along? Or were we so eager to 'take politics out of administration' that we threw the baby out with the bathwater?"[25]

It is possible to get the impression that during this formative period of public administration, most of the focus was on internal issues: management practices and problems; organizational behavior and structures; and budgeting and personnel issues. However, there was also ongoing a profound discussion, indeed a debate, over external issues—specifically the concept of administrative responsibility. Basically the issues involved were how can we ensure that governmental administration, in pursuit of being responsive to interest groups, executive and legislative forces, and constituencies, will act legally and responsibly?

These issues were hotly discussed in the late 1930s and early 1940s by Carl J. Friedrich (1901–) and Herman Finer (1898–1969). A lively debate ensued between the two. Friedrich argued that administrative responsibility is best assured internally, through professionalism or professional standards or codes. Internal checks and balances were necessary because the modern bureaucrat's policy expertise and specialized abilities were so extensive (necessarily so because of the increasing complexities of modern policies). Consequently, there was little real possibility for adequate review by an outside political or legislative source.[26]

Finer argued, on the other hand, that administrative responsibility could only be maintained externally through legislative or popular controls. External checks and balances were the only way to ensure subordination of bureaucrats because internal power of control would, ultimately, lead to corruption. In Finer's view, some form of electoral or legislative review was the only possible way to avoid abuses of bureaucratic power.[27]

But the classic overview of this problem of administrative responsibility and accountability comes from E. Pendleton Herring's (1903–)[28] 1937 book *Public Administration and the Public Interest.* Herring examines the problems posed by the dramatic increase in the scope of government and the influence of administrative discretion. He accepts that laws passed by legislatures, institutions designed for compromise, are necessarily the products of legislative compromise and thus often so vague that they are in need of further definition. The bureaucrat, by default, has the job of providing definition to the general principles embodied in a statute by issuing supplemental rules and regulations. "Upon the shoulders of the bureaucrat has been placed in large part the burden of reconciling group differences and making effective and workable the economic and social compromises arrived at through the legislative process." In effect, it becomes the job of the bureaucrat to ethically define the public interest.

Herring's discussion of the public interest and the critical roles played by bureaucrats and interest groups in public policy formulation correctly anticipated many of the critical issues still being grappled with in schools of public policy and administration today. Herring is a significant voice in what political science calls group theory, a school of thought that views government as representing various group interests and negotiating policy outcomes among them. According to Herring, the most basic task of a bureaucrat was to establish working relationships with the various special interests so that their concerns could be more efficiently brokered. While Herring looked upon this process as highly desirable, a quarter century later Theodore J. Lowi (see Chapter IV) would provide a devastating critique of why modern bureaucracy's penchant for establishing such harmonious working relationships is paralyzing modern government.

Accompanying the growing repudiation of scientific management as the sole body of administrative wisdom was a challenge to Weber's "ideal-type" bureaucracy. Even before it was widely available in an English translation, it sired a lively debate about its underlying premises. In a 1940 issue of the journal *Social Forces,* Robert K. Merton (1910–), one of the most influential of modern sociologists, published an article, "Bureaucratic Structure and Personality," which proclaimed that the "ideal-type" bureaucracy espoused by Weber had inhibiting dysfunctions—characteristics that prevented it from being optimally efficient. This is a theme that has been echoed equally by subsequent empirical studies and the polemics of politicians. In the 1950s, Merton slightly revised the article for inclusion in his collection of essays, *Social Theory and Social Structure.* The revision is reprinted here.

The 1930s saw the advent of increasingly larger government domestic programs and concomitant expenditures. Consequently, budgeting became of increasing importance. However, budgetary theory—that is, how to rationally allocate government resources—was woefully inadequate. The emphasis was on process and line-item budgeting, which stressed accountability and control. Performance budgeting, which stressed work measurement, much as scientific management, was increasingly advanced and used as an appropriate management-oriented budgetary process. Nevertheless, there remained little integration of the budgetary process with rational policy making and decision making. In 1940, V. O. Key, Jr. (1908–1963), the political scientist who was to play a leading role in the development of the behavioral approach to the study of American politics,[29] wrote an article bemoaning "The Lack of a Budgetary Theory." Greatly concerned about the overemphasis on mechanics, he posed what was soon acknowledged as the central question of budgeting—"On what basis shall it be decided to allocate X dollars to activity A instead of activity B?" Key then goes on to elaborate on what he felt were the major areas of inquiry that should be researched to develop a budgeting theory. This along with continuing pressure for even greater increases in the size of government programs would set the stage for the major advances to come in this critical subfield of public administration.

In the two decades plus that span the period between the world wars, American government changed dramatically. At the federal level, the New Deal's efforts to cope with a worldwide depression significantly and rapidly altered the traditional roles of government. Reforms in state government and city management were equally significant. Reactive roles gave way to proactive roles. Government organization would be dominated by new themes: centralization, management planning, performance measurement, and new forms of social programs. Still, there was uncertainty, both to the future of government and the focus of the field of public administration. In 1939, Leonard D. White published a revised edition of his pioneering textbook. His opening statement provides a fitting summary of the state of public administration at the end of this period of immense transformation:

> The decade which has passed since the first edition of this book has shaken the economic and political foundations of the contemporary world. The effect of the repeated crises of these years upon public administration has been great, exactly how great we cannot yet be sure. As a nation we are, however, slowly accepting the fact that the loose-jointed, easy-going somewhat irresponsible system of administration which we carried over from our rural agricultural background is no longer adequate for present and future needs. The council-manager form of municipal government, the reconstruction of state governments and their administrative disciplining by federal authorities, and the pending reform of the federal structure itself are unmistakable signs of adaption to new necessities.[30]

NOTES

1. For explanations for the growth of government during the 1920s, see: Geoffrey Perrett, *America in the Twenties: A History* (New York: Simon & Schuster, 1982), pp. 251–252, 426, 429, 431, 463, 490.
2. Dwight Waldo, *The Administrative State: A Study of the Political Theory of American Public Administration* (New York: Ronald Press, 1948), p. 206–207.
3. Vincent Ostrom, *The Intellectual Crisis in American Public Administration,* rev. ed. (University of Alabama Press, 1974), p. 36.
4. Nicholas Henry, *Public Administration and Public Affairs* (Englewood Cliffs, N.J.: Prentice-Hall, 1975), pp. 8–9.
5. Howard E. McCurdy, *Public Administration: A Bibliographic Guide to the Literature* (New York: Marcel Dekker, 1986), p. 22.
6. Waldo, p. 206.
7. For appreciations of White's varied intellectual contributions to public administration, see: John M. Gaus, "Leonard Dupree White 1891–1958," *Public Administration Review* 18 (Summer 1958); Herbert J. Storing, "Leonard D. White and the Study of Public Administration," *Public Administration Review* 25 (March 1965).
8. Leonard D. White, *Introduction to the Study of Public Administration* (New York: Macmillan, 1926), p. viii.

9. The fourth and last edition would be published in 1955.
10. White, p. 2.
11. Sometimes called the "Dean of American Public Administration," Gulick was the Eaton Professor of Municipal Science and Administration at Columbia University from 1931–1942; a close adviser to President Franklin D. Roosevelt from even before he became Governor of New York; and a founder of the Institute of Public Administration, the American Society for Public Administration, and the National Academy of Public Administration. For an appreciation of his career, see: Stephen K. Blumberg, "Seven Decades of Public Administration: A Tribute to Luther Gulick." *Public Administration Review* 41 (March–April 1981).
12. For her collected papers, see: Henry C. Metcalf and Lyndall Urwick, eds., *Dynamic Administration: The Collected Papers of Mary Parker Follett* (New York: Harper & Bros., 1942); For an appreciation of her contributions, see: Elliot M. Fox, "Mary Parker Follett: The Enduring Contribution," *Public Administration Review* 28 (December 1968).
13. For a biography, see: Lyndall F. Urwick, *The Life and Work of Elton Mayo* (London: Urwick, Orr & Partners, Ltd., 1960).
14. The definitive account of the studies themselves is to be found in F. J. Roethlisberger and William J. Dickson's *Management and the Worker* (Cambridge, Mass.: Harvard University Press, 1939).
15. Cambridge, Mass.: Harvard University Press, 1938). Barnard's only other book was *Organization and Management: Selected Papers* (Cambridge, Mass.: Harvard University Press, 1948).
16. For biographical information, see: William B. Wolf, *The Basic Barnard: An Introduction to Chester I. Barnard and His Theories of Organization and Management* (Ithaca, N.Y.: New York State School of Industrial and Labor Relations, Cornell University, 1974).
17. Harold Seidman, *Politics, Position, and Power: The Dynamics of Federal Organization,* 3rd ed. (New York: Oxford University Press, 1980).
18. Frederick C. Mosher, *Government Reorganization: Cases and Commentary* (Indianapolis, Ind.: Bobbs-Merrill, 1967).
19. Peter L. Szanton, ed., *Federal Reorganization: What Have We Learned?* (Chatham, N.J.: Chatham House, 1981).
20. For Brownlow's autobiography, see: *A Passion for Politics: The Autobiography of Louis Brownlow, First Half* (Chicago: University of Chicago Press, 1955); *A Passion for Anonymity: The Autobiography of Louis Brownlow, Second Half* (Chicago: University of Chicago Press, 1958). For a more objective appreciation, see: Barry D. Karl, "Louis Brownlow," *Public Administration Review* 39 (November–December 1979).
21. For histories of the Brownlow Committee and executive reorganization in the New Deal, see: Barry Karl, *Executive Reorganization and Reform in the New Deal* (Cambridge, Mass.: Harvard University Press, 1963); Richard Polenberg, *Reorganizing Roosevelt's Government: The Controversy over Executive Reorganization, 1936–1939* (Cambridge, Mass.: Harvard University Press, 1966).
22. In the 1983 case of *Immigration and Naturalization Service v. Chadha* the U.S. Supreme Court questioned the constitutionality of congressional vetoes.
23. For example, the Committee recommended "the reorganization of the Civil Service Commission as a central personnel agency." This would not happen until the Civil Service Reform Act of 1978.
24. Meriam, a Brookings Institution staff member, was the liaison between the Brownlow Committee and Brookings, which at the time was working for a congressional committee that was largely opposed to the Brownlow Committee's call for enhanced executive powers. For a biographical portrait, see: Donald T. Critchlow, "Lewis Meriam, Expertise, and Indian Reform," *The Historian* 43 No. 4 (May 1981).
25. Blumberg, p. 247.
26. Carl J. Friedrich, "The Nature of Administrative Responsibility," in *Public Policy,* ed. Carl J. Friedrich (Cambridge, Mass.: Harvard University Press, 1940).
27. Herman Finer, "Administrative Responsibility in Democratic Government," *Public Administration Review* 1 (Autumn 1941).

28. Herring, a Harvard professor who would later spend twenty years as president of the Social Science Research Council (1948–1968), also wrote a pioneering study on the role of pressure groups, *Group Representation Before Congress* (New York: Russell & Russell, 1929), and one of the first studies on the relationship between a manager's background and behavior in office, *Federal Commissioners: A Study of Their Careers and Qualifications* (Cambridge, Mass.: Harvard University Press, 1936).
29. Key's major works included: *Politics, Parties and Pressure Groups* (New York: Crowell, 1942; 5th ed., 1964); *Southern Politics in State and Nation* (New York: Alfred A. Knopf, 1949); *American State Politics: An Introduction* (New York: Alfred A. Knopf, 1956); *Public Opinion and American Democracy* (New York: Alfred A. Knopf, 1961).
30. Leonard D. White, *Introduction to the Study of Public Administration,* rev. ed. (New York: Macmillan, 1939), p. xiv.

A CHRONOLOGY OF PUBLIC ADMINISTRATION: 1918–1941

1918 William F. Willoughby in *The Movement Towards Budgetary Reform in the States* outlined developments that were leading to the creation of modern budget systems.

1919 The failure of the Boston police strike sets back municipal unionization and makes Calvin Coolidge, the governor of Massachusetts, a national hero.

The Eighteenth Amendment, Prohibition, is ratified; the Volstead Act is passed to enforce it.

1920 The Retirement Act creates the first federal service pension system.

The Nineteenth Amendment giving women the right to vote is ratified.

1921 The Budget and Accounting Act establishes the Bureau of the Budget in the Department of the Treasury and the General Accounting Office as an agency of the Congress.

The Port of New York Authority is created by the states of New York and New Jersey.

1922 Max Weber's structural definition of bureaucracy is published posthumously; it uses an "ideal-type" approach to extrapolate from the real world the central core of features that characterizes the most fully developed form of bureaucratic organization.

1923 The Classification Act brings position classification to Washington-based federal employees and establishes the principle of equal pay for equal work.

The Teapot Dome scandals reveal widespread corruption in the Harding administration.

1924 The Maxwell School of Citizenship and Public Affairs is established at Syracuse University to offer graduate work in the social sciences and public administration.

Hawthorne studies began at the Hawthorne Works of the Western Electric Company in Chicago; they will last until 1932 and lead to new thinking about the relationship of work environment to productivity.

Rogers Act creates merit-based career system for the Department of State.

1926 Leonard D. White's *Introduction to the Study of Public Administration* is the first text in public administration.

The first factor comparison position classification system was installed by Eugene J. Benge at the Philadelphia Transit Company (the federal government would adopt this kind of system in 1975).

Mary Parker Follett in calling for "power with" as opposed to "power over" anticipates the movement toward more participatory management styles.

1927 The Brookings Institution is formed.

1929 The University of Southern California establishes the first independent professional school of public administration.

1930 Durham County, South Carolina, is first to install county-manager form of county government.

1931 Mooney and Reiley in *Onward Industry* (republished in 1939 as *The Principles of Organization*) show how the newly discovered "principles of organization" have really been known since ancient times.

Congress designates "The Star Spangled Banner" as the national anthem.

1932 Wisconsin passes the nation's first unemployment insurance law.

1933 President Franklin D. Roosevelt's New Deal begins.

Francis Perkins, the first woman in a president's cabinet, is appointed Secretary of Labor.

The Eighteenth Amendment, Prohibition, is repealed.

Elton Mayo's *The Human Problems of an Industrial Civilization* is the first major report on the Hawthorne studies; the first significant call for a human relations movement.

The Tennessee Valley Authority (TVA) is established by Congress as an independent public corporation.

1935 The National Labor Relations (Wagner) Act establishes the right of private sector employees to organize and bargain collectively.

Social Security program is created.

The Commission of Inquiry on Public Service Personnel publishes a major study of government personnel practices, *Better Government Personnel;* many of the Commission's recommendations would find their way into the 1939 Brownlow Committee report.

1936 J. Donald Kingsley and William E. Mosher's *Public Personnel Administration* becomes the first text in this field.

John Maynard Keynes publishes his *General Theory of Employment, Interest and Money,* which calls for using a government's fiscal and monetary policies to positively influence a capitalistic economy.

The President's Committee on Administrative Management is established; known as the Brownlow Committee after its chairman, Louis Brownlow (the other two members were Charles Merriam and Luther Gulick), it will examine the organization of the executive branch.

E. Pendleton Herring in *Public Administration and the Public Interest* asserts that bureaucrats, by default, must often be the arbiters of the public interest.

1937 The Brownlow Committee's report says that the "President needs help" and calls for the reorganization of the executive branch.

Luther Gulick and Lyndall Urwick edit the *Papers on the Science of Administration,* an attempt to summarize the state of the art of organization theory that is now considered to be the high water mark of public administration's "period of orthodoxy"; Gulick's "Notes on the Theory of Organization," which calls attention to the various functional elements of the work of an executive with his mnemonic device POSDCORB, was first published in this collection.

1938 The Fair Labor Standards Act provides minimum wages, overtime pay, and limits on child labor.

Chester I. Barnard's *The Functions of the Executive,* his sociological analysis of organizations, encourages and foreshadows the postwar revolution in thinking about organizational behavior.

1939 American Society for Public Administration is founded.

The Reorganization Act enables the creation of the Executive Office of the President and the transfer of the Bureau of the Budget from the Treasury to the White House.

Lewis Meriam's *Reorganization of the National Government* offers arguments against the expansion of executive powers at the expense of the Congress.

The Hatch Act passed to prohibit political activities by federal employees (the next year it was amended to also prohibit political activities by state and local government employees who were paid with federal funds).

Roethlisberger and Dickson publish *Management and the Worker,* the definitive account of the Hawthorne studies.

The federal government first requires the states to have merit systems for employees in programs aided by federal funds.

1940 Robert K. Merton's article "Bureaucratic Structure and Personality" proclaimed that Max Weber's "ideal-type" bureaucracy had inhibiting dysfunctions leading to inefficiency and worse.

Carl J. Friedrich in "The Nature of Administrative Responsibility" asserts that accountability and responsibility are best assured internally through professionalism and professional standards.

Public Administration Review is first published; Leonard D. White is its first editor.

V. O. Key, Jr., bemoans "The Lack of a Budgetary Theory" in the *American Political Science Review.*

1941 James Burnham in *The Managerial Revolution* asserts that as the control of large organizations passes from the hands of the owners into the hands of professional administrators, the society's new governing class will be the possessors not of wealth but of technical expertise.

Herman Finer in "Administrative Responsibility in Democratic Government" argues that accountability and responsibility can only be maintained externally through legislative or popular controls.

Japanese sneak attack on Pearl Harbor brings the United States into World War II.

5
Bureaucracy
Max Weber

1. CHARACTERISTICS OF BUREAUCRACY

Modern officialdom functions in the following specific manner:

I. *There is the principle of fixed and official jurisdictional areas, which are generally ordered by rules, that is, by laws or administrative regulations.* [Italics added]

1. The regular activities required for the purposes of the bureaucratically governed structure are distributed in a fixed way as official duties.
2. The authority to give the commands required for the discharge of these duties is distributed in a stable way and is strictly delimited by rules concerning the coercive means, physical, sacerdotal, or otherwise, which may be placed at the disposal of officials.
3. Methodical provision is made for the regular and continuous fulfillment of these duties and for the execution of the corresponding rights; only persons who have the generally regulated qualifications to serve are employed.

In public and lawful government these three elements constitute "bureaucratic authority." In private economic domination, they constitute bureaucratic "management." Bureaucracy, thus understood, is fully developed in political and ecclesiastical communities only in the modern state, and, in the private economy, only in the most advanced institutions of capitalism. Permanent and public office authority, with fixed jurisdiction, is not the historical rule but rather the exception. This is so even in large political structures such as those of the ancient Orient, the Germanic and Mongolian empires of conquest, or of many feudal structures of state. In all these cases, the ruler executes the most important measures through personal trustees, table-companions, or court-servants. Their commissions and authority are not precisely delimited and are temporarily called into being for each case.

II. *The principles of office hierarchy and of levels of graded authority mean a firmly ordered system of super- and subordination in which there is a supervision of the lower offices by the higher ones.* Such a system offers the governed the possibility of appealing the decision of a lower office to its higher authority, in a definitely regulated manner. With the full development of the bureaucratic type, the office hierarchy is monocratically organized. The principle of hierarchical office authority is found in all bureaucratic structures: in state and ecclesiastical structures as well as in large party organizations and private enterprises. It does not matter for the character of bureaucracy whether its authority is called "private" or "public."

When the principle of jurisdictional "competency" is fully carried through, hierarchical subordination—at least in public office—does not mean that the "higher" authority is simply authorized to take over the business of the "lower." Indeed, the opposite is the rule. Once established and having fulfilled its task, an office tends to continue in existence and be held by another incumbent.

III. *The management of the modern office is based upon written documents ("the files"), which are preserved in their original or draught form.* There is, therefore, a staff of subaltern officials and scribes of all sorts. The body of officials actively engaged in a "public" office, along with the respective apparatus of material implements and the files, make up a "bureau." In private enterprise, "the bureau" is often called "the office."

In principle, the modern organization of the civil service separates the bureau from the private domicile of the official, and, in general, bureaucracy segregates official activity as something distinct from the sphere of private life. Public monies and equipment are divorced from the private property of the official. This condition is everywhere the product of a long development. Nowadays, it is found in public as well as in private enterprises; in the latter, the principle extends even to the leading entrepreneur. In principle, the executive office is separated from the household, business from private correspondence, and business assets from private fortunes. The more consistently the modern type of business management has been carried through the more are these separations the case. The beginnings of this process are to be found as early as the Middle Ages.

It is the peculiarity of the modern entrepreneur that he conducts himself as the "first official" of his enterprise, in the very same way in which the ruler of a specifically modern bureaucratic state spoke of himself as "the first servant" of the state. The idea that the bureau activities of the state are intrinsically different in character from the management of private economic offices is a continental European notion and, by way of contrast, is totally foreign to the American way.

IV. *Office management, at least all specialized office management—and such management is distinctly modern—usually presupposes thorough and expert training.* This increasingly holds for the modern executive and employee of private enterprises, in the same manner as it holds for the state official.

V. *When the office is fully developed, official activity demands the full working capacity of the official, irrespective of the fact that his obligatory time in the bureau may be firmly delimited.* In the normal case, this is only the product of a long development, in the public as well as in the private office. Formerly, in all cases, the normal state of affairs was reversed: official business was discharged as a secondary activity.

VI. *The management of the office follows general rules, which are more or less stable, more or less exhaustive, and which can be learned.* Knowledge of these rules represents a special technical learning which the officials possess. It involves jurisprudence, or administrative or business management.

The reduction of modern office management to rules is deeply embedded in its very nature. The theory of modern public administration, for instance, assumes that the authority to order certain matters by decree—which as been legally granted to public authorities—does not entitle the bureau to regulate the matter by commands given for each case, but only to regulate the matter abstractly. This stands in extreme contrast to the regulation of all relationships through individual privileges and bestowals of favor, which is absolutely dominant in patrimonialism, at least in so far as such relationships are not fixed by sacred tradition.

2. THE POSITION OF THE OFFICIAL

All this results in the following for the internal and external position of the official:

I. *Office holding is a "vocation."* This is shown, first, in the requirement of a firmly prescribed course of training, which demands the entire capacity for work for a long period of time, and in the generally prescribed and special examinations which are prerequisites of employment. Furthermore, the position of the official is in the nature of a duty. This determines the internal structure of his relations, in the following manner: Legally and actually, office holding is not considered a source to be exploited for rents or emoluments, as was normally the case during the Middle Ages and frequently up to the threshold of recent times. Nor is office holding considered a usual exchange of services for equivalents, as is the case with free labor contracts. Entrance into an office, including one in the private economy, is considered an acceptance of a specific obligation of faithful management in return for a secure existence. It is decisive for the specific nature of modern loyalty to an office that, in the pure type, it does not establish a relationship to a *person,* like the vassal's or disciple's faith in feudal or in patrimonial relations of authority. Modern loyalty is devoted to impersonal and functional purposes. Behind the functional purposes, of course, "ideas of culture-values" usually stand. These are *ersatz* for the earthly or supra-mundane personal master: ideas such as "state," "church," "community," "party," or "enterprise" are thought of as being realized in a community; they provide an ideological halo for the master.

The political official—at least in the fully developed modern state—is not considered the personal servant of a ruler. Today, the bishop, the priest, and the preacher are in fact no longer, as in early Christian times, holders of purely personal charisma. The supra-mundane and sacred values which they offer are given to everybody who seems to be worthy of them and who asks for them. In former times, such leaders acted upon the personal command of their master; in principle, they were responsible only to him. Nowadays, in spite of the partial survival of the old theory, such religious leaders are officials in the service of a functional purpose, which in the present-day "church" has become routinized and, in turn, ideologically hallowed.

II. *The personal position of the official is patterned in the following way:*

1. Whether he is in a private office or a public bureau, the modern official always strives and usually enjoys a distinct *social esteem* as compared with the governed. His social position is guaranteed by the prescriptive rules of rank order and, for the political official, by special definitions of the criminal code against "insults of officials" and "contempt" of state and church authorities.

The actual social position of the official is normally highest where, as in old civilized countries, the following conditions prevail: a strong demand for administration by trained experts; a strong and stable social differentiation, where the official predominantly derives from socially and economically privileged strata because of the social distribution of power; or where the costliness of the required training and status conventions are binding upon him. The possession of educational certificates—to be discussed elsewhere—are usually linked with qualification for office. Naturally, such certificates or patents enhance the "status element" in the social position of the official. For the rest this status factor in individual cases is explicitly and impassively acknowledged; for example, in the prescription that the acceptance or rejection of an aspirant to an official career depends upon the consent ("election") of the members of the official body. This is the case in the German army with the officer corps. Similar phenomena, which promote this guild-like closure of officialdom, are typically found in patrimonial and, particularly, in prebendal officialdoms of the past. The desire to resurrect such phenomena in changed forms is by no means infrequent among modern bureaucrats. For instance, they have played a role among the demands of the quite proletarian and expert officials (the *tretyj* element) during the Russian revolution.

Usually the social esteem of the officials as such is especially low where the demand for expert administration and the dominance of status conventions are weak. This is especially the case in the United States; it is often the case in new settlements by virtue of their wide fields for profitmaking and the great instability of their social stratification.

2. The pure type of bureaucratic official is *appointed* by a superior authority. An official elected by the governed is not a purely bureaucratic figure. Of course, the formal existence of an election does not by itself mean that no appointment hides behind the election—in the state, especially, appointment by party chiefs. Whether or not this is the case does not depend upon legal statutes but upon the way in which the party mechanism functions. Once firmly organized, the parties can turn a formally free election into the mere acclamation of a candidate designated by the party chief. As a rule, however, a formally free election is turned into a fight, conducted according to definite rules, for votes in favor of one of two designated candidates.

In all circumstances, the designation of officials by means of an election among the governed modifies the strictness of hierarchical subordination. In principle, an official who is so elected has an autonomous position opposite the superordinate official. The elected official does not derive his position "from above" but "from below" or at least not from a superior authority of the official hierarchy but from powerful party men ("bosses"), who also determine his further career. The career of the elected official is not, or at least not primarily, dependent upon his chief in the administration. The official who is not elected but appointed by a chief normally functions more exactly, from a technical point of view, because, all other circumstances being equal, it is more likely that purely functional points of consideration and qualities will determine his selection and career. As laymen, the governed can become acquainted with the extent to which a candidate is expertly qualified for office only in terms of experience, and hence only after his service. Moreover, in every sort of selection of officials by election, parties quite naturally give decisive weight not to expert considerations but to the services a follower renders to the party boss. This holds for all kinds of procurement of officials by elections, for the designation of formally free, elected officials by party bosses when they determine the slate of candidates, or the free appointment by a chief who has himself been elected. The contrast, however, is relative: substantially similar conditions hold where legitimate monarchs and their subordinates appoint officials, except that the influence of the followings are then less controllable.

Where the demand for administration by trained experts is considerable, and the party followings have to recognize an intellectually developed, educated, and freely moving "public opinion," the use of unqualified officials falls back upon the party in power at the next election. Naturally, this is more likely to happen when the officials are appointed by the chief. The demand for a trained administration now exists in the United States, but in the large cities, where immigrant votes are "corraled," there is, of course, no educated public opinion. Therefore, popular elections of the administrative chief and also of his subordinate officials usually endanger the expert qualification of the official as well as the precise functioning of the bureaucratic mechanism. It also weakens the dependence of the officials upon the hierarchy. This holds at least for the large administrative bodies that are difficult to supervise. The superior qualification and integrity of federal judges, appointed by the President, as over against elected judges in the United States is well known, although both types of officials have been selected primarily in terms of party considerations. The great changes in American metropolitan administrations demanded by reformers have proceeded essentially from elected mayors working with an apparatus of officials who were appointed by them. These reforms have thus come about in a "Caesarist" fashion. Viewed technically, as an organized form of authority, the efficiency of "Caesarism," which often grows out of democracy, rests in general upon the position of the "Caesar" as a free trustee of the masses (of the army or of the citizenry), who is unfettered by tradition. The "Caesar" is thus the unrestrained master of a body of highly qualified military officers and officials whom he selects freely and personally without regard to tradition or to any other considerations. This "rule of the personal genius," however, stands in contradiction to the formally "democratic" principle of a universally elected officialdom.

3. Normally, the position of the official is held for life, at least in public bureaucracies; and this is increasingly the case for all similar structures. As a factual rule, *tenure for life* is presupposed, even where the giving of notice or periodic reappointment occurs. In contrast to the worker in a private enterprise, the official normally holds tenure. Legal or actual life-tenure, however, is not recognized as the official's right to the possession of office, as was the case with many structures of authority in the past. Where legal guarantees against arbitrary dismissal or transfer are developed, they merely serve to guarantee a strictly objective discharge of specific office duties free from all personal considerations. In Germany, this is the case for all juridical and, increasingly, for all administrative officials.

Within the bureaucracy, therefore, the measure of "independence," legally guaranteed by tenure, is not always a source of increased status for the official whose position is thus secured. Indeed, often the reverse holds, especially in old cultures and communities that are highly differentiated. In such communities, the stricter the subordination under the arbitrary rule of the master, the more it guarantees the maintenance of the conventional seigneurial style of living for the official. Because of the very absence of these legal guarantees of tenure, the conventional esteem for the official may rise in the same way as, during the Middle Ages, the esteem of the nobility of office rose at the expense of esteem for the freemen, and as the king's judge surpassed that of the people's judge. In Germany, the military officer or the administrative official can be removed from office at any time, or at least far more readily than the "independent judge," who never pays with loss of his office for even the grossest offense against the "code of honor" or against social conventions of the salon. For this very reason, if other things are equal, in the eyes of the master stratum the judge is considered less qualified for social intercourse than are officers and administrative officials, whose greater dependence on the master is a greater guarantee of their conformity with status conventions. Of course, the average official strives for a civil-service law, which would materially secure his old age and provide increased guarantees against his arbitrary removal from office. This striving, however, has its limits. A very strong development of the "right to the office" naturally makes it more difficult to staff them with regard to technical efficiency, for such a development decreases the career-opportunities of ambitious candidates for office. This makes for the fact that officials, on the whole, do not feel their dependency upon those at the top. This lack of a feeling of dependency, however, rests primarily upon the inclination to depend upon one's equals rather than upon the socially inferior and governed strata. The present conservative movement among the Badenia clergy, occasioned by the anxiety of a presumably threatening separation of church and state, has been expressly determined by the desire not to be turned "from a master into a servant of the parish."

4. The official receives the regular *pecuniary* compensation of a normally fixed *salary* and the old age security provided by a pension. The salary is not measured like a wage in terms of work done, but according to "status," that is, according to the kind of function (the "rank") and, in addition, possibly, according to the length of service. The relatively great security of the official's income, as well as the rewards of social esteem, make the office a sought-after position, especially in countries which no longer provide opportunities for colonial profits. In such countries, this situation permits relatively low salaries for officials.
5. The official is set for a "*career*" within the hierarchical order of the public service. He moves from the lower, less important, and lower paid to the higher positions. The average official naturally desires a mechanical fixing of the conditions of promotion: if not of the offices, at least of the salary levels. He wants these conditions fixed in terms of "seniority," or possibly according to grades achieved in a developed system of expert examinations. Here and there, such examinations actually form character *indelebilis* of the official and have lifelong effects on his career. To this is joined the desire to qualify the right to office and the increasing tendency toward status group closure and economic security. All of this makes for a tendency to consider the offices as "prebends" of those who are qualified by educational certificates. The necessity of taking general personal and intellectual qualifications into consideration, irrespective of the often subaltern character of the educational certificate, has led to a condition in which the highest political offices, especially the positions of "ministers," are principally filled without reference to such certificates.

6

Introduction to the Study of Public Administration

Leonard D. White

PREFACE

Curiously enough, commentators on American political institutions have never produced a systematic analysis of our administrative system except from the point of view of the lawyer. Until the last few years even the text books have obstinately closed their eyes to this enormous terrain, studded with governmental problems of first magnitude and fascinating interest; and even today they dismiss the subject with a casual chapter. But certainly no one pretends that administration can still be put aside "as a practical detail which clerks could arrange after doctors had agreed upon principles."

The fact is that the last two decades have produced a voluminous literature dealing with the business side of government. The present volume represents an attempt to bring together the salient facts of American experience and observation and to deal with them analytically and critically. To accomplish this within the limits of a single volume is no easy task, implying as it does a constant danger of falling prey either to the Scylla of indiscriminate detail or the Charybdis of unsupported generalization. The total lack of any charted passage through these unexplored waters adds much to the hazards of the venture.

The book rests upon at least four assumptions. It assumes that administration is a single process, substantially uniform in its essential characteristics wherever observed, and therefore avoids the study of municipal administration, state administration, or federal administration as such. It assumes that the study of administration should start from the base of management rather than the foundation of law, and is therefore more absorbed in the affairs of the American Management Association than in the decisions of the courts. It assumes that administration is still primarily an art but attaches importance to the significant tendency to transform it into a science. It assumes that administration has become, and will continue to be the heart of the problem of modern government.

CHAPTER ONE ADMINISTRATION AND THE MODERN STATE

Management has gradually become a profession. Its task has increased in difficulty, responsibility, and complexity, until today it touches all the sciences, from chemistry and mechanics to psychology and medicine. It calls to its service, therefore, men and women with tact and ideals, with the highest scientific qualifications and with a strong capacity for organization and leadership. It is employing lawyers and doctors, accountants and artists, and by directing their professions, is forming a supreme profession of its own, with all the implications consequent upon such a line of progress of standards, qualifications, apprenticeship, and technique.

OLIVER SHELDON: *Philosophy of Management.*

1. The Scope and Nature of Public Administration

There is an essential unity in the process of administration, whether it be observed in city, state, or federal governments, that precludes a "stratified" classification of the subject. To treat it in terms of municipal administration, state administration, or national administration, is to imply a distinction that in reality does not exist. The fundamental problems such as the development of personal initiative, the assurance of individual competence and integrity, responsibility, coordination, fiscal supervision, leadership, morale are in fact the same; and most of the subjects of administration defy the political boundaries of local and state government. Health administration, the licensing of medical practitioners, the control of trade, the reclamation of waste lands, have little fact relation to cities or counties or states as such. Nor do the respective phases of city, state, or federal government present any significant variation in the technique of their administration. At the outset, therefore, it seems important to insist that the administrative process is a unit, and to conceive it not as municipal administration, or state administration, or federal administration, but as a process common to all levels of government.

Public administration is the management of men and materials in the accomplishment of the purposes of the state. This definition emphasizes the managerial phase of administration and minimizes its legalistic and formal aspect.

It relates the conduct of government business to the conduct of the affairs of any other social organization, commercial, philanthropic, religious, or educational, in all of which good management is recognized as an element essential to success. It leaves open the question to what extent the administration itself participates in formulating the purposes of the state, and avoids any controversy as to the precise nature of administrative action.[1]

The objective of public administration is the most efficient utilization of the resources at the disposal of officials and employees. These resources include not only current appropriations and material equipment in the form of public buildings, machinery, highways and canals, but also the human resources bound up in the hundreds of thousands of men and women who work for the state. In every direction good administration seeks the elimination of waste, the conservation of material and energy, and the most rapid and complete achievement of public purposes consistent with economy and the welfare of the workers.

The actual functioning of this branch of government may perhaps be made more realistic by an account of what takes place in a great department in the course of a day. For purposes of illustration a health department in a large city will suffice. Business commences at nine o'clock, when most of the employees are presumably at their desks. As they enter the office, they sign a time sheet or punch a time clock, dispose of their outer garments in lockers, exchange comment with their neighbors and settle down for the day's work. A steady stream of business develops; telephone calls from citizens, from field inspectors, and from special detail; window calls on a great variety of topics large and small; telegraphic reports from a neighboring city in which an epidemic is threatening; conferences within the bureaus; conferences between bureaus; messengers hurrying back and forth; policemen from local health stations bringing in samples for analysis, and anxious citizens seeking the results of samples brought in yesterday; a deputation from the undertakers protesting against the condition of the hospital morgues; an alderman seeking appointment for a local supporter; a score of prostitutes waiting in the anteroom for examination before appearing in the courtroom; a salesman protesting against the award of a contract for laboratory supplies; a handful of loiterers whispering in casual groups in the corridors, all seeming to the uninitiated observer the height of confusion and disorder. Further observation, however, dispels the first impression; the various kinds of work are segregated and assigned to specially trained men and women; certain types of inquiry or complaint are handled by a standardized method; forms are made out and sent on the proper route for final disposition; some business is transacted by a clerk, other business is referred to the assistant bureau chief, so that by a process of selection routine work is disposed of by the lower ranks of the service, while matters of importance are brought to the attention of the higher officials. Thus proceeds in an orderly fashion all the complicated business of the office; some spend the day making out forms, others filing correspondence, some answering telephone complaints and directing inspectors, others dictating correspondence, making bacteriological analyses, inspecting ventilation systems, granting licenses, making blue prints, while at the head of the service, the commissioner of public health maintains the necessary connections of the department with the city council and the mayor, with the party organization, with the finance committee, with the public, and with the health authorities of the state and the United States, not neglecting meanwhile to assure himself of the proper operation of the many phases of the work of the department itself.

All of this is a far cry from the Egyptian scribe who laboriously copied accounts on his roll of papyrus, but the natural history of administration connects its ancient and modern forms in an unbroken sequence of development. The process of specialization has indeed wrought a prodigious transformation in methods, but the essential administrative duties connected with military affairs, with finance, with the "king's" household are still performed with the same objectives as in ages past. What differentiates the modern public official from the scribe of antiquity is the marvelous material equipment with which he works, and the contribution which science has made, and continues to make, to his profession.

Public administration is, then, the execution of the public business; the goal of administrative activity the most expeditious, economical, and complete achievement of public programs. This obviously is not the sole objective of the state as an organized unit; the protection of private rights, the development of civic capacity and sense of civic responsibility, the due recognition of the manifold phases of public opinion, the maintenance of order, the provision of a national minimum of welfare, all bespeak the constant solicitude of the state. Administration must be correlated with other branches of government, as well as adjusted to the immense amount of private effort which in America far more than elsewhere supplements public enterprise. The following chapter deals with these adjustments, but here it is desirable to differentiate the adjacent fields of administration and administrative law.

It is said that "administrative law is that part of the public law which fixes the organization and determines the competence of the administrative authorities, and indicates to the individual remedies for the violation of his rights."[2] This definition rightly indicates that the subject matter belongs to the field of law, and points to its major objective, the protection of private rights. The objective of public administration is the efficient conduct of public business.

These two goals are not only different, but may at times conflict. Administration is of course bound by the rules of administrative law, as well as by the prescriptions of constitutional law; but within the boundaries thus set, it seeks the most effective accomplishment of public purposes. The whole matter is tersely set forth by Professor Freund.[3]

> The thought of those interested in public administration seems at the present time to be mainly concerned with problems of efficiency. This is easy to understand. With the rapid expansion of governmental control over all kinds of important interests we have, on the whole, held fast to the self-governmental theory of administrative organization which is not productive of the highest degree of expert knowledge and skill.
>
> Yet increased administrative powers call for increased safeguards against their abuses, and as long as there is the possibility of official error, partiality or excess of zeal, the protection of private right is as important an object as the effectuation of some governmental policy.

Students of government are familiar with the traditional division of governmental activities into the legislative, executive, and judicial.[4] It is important to understand that the work of the administration involves all three types of activity, although a strict application of the theory of separation of power would seem to confine it to "executive" business. After pointing out that the administrative commission exercises an authority which is in part executive, in part legislative, and in part judicial, Croly asserts "it is simply a means of consolidating the divided activities of government for certain practical social purposes," and proceeds to give a reasoned defense of this fusion of powers.[5] Administration more and more tends in fact to reach into the established fields of legislation and adjudication, raising important problems which will be the subject of study in later chapters.

Students of public affairs are gradually discerning, in fact, that administration has become the heart of the modern problem of government. In an earlier and simpler age, legislative bodies had the time to deal with the major issues, the character of which was suited to the deliberations of the lay mind; they were primarily problems involving judgments on important questions of political ethics, such as the enfranchisement of citizens by abolishing property qualifications, the disposition of the public land, the disestablishment of the Anglican Church, or the liberalization of a monarchist state. The problems which crowd upon legislative bodies today are often entangled with, or become exclusively technical questions which the layman can handle only by utilizing the services of the expert. The control of local government, the regulation of utilities, the enforcement of the prohibition amendment, the appropriation for a navy, the organization of a health department, the maintenance of a national service of agricultural research, are all matters which can be put upon the statute book only with the assistance of men who know the operating details in each case. So we discover in the administrative service one official who knows all that can be known about the control of water-borne diseases, another who has at his fingertips the substance of all available information on wheat rust, and another who cannot be "stumped" on appropriations for the national park service. These men are not merely useful to legislators overwhelmed by the increasing flood of bills; they are simply indispensable. They are the government. One may indeed suggest that the traditional assignment of the legislature as the pivotal agency in the governmental triumvirate is destined at no distant date to be replaced by a more realistic analysis which will establish government as the task of administration, operating within such areas as may be circumscribed by legislatures and courts.

2. The Emergence of Administration

It is from Great Britain of course that the United States derived its administrative institutions. Our local governments were patterned after the English model in the seventeenth century. Decentralized, self-governmental, dominated by the "squirearchy," they proved to be readily adaptable to the economic and social conditions of the New World. Even today the main lines of our administrative structure are profoundly influenced by their English origin; nowhere in the American commonwealths can be found the prototype of the continental intendant or his successor, the prefect.

But the modern social and economic environment in which administration operates, and the insistent demand for a greater and greater degree of state intervention are destined to force the issue whether a modern industrial, interventionist state can possibly operate on the restricted base of voluntary and substantially amateur effort which characterizes our administrative inheritance. The problems with which officials must grapple are now so varied in scope, so technical in character, so insistent for solution that it hardly seems possible that the state can hold its own except by adopting at least some of the essentials of bureaucratic administration. Is it not now imperative for democratic states to derive the advantage of a civil service characterized by permanence of tenure, special training for official position, professional interest on the part of the public official, undivided loyalty to the interests of the state? No one will understand that this suggestion is in favor of autocratic as contrasted with democratic institutions. But democracies can fruitfully borrow from more highly organized administrative systems those elements which can be properly adapted to their fundamental political institutions in order to make more effective the achievement of their own purposes and programs.

The fact is that the role of administration in the modern state is profoundly affected by the general political and cultural environment of the age. The *laissez faire* school of social philosophy, demanding the restriction of state activities to the bare minimum of external protection and police, created a situation in which administration was restricted in scope and feeble in operation. Officialdom was thought a necessary evil, bureaucracy an ever-present danger. On the continent irresponsible governments, able within large limits to defy the wishes of the people, and themselves often without programs of social betterment, contributed powerfully to the philosophic argument in favor of nonintervention by the state.

The industrial revolution and its many social, economic, and political implications are fundamentally responsible for the new social philosophy and the new concept of public administration. *Laissez faire* has been abandoned by philosophers and statesmen alike, and a new era of collective activity has been ushered in by the twentieth century. The expansion of industry on a national and international scale, the growth of transportation by railroad, motor truck and airplane, the transformation of communication by modern postal systems, the press, the telegraph, telephone, wireless and radio, the enormously increasing mobility of persons and ideas, the urbanization of industrial states and the crystallization of powerful social classes and economic interests have not only increased the area and intensity of administrative activity, but also have added new types of problems and magnified the importance and the difficulty of the old.

The industrial revolution has necessitated, in short, a degree of social cooperation in which *laissez faire* has become impossible; and gradually the new environment is building up in men's minds a conception of the rôle of the state which approximates the function assigned to it by the conditions of modern life. These new ideas involve the acceptance of the state as a great agency of social cooperation, as well as an agency of social regulation. The state becomes therefore an important means by which the program of social amelioration is effected. "The power of the civil service is increasing," writes an English scholar, "for the state has given up its old rôle of acting, in Lassalle's phrase, as night-watchman, as a mere dispenser of justice in the strictest sense of the word. Today it acts on the theory that the good of the individual and of society may be discovered by the processes of social reason and action, and be implemented through statutes."[6]

The enlarging positive program of the state does not imply by any means a corresponding diminution of its repressive and regulative activities. The struggle of classes over the distribution of the social surplus has led to the intervention of the state on behalf of the economically weak (children, women, laboring classes) by insistence on minimum wage, limited hours of labor, and healthful working conditions; the persistence of various groups of "reformers" has brought about prohibitions and regulations of divers kinds (sale of cigarettes, narcotics, alcohol, censorship of motion pictures); the need for guaranteeing so far as possible the integrity of the processes of self-government has led to the regulation of elections and political parties, and the elaboration of such repressive legislation as corrupt practice acts.

In every direction, therefore, the task of the modern state is enlarging. In every direction likewise the range of public administration is being extended, for every phase of the new program of the state is reflected in additional administrative activity.

For these reasons it is not surprising that in the last two decades increasing attention has been given to the business side of government. The remarkable thing is that for over a hundred years of our national existence, the only phase of administration to emerge in the arena of national issues was the spoils system. In a brilliant essay Wilson explained the American failure to grasp the importance of sound administration. Writing in the *Political Science Quarterly*, he pointed out:

> No one wrote systematically of administration as a branch of the science of government until the present century had passed its first youth and had begun to put forth its characteristic flower of systematic knowledge. Up to our own day all the political writers whom we now read had thought, argued, dogmatized, only about the *constitution* of governments; about the nature of the state, the essence and seat of sovereignty, popular power and kingly prerogative. . . . The central field of controversy was that great field of theory in which monarchy rode tilt against democracy, in which oligarchy would have built for itself strongholds of privilege, and in which tyranny sought opportunity to make good its claim to receive submission from all competitors. The question, how law should be administered with enlightenment, with equity, with speed, and without friction, was put aside as a practical detail which clerks could arrange after doctors had agreed upon principles.

Unfortunately the future President of Princeton University and the United States never carried his penetrating researches beyond this preliminary study.

The interest of the twentieth century in public administration is due to a variety of causes. Of these the rapidly increasing cost of government, "the unprecedented cataclysm of public expenditure," is one of the most important.[7] The statement is made that the total revenues raised for municipal, county, state, and national purposes increased from $2,131,402,000 in 1912 to $6,346,332,000 in 1922, an increase of 198 percent; and the per capita revenues in 1912 increased from $21.96 to $58.37 in 1922.[8] The total net expenditures of the federal government reached their peak in the fiscal year 1920, at $5,687,712,849, since when there has been a progressive decline to an annual expenditure of about $3,000,000,000. The expenditures of the state governments, however, show a rapid increase since the war. In 1913 they were $3.95 per capita, and in 1922, $11.82.[9] Municipal expenditures show a per capita increase for all general departments from $17.34 in 1912 to $33.15 in 1922.[10] Dr. Mitchell and his associates estimate an increase in national income, 1913 to 1919, from 33.3 billions to 66.0 billions of dollars, or approximately two hundred per cent. This indicates that national income is not burdened by governmental expenditure to any substantially greater degree in recent years than before the war, but the outcry against high taxes is none the less real.[11] The wide publicity given to the rising tide of expenditure, the heavy burden of taxation, and the dramatic efforts of the national administration in favor of economy, have all emphasized the demand for greater efficiency. The pressure for more effective use of public resources is unremitting, and so long as existing high levels of taxation remain, every avenue will need to be explored in order to secure maximum results for every expenditure.

The World War brought into vivid contrast the administrative methods of democratic and autocratic governments, and gave rise to sharp criticisms of the time-honored plan of "muddling through." At an early date the war was declared to be one between democracy and autocracy, but at a later date there was general agreement that democracy had been forced to adopt the administrative methods of autocracy to gain its end.[12] The various administrative methods employed in the belligerent countries to control the food supply, however, furnish interesting illustrations of the democratic and autocratic approach to specific problems.

On a less dramatic scale, international competition in trade and industry continues to sharpen the demand for efficiency in government. The United States Chamber of Commerce has taken an active interest in greater efficiency "because as business men they already believed in efficiency and economy and wanted to see it applied to the municipal, state, and national governments; because they realized that efficient and economical government was a prime requisite for prosperity and business success; and because as good citizens, they desired to see an honest, sound and intelligent administration." In 1912 at the first annual meeting of the Chamber of Commerce there was discussion of budget reform for the federal government, followed by a referendum which almost unanimously adopted a specific proposal. Year after year the Chamber of Commerce has pressed the matter upon the attention of Congress.

This organization has also urged federal grants for the assistance of vocational schools, a federal department of public works, a general reorganization of the administrative system, improved methods of personnel management, and a permanent planning department in the post office. The New York Chamber of Commerce has also taken an active part in proposing better administration, both state and federal. The reorganization of the consular and diplomatic services achieved by the Rogers Act was urged by business interests. Secretary Hoover's recent revelations of monopolies in rubber, coffee, sisal, and other commodities controlled by foreign governments point to a new phase of international commercial competition which may have important reactions on the problems of our administrative organization. The fact of the matter is that American business has reached the point where it cannot continue to reap profits merely by enlarging its productivity to catch up with a home market protected by a high tariff wall. It is now a competitor in the world market, and is faced with the necessity of maintaining profits largely by reductions in the cost of production through better management and more effective use of resources. That is, it has been forced to consider on a large scale the reduction of expenses, and the most efficient utilization of its equipment. In this it has preceded government.

The insistence of powerful social groups upon the practical realization of their legislative programs is a constant spur to improved administrative methods. The enforcement of the eighteenth amendment is a significant illustration of the point. The advocates of stringent enforcement legislation failed to insist upon the selection of prohibition officials by merit. The lax and feeble enforcement of the Volstead Act quickly caused the Anti-Saloon League to demand better execution of the law; the issue shifted from policy to administration. This illustrates a universal transfer of interest, for when once a policy has received legislative sanction, the chief problem becomes one of administration. Similarly the agencies interested in limitation of the hours of labor, minimum wage, tax reform, and other issues become powerful exponents of sound administrative methods.

The scientific management movement has had a very important share in stimulating improvement in the methods of carrying on public business.[13] Commencing with the pioneer work of Frederick W. Taylor, the movement has developed constantly widening interests, and has eventually built up the outlines of a whole philosophy of social betterment on the basis of scientific control of the productive process.

The enormous improvements which have been made by scientific management in some industries have raised the question whether or not equally striking improvements are feasible in government. Whatever answer be given to this question, there can be no doubt that the achievements of scientific management have aroused a vast amount of dissatisfaction with the antiquated methods which have characterized many public offices. More and more clearly it is being understood that the promise of American life will never be realized until American administration has been lifted out of the ruts in which it has been left by a century of neglect.

NOTES

1. One of the earliest definitions by an American author is found in the following lines written by Woodrow Wilson: "The field of administration is the field of business. . . . The object of administrative study is to rescue executive methods from the confusion and costliness of empirical experiment and set them upon foundation laid deep in stable principle. . . . Public administration is the detailed and systematic execution of public law. Every particular application of general law is an act of administration." "The Study of Administration," *Political Science Quarterly* 2, pp. 210, 212.

   Goodnow defined the field in these terms: "Such then is what is meant in these pages by the function of administration—the execution, in nonjudicial matters, of the law or will of the state as expressed by the competent authority." *Principles of Administrative Law of the United States*, p. 14 (1905). Goodnow's writings, however, do not make a clear distinction between administration and administrative law. This distinction is only now emerging in fact. It is recognized by the French phrases, *droit administratif* and *doctrine administrative*, by the German words *Verwaltungsrecht* and *Verwaltungskunde*, or *Verwaltungspolitik*. Note also the words "*les sciences administratives.*" See below for the author's differentiation.

2. Frank J. Goodnow, *Comparative Administrative Law* 1 pp. 8–9 (1893). The contrast is well brought forth by comparing two articles dealing with the two fields, respectively: J. D. Barnett, "Public Agencies and Private Agencies," *Am. Pol. Sci. Rev.* 18, pp. 34–48 (1924); and J. C. Logan, "Cooperation of Public and Private Welfare Agencies," *Annals*, 105, pp. 88–92 (1923).

3. *Proceedings, Am. Pol. Sci. Assoc.* 6, p. 58 (1909).

4. A careful definition of terms is to be found from the pen of the editor in the *Illinois Law Review* 15, pp. 108–18. He writes: "Legislation is the declaration, independently of their application, of new rules of compulsory conduct, by an organ of the state, whose powers are specialized to exclude other functions except as incidental. Adjudication is the determination of a specific controversy, by the application of a rule of compulsory conduct, by an organ of the state, whose powers are specialized to exclude other functions except as incidental. The

executive function is the factual and ultimate realization of a rule of compulsory conduct through an organ of the state, whose powers are specialized to exclude other functions except as incidental. Administrative power is a fourth term; its functions in pure theory must always be one of the three kinds of powers enumerated, but in practice may be and usually are a combination of two or more of these powers. Clear examples of this combination of powers are the Interstate Commerce Commission, the Federal Trade Board, and the numerous state public utility commissions."

5. Herbert A. Croly, *Progressive Democracy*, ch. 17 (1914).
6. Herman Finer, "The Civil Service in the Modern State," *Am. Pol. Sci. Rev.* 19, pp. 277–289 (1925).
7. *See* Henry J. Ford, *Cost of our National Government* (1910); Edward B. Rosa, "Expenditures and Revenues of the Federal Government," *Annals* 95, p. 1 (1921); Herbert D. Brown, "The Historical Development of National Expenditures," *Proceedings of the Academy of Political Science* 9, pp. 336–346 (1921).
8. "The Trend in Public Expenditures," *Annals* 113, part 1 (1924).
9. Austin F. MacDonald, "The Trend in Recent State Expenditures," *Annals* 113, pp. 8–15; *cf.* Minnesota Tax Commission, "Cost of Government in Minnesota," *Biennial Report,* 1918. "The economic fact which is going to force good municipal government—even scientific management in city affairs—is the growing cost of the undertaking. It is only because we do not have the figures which represent the difficulty of the task ahead of us that we are not appalled by it." Morris L. Cooke, "Scientific Management of the Public Business," *Am. Pol. Sci. Rev.* 9, pp. 488–495 (1915); cf. "The Cost of Government, City of Detroit," *Public Business* 80, 97, published by the Detroit Bureau of Governmental Research.
10. Lane W. Lancaster, "The Trend in City Expenditures," *Annals* 113, pp. 15–22 (1924).
11. National Bureau of Economic Research, *Income in the United States,* 1, p. 13 (1921).
12. Cf. Charles G. Fenwick, "Democracy and Efficient Government—Lessons of the War," *Am. Pol. Sci. Rev.* 14, pp. 565–86. (1920).
13. *See* Frank B. Copley, *Frederic W. Taylor, the Father of Scientific Management* (1923); Horace B. Drury, *Scientific Management, a History and Criticism* (1915); Edward E. Hunt, *Scientific Management since Taylor* (1924); General William Crozier, "Scientific Management in Government Establishments," *Bulletin of the Taylor Society* 1 (1915); C. B. Thompson, "Literature of Scientific Management," *Quarterly Journal of Economics* 28, pp. 506–557 (1913–14); Henry H. Farquhar, "Positive Contributions of Scientific Management," *Ibid* 33, pp. 466–503 (1918–19), and "Critical Analysis of Scientific Management," *Bulletin of the Taylor Society* 9, pp. 16–30 (1924); Frederick A. Cleveland, "The Application of Scientific Management to the Activities of the State," *Tuck School Conference on Scientific Management,* pp. 313–35 (1912); Morris L. Cooke, "The Influence of Scientific Management upon Government," *Bulletin of the Taylor Society* 9, pp. 31–38 (1924).

   Note also William H. Leffingwell, *Office Management* (1915); Richard H. Lansburgh, *Industrial Management* (1923).

   For a very significant change in the attitude of organized labor toward management read "Labor's Ideals Concerning Management," by President William A. Green of the American Federation of Labor, *Bulletin of the Taylor Society* 10, pp. 241–53 (1925).

7
The Giving of Orders
Mary Parker Follett

To some men the matter of giving orders seems a very simple affair; they expect to issue their own orders and have them obeyed without question. Yet, on the other hand, the shrewd common sense of many a business executive has shown him that the issuing of orders is surrounded by many difficulties; that to demand an unquestioning obedience to orders not approved, not perhaps even understood, is bad business policy. Moreover, psychology, as well as our own observation, shows us not only that you cannot get people to do things most satisfactorily by ordering them or exhorting them; but also that even reasoning with them, even convincing them intellectually, may not be enough. Even the "consent of the governed" will not do all the work it is supposed to do, an important consideration for those who are advocating employee representation. For all our past life, our early training, our later experience, all our emotions, beliefs, prejudices, every desire that we have, have formed certain habits of mind that the psychologists call habit-patterns, action-patterns, motor-sets.

Therefore it will do little good merely to get intellectual agreement; unless you change the habit-patterns of people, you have not really changed your people. Business administration, industrial organization, should build up certain habit-patterns, that is, certain mental attitudes. For instance, the farmer has a general disposition to "go it alone," and this is being changed by the activities of the co-operatives, that is, note, *by the farmer's own activities.* So the workman has often a general disposition of antagonism to his employers which cannot be changed by argument or exhortation, but only through certain activities which will create a different disposition. One of my trade union friends told me that he remembered when he was a quite small boy hearing his father, who worked in a shoe-shop, railing daily against his boss. So he grew up believing that it was inherent in the nature of things that the workman should be against his employer. I know many working men who have a prejudice against getting college men into factories. You could all give me examples of attitudes among your employees which you would like to change. We want, for instance, to create an attitude of respect for expert opinion.

If we analyse this matter a little further we shall see that we have to do three things. I am now going to use psychological language: (1) build up certain attitudes; (2) provide for the release of these attitudes; (3) augment the released response as it is being carried out. What does this mean in the language of business? A psychologist has given us the example of the salesman. The salesman first creates in you the attitude that you want his article; then, at just the "psychological" moment, he produces his

Source: Henry C. Metcalf, ed., *Scientific Foundations of Business Administration* (Baltimore: Williams & Wilkins Co., 1926). Footnotes omitted.

contract blank which you may sign and thus release that attitude; then if, as you are preparing to sign, some one comes in and tells you how pleased he has been with his purchase of this article, that augments the response which is being released.

If we apply this to the subject of orders and obedience, we see that people can obey an order only if previous habit-patterns are appealed to or new ones created. When the employer is considering an order, he should also be thinking of the way to form the habits which will ensure its being carried out. We should first lead the salesmen selling shoes or the bank clerk cashing cheques to see the desirability of a different method. Then the rules of the store or bank should be so changed as to make it possible for salesman or cashier to adopt the new method. In the third place they could be made more ready to follow the new method by convincing in advance some one individual who will set an example to the others. You can usually convince one or two or three ahead of the rank and file. This last step you all know from your experience to be good tactics; it is what the psychologists call intensifying the attitude to be released. But we find that the released attitude is not by one release fixed as a habit; it takes a good many responses to do that.

This is an important consideration for us, for from one point of view business success depends largely on this—namely, whether our business is so organized and administered that it tends to form certain habits, certain mental attitudes. It has been hard for many old-fashioned employers to understand that *orders will not take the place of training.* I want to italicize that. Many a time an employer has been angry because, as he expressed it, a workman "wouldn't" do so and so, when the truth of the matter was that the workman couldn't, actually couldn't, do as ordered because he could not go contrary to life-long habits. This whole subject might be taken up under the heading of education, for there we could give many instances of the attempt to make arbitrary authority take the place of training. In history, the aftermath of all revolutions shows us the results of the lack of training.

In this matter of prepared-in-advance behaviour patterns—that is, in preparing the way for the reception of orders, psychology makes a contribution when it points out that the same words often rouse in us a quite different response when heard in certain places and on certain occasions. A boy may respond differently to the same suggestion when made by his teacher and when made by his schoolmate. Moreover, he may respond differently to the same suggestion made by the teacher in the schoolroom and made by the teacher when they are taking a walk together. Applying this to the giving of orders, we see that the place in which orders are given, the circumstances under which they are given, may make all the difference in the world as to the response which we get. Hand them down a long way from President or Works Manager and the effect is weakened. One might say that the strength of favourable response to an order is in inverse ratio to the distance the order travels. Production efficiency is always in danger of being affected whenever the long-distance order is substituted for the face-to-face suggestion. There is, however, another reason for that which I shall consider in a moment.

All that we said in the foregoing paper of integration and circular behaviour applies directly to the anticipation of response in giving orders. We spoke then of what the psychologists call linear and circular behaviour. Linear behaviour would be, to quote from Dr. Cabot's review of my book, *Creative Experience,* when an order is accepted as passively as the woodshed accepts the wood. In circular behaviour you get a "come-back." But we all know that we get the come-back every day of our life, and we must certainly allow for it, or for what is more elegantly called circular behaviour, in the giving of orders. Following out the thought of the previous paper, I should say that the giving of orders and the receiving of orders ought to be a matter of integration through circular behaviour, and that we should seek methods to bring this about.

Psychology has another important contribution to make on this subject of issuing orders or giving directions: before the integration can be made between order-giver and order-receiver, there is often an integration to be made within one or both of the individuals concerned. There are often two dissociated paths in the individual; if you are clever enough to recognize these, you can sometimes forestall a Freudian conflict, make the integration appear before there is an acute stage.

To explain what I mean, let me run over briefly a social worker's case. The girl's parents had been divorced and the girl placed with a jolly, easy-going, slack and untidy family, consisting of the father and mother and eleven children, sons and daughters. Gracie was very happy here, but when the social worker in charge of the case found that the living conditions involved a good deal of promiscuity, she thought the girl should be placed elsewhere. She therefore took her to call on an aunt who had a home with some refinement of living, where they had "high tastes," as one of the family said. This aunt wished to have Gracie live with her, and Gracie decided that she would like to do so. The social worker, however, in order to test her, said, "But I thought you were so happy where you are." "Can't I be happy and high, too?" the girl replied. There were two wishes here, you see. The social worker by removing the girl to the aunt may have forestalled a Freudian conflict, the dissociated paths may have been united. I do not know the outcome of this story, but it indicates a method of dealing with our co-directors—make them "happy and high, too."

Business administration has often to consider how to deal with the dissociated paths in individuals or groups, but the methods of doing this successfully have been developed much further in some departments than in others. We have as yet hardly recognized this as part of the technique of dealing with employees, yet the clever salesman knows that it is the chief part of his job. The prospective buyer wants the article and does not want it. The able salesman does not suppress the arguments in the mind of the purchaser against buying, for then the purchaser might be sorry afterwards for his purchase, and that would not be good salesmanship. Unless he can unite, integrate, in the purchaser's mind, the reasons for buying and the reasons for not buying, his future sales will be imperilled, he will not be the highest grade salesman.

Please note that this goes beyond what the psychologist whom I quoted at the beginning of this section told us. He said, "The salesman must create in you the attitude that you want his article." Yes, but only if he creates this attitude by integration, not by suppression.

Apply all this to orders. An order often leaves the individual to whom it is given with two dissociated paths; an order should seek to unite, to integrate, dissociated paths. Court decisions often settle arbitrarily which of two ways is to be followed without showing a possible integration of the two, that is, the individual is often left with an internal conflict on his hands. This is what both courts and business administration should try to prevent, the internal conflicts of individuals or groups.

In discussing the preparation for giving orders, I have not spoken at all of the appeal to certain instincts made so important by many writers. Some writers, for instance, emphasize the instinct of self-assertion; this would be violated by too rigid orders or too clumsily-exercised authority. Other writers, of equal standing, tell us that there is an instinct of submission to authority. I cannot discuss this for we should first have to define instincts, too long an undertaking for us now. Moreover, the exaggerated interest in instincts of recent years, an interest which in many cases has received rather crude expression, is now subsiding. Or, rather, it is being replaced by the more fruitful interest in habits.

There is much more that we could learn from psychology about the forming of habits and the preparation for giving orders than I can even hint at now. But there is one point, already spoken of by implication, that I wish to consider more explicitly—namely, the manner of giving orders. Probably more industrial trouble has been caused by the manner in which orders are given than in any other way. In the *Report on Strikes and Lockouts,* a British Government publication, the cause of a number of strikes is given as "alleged harassing conduct of the foreman," "alleged tyrannical conduct of an under-foreman," "alleged overbearing conduct of officials." The explicit statement, however, of the tyranny of superior officers as the direct cause of strikes is I should say, unusual, yet resentment smoulders and breaks out in other issues. And the demand for better treatment is often explicit enough. We find it made by the metal and woodworking trades in an aircraft factory, who declared that any treatment of men without regard to their feelings of self-respect would be answered by a stoppage of work. We find it put in certain agreements with employers that "the men must be treated with proper respect, and threats and abusive language must not be used."

What happens to man, *in* a man, when an order is given in a disagreeable manner by foreman, head of department, his immediate superior in store, bank or factory? The man addressed feels that his self-respect is attacked, that one of his most inner sanctuaries is invaded. He loses his temper or becomes sullen or is on the defensive; he begins thinking of his "rights"—a fatal attitude for any of us. In the language we have been using, the wrong behaviour pattern is aroused, the wrong motor-set; that is, he is now "set" to act in a way which is not going to benefit the enterprise in which he is engaged.

There is a more subtle psychological point here, too; the more you are "bossed" the more your activity of thought will take place within the bossing-pattern, and your part in that pattern seems usually to be opposition to the bossing.

This complaint of the abusive language and the tyrannical treatment of the one just above the worker is an old story to us all, but there is an opposite extreme which is far too little considered. The immediate superior officer is often so close to the worker that he does not exercise the proper duties of his position. Far from taking on himself an aggressive authority, he has often evaded one of the chief problems of his job: how to do what is implied in the fact that he has been put in a position over others. The head of the woman's cloak department in a store will call out, "Say, Sadie, you're 36, aren't you? There's a woman down in the Back Bay kicking about something she says you promised yesterday." "Well, I like that," says Sadie, "Some of those Back Bay women would kick in Heaven." And that perhaps is about all that happens. Of course, the Back Bay lady has to be appeased, but there is often no study of what has taken place for the benefit of the store. I do not mean that a lack of connection between such incidents and the improvement of store technique is universal, but it certainly exists far too often and is one of the problems of those officials who are just above the heads of departments. Naturally, a woman does not want to get on bad terms with her fellow employees with whom she talks and works all day long. Consider the chief operator of the telephone exchanges, remembering that the chief operator is a member of the union, and that the manager is not.

Now what is our problem here? How can we avoid the two extremes: too great bossism in giving orders, and practically no orders given? I am going to ask how *you* are avoiding these extremes. My solution is to depersonalize the giving of orders, to unite all concerned in a study of the situation, to discover the law of the situation and obey that. Until we do this I do not think we shall have the most successful business administration. This is what does take place, what has to take place, when there is a question between two men in positions of equal authority. The head of the sales departments does not give orders to the head of the production department, or vice versa. Each studies the market and the final decision is made as the market demands. This is, ideally, what should take place between foremen and rank and file, between any head and his subordinates. One *person* should not give orders to another *person*, but both should agree to take their orders from the situation. If orders are simply part of the situation, the question of someone giving and someone receiving does not come up. Both accept the orders given by the situation. Employers accept the orders given by the situation; employees accept the orders given by the situation. This gives, does it not, a slightly different aspect to the whole of business administration through the entire plant?

We have here, I think, one of the largest contributions of scientific management: it tends to depersonalize orders. From one point of view, one might call the essence of scientific management the attempt to find the law of the situation. With scientific management the managers are as much under orders as the workers, for both obey the law of the situation. Our job is not how to get people to obey orders, but how to devise methods by which we can best *discover* the order integral to a particular situation. When that is found, the employee can issue it to the employer, as well as employer to employee. This often happens easily and naturally. My cook or my stenographer points out the law of the situation, and I, if I recognize it as such, accept it, even although it may reverse some "order" I have given.

If those in supervisory positions should depersonalize orders, then there would be no overbearing authority on the one hand, nor on the other that dangerous *laissez-aller* which comes from the fear of exercising authority. Of course we should exercise authority, but always the authority of the situation. I do not say that we have found the way to a frictionless existence, far from it, but we now understand the place which we mean to give to friction. We intend to set it to work for us as the engineer does when he puts the belt over the pulley. There will be just as much, probably more, room for disagreement in the method I am advocating. The situation will often be seen differently, often be interpreted differently. But we shall know what to do with it, we shall have found a method of dealing with it.

I call it depersonalizing because there is not time to go any further into the matter. I think it really is a matter of *repersonalizing*. We, persons, have relations with each other, but we should find them in and through the whole situation. We cannot have any sound relations with each other as long as we take them out of that setting which gives them their meaning and value. This divorcing of persons and the situation does a great deal of harm. I have just said that scientific management depersonalizes; the deeper philosophy of scientific management shows us personal relations within the whole setting of that thing of which they are a part.

There is much psychology, modern psychology particularly, which tends to divorce person and situation. What I am referring to is the present zest for "personality studies." When some difficulty arises, we often hear the psychologist whose specialty is personality studies say, "Study the psychology of that man." And this is very good advice, but only if at the same time we study the entire situation. To leave out the whole situation, however, is so common a blunder in the studies of these psychologists that it constitutes a serious weakness in their work. And as those of you who are personnel directors have more to do, I suppose, with those psychologists who have taken personality for their specialty than with any others, I wish you would watch and see how often you find that this limitation detracts from the value of their conclusions.

I said above that we should substitute for the long-distance order the face-to-face suggestion. I think we can now see a more cogent reason for this than the one then given. It is not the face-to-face suggestion that we want so much as the joint study of the problem, and such joint study can be made best by the employee and his immediate superior or employee and special expert on that question.

I began this talk by emphasizing the advisability of preparing in advance the attitude necessary for the carrying out of orders, as in the previous paper we considered preparing the attitude for integration; but we have now, in our consideration of the joint study of situations, in our emphasis on obeying the law of the situation, perhaps got a little beyond that, or rather we have now to consider in what sense we wish to take the psychologist's doctrine of prepared-in-advance attitudes. By itself this would not take us far, for everyone is studying psychology nowadays, and our employees are going to be just as active in preparing us as we in preparing them! Indeed, a girl working in a factory said to me, "We had a course in psychology last winter, and I see now that you have to be pretty careful how you put things to the managers if you want them to consider favourably what you're asking for." If this prepared-in-advance idea were all that the psychologists think it, it would have to be printed privately as secret doctrine. But the truth is that the best preparation for integration in the matter of orders or in anything else, is a joint study of the situation. We should not try to create the attitude we *want*, although that is the usual phrase, but the attitude required for cooperative study and decision. This holds good even for the salesman. We said above that when the salesman is told that he should create in the prospective buyer the attitude that he wants the article, he ought also to be told that he should do this by integration rather than by suppression. We have now a hint of *how* he is to attain this integration.

I have spoken of the importance of changing some of the language of business personnel relations. We considered whether the words "grievances," "complaints," or Ford's "trouble specialists" did not arouse the wrong behaviour-patterns. I think "order" certainly does. If that word is not to mean any longer external authority, arbitrary authority, but the law of the situation, then we need a new word for it. It is often the order that people resent as much as the thing ordered. People do not like to be ordered even to take a holiday. I have often seen instances of this. The wish to govern one's own life is, of course, one of the most fundamental feelings in every human being. To call this "the instinct of self-assertion," "the instinct of initiative," does not express it wholly. I think it is told in the life of some famous American that when he was a boy and his mother said, "Go get a pail of water," he always replied, "I won't," before taking up the pail and fetching the water. This is significant; he resented the command, the command of a person; but he went and got the water, not, I believe, because he had to, but because he recognized the demand of the situation. *That*, he knew he had to obey; *that*, he was willing to obey. And this kind of obedience is not opposed to the wish to govern one's self, but each is involved in the other; both are part of the same fundamental urge at the root of one's being. We have here something far more profound than "the egoistic impulse" or "the instinct of self-assertion." We have the very essence of the human being.

This subject of orders has led us into the heart of the whole question of authority and consent. When we conceive of authority and consent as parts of an inclusive situation, does that not throw a flood of light on this question? The point of view here presented gets rid of several dilemmas which have seemed to puzzle people in dealing with consent. The feeling of being "under" someone, of "subordination," of "servility," of being "at the will of another," comes out again and again in the shop stewards movement and in the testimony before the Coal Commission. One man said before the Coal Commission, "It is all right to work *with* anyone; what is disagreeable is to feel too distinctly that you are working *under* anyone." *With* is a pretty good preposition, not because it connotes democracy, but because it connotes functional unity, a much more profound conception than that of democracy as usually held. The study of the situation involves the *with* preposition. Then Sadie is not left alone by the head of the cloak department, nor does she have to obey her. The head of the department says, "Let's see how such cases had better be handled, then we'll abide by that." Sadie is not under the head of the department, but both are *under* the situation.

Twice I have had a servant applying for a place ask me if she would be treated as a menial. When the first woman asked me that, I had no idea what she meant, I though perhaps she did not want to do the roughest work, but later I came to the conclusion that to be treated as a menial meant to be obliged to be under someone, to follow orders without using one's own judgment. If we believe that what heightens self-respect increases efficiency, we shall be on our guard here.

Very closely connected with this is the matter of pride in one's work. If an order goes against what the craftsman or the clerk thinks is the way of doing his work which will bring the best results, he is justified in not wishing to obey that order. Could not that difficulty be met by a joint study of the situation? It is said that it is characteristic of the British workman to feel, " I know my job and won't be told how." The peculiarities of the British workman might be met by a joint study of the situation, it being understood that he probably has more to contribute to that study than anyone else. . . .

There is another dilemma which has to be met by everyone who is in what is called a position of authority: how can you expect people merely to obey orders and at the same time to take that degree of responsibility which they should take? Indeed, in my experience, the people who enjoy following orders blindly, without any thought on their own part, are those who like thus to get rid of responsibility. But the taking of responsibility, each according to his capacity, each according to his function in the whole . . . , this taking of responsibility is usually the most vital matter in the life of every human being, just as the allotting of responsibility is the most important part of business administration.

A young trade unionist said to me, "How much dignity can I have as a mere employee?" He can have all the dignity in the world if he is allowed to make his fullest contribution to the plant *and to assume definitely the responsibility therefor.*

I think one of the gravest problems before us is how to make the reconciliation between receiving orders and taking responsibility. And I think the reconciliation can be made through our conception of the law of the situation. . . .

We have considered the subject of symbols. It is often very apparent that an order is a symbol. The referee in the game stands watch in hand, and says, "Go." It is an order, but order only as symbol. I may say to an employee, "Do so and so," but I should say it only because we have both agreed, openly or tacitly, that that which I am ordering done is the best thing to be done. The order is then a symbol. And if it is a philosophical and psychological truth that we owe obedience only to a functional unity to which we are contributing, we should remember that a more accurate way of stating that would be to say that our obligation is to a unifying, to a process.

This brings us now to one of our most serious problems in this matter of orders. It is important, but we can touch on it only briefly; it is what we spoke of . . . as the evolving situation. I am trying to show here that the order must be integral to the situation and must be recognized as such. But we saw that the situation was always developing. If the situation is never stationary, then the order should never be stationary, so to speak; how to prevent it from being so is our problem. The situation is changing while orders are being carried out, because, by and through orders being carried out. How is the order to keep up with the situation? External orders never can, only those drawn fresh from the situation.

Moreover, if taking a *responsible* attitude toward experience involves recognizing the evolving situation, a *conscious* attitude toward experience means that we note the change which the developing situation makes in ourselves; the situation does not change without changing us.

To summarize, . . . integration being the basic law of life, orders should be the composite conclusion of those who give and those who receive them; more than this, that they should be the integration of the people concerned and the situation; even more than this, that they should be the integration involved in the evolving situation. If you accept my three fundamental statements on this subject: (1) that the order should be the law of the situation; (2) that the situation is always evolving; (3) that orders should involve circular not linear behaviour—then we see that our old conception of orders has somewhat changed, and that there should therefore follow definite changes in business practice.

There is a problem so closely connected with the giving of orders that I want to put it before you for future discussion. After we have decided on our orders, we have to consider how much and what kind of supervision is necessary or advisable in order that they shall be carried out. We all know that many workers object to being watched. What does that mean, how far is it justifiable? How can the objectionable element be avoided and at the same time necessary supervision given? I do not think that this matter has been studied sufficiently. When I asked a very intelligent girl what she thought would be the result of profit sharing and employee representation in the factory where she worked, she replied joyfully, "We shan't need foremen any more." While her entire ignoring of the fact that the foreman has other duties than keeping workers on their jobs was amusing, one wants to go beyond one's amusement and find out what this objection to being watched really means.

In a case in Scotland arising under the Minimum Wage Act, the overman was called in to testify whether or not a certain workman did his work properly. The examination was as follows:

> *Magistrate:* "But isn't it your duty under the Mines Act to visit each working place twice a day?"
>
> *Overman:* "Yes."
>
> *Magistrate:* "Don't you do it?"
>
> *Overman:* "Yes."
>
> *Magistrate:* "Then why didn't you ever see him work?"
>
> *Overman:* "They always stop work when they see an overman coming and sit down and wait till he's gone—even take out their pipes, if it's a mine free from gas. They won't let anyone watch them."

An equally extreme standard was enforced for a part of the war period at a Clyde engineering works. The chairman of shop stewards was told one morning that there was a grievance at the smithy. He found one of the blacksmiths in a rage because the managing director in his ordinary morning's walk through the works had stopped for five minutes or so and watched this man's fire. After a shop meeting the chairman took up a deputation to the director and secured the promise that this should not happen again. At the next works meeting the chairman reported the incident to the body of workers, with the result that a similar demand was made throughout the works and practically acceded to, so that the director hardly dared to stop at all in his morning's walk.

I have seen similar instances cited. Many workmen feel that being watched is unbearable. What can we do about it? How can we get proper supervision without this watching which a worker resents? Supervision is necessary; supervision is resented—how are we going to make the integration there? Some say, "Let the workers elect the supervisors." I do not believe in that.

There are three other points closely connected with the subject of this paper which I should like merely to point out. First, when and how do you point out mistakes, misconduct? One principle can surely guide us here: don't blame for the sake of blaming, make what you have to say accomplish something; say it in that form, at that time, under those circumstances, which will make it a real education to your subordinate. Secondly, since it is recognized that the one who gives the orders is not as a rule a very popular person, the management sometimes tries to offset this by allowing the person who has this onus upon him to give any pleasant news to the workers, to have the credit of any innovation which the workers very much desire. One manager told me that he always tried to do this. I suppose that this is good behaviouristic psychology, and yet I am not sure that it is a method I wholly like. It is quite different, however, in the case of a mistaken order having been given; then I think the one who made the mistake should certainly be the one to rectify it, not as a matter of strategy, but because it is better for him too. It is better for all of us not only to acknowledge our mistakes, but to do something about them. If a foreman discharges someone and it is decided to reinstate the man, it is obviously not only good tactics but a square deal to the foreman to allow him to do the reinstating.

There is, of course, a great deal more to this matter of giving orders than we have been able to touch on; far from exhausting the subject, I feel that I have only given hints. I have been told that the artillery men suffered more mentally in the war than others, and the reason assigned for this was that their work was directed from a distance. The combination of numbers by which they focused their fire was telephoned to them. The result was also at a distance. Their activity was not closely enough connected with the actual situation at either end.

8 Public Administration and the Public Interest

E. Pendleton Herring

Upon the shoulders of the bureaucrat has been placed in large part the burden of reconciling group differences and making effective and workable the economic and social compromises arrived at through the legislative process. Thus Congress passes a statute setting forth a general principle. The details must be filled in by supplemental regulation. The bureaucrat is left to decide as to the conditions that necessitate the law's application. He is in a better position than the legislators to perform these duties. His daily occupation brings him into direct contact with the situation the law is intended to meet. He knows what can be enforced and he can better envisage the limits of legislative fiats. This increase in administrative discretion, while making possible the more understanding application of rules to concrete situations, nevertheless places a heavy duty on the administrator. The words of the statute delimit his scope, but within the margin of his discretion he must write his interpretation of state purpose.

The social and economic aspects of this process must be left to others. The political result has been the preservation thus far of the liberal democratic state as the agency of control and the transfer from Congress of much of the direct superintendence of reconciling the conflicting groups within the state. The governmental result has been the creation of a great bureaucracy with wide powers to carry on these functions. Great public services are needed all the way

Source: E. Pendleton Herring, *Public Administration and the Public Interest* (New York: McGraw-Hill Book Company, 1936), pp. 7–11, 23–25. Reprinted with permission.

from the primary functions relating to police, sanitation, and the care of paupers to official enterprises that compete with private business. There are huge public-relief projects financed by taxing one class in order to alleviate the hunger pangs of another. The extent to which these activities are carried cannot be fixed but will vary in accordance with the character of the economic groups that have succeeded in attaining control of the government at any given time. There persists, nevertheless, a residue of responsibility no matter what combination is in control of the government. The mere existence of a great administrative organization necessitates a certain continuity that has little reference to political overturns. Groups must be willing to recognize that the state has a purpose which transcends their own immediate ends. The bureaucracy cannot assert a state purpose against the united hostility of groups that basically comprise the source whence authority springs.

In the United States the bureaucracy suffers for want of a hierarchical organization and a personnel united by a harmonious concept of state service. But a bureaucracy in these terms arouses the suspicion and criticism of interest groups, who regard the administration as designed to serve them or at least *not to interfere* with their group purposes. And it is these interest groups that wield political authority under a representative system. Such interests criticize "bureaucracy" as inimical to popular government. Yet only through developing a proper administrative organization can democracy survive.

We conclude, then, that the purpose of the democratic state is the free reconciliation of group interests and that the attainment of this end necessitates the development of a great administrative machine. Thus, paradoxical as it may seem to Jeffersonian Democrats, the liberal democratic state must be sustained by a huge bureaucracy. This viewpoint, however, has not won general acceptance.

Groups of citizens, seeking to advance their own interests or to protect themselves from the onslaughts of rivals, have turned to the government for aid. Yet the citizen distrusts the state at the same time that he appeals to it for help. He desires to use the facilities of the government; but he does not wish the government to direct or control his activities. As a result the federal administrative services have not been fused into a unified and responsible whole. They are a conglomeration of service agencies, independent regulatory commissions, and ill-proportioned bureaus and departments.

The present tangle of alphabetical monstrosities is not a new phenomenon. The confusion is greater because the variety of federal functions is greater. If the government is to become responsible for the economic security of various classes, the administrative machinery must be made adequate to the burden imposed. This does not mean creating more bureaus and commissions but rather reorganizing those that exist. The federal administration must be viewed as a whole: it must be developed into an institution for executing policy in the public interest and for promoting the general welfare. This will require a change in attitude on the part of most citizens. Groups have demanded special consideration from the federal government for themselves while condemning the general encroachment of the state into private affairs. The establishment of an adequate administrative structure and personnel must be undertaken if the state is to carry its ever-increasing load. The problem of bureaucracy must be faced directly.

No civil servant, however, wrapt in the bindings of official red tape, can regard himself as insulated from the currents of opinion generated by the groups with which his bureau comes into contact. The citizen for his part must feel that his experience and his special competence have some place in governance. How can a mutually advantageous connection be made?

The adjustment is not easy. "In every country," Herman Finer states, "the public is hostile to the official because at some time or other, as an inspector or a tax collector or a medical officer, or what not, he comes to take away, not to give—it is in the nature of his task to limit one's freedom and property."[1] The suspicion of bureaucracy is particularly keen in the United States, and not without just cause. "Political pull" remains the citizen's chief defense against officialdom in this country. This faulty resource is all the more necessary under a system where ministerial responsibility is lacking and public integrity is often wanting in official circles. Moreover, we have a tradition of distrust for government that harks back to Colonial and Revolutionary days. Official interference has long been regarded as irksome and unfriendly. Conditions of pioneer life doubtless intensified this feeling. We accepted bureaucratic incompetence as an inevitable characteristic of an institution from which little good was to be expected in any case. Our confidence was placed in the courts where the justice of the rule of the law would protect us, we hoped, from the caprice of a government by men.[2]

The courts are often found taking the part of the citizen against the powers of officialdom. Their verdict time and again delimits or restricts bureaucratic competence. In the elected executive and legislature the citizen feels that some degree of control is attainable through political channels. The tradition of a rule of law gives him confidence in the courts. But how can he affect the course of administrative action?[3] Underlying such criticism is the uneasy feeling that the force of the government is turned to purposes contrary to those of his group. It often happens that a regulatory measure is enacted over the urgent protest of those thereby affected. The legislature, supported by a momentary public enthusiasm, discharges its duty in passing the law and turns to other matters. The bureaucrat is left to enforce the law over the disgruntled group thus brought under his jurisdiction. Governmental activity is unobjectionable to special interests when in accord with their aims, but when it is directed to other ends the cry of bureaucratic interference is raised.

The legislature, often because of a fortuitous combination of political factors, enacts a law. An administrative agency becomes responsible for its execution, and the legislative will is thus in a sense institutionalized and personified. Except for the relatively rare instances where a statute is rendered innocuous by nonenforcement, the legislative will is "frozen" until the law is changed. Meanwhile, a change of economic or political conditions may alter the alignment of social forces in the community and thereby bring the statute into disfavor, without necessarily forcing legislative amendment in response to criticisms. The legal responsibility of the official remains the same and the censure he incurs is the price of discharging his manifest duties.

• • •

Government today is largely a matter of expert administration. Increasing authority and discretion are granted the executive branch. The state has undertaken a great number of services left in the past to private enterprise or scarcely attempted at all. These activities have given special interests a stake in the government. The actual point at which their right to pursue freely their own aims comes into conflict with the fulfillment of the broader aims of the community is a matter for judgment as particular cases arise. But the civil servant has no clear standard upon which to act. In a word, our present bureaucracy has accumulated vast authority but it lacks direction and coördination.

The President is nominal head of the "administration," but under present conditions the task of coördination is beyond the capacities of the transient occupants of this position. A system of administrative law might in time indicate the limits of bureaucratic responsibility and develop the conception of public interest. But the official today finds himself largely isolated except for the presence of those interests directly affected by the consequences of his action. These loom largest in the context of his administrative surroundings.

What criteria are to guide him? The *public interest* is the standard that guides the administrator in executing the law. This is the verbal symbol designed to introduce unity, order, and objectivity into administration.

This concept is to the bureaucracy what the "due process" clause is to the judiciary. Its abstract meaning is vague but its application has far-reaching effects. The radio commissioners were to execute the law in the "public interest, convenience or necessity." The trade commissioners are to apply the law when they deem such action "to the interest of the public." Congress has frequently authorized boards and quasi-judicial commissions to determine the public interest.

Although it is clear that the official must balance the interests of the conflicting groups before him, by what standards is he to weigh their demands? To hold out the *public interest* as a criterion is to offer an imponderable. Its value is psychological and does not extend beyond the significance that each responsible civil servant must find in the phrase for himself. Acting in accordance with this subjective conception and bounded by his statutory competence, the bureaucrat selects from the special interests before him a combination to which he gives official sanction. Thus inescapably in practice the concept of public interest is given substance by its identification with the interests of certain groups. The bureaucrat is placed in a situation similar to the plight of Rousseau's citizen. The latter was to vote in accordance with the general will. If he found himself in the minority when the votes were counted, he knew that he had guessed incorrectly as to the *volonté générale*. The official, however, must endeavor to act in the public interest, but without the consolation of testing his judgment in a bureaucratic plebiscite. He must follow his star with but little light on the immediate pitfalls in his path.

The administrator has certain guiding criteria supplied by statutes, but inevitably a margin of discretion remains inherent in the administrative process. He can build up support for his policies and to some extent choose his adversaries. The choice may be of crucial importance. By supporting the groups demanding a strict interpretation of the law, he may bring about an ultimate effect quite different to the outcome resulting from coöperation with those who favor a liberal reading of the statute. He may even reach out for the opinions held by groups less well organized or aggressively directed.

The predicament of the bureaucrat now becomes clear. Special interests cannot be denied a voice in the councils of state since it is their concerns that provide substance out of which the public welfare is formulated. On the other hand, a well-coördinated and responsible bureaucracy is essential if the purpose of the state is to be attained.[4] The solution of the liberal democratic state must lie in establishing a working relationship between the bureaucrats and special interests—a relationship that will enable the former to carry out the purpose of the state and the latter to realize their own ends.

Such a harmonious relationship is made all the more difficult in the United States by the diversity of conditions over the country and by the variety of activities undertaken by the government. Moreover, federal officials concern themselves with some problems over which they can exercise no coercive authority. The successful administration of many federal services depends upon the cooperation of state and local authorities with the national government. The ties between the community and the federal bureaucracy can best be described and evaluated in terms of the particular situations they are designed to meet. It is difficult to discuss these developments in general terms. Officials working in their own domains have used their ingenuity and found their own solutions.

Public administration in actual practice is a process whereby one individual acting in an official capacity and in accordance with his interpretation of his legal responsibility applies a statute to another individual who is in a legally subordinate position. The public as such is not concerned in this process.

To the officer executing the law, the public is simply an abstraction. Law is applied by one man to another. In the realm of discussion, the public is treated as a reality and words are directed to the populace. But this is a one-sided relationship. Officials receive many responses from individuals but the only reaction they receive from the public is that which they may choose to read into a collection of individual reactions.

Generally these responses may be arranged in more precise categories built around an occupational or economic interest. When this happens, the official finds it possible to negotiate with groups articulate and self-conscious because of a common concern.

Thus law is not administered in a vacuum, but in an environment composed of all those who have an interest in the application or the nonenforcement of the statute. The official is surrounded by a web of interests—and a web often dominated by an unpredictable spider. This ultimate determinator may be the courts, the legislature, an administrative superior, or a powerful economic interest. The administrator is one strand in a complicated mesh of forces, political, social, and economic. The public, viewed in the mass, is of relatively little importance in this context.

NOTES

1. Herman Finer, *Theory and Practice of Modern Government*, (Dial Press, 1932) p. 1500.
2. John Dickinson, "Administrative Law and the Fear of Bureaucracy," parts I and 2, *American Bar Association Journal* (October-November, 1928), and "The Perennial Cry of Bureaucracy," *Yale Review* (Spring, 1935). For recent discussions of interest, see E. Watkins, "Dangerous By-products of Bureaucracy," and S. E. Edmunds, "The Growth of Federal Bureaucratic Tyranny," *Lawyer and Banker* (January, 1933); Charles and William Beard, "The Case for Bureaucracy," *Scribner's* (April, 1933); Lawrence Sullivan, "The Dead Hand of Bureaucracy," *Forum* (January, 1933).
3. The attitude of many businessmen is reflected in the following words taken down during a discussion at the annual meeting of an important association: "We can hardly say that we today live under a government of law. We rather live under a government of bureaus and commissions. Personally I would prefer to have my rights fixed by law to having my interests always subject to the discretionary control of bureaus

and commissions. Yet that is exactly what Government regulation means. The Government, of course, has certain functions like that of experimentation, the increase of human knowledge, with which we cannot quarrel, but when it comes to a proposition of regulating all business by people located in Washington it is time to protest. They proceed upon the assumption of omniscience on the part of these people and then wish to clothe them with omnipotence. They like to have the laws so formulated that there is no appeal from their decision." *Tenth Annual Meeting of the National Coal Association*, June 15–17, 1927, p. 63.

4. As Professor C. J. Friedrich has so cogently stated: "If a popular government is incapable of maintaining a bureaucratic hierarchy, it is bound to give way to a form of government which will accomplish that, whether it be the dictatorship of an individual or of a small group in the name of the nation, the people, or the proletariat." *Responsible Bureaucracy*, (Harvard University Press, 1932), p. 28.

9

Notes on the Theory of Organization

Luther Gulick

Every large-scale or complicated enterprise requires many men to carry it forward. Wherever many men are thus working together the best results are secured when there is a division of work among these men. The theory of organization, therefore, has to do with the structure of co-ordination imposed upon the work-division units of an enterprise. Hence it is not possible to determine how an activity is to be organized without, at the same time, considering how the work in question is to be divided. Work division is the foundation of organization; indeed, the reason for organization.

1. THE DIVISION OF WORK

It is appropriate at the outset of this discussion to consider the reasons for and the effect of the division of work. It is sufficient for our purpose to note the following factors.

Why Divide Work?

Because men differ in nature, capacity and skill, and gain greatly in dexterity by specialization; Because the same man cannot be at two places at the same time; Because the range of knowledge and skill is so great that a man cannot within his life-span know more than a small fraction of it. In other words, it is a question of human nature, time, and space.

In a shoe factory it would be possible to have 1,000 men each assigned to making complete pairs of shoes. Each man would cut his leather, stamp in the eyelets, sew up the tops, sew on the bottoms, nail on the heels, put in the laces, and pack each pair in a box. It might take two days to do the job. One thousand men would make 500 pairs of shoes a day. It would also be possible to divide the work among these same men, using the identical hand methods, in an entirely different way. One group of men would be assigned to cut the leather,

Source: Luther Gulick and Lyndall Urwick, eds., *Papers on the Science of Administration* (New York: Institute of Public Administration, 1937), pp. 3–13.

another to putting in the eyelets, another to stitching up the tops, another to sewing on the soles, another to nailing on the heels, another to inserting the laces and packing the pairs of shoes. We know from common sense and experience that there are two great gains in this latter process: first, it makes possible the better utilization of the varying skills and aptitudes of the different workmen, and encourages the development of specialization; and second, it eliminates the time that is lost when a workman turns from a knife, to a punch, to a needle and awl, to a hammer, and moves from table to bench, to anvil, to stool. Without any pressure on the workers, they could probably turn out twice as many shoes in a single day. There would be additional economies, because inserting laces and packing could be assigned to unskilled and low-paid workers. Moreover, in the cutting of the leather there would be less spoilage because the less skillful pattern cutters would all be eliminated and assigned to other work. It would also be possible to cut a dozen shoe tops at the same time from the same pattern with little additional effort. All of these advances would follow, without the introduction of new labor saving machinery.

The introduction of machinery accentuates the division of work. Even such a simple thing as a saw, a typewriter, or a transit requires increased specialization, and serves to divide workers into those who can and those who cannot use the particular instrument effectively. Division of work on the basis of the tools and machines used in work rests no doubt in part on aptitude, but primarily upon the development and maintenance of skill through continued manipulation.

Specialized skills are developed not alone in connection with machines and tools. They evolve naturally from the materials handled, like wood, or cattle, or paint, or cement. They arise similarly in activities which center in a complicated series of interrelated concepts, principles, and techniques. These are most clearly recognized in the professions, particularly those based on the application of scientific knowledge, as in engineering, medicine, and chemistry. They are none the less equally present in law, ministry, teaching, accountancy, navigation, aviation, and other fields.

The nature of these subdivisions is essentially pragmatic, in spite of the fact that there is an element of logic underlying them. They are therefore subject to a gradual evolution with the advance of science, the invention of new machines, the progress of technology and the change of the social system. In the last analysis, however, they appear to be based upon differences in individual human beings. But it is not to be concluded that the apparent stability of "human nature," whatever that may be, limits the probable development of specialization. The situation is quite the reverse. As each field of knowledge and work is advanced, constituting a continually larger and more complicated nexus of related principles, practices and skills, any individual will be less and less able to encompass it and maintain intimate knowledge and facility over the entire area, and there will thus arise a more minute specialization because knowledge and skill advance while man stands still. Division of work and integrated organization are the bootstraps by which mankind lifts itself in the process of civilization.

The Limits of Division

There are three clear limitations beyond which the division of work cannot to advantage go. The first is practical and arises from the volume of work involved in man-hours. Nothing is gained by subdividing work if that further subdivision results in setting up a task which requires less than the full time of one man. This is too obvious to need demonstration. The only exception arises where space interferes, and in such cases the part-time expert must fill in his spare time at other tasks, so that as a matter of fact a new combination is introduced.

The second limitation arises from technology and custom at a given time and place. In some areas nothing would be gained by separating undertaking from the custody and cleaning of churches, because by custom the sexton is the undertaker; in building construction it is extraordinarily difficult to redivide certain aspects of electrical and plumbing work and to combine them in a more effective way, because of the jurisdictional conflicts of craft unions; and it is clearly impracticable to establish a division of cost accounting in a field in which no technique of costing has yet been developed.

This second limitation is obviously elastic. It may be changed by invention and by education. If this were not the fact, we should face a static division of labor. It should be noted, however, that a marked change has two dangers. It greatly restricts the labor market from which workers may be drawn and greatly lessens the opportunities open to those who are trained for the particular specialization.

The third limitation is that the subdivision of work must not pass beyond physical division into organic division. It might seem far more efficient to have the front half of the cow in the pasture grazing and the rear half in the barn being milked all of the time, but this organic division would fail. Similarly there is no gain from splitting a single movement or gesture like licking an envelope, or tearing apart a series of intimately and intricately related activities.

It may be said that there is in this an element of reasoning in a circle; that the test here applied as to whether an activity is organic or not is whether it is divisible or not—which is what we set out to define. This charge is true. It must be a pragmatic test. Does the division work out? Is something vital destroyed and lost? Does it bleed?

The Whole and the Parts

It is axiomatic that the whole is equal to the sum of its parts. But in dividing up any "whole," one must be certain that every part, including unseen elements and relationships, is accounted for. The marble sand to which the Venus de Milo may be reduced by a vandal does not equal the statue, though every last grain be preserved; nor is a thrush just so much feathers, bones, flesh and blood; nor a typewriter merely so much steel, glass, paint and rubber. Similarly a piece of work to be done cannot be subdivided into the obvious component parts without great danger that the central design, the operating relationships, the imprisoned idea, will be lost.

A simple illustration will make this clear. One man can build a house. He can lay the foundation, cut the beams and boards, make the window frames and doors, lay the floors, raise the roof, plaster the walls, fit in the heating and water systems, install the electric wiring, hang the paper, and paint the structure. But if he did, most of the work would be done by hands unskilled in the work; much material would be spoiled, and the work would require many months of his time. On the other hand, the whole job of building the house might be divided among a group of men. One man could do the foundation, build the chimney, and plaster the walls; another could erect the frame, cut the timbers and the boards, raise the roof, and do all the carpentry; another all the plumbing; another all the paper hanging and painting; another all the electric wiring. But this would not make a house unless someone—an architect—made a plan for the house, so that each skilled worker could know what to do and when to do it.

When one man builds a house alone he plans as he works; he decides what to do first and what next, that is, he "co-ordinates the work." When many men work together to build a house this part of the work, the co-ordinating, must not be lost sight of.

In the "division of the work" among the various skilled specialists, a specialist in planning and co-ordination must be sought as well. Otherwise, a great deal of time may be lost, workers may get in each other's way, material may not be on hand when needed, things may be done in the wrong order, and there may even be a difference of opinion as to where the various doors and windows are to go. It is self-evident that the more the work is subdivided, the greater is the danger of confusion, and the greater is the need of overall supervision and co-ordination. Co-ordination is not something that develops by accident. It must be won by intelligent, vigorous, persistent and organized effort.

2. THE CO–ORDINATION OF WORK

If subdivision of work is inescapable, co-ordination becomes mandatory. There is, however, no one way to co-ordination. Experience shows that it may be achieved in two primary ways. These are:

1. By organization, that is, by interrelating the subdivisions of work by allotting them to men who are placed in a structure of authority, so that the work may be co-ordinated by orders of superiors to subordinates, reaching from the top to the bottom of the entire enterprise.
2. By the dominance of an idea, that is, the development of intelligent singleness of purpose in the minds and wills of those who are working together as a group, so that each worker will of his own accord fit his task into the whole with skill and enthusiasm.

These two principles of co-ordination are not mutually exclusive, in fact, no enterprise is really effective without the extensive utilization of both.

Size and time are the great limiting factors in the development of co-ordination. In a small project, the problem is not difficult; the structure of authority is simple, and the central purpose is real to every worker. In a large complicated enterprise, the organization becomes involved, the lines of authority tangled, and there is danger that the workers will forget that there is any central purpose, and so devote their best energies only to their own individual advancement and advantage.

The interrelated elements of time and habit are extraordinarily important in co-ordination. Man is a creature of habit. When an enterprise is built up gradually from small beginnings the staff can be "broken in" step by step. And when difficulties develop, they can be ironed out, and the new method followed from that point on as a matter of habit, with the knowledge that that particular difficulty will not develop again. Routines may even be mastered by drill as they are in the army. When, however, a large new enterprise must be set up or altered overnight, then the real difficulties of co-ordination make their appearance. The factor of habit, which is thus an important foundation of co-ordination when time is available, becomes a serious handicap when time is not available, that is, when change rules. The question of co-ordination therefore must be approached with different emphasis in small and in large enterprises; in simple and in complex situations; in stable and in new or changing organizations.

Co-ordination through Organization

Organization as a way of co-ordination requires the establishment of a system of authority whereby the central purpose or objective of an enterprise is translated into reality through the combined efforts of many specialists, each working in his own field at a particular time and place.

It is clear from long experience in human affairs that such a structure of authority requires not only many men at work in many places at selected times, but also a single directing executive authority.[1] The problem of organization thus becomes the problem of building up between the executive at the center and the subdivisions of work on the periphery an effective network of communication and control.

The following outline may serve further to define the problem:

I. First Step: Define the job to be done, such as the furnishing of pure water to all of the people and industries within a given area at the lowest possible cost;

II. Second Step: Provide a director to see that the objective is realized;

III. Third Step: Determine the nature and number of individualized and specialized work units into which the job will have to be divided. As has been seen above, this subdivision depends partly upon the size of the job (no ultimate subdivision can generally be so small as to require less than the full time of one worker) and upon the status of technological and social development at a given time;

IV. Fourth Step: Establish and perfect the structure of authority between the director and the ultimate work subdivisions.

It is this fourth step which is the central concern of the theory of organization. It is the function of this organization (IV) to enable the director (II) to co-ordinate and energize all of the sub-divisions of work (III) so that the major objective (I) may be achieved efficiently.

The Span of Control

In this undertaking we are confronted at the start by the inexorable limits of human nature. Just as the hand of man can span only a limited number of notes on the piano, so the mind and will of man can span but a limited number of immediate managerial contacts. The problem has been discussed brilliantly by Graicunas in his paper included in this collection. The limit of control is partly a matter of the limits of knowledge, but even more is it a matter of the limits of time and of energy. As a result the executive of any enterprise can personally direct only a few persons. He must depend upon these to direct others, and upon them in turn to direct still others, until the last man in the organization is reached.

This condition placed upon all human organization by the limits of the span of control obviously differs in different kinds of work and in organizations of different sizes. Where the work is of a routine, repetitive, measurable and homogeneous character, one man can perhaps direct several score workers. This is particularly true when the workers are all in a single room. Where the work is diversified, qualitative, and particularly when the workers are scattered, one man can supervise only a few. This diversification, dispersion, and non-measurability is of course most evident at the very top of any organization. It follows that the limitations imposed by the span of control are most evident at the top of an organization, directly under the executive himself.

But when we seek to determine how many immediate subordinates the director of an enterprise can effectively supervise, we enter a realm of experience which has not been brought under sufficient scientific study to furnish a final answer. Sir Ian Hamilton says, "The nearer we approach the supreme head of the whole organization, the more we ought to work towards groups of three; the closer we get to the foot of the whole organization (the Infantry of the Line), the more we work towards groups of six."[2]

The British Machinery of Government Committee of 1918 arrived at the conclusion that "The Cabinet should be small in number—preferably ten or, at most, twelve."[3]

Henri Fayol said "[In France] a minister has twenty assistants, where the Administrative Theory says that a manager at the head of a big undertaking should not have more than five or six."[4]

Graham Wallas expressed the opinion that the Cabinet should not be increased "beyond the number of ten or twelve at which organized oral discussion is most efficient."[5]

Léon Blum recommended for France a Prime Minister with a technical cabinet modelled after the British War Cabinet, which was composed of five members.[6]

It is not difficult to understand why there is this divergence of statement among authorities who are agreed on the fundamentals. It arises in part from the differences in the capacities and work habits of individual executives observed, and in part from the non-comparable character of the work covered. It would seem that insufficient attention has been devoted to three factors, first, the element of diversification of function; second, the element of time; and third, the element of space. A chief of public works can deal effectively with more direct subordinates than can the general of the army, because all of his immediate subordinates in the department of public works will be in the general field of engineering, while in the army there will be many different elements, such as communications, chemistry, aviation, ordnance, motorized service, engineering, supply, transportation, etc., each with its own technology. The element of time is also of great significance as has been indicated above. In a stable organization the chief executive can deal with more immediate subordinates than in a new or changing organization. Similarly, space influences the span of control. An organization located in one building can be supervised through more immediate subordinates than can the same organization if scattered in several cities. When scattered there is not only need for more supervision, and therefore more supervisory personnel, but also for a fewer number of contacts with the chief executive because of the increased difficulty faced by the chief executive in learning sufficient details about a far-flung organization to do an intelligent job. The failure to attach sufficient importance to these variables has served to limit the scientific validity of the statements which have been made that one man can supervise but three, or five, or eight, or twelve immediate subordinates.

These considerations do not, however, dispose of the problem. They indicate rather the need for further research. But without further research we may conclude that the chief executive of an organization can deal with only a few immediate subordinates; that this number is determined not only by the nature of the work, but also by the nature of the executive; and that the number of immediate subordinates in a large, diversified and dispersed organization must be even less than in a homogeneous and unified organization to achieve the same measure of co-ordination.

One Master

From the earliest times it has been recognized that nothing but confusion arises under multiple command. "A man cannot serve two masters" was adduced as a theological argument because it was already accepted as a principle of human relation in everyday life. In administration this is known as the principle of "unity of command."[7] The principle may be stated as follows: A workman subject to orders from several superiors will be confused, inefficient, and irresponsible; a workman subject to orders from but one superior may be methodical, efficient, and responsible. Unity of command thus refers to those who are commanded, not to those who issue the commands.[8]

The significance of this principle in the process of co-ordination and organization must not be lost sight of. In building a structure of co-ordination, it is often tempting to set up more than one boss for a man who is doing work which has more than one relationship. Even as great a philosopher of management as Taylor fell into this error in setting up separate foremen to deal with machinery, with materials, with speed, etc., each with the power of giving orders directly to the individual workman.[9] The rigid adherence to the principle of unity of command may have its absurdities; these are, however, unimportant in comparison with the certainty of confusion, inefficiency and irresponsibility which arise from the violation of the principle.

Technical Efficiency

There are many aspects of the problem of securing technical efficiency. Most of these do not concern us here directly. They have been treated extensively by such authorities as Taylor, Dennison, and Kimball, and their implications for general organization by Fayol, Urwick, Mooney, and Reiley. There is, however, one efficiency concept which concerns us deeply in approaching the theory of organization. It is the principle of homogeneity.

It has been observed by authorities in many fields that the efficiency of a group working together is directly related to the homogeneity of the work they are performing, of the processes they are utilizing, and of the purposes which actuate them. From top to bottom, the group must be unified. It must work together.

It follows from this (1) that any organizational structure which brings together in a single unit work divisions which are non-homogeneous in work, in technology, or in purpose will encounter the danger of friction and inefficiency; and (2) that a unit based on a given specialization cannot be given technical direction by a layman.

In the realm of government it is not difficult to find many illustrations of the unsatisfactory results of non-homogeneous administrative combinations. It is generally agreed that agricultural development and education cannot be administered by the same men who enforce pest and disease control, because the success of the former rests upon friendly co-operation and trust of the farmers, while the latter engenders resentment and suspicion. Similarly, activities like drug control established in protection of the consumer do not find appropriate homes in departments dominated by the interests of the producer. In the larger cities and in states it has been found that hospitals cannot be so well administered by the health department directly as they can be when set up independently in a separate department, or at least in a bureau with extensive autonomy, and it is generally agreed that public welfare administration and police administration require separation, as do public health administration and welfare administration, though both of these combinations may be found in successful operation under special conditions. No one would think of combining water supply and public education, or tax administration and public recreation. In every one of these cases, it will be seen that there is some element either of work to be done, or of the technology used, or of the end sought which is non-homogeneous.

Another phase of the combination of incompatible functions in the same office may be found in the common American practice of appointing unqualified laymen and politicians to technical positions or to give technical direction to highly specialized services. As Dr. Frank J. Goodnow pointed out a generation ago, we are faced here by two heterogeneous functions, "politics" and "administration," the combination of which cannot be undertaken within the structure of the administration without producing inefficiency.

Caveamus Expertum

At this point a word of caution is necessary. The application of the principle of homogeneity has its pitfalls. Every highly trained technician, particularly in the learned professions, has a profound sense of omniscience and a great desire for complete independence in the service of society. When employed by government he knows exactly what the people need better than they do themselves, and he knows how to render this service. He tends to be utterly oblivious of all other needs, because, after all, is not his particular technology the road to salvation? Any restraint applied to him is "limitation of freedom," and any criticism "springs from ignorance and jealousy." Every budget increase he secures is "in the public interest," while every increase secured elsewhere is "a sheer waste." His efforts and maneuvers to expand are "public education" and "civic organization," while similar efforts by others are "propaganda" and "politics."

Another trait of the expert is his tendency to assume knowledge and authority in fields in which he has no competence. In this particular, educators, lawyers, priests, admirals, doctors, scientists, engineers, accountants, merchants and bankers are all the same—having achieved technical competence or "success" in one field, they come to think this competence is a general quality detachable from the field and inherent in themselves. They step without embarrassment into other areas. They do not remember that the robes of authority of one kingdom confer no sovereignty in another; but that there they are merely a masquerade.

The expert knows his "stuff." Society needs him, and must have him more and more as man's technical knowledge becomes more and more extensive. But history shows us that the common man is a better judge of his own needs in the long run than any cult of experts. Kings and ruling classes, priests and prophets, soldiers and lawyers, when permitted to rule rather than serve mankind, have in the end done more to check the advance of human welfare than they have to advance it. The true place of the expert is, as A. E. said so well, "on tap, not on top." The essential validity of democracy rests upon this philosophy, for democracy is a way of government in which the common man is the final judge of what is good for him.

Efficiency is one of the things that is good for him because it makes life richer and safer. That efficiency is to be secured more and more through the use of technical specialists. These specialists have no right to ask for, and must not be given freedom from supervisory control, but in establishing that control, a government which ignores the conditions of efficiency cannot expect to achieve efficiency.

3. ORGANIZATIONAL PATTERNS

Organization Up or Down?

One of the great sources of confusion in the discussion of the theory of organization is that some authorities work and think primarily from the top down, while others work and think from the bottom up. This is perfectly natural because some authorities are interested primarily in the executive and in the problems of central management, while others are interested primarily in individual services and activities. Those who work from the top down regard the organization as a system of subdividing the enterprise under the chief executive, while those who work from the bottom up, look upon organization as a system of combining the individual units of work into aggregates which are in turn subordinated to the chief executive. It may be argued that either approach leads to a consideration of the entire problem, so that it is of no great significance which way the organization is viewed. Certainly it makes this very important practical difference: those who work from the top down must guard themselves from the danger of sacrificing the effectiveness of the individual services in their zeal to achieve a model structure at the top, while those who start from the bottom, must guard themselves from the danger of thwarting coordination in their eagerness to develop effective individual services.

In any practical situation the problem of organization must be approached from both top and bottom. This is particularly true in the reorganization of a going concern. May it not be that this practical necessity is likewise the sound process theoretically? In that case one would develop the plan of an organization or reorganization both from the top downward and from the bottom upward, and would reconcile the two at the center. In planning the first subdivisions under the chief executive, the principle of the limitation of the span of control must apply; in building up the first aggregates of specialized functions, the principle of homogeneity must apply. If any enterprise has such an array of functions that the first subdivisions from the top down do not readily meet the first aggregations from the bottom up, then additional divisions and additional aggregates must be introduced, but at each further step there must be a less and less rigorous adherence to the two conflicting principles until their juncture is effected.

An interesting illustration of this problem was encountered in the plans for the reorganization of the City of New York. The Charter Commission of 1934 approached the problem with the determination to cut down the number of departments and separate activities from some 60 to a manageable number. It was equally convinced after conferences with officials from the various city departments that the number could not be brought below 25 without bringing together as "departments" activities which had nothing in common or were in actual conflict. This was still too many for effective supervision by the chief executive. As a solution it was suggested by the author that the charter provide for the subdividing of the executive by the appointment of three or four assistant mayors to whom the mayor might assign parts of his task of broad supervision and co-ordination. Under the plan the assistant mayors would bring all novel and important matters to the mayor for decision, and through continual intimate relationship know the temper of his mind on all matters, and thus be able to relieve him of great masses of detail without in any way injecting themselves into the determination of policy. Under such a plan one assistant mayor might be assigned to give general direction to agencies as diverse as police, parks, hospitals, and docks without violating the principle of homogeneity any more than is the case by bringing these activities under the mayor himself, which is after all a paramount necessity under a democratically controlled government. This is not a violation of the principle of homogeneity *provided* the assistant mayors keep out of the technology of the services and devote themselves to the broad aspects of administration and co-ordination, as would the mayor himself. The assistants were conceived of as parts of the mayoralty, not as parts of the service departments. That is, they represented not the apex of a structure built from the bottom up, but rather the base of a structure extended from the top down, the object of which was to multiply by four the points of effective contact between the executive and the service departments.[10]

Organizing the Executive

The effect of the suggestion presented above is to organize and institutionalize the executive function as such so that it may be more adequate in a complicated situation. This is in reality not a new idea. We do not, for example, expect the chief executive to write his own letters. We give him a private secretary, who is part of his office and assists him to do this part of his job. This secretary is not a part of any department; he is a subdivision of the executive himself. In just this way, though on a different plane, other phases of the job of the chief executive may be organized.

Before doing this, however, it is necessary to have a clear picture of the job itself. This brings us directly to the question, "What is the work of the chief executive? What does he do?"

The answer is POSDCORB.

POSDCORB is, of course, a made-up word designed to call attention to the various functional elements of the work of a chief executive because "administration" and "management" have lost all specific content.[11] POSDCORB is made up of the initials and stands for the following activities:

Planning, that is working out in broad outline the things that need to be done and the methods for doing them to accomplish the purpose set for the enterprise;

Organizing, that is the establishment of the formal structure of authority through which work subdivisions are arranged, defined and co-ordinated for the defined objective;

Staffing, that is the whole personnel function of bringing in and training the staff and maintaining favorable conditions of work;

Directing, that is the continuous task of making decisions and embodying them in specific and general orders and instructions and serving as the leader of the enterprise;

Co-ordinating, that is the all important duty of interrelating the various parts of the work;

Reporting, that is keeping those to whom the executive is responsible informed as to what is going on, which thus includes keeping himself and his subordinates informed through records, research and inspection;

Budgeting, with all that goes with budgeting in the form of fiscal planning, accounting and control.

This statement of the work of a chief executive is adapted from the functional analysis elaborated by Henri Fayol in his "Industrial and General Administration." It is believed that those who know administration intimately will find in this analysis a valid and helpful pattern, into which can be fitted each of the major activities and duties of any chief executive.

If these seven elements may be accepted as the major duties of the chief executive, it follows that they *may* be separately organized as subdivisions of the executive. The need for such subdivision depends entirely on the size and complexity of the enterprise. In the largest enterprises, particularly where the chief executive is as a matter of fact unable to do the work that is thrown upon him, it may be presumed that one or more parts of POSDCORB should be suborganized.

NOTES

1. I.e., when *organization is the basis of co-ordination.* Wherever the central executive authority is composed of several who exercise their functions jointly by majority vote, as on a board, this is from the standpoint of organization still a "single authority"; where the central executive is in reality composed of several men acting freely and independently, then organization cannot be said to be the basis of co-ordination; it is rather the dominance of an idea and falls under the second principle stated above.
2. Sir Ian Hamilton, *The Soul and Body of an Army* (Arnold: London, 1921), p. 230.
3. Great Britain. Ministry of Reconstruction. Report of the Machinery of Government Committee. H. M. Stationery Office, London, 1918, p. 5.
4. Henri Fayol, "The Administrative Theory in the State." Address before the Second International Congress of Administrative Science at Brussels, September 13, 1923. Paper IV in this collection.
5. Graham Wallas, *The Great Society* (Macmillan: London and New York, 1919), p. 264.
6. Léon Blum, *La Réforme Gouvernementale* (Grasset: Paris, 1918; reprint, 1936), p. 59.
7. Henri Fayol, *Industrial and General Administration* trans. J. A. Coubrough (International Management Association: Geneva, 1930).
8. Fayol terms the latter "unity of direction."
9. Frederick Winslow Taylor, *Shop Management* (Harper & Row, New York and London, 1911), p. 99.
10. This recommendation was also presented to the Thatcher Charter Commission of 1935, to which the author was a consultant. A first step in this direction was taken in Sec. 9, Chap. I of the new charter which provides for a deputy mayor, and for such other assistance as may be provided by ordinance.
11. See Minutes of the Princeton Conference on Training for the Public Service, 1935, p. 35. See also criticism of this analysis in Lewis Meriam, *Public Service and Special Training* (University of Chicago Press, 1936), pp. 1, 2, 10 and 15, where this functional analysis is misinterpreted as a statement of qualifications for appointment.

10
Report of the President's Committee on Administrative Management

Louis Brownlow, Charles E. Merriam & Luther Gulick

THE AMERICAN EXECUTIVE

The need for action in realizing democracy was as great in 1789 as it is today. It was thus not by accident but by deliberate design that the Founding Fathers set the American executive in the Constitution on a solid foundation. Sad experience under the Articles of Confederation, with an almost headless government and committee management, had brought the American Republic to the edge of ruin. Our forefathers had broken away from hereditary government and pinned their faith on democratic rule, but they had not found a way to equip the new democracy for action. Consequently, there was grim purpose in resolutely providing for a presidency which was to be a national office. The president is indeed the one and only national officer representative of the entire nation. There was hesitation on the part of some timid souls in providing the president with an election independent of the Congress; with a longer term than most governors of that day; with the duty of informing the Congress as to the state of the Union and of recommending to its consideration "such Measures as he shall judge necessary and expedient"; with a two-thirds veto; with a wide power of appointment; and with military and diplomatic authority. But this reluctance was overcome in the face of need and a democratic executive established.

Equipped with these broad constitutional powers, reenforced by statute, by custom, by general consent, the American executive must be regarded as one of the very greatest contributions made by our nation to the development of modern democracy—a unique institution the value of which is as evident in times of stress and strain as in periods of quiet.

As an instrument for carrying out the judgment and will of the people of a nation, the American executive occupies an enviable position among the executives of the states of the world, combining as it does the elements of popular control and the means for vigorous action and leadership—uniting stability and flexibility. The American executive as an institution stands across the path of those who mistakenly assert that democracy must fail because it can neither decide promptly nor act vigorously.

Our presidency unites at least three important functions. From one point of view the president is a political leader—leader of a party, leader of the Congress, leader of a people. From another point

Source: President's Committee on Administrative Management, *Administrative Management in the Government of the United States, January 8, 1937* (Washington, D.C.: United States Government Printing Office, 1937), pp. 1–6.

of view he is head of the nation in the ceremonial sense of the term, the symbol of our American national solidarity. From still another point of view the president is the chief executive and administrator within the federal system and service. In many types of government these duties are divided or only in part combined, but in the United States they have always been united in one and the same person whose duty it is to perform all of these tasks.

Your Committee on Administrative Management has been asked to investigate and report particularly upon the last function; namely, that of administrative management—the organization for the performance of the duties imposed upon the president in exercising the executive power vested in him by the Constitution of the United States.

IMPROVING THE MACHINERY OF GOVERNMENT

Throughout our history we have paused now and then to see how well the spirit and purpose of our nation is working out in the machinery of everyday government with a view to making such modifications and improvements as prudence and the spirit of progress might suggest. Our government was the first to set up in its formal Constitution a method of amendment, and the spirit of America has been from the beginning of our history the spirit of progressive changes to meet conditions shifting perhaps more rapidly here than elsewhere in the world.

Since the Civil War, as the tasks and responsibilities of our government have grown with the growth of the nation in sweep and power, some notable attempts have been made to keep our administrative system abreast of the new times. The assassination of President Garfield by a disappointed office seeker aroused the nation against the spoils system and led to the enactment of the civil-service law of 1883. We have struggled to make the principle of this law effective for half a century. The confusion in fiscal management led to the establishment of the Bureau of the Budget and the budgetary system in 1921. We still strive to realize the goal set for the nation at that time. And, indeed, many other important forward steps have been taken.

Now we face again the problem of governmental readjustment, in part as the result of the activities of the nation during the desperate years of the industrial depression, in part because of the very growth of the nation, and in part because of the vexing social problems of our times. There is room for vast increase in our national productivity and there is much bitter wrong to set right in neglected ways of human life. There is need for improvement of our governmental machinery to meet new conditions and to make us ready for the problems just ahead.

Facing one of the most troubled periods in all the troubled history of mankind, we wish to set our affairs in the very best possible order to make the best use of all of our national resources and to make good our democratic claims. If America fails, the hopes and dreams of democracy over all the world go down. We shall not fail in our task and our responsibility, but we cannot live upon our laurels alone.

We seek modern types of management in national government best fitted for the stern situations we are bound to meet, both at home and elsewhere. As to ways and means of improvement, there are naturally sincere differences of judgment and opinion, but only a treasonable design could oppose careful attention to the best and soundest practices of government available for the American nation in the conduct of its heavy responsibilities.

THE FOUNDATIONS OF GOVERNMENTAL EFFICIENCY

The efficiency of government rests upon two factors: the consent of the governed and good management. In a democracy consent may be achieved readily, though not without some effort, as it is the cornerstone of the Constitution. Efficient management in a democracy is a factor of peculiar significance.

Administrative efficiency is not merely a matter of paper clips, time clocks, and standardized economies of motion. These are but minor gadgets. Real efficiency goes much deeper down. It must be built into the structure of a government just as it is built into a piece of machinery.

Fortunately the foundations of effective management in public affairs, no less than in private, are well known. They have emerged universally wherever men have worked together for some common purpose, whether through the state, the church, the private association, or the commercial enterprise. They have been written into constitutions, charters, and articles of incorporation, and exist as habits of work in the daily life of all organized peoples. Stated in simple terms these canons of efficiency require the establishment of a responsible and effective chief executive as the center of energy, direction, and administrative management; the systematic organization of all activities in the hands of a qualified personnel under the direction of the chief executive; and to aid him in this, the establishment of appropriate managerial and staff agencies. There must also be provision for planning, a complete fiscal system, and means for holding the executive accountable for his program.

Taken together, these principles, drawn from the experience of mankind in carrying on large-scale enterprises, may be considered as the first requirement of good management. They comprehend the subject matter of administrative management as it is dealt with in this report. Administrative management concerns itself in a democracy with the executive and his duties, with managerial and staff aides, with organization, with personnel, and with the fiscal system because these are the indispensable means of making good the popular will in a people's government.

MODERNIZING OUR GOVERNMENTAL MANAGEMENT

In the light of these canons of efficiency, what must be said of the government of the United States today? Speaking in the broadest terms at this point, and in detail later on, we find in the American government at the present time that the effectiveness of the chief executive is limited and restricted, in spite of the clear intent of the Constitution to the contrary; that the work of the executive branch is badly organized; that the managerial agencies are weak and out of date; that the public service does not include its share of men and women of outstanding capacity and character; and that the fiscal and auditing systems are inadequate. These weaknesses are found at the center of our government and involve the office of the chief executive itself.

While in general principle our organization of the presidency challenges the admiration of the world, yet in equipment for administrative management our Executive Office is not fully abreast of the trend of our American times, either in business or in government. Where, for example, can there be found an executive in any way comparable upon whom so much petty work is thrown? Or who is forced to see so many persons on unrelated matters and to make so many decisions on the basis of what may be, because of the very press of work, incomplete information? How is it humanly possible to know fully the affairs and problems of over 100 separate major agencies, to say nothing of being responsible for their general direction and coordination?

These facts have been known for many years and are so well appreciated that it is not necessary for us to prove again that the president's administrative equipment is far less developed than his responsibilities, and that a major task before the American government is to remedy this dangerous situation. What we need is not a new principle, but a modernizing of our managerial equipment.

This is not a difficult problem in itself. In fact, we have already dealt with it successfully in state governments, in city governments, and in large-scale private industry. Gov. Frank O. Lowden in Illinois, Gov. Alfred E. Smith in New York, Gov. Harry F. Byrd in Virginia, and Gov. William Tudor Gardiner in Maine, among others, have all shown how similar problems can be dealt with in large governmental units. The federal government is more extensive and more complicated, but the principles of reorganization are the same. On the basis of this experience and our examination of the executive branch we conclude that the following steps should now be taken:

1. To deal with the greatly increased duties of executive management falling upon the president the White House staff should be expanded.
2. The managerial agencies of the government, particularly those dealing with the budget, efficiency research, personnel, and planning, should be greatly strengthened and developed as arms of the chief executive.
3. The merit system should be extended upward, outward, and downward to cover all non-policy-determining posts, and the civil service system should be reorganized and opportunities established for a career system attractive to the best talent of the nation.
4. The whole executive branch of the government should be overhauled and the present 100 agencies reorganized under a few large departments in which every executive activity would find its place.
5. The fiscal system should be extensively revised in the light of the best governmental and private practice, particularly with reference to financial records, audit, and accountability of the executive to the Congress.

These recommendations are explained and discussed in the following sections of this report.

THE PURPOSE OF REORGANIZATION

In proceeding to the reorganization of the government it is important to keep prominently before us the ends of reorganization. Too close a view of machinery must not cut off from sight the true purpose of efficient management. Economy is not the only objective, though reorganization is the first step to savings; the elimination of duplication and contradictory policies is not the only objective, though this will follow; a simple and symmetrical organization is not the only objective, though the new organization will be simple and symmetrical; higher salaries and better jobs are not the only objectives, though these are necessary; better business methods and fiscal controls are not the only objectives, though these too are demanded. There is but one grand purpose, namely, to make democracy work today in our national government; that is, to make our government an up-to-date, efficient, and effective instrument for carrying out the will of the nation. It is for this purpose that the government needs thoroughly modern tools of management.

As a people we congratulate ourselves justly on our skill as managers—in the home, on the farm, in business big and little—and we properly expect that management in government shall be of the best American model. We do not always get these results, and we must modestly say "we count not ourselves to have attained," but there is a steady purpose in America to press forward until the practices of our governmental administration are as high as the purpose and standards of our people. We know that bad management may spoil good purposes, and that without good management democracy itself cannot achieve its highest goals.

THE WHITE HOUSE STAFF

In this broad program of administrative reorganization the White House itself is involved. The president needs help. His immediate staff assistance is entirely inadequate. He should be given a small number of executive assistants who would be his direct aides in dealing with the managerial agencies and administrative departments of the government. These assistants, probably not exceeding six in number, would be in addition to his present secretaries, who deal with the public, with the Congress, and with the press and the radio. These aides would have no power to make decisions or issue instructions in their own right. They would not be interposed between the president and the heads of his departments. They would not be assistant presidents in any sense. Their function would be, when any matter was presented to the president for action affecting any part of the administrative work of the government, to assist him in obtaining quickly and without delay all pertinent information possessed by any of the executive departments so as to guide him in making his responsible decisions; and then when decisions have been made, to assist him in seeing to it that every administrative department and agency affected is promptly informed. Their effectiveness in assisting the president will, we think, be directly proportional to their ability to discharge their functions with restraint. They would remain in the background, issue no orders, make no decisions, emit no public statements. Men for these positions should be carefully chosen by the president from within and without the government. They should be men in whom the president has personal confidence and whose character and attitude is such that they would not attempt to exercise power on their own account. They should be possessed of high competence, great physical vigor, and a passion for anonymity. They should be installed in the White House itself, directly accessible to the president. In the selection of these aides the president should be free to call on departments from time to time for the assignment of persons who, after a tour of duty as his aides, might be restored to their old positions.

This recommendation arises from the growing complexity and magnitude of the work of the president's office. Special assistance is needed to insure that all matters coming to the attention of the president have been examined from the over-all managerial point of view, as well as from all standpoints that would bear on policy and operation. It also would facilitate the flow upward to the president of information upon which he is to base his decisions and the flow downward from the president of the decisions once taken for execution by the department or departments affected. Thus such a staff would not only aid the president but would also be of great assistance to the several executive departments and to the managerial agencies in simplifying executive contacts, clearance, and guidance.

The president should also have at his command a contingent fund to enable him to bring in from time to time particular persons possessed of particular competency for a particular purpose and whose services he might usefully employ for short periods of time.

The president in his regular office staff should be given a greater number of positions so that he will not be compelled, as he has been compelled in the past, to use for his own necessary work persons carried on the pay rolls of other departments.

If the president be thus equipped he will have but the ordinary assistance that any executive of a large establishment is afforded as a matter of course.

In addition to this assistance in his own office the president must be given direct control over and be charged with immediate responsibility for the great managerial functions of the government which affect all of the administrative departments. . . . These functions are personnel management, fiscal and organizational management, and planning management. Within these three groups may be comprehended all of the essential elements of business management.

The development of administrative management in the federal government requires the improvement of the administration of these managerial activities, not only by the central agencies in charge, but also by the departments and bureaus. The central agencies need to be strengthened and developed as managerial arms of the chief executive, better equipped to perform their central responsibilities and to provide the necessary leadership in bringing about improved practices throughout the government.

The three managerial agencies, the Civil Service Administration, the Bureau of the Budget, and the National Resources Board should be a part and parcel of the Executive Office. Thus the president would have reporting to him directly the three managerial institutions whose work and activities would affect all of the administrative departments.

The budgets for the managerial agencies should be submitted to the Congress by the president as a part of the budget for the Executive Office. This would distinguish these agencies from the operating administrative departments of the government, which should report to the president through the heads of departments who collectively compose his cabinet. Such an arrangement would materially aid the president in his work of supervising the administrative agencies and would enable the Congress and the people to hold him to strict accountability for their conduct.

11
Informal Organizations and Their Relation to Formal Organizations

Chester I. Barnard

I. WHAT INFORMAL ORGANIZATIONS ARE

It is a matter of general observation and experience that persons are frequently in contact and interact with each other when their relationships are not a part of or governed by any formal organization. The magnitude of the numbers involved varies from two persons to that of a large mob or crowd. The characteristic of these contacts or interactions is that they occur and continue or are repeated without any specific conscious *joint* purpose. The contact may be accidental, or incidental to organized activities, or arise from some personal desire or gregarious instinct; it may be friendly or hostile. But whatever the origins, the fact of such contacts, interactions, or groupings changes the experience, knowledge, attitudes, and emotions of the individuals affected. Sometimes we are aware of the fact that our emotions are affected, for example, by being in a crowd; more often we observe effects of such relationships in others; still more frequently we are not aware of any permanent effects either in ourselves or in others by direct observation. But we nevertheless currently show that we infer such effects by using the phrase "mob psychology," by recognizing imitation and emulation, by understanding that there are certain attitudes commonly held, and very often by our use of the phrases "consensus of opinion" and "public opinion." The persistence of such effects is embodied in "states of mind" and habits of action which indicate the capacities of memory, experience, and social conditioning. As a result of these capacities some of the effects of contacts of persons with limited numbers of persons can spread through very large numbers in a sort of endless chain of interaction over wide territories and through long periods of time.

By informal organization I mean the aggregate of the personal contacts and interactions and the associated groupings of people that I have just described. Though common or joint purposes are excluded by definition, common or joint results of important character nevertheless come from such organization.

Now it is evident from this description that informal organization is indefinite and rather structureless, and has no definite subdivision. It may be regarded as a shapeless mass of quite varied densities, the variations in density being a result of external factors affecting the closeness of people geographically or of formal purposes which bring them specially into contact for conscious joint accomplishments. These areas of special density I call informal organizations, as distinguished from societal or general organization in its informal aspects. Thus there is an informal organization of a community, of a state. For our purposes, it is important that there are informal organizations related to formal organizations everywhere.

II. CONSEQUENCES OF INFORMAL ORGANIZATIONS

Informal organization, although comprising the processes of society which are unconscious as contrasted with those of formal organization which are conscious, has two important classes of effects: *(a)* it establishes certain attitudes, understandings, customs, habits, institutions; and *(b)* it creates the condition under which formal organization may arise.

(a) The most general direct effects of informal organization are customs, mores, folklore, institutions, social norms and ideals—a field of importance in general sociology and especially in social psychology and in social anthropology. No discussion of these effects is necessary here, except on two points. The first is that as a result, as I think, of the inadequate attention to formal organization there is much confusion between formal institutions, resulting directly from formal organizational processes, and informal institutions resulting from informal organization; for example, a practice established by legal enactment, and a custom, the latter usually prevailing in the event of conflict. Not only locally, in restricted collectivities, but in broad areas and large collectivities, there is a divergence, and a corrective interaction, between institutions informally developed and those elaborated through formal organization practices. The first correspond to the unconscious or nonintellectual actions and habits of individuals, the second to their reasoned and calculated actions and policies. The actions of formal organizations are relatively quite logical.

(b) Informal association is rather obviously a condition which necessarily precedes formal organization. The possibility of accepting a common purpose, of communicating, and of attaining a state of mind under which there is willingness to coöperate, requires prior contact and preliminary interaction. This is especially clear in those cases where the origin of formal organization is spontaneous. The informal relationship in such cases may be exceedingly brief, and of course conditioned by previous experience and knowledge of both informal and formal organization.

The important consideration for our purposes, however, is that informal organization compels a certain amount of formal organization, and probably cannot persist or become extensive without the emergence of formal organization. This partly results from the recognition of similarity of needs and interests which continuation of contact implies. When these needs and interests are material and not social, either combination and coöperation—at least to the extent of the development of a distributive purpose—or conflict of interest, antagonism, hostility, and disorganization ensue.

Even when the needs and interests are not material but are social—that is, there is a gregarious need of interaction for its own sake—it likewise requires a considerable concentration upon definite purposes or ends of action to maintain the association. This is especially true if instead of gregarious impulses one goes back to a *need of action* as a primary propensity or instinct. It is an observable fact that men are universally active, and that they seek objects of activity. Correlative with this is the observation that enduring social contact, even when the object is exclusively social, seems generally impossible without activity. It will be generally noted that a purely passive or bovine kind of association among men is of short duration. They seem impelled to *do something.* It is frequently the case that the existence of organizations depends upon satisfactions in mere association, and that this is the uniform and only motive of all participants. In these cases, nevertheless, we can, I think, always observe a purpose, or concrete object of action, which may be of minor importance or even trivial. In these cases it may make no difference in a direct and substantial sense whether the objective is accomplished or not. For example, the discussion of some subject (or subjects) is essential to conversation which is socially desirable, yet the participants may be and frequently are rather indifferent to the subject itself. But the personal associations which give the satisfactions depends upon discussing *something.* This is easily observed in ordinary social affairs.

Thus a concrete object of action is necessary to social satisfactions. The simplest form of doing something together is, of course, conversation, but it is evident that any particular form of activity for one reason or another is exhausted usually in a short time and that alternative methods of activity are on the whole not easy to devise either by individuals or groups. Hence, the great importance of established patterns of activity. Where circumstances develop so that a variety of outlets for activity involving associations are not readily available—as is often the case, for example, with unemployed persons—the situation is one in which the individual is placed in a sort of social vacuum, producing a feeling and also objective behavior of being "lost." I have seen this a number of times. Where the situation affects a number of persons simultaneously they are likely to do any sort of mad thing. The necessity for action where a group of persons is involved seems to be almost overwhelming. I think this necessity underlies such proverbs as "Idle hands make mischief," and I have no doubt that it may be the basis for a great deal of practice within armies.

The opposite extreme to lack of concrete objectives of action is a condition of social complexity such that action may take a great many different forms involving the possibilities of association with many different groups. In such situations the individual may be unable to decide which activity he wishes to indulge in, or what groups he wishes to be associated with. This may induce a sort of paralysis of action through inability to make choice, or it may be brought about by conflict of obligations. The resulting condition was described by the French sociologist Durkheim as "anomie." This I take to be a state of individual paralysis of social action due to the absence of effective norms of conduct.

The activities of individuals necessarily take place within local immediate groups. The relation of a man to a large organization, or to his nation, or to his church, is necessarily through those with whom he is in *immediate* contact. Social activities cannot be action at a distance. This seems not to have been sufficiently noted. It explains, or justifies, a statement made to me that comradeship is much more powerful than patriotism, etc., in the behavior of soldiers. The essential need of the individual is association, and that requires local activity or immediate interaction between individuals. Without it the man is lost. The willingness of men to endure onerous routine and dangerous tasks which they could avoid is explained by this necessity for action at all costs in order to maintain the sense of social integration, whether the latter arises from "instinct," or from social conditioning, or from physiological necessity, or all three. Whether this necessity for action in a social setting arises exclusively from biological factors, or is partly inherent in gregarious association, need not be considered.

Finally, purposive coöperation is the chief outlet for the logical or scientific faculties of men, and is the principal source of them as well. Rational action is chiefly a purposive coöperative action, and the personal capacity of rational action is largely derived from it.

For these reasons, either small enduring informal organizations or large collectivities seem always to possess a considerable number of formal organizations. These are the definite structural material of a society. They are the poles around which personal associations are given sufficient consistency to retain continuity. The alternative is disintegration into hostile groups, the hostility itself being a source of integrating purposes (defense and offense) of the groups which are differentiated by hostility. Thus as formal organization becomes extended in scope it permits and requires an expansion of societal cohesiveness. This is most obviously the case when formal organization complexes of government expand—government itself is insufficient, except where economic and religious functions are included in it. Where with the expansion of formal government complexes there is correlative expansion of religious, military, economic, and other formal organizations, the structure of a large-scale society is present. When these formal complexes fail or contract, social disintegration sets in. There appear to be no societies which in fact are not completely structured by formal organizations—beginning with families and ending in great complexes of states and religions.

This is not to deny, but to reaffirm, that the attitudes, institutions, customs, of informal society affect and are partly expressed through formal organization. They are interdependent aspects of the same phenomena—a society is structured by formal organizations, formal organizations are vitalized and conditioned by informal organization. What is asserted is that there cannot be one without the other. If one fails the other disintegrates. Nor is this to say that when disintegrated the separated or conflicting societies (except isolated societies) have no affect upon each other. Quite the contrary; but the effect is not coöperative but polemic; and even so requires formal organization within the conflicting societies. Complete absence of formal organization would then be a state of nearly complete individualism and disorder.

III. THE CREATION OF INFORMAL BY FORMAL ORGANIZATIONS

Formal organizations arise out of and are necessary to informal organization; but when formal organizations come into operation, they create and require informal organizations.

It seems not easily to be recognized without long and close observation that an important and often indispensable part of a formal system of cooperation is informal. In fact, more often than not those with ample experience (officials and executives of all sorts of formal organizations) will deny or neglect the existence of informal organizations within their "own" formal organizations. Whether this is due to excessive concentration on the problems of formal organization, or to reluctance to acknowledge the existence of what is difficult to define or describe, or what lacks in concreteness, it is unnecessary to consider. But it is undeniable that major executives and even entire executive organizations are often completely unaware of wide-spread influences, attitudes, and agitations within their organizations. This is true not only of business organizations but also of political organizations, governments, armies, churches, and universities.

Yet one will hear repeatedly that "you can't understand an organization or how it works from its organization chart, its charter, rules and regulations, nor from looking at or even watching its personnel." "Learning the organization ropes" in most organizations is chiefly learning who's who, what's what, why's why, of its informal society. One could not determine very closely how the government of the United States works from reading its Constitution, its court decisions, its statutes, or its administrative regulations. Although ordinarily used in a derogatory sense, the phrase "invisible government" expresses a recognition of informal organization.

Informal organizations as associated with formal organization, though often understood intuitively by managers, politicians, and other organization authorities, have only been definitely studied, so far as I know, at the production level of industrial organizations. In fact, informal organization is so much a part of our matter-of-course intimate experience of everyday association, either in connection with formal organizations or not, that we are unaware of it, seeing only a part of the specific interactions involved. Yet it is evident that association of persons in connection with a formal or specific activity inevitably involves interactions that are incidental to it.

IV. THE FUNCTIONS OF INFORMAL IN FORMAL ORGANIZATIONS

One of the indispensable functions of informal organizations in formal organizations—that of communication—has already been indicated. Another function is that of the maintenance of cohesiveness in formal organizations through regulating the willingness to serve and the stability of objective authority. A third function is the maintenance of the feeling of personal integrity, of self-respect, of independent choice. Since the interactions of informal organization are not consciously dominated by a given impersonal objective or by authority as the organization expression, the interactions are apparently characterized by choice, and furnish the opportunities often for reinforcement of personal attitudes. Though often this function is deemed destructive of formal organization, it is to be regarded as a means of maintaining the personality of the individual against certain effects of formal organizations which tend to disintegrate the personality.

The purpose of this chapter has been to show (1) that those interactions between persons which are based on personal rather than on joint or common purposes, because of their repetitive character become systematic and organized through their effect upon habits of action and thought and through their promotion of uniform states of mind; (2) that although the number of persons with whom any individual may have interactive experience is limited, nevertheless the endless-chain relationship between persons in a society results in the development, in many respects, over wide areas and among many persons, of uniform states of mind which crystallize into what we call mores, customs, institutions; (3) that informal organization gives rise to formal organizations, and that formal organizations are necessary to any large informal or societal organization; (4) that formal organizations also make explicit many of the attitudes, states of mind, and institutions which develop directly through informal organizations, with tendencies to divergence, resulting in interdependence and mutual correction of these results in a general and only approximate way; (5) that formal organizations, once established, in their turn also create informal organizations; and (6) that informal organizations are necessary to the operation of formal organizations as a means of communication, of cohesion, and of protecting the integrity of the individual.

12 Concepts of Reorganization

Lewis Meriam

Economy and efficiency in the national government are the almost universally accepted objectives of reorganization. Some proponents of reorganization would define economy as an actual reduction in expenditures, whereas others would accept more efficient service for a given expenditure as constituting economy in administration. The members of this latter school of thought, as a matter of fact, seem almost to regard economy and efficiency as identical terms, whereas the former group regards actual savings as essential to real economy.

Important differences among proponents of reorganization arise over the devices that should be used for securing economy and efficiency and the governmental machinery and procedures that are necessary for applying these devices. The significant differences of opinion which exist arise in large measure out of varying conceptions as to the proper spheres of power and action as between the President on the one hand and the Congress on the other. In reality, there appear to be four more or less distinct concepts of reorganization and reorganization procedure. Some proponents of reorganization appear to have only one of these concepts in mind, whereas the thinking of others embraces two or more of them. Accordingly the term "reorganization" as currently used involves basically different meanings, and the resulting confusion serves greatly to complicate the practical problem of effecting a satisfactory overhauling of federal government machinery.

In the present chapter an effort will be made to clarify these various concepts. Then, after the basic statistical data that constitute the factual background of the entire problem have been presented in Chapter II, each of the major concepts will be considered in some detail in a separate chapter.

Source: Lewis Meriam, "Part I. An Analysis of the Problem," in *Reorganization of the National Government: What Does It Involve?* by Lewis Meriam and Laurence F. Schmeckebier (Washington, D.C.: Brookings Institution, 1939), pp. 11–21.

STRUCTURAL REORGANIZATION

Students of both public and private enterprises are familiar with organization charts that show the structure or anatomy of the institution or agency under consideration. In the national government the first of the organization charts ordinarily shows the President as the chief of the administrative branch, under him the ten Cabinet members who head the executive departments, and the heads of such independent establishments as report directly to the President. Then come the charts for departmental and independent establishments, showing the bureaus or other major divisions thereof. Next come the bureau or other major division charts, showing how each bureau or major division is made up of distinctive structural working units. In the case of large or complicated agencies there may be charts showing the division of the working units into sections or even subsections. Taken altogether the charts show the anatomical structure of the administrative branch of the government, or as some express it, the administrative hierarchy which extends from the most humble worker at the base of the administrative pyramid to the President at its apex.

This administrative structure was never planned in advance nor were any definite principles laid down which were to govern its development. A favorite remark is that like Topsy "it just growed." This remark is not entirely fair, for although there never was either a master plan or a body of established guiding principles, both the Congress and the Presidents in establishing new agencies have given much time and thought to matters of organization: where the new agency shall be placed with relation to the President and to existing agencies and often as to what its internal structure should be; what position or positions should head it; and perhaps how it should be subdivided into working units.

Since the administrative structure has thus developed piecemeal over practically a century and a half and has never been completely and systematically overhauled, many people naturally believe that material advances in economy and efficiency could be secured by its radical revision. They cite its obvious complexity and give instances of overlapping, duplications, and even conflicts among different administrative agencies. They believe that through structural reorganization the whole administrative machine may be greatly simplified and that by departmentalization the overlappings may be materially reduced, conflicts practically eliminated, and duplications reduced to the vanishing point. Persons who hold this concept think of reorganization simply as organizing again the whole structure from bottom to top. They seek unification and coordination.

THE CURTAILMENT OF FUNCTIONS AND ACTIVITIES

Many individuals who have been interested in administrative reorganization focus attention upon the elimination of useless or unimportant services. It is argued that once a government has undertaken to perform a function, to conduct an activity, or to render a service, there is an inevitable tendency to continue to do so even though changes in economic and social conditions may have profoundly altered the significance of the service. It is also pointed out that many activities have been undertaken merely because some particular Cabinet official or bureau head has at some time manifested an interest, perhaps only tentative or experimental in character, in a particular problem, and that inertia or the vested interests of staff personnel serves to perpetuate the activity indefinitely. Accordingly, it is believed that during the course of the last 150 years the national government must have accumulated many functions and activities that are no longer essential or justifiable, the elimination or curtailment of which would yield substantial reductions in expenditure.

Some who hold the concept that reorganization means, not structural changes which would allow the present functions and activities to be carried out with greater economy and efficiency, but actual reductions and curtailments in services, contend that a government, like an individual, should adjust its activities to its income. In times of prosperity when income is high, activities that partake of the nature of luxuries may well be afforded; when income falls off, all unnecessary activities should be curtailed or abandoned. Only thus, it is urged, can the nation's budget be kept in balance.

A practical difficulty in the application of this concept of course lies in the difficulty of securing agreement among its advocates as to the particular functions and activities that are outmoded or that fall in the luxury class. It is a matter of common knowledge that our national government has, over the years, undertaken many functions and activities at the behest of particular sections of the country or of certain special interests or, to use the popular term, "pressure groups." Persons who are not interested in these regional or group interests are, of course, prone to classify such activities as subject to curtailment or elimination, whereas the beneficiaries consider their maintenance as vitally essential. Naturally the officers and employees of the governmental agency in question join with the specially benefited groups in resisting either abolition or serious curtailment.

This type of reorganization thus involves a wide range of interests as well as major issues of public policy. It not only meets with a maximum of resistance from the groups which would be adversely affected, but it enters the field of substantive governmental policy, and thus involves a wider range of considerations than does structural reorganization.

EXECUTIVE CONTROL

Many proponents of reorganization believe that efficiency in administration can only be attained through providing for greater executive control by the President. Despite a good deal of agreement on that general statement, there is wide and fundamental disagreement as to the devices for providing that control. In the present chapter, which deals only with concepts of reorganization, the three major devices which have been advocated will be briefly outlined. Then a supposed parallel between state reorganization and national reorganization will be examined. Finally a few words will be said regarding the European background against which this subject of executive control and executive powers is today inevitably viewed. The principal discussion will, of course, come in the chapter devoted to the subject of executive control.

The three major proposals arranged in descending order according to their degree of radicalism from one point of view are:

1. To increase materially the actual power of the President without any increase whatever in the congressional control over the President. In fact the increase in power would be achieved under the Constitution by having the Congress

delegate some of its powers to the President and by having it forego the exercise of some of the power it now possesses. The argument advanced in support of this change is briefly that the President alone represents all the people; the people hold the President responsible for the success of the government; and consequently the President should have power commensurate with his responsibility. Some advocates of this proposal contend that the American people should be far more concerned about the power to govern than about preserving the constitutional system of the division of powers.

2. To increase materially the power of the President but at the same time, possibly through constitutional amendments, to increase the power of the Congress to hold him responsible for the manner in which he uses his increased power. Persons who hold these views see distinct advantages in the parliamentary system under which the executive is directly responsible to the legislature and may be removed from office if he fails to retain the support of a majority of its members. They agree with the group described in the preceding paragraph that the President should have sufficient powers so that he may fairly be held responsible for results, but they would not give him increased powers until compensating increases have been made in the devices for holding him responsible to the people through their chosen representatives in the Congress. They do not regard election once in four years as a sufficient device, since they fear that some President might use the increased powers of his office to build a national political machine to insure the continuance of his control of the government.
3. To make no change in the powers of the President as they are set forth in the Constitution, to preserve the division of powers as the Constitution provides, but to furnish the President with better mechanisms, particularly through the establishment of adequate staff agencies, to enable him more easily to perform his functions as general manager of the executive branch of the government. At the same time some advocates of this method would strengthen the staff agencies, which serve the Congress so that it could have better detailed factual material as a basis for the exercise of its present constitutional powers for controlling administration both through general legislation and through appropriation acts. This group points out that under the Constitution all executive power is vested in the President and that he has power to remove any officer in the executive branch of the government, exclusive of certain officers in independent quasi-legislative and quasi-judicial agencies, if with respect to them the Congress has exercised its constitutional right to restrict the removal power. They believe that the power is sufficient—that what is needed is greatly improved mechanisms for the exercise of the power.

Some advocates of increasing the power of the executive maintain that state governments have been effectively reorganized through increasing the power and responsibility of the governor and that a like course should be followed to secure administrative efficiency in the national government. Two points deserve brief mention in connection with this line of thinking.

The evidence as to the effect of increasing the power of the governor on the efficiency of the state governments is by no means conclusive. Observers in certain states that have thus been reorganized maintain that the efficiency and the quality of state government has actually deteriorated; but it is by no means certain that the admitted deterioration has resulted from increasing the power of the governor. More basic political forces may have been responsible. It seems reasonably certain, however, that the result of increasing the power of the governor depends on the kind of governor the people elect. An excellent governor can use his increased power in the interests of good administration; a poor governor, interested primarily in partisan politics, patronage, and his own political advancement, can abuse the power that has been entrusted to him.

The second point is that the national executive organization has never been in the least comparable with that of the state governments. Being fearful of executive encroachment, many of the states in drafting their early constitutions made the governorship weak and ornamental rather than powerful. They provided many elected administrative officers, each dominant in his particular field, and the governor had no real power or control over these elected officials. Often, moreover, the state legislatures set up departments, agencies, even separate eleemosynary or penal institutions, under independent boards which the governor could not control. Thus the governor was only first among many elected and appointed administrative officials. To remedy this situation and to make possible a coordinated state administrative program, the reorganizers went as far as they could in copying the national system, which provides for only one elected officer in the executive branch, in whom is vested all executive power, including the power to remove any officer in the executive branch of the government. Thus the differences between the structure of the national government and that of many of the states before reorganization are so great that in the ensuing chapters no attempt will be made to argue that what has been done in the states furnishes a pattern for what should be done in the national government.

Because of political developments in continental Europe since the World War this whole question of increasing the power of the President and the division of powers between the executive, the legislature, and the courts will necessarily be viewed against the European background. Here again opinion is sharply divided. One group attributes the rise of dictatorships to the weaknesses of legislative bodies, to the inability of legislatively controlled governments to get things done. To escape dictatorships democratic government must be made efficient. Efficiency is to be secured by vesting great power in an elected executive, chosen through democratic process. The second group, noting Hitler's rise to power within constitutional forms and his subsequent ability to command almost universal support through popular elections, regards proposals to vest great powers in the executive as a device not to preserve democracy as we have known it but seriously to endanger it. It is the existence of problems such as these that has made reorganization of the executive branch of the government a really major issue.

CONTINUOUS REORGANIZATION

The three concepts of reorganization thus far discussed assume that reorganization is to be brought about in the main by a single reorganization act which will partake of the nature of a surgical operation. The administrative branch of the national government will go under the surgeon's knife for a year or two and will emerge at the end completely reorganized, modernized, and efficient. Holders of the fourth concept of reorganization question the practicability of the surgical operation type of approach as the major device for solving the problem. They believe that the national government is far too large and too complex a going concern to be dealt with in that way.

Persons with this conception believe, moreover, that organization is not at all a static thing which once set right will stay right; rather it is a living organism that must change from time to time as conditions change. Thus they seek not for a reorganization bill which will streamline the administrative branch of government but for one which will perfect the machinery for a regular, orderly consideration of organization problems as they arise. They see no reason for attempting to solve all the problems at once when they believe that with adequate procedure it would be entirely possible to take up the major problems separately and to deal with each according to sound democratic legislative process. They emphasize the fact that each year the Congress reviews the work of practically all the administrative agencies in connection with the annual appropriation bills. They believe that with the amplification of existing governmental machinery, both executive and legislative, the desired ends of reorganization could be better achieved within a reasonable period and that, moreover, the devices would be effective in continuing to keep the organization in good condition.

They contend that structural organization is only one factor in economy and efficiency, a factor the importance of which has been greatly overestimated. Far more important in eliminating overlapping and duplication, preventing conflicts, and promoting coordination and co-operation, is day-to-day management. Hence, those who hold this conception of reorganization stress the importance of developing, through legislation, sound mechanisms and procedures for doing a good, continuous job, with the President and the Congress both performing their constitutional functions; and they question the wisdom and practicability of achieving the desired ends in a bill which attempts the surgical operation.

13
Bureaucratic Structure and Personality

Robert K. Merton

A formal, rationally organized social structure involves clearly defined patterns of activity in which, ideally, every series of actions is functionally related to the purposes of the organization.[1] In such an organization there is integrated a series of offices, of hierarchized statuses, in which inhere a number of obligations and privileges closely defined by limited and specific rules. Each of these offices contains an area of imputed competence and responsibility. Authority, the power of control which derives from an acknowledged status, inheres in the office and not in the particular person who performs the official role. Official action ordinarily occurs within the framework of preexisting rules of the organization. The system of prescribed relations between the various offices involves a considerable degree of formality and clearly defined social distance between the occupants of these positions. Formality is manifested by means of a more or less complicated social ritual which symbolizes and supports the pecking order of the various offices. Such formality, which is integrated with the distribution of authority within the system, serves to minimize friction by largely restricting (official) contact to modes which are previously defined by the rules of the organization. Ready calculability of others' behavior and a stable set of mutual expectations is thus built up. Moreover, formality facilitates the interaction of the occupants of offices despite their (possibly hostile) private attitudes toward one another. In this way, the subordinate is protected from the arbitrary action of his superior, since the actions of both are constrained by a mutually recognized set of rules. Specific procedural devices foster objectivity and restrain the "quick passage of impulse into action."[2]

THE STRUCTURE OF BUREAUCRACY

The ideal type of such formal organization is bureaucracy and, in many respects, the classical analysis of bureaucracy is that by Max Weber.[3] As Weber indicates, bureaucracy involves a clear-cut division of integrated activities which are regarded as duties inherent in the office. A system of differentiated controls and sanctions is stated in the regulations. The assignment of roles occurs on the basis of technical qualifications which are ascertained through formalized, impersonal procedures (*e.g.*, examinations). Within the structure of hierarchically arranged authority, the activities of "trained and salaried experts" are governed by general, abstract, and clearly defined rules which preclude the necessity for the issuance of specific instructions for each specific case. The

Source: Reprinted with permission of Macmillan Publishing Co., Inc., from *Social Theory and Social Structure* (revised and enlarged edition) by Robert K. Merton. Copyright © 1957 by The Free Press, a Corporation. This is a revised version of an article of the same title that appeared in *Social Forces*, vol. 18 (1940).

generality of the rules requires the constant use of *categorization*, whereby individual problems and cases are classified on the basis of designated criteria and are treated accordingly. The pure type of bureaucratic official is appointed, either by a superior or through the exercise of impersonal competition; he is not elected. A measure of flexibility in the bureaucracy is attained by electing higher functionaries who presumably express the will of the electorate (*e.g.*, a body of citizens or a board of directors). The election of higher officials is designed to affect the purposes of the organization, but the technical procedures for attaining these ends are carried out by continuing bureaucratic personnel.[4]

Most bureaucratic offices involve the expectation of life-long tenure, in the absence of disturbing factors which may decrease the size of the organization. Bureaucracy maximizes vocational security.[5] The function of security of tenure, pensions, incremental salaries and regularized procedures for promotion is to ensure the devoted performance of official duties, without regard for extraneous pressures.[6] The chief merit of bureaucracy is its technical efficiency, with a premium placed on precision, speed, expert control, continuity, discretion, and optimal returns on input. The structure is one which approaches the complete elimination of personalized relationships and nonrational considerations (hostility, anxiety, affectual involvements, etc.).

With increasing bureaucratization, it becomes plain to all who would see that man is to a very important degree controlled by his social relations to the instruments of production. This can no longer seem only a tenet of Marxism, but a stubborn fact to be acknowledged by all, quite apart from their ideological persuasion. Bureaucratization makes readily visible what was previously dim and obscure. More and more people discover that to work, they must be employed. For to work, one must have tools and equipment. And the tools and equipment are increasingly available only in bureaucracies, private or public. Consequently, one must be employed by the bureaucracies in order to have access to tools in order to work in order to live. It is in this sense that bureaucratization entails separation of individuals from the instruments of production, as in modern capitalistic enterprise or in state communistic enterprise (of the midcentury variety), just as in the postfeudal army, bureaucratization entailed complete separation from the instruments of destruction. Typically, the worker no longer owns his tools nor the soldier, his weapons. And in this special sense, more and more people become workers, either blue collar or white collar or stiff shirt. So develops, for example, the new type of scientific worker, as the scientist is "separated" from his technical equipment—after all, the physicist does not ordinarily own his cyclotron. To work at his research, he must be employed by a bureaucracy with laboratory resources.

Bureaucracy is administration which almost completely avoids public discussion of its techniques, although there may occur public discussion of its policies.[7] This secrecy is confined neither to public nor to private bureaucracies. It is held to be necessary to keep valuable information from private economic competitors or from foreign and potentially hostile political groups. And though it is not often so called, espionage among competitors is perhaps as common, if not as intricately organized, in systems of private economic enterprise as in systems of national states.

Cost figures, lists of clients, new technical processes, plans for production—all these are typically regarded as essential secrets of private economic bureaucracies which might be revealed if the bases of all decisions and policies had to be publicly defended.

THE DYSFUNCTIONS OF BUREAUCRACY

In these bold outlines, the positive attainments and functions of bureaucratic organization are emphasized and the internal stresses and strains of such structures are almost wholly neglected. The community at large, however, evidently emphasizes the imperfections of bureaucracy, as is suggested by the fact that the "horrid hybrid," bureaucrat, has become an epithet, a *Schimpfwort*.

The transition to a study of the negative aspects of bureaucracy is afforded by the application of Veblen's concept of "trained incapacity," Dewey's notion of "occupational psychosis" or Warnotte's view of "professional deformation." Trained incapacity refers to that state of affairs in which one's abilities function as inadequacies or blind spots. Actions based upon training and skills which have been successfully applied in the past may result in inappropriate responses *under changed conditions*. An inadequate flexibility in the application of skills, will, in a changing milieu, result in more or less serious maladjustments.[8] Thus, to adopt a barnyard illustration used in this connection by Burke, chickens may be readily conditioned to interpret the sound of a bell as a signal for food. The same bell may now be used to summon the trained chickens to their doom as they are assembled to suffer decapitation. In general, one adopts measures in keeping with one's past training and, under new conditions which are not recognized as *significantly* different, the very soundness of this training may lead to the adoption of the wrong procedures. Again, in Burke's almost echolalic phrase, "people may be unfitted by being fit in an unfit fitness"; their training may become an incapacity.

Dewey's concept of occupational psychosis rests upon much the same observations. As a result of their day to day routines, people develop special preferences, antipathies, discriminations and emphases.[9] (The term psychosis is used by Dewey to denote a "pronounced character of the mind.") These psychoses develop through demands put upon the individual by the particular organization of his occupational role.

The concepts of both Veblen and Dewey refer to a fundamental ambivalence. Any action can be considered in terms of what it attains or what it fails to attain. "A way of seeing is also a way of not seeing—a focus upon object *A* involves a neglect of object *B*."[10] In his discussion, Weber is almost exclusively concerned with what the bureaucratic structure attains: precision, reliability, efficiency. This same structure may be examined from another perspective provided by the ambivalence. What are the limitations of the organizations designed to attain these goals?

For reasons which we have already noted, the bureaucratic structure exerts a constant pressure upon the official to be "methodical, prudent, disciplined." If the bureaucracy is to operate successfully, it must attain a high degree of reliability of behavior, an unusual degree of conformity with prescribed patterns of action. Hence, the fundamental importance of discipline which may be as highly developed in a religious or economic bureaucracy as in the army. Discipline can be effective only if the ideal patterns are buttressed by strong sentiments which entail devotion to one's duties, a keen sense of the limitation of one's authority and competence, and methodical performance of routine activities. The efficacy of social structure depends ultimately upon infusing group participants with appropriate attitudes and sentiments. As we shall see, there are definite arrangements in the bureaucracy for inculcating and reinforcing these sentiments.

At the moment, it suffices to observe that in order to ensure discipline (the necessary reliability of response), these sentiments are often more intense than is technically necessary. There is a margin of safety, so to speak, in the pressure exerted by these sentiments upon the bureaucrat to conform to his patterned obligations, in much the same sense that added allowances (precautionary overestimations) are made by the engineer in designing the supports for a bridge. But this very emphasis leads to a transference of the sentiments from the *aims* of the organization onto the particular details of behavior required by the rules. Adherence to the rules, originally conceived as a means, becomes transformed into an end-in-itself; there occurs the familiar process of *displacement of goals* whereby "an instrumental value becomes a terminal value."[11] Discipline, readily interpreted as conformance with regulations, whatever the situation, is seen not as a measure designed for specific purposes but becomes an immediate value in the life-organization of the bureaucrat. This emphasis, resulting from the displacement of the original goals, develops into rigidities and an inability to adjust readily. Formalism, even ritualism, ensues with an unchallenged insistence upon punctilious adherence to formalized procedures.[12] This may be exaggerated to the point where primary concern with conformity to the rules interferes with the achievement of the purposes of the organization, in which case we have the familiar phenomenon of the technicism or red tape of the official. An extreme product of this process of displacement of goals is the bureaucratic virtuoso, who never forgets a single rule binding his action and hence is unable to assist many of his clients.[13] A case in point, where strict recognition of the limits of authority and literal adherence to rules produced this result, is the pathetic plight of Bernt Balchen, Admiral Byrd's pilot in the flight over the South Pole.

> According to a ruling of the department of labor Bernt Balchen . . . cannot receive his citizenship papers. Balchen, a native of Norway, declared his intention in 1927. It is held that he has failed to meet the condition of five years' continuous residence in the United States. The Byrd antarctic voyage took him out of the country, although he was on a ship carrying the American flag, was an invaluable member of the American expedition, and in a region to which there is an American claim because of the exploration and occupation of it by Americans, this region being Little America.
>
> The bureau of naturalization explains that it cannot proceed on the assumption that Little America is American soil. That would be *trespass on international questions* where it has no sanction. So far as the bureau is concerned, Balchen was out of the country and *technically* has not complied with the law of naturalization.[14]

STRUCTURAL SOURCES OF OVERCONFORMITY

Such inadequacies in orientation which involve trained incapacity clearly derive from structural sources. The process may be briefly recapitulated. (1)

An effective bureaucracy demands reliability of response and strict devotion to regulations. (2) Such devotion to the rules leads to their transformation into absolutes; they are no longer conceived as relative to a set of purposes. (3) This interferes with ready adaptation under special conditions not clearly envisaged by those who drew up the general rules. (4) Thus, the very elements which conduce toward efficiency in general produce inefficiency in specific instances. Full realization of the inadequacy is seldom attained by members of the group who have not divorced themselves from the meanings which the rules have for them. These rules in time become symbolic in cast, rather than strictly utilitarian.

Thus far, we have treated the ingrained sentiments making for rigorous discipline simply as data, as given. However, definite features of the bureaucratic structure may be seen to conduce to these sentiments. The bureaucrat's official life is planned for him in terms of a graded career, through the organizational devices of promotion by seniority, pensions, incremental salaries, etc., all of which are designed to provide incentives for disciplined action and conformity to the official regulations.[15] The official is tacitly expected to and largely does adapt his thoughts, feelings and actions to the prospect of this career. But *these very devices* which increase the probability of conformance also lead to an over-concern with strict adherence to regulations which induces timidity, conservatism, and technicism. Displacement of sentiments from goals onto means is fostered by the tremendous symbolic significance of the means (rules).

Another feature of the bureaucratic structure tends to produce much the same result. Functionaries have the sense of a common destiny for all those who work together. They share the same interests, especially since there is relatively little competition in so far as promotion is in terms of seniority. In-group aggression is thus minimized and this arrangement is therefore conceived to be positively functional for the bureaucracy. However, the *esprit de corps* and informal social organization which typically develops in such situations often leads the personnel to defend their entrenched interests rather than to assist their clientele and elected higher officials. As President Lowell reports, if the bureaucrats believe that their status is not adequately recognized by an incoming elected official, detailed information will be withheld from him, leading him to errors for which he is held responsible. Or, if he seeks to dominate fully, and thus violates the sentiment of self-integrity of the bureaucrats, he may have documents brought to him in such numbers that he cannot manage to sign them all, let alone read them.[16] This illustrates the defensive informal organization which tends to arise whenever there is an apparent threat to the integrity of the group.[17]

It would be much too facile and partly erroneous to attribute such resistance by bureaucrats simply to vested interests. Vested interests oppose any new order which either eliminates or at least makes uncertain their differential advantage deriving from the current arrangements. This is undoubtedly involved in part in bureaucratic resistance to change but another process is perhaps more significant. As we have seen, bureaucratic officials affectively identify themselves with their way of life. They have a pride of craft which leads them to resist change in established routines; at least, those changes which are felt to be imposed by others. This nonlogical pride of craft is a familiar pattern found even, to judge from Sutherland's

Professional Thief, among pickpockets who, despite the risk, delight in mastering the prestige-bearing feat of "beating a left breech" (picking the left front trousers pocket).

In a stimulating paper, Hughes has applied the concepts of "secular" and "sacred" to various types of division of labor; "the sacredness" of caste and *Stände* prerogatives contrasts sharply with the increasing secularism of occupational differentiation in our society.[18] However, as our discussion suggests, there may ensue, in particular vocations and in particular types of organization, the *process of sanctification* (viewed as the counterpart of the process of secularization). This is to say that through sentiment-formation, emotional dependence upon bureaucratic symbols and status, and affective involvement in spheres of competence and authority, there develop prerogatives involving attitudes of moral legitimacy which are established as values in their own right, and are no longer viewed as merely technical means for expediting administration. One may note a tendency for certain bureaucratic norms, originally introduced for technical reasons, to become rigidified and sacred, although, as Durkheim would say, they are *laïque en apparence.*[19] Durkheim has touched on this general process in his description of the attitudes and values which persist in the organic solidarity of a highly differentiated society.

PRIMARY VERSUS SECONDARY RELATIONS

Another feature of the bureaucratic structure, the stress on depersonalization of relationships, also plays its part in the bureaucrat's trained incapacity. The personality pattern of the bureaucrat is nucleated about this norm of impersonality. Both this and the categorizing tendency, which develops from the dominant role of general, abstract rules, tend to produce conflict in the bureaucrat's contacts with the public or clientele. Since functionaries minimize personal relations and resort to categorization, the peculiarities of individual cases are often ignored. But the client who, quite understandably, is convinced of the special features of *his* own problem often objects to such categorical treatment. Stereotyped behavior is not adapted to the exigencies of individual problems. The impersonal treatment of affairs which are at times of great personal significance to the client gives rise to the charge of "arrogance" and "haughtiness" of the bureaucrat. Thus, at the Greenwich Employment Exchange, the unemployed worker who is securing his insurance payment resents what he deems to be "the impersonality and, at times, the apparent abruptness and even harshness of his treatment by the clerks. . . . Some men complain of the superior attitude which the clerks have."[20]

Still another source of conflict with the public derives from the bureaucratic structure. The bureaucrat, in part irrespective of his position with*in* the hierarchy, acts as a representative of the power and prestige of the entire structure. In his official role he is vested with definite authority. This often leads to an actually or apparently domineering attitude, which may only be exaggerated by a discrepancy between his position within the hierarchy and his position with reference to the public.[21] Protest and recourse to other officials on the part of the client are often ineffective or largely precluded by the previously mentioned *esprit de corps* which joins the officials into a more or less solidary in-group. This source of conflict *may* be minimized in private enterprise since the client can register an effective protest by transferring his trade to another organization within the competitive system. But with the monopolistic nature of the public organization, no such alternative is possible. Moreover, in this case, tension is increased because of a discrepancy between ideology and fact: the governmental personnel are held to be "servants of the people," but in fact they are often superordinate, and release of tension can seldom be afforded by turning to other agencies for the necessary service.[22] This tension is in part attributable to the confusion of the status of bureaucrat and client; the client may consider himself socially superior to the official who is at the moment dominant.[23]

Thus, with respect to the relations between officials and clientele, one structural source of conflict is the pressure for formal and impersonal treatment when individual, personalized consideration is desired by the client. The conflict may be viewed, then, as deriving from the introduction of inappropriate attitudes and relationships. Conflict with*in* the bureaucratic structure arises from the converse situation, namely, when personalized relationships are substituted for the structurally required impersonal relationships. This type of conflict may be characterized as follows.

The bureaucracy, as we have seen, is organized as a secondary, formal group. The normal responses involved in this organized network of social expectations are supported by affective attitudes of members of the group. Since the group is oriented toward secondary norms of impersonality, any failure to conform to these norms will arouse antagonism from those who have identified themselves with the legitimacy of these rules. Hence, the substitution of personal for impersonal treatment within the structure is met with widespread disapproval and is characterized by such epithets as graft, favoritism, nepotism, apple-polishing, etc. These epithets are clearly manifestations of injured sentiments.[24] The function of such virtually automatic resentment can be clearly seen in terms of the requirements of bureaucratic structure.

Bureaucracy is a secondary group structure designed to carry on certain activities which cannot be satisfactorily performed on the basis of primary group criteria.[25] Hence behavior which runs counter to these formalized norms becomes the object of emotionalized disapproval. This constitutes a functionally significant defence set up against tendencies which jeopardize the performance of socially necessary activities. To be sure, these reactions are not rationally determined practices explicitly designed for the fulfillment of this function. Rather, viewed in terms of the individual's interpretation of the situation, such resentment is simply an immediate response opposing the "dishonesty" of those who violate the rules of the game. However, this subjective frame of reference notwithstanding, these reactions serve the latent function of maintaining the essential structural elements of bureaucracy by reaffirming the necessity for formalized, secondary relations and by helping to prevent the disintegration of the bureaucratic structure which would occur should these be supplanted by personalized relations. This type of conflict may be generically described as the intrusion of primary group attitudes when secondary group attitudes are institutionally demanded, just as the bureaucrat-client conflict often derives from interaction on impersonal terms when personal treatment is individually demanded.[26]

PROBLEMS FOR RESEARCH

The trend towards increasing bureaucratization in Western Society, which Weber had long since foreseen, is not the sole reason for sociologists to turn their attention to this field. Empirical studies of the interaction of bureaucracy and personality should especially increase our understanding of social structure. A large number of specific questions invite our attention. To what extent are particular personality types selected and modified by the various bureaucracies (private enterprise, public service, the quasi-legal political machine, religious orders)? Inasmuch as ascendancy and submission are held to be traits of personality, despite their variability in different stimulus-situations, do bureaucracies select personalities of particularly submissive or ascendant tendencies? And since various studies have shown that these traits can be modified, does participation in bureaucratic office tend to increase ascendant tendencies? Do various systems of recruitment (*e.g.*, patronage, open competition involving specialized knowledge or general mental capacity, practical experience) select different personality types?[27] Does promotion through seniority lessen competitive anxieties and enhance administrative efficiency? A detailed examination of mechanisms for imbuing the bureaucratic codes with affect would be instructive both sociologically and psychologically. Does the general anonymity of civil service decisions tend to restrict the area of prestige-symbols to a narrowly defined inner circle? Is there a tendency for differential association to be especially marked among bureaucrats?

The range of theoretically significant and practically important questions would seem to be limited only by the accessibility of the concrete data. Studies of religious, educational, military, economic, and political bureaucracies dealing with the interdependence of social organization and personality formation should constitute an avenue for fruitful research. On that avenue, the functional analysis of concrete structures may yet build a Solomon's House for sociologists.

NOTES

1. For a development of the concept of "rational organization," see Karl Mannheim, *Mensch und Gesellschaft im Zeitalter des Umbaus* (Leiden: A. W. Sijthoff, 1935), esp. 28 ff.
2. H. D. Lasswell, *Politics* (New York: McGraw-Hill, 1936), 120–21.
3. Max Weber, *Wirtschaft und Gesellschaft* (Tübingen: J. C. B. Mohr, 1922), Pt. III, chap. 6; 650–678. For a brief summary of Weber's discussion, see Talcott Parsons, *The Structure of Social Action*, esp. 506 ff. For a description, which is not a caricature, of the bureaucrat as a personality type, see C. Rabany, "Les types sociaux: le fonctionnaire," *Revue générale d'administration* 88 (1907), 5–28.
4. Karl Mannheim, *Ideology and Utopia* (New York: Harcourt Brace Jovanovich, 1936), 18n., 105 ff. See also Ramsay Muir, *Peers and Bureaucrats* (London: Constable, 1910), 12–13.
5. E. G. Cahen-Salvador suggests that the personnel of bureaucracies is largely constituted by those who value security above all else. See his "La situation matérielle et morale des fonctionnaires," *Revue politique et parlementaire* (1926), 319.
6. H. J. Laski, "Bureaucracy," *Encyclopedia of the Social Sciences*. This article is written primarily from the standpoint of the political scientist rather than that of the sociologist.
7. Weber, *op. cit.*, 671.
8. For a stimulating discussion and application of these concepts, see Kenneth Burke, *Permanence and Change* (New York: New Republic, 1935), pp. 50 ff.; Daniel Warnotte, "Bureaucratie et Fonctionnarisme," *Revue de l'Institut de Sociologie* 17 (1937), 245.
9. *Ibid.*, 58–59.
10. *Ibid.*, 70.
11. This process has often been observed in various connections. Wundt's *heterogony of ends* is a case in point; Max Weber's *Paradoxie der Folgen* is another. See also MacIver's observations on the transformation of civilization into culture and Lasswell's remark that "the human animal distinguishes himself by his infinite capacity for making ends of his means." See Merton, "The unanticipated consequences of purposive social action," *American Sociological Review* 1 (1936), 894–904. In terms

of the psychological mechanisms involved, this process has been analyzed most fully by Gordon W. Allport, in his discussion of what he calls "the functional autonomy of motives." Allport emends the earlier formulations of Woodworth, Tolman, and William Stern, and arrives at a statement of the process from the standpoint of individual motivation. He does not consider those phases of the social structure which conduce toward the "transformation of motives." The formulation adopted in this paper is thus complementary to Allport's analysis; the one stressing the psychological mechanisms involved, the other considering the constraints of the social structure. The convergence of psychology and sociology toward this central concept suggests that it may well constitute one of the conceptual bridges between the two disciplines. See Gordon W. Allport, *Personality* (New York: Henry Holt & Co., 1937), chap. 7.

12. See E. C. Hughes, "Institutional office and the person," *American Journal of Sociology*, 43 (1937), 404–413; E. T. Hiller, "Social structure in relation to the person," *Social Forces* 16 (1937), 34–4.

13. Mannheim, *Ideology and Utopia*, 106.

14. Quoted from the *Chicago Tribune* (June 24, 1931, p. 10) by Thurman Arnold, *The Symbols of Government* (New Haven: Yale University Press, 1935), 201–2. (My italics.)

15. Mannheim, *Mensch und Gesellschaft*, 32–33. Mannheim stresses the importance of the "Lebensplan" and the "Amtskarriere." See the comments by Hughes, *op. cit.*, 413.

16. A. L. Lowell, *The Government of England* (New York, 1908), I, 189 ff.

17. For an instructive description of the development of such a defensive organization in a group of workers, see F. J. Roethlisberger and W. J. Dickson, *Management and the Worker* (Boston: Harvard School of Business Administration, 1934).

18. E. C. Hughes, "Personality types and the division of labor," *American Journal of Sociology* 33 (1928), 754–768. Much the same distinction is drawn by Leopold von Wiese and Howard Becker, *Systematic Sociology* (New York: John Wiley & Sons, 1932), 222–25 *et passim.*

19. Hughes recognizes one phase of this process of sanctification when he writes that professional training "carries with it as a by-product assimilation of the candidate to a set of professional attitudes and controls, *a professional conscience and solidarity. The profession claims and aims to become a moral unit.*" Hughes, *op. cit.*, 762, (italics inserted). In this same connection, Sumner's concept of *pathos*, as the halo of sentiment which protects a social value from criticism, is particularly relevant, inasmuch as it affords a clue to the mechanism involved in the process of sanctification. See his *Folkways*, 180–181.

20. " 'They treat you like a lump of dirt they do. I see a navvy reach across the counter and shake one of them by the collar the other day. The rest of us felt like cheering. Of course he lost his benefit over it. . . . But the clerk deserved it for his sassy way.' " (E. W. Bakke, *The Unemployed Man*, 79–80). Note that the domineering attitude was *imputed* by the unemployed client who is in a state of tension due to his loss of status and self-esteem in a society where the ideology is still current that an "able man" can always find a job. That the imputation of arrogance stems largely from the client's state of mind is seen from Bakke's own observation that "the clerks were rushed, and had no time for pleasantries, but there was little sign of harshness or a superiority feeling in their treatment of the men." In so far as there is an objective basis for the imputation of arrogant behavior to bureaucrats, it may possibly be explained by the following juxtaposed statements. "Auch der moderne, sei es öffentliche, sei es private, Beamte erstrebt immer und geniesst meist den Beherrschten gegenüber eine spezifisch gehobene, 'ständische' soziale Schätzung." (Weber, *op. cit.*, 652.) "In persons in whom the craving for prestige is uppermost, hostility usually takes the form of a desire to humiliate others." K. Horney, *The Neurotic Personality of Our Time*, 178–79.

21. In this connection, note the relevance of Koffka's comments on certain features of the pecking-order of birds. "If one compares the behavior of the bird at the top of the pecking list, the despot, with that of one very far down, the second or third from the last, then one finds the latter much more cruel to the few others over whom he lords it than the former in his treatment of all members. As soon as one removes from the group all members above the penultimate, his behavior becomes milder and may even become very friendly. . . . It is not difficult to find analogies to this in human societies, and therefore one side of such behavior must be primarily the effects of the social groupings, and not of individual characteristics." K. Koffka, *Principles of Gestalt Psychology* (New York: Harcourt Brace Jovanovich, 1935), 668–9.

22. At this point the political machine often becomes functionally significant. As Steffens and others have shown, highly personalized relations and the abrogation of formal rules (red tape) by the machine often satisfy the needs of individual "clients" more fully than the formalized mechanism of governmental bureaucracy. See the slight elaboration of this as set forth in Chapter I.

23. As one of the unemployed men remarked about the clerks at the Greenwich Employment Exchange: " 'And the bloody blokes wouldn't have their jobs if it wasn't for us men out of a job either. That's what gets me about their holding their noses up.' " Bakke, *op. cit.*, 80. See also H. D. Lasswell and G. Almond, "Aggressive behavior by clients towards public relief administrators," *American Political Science Review* 28 (1934), 643–55.

24. The diagnostic significance of such linguistic indices as epithets has scarcely been explored by the sociologist. Sumner properly observes that epithets produce "summary criticisms" and definitions of social situations. Dollard also notes that "epithets frequently define the central issues in a society," and Sapir has rightly emphasized the importance of context of situations in appraising the significance of epithets. Of equal relevance is Linton's observation that "in case histories the way in which the community felt about a particular episode is, if anything, more important to our study than the actual behavior. . . ." A sociological study of "vocabularies of encomium and opprobrium" should lead to valuable findings.

25. *Cf.* Ellsworth Faris, *The Nature of Human Nature* (New York: McGraw-Hill, 1937), 41 ff.

26. Community disapproval of many forms of behavior may be analyzed in terms of one or the other of these patterns of substitution of culturally inappropriate types of relationship. Thus, prostitution constitutes a type-case where coitus, a form of intimacy which is institutionally defined as symbolic of the most "sacred" primary group relationship, is placed within a contractual context, symbolized by the exchange of that most impersonal of all symbols, money. See Kingsley Davis, "The sociology of prostitution," *American Sociological Review* 2 (1937), 744–55.

27. Among recent studies of recruitment to bureaucracy are: Reinhard Bendix, *Higher Civil Servants in American Society* (Boulder: University of Colorado Press, 1949); Dwaine Marwick, *Career Perspectives in a Bureaucratic Setting* (Ann Arbor: University of Michigan Press, 1954); R. K. Kelsall, *Higher Civil Servants in Britain* (London: Routledge & Kegan Paul, 1955); W. L. Warner and J. C. Abegglen, *Occupational Mobility in American Business and Industry* (Minneapolis: University of Minnesota Press, 1955).

14
The Lack of a Budgetary Theory

V. O. Key, Jr.

On the most significant aspect of public budgeting, i.e., the allocation of expenditures among different purposes so as to achieve the greatest return, American budgetary literature is singularly arid. Toilers in the budgetary field have busied themselves primarily with the organization and procedure for budget preparation, the forms for the submission of requests for funds, the form of the budget document itself, and like questions.[1] That these things have deserved the consideration given them cannot be denied when the unbelievable resistance to the adoption of the most rudimentary essentials of budgeting is recalled and their unsatisfactory condition in many jurisdictions even now is observed. Nevertheless, the absorption of energies in the establishment of the mechanical

Source: American Political Science Review 34 (December 1940).

foundations for budgeting has diverted attention from the basic budgeting problem (on the expenditure side), namely: On what basis shall it be decided to allocate x dollars to activity A instead of activity B?

Writers on budgeting say little or nothing about the purely economic aspects of public expenditure. "Economics," says Professor Robbins, "is the science which studies human behavior as a relationship between ends and scarce means which have alternative uses."[2] Whether budgetary behavior is economic or political is open to fruitless debate; nevertheless, the point of view and the mode of thought of the economic theorist are relevant, both in the study of and action concerning public expenditure. The budget-maker never has enough revenue to meet the requests of all spending agencies, and he must decide (subject, of course, to subsequent legislative action) how scarce means shall be allocated to alternative uses. The completed budgetary document (although the budget-maker may be quite unaware of it) represents a judgment upon how scarce means should be allocated to bring the maximum return in social utility.[3]

In their discussions of the review of estimates, budget authorities rarely go beyond the question of how to judge the estimates for particular functions, i.e., ends; and the approach to the review of the estimate of the individual agency is generally directed toward the efficiency with which the particular end is to be achieved.[4] Even in this sort of review, budget-makers have developed few standards of evaluation, acting, rather, on the basis of their impressionistic judgment, of a rudimentary cost accounting, or perhaps, of the findings of administrative surveys. For decisions on the requests of individual agencies, the techniques have by no means reached perfection.[5] It is sometimes possible to compute with fair accuracy whether the increased efficiency from new public works, such as a particular highway project, will warrant the capital outlay. Or, given the desirability of a particular objective, it may be feasible to evaluate fairly precisely alternative means for achieving that end. Whether a particular agency is utilizing, and plans to utilize, its resources with the maximum efficiency is of great importance, but this approach leaves untouched a more fundamental problem. If it is assumed that an agency is operating at maximum efficiency, the question remains whether the function is worth carrying out at all, or whether it should be carried out on a reduced or enlarged scale, with resulting transfers of funds to or from other activities of greater or lesser social utility.

Nor is there found in the works of the public finance experts much enlightenment on the question herein considered. They generally dispose of the subject of expenditures with a few perfunctory chapters and hurry on to the core of their interest—taxation and other sources of revenue. On the expenditure side, they differentiate, not very plausibly, between productive and unproductive expenditure; they consider the classification of public expenditures; they demonstrate that public expenditures have been increasing; and they discuss the determination of the optimum aggregate of public expenditure; but they do not generally come to grips with the question of the allocation of public revenues among different objects of expenditure.[6] The issue is recognized, as when Pigou says: "As regards the distribution, as distinct from the aggregate cost, of optional government expenditure, it is clear that, just as an individual will get more satisfaction out of his income by maintaining a certain balance between different sorts of expenditure, so also will a community through its government. The principle of balance in both cases is provided by the postulate that resources should be so distributed among different uses that the marginal return of satisfaction is the same for all of them. . . . Expenditure should be distributed between battleships and poor relief in such wise that the last shilling devoted to each of them yields the same real return. We have here, so far as theory goes, a test by means of which the distribution of expenditure along different lines can be settled."[7] But Pigou dismisses the subject with a paragraph, and the discussion by others is not voluminous.[8]

The only American writer on public finance who has given extended attention to the problem of the distribution of expenditures is Mabel Walker. In her *Municipal Expenditures,* she reviews the theories of public expenditure and devises a method for ascertaining the tendencies in distribution of expenditures on the assumption that the way would be pointed to "a norm of expenditures consistent with the state of progress at present achieved by society." While her method would be inapplicable to the federal budget,[9] and would probably be of less relevance in the analysis of state than of municipal expenditures, her study deserves reflective perusal by municipal budget officers and by students of the problem.[10]

Literature skirting the edges of the problem is found in the writings of those economists who have concerned themselves with the economic problems of the socialist state. In recent years, a new critique of socialism has appeared.[11] This attack, in the words of one who attempts to refute it, is ". . . more subtle and technical than the previous ones, based on the supposed inability of a socialist community to solve purely economic problems. . . . What is asserted is that, even with highly developed technique, adequate incentives to activity, and rational control of population, the economic directors of a socialist commonwealth would be unable to balance against each other the worthwhileness of different lines of production or the relative advantages of different ways of producing the same good."[12] Those who believe this problem not insoluble in a socialist economy set out to answer the question: "What is the proper method of determining just what commodities shall be produced from the economic resources at the disposal of a given community?"[13] One would anticipate from those seeking to answer this question some light on the problems of the budget-maker in a capitalist state. But they are concerned only with the pricing of state-produced goods for sale to individuals in a socialist economy. Professor Dickinson, for example, excludes from his discussion goods and services provided in a socialist economy "free of charge to all members of society, as the result of a decision, based on other grounds than market demands, made by some authoritative economic organ of the community."[14] That exclusion removes from consideration the point at issue. Nevertheless, the critics of socialist theory do at least raise essentially the same problem as that posed in the present discussion; and their comment is suggestive.

Various studies of the economics of public works touch the periphery of the problem concerning the allocation of public expenditures. The principal inquiries have been prosecuted under the auspices of the National Resources Planning Board and its predecessor organizations. These reports, however, are concerned in the main with the question of how much in the aggregate should be spent, and when, in order to function as the most effective absorber of the shocks incidental to cyclical fluctuations. Two studies, by Arthur D. Gayer and John M. Clark, deal with public works outlays as stabilizers of the economic order and with related matters.[15] These works suggest factors relevant in the determination of the total amount of the capital budget; but in them the problem of selection among alternative public works projects is not tackled. In another study, the latter issue is approached by Russell V. Black from a rich background of city planning experience, and he formulates a suggestive but tentative set of criteria for the selection and programming of public works projects.[16]

Planning agencies and professional planners have been more interested in the abstract problem of ascertaining the relative utility of public outlays than has any other group. The issue is stated theoretically in a recent report: "The problem is essentially one of the development of criteria for selecting the objects of public expenditure. As a larger and larger proportion of the national income is spent for public purposes, the sphere of the price system with its freedom of choice of objects of expenditure is more and more restricted. Concurrently, the necessity for developing methods by which public officials may select objects of expenditure which will bring the greatest utility or return and most accurately achieve social aspirations becomes more pressing. In a sense, this constitutes the central problem of the productive state. If planning is to be 'over-all' planning, it must devise techniques for the balancing of values within a framework that gives due regard both to the diverse interests of the present and to the interests of the future."[17] Planning agencies have not succeeded in formulating any convincing principles, either descriptive or normative, concerning the allocation of public funds, but they have, within limited spheres, created governmental machinery facilitating the consideration of related alternative expenditures. The most impressive example is the Water Resources Committee (of the National Resources Planning Board) and its subsidiary drainage-basin committees.[18] Through this machinery, it is possible to consider alternatives in objectives and sequences of expenditure—questions that would not arise concretely without such machinery. Perhaps the approach toward the practical working out of the issue lies in the canalizing of decisions through the governmental machinery so as to place alternatives in juxtaposition and compel consideration of relative values. This is the effect of many existing institutional arrangements; but the issue is rarely so stated, and the structure of government, particularly the federal-state division, frequently prevents the weighing of alternatives.

It may be argued that for the best performance of individual public functions a high degree of stability in the amount of funds available year after year is desirable, and that the notion that there is, or needs to be, mobility of resources as among functions is erroneous. Considerable weight is undoubtedly to be attached to this view. Yet over periods of a few years important shifts occur in relative financial emphasis on different functions of government. Even in minor adjustments, the small change up or down at the margin may be of considerable significance. Like an individual consumer, the state may have certain minimum expenditures generally agreed upon, but care in weighing the relative utility of alternative expenditures becomes more essential as the point of marginal utility is approached. Moreover, within the public economy, frictions (principally institutional in character) exist to obstruct and delay adjustments in the allocation of resources in keeping with changing wants probably to a greater extent than in the private economy.

Efforts to ascertain more precisely the relative "values" of public services may be thought fruitless because of the influence of pressure groups in the determination of the allocation of funds. Each spending agency has its clientele, which it marshals for battle before budgetary and appropriating agencies.[19] And there are those who might contend that the pattern of expenditures resultant from the interplay of these forces constitutes a maximization of return from public expenditure, since it presumably reflects the social consensus on the relative values of different services. If this be true, the more efficient utilization of resources would be promoted by the devising of means more accurately to measure the political strength of interests competing for appropriations. That the appropriation bill expresses a social consensus sounds akin to the mystic doctrine of the "general will." Constantly, choices have to be made between the demands of different groups; and it is probably true that factors other than estimates of the relative political strength of contending groups frequently enter into the decisions. The pressure theory suggests the potential development in budget bureaus and related agencies of a strong bureaucracy strategically situated, and with a vested interest in the general welfare, in contrast with the particularistic drives of the spending agencies.

It is not to be concluded that by excogitation a set of principles may be formulated on the basis of which the harassed budget official may devise an automatic technique for the allocation of financial resources. Yet the problem needs study in several directions. Further examination from the viewpoints of economic theory and political philosophy could produce valuable results. The doctrine of marginal utility, developed most finely in the analysis of the market economy, has a ring of unreality when applied to public expenditures. The most advantageous utilization of public funds[20] resolves itself into a matter of value preferences between ends lacking a common denominator. As such, the question is a problem in political philosophy; keen analyses in these terms would be of the utmost importance in creating an awareness of the problems of the budgetary implementation of programs of political action of whatever shade. The discussion also suggests the desirability of careful and comprehensive analyses of the budgetary process. In detail, what forces go into the making of state budgets? What factors govern decisions of budgetary officials? Precisely what is the rôle of the legislature? On the federal level, the field for inquiry is broader, including not only the central budgetary agency, but departmental budget offices as well. Studies of congressional appropriating processes are especially needed.[21] For the working budget official, the implications of the discussion rest primarily in a point of view in the consideration of estimates in terms of alternatives—decisions which are always made, but not always consciously. For the personnel policy of budget agencies, the question occurs whether almost sole reliance on persons trained primarily in accounting and fiscal procedure is wise. The thousands of little decisions made in budgetary agencies grow by accretion into formidable budgetary documents which from their sheer mass are apt often to overwhelm those with the power of final decision. We need to look carefully at the training and working assumptions of these officials, to the end that the budget may most truly reflect the public interest.[22]

NOTES

1. See A. E. Buck, *Public Budgeting* (New York, 1929); J. Wilner Sundelson, *Budgetary Methods in National and State Governments* (New York State Tax Commission, Special Report No. 14, 1938); *ibid.*, "Budgetary Principles," *Political Science Quarterly* 50 (1935): 236–263.
2. Lionel Robbins, *An Essay on the Nature and Significance of Economic Science* (2nd ed., London, 1935), p. 16.
3. If the old saying that the state fixes its expenditures and then raises sufficient revenues to meet them were literally true, the budget officer would not be faced by a problem of scarcity. However, there is almost invariably a problem of scarcity in the public economy—to which all budget officers, besieged by spending departments, will testify.
4. See Buck, *op. cit.*, Chap. 11.
5. The development of standards for the evaluation of the efficiency of performance of particular functions—entirely apart from the value of the functions—is as yet in a primitive stage. Such standards, for budgetary purposes at least, require cost accounting, which implies a unit of measurement. A standard of comparison is also implied, such as the performance of the same agency during prior fiscal periods, or the performance of other agencies under like conditions. In the absence of even crude measurement devices, budgetary and appropriating authorities are frequently thrown back upon the alternative of passing on individual items—three clerks, two messengers, seven stenographers, etc.—a practice which often causes exasperation among operating officials. Although our knowledge of budgetary behavior is slight, the surmise is probably correct that questions of the efficiency of operation in achieving a particular end are generally hopelessly intermingled with the determination of the relative value of different ends. Operating officials often shy away from experimentation with devices of measurement, but it may be suggested that measures of the efficiency of performance should tend to divert the attention of budgetary and appropriating officials from concern with internal details to the pivotal question of the relative value of services.
6. See, for example, H. L. Lutz, *Public Finance.*
7. *A Study in Public Finance* (London, 1928), p. 50. See also E. R. A. Seligman, "The Social Theory of Fiscal Science," *Political Science Quarterly* 41 (1926): 193–218, 354–383, and Gerhard Colm, "Theory of Public Expenditures," *Annals of the American Academy of Political and Social Science* 183 (1930): 1–11.
8. For a review of the literature, see Mabel L. Walker, *Municipal Expenditures* (Baltimore, 1930), Chap. 3.
9. In this connection, see C. H. Wooddy, *The Growth of the Federal Government, 1915–1932* (New York, 1934).
10. In the field of state finance, a valuable study has been made by I. M. Labovitz in *Public Policy and State Finance in Illinois* (Social Science Research Committee, University of Chicago. Publication pending.
11. See F. A. von Hayek, ed., *Collectivist Economic Planning* (London, 1935).
12. H. D. Dickinson, "Price Formation in a Socialist Community," *Economic Journal* 43: 237–250. See also, E. F. M. Durbin, "Economic Calculus in a Planned Economy," *Economic Journal* 46 (1936): 676–690 and A. R. Sweezy, "The Economist in a Socialist Economy," in *Explorations in Economics; Notes and Essays Contributed in Honor of F. W. Taussig* (1936), 422–433.
13. F. M. Taylor, "The Guidance of Production in a Socialist State," *American Economic Review* 19 (1929): 1–8.
14. *Op. cit.*, 238. Of Soviet Russia, Brown and Hinrichs say: "In a planned economy, operating if necessary under pressure to accomplish a predetermined production, the decision with regard to major prices is essentially a political one." "The Planned Economy of Soviet Russia," *Political Science Quarterly* 46 (1931): 362–402.
15. J. M. Clark, *Economics of Planning Public Works* (Washington, D.C.: Government Printing Office, 1935); A. D. Gayer, *Public Works in Prosperity and Depression* (New York: National Bureau of Economic Research, 1935). See also the essay by Simeon E. Leland in National Resources Committee, *Public Works Planning* (Washington, D.C.: Government Printing Office, 1936).
16. *Criteria and Planning for Public Works* (Washington, D.C.: National Resources Board, mimeographed, 1934). See especially pp. 165–168.
17. National Resources Committee, *The Future of State Planning* (Washington, D.C.: Government Printing Office, 1938), p. 19. Mr. J. Reeve has called my attention to the fact that

the problem of allocation of public expenditures has come to be more difficult also because of the increasingly large number of alternative purposes of expenditure.

18. For an approach to the work of the Water Committee in terms somewhat similar to those of this paper, see National Resources Committee, *Progress Report,* December, 1938, pp. 29–36. For an example of the work, see National Resources Committee, *Drainage Basin Problems and Programs, 1937 Revision* (Washington, D.C.: Government Printing Office, 1938).

19. E. B. Logan, "Group Pressures and State Finance," *Annals of the American Academy of Political and Social Science* 179 (1935): 131–135, and Dayton David McKean, *Pressures on the Legislature of New Jersey* (New York, 1938), Chap. 5.

20. This matter is really another facet of the problem of the determination of the "public interest" with which E. P. Herring grapples in *Public Administration and the Public Interest.*

21. For such studies, useful methodological ideas might be gleaned from Professor Schattschneider's *Politics, Pressures, and the Tariff.*

22. Helpful comments by I. M. Labovitz and Homer Jones on a preliminary draft of this paper are hereby acknowledged.

CHAPTER III

The Postwar Period

By the end of the Second World War, American public administration had completed its transformation into a modern bureaucratic state. But the principles of administration as espoused by scientific management proved to be increasingly inadequate when gauged against the size and complexity of modern governments. In the postwar period, which is used broadly here to cover most of the 1940s and all of the 1950s, new challenges to the traditional themes of administration prevailed. Most prominent were the familiar issues of the nature and effects of bureaucratic organizations and the political dimensions of the new administrative state.

The Hawthorne experiments of the 1930s had provided the first major empirical challenge to the scientific management notion that the worker was primarily an economic animal who would work solely for money. Abraham H. Maslow (1908–1970),[1] a psychologist, took the basic Hawthorne finding that workers are as much social as economic creatures a step further when he first proposed his famous "needs hierarchy" in his 1943 *Psychological Review* article, "A Theory of Human Motivation." Maslow asserted that humans had five sets of goals or basic needs arranged in a hierarchy of prepotency: physiological needs (food, water, shelter, etc.), safety needs, love or affiliation needs, esteem needs, and the final need for self-actualization—when an individual theoretically reaches self-fulfillment and becomes all that he or she is capable of becoming.[2] Once the lower needs are satisfied, they cease to be motivators of behavior. Conversely, higher needs cannot motivate until lower needs are satisfied. Maslow's psychological analysis of motivation proved to be the foundation for much subsequent research in organizational behavior. Others, such as Herzberg,[3] McGregor,[4] and Argyris,[5] would take Maslow's concepts and develop them into more comprehensive theories of motivation and organizational behavior. Still, Maslow's work, much as with Weber's analysis of bureaucratic structure, would be the point of departure.

The New Deal and World War II were significant influences on the theory and practice of public administration. While those wars against depression and oppression were primarily economic and military operations, they were also immense managerial undertakings. The experience of those years called into question much of what was then the conventional wisdom of public administration. The politics-administration dichotomy of the reform movement lost its viability amid the New Deal and the war effort. It was simply not possible to take value-free processes of business and apply them to government. Government, in spite of the best efforts of many reformers, was not a business and was not value free.[6]

The attack on the politics-administration dichotomy came from many quarters at once. David E. Lilienthal (1899–1981), in "Planning and Planners," a chapter from his 1944 book, *TVA: Democracy on the March*[7], wrote of his experiences with the Tennessee Valley Authority.[8] He found the planning process of government to be a blatantly political enterprise—one that was, not incidently, both healthy and beneficial for a democratic society.

Lilienthal's examination of planning and its effects at the TVA, which we have reprinted here, contains another critical dimension that would not take root until the 1970s. In voicing great concern about the responsibility of executing the actual plans, he was addressing the problem of implementation. His questions still form much of the crux of our concerns in public policy today—how does planning join the designer and implementor inside the organization? And how does planning ensure the participation of, and not the coercion of, the outside public to accept the plan?

Paul Appleby (1891–1963), a prominent New Deal administrator and Dean of the Maxwell School at Syracuse University,[9] wrote perhaps the most skillful polemic of the era, which asserted that this theoretical insistence on apolitical governmental processes went against the grain of the American experience. Appleby in *Big Democracy*[10] compared government to business. In his chapter "Government is Different," reprinted here, he emphatically shattered public administration's self-imposed demarcation between politics and administration. He held that it was a myth that politics was separate and could somehow be taken out of administration. Political involvement was good—not evil as many of the progressive reformers had claimed—because political involvement in administration acted as a check on the arbitrary exercise of bureaucratic power.

It seems fair to say that Appleby's work was the obituary for the politics-administration dichotomy. In the future those who would describe the political ramifications and issues of administration would not begin by contesting the politics-administration dichotomy as incorrect or irrelevant; rather, they would begin from the premise, so succinctly put by Appleby, that "government is different because government is politics."

Perhaps the most significant landmark in the public administration world of the 1940s was Herbert Simon's (1916–) 1947 book, *Administrative Behavior*, which urged that a true scientific method be used in the study of administrative phenomena, that the perspective of logical positivism should be used in dealing with questions of policy making, and that decision making is the true heart of administration. It was here that Simon refuted the principles approach to public administration that then dominated administrative thinking. In "The Proverbs of Administration," his 1946 *Public Administration Review* article that was later incorporated into his book and which is reprinted here, Simon examined Gulick's POSDCORB and its associated components and found them to be inconsistent, conflicting, and inapplicable to many of the administrative situations facing public administrators. Overall, Simon concluded that the so-called principles of administration are really "proverbs of administration."

In the last section of Simon's article there is a brief discussion of the limitations on decision making, using the context of rationality. Simon presents a number of questions about how organizations make administrative decisions. His subsequent book presents the beginning of his concept of "bounded rationality"[11] and goes on to build upon the theoretical foundations of Chester I. Barnard to advocate a systems approach for examining the various facets of administrative behavior. This initial work and his subsequent research on models and systems of decision making would, more than three decades later, make Simon the only noneconomist to win the Nobel Prize for Economics.

With the devastation of the politics-administration dichotomy, the neat subdivision of what was political science and what was public administration was destroyed. Robert A. Dahl (1915–), one of the most significant of the early behavioralists in political science,[12] analyzed the state of the art of the discipline of public administration in his 1947 *Public Administration Review* article, "The Science of Public Administration," reprinted here. He prescribed some courses of action for a discipline that had to rapidly emerge on its own terms. But more significantly, Dahl was serving notice to public administration theorists that to be accepted as political science (which was the field of study of most public administration academics), the accepted doctrine that administration is politics would have to move beyond mere revelation. A science of public administration should be created, he argued, that "states ends honestly" and (1) recognizes the complexities of human behavior, (2) deals with the problems of normative values in administrative situations, and (3) takes into account the relationship between public administration and its social setting. Dahl expanded this last point saying that "as long as the study of public administration is not comparative, claims for a 'science of public administration' sound rather hollow." Over the next two decades comparative public administration would emerge as a major subset of the field,[13] but even today the subject is not taught in most programs.

Dahl anticipated some of the difficulties in store for public administration if it wished to stay as a branch of political science. Ultimately, in the 1970s public administration would begin to emerge out of both political science and business administration and become a field of study in its own right. Nevertheless, no matter where the field is as an intellectual subset of knowledge, in American universities it is still housed mostly with departments of political science and schools of business.

Philip Selznick (1919–), a sociologist, looked at the processes that Lilienthal and his associates used to gain local support for Tennessee Valley Authority programs and made famous a new buzzword, "cooptation," which described the efforts of an organization to bring and subsume new elements into its policy-making process in order to prevent such elements from being a threat to the organization or its mission. Reprinted here is that portion of Selznick's 1944 book, *TVA and the Grass Roots,*[14] which contains his analysis of the process, results, and implications of using "The

Cooptative Mechanism." It was the first major sociological treatment of the "powers" of administrative organizations and their impacts upon democratic society and public participation in the policy-making process.

Selznick argued that in bureaucratic organizations cooptation would reflect "a state of tension between formal authority and social power." A decade later in his *Leadership in Administration*[15] he would examine more comprehensively the various facets of the use of bureaucratic power by administrative organizations and the process of selecting and fulfilling policy goals. Selznick anticipated many of the 1980s notions of "transformational leadership"[16] when he asserted that the function of an institutional leader is to help shape the environment in which the institution operates and to define new institutional directions through recruitment, training, and bargaining.

Norton Long (1910–), in his 1947 *Public Administration Review* article, "Power and Administration," dealt with the ramifications of executive power and responsibility by mimicking Machiavelli[17] in stressing the significance of prestige and appearance and the wisdom of sacrificing subordinates to these ends. In a sense, Long's article, reprinted here, completes the political dimensions of public administration since it describes the application of political tactics to internal operations and personnel considerations. By the end of the 1940s, virtually all aspects of the administrative process had found their place in the political perspective.

After dealing with the internal dimensions of executive power, such matters as organizational authority and agency coordination, Long considered some of the external dimensions. The extraordinary concentration of power, mandated by emergency conditions (the Great Depression and the Second World War) in the executive branch left unresolved the question of control for the future. Building upon Herring's work, they asked in whose interest and to what purpose would government bureaus serve? Would they not, placed in a political vacuum, pursue their own goals and objectives? Long provided searching questions and expressed considerable skepticism about the current abilities of legislatures and executives to insure adequate safeguards, much less direction. Long's writings[18] also anticipated the "power and politics" school of organization theory[19] by a generation.

For the emerging field of budgeting the postwar period was a period both of consolidation and of the development of new techniques. Performance budgeting, which was in its prime, after being officially sanctioned by the Hoover Commission of 1949, stressed using the budget process as a tool for work measurement and efficiency analysis. But Verne B. Lewis (1913–), a federal budget officer,[20] continued the quest for the development of a theory of budgeting that V. O. Key, Jr., had sought a dozen years earlier. In his "Toward a Theory of Budgeting," Lewis presented a theory of alternative budgeting. His analysis marked an important link to the PPB systems of the 1960s and especially to the zero-base budgeting systems of the 1970s.

Lewis' analysis is comprehensive—beginning with his recognition of V. O. Key's budget questions from the previous decade to arguing the merits for an economic theory of budgeting. He advocated budget submissions prepared in a manner that would facilitate comparison and demonstrate a range of choices for service and funding levels, and at the same time have the final choice provide realistic contracts, that is, specific, realistic expectations for the individual program managers. The implied rationale for this process almost seems a restating of V. O. Key's classic budgeting equation: For X level of funding, Y level of service can be provided; for X + 1 funding, Y + Z services, and so on.

Alternative budgeting, Lewis's preferred solution, was a means to overcome traditional budgetary review techniques that focus on item by item control. Rather, the focus would be on scaling levels of program services and goals to varying levels of funding. Lewis, a realist, saw clearly the influence of other factors such as "price and prejudice, provincialism, and politics" in budgetary decisions. His hope was for the advent of budgeting systems that could overcome these noneconomic and nonrational factors.

Many who were concerned with developing public administration as an academic discipline faced the problem of definition. If one were to review all of the basic public administration texts of the last thirty years, one would find two basic approaches toward defining the discipline. One approach attempted to present a comprehensive definition. The other asserted that the concerns of public administration were too broad to seek a definition, that any definition would tend to limit the boundaries of this seemingly boundless field. If we must have a definition, the best (which we have reprinted here) is Dwight Waldo's (1913–   ) "What is Public Administration?"[21]

In part, Waldo's definition is so significant because it is by Waldo, who is widely considered the preeminent historian of the discipline of public administration.[22] Note how he expands upon the concept of rational action that was earlier developed by Herbert A. Simon in *Administrative Behavior*. Waldo also anticipates the systems approach to defining organizations when he discusses structural-functional analysis. This approach to studying societies, communities, or organizations was pioneered by the sociologist Talcott Parsons.[23] Structural functionalism views these social units as systems; their particular features are explained in terms of their contributions—their functions—in maintaining the system. Waldo also seeks to define public administration in terms of culture. Only in the 1980s would this concern of organizational definition come into its own.[24] But Waldo's overall perspective held that public administration was a subset of political science, that the longstanding art of public administration would have to be fused with the newly emerging science of public administration.

As the postwar period drew to a close, there were several voices reinterpreting the principles approach to public administration. Scientific management and principles gave way to administrative management science. Foremost among these was Catheryn Seckler-Hudson (1902–1963) of The American University. In the postwar period, she edited or wrote numerous key works on planning, organization, and management,[25] including a six-volume set of papers on budgeting.[26] She recognized the policy and political implications within the "setting of public administration" but gave primary weight to the problems of public management.

"Management," she argued, "will be regarded as the effective utilization of human resources and material to reach the known goal." Much of her work was exceptionally technical. Using an outline approach at times, she provided extensive detail about management techniques and methods. To a great extent, her work nicely predicts what is only now emerging in the 1980s—a renewed emphasis on technique and management technology or "nuts and bolts," which is loosely regarded as public management. As an example of her "technical" approach to public management, we have reprinted her "Basic Concepts in Study of Public Management," the first chapter from her book, *Organization and Management: Theory and Practice*.

C. Northcote Parkinson's (1909–   ) famous law that "work expands so as to fill the time available for its completion" first appeared in 1957. Parkinson (an otherwise serious naval, military, and economic historian) practically overnight became popular as the administrative theorist of the masses. The popularity of his "law" has been rivaled only by that of Laurence J. Peter and his "principle" (see Chapter IV). While Parkinson's essay, "Parkinson's Law or the Rising Pyramid," which is reprinted here from the book of the same title, was intentionally satirical, it nevertheless offered valuable insights into the pathologies of bureaucratic organizations. Parkinson himself has become a significant role model for other writers in the field of management, because he took information that, in other hands, would have been a dull administrative analysis of organizations and made it into an international best-seller.[27]

Few authors have done more to popularize the new industrial humanism than Douglas M. McGregor (1906–1964)[28] by his abstraction of the contending traditional and humanistic managerial philosophies into his now famous Theory X and Theory Y sets of assumptions. Like Herbert Simon before him, McGregor pointed out the absurdity of maintaining universal principles of organizational arrangements. While such laws, principles, or proverbs may be appropriate in a highly disciplined hierarchical organization, such as an army, they may become ineffective and even dysfunctional when applied to modern organizations—especially governmental organizations, where a lack of hierarchical discipline is frequently considered to be a valuable check against autocratic tendencies. McGregor's 1957 article, "The Human Side of Enterprise," reprinted here, presented the main themes of his more famous 1960 book with the same title.[29]

Charles E. Lindblom's (1917–   ) 1959 *Public Administration Review* article, "The Science of Muddling Through," took a hard look at the rational models of the decisional processes of government. Lindblom rejected the notion that most decisions are made by rational—total information—processes. Instead he saw such decisions—indeed, the whole policy-making process—dependent upon small incremental decisions that tended to be made in response to short-term political conditions. Lindblom's thesis, essentially, held that decision making was controlled infinitely more by events and circumstances than by the will of those in policy-making positions. His analysis encouraged considerable work in that area of the discipline that sits most on the boundary between political science and public administration—public policy.[30]

It is fitting that Lindblom's work marks the closing of the postwar period. A major reason that politics, policy, and decision making were so important was the sheer significance of government effort itself. By 1960, there were over 2.4 million federal civil employees, 1.5 million state government employees, and 4.8 million local government employees. Government outlays or expenditures at the federal level had now reached 92 billion (the first 100 billion dollar budget would occur in 1962). State and local government expenditures totaled another 60 billion dollars. To put this into context, consider that federal government expenditures in 1940 were approximately 9.5 billion or ten percent of the gross national product (GNP); 92.5 billion in 1960 represented almost nineteen percent of the nation's GNP. Even a conservative president such as Eisenhower would have little impact on slowing the size and growth of government. The modern administrative state by 1960 was complete.

NOTES

1. For an intellectual biography, see: Frank G. Goble, *The Third Force: The Psychology of Abraham Maslow* (New York: Grossman Publishers, 1970). Maslow would later provide a more expansive analysis of his "needs hierarchy" in his text *Motivation and Personality*, 2nd ed. (New York: Harper & Row, 1970).
2. The importance of the concept of self-actualization was established long before Maslow gave it voice. The nineteenth-century poet, Robert Browning, described its essence when he wrote that "a man's reach should exceed his grasp, or what's a heaven for?"
3. See the "motivation-hygiene" theory in Frederick Herzberg, Bernard Mausner, and Barbara Snyderman, *The Motivation to Work* (New York: John Wiley & Sons, 1959).
4. See Theory X and Theory Y in Douglas M. McGregor, *The Human Side of Enterprise* (New York: McGraw-Hill, 1960).
5. See the "personality versus organization" hypothesis in Chris Argyris, *Personality and Organization* (New York: Harper & Row, 1957).
6. The most comprehensive analysis of the values of public administration from this period is Dwight Waldo's *The Administrative State: A Study of the Political Theory of American Public Administration* (New York: Ronald Press, 1948) which attacked the "gospel of efficiency" that so dominated administrative thinking prior to World War II.
7. (New York: Harper & Bros. 1944).
8. Lilienthal was chairman of the TVA and later of the Atomic Energy Commission. He kept and later published comprehensive diaries of his experiences. See: *The Journals of David E. Lilienthal* (New York: Harper & Row, vols. I & II, 1964; vol. III, 1966; vol. IV, 1969; vol. V, 1971; vol. VI, 1976).
9. For a review of Appleby's work and influence, see: Roscoe C. Martin, ed. *Public Administration and Democracy: Essays in Honor of Paul H. Appleby* (Syracuse: Syracuse University Press, 1965).
10. (New York: Alfred A. Knopf, 1945).
11. Because truly rational research on any problem can never be completed, humans put "bounds" on their rationality and make decisions, not on the basis of optimal information, but on the basis of satisfactory information. Thus, humans tend to make their decisions by "satisficing"—choosing a course of action that meets one's minimum standards for satisfaction. Simon, with James March, expands upon these notions in *Organizations* (New York: John Wiley & Sons, 1958).

12. Dahl was a prime exponent of pluralism and interest group participation in the political process. His major works include: with Charles E. Lindblom, *Politics, Economics and Welfare* (New York: Harper & Bros., 1953); *A Preface to Democratic Theory* (Chicago: University of Chicago Press, 1956); *Who Governs? Democracy and Power in an American City* (New Haven, Conn.: Yale University Press, 1961); *Modern Political Analysis,* 3rd ed. (Englewood Cliffs, N.J.: Prentice-Hall, 1976).
13. The major text in comparative public administration is: Ferrel Heady, *Public Administration: A Comparative Perspective,* 3rd ed. (New York: Marcel Dekker, 1984).
14. (Berkeley, Calif.: University of California Press, 1949).
15. (New York: Row, Peterson, 1957).
16. See for example: Waren G. Bennis, "Transformative Power and Leadership," in *Leadership and Organizational Culture,* ed. T. J. Sergiovanni and J. E. Corbally (Urbana, Ill.: University of Illinois Press, 1984); Noel M. Tichy and David O. Ulrich, "The Leadership Challenge—A Call for the Transformational Leader," *Sloan Management Review* 26 (Fall 1984).
17. Niccolo Machiavelli (1469–1527) is the most famous management and political analyst of the Italian Renaissance. His book of advice to would-be leaders, *The Prince,* is the progenitor of all "how to succeed" books that advocate practical rather than moral actions.
18. For his collected essays, see: *The Polity* (Chicago: Rand McNally, 1962).
19. This school of thought views organizations as complex systems of individuals and coalitions, each having its own interests, beliefs, values, preferences, perspectives, and perceptions. The coalitions compete with each other continuously for scarce organizational resources. Conflict is inevitable. Influence, and the power and political activities through which influence is acquired and maintained, is the primary "weapon" for use in competition and conflicts. For analyses, see: Antony Jay, *Management and Machiavelli: An Inquiry Into the Politics of Corporate Life* (New York: Holt, Rinehart & Winston, 1967); Jeffrey Pfeffer, *Power in Organizations* (Marshfield, Mass. Pitman Publishing 1981); Henry Mintzberg, *Power in and Around Organizations* (Englewood Cliffs, N.J.: Prentice-Hall, 1983).
20. Lewis, after more than a decade with the Atomic Energy Commission, was the Director of Budget and Finance for the Department of State from 1961 to 1971. After his retirement from the federal service, he joined the faculty of the Graduate School of Public Affairs of the University of Washington.
21. This is the first chapter from his *The Study of Public Administration* (New York: Random House, 1955).
22. For a history of Waldo's intellectual influence and career, see: Brack Brown and Richard J. Stillman II, *The Search for Public Administration: The Ideas and Career of Dwight Waldo* (College Station, Texas: Texas A & M University Press, 1986).
23. See his *The Social System* (New York: Free Press, 1951).
24. See as examples: Edgar H. Schein, *Organizational Culture and Leadership* (San Francisco: Jossey-Bass, 1985); Vijay Sathe, ed. *Culture and Corporate Realities* (Homewood, Ill.: Richard D. Irwin, 1985).
25. For example, *Papers on Organization and Management* (Washington, D.C.: The American University Press, 1945); *Processes on Organization and Management* (Washington, D.C.: The American University Press, 1948); *Organization and Management: Theory and Practice* (Washington, D.C.: The American University Press, 1955).
26. *Budgeting: An Instrument of Planning and Management,* 6 vols. (Washington, D.C.: The American University Press, 1955).
27. Parkinson has continued with his "legal" studies, but has never duplicated his initial success. See his: *The Law and the Profits* (Boston: Houghton Mifflin, 1960); *Mrs. Parkinson's Law* (Boston: Houghton Mifflin, 1968); *The Law of Delay* (Boston: Houghton Mifflin, 1971).
28. For an evaluation of McGregor's impact and contributions by a colleague of his at M.I.T.'s Sloan School of Management, see: Warren G. Bennis, "Chairman Mac in Perspective, *Harvard Business Review* (September–October, 1972).
29. (New York: McGraw-Hill, 1960).

30. Lindblom's article created a new subfield in public administration—muddle analysis. See: Yehezkel Dror, "Muddling Through—Science or Inertia?" *Public Administration Review* 24 (September 1964); John J. Bailey and Robert J. O'Conner, "Operationalizing Incrementalism: Measuring the Muddles," *Public Administration Review* 35 (January–February 1975); Anthony J. Balzer, "Reflections on Muddling Through," *Public Administration Review* 39 (November–December 1979); Bruce Adams, "The Limitations of Muddling Through: Does Anyone in Washington Really Think Anymore?" *Public Administration Review* 39 (November–December 1979); Charles E. Lindblom, "Still Muddling, Not Yet Through," *Public Administration Review* 39 (November–December 1979).

A CHRONOLOGY OF PUBLIC ADMINISTRATION: 1943–1959

1943 Abraham Maslow's "needs hierarchy" first appears in his article, "A Theory of Human Motivation" in *Psychological Review.*

Withholding for federal income tax begins as a temporary wartime measure.

1944 J. Donald Kingsley's *Representative Bureaucracy* develops the concept that all social groups have a right to participate in their governing institutions in proportion to their numbers in the population.

David E. Lilienthal in *TVA: Democracy on the March* writes that the planning process of government is a blatantly political enterprise, a situation that is both healthy and beneficial for a democratic society.

1945 Paul Appleby leads the postwar attack on the politics-administration dichotomy by insisting in *Big Democracy* that apolitical governmental processes went against the grain of the American experience.

With the dropping of the atomic bomb and the end of World War II, the suddenly public Manhattan Project marks the federal government's first major involvement with science in a policy-making role.

1946 The Employment Act creates the Council of Economic Advisors and asserts that it is the policy of the federal government to maintain full employment.

The Administrative Procedure Act standardized many federal government administrative practices across agencies.

Herbert A. Simon's "The Proverbs of Administration" attacks the principles approach to management for being inconsistent and often inapplicable.

1947 National Training Laboratory for Group Development (now called the NTL Institute for Applied Behavioral Science) is established to do research on group dynamics and later sensitivity training.

The First Hoover Commission (1947–1949) recommends increased managerial capacity in the Executive Office of the President.

The National Security Act creates the Department of Defense.

Robert A. Dahl in "The Science of Public Administration" argues that public administration needs to deal with its normative aspects, that the study of it has become too parochial, and that workers can no longer be viewed in the scientific management tradition as human interchangeable parts in a bureaucratic machine.

Herbert A. Simon's *Administrative Behavior* urges that a true scientific method be used in the study of administrative phenomena, that the perspective of logical positivism should be used in dealing with questions of policy making, and that decision making is really the true heart of administration.

President Harry S. Truman's Executive Order 9835 launches the federal government's loyalty program designed to root out subversives in the bureaucracy.

1948 Dwight Waldo publishes *The Administrative State,* which attacks the "gospel of efficiency" that dominated administrative thinking prior to World War II.

Inter-University Case Program started to encourage the development and dissemination of case studies in public administration.

Wallace S. Sayre in *Public Administration Review* attacks public personnel administration as the "triumph of techniques over purpose."

President Harry S. Truman orders the integration of the armed forces.

1949 Philip Selznick in *TVA and the Grass Roots* discovers "cooptation" when he examines how the Tennessee Valley Authority subsumed new elements into its policy making process in order to prevent those elements from being a threat to the organization.

In his *Public Administration Review* article, "Power and Administration," Norton E. Long finds that the lifeblood of administration is power and that managers had to do more than just apply the scientific method to problems—they had to attain, maintain, and increase their power or risk failing in their mission.

Rufus E. Miles, Jr., of the Bureau of the Budget first states Miles' Law: "Where you stand depends on where you sit."

Air Force Captain Edsel Murphy first states Murphy's Law: "If anything can go wrong, it will."

1950 The Budgeting and Accounting Procedures Act mandated the performance budgeting concepts called for by the first Hoover Commission.

George C. Homans publishes *The Human Group,* the first major application of "systems" to organizational analysis.

Senator Joseph McCarthy in a speech in Wheeling, West Virginia, holds up a list that he claims contains the names of 205 people known to be communists but still employed in the State Department; McCarthyism, recklessly charging that individuals are communists or communist influenced, flourished.

1951 David Truman's *The Governmental Process* calls for viewing interest groups as the real determinant of, and focal point of study on, public policy.

Kurt Lewin proposes a general model of change consisting of three phases, "unfreezing, change, refreezing" in his *Field Theory in Social Science;* this model becomes the conceptual frame for organization development.

Ludwig von Bertalanffy's article "General Systems Theory: A New Approach to the Unity of Science" is published in *Human Biology;* his concepts will become *the* intellectual basis for the systems approach to organizational thinking.

1952 Harold Stein edits the first major casebook, *Public Administration and Policy Development.*

Verne B. Lewis' "Toward a Theory of Budgeting" presents a theory of alternative budgeting that will be an important link to the PPB systems of the 1960s and the ZBB systems of the 1970s.

1953 The Second Hoover Commission (1953–1955) recommends the curtailment and abolition of federal government activities that are competitive with private enterprise.

Department of Health, Education and Welfare (HEW) is created.

1954 Peter Drucker's book, *The Practice of Management,* popularizes the concept of management by objectives.

The Supreme Court in *Brown v. Board of Education of Topeka Kansas* held that racially separate educational facilities were inherently unequal and therefore violated the equal protection clause of the Fourteenth Amendment.

Senator Joseph McCarthy (and in effect McCarthyism) is censured by the U.S. Senate.

Lakewood, California, pioneers the service contract whereby a small jurisdiction (such as Lakewood) buys government services such as police and fire protection from a neighboring large jurisdiction (such as Los Angeles).

Alvin Gouldner's *Patterns of Industrial Bureaucracy* describes three possible responses to a formal bureaucratic structure: "mock" where the formal rules are ignored by both management and labor, "punishment-centered" where management seeks to enforce rules that workers resist, and "representative" where rules are both enforced and obeyed.

1955 Kestnbaum Commission on Intergovernmental Relations recommends the establishment of a "permanent center for overall attention to the problems of inter-level relationships."

AFL–CIO is formed by the merger of the American Federation of Labor and the Congress of Industrial Organization.

Marver Bernstein in *Regulating Business by Independent Commission* develops a life cycle theory of regulatory commissions with these stages: gestation, youth, maturity, and decline.

Catheryn Seckler-Hudson takes a technical approach to her development of "Basic Concepts in the Study of Public Management."

Dwight Waldo's *The Study of Public Administration* seeks a fusion of the longstanding art of public administration with the newly emerging science of public administration.

1956 William H. Whyte, Jr., first profiles *The Organization Man* as an individual within an organization who accepts its values and finds harmony in conforming to its policies.

1957 C. Northcote Parkinson discovers his law that "work expands so as to fill the time available for its completion."

Chris Argyris asserts in his first major book, *Personality and Organization,* that there is an inherent conflict between the personality of a mature adult and the needs of modern organizations.

Douglas M. McGregor's article, "The Human Side of Enterprise," distills the contending traditional (authoritarian) and humanistic managerial philosophies into Theory X and Theory Y.

Program Evaluation and Review Technique (PERT) is developed by the Navy during planning for the Polaris ballistic missile system.

Anthony Downs' *An Economic Theory of Democracy* establishes the intellectual framework for "public choice" economics.

Philip Selznick in *Leadership in Administration* anticipated many of the 1980s notions of "transformational leadership" when he asserted that the function of an institutional leader is to help shape the environment in which the institution operates and to define new institutional directions through recruitment, training, and bargaining.

1958 March and Simon in *Organizations* seek to inventory all that is worth knowing about the behavioral revolution in organization theory.

Wallace S. Sayre in "Premises of Public Administration: Past and Emerging" predicts that a "new orthodoxy" in public administration will evolve to replace the "old orthodoxy."

The Government Employees Training Act allows federal agencies for the first time to spend significant sums for employee training and development.

1959 New York City is the first major city to allow for collective bargaining with its employee unions.

Wisconsin is the first state to enact a comprehensive law governing public sector labor relations.

The Advisory Commission on Intergovernmental Relations is established.

Charles A. Lindblom's "The Science of 'Muddling Through' " rejects the rational model of decision making in favor of incrementalism.

Herzberg, Mausner, and Snyderman's *The Motivation to Work* puts forth the motivation-hygiene theory.

15
A Theory of Human Motivation

A. H. Maslow

I. INTRODUCTION

In a previous paper[1] various propositions were presented which would have to be included in any theory of human motivation that could lay claim to being definitive. These conclusions may be briefly summarized as follows:

1. The integrated wholeness of the organism must be one of the foundation stones of motivation theory.
2. The hunger drive (or any other physiological drive) was rejected as a centering point or model for a definitive theory of motivation. Any drive that is somatically based and localizable was shown to be atypical rather than typical in human motivation.
3. Such a theory should stress and center itself upon ultimate or basic goals rather than partial or superficial ones, upon ends rather than means to these ends. Such a stress would imply a more central place for unconscious than for conscious motivations.
4. There are usually available various cultural paths to the same goal. Therefore conscious, specific, local-cultural desires are not as fundamental in motivation theory as the more basic, unconscious goals.
5. Any motivated behavior, either preparatory or consummatory, must be understood to be a channel through which many basic needs may be simultaneously expressed or satisfied. Typically an act has *more* than one motivation.
6. Practically all organismic states are to be understood as motivated and as motivating.
7. Human needs arrange themselves in hierarchies of prepotency. That is to say, the appearance of one need usually rests on the prior satisfaction of another, more prepotent need. Man is a perpetually wanting animal. Also no need or drive can be treated as if it were isolated or discrete; every drive is related to the state of satisfaction or dissatisfaction of other drives.
8. *Lists* of drives will get us nowhere for various theoretical and practical reasons. Furthermore any classification of motivations must deal with the problem of levels of specificity or generalization of the motives to be classified.
9. Classifications of motivations must be based upon goals rather than upon instigating drives or motivated behavior.
10. Motivation theory should be human-centered rather than animal-centered.
11. The situation or the field in which the organism reacts must be taken into account, but the field alone can rarely serve as an exclusive explanation for behavior. Furthermore the field itself must be interpreted in terms of the organism. Field theory cannot be a substitute for motivation theory.
12. Not only the integration of the organism must be taken into account, but also the possibility of isolated,

Source: Psychological Review 50 (July 1943), pp. 370–396. Footnotes and pertinent references combined and renumbered; references not appearing in text have been omitted.

specific, partial or segmental reactions.

It has since become necessary to add to these another affirmation.

13. Motivations theory is not synonymous with behavior theory. The motivations are only one class of determinants of behavior. While behavior is almost always motivated, it is also almost always biologically, culturally, and situationally determined as well.

The present paper is an attempt to formulate a positive theory of motivation which will satisfy these theoretical demands and at the same time conform to the known facts, clinical and observational as well as experimental. It derives most directly, however, from clinical experience. This theory is, I think, in the functionalist tradition of James and Dewey, and is fused with the holism of Wertheimer,[2] Goldstein,[3] and Gestalt Psychology and with the dynamicism of Freud[4] and Adler.[5] This fusion or synthesis may arbitrarily be called a "general-dynamic" theory.

It is far easier to perceive and to criticize the aspects in motivation theory than to remedy them. Mostly this is because of the very serious lack of sound data in this area. I conceive this lack of sound facts to be due primarily to the absence of a valid theory of motivation. The present theory then must be considered to be a suggested program or framework for future research and must stand or fall, not so much on facts available or evidence presented, as upon researches yet to be done, researches suggested perhaps, by the questions raised in this paper.

II. THE BASIC NEEDS

The "Physiological" Needs. The needs that are usually taken as the starting point for motivation theory are the so-called physiological drives. Two recent lines of research make it necessary to revise our customary notions about these needs: first, the development of the concept of homeostasis, and second, the finding that appetites (preferential choices among foods) are a fairly efficient indication of actual needs or lacks in the body.

Homeostasis refers to the body's automatic efforts to maintain a constant, normal state of the blood stream. Cannon[6] has described this process for (1) the water content of the blood, (2) salt content, (3) sugar content, (4) protein content, (5) fat content, (6) calcium content, (7) oxygen content, (8) constant hydrogen-ion level (acid-base balance) and (9) constant temperature of the blood. Obviously this list can be extended to include other minerals, the hormones, vitamins, etc.

Young in a recent article[7] has summarized the work on appetite in its relation to body needs. If the body lacks some chemical, the individual will tend to develop a specific appetite or partial hunger for that food element.

Thus it seems impossible as well as useless to make any list of fundamental physiological needs for they can come to almost any number one might wish, depending on the degree of specificity of description. We can not identify all physiological needs as homeostatic. That sexual desire, sleepiness, sheer activity and maternal behavior in animals, are homeostatic, has not yet been demonstrated. Furthermore, this list would not include the various sensory pleasures (tastes, smells, tickling, stroking) which are probably physiological and which may become the goals of motivated behavior.

In a previous paper[8] it has been pointed out that these physiological drives or needs are to be considered unusual rather than typical because they are isolable, and because they are localizable somatically. That is to say, they are relatively independent of each other, of other motivations and of the organism as a whole, and secondly, in many cases, it is possible to demonstrate a localized, underlying somatic base for the drive. This is true less generally than has been thought (exceptions are fatigue, sleepiness, maternal responses) but it is still true in the classic instances of hunger, sex, and thirst.

It should be pointed out again that any of the physiological needs and the consummatory behavior involved with them serve as channels for all sorts of other needs as well. That is to say, the person who thinks he is hungry may actually be seeking more for comfort, or dependence, than for vitamins or proteins. Conversely, it is possible to satisfy the hunger need in part by other activities such as drinking water or smoking cigarettes. In other words, relatively isolable as these physiological needs are, they are not completely so.

Undoubtedly these physiological needs are the most prepotent of all needs. What this means specifically is, that in the human being who is missing everything in life in an extreme fashion, it is most likely that the major motivation would be the physiological needs rather than any others. A person who is lacking food, safety, love, and esteem would most probably hunger for food more strongly than for anything else.

If all the needs are unsatisfied, and the organism is then dominated by the physiological needs, all other needs may become simply non-existent or be pushed into the background. It is then fair to characterize the whole organism by saying simply that it is hungry, for consciousness is almost completely preempted by hunger. All capacities are put into the service of hunger-satisfaction, and the organization of these capacities is almost entirely determined by the one purpose of satisfying hunger. The receptors and effectors, the intelligence, memory, habits, all may now be defined simply as hunger-gratifying tools. Capacities that are not useful for this purpose lie dormant, or are pushed into the background. The urge to write poetry, the desire to acquire an automobile, the interest in American history, the desire for a new pair of shoes are, in the extreme case, forgotten or become of secondary importance. For the man who is extremely and dangerously hungry, no other interests exist but food. He dreams food, he remembers food, he thinks about food, he emotes only about food, he perceives only food and he wants only food. The more subtle determinants that ordinarily fuse with the physiological drives in organizing even feeding, drinking or sexual behavior, may now be so completely overwhelmed as to allow us to speak at this time (but *only* at this time) of pure hunger drive and behavior, with the one unqualified aim of relief.

Another peculiar characteristic of the human organism when it is dominated by a certain need is that the whole philosophy of the future tends also to change. For our chronically and extremely hungry man, Utopia can be defined very simply as a place where there is plenty of food. He tends to think that, if only he is guaranteed food for the rest of his life, he will be perfectly happy and will never want anything more. Life itself tends to be defined in terms of eating. Anything else will be defined as unimportant. Freedom, love, community feeling, respect, philosophy, may all be waved aside as fripperies which are useless since they fail to fill the stomach. Such a man may fairly be said to live by bread alone.

It cannot possibly be denied that such things are true, but their *generality* can be denied. Emergency conditions are, almost by definition, rare in the normally functioning peaceful society. That this truism can be forgotten is due mainly to two reasons. First, rats have few motivations other than physiological ones, and since so much of the research upon motivation has been made with these animals, it is easy to carry the rat-picture over to the human being. Secondly, it is too often not realized that culture itself is an adaptive tool, one of whose main functions is to make the physiological emergencies come less and less often. In most of the known societies, chronic extreme hunger of the emergency type is rare, rather than common. In any case, this is still true in the United States. The average American citizen is experiencing appetite rather than hunger when he says "I am hungry." He is apt to experience sheer life-and-death hunger only by accident and then only a few times through his entire life.

Obviously a good way to obscure the "higher" motivations, and to get a lopsided view of human capacities and human nature, is to make the organism extremely and chronically hungry or thirsty. Anyone who attempts to make an emergency picture into a typical one, and who will measure all of man's goals and desires by his behavior during extreme physiological deprivation is certainly being blind to many things. It is quite true that man lives by bread alone—when there is no bread. But what happens to man's desires when there *is* plenty of bread and when his belly is chronically filled?

At once other (and "higher") needs emerge and these, rather than physiological hungers, dominate the organism. And when these in turn are satisfied, again new (and still "higher") needs emerge and so on. This is what we mean by saying that the basic human needs are organized into a hierarchy of relative prepotency.

One main implication of this phrasing is that gratification becomes as important a concept as deprivation in motivation theory, for it releases the organism from the domination of a relatively more physiological need, permitting thereby the emergence of other more social goals. The physiological needs, along with their partial goals, when chronically gratified cease to exist as active determinants or organizers of behavior. They now exist only in a potential fashion in the sense that they may emerge again to dominate the organism if they are thwarted. But a want that is satisfied is no longer a want. The organism is dominated and its behavior organized only by unsatisfied needs. If hunger is satisfied, it becomes unimportant in the current dynamics of the individual.

This statement is somewhat qualified by a hypothesis to be discussed more fully later, namely that it is precisely those individuals in whom a certain need has always been satisfied who are best equipped to tolerate deprivation of that need in the future, and that furthermore, those who have been deprived in the past will react differently to current satisfactions than the one who has never been deprived.

The Safety Needs. If the physiological needs are relatively well gratified, there then emerges a new set of needs, which we may categorize roughly as the safety needs. All that has been said of the physiological needs is equally true, although in lesser degree, of these desires. The organism may equally well be wholly dominated by them. They may serve as the almost exclusive organizers of behavior, recruiting all the capacities of the organism in their service, and we may then fairly describe the whole organism as a safety-seeking mechanism. Again we may say of the receptors, the effectors, of the intellect and the other capacities that they are primarily safety-seeking tools. Again, as in the hungry man, we find that the dominating goal is a strong determinant not only of his current world-outlook and philosophy but also of his philosophy of the future. Practically everything looks less important than safety, (even sometimes the physiological needs which being satisfied, are now underestimated). A man, in this state, if it is extreme enough and chronic enough, may be characterized as living almost for safety alone.

Although in this paper we are interested primarily in the needs of the adult, we can approach an understanding of his safety needs perhaps more efficiently by observation of infants and children, in whom these needs are much more simple and obvious. One reason for the clearer appearance of the threat or danger reaction in infants is that they do not inhibit this reaction at all, whereas adults in our society have been taught to inhibit it at all costs. Thus even when adults do feel their safety to be threatened, we may not be able to see this on the surface. Infants will react in a total fashion and as if they were endangered, if they are disturbed or dropped suddenly, startled by loud noises, flashing light, or other unusual sensory stimulation, by rough handling, by general loss of support in the mother's arms, or by inadequate support.[9]

In infants we can also see a much more direct reaction to bodily illnesses of various kinds. Sometimes these illnesses seem to be immediately and *per se* threatening and seem to make the child feel unsafe. For instance, vomiting, colic or other sharp pains seem to make the child look at the whole world in a different way. At such a moment of pain, it may be postulated that, for the child, the appearance of the whole world suddenly changes from sunniness to darkness, so to speak, and becomes a place in which anything at all might happen, in which previously stable things have suddenly become unstable. Thus a child who because of some bad food is taken ill may, for a day or two, develop fear, nightmares, and a need for protection and reassurance never seen in him before his illness.

Another indication of the child's need for safety is his preference for some kind of undisrupted routine or rhythm. He seems to want a predictable, orderly world. For instance, injustice, unfairness, or inconsistency in the parents seems to make a child feel anxious and unsafe. This attitude may be not so much because of the injustice *per se* or any particular pains involved, but rather because this treatment threatens to make the world look unreliable, or unsafe, or unpredictable. Young children seem to thrive better under a system which has at least a skeletal outline of rigidity, in which there is a schedule of a kind, some sort of routine, something that can be counted upon, not only for the present but also far into the future. Perhaps one could express this more accurately by saying that the child needs an organized world rather than an unorganized or unstructured one.

The central role of the parents and the normal family setup are indisputable. Quarreling, physical assault, separation, divorce or death within the family may be particularly terrifying. Also parental outbursts or rage or threats of punishment directed to the child, calling him names, speaking to him harshly, shaking him, handling him roughly, or actual physical punishment sometimes elicit such total panic and terror in the child that we must assume more is involved than the physical pain alone.

While it is true that in some children this terror may represent also a fear of loss of parental love, it can also occur in completely rejected children, who seem to cling to the hating parents more for sheer safety and protection than because of hope of love.

Confronting the average child with new, unfamiliar, strange, unmanageable stimuli or situations will too frequently elicit the danger or terror reaction, as for example, getting lost or even being separated from the parents for a short time, being confronted with new faces, new situations or new tasks, the sight of strange, unfamiliar or uncontrollable objects, illness or death. Particularly at such times, the child's frantic clinging to his parents is eloquent testimony to their role as protectors (quite apart from their roles as food-givers and love-givers).

From these and similar observations, we may generalize and say that the average child in our society generally prefers a safe, orderly, predictable, organized world, which he can count on, and in which unexpected, unmanageable or other dangerous things do not happen, and in which, in any case, he has all-powerful parents who protect and shield him from harm.

That these reactions may so easily be observed in children is in a way a proof of the fact that children in our society, feel too unsafe (or, in a word, are badly brought up). Children who are reared in an unthreatening, loving family do *not* ordinarily react as we have described above.[10] In such children the danger reactions are apt to come mostly to objects or situations that adults too would consider dangerous.[11]

The healthy, normal, fortunate adult in our culture is largely satisfied in his safety needs. The peaceful, smoothly running "good" society ordinarily makes its members feel safe enough from wild animals, extremes of temperature, criminals, assault and murder, tyranny, etc. Therefore, in a very real sense, he no longer has any safety needs as active motivators. Just as a sated man no longer feels hungry, a safe man no longer feels endangered. If we wish to see these needs directly and clearly we must turn to neurotic or near-neurotic individuals, and to the economic and social underdogs. In between these extremes, we can perceive the expressions of safety needs only in such phenomena as, for instance, the common preference for a job with tenure and protection, the desire for a savings account, and for insurance of various kinds (medical, dental, unemployment, disability, old age).

Other broader aspects of the attempt to seek safety and stability in the world are seen in the very common preference for familiar rather than unfamiliar things, or for the known rather than the unknown. The tendency to have some religion or world-philosophy that organizes the universe and the men in it into some sort of satisfactorily coherent, meaningful whole is also in part motivated by safety-seeking. Here too we may list science and philosophy in general as partially motivated by the safety needs (we shall see later that there are also other motivations to scientific, philosophical or religious endeaver).

Otherwise the need for safety is seen as an active and dominant mobilizer of the organism's resources only in emergencies, e.g., war, disease, natural catastrophes, crime waves, societal disorganization, neurosis, brain injury, chronically bad situation.

Some neurotic adults in our society are, in many ways, like the unsafe child in their desire for safety, although in the former it takes on a somewhat special appearance. Their reaction is often to unknown, psychological dangers in a world that is perceived to be hostile, overwhelming and threatening. Such a person behaves as if a great catastrophe were almost always impending, *i.e.*, he is usually responding as if to an emergency. His safety needs often find specific expression in a search for a protector, or a stronger person on whom he may depend, or perhaps, a Fuehrer.

The neurotic individual may be described in a slightly different way with some usefulness as a grown-up person who retains his childish attitudes toward the world. That is to say, a neurotic adult may be said to behave "as if" he were actually afraid of a spanking, or of his mother's disapproval, or of being abandoned by his parents, or having his food taken away from him. It is as if his childish attitudes of fear and threat reaction to a dangerous world had gone underground, and untouched by the growing up and learning processes, were now ready to be called out by any stimulus that would make a child feel endangered and threatened.[12]

The neurosis in which the search for safety takes its clearest form is in the compulsive-obsessive neurosis. Compulsive obsessives try frantically to order and stabilize the world so that no unmanageable, unexpected or unfamiliar dangers will ever appear.[13] They hedge themselves about with all sorts of ceremonials, rules and formulas so that every possible contingency may be provided for and so that no new contingencies may appear. They are much like the brain-injured cases, described by Goldstein,[14] who manage to maintain their equilibrium by avoiding everything unfamiliar and strange and by ordering their restricted world in such a neat, disciplined, orderly fashion that everything in the world can be counted upon. They try to arrange the world so that anything unexpected (dangers) cannot possibly occur. If, through no fault of their own, something unexpected does occur, they go into a panic reaction as if this unexpected occurrence constituted a grave danger. What we can see only as a none-too-strong preference in the healthy person, *e.g.*, preference for the familiar, becomes a life-and-death necessity in abnormal cases.

The Love Needs. If both the physiological and the safety needs are fairly well gratified, then there will emerge the love and affection and belongingness needs, and the whole cycle already described will repeat itself with this new center. Now the person will feel keenly, as never before, the absence of friends, or a sweetheart, or a wife, or children. He will hunger for affectionate relations with people in general, namely, for a place in his group, and he will strive with great intensity to achieve this goal. He will want to attain such a place more than anything else in the world and may even forget that once, when he was hungry, he sneered at love.

In our society the thwarting of these needs is the most commonly found core in cases of maladjustment and more severe psychopathology. Love and affection, as well as their possible expression in sexuality, are generally looked upon with ambivalence and are customarily hedged about with many restrictions and inhibitions. Practically all theorists of psychopathology have stressed thwarting of the love needs as basic in the picture of maladjustment. Many clinical studies have therefore been made of this need and we know more about it perhaps than any of the other needs except the physiological ones.[15]

One thing that must be stressed at this point is that love is not synonymous with sex. Sex may be studied as a purely physiological need. Ordinarily sexual behavior is multi-determined, that is to say, determined not only by sexual but also by other needs, chief among which are the love and affection needs. Also not to be overlooked is the fact that the love needs involve both giving *and* receiving love.[16]

The Esteem Needs. All people in our society (with a few pathological exceptions) have a need or desire for a stable, firmly based, (usually) high evaluation of themselves, for self-respect, or self-esteem, and for the esteem of others. By firmly based self-esteem, we mean that which is soundly based upon real capacity, achievement and respect from others. These needs may be classified into two subsidiary sets. These are, first, the desire for strength, for achievement, for adequacy, for confidence in the face of the world, and for independence and freedom.[17] Secondly, we have what we may call the desire for reputation or prestige (defining it as respect or esteem from other people), recognition, attention, importance or appreciation.[18] These needs have been relatively stressed by Alfred Adler and his followers, and have been relatively neglected by Freud and the psychoanalysts. More and more today however there is appearing widespread appreciation of their central importance.

Satisfaction of the self-esteem need leads to feelings of self-confidence, worth, strength, capability and adequacy of being useful and necessary in the world. But thwarting of these needs produces feelings of inferiority, of weakness and of helplessness. These feelings in turn give rise to either basic discouragement or else compensatory or neurotic trends. An appreciation of the necessity of basic self-confidence and an understanding of how helpless people are without it, can be easily gained from a study of severe traumatic neurosis.[19]

The Need for Self-Actualization. Even if all these needs are satisfied, we may still often (if not always) expect that a new discontent and restlessness will soon develop, unless the individual is doing what he is fitted for. A musician must make music, an artist must paint, a poet must write, if he is to be ultimately happy. What a man *can* be, he *must* be. This need we may call self-actualization.

This term, first coined by Kurt Goldstein, is being used in this paper in a much more specific and limited fashion. It refers to the desire for self-fulfillment, namely, to the tendency for him to become actualized in what he is potentially. This tendency might be phrased as the desire to become more and more what one is, to become everything that one is capable of becoming.

The specific form that these needs will take will of course vary greatly from person to person. In one individual it may take the form of the desire to be an ideal mother, in another it may be expressed athletically, and in still another it may be expressed in painting pictures or in inventions. It is not necessarily a creative urge although in people who have any capacities for creation it will take this form.

The clear emergence of these needs rests upon prior satisfaction of the physiological, safety, love and esteem needs. We shall call people who are satisfied in these needs, basically satisfied people, and it is from these that we may expect the fullest (and healthiest) creativeness.[20] Since, in our society, basically satisfied people are the exception, we do not know much about self-actualization, either experimentally or clinically. It remains a challenging problem for research.

The Preconditions for the Basic Need Satisfactions. There are certain conditions which are immediate prerequisites for the basic need satisfactions. Danger to these is reacted to almost as if it were a direct danger to the basic needs themselves. Such conditions as freedom to speak, freedom to do what one wishes so long as no harm is done to others, freedom to express one's self, freedom to investigate and seek for information, freedom to defend one's self, justice, fairness, honesty, orderliness in the group are examples of such preconditions for basic need satisfactions. Thwarting in these freedoms will be reacted to with a threat or emergency response. These conditions are not ends in themselves but they are *almost* so since they are so closely related to the basic needs, which are apparently the only ends in themselves. These conditions are defended because without them the basic satisfactions are quite impossible, or at least, very severely endangered.

If we remember that the cognitive capacities (perceptual, intellectual, learning) are a set of adjustive tools, which have, among other functions, that of satisfaction of our basic needs, then it is clear that any danger to them, any deprivation or blocking of their free use, must also be indirectly threatening to the basic needs themselves. Such a statement is a partial solution of the general problems of curiosity, the search for knowledge, truth and wisdom, and the ever-persistent urge to solve the cosmic mysteries.

We must therefore introduce another hypothesis and speak of degrees of closeness to the basic needs, for we have already pointed out that *any* conscious desires (partial goals) are more or less important as they are more or less close to the basic needs. The same statement may be made for various behavior acts. An act is psychologically important if it contributes directly to satisfaction of basic needs. The less directly it so contributes, or the weaker this contribution is, the less important this act must be conceived to be from the point of view of dynamic psychology. A similar statement may be made for the various defense or coping mechanisms. Some are very directly related to the protection or attainment of the basic needs, others are only weakly and distantly related. Indeed if we wished, we could speak of more basic and less basic defense mechanisms, and then affirm that danger to the more basic defenses is more threatening than danger to less basic defenses (always remembering that this is so only because of their relationship to the basic needs).

The Desires to Know and to Understand. So far, we have mentioned the cognitive needs only in passing. Acquiring knowledge and systematizing the universe have been considered as, in part, techniques for the achievement of basic safety in the world, or, for the intelligent man, expressions of self-actualization. Also freedom of inquiry and expression have been discussed as preconditions of satisfactions of the basic needs. True though these formulations may be, they do not constitute definitive answers to the question as to the motivation role of curiosity, learning, philosophizing, experimenting, etc. They are, at best, no more than partial answers.

This question is especially difficult because we know so little about the facts. Curiosity, exploration, desire for the facts, desire to know may certainly be observed easily enough. The fact that they often are pursued even at great cost to the individual's safety is an earnest of the partial character of our previous discussion. In addition, the writer must admit that, though he has sufficient clinical evidence to postulate the desire to know as a very strong drive in intelligent people, no data are available for unintelligent people. It may then be largely a function of relatively high intelligence. Rather tentatively, then, and largely in the hope of stimulating discussion and research, we shall postulate a basic desire to know, to be aware of reality, to get the facts, to satisfy curiosity, or as Wertheimer phrases it, to see rather than to be blind.

This postulation, however, is not enough. Even after we know, we are impelled to know more and more minutely and microscopically on the one hand, and on the other, more and more extensively in the direction of world philosophy, religion, etc. The facts that we acquire, if they are isolated or atomistic, inevitably get theorized about, and either analyzed or organized or both. This process has been phrased by some as the search for "meaning." We shall then postulate a desire to understand, to systematize, to organize, to analyze, to look for relations and meanings.

Once these desires are accepted for discussion, we see that they too form themselves into a small hierarchy in which the desire to know is prepotent over the desire to understand. All the characteristics of a hierarchy of prepotency that we have described above seem to hold for this one as well.

We must guard ourselves against the too easy tendency to separate these desires from the basic needs we have discussed above, *i.e.*, to make a sharp dichotomy between "cognitive" and "conative" needs. The desire to know and to understand are themselves conative, *i.e.*, have a striving character, and are as much personality needs as the "basic needs" we have already discussed.[21]

III. FURTHER CHARACTERISTICS OF THE BASIC NEEDS

The Degree of Fixity of the Hierarchy of Basic Needs. We have spoken so far as if this hierarchy were a fixed order but actually it is not nearly as rigid as we may have implied. It is true that most of the people with whom we have worked have seemed to have these basic needs in about the order that has been indicated. However, there have been a number of exceptions.

1. There are some people in whom, for instance, self-esteem seems to be more important than love. This most common reversal in the hierarchy is usually due to the development of the notion that the person who is most likely to be loved is a strong or powerful person, one who inspires respect or fear, and who is self confident or aggressive. Therefore such people who lack love and seek it, may try hard to put on a front of aggressive, confident behavior. But essentially they seek high self-esteem and its behavior expressions more as a means-to-an-end than for its own sake; they seek self-assertion for the sake of love rather than for self-esteem itself.
2. There are other, apparently innately creative people in whom the drive to creativeness seems to be more important than any other counterdeterminant. Their creativeness might appear not as self-actualization released by basic satisfaction, but in spite of lack of basic satisfaction.
3. In certain people the level of aspiration may be permanently deadened or lowered. That is to say, the less prepotent goals may simply be lost, and may disappear forever, so that the person who has experienced life at a very low level, *i.e.*, chronic unemployment, may continue to be satisfied for the rest of his life if only he can get enough food.
4. The so-called "psychopathic personality" is another example of permanent loss of the love needs. These are people who, according to the best data available,[22] have been starved for love in the earliest months of their lives and have simply lost forever the desire and

the ability to give and to receive affection (as animals lose sucking or pecking reflexes that are not exercised soon enough after birth).

5. Another cause of reversal of the hierarchy is that when a need has been satisfied for a long time, this need may be underevaluated. People who have never experienced chronic hunger are apt to underestimate its effects and to look upon food as a rather unimportant thing. If they are dominated by a higher need, this higher need will seem to be the most important of all. It then becomes possible, and indeed does actually happen, that they may, for the sake of this higher need, put themselves into the position of being deprived in a more basic need. We may expect that after a long-time deprivation of the more basic need there will be a tendency to reevaluate both needs so that the more prepotent need will actually become consciously prepotent for the individual who may have given it up very lightly. Thus, a man who has given up his job rather than lose his self-respect, and who then starves for six months or so, may be willing to take his job back even at the price of losing his self-respect.
6. Another partial explanation of *apparent* reversals is seen in the fact that we have been talking about the hierarchy of prepotency in terms of consciously felt wants or desires rather than of behavior. Looking at behavior itself may give us the wrong impression. What we have claimed is that the person will *want* the more basic of two needs when deprived in both. There is no necessary implication here that he will act upon his desires. Let us say again that there are many determinants of behavior other than the needs and desires.
7. Perhaps more important than all these exceptions are the ones that involve ideals, high social standards, high values and the like. With such values people become martyrs; they will give up everything for the sake of a particular ideal, or value. These people may be understood, at least in part, by reference to one basic concept (or hypothesis) which may be called "increased frustration-tolerance through early gratification." People who have been satisfied in their basic needs throughout their lives, particularly in their earlier years, seem to develop exceptional power to withstand present or future thwarting of these needs simply because they have strong, healthy character structure as a result of basic satisfaction. They are the "strong" people who can easily weather disagreement or opposition, who can swim against the stream of public opinion and who can stand up for the truth at great personal cost. It is just the ones who have loved and been well loved, and who have had many deep friendships who can hold out against hatred, rejection or persecution.

   I say all this in spite of the fact that there is a certain amount of sheer habituation which is also involved in any full discussion of frustration tolerance. For instance, it is likely that those persons who have been accustomed to relative starvation for a long time, are partially enabled thereby to withstand food deprivation. What sort of balance must be made between these two tendencies, of habituation on the one hand, and of past satisfaction breeding present frustration tolerance on the other hand, remains to be worked out by further research. Meanwhile we may assume that they are both operative, side by side, since they do not contradict each other. In respect to this phenomenon of increased frustration tolerance, it seems probable that the most important gratifications come in the first two years of life. That is to say, people who have been made secure and strong in the earliest years, tend to remain secure and strong thereafter in the face of whatever threatens.

Degrees of Relative Satisfaction. So far, our theoretical discussion may have given the impression that these five sets of needs are somehow in step-wise, all-or-none relationships to each other. We have spoken in such terms as the following: "If one need is satisfied, then another emerges." This statement might give the false impression that a need must be satisfied 100 percent before the next need emerges. In actual fact, most members of our society who are normal, are partially satisfied in all their basic needs and partially unsatisfied in all their basic needs at the same time. A more realistic description of the hierarchy would be in terms of decreasing percentages of satisfaction as we go up the hierarchy of prepotency. For instance, if I may assign arbitrary figures for the sake of illustration, it is as if the average citizen is satisfied perhaps 85 percent in his physiological needs, 70 percent in his safety needs, and 10 percent in his self-actualization needs.

As for the concept of emergence of a new need after satisfaction of the prepotent need, this emergence is not a sudden, saltatory phenomenon but rather a gradual emergence by slow degrees from nothingness. For instance, if prepotent need A is satisfied only 10 percent, then need B may not be visible at all. However, as this need A becomes satisfied 25 percent, need B may emerge 5 percent, as need A becomes satisfied 75 percent need B may emerge 90 percent, and so on.

Unconscious Character of Needs. These needs are neither necessarily conscious nor unconscious. On the whole, however, in the average person, they are more often unconscious rather than conscious. It is not necessary at this point to overhaul the tremendous mass of evidence which indicates the crucial importance of unconscious motivation. It would by now be expected, on a priori grounds alone, that unconscious motivations would on the whole be rather more important than the conscious motivations. What we have called the basic needs are very often largely unconscious although they may, with suitable techniques, and with sophisticated people become conscious.

Cultural Specificity and Generality of Needs. This classification of basic needs makes some attempt to take account of the relative unity behind the superficial differences in specific desires from one culture to another. Certainly in any particular culture an individual's conscious motivational content will usually be extremely different from the conscious motivational content of an individual in another society. However, it is the common experience of anthropologists that people, even in different societies, are much more alike than we would think from our first contact with them, and that as we know them better we seem to find more and more of this commonness. We then recognize the most startling differences to be superficial rather than basic, *e.g.*, differences in style of hairdress, clothes, tastes in food, etc. Our classification of basic needs is in part an attempt to account for this unity behind the apparent diversity from culture to culture. No claim is made that it is ultimate or universal for all cultures. The claim is made only that it is relatively *more* ultimate, more universal, more basic, than the superficial conscious desires from culture to culture, and makes a somewhat closer approach to common-human characteristics. Basic needs are *more* common-human than superficial desires or behaviors.

Multiple Motivations of Behavior. These needs must be understood *not* to be *exclusive* or single determiners of certain kinds of behavior. An example may be found in any behavior that seems to be physiologically motivated, such as eating, or sexual play or the like. The clinical psychologists have long since found that any behavior may be a channel through which flow various determinants. Or to say it in another way, most behavior is multi-motivated. Within the sphere of motivational determinants any behavior tends to be determined by several or *all* of the basic needs simultaneously rather than by only one of them. The latter would be more an exception than the former. Eating may be partially for the sake of filling the stomach, and partially for the sake of comfort and amelioration of other needs. One may make love not only for pure sexual release, but also to convince one's self of one's masculinity, or to make a conquest, to feel powerful, or to win more basic affection. As an illustration, I may point out that it would be possible (theoretically if not practically) to analyze a single act of an individual and see in it the expression of his physiological needs, his safety needs, his love needs, his esteem needs and self-actualization. This contrasts sharply with the more naive brand of trait psychology in which one trait or one motive accounts for a certain kind of act, *i.e.*, an aggressive act is traced solely to a trait of aggressiveness.

Multiple Determinants of Behavior. Not all behavior is determined by the basic needs. We might even say that not all behavior is motivated. There are many determinants of behavior other than motives.[23] For instance, one other important class of determinants is the so-called "field" determinants. Theoretically, at least, behavior may be determined completely by the field, or even by specific isolated external stimuli, as in association of ideas, or certain conditioned reflexes. If in response to the stimulus word "table" I immediately perceive a memory image of a table, this response certainly has nothing to do with my basic needs.

Secondly, we may call attention again to the concept of "degree of closeness to the basic needs" or "degree of motivation." Some behavior is highly motivated, other behavior is only weakly motivated. Some is not motivated at all (but all behavior is determined).

Another important point[24] is that there is a basic difference between expressive behavior and coping behavior (functional striving, purposive goal seeking). An expressive behavior does not try to do anything; it is simply a reflection of the personality. A stupid man behaves stupidly, not because he wants to, or tries to, or is motivated to, but simply because he *is* what he is. The same is true when I speak in a bass voice rather than tenor or soprano. The random movements of a healthy child, the smile on the face of a happy man even when he is alone, the springiness of the healthy man's walk, and the erectness of his carriage are other examples of expressive, non-functional behavior. Also the *style* in which a man carries out almost all his behavior, motivated as well as unmotivated, is often expressive.

We may then ask, is *all* behavior expressive or reflective of the character structure? The answer is "No." Rote, habitual, automatized, or conventional behavior may or may not be expressive. The same is true for most "stimulus-bound" behaviors.

It is finally necessary to stress that expressiveness of behavior, and goal-directedness of behavior are not mutually exclusive categories. Average behavior is usually both.

Goals as Centering Principle in Motivation Theory. It will be observed that the basic principle in our classification has been neither the instigation nor the motivated behavior but rather the functions, effects, purposes, or goals of the behavior. It has been proven sufficiently by various people that this is the most suitable point for centering in any motivation theory.[25]

Animal- and Human-Centering. This theory starts with the human being rather than any lower and presumably "simpler" animal. Too many of the findings that have been made in animals have been proven to be true for animals but not for the human being. There is no reason whatsoever why we should start with animals in order to study human motivation. The logic or rather illogic behind this general fallacy of "pseudo-simplicity" has been exposed often enough by philosophers and logicians as well as by scientists in each of the various fields. It is no more necessary to study animals before one can study man than it is to study mathematics before one can study geology or psychology or biology.

We may also reject the old, naive behaviorism which assumed that it was somehow necessary, or at least more "scientific" to judge human beings by animal standards. One consequence of this belief was that the whole notion of purpose and goal was excluded from motivational psychology simply because one could not ask a white rat about his purposes. Tolman[26] has long since proven in animal studies themselves that this exclusion was not necessary.

Motivation and the Theory of Psychopathogenesis. The conscious motivational content of everyday life has, according to the foregoing, been conceived to be relatively important or unimportant accordingly as it is more or less closely related to the basic goals. A desire for an ice cream cone might actually be an indirect expression of a desire for love. If it is, then this desire for the ice cream cone becomes extremely important motivation. If however the ice cream is simply something to cool the mouth with, or a casual appetitive reaction, then the desire is relatively unimportant. Everyday conscious desires are to be regarded as symptoms, as *surface indicators of more basic needs.* If we were to take these superficial desires at their face value we would find ourselves in a state of complete confusion which could never be resolved, since we would be dealing seriously with symptoms rather than with what lay behind the symptoms.

Thwarting of unimportant desires produces no psychopathological results; thwarting of a basically important need does produce such results. Any theory of psychopathogenesis must then be based on a sound theory of motivation. A conflict or a frustration is not necessarily pathogenic. It becomes so only when it threatens or thwarts the basic needs, or partial needs that are closely related to the basic needs.[27]

The Role of Gratified Needs. It has been pointed out above several times that our needs usually emerge only when more prepotent needs have been gratified. Thus gratification has an important role in motivation theory. Apart from this, however, needs cease to play an active determining or organizing role as soon as they are gratified.

What this means is that, *e.g.*, a basically satisfied person no longer has the needs for esteem, love, safety, etc. The only sense in which he might be said to have them is in the almost metaphysical sense that a sated man has hunger, or a filled bottle has emptiness. If we are interested in what *actually* motivates us, and not in what has, will, or might motivate us, then a satisfied need is not a motivator. It must be considered for all practical purposes simply not to exist, to have disappeared. This point should be emphasized because it has been either overlooked or contradicted in every theory of motivation I know.[28] The perfectly healthy, normal, fortunate man has no sex needs or hunger needs, or needs for safety, or for love, or for prestige, or self-esteem, except in stray moments of quickly passing threat. If we were to say otherwise, we should also have to aver that every man had all the pathological reflexes, *e.g.*, Babinski, etc., because if his nervous system were damaged, these would appear.

It is such considerations as these that suggest the bold postulation that a man who is thwarted in any of his basic needs may fairly be envisaged simply as a sick man. This is a fair parallel to our designation as "sick" of the man who lacks vitamins or minerals. Who is to say that a lack of love is less important than a lack of vitamins? Since we know the pathogenic effects of love starvation, who is to say that we are invoking value-questions in an unscientific or illegitimate way, any more than the physician does who diagnoses and treats pellagra or scurvy? If I were permitted this usage, I should then say simply that a healthy man is primarily motivated by his needs to develop and actualize his fullest potentialities and capacities. If a man has any other basic needs in any active, chronic sense, then he is simply an unhealthy man. He is as surely sick as if he had suddenly developed a strong salt-hunger or calcium hunger.[29]

If this statement seems unusual or paradoxical, the reader may be assured that this is only one among many such paradoxes that will appear as we revise our ways of looking at man's deeper motivations. When we ask what man wants of life, we deal with his very essence.

IV. SUMMARY

1. *There are at least five sets of goals, which we may call basic needs.* These are briefly physiological, safety, love, esteem, and self-actualization. In addition, we are motivated by the desire to achieve or maintain the various conditions upon which these basic satisfactions rest and by certain more intellectual desires.
2. *These basic goals are related to each other, being arranged in a hierarchy of prepotency.* This means that the most prepotent goal will monopolize consciousness and will tend of itself to organize the recruitment of the various capacities of the organism. The less prepotent needs are minimized, even forgotten or denied. But when a need is fairly well satisfied, the next prepotent ("higher") need emerges, in turn to dominate the conscious life and to serve as the center of organization of behavior, since gratified needs are not active motivators.

   Thus man is a perpetually wanting animal. Ordinarily the satisfaction of these wants is not altogether mutually exclusive, but only tends to be. The average member of our society is most often partially satisfied and partially unsatisfied in all of his wants. The hierarchy principle is usually empirically observed in terms of increasing percentages of non-satisfaction as we go up the hierarchy. Reversals of the average order of the hierarchy are sometimes observed. Also it has been observed that an individual may permanently lose the higher wants in the hierarchy under special conditions. There are not only ordinarily multiple motivations for usual behavior, but in addition many determinants other than motives.
3. *Any thwarting or possibility of thwarting of these basic human goals, or danger to the defenses which protect them, or to the conditions upon which they rest, is considered to be a psychological threat.* With a few exceptions, all psychopathology may be partially traced to such threats. A basically thwarted man may actually be defined as a "sick" man, if we wish.
4. *It is such basic threats which bring about the general emergency reactions.*
5. *Certain other basic problems have not been dealt with because of limitations of space.* Among these are (*a*) the problem of

values in any definitive motivation theory, (*b*) the relation between appetites, desires, needs and what is "good" for the organism, (*c*) the etiology of the basic needs and their possible derivation in early childhood, (*d*) redefinition of motivational concepts, *i.e.*, drive, desire, wish, need, goal, (*e*) implication of our theory for hedonistic theory, (*f*) the nature of the uncompleted act, or success and failure, and of aspiration-level, (*g*) the role of association, habit and conditioning, (*h*) relation to the theory of interpersonal relations, (*i*) implications for psychotherapy, (*j*) implication for theory of society, (*k*) the theory of selfishness, (*l*) the relation between needs and cultural patterns, (*m*) the relation between this theory and Allport's theory of functional autonomy. These as well as certain other less important questions must be considered as motivation theory attempts to become definitive.

NOTES

1. A. H. Maslow, "A preface to motivation theory." *Psychosomatic Med.* 5 (1943):85–92.
2. M. Wertheimer, Unpublished lectures at the New School for Social Research.
3. K. Goldstein, *The organism* (New York: American Book Co., 1939).
4. S. Freud, *New introductory lectures on psychoanalysis* (New York: Norton, 1933).
5. A. Adler, *Social interest* (London: Faber & Faber, 1938).
6. W. B. Cannon, *Wisdom of the body* (New York: Norton, 1932).
7. P. T. Young, "The experimental analysis of appetite," *Psychol. Bull.* 38: (1941) 129–164.
8. Maslow, A preface to motivation theory, *op cit.*
9. As the child grows up, sheer knowledge and familiarity as well as better motor development make these "dangers" less and less dangerous and more and more manageable. Throughout life it may be said that one of the main conative functions of education is this neutralizing of apparent dangers through knowledge, *e.g.*, I am not afraid of thunder because I know something about it.
10. M. Shirley, "Children's adjustments to a strange situation," *J. abnorm. (soc.) Psychol.* 37 (1942):201–217.
11. A "test battery" for safety might be confronting the child with a small exploding firecracker, or with a bewhiskered face, having the mother leave the room, putting him upon a high ladder, a hypodermic injection, having a mouse crawl up to him, etc. Of course I cannot seriously recommend the deliberate use of such "tests" for they might very well harm the child being tested. But these and similar situations come up by the score in the child's ordinary day-to-day living and may be observed. There is no reason why these stimuli should not be used with, for example, young chimpanzees.
12. Not all neurotic individuals feel unsafe. Neurosis may have at its core a thwarting of the affection and esteem needs in a person who is generally safe.
13. A. H. Maslow and B. Mittelmann, *Principles of abnormal psychology* (New York: Harper & Row, 1941).
14. Goldstein, *op cit.*
15. Maslow and Mittelmann, *op cit.*
16. For further details, see A. H. Maslow, "The dynamics of psychological security-insecurity," *Character & Pers.* 10 (1942):331–344 and J. Plant, *Personality and the cultural pattern* (New York: Commonwealth Fund, 1937), Chapter 5.
17. Whether or not this particular desire is universal we do not know. The crucial question, especially important today, is "Will men who are enslaved and dominated inevitably feel dissatisfied and rebellious?" We may assume on the basis of commonly known clinical data that a man who has known true freedom (not paid for by giving up safety and security but rather built on the basis of adequate safety and security) will not willingly or easily allow his freedom to be taken away from him. But we do not know that this is true for the person born into slavery. The events of the next decade should give us our answer. See discussion of this problem in E. Fromm, *Escape from freedom* (New York: Farrar and Rinehart, 1941).
18. Perhaps the desire for prestige and respect from others is subsidiary to the desire for self-esteem or confidence in oneself. Observation of children seems to indicate that this is so, but

clinical data give no clear support for such a conclusion.

19. A. Kardiner, *The traumatic neuroses of our time* (New York: Hoeber, 1941). For more extensive discussion of normal self-esteem, as well as for reports of various researchers, see A. H. Maslow, "Dominance, personality and social behavior in women," *J. soc. Psychol.* 10 (1939):3–39.

20. Clearly creative behavior, like painting, is like any other behavior in having multiple determinants. It may be seen in "innately creative" people whether they are satisfied or not, happy or unhappy, hungry or sated. Also it is clear that creative activity may be compensatory, ameliorative or purely economic. It is my impression (as yet unconfirmed) that it is possible to distinguish the artistic and intellectual products of basically satisfied people by inspection alone. In any case, here too we must distinguish, in a dynamic fashion, the overt behavior itself from its various motivations or purposes.

21. Wertheimer, *op cit.*

22. D. M. Levy, "Primary affect hunger," *Amer. J. Psychiat.* 94 (1937):643–652.

23. I am aware that many psychologists and psychoanalysts use the terms *motivated* and *determined* synonymously, *e.g.*, Freud. But I consider this an obfuscating usage. Sharp distinctions are necessary for clarity of thought, and precision in experimentation.

24. To be discussed fully in a subsequent publication.

25. The interested reader is referred to the very excellent discussion of this point in H. A. Murray, *et al*, *Explorations in personality* (New York: Oxford University Press, 1938).

26. E. C. Tolman, *Purposive behavior in animals and men* (New York: Century, 1932).

27. A. H. Maslow, "Conflict, frustration, and the theory of threat," *J. abnorm. (soc.) Psychol.* 38 (1943):81–86.

28. Note that acceptance of this theory necessitates basic revision of the Freudian theory.

29. If we were to use the word *sick* in this way, we should then also have to face squarely the relations of man to his society. One clear implication of our definition would be that (1) since a man is to be called sick who is basically thwarted, and (2) since such basic thwarting is made possible ultimately only by forces outside the individual, then (3) sickness in the individual must come ultimately from a sickness in the society. The "good" or healthy society would then be defined as one that permitted man's highest purposes to emerge by satisfying all his prepotent basic needs.

16
Planning and Planners
David E. Lilienthal

TVA is supposed to be a planning agency for this region. Yet nowhere on your organization chart do I find a Department of Planning; and when I ask for a copy of the TVA Plan no one can produce it: Some such comment has been made many times by friendly and earnest visitors to TVA.

The reason *the* TVA Plan is not available is that there is no such document. Nor is there one separate department set off by itself, where planners exercise their brains. To one who has read thus far in this account, it is evident this does not constitute the TVA idea of planning.

Source: Chapter 18 "Planning and Planners" from *TVA: Democracy on the March* by David E. Lilienthal.

The TVA *is* a planning agency. The great change going on in this valley is an authentic example of modern democratic planning; this was the expressed intent of Congress, by whose authority the TVA acts. But through the years the TVA has deliberately been sparing in the use of the terminology of "plans" and "planning" within TVA and outside, and those terms have appeared infrequently thus far in this book. For the term "planning" has come to be used in so many different senses that the nomenclature has almost lost usefulness, has even come to be a source of some confusion.

It is necessary, however, to attempt to translate the ideas of this book into the terminology of planning and the language that planners employ.

To some the content of the word "planning" has been pared down until it means merely ordinary foresight, and thereby the term has lost any broad significance. Others have gone to the other extreme; they approve or violently condemn "planning" because to them it means a complete reconstitution of our social system, comprehensive state socialism, or overall centralized economic planning with powers of enforcement.

The term "planning," however various are the meanings ascribed to it, is here to stay; but, since it has apparently come to mean all things to all men, I have, in preceding chapters, set out just what I have in mind in using the word, and what planning means in this valley. "Unified development" as I have described the idea in action is, in substance, the valley's synonym for "planning."

We have always made plans in America. The questions for us is not: Should we plan? but: *What kind of plans* should we make? What kind of planners? What method of "enforcement of plans?" On these matters what has transpired in the Tennessee Valley, as I have tried to describe it, casts the light of actual experience.

Economic and social planning in America is by no means new and strange, but is indeed as old as the Republic. Generally speaking, planning in this country in the past has been practiced by two great groups: first, by elected public officials, variously called "politicians" or "statesmen"; and, second, by businessmen, called by some "empire builders," by others "exploiters of our resources."

Let us look for a moment at some of the instances of planning carried on by public men, selected to represent the economic interests and the social point of view of their constituents. Land planning, for example. By Royal Proclamation in 1763 the colonists were barred from free access to the western lands. Then, by the Ordinance of 1787, the politicians established a different conception of land planning: the opening of the western lands to settlers. The economic and social views of the people of that time called for land planning which would encourage and stimulate the settlement of the West.

Or take another illustration of public planning by elected officials, industrial planning. In the early days of American manufacturing, a plan was devised to stimulate industry. Certain of the public men of that day, like Hamilton and Webster and their sectional constituents, wanted a particular result: manufacturing in the Northeastern States. With the home market "protected," they planned an industrial future for the Northeast, and the method they used to effectuate the plan was the protective tariff.

The Homestead Act of 1862, the Income Tax Amendment, the Sherman Anti-Trust Act, the Granger

Laws—one can recite instance after instance of public planning through our political institutions, through acts of Congress, acts of state legislatures, local ordinances. One thing particularly characteristic of such planning by elected representatives is that they did not as a regular practice call into their councils the assistance of technically trained men—scientists, economists, engineers, administrators—to assist them in formulating these plans.

How well did these early planners do their job? Were the plans well conceived and in the public interest? This much is certain: their plans were not sterile, they were not merely reports and recommendations, written to be filed away and to gather dust. They were put into action, and out of that action in less than 150 years grew the greatest industrial and agricultural nation of all time.

Great as were some of the accomplishments of public planners in the past, we know that we suffer today from the consequences of some of those plans. The state of our natural resources has become a national emergency, grave and critical. Hindsight tells us that some of the public land policies embodied in such planning as the Homestead laws were extravagant and wasteful. Such piecemeal planning for the immediate year-to-year demands of particular groups of constituents we now know was not wise planning. Catastrophic floods, denuded forests, soil exhaustion—these are part of the price we are paying. For more than a generation a change in those plans has been urged. Overtones prophetic of President Roosevelt's message to Congress concerning TVA were heard, faintly it is true, as early as 1909 when President Theodore Roosevelt's Conservation Commission made this recommendation:

> Broad plans should be adopted providing for a system of waterway improvement extending to all uses of the waters and benefits to be derived from their control, including the clarification of the water and abatement of floods for the benefit of navigation; the extension of irrigation; the development and application of power; the prevention of soil wash; the purification of streams for water supply; and the drainage and utilization of the waters of swamp and overflow lands.

As in the case of planning by public men, we should remember that when businessmen become planners they are not venturing into new and strange fields. Long-range planning is a familiar and established practice of progressive business. Perhaps the best-known example is that of the American Telephone and Telegraph Company. This vast communication service has expended large sums of money in continuous and intensive study of the future, and on the basis of such study develops plans five years, ten years, and even longer in advance—plans for new construction, for the revision of its exchanges, for the building of additional capacity. In other businesses there has long been comparable economic planning with substantial organizations devoted to the task. Surveys are made of the market, financial trends, technological changes, all the complex factors which will affect the future activities of a great business enterprise.

Planning by businessmen, often under some other name, is recognized as necessary to the conduct of private enterprise. It has the virtue of a single and direct objective, one that can be currently measured that is producing and marketing goods or services at a profit. A plan that is impressive in the form of a report but which does not work, as judged by the financial reports of the company, is an unsuccessful plan. It has been just as simple as that. The business planner has rarely felt it necessary to complicate his problem by trying to determine whether the making of profit under his plan benefits the whole of society, or injures it. And, as I have said, it is not often that a single business or even an entire industry is in a position to pass intelligently upon such a question.

This is admittedly a grave defect of planning by the businessman. For his legitimate and essential object, namely a profitable business, is not necessarily consistent with the object of society, that is, a prosperous and happy people. The plans of the AT&T and of the small manufacturer may both be quite effective within those enterprises. But factors affecting the plans of the AT&T and the small manufacturer go far beyond their businesses. Over this multitude of external factors the businessman has little or no effective control. As this and a thousand valleys demonstrate so tragically, private planning, even when temporarily sound from the viewpoint of a particular enterprise, has often resulted in great injury to many other enterprises, and therefore to the public welfare.

The idea of unified resource development is based upon the premise that by democratic planning the individual's interest, the interest of private undertakings, can increasingly be made one with the interest of all of us, i.e., the community interest. By and large, things are working out that way in the Tennessee Valley. The income of the private business of farming has increased, largely as a result of a program of aiding the region's soil. Sales by private fertilizer companies have increased more rapidly than at any other time in their history, a result attributed largely to TVA's development and demonstration of new fertilizer products designed to further the overall public interest in the land. Promotion of education in forest-fire protection and scientific cutting methods has furthered conservation and at the same time aided the private business of lumbering, and chemical industries dependent upon a permanent supply of forest products. Community planning has made towns more attractive and pleasant for everyone, and at the same time increased land values for individual owners. These results and many others I have described have been in the general public interest; all have furthered the interest of particular business enterprises.

Effective planners must understand and believe in people. The average man is constantly in the mind of the effective planning expert. Planners, whether they are technicians or administrators, must recognize that they are not dealing with philosophical abstractions, or mere statistics or engineering data or legal principles, and that planning is not an end in itself.

In the last analysis, in democratic planning it is human beings we are concerned with. Unless plans show an understanding and recognition of the aspirations of men and women, they will fail. Those who lack human understanding and cannot share the emotions of men can hardly forward the objectives of realistic planning. Thurman Arnold, in *The Symbols of Government,* has well described this type of earnest but unrealistic person:

> They usually bungle their brief opportunities in power because they are too much in love with an ideal society to treat the one actually before them with skill and understanding. Their constant and futile cry is reiterated through the ages: "Let us educate the people so that they can understand and appreciate us."

A great plan, a moral and indeed a religious purpose, deep and fundamental, is democracy's answer both to our own homegrown would-be dictators and foreign anti-democracy alike. In the unified development of resources there is such a great plan: the unity of nature and mankind. Under such a plan this valley moves forward. True, it is but a step at a time. But under democratic planning responsibility by each citizen is assumed not simply for the little advance made each day, but for that vast and all-pervasive end and purpose of all our labors, the material well-being of all men and the opportunity for them to build for themselves spiritual strength.

Here is the life principle of democratic planning—an awakening in the whole people of a sense of this common moral purpose. Not one goal, but a direction. Not one plan, once and for all, but *the conscious selection by the people of successive plans.* It was Whitman the democrat who warned that "the goal that was named cannot be countermanded."

If this conception of planning is sound, as I believe, then it is plain that in a democracy we always must rest our plans upon "here and now," upon "things as they are." How many are the bloody casualties of efforts to improve the lot of man, how bitter the lost ground and disillusionment because of failure to understand so simple and yet so vital an issue of human strategy. So frequently have men sought an escape from the long task of education, the often prosaic day-by-day steps to "do something about it," by pressing for a plan—usually in the form of a law—without considering whether the people understand the reason for the law's plan, or how they are to benefit by it.

An unwillingness to start from where you are ranks as a fallacy of historic proportions; present-day planning, anywhere in the world for that matter, will fall into the same pit if it makes the same gigantic error. It is because the lesson of the past seems to me so clear on this score, because the nature of man so definitely confirms it, that there has been this perhaps tiresome repetition throughout this record: the people must be in on the planning; their existing institutions must be made part of it; self-education of the citizenry is more important than specific projects or physical changes.

And it is because of this conviction that the TVA has never attempted by arbitrary action to "eliminate" or to force reform upon those factors or institutions in the valley's life which are vigorously antagonistic to a plan for unified development.

We move step by step—from where we are. Everyone has heard the story of the man who was asked by a stranger how he could get to Jonesville; after long thought and unsuccessful attempts to explain the several turns that must be made, he said, so the anecdote runs: "My friend, I tell you; if I were you, I wouldn't start from here." Some planning is just like that; it does not start from here; it assumes a "clean slate" that never has and never can exist.

The TVA idea of planning sees action and planning not as things separate and apart, but as one single and continuous process. In the President's message to the Congress in 1933, this fact was stressed. The words bear repetition here: The TVA, he said, "should be charged with the broadest duty of planning for the proper use, conservation, and development of the natural resources of the Tennessee River drainage basin and its adjoining territory for the general social and economic welfare of the Nation." Then follows this sentence: "This Authority should also be clothed with the necessary power to carry these plans into effect." And the law enacted this principle.

This is fundamental. And yet it is here that much of the disagreement with TVA has arisen from outside, and in its first years internal disagreement as well. The idea that planning and responsibility for action may and should be divorced—the maker of plans having little or nothing to do with their execution—follows the analogy of the planning of a house, an office building, any fixed structure. But the analogy is a mistaken one. For the development of a region is a course of action; it has no arbitrary point of beginning and goes on and on with no point of completion. The individual acts that make up regional development are the day-to-day activities of plowing a particular field, harvesting timber from a particular tract, the building of a factory, a church, a house, a highway. TVA's purpose was not the making of plans but that a valley be developed.

Plans had to be made, of course, many of them. But plans and action are part of one responsibility. TVA is responsible not alone for plans but for results. Those results depend chiefly upon the people's participation. Getting that participation was to be almost wholly on a voluntary basis. To get a job done in this way was a unique assignment, one that required the invention of new devices and new methods. If TVA had been a "planning agency" in the sense that its responsibility had been limited to the making of plans—the usual meaning of the term—those plans would probably have met the fate of so many other plans: brochures decorating bookshelves, adornments of what is so often mere sterile learning.

In *The Coming Victory of Democracy*, Thomas Mann put his finger on this deep-lying error of intellectualism that treats planning apart from action. His words are moving, for they tell much of the causes beneath the catastrophe of European culture:

> Democracy is thought; but it is thought related to life and action. . . . No intellectual of the pre-democratic era ever thought of action, nor of what kind of action would result if his thinking were put into practice. It is characteristic of undemocratic or of democratically uneducated nations that their thinking goes on without reference to reality, in pure abstraction, in complete isolation of the mind from life itself, and without the slightest consideration for the realistic consequences of thought.

In the TVA the merging of planning and responsibility for the carrying out of those plans forces our technicians to make them a part of the main stream of living in the region or community; this it is that breathes into plans the breath of life. For in the Tennessee Valley the expert cannot escape from the consequences of his planning, as he can and usually does where it is divorced from execution. This has a profound effect on the experts themselves. Where planning is conceived of in this way, the necessity that experts should be close to the problems with which they are dealing is evident.

In my opinion the idea of planning is still struggling for popular support in America in part for this reason: that many of the most spectacular plans have been drawn by men who did not have the responsibility for carrying them out. They did not have the salutary discipline which the experts of this valley had who have had to ask themselves: "Is this a plan that I can take responsibility for seeing carried out? Will the people understand it, will the people help to make it effective? Will they make the plan their own?"

In the work of the TVA we have taken to heart and sought to put into practice what seems to me one of the most profound utterances upon the problem of freedom through democracy.

They are the words of the late John Dewey.

> The conflict as it concerns the democracy to which our history commits us [he wrote] is *within* our own institutions and attitudes. It can be won only by extending the application of democratic methods, methods of consultation, persuasion, negotiation, communication, cooperative intelligence, in the task of making our own politics, industry, education, our cultures generally, a servant and an evolving manifestation of democratic ideas. . . .
>
> . . .democratic ends demand democratic methods for their realization. . . . Our first defense is to realize that democracy can be served only by the slow day-by-day adoption and contagious diffusion in every phase of our common life of methods that are identical with the ends to be reached. . . . An American democracy can serve the world only as it demonstrates in the conduct of its own life the efficacy of plural, partial, and experimental methods in securing and maintaining an ever-increasing release of the powers of human nature, in service of a freedom which is co-operative and a co-operation which is voluntary.[1]

What of the enforcement of economic and social plans in this valley? In the building of dams and other structures, TVA of course has the power which even private utilities and railroads have, to take property of landowners who are unwilling to sell, at a price fixed by court proceedings. It can refuse to sell power except under the policies set out in the TVA Act. But, beyond such things, in no significant particular is TVA planning for the development of this region enforceable by law. And this, in my opinion, has not been a handicap.

This is not to say dogmatically that there is never any justification whatever for regulatory measures, or that voluntary methods have not resulted in a good many mistakes and waste that good planning would have avoided, if the people who made those decisions had been persuaded to make different ones. It is pointed out to us constantly that the course of education and voluntary action is too slow, that only the force of law will meet the crisis of soil depletion. Critics, admitting that not a little progress has been made by the TVA methods, point to the many farmers who still persist in plowing higher and higher on their hills, planting more corn and cotton, destroying more and more land; to the timber interests which continue to spurn the advice of forest technicians that would sustain the yield of lumber; to the manufacturers who still pollute the streams with waste and show scant interest in technical means of ending this contamination. More than once industries have been located at points where it seemed clear that sound planning should discourage industrial location.

This lack of power to enforce plans has disturbed a good many observers and students of the enterprise, especially in the early years, and still mystifies and irritates some of them. But the TVA has continued to rely upon and to emphasize the methods described in this book, the ways of contract, persuasion, incentives, encouragement, methods based on the people's confidence in TVA's comprehension, its good faith, and the quality of its technical leadership. I feel strongly that the admitted limitations of voluntary methods, distressing and tragic as their consequences sometimes are, do not invalidate the wisdom of a *minimum of coercion* in carrying out plans for resource development. For coercion is insatiable. In whatever guise, once coercion becomes the accepted reliance for making planning effective, more and more coercion is needed. I am deeply persuaded that high as the price of voluntary methods may be, in delays and errors, in the end the price of arbitrary enforcement of planning is nothing less than our freedom.

NOTE

1. *Freedom and Culture* (New York: G. P. Putnam's Sons, 1939), pp. 175–6.

17 Government Is Different

Paul Appleby

It is exceedingly difficult clearly to identify the factors which make government different from every other activity in society. Yet this difference is a fact and I believe it to be so big a difference that the dissimilarity between government and all other forms of social action is greater than any dissimilarity among those other forms themselves. Without a willingness to recognize this fact, no one can even begin to discuss public affairs to any good profit or serious purpose.

ANALYSIS OF DIFFERENCES

Some of the less important of these differences are generally acknowledged and accepted. For example, the public recognizes without much thought or question that a good lawyer will not necessarily make a good judge. Dimly, except by those who have paid special attention to the matter, it is seen that the function of a judge, even though it has to do with law, is very different from the function of a lawyer. Attorneys treat specific situations in terms of the interests of their clients except only for the making of necessary adjustments to legal, ethical, and public-relations considerations. To have a society made up entirely of persons thinking like lawyers and clients, no matter how well intentioned, would be plainly impractical if not impossible. We must also have persons thinking and acting like judges. Yet many of us fail to recognize the need of having persons thinking and acting like government officials. To elevate an excellent lawyer to the bench will not guarantee society even a tolerably good judge. It should be equally patent that men with excellent records in private business will not necessarily make competent government officials.

In both cases, particularly in the lower brackets, there is through self-selection a certain automatic correction that limits the number of major errors in appointments. Many lawyers are not attracted to the bench. Their disinterest usually reflects some missing qualification. Should an opportunity for appointment to a very high court be offered, there would be some tendency for the thought of honor and prestige to outweigh other considerations. But, in general, individual tastes and interests furnish material evidence of qualification and play a positive role in the process of selection. So in the choosing of government personnel. In ordinary periods many persons have little inclination to enter government, while others are strongly attracted to it. These inclinations and disinclinations are significant, and sometimes controlling, factors in the determination of the general result. In extraordinary times, however, new factors such as patriotism, desire for adventure, or other considerations may come into play and cause proportionately a far greater number of people to aspire to positions in the public service. Many of these persons will, by reason of temperament, outlook, and experience, be utterly unqualified for government work. Others will be qualified only to advise; in government they are technicians—experts in specific nongovernmental enterprises. By and large, those who do not normally and consistently feel a great interest in government will not be good prospects. In general, the more they have succeeded in nongovernmental fields, the more they have developed interests and habits of thought that will unfit them for government. Obviously the more delicate and difficult distinctions have to do with upper-bracket positions. There, surely, patriotism, zeal, and intelligence could never be enough—any more than they could be accepted as adequate criteria in selecting candidates for the bench from the ranks of the bar, or in selecting army generals from nonmilitary ranks.

Admittedly there are many positions in government in which persons may function very much as they would outside of government. This is true chiefly in such lower-bracket jobs as those of charwomen, elevator operators, messengers, clerks, and typists. Yet even with respect to these there are countless instances where the employee works for the government because he definitely prefers public employment and where that preference has served the public interest. The public would be gratified and moved if it could know of them. Some day it will. For, sooner or later, regard for self-interest, coupled with a sense of justice, will cause the public to be concerned far beyond what it is today over contemptuous attitudes toward lowly government "clerks" and bureaucrats.

Government is not different, however, simply in respect of personnel. The temperament and attitude of a judge do not furnish a complete basis for understanding the character and functioning of our judicial system. Courts are not simply assemblages of judges. Neither are they simply a succession of judicial procedures. Both of these and something over are required to make a judicial *system*. Hence the importance of popular attitudes regarding what is expected in and from a judge. All these things together, expressed in individually well-selected judges, are essential to an effective judiciary. So it is with government in general. It, too, is a *system*, and the system cannot be understood except in terms of the public employees themselves, their conceptions of their positions, and the attitudes of the public about what is required in and from our civil servants. These elements together are what make government a system, for in combination they comprise what we call a bureaucracy.

The qualifications for judges differ from those for other governmental people because their functions differ. Yet these qualifications may be used to illustrate a fundamental distinction between governmental and nongovernmental tasks. In common speech reference is made to the "judicial temperament." One might similarly refer to the governmental temperament. But temperament seems to me to be less satisfactory as a common denominator than attitude. Consequently I shall speak of the "governmental attitude."

SIGNIFICANCE OF ATTITUDES

In my judgment no one can serve the public as it should be served by a governmental official unless he has a public-interest attitude with certain special characteristics. The carrying on of government involves action. No matter how many studies may be required, government in the final analysis is action—organized action. Persons in high positions must have a sense of action. They must have a feeling of the need for decisions to get things done. They must be able to organize resources whether of personnel, material, or information so that contemplation of objectives will be translated into accomplishment.

What has been said with reference to action is familiar to the field of business no less than government. I have, one might say, portrayed the executive, particularly the big business executive. But what I have said up to this point is, of itself, no more adequate to make a governmental administrator than knowledge of the law alone is adequate qualification for a judge. Even possessed of patriotism and zeal, the most capable business executive in the country might be a most dismal failure in government. Indeed, in actual fact many such persons do fail in government. The press, however, ordinarily treats them with such special favor, and their prestige generally is so great, that the public rarely learns of their failure. Strangely enough, their actual induction into government is often political rather than the opposite, as is commonly supposed. Frequently they are appointed to official positions as a means for securing additional support for governmental action. Or they are sought for their prestige, which, since government has the job of maintaining and developing political unity, is always a factor for legitimate consideration.

This feeling for action and this ability to organize resources for action do, of course, resemble corresponding talents that are essential for nongovernmental executives. There are business executives who can serve government well, and vice versa. But just as there are successful business executives who could not do well in government, so it is true that some governmental executives who are able to administer public affairs with distinction would probably fail if transferred to private enterprise.

It is instructive to observe that big businessmen who have inherited large business interests seem, on the average, to be better bets for government service than those of the self-made variety. This is probably the result of the development of a special attitude of public responsibility inculcated by parents who were especially conscientious or concerned about what inherited wealth might do to their children. It may derive, too, from some special stimulation to self-questioning and reflection forced by their station of privilege on especially responsible young people. Or it may be the result of their being able or, for that matter, obliged to deal with their affairs more *generally*—that is, with less concentration on the ordinary objective of managing things with an eye to monthly earnings and profits.

Many businessmen, especially those of the self-made variety, have the disadvantage for government service of being prima donnas, with strong personalities too little adjustable to situations other than the ones they have come to dominate. This is true also, to be sure, of some types of vivid politicians who are effective as spokesmen but unable to function as administrators. It seems to be true both of businessmen and politicians that the spread of their activity—their participation in more than one field, and preferably in many more than one—has something to do with their ability to *manage* governmental organizations. Politicians inevitably rub up against more considerations; they tend to be more broadly stimulated. Thus any man of political inclinations who has had organizational and executive experience would be a superior prospect for success as a public official for the reason that he would, almost inevitably, have developed breadth of view and a public-interest attitude.

HOW BUSINESS LOOKS AT GOVERNMENT

It may be unfortunate, but it is nevertheless a fact that, because of factors beyond its control, no industry can realize its own social aspirations. It is also true that no industry can regard public interest equally with industrial interest. That cannot be its function; it must have a different and narrower one. Governments exist precisely for the reason that there is a need to have special persons in society charged with the function of promoting and protecting the public interest.

People tend to develop a sense of responsibility with respect to the functions for which officially they are responsible. Ordinary people brought into government tend to develop some special degree of public responsibility. Yet there are wide ranges of differences in this respect, as everyone knows. Long concentration on other functions unfits a great many people for governmental service. I have seen scores of businessmen in government who were not able to sense the differences between government and business. Without being venal, some thought their positions in government simply a fortunate special privilege, like being the cousin of a purchasing agent. Others again had the fixed idea that the best possible way of promoting the public welfare would be to help private business and assumed accordingly that doing favors for private business was their simple governmental duty.

Business itself, however, does not feel that way in its general attitude toward government. In all things other than those that make for its own profit, a business concern expects government to be guided by a public-interest point of view. The brevity of cabled news sometimes makes such things clearer than does the lengthier reporting of news at home. Consider, for example, this dispatch in the Paris edition of the *New York Herald-Tribune* for the year 1934:

> U.S. INVESTMENT BANKERS
> ENDORSE ROOSEVELT POLICY
>
> White Sulphur Springs, W. Va., Oct. 31—The Convention of the Investment Bankers Association, meeting here, offered today its full assistance to President Roosevelt in his recovery program.
>
> A resolution was passed in which it was stated that the members of the association would stand behind the President *in all measures which were not calculated to infringe on their own interests.* The bankers offered Roosevelt their *whole-hearted support in particular in all his efforts on their behalf.*

The italics are mine.

Since most governmental actions affect other persons more than they do us as individuals, we all wish governmental action to be what it needs to be with respect to others, while yet, of course, being considerate of us. The truly governmental official in a democracy comes in the course of time to appreciate this. Under the impact of popular demands and lamentations he comes to realize that he must try to operate in a governmental way; that is, through action which is as fair as possible, and as uniform as possible, and which can be taken publicly and publicly explained.

ESSENTIAL CHARACTER OF GOVERNMENT

In broad terms the governmental function and attitude have at least three complementary aspects that go to differentiate government from all other institutions and activities: breadth of scope, impact, and consideration; public accountability; political character. No nongovernmental institution has the breadth of government. Nothing the national government does in New England can be separated from what it does in New Mexico. Other enterprises may ignore factors remotely related to their central purposes but not the government of the United States; it is supported, tolerated, or evicted on the basis of a balance involving the sum total of everything in the nation. No other institution is so publicly accountable. No action taken or contemplated by the government of a democracy is immune to public debate, scrutiny, or investigation. No other enterprise has such equal appeal or concern for everyone, is so equally dependent on everyone, or deals so vitally with those psychological intangibles which reflect popular economic needs and social aspirations. Other institutions, admittedly, are not free from politics, but government *is* politics.

Government administration differs from all other administrative work to a degree not even faintly realized outside, by virtue of its public nature, the way in which it is subject to public scrutiny and public outcry. An administrator coming into government is struck at once, and continually thereafter, by the press and public interest in every detail of his life, personality, and conduct. This interest often runs to details of administrative action that in private business would never be of concern other than inside the organization. Each employee hired, each one demoted, transferred, or discharged, every efficiency rating, every assignment of responsibility, each change in administrative structure, each conversation, each letter, has to be thought about in terms of possible public agitation, investigation, or judgment. Everything has to be considered in terms of what any employee anywhere may make of it, for any employee may be building a file of things that could be made publicly embarrassing. Any employee who later may be discharged is a potentially powerful enemy, for he can reach the press and Congress with whatever charges his knothole perspective may have invited. Charges of wrongdoing on the part of a government official are always news, no matter who makes the charge, for every former employee is regarded as a source of authoritative and inside information.

In private business the same employee would be discredited by the very fact of having been discharged. Government employees number far less than nongovernment employees, but the cases of discharged government workers getting into the public prints with denunciations of their former chiefs must be at least a thousand times more frequent. A person discharged is always offended. But whereas a person discharged from a private job is of little interest to the press, the dismissal of a person from a public job is regarded as public business.

This is not to say that I would have it otherwise. I am simply calling attention to it as a fact that greatly differentiates government from business. But the public would do well in judging such reports to consider them in perspective with similar, unaired situations in nongovernmental fields.

Because of these circumstances, every governmental executive lives and moves and has his being in the presence of public dynamite. Every action he may take is influenced by this condition—whether before or after an explosion.

Millions of dollars are spent every year in government because of this situation—millions that would not have to be spent in private organizations. In a narrow sense government tends therefore to be less efficient because of its public nature. But since government operates more in the public interest because of such special attention and scrutiny, the net effect is to make it more efficient in terms of its central purpose.

As an illustration of the way in which disgruntled or dismissed employees cause expenditures of millions of dollars a year, let me cite the case of a man whom I have never seen, but whose activities I had occasion to follow for a full decade. During this entire period (and also for ten years preceding it) he carried on a continuous series of campaigns against a half-dozen of the ablest executives in the government. He talked ad hominem and ad infinitum to writers of gossip columns. He wrote to the Director of the Bureau of the Budget, to other administrative officials, and to members of the Congress. He made hundreds of charges of misconduct, not one of which was warranted. Each one, however, had to be carefully investigated and duly reported. His superiors were reluctant to discharge him for communicating with members of Congress because to do so would perhaps have convinced hostile Congressmen of the truth of the charges. He cost the government hundreds of times more than his salary, and he stayed on the job until he reached retirement age.

The public nature of the government's business thus makes for a great difference in organizational discipline. Government employees often discuss their work with others in a way that would cause immediate discharge were they on the payroll of a private organization. Press and public both expect and induce that kind of talk. Business executives coming into government with no experience to prepare them for such a situation often find it extremely hard to adjust themselves to it. Yet some adjustment is an absolute necessity.

Generally the bigger a corporation, the more complex it is. An outsider can easily get lost in any of its fields of operations—raw materials, marketing, production, labor relations, finance, and management. Yet in relation to the United States government even the very largest corporation is small and simple. And the more big corporations we have, the more complex must the government become. Government, dealing in one way or another with almost everything, requires in its highest officials a special competence in handling relationships among all the varied and powerful forces, activities, and elements in the country. At the top the job is that of managing relationships between the complex parts of the entire nation, of giving both form and leadership to the life of the whole people. At that level it is an art—the art of politics. Only a politician can be President. The President needs economic understanding, but he should not function as an economist; he needs legal understanding, but he should not function as a lawyer; he needs business understanding, but he should not function as a businessman; he needs social understanding, but he should not function as a sociologist; he needs understanding of research, but he should not function as a scientist; he needs understanding of agriculture, labor, finance, but he should not function as a farmer, laborer, or banker. He needs to understand these *broadly* in order to understand politics: his success or failure as President depends on how he functions as a politician. At its best, politics is statesmanship.

Statecraft—government—is different from all other professions because it is broader than anything else in the field of action. Purely speculative thought and emotion may range a wider field, yet even this may be doubted, for government must be concerned with intellectual and emotional outreachings too. Government is different because it must take account of all the desires, needs, actions, thoughts, and sentiments of 140,000,000 people. Government is different because government is politics.

18
The Proverbs of Administration

Herbert A. Simon

A fact about proverbs that greatly enhances their quotability is that they almost always occur in mutually contradictory pairs. "Look before you leap!"—but "He who hesitates is lost."

This is both a convenience and a serious defect—depending on the use to which one wishes to put the proverbs in question. If it is a matter of rationalizing behavior that has already taken place or justifying action that has already been decided upon, proverbs are ideal. Since one is never at a loss to find one that will prove his point—or the precisely contradictory point, for that matter—they are a great help in persuasion, political debate, and all forms of rhetoric.

But when one seeks to use proverbs as the basis of a scientific theory, the situation is less happy. It is not that the propositions expressed by the proverbs are insufficient; it is rather that they prove too much. A scientific theory should tell what is true but also what is false. If Newton had announced to the world that particles of matter exert either an attraction or a repulsion on each other, he would not have added much to scientific knowledge. His contribution consisted in showing that an attraction was exercised and in announcing the precise law governing its operation.

Most of the propositions that make up the body of administrative theory today share, unfortunately, this defect of proverbs. For almost every principle one can find an equally plausible and acceptable contradictory principle. Although the two principles of the pair will lead to exactly opposite organizational recommendations, there is nothing in the theory to indicate which is the proper one to apply.[1]

It is the purpose of this paper to substantiate the sweeping criticism of administrative theory, and to present some suggestions—perhaps less concrete than they should be—as to how the existing dilemma can be solved.

SOME ACCEPTED ADMINISTRATIVE PRINCIPLES

Among the more common principles that occur in the literature of administration are these:

Source: From *Public Administration Review,* 6 (Winter 1946), pp. 53–67. Footnotes renumbered.

1. Administrative efficiency is increased by a specialization of the task among the group.
2. Administrative efficiency is increased by arranging the members of the group in a determinate hierarchy of authority.
3. Administrative efficiency is increased by limiting the span of control at any point in the hierarchy to a small number.
4. Administrative efficiency is increased by grouping the workers, for purposes of control, according to *(a)* purpose, *(b)* process, *(c)* clientele, or *(d)* place. (This is really an elaboration of the first principle but deserves separate discussion.)

Since these principles appear relatively simple and clear, it would seem that their application to concrete problems of administrative organization would be unambiguous and that their validity would be easily submitted to empirical test. Such, however, seems not to be the case. To show why it is not, each of the four principles just listed will be considered in turn.

Specialization. Administrative efficiency is supposed to increase with an increase in specialization. But is this intended to mean that *any* increase in specialization will increase efficiency? If so, which of the following alternatives is the correct application of the principle in a particular case?

1. A plan of nursing should be put into effect by which nurses will be assigned to districts and do all nursing within that district, including school examinations, visits to homes or school children, and tuberculosis nursing.
2. A functional plan of nursing should be put into effect by which different nurses will be assigned to school examinations, visits to homes of school children, and tuberculosis nursing. The present method of generalized nursing by districts impedes the development of specialized skills in the three very diverse programs.

Both of these administrative arrangements satisfy the requirement of specialization—the first provides specialization by place; the second, specialization by function. The principle of specialization is of no help at all in choosing between the two alternatives.

It appears that the simplicity of the principle of specialization is a deceptive simplicity—a simplicity which conceals fundamental ambiguities. For "specialization" is not a condition of efficient administration; it is an inevitable characteristic of all group effort, however efficient or inefficient that effort may be. Specialization merely means that different persons are doing different things—and since it is physically impossible for two persons to be doing the same thing in the same place at the same time, two persons are always doing different things.

The real problem of administration, then, is not to "specialize," but to specialize in that particular manner and along those particular lines which will lead to administrative efficiency. But, in thus rephrasing this "principle" of administration, there has been brought clearly into the open its fundamental ambiguity: "Administrative efficiency is increased by a specialization of the task among the group in the direction which will lead to greater efficiency."

Further discussion of the choice between competing bases of specialization will be undertaken after two other principles of administration have been examined.

Unity of Command. Administrative efficiency is supposed to be enhanced by arranging the members of the organization in a determinate hierarchy of authority in order to preserve "unity of command."

Analysis of this "principle" requires a clear understanding of what is meant by the term "*authority.*" A subordinate may be said to accept authority whenever he permits his behavior to be guided by a decision reached by another, irrespective of his own judgment as to the merits of that decision.

In one sense the principle of unity of command, like the principle of specialization, cannot be violated; for it is physically impossible for a man to obey two contradictory commands—that is what is meant by "contradictory commands." Presumably, if unity of command is a principle of administration, it must assert something more than this physical impossibility. Perhaps it asserts this: that it is undesirable to place a member of an organization in a position where he receives orders from more than one superior. This is evidently the meaning that Gulick attaches to the principle when he says,

> The significance of this principle in the process of co-ordination and organization must not be lost sight of. In building a structure of co-ordination, it is often tempting to set up more than one boss for a man who is doing work which has more than one relationship. Even as great a philosopher of management as Taylor fell into this error in setting up separate foremen to deal with machinery with materials, with speed, etc., each with the power of giving orders directly to the individual workman. The rigid adherence to the principle of unity of command may have its absurdities; these are, however, unimportant in comparison with the certainty of confusion, inefficiency and irresponsibility which arise from the violation of the principle.[2]

Certainly the principle of unity of command, thus interpreted, cannot be criticized for any lack of clarity or any ambiguity. The definition of authority given above should provide a clear test whether, in any concrete situation, the principle is observed. The real fault that must be found with this principle is that it is incompatible with the principle of specialization. One of the most important uses to which authority is put in organization is to bring about specialization in the work of making decisions, so that each decision is made at a point in the organization where it can be made most expertly. As a result, the use of authority permits a greater degree of expertness to be achieved in decision making than would be possible if each operative employee had himself to make all the decisions upon which his activity is predicated. The individual fireman does not decide whether to use a two-inch hose or a fire extinguisher; that is decided for him by his officers, and the decision is communicated to him in the form of a command.

However, if unity of command, in Gulick's sense, is observed, the decisions of a person at any point in the administrative hierarchy are subject to influence through only one channel of authority; and if his decisions are of a kind that require expertise in more than one field of knowledge, then advisory and informational services must be relied upon to supply those premises which lie in a field not recognized by the mode of specialization in the organization. For example, if an accountant in a school department is subordinate to an educator, and if unity of command is observed, then the finance department cannot issue direct orders to him regarding the technical, accounting aspects of his work. Similarly, the director of motor vehicles in the public works department will be unable to issue direct orders on care of motor equipment to the fire-truck driver.[3]

Gulick, in the statement quoted above, clearly indicates the difficulties to be faced if unity of command is not observed. A certain amount of irresponsibility and confusion are almost certain to ensue. But perhaps this is not too great a price to pay for the increased expertise that can be applied to decisions. What is needed to decide the issue is a principle of administration that would enable one to weigh the relative advantages of the two courses of action. But neither the principle of unity of command nor the principle of specialization is helpful in adjudicating the controversy. They merely contradict each other without indicating any procedure for resolving the contradiction.

If this were merely an academic controversy—if it were generally agreed and had been generally demonstrated that unity of command must be preserved in all cases, even with a loss in expertise—one could assert that in case of conflict between the two principles, unity of command should prevail. But the issue is far from clear, and experts can be ranged on both sides of the controversy. On the side of unity of command there may be cited the dictums of Gulick and others.[4] On the side of specialization there are Taylor's theory of functional supervision, Macmahon and Millett's idea of "dual supervision," and the practice of technical supervision in military organization.[5]

It may be, as Gulick asserts, that the notion of Taylor and these others is an "error." If so, the evidence that it is an error has never been marshalled or published—apart from loose heuristic arguments like that quoted above. One is left with a choice between equally eminent theorists of administration and without any evidential basis for making that choice.

What evidence there is of actual administrative practice would seem to indicate that the need for specialization is to a very large degree given priority over the need for unity of command. As a matter of fact, it does not go too far to say that unity of command, in Gulick's sense, never has existed in any administrative organization. If a line officer accepts the regulations of an accounting department with regard to the procedure for making requisitions, can it be said that, in this sphere, he is not subject to the authority of the accounting department? In any actual administrative situation authority is zoned, and to maintain that this zoning does not contradict the principle of unity of command requires a very different definition of authority from that used here. This subjection of the line officer to the accounting department is no different, in principle, from Taylor's recommendation that in the matter of work programming a workman be subject to one foreman, in the matter of machine operation to another.

The principle of unity of command is perhaps more defensible if narrowed down to the following: In case two authoritative commands conflict, there should be a single determinate person whom the subordinate is expected to obey; and the sanctions of authority should be applied against the subordinate only to enforce his obedience to that one person.

If the principle of unity of command is more defensible when stated in this limited form, it also solves fewer problems. In the first place, it no longer requires, except for settling conflicts of authority, a single hierarchy of authority. Consequently, it leaves unsettled the very important question of how authority should be zoned in a particular organization (i.e., the modes of specialization) and through what channels it should be exercised. Finally, even this narrower concept of unity of command conflicts with the principle of specialization, for whenever disagreement does occur and the organization members revert to the formal lines of authority, then only those types of specialization which are represented in the hierarchy of authority can impress themselves on decision. If the training officer of a city exercises only functional supervision over the police training officer, then in case of disagreement with the police chief, specialized knowledge of police problems will determine the outcome while specialized knowledge of training problems will be subordinated or ignored. That this actually occurs is shown by the frustration so commonly expressed by functional supervisors at their lack of authority to apply sanctions.

Span of Control. Administrative efficiency is supposed to be enhanced by limiting the number of subordinates who report directly to any one administrator to a small number—say six. This notion that the "span of control" should be narrow is confidently asserted as a third incontrovertible principle of administration. The usual common-sense arguments for restricting the span of control are familiar and need not be repeated here. What is not so generally recognized is that a contradictory proverb of administration can be stated which, though it is not so familiar as the principle of span of control, can be supported by arguments of equal plausibility. The proverb in question is the following: Administrative efficiency is enhanced by keeping at a minimum the number of organizational levels through which a matter must pass before it is acted upon.

This latter proverb is one of the fundamental criteria that guide administrative analysis in procedures simplification work. Yet in many situations the results to which this principle leads are in direct contradiction to the requirements of the principle of span of control, the principle of unity of command, and the principle of specialization. The present discussion is concerned with the first of these conflicts. To illustrate the difficulty, two alternative proposals for the organization of a small health department will be presented—one based on the restriction of span of control, the other on the limitation of number of organization levels:

1. The present organization of the department places an administrative overload on the health officer by reason of the fact that all eleven employees of the department report directly to him and the further fact that some of the staff lack adequate technical training. Consequently, venereal disease clinic treatments and other details require an undue amount of the health officer's personal attention.

   It has previously been recommended that the proposed medical officer be placed in charge of the venereal disease and chest clinics and all child hygiene work. It is further recommended that one of the inspectors be designated chief inspector and placed in charge of all the department's inspectional activities and that one of the nurses be designated as head nurse. This will relieve the health commissioner of considerable detail and will leave him greater freedom to plan and supervise the health program as a whole, to conduct health education, and to coordinate the work of the department with that of other community agencies. If the department were thus organized, the effectiveness of all employees could be substantially increased.
2. The present organization of the department leads to inefficiency and excessive red tape by reason of the fact that an unnecessary supervisory level intervenes between the health officer and the operative employees, and that those four of the twelve employees who are best trained technically are engaged largely in "overhead" administrative duties. Consequently, unnecessary delays occur in securing the approval of the health officer on matters requiring his attention, and too

> many matters require review and re-review.
>
> The medical officer should be left in charge of the venereal disease and chest clinics and child hygiene work. It is recommended, however, that the position of chief inspector and head nurse be abolished and that the employees now filling these positions perform regular inspectional and nursing duties. The details of work scheduling now handled by these two employees can be taken care of more economically by the secretary to the health officer, and, since broader matters of policy have, in any event, always required the personal attention of the health officer, the abolition of these two positions will eliminate a wholly unnecessary step in review, will allow an expansion of inspectional and nursing services, and will permit at least a beginning to be made in the recommended program of health education. The number of persons reporting directly to the health officer will be increased to nine, but since there are few matters requiring the coordination of these employees, other than the work schedules and policy questions referred to above, this change will not materially increase his work load.

The dilemma is this: in a large organization with complex interrelations between members, a restricted span of control inevitably produces excessive red tape, for each contact between organization members must be carried upward until a common superior is found. If the organization is at all large, this will involve carrying all such matters upward through several levels of officials for decision and then downward again in the form of orders and instructions—a cumbersome and time-consuming process.

The alternative is to increase the number of persons who are under the command of each officer, so that the pyramid will come more rapidly to a peak, with fewer intervening levels. But this, too, leads to difficulty, for if an officer is required to supervise too many employees, his control over them is weakened.

If it is granted, then, that both the increase and the decrease in span of control has some undesirable consequences, what is the optimum point? Proponents of a restricted span of control have suggested three, five, even eleven, as suitable numbers, but nowhere have they explained the reasoning which led them to the particular number they selected. The principle as stated casts no light on this very crucial question. One is reminded of current arguments about the proper size of the national debt.

Organization by Purpose, Process, Clientele, Place. Administrative efficiency is supposed to be increased by grouping workers according to *(a)* purpose, *(b)* process, *(c)* clientele, or *(d)* place. But from the discussion of specialization it is clear that this principle is internally inconsistent; for purpose, process, clientele, and place are competing bases of organization, and at any given point of division the advantages of three must be sacrificed to secure the advantages of the fourth. If the major departments of a city, for example, are organized on the basis of major purpose, then it follows that all the physicians, all the lawyers, all the engineers, all the statisticians will not be located in a single department exclusively composed of members of their profession but will be distributed among the various city departments needing their services. The advantages of organization by process will thereby be partly lost.

Some of these advantages can be regained by organizing on the basis of process *within* the major departments. Thus there may be an engineering bureau within the public works department, or the board of education may have a school health service as a major division of its work. Similarly, within smaller units there may be division by area or by clientele: e.g., a fire department will have separate companies located throughout the city, while a welfare department may have intake and case work agencies in various locations. Again, however, these major types of specialization cannot be simultaneously achieved, for at any point in the organization it must be decided whether specialization at the next level will be accomplished by distinction of major purpose, major process, clientele, or area.

The conflict may be illustrated by showing how the principle of specialization according to purpose would lead to a different result from specialization according to clientele in the organization of a health department.

1. Public health administration consists of the following activities for the prevention of disease and the maintenance of healthful conditions: (1) vital statistics; (2) child hygiene—prenatal, maternity, postnatal, infant, preschool, and school health programs; (3) communicable disease control; (4) inspection of milk, foods, and drugs; (5) sanitary inspection; (6) laboratory service; (7) health education.

   One of the handicaps under which the health department labors is the fact that the department has no control over school health, that being an activity of the county board of education, and there is little or no coordination between that highly important part of the community health program and the balance of the program which is conducted by the city-county health unit. It is recommended that the city and county open negotiations with the board of education for the transfer of all school health work and the appropriation therefor to the joint health unit. . . .

2. To the modern school department is entrusted the care of children during almost the entire period that they are absent from the parental home. It has three principal responsibilities toward them: (1) to provide for their education in useful skills and knowledge and in character; (2) to provide them with wholesome play activities outside school hours; (3) to care for their health and to assure the attainment of minimum standards of nutrition.

   One of the handicaps under which the school board labors is the fact that, except for school lunches, the board has no control over child health and nutrition, and there is little or no coordination between that highly important part of the child development program and the balance of the program which is conducted by the board of education. It is recommended that the city and county open negotiations for the transfer of all health work for children of school age to the board of education.

Here again is posed the dilemma of choosing between alternative, equally plausible, administrative principles. But this is not the only difficulty in the present case, for a closer study of the situation shows there are fundamental ambiguities in the meanings of the key items—"purpose," "process," "clientele," and "place."

"Purpose" may be roughly defined as the objective or end for which an activity is carried on; "process" as a means for accomplishing a purpose. Processes, then, are carried on in order to achieve purposes. But purposes themselves may generally be arranged in some sort of hierarchy. A typist moves her fingers in order to type; types in order to reproduce a letter; reproduces a letter in order that an inquiry may be answered. Writing a letter is then the purpose for which the typing is performed; while writing a letter is also the process whereby the purpose of replying to an inquiry is achieved. It follows that the same activity may be described as purpose or as process.

This ambiguity is easily illustrated for the case of an administrative organization. A health department conceived as a unit whose task it is to care for the health of the community is a purpose organization; the same department conceived as a unit which makes use of the medical arts to carry on its work is a process organization. In the same way, an education department may be viewed as a purpose (to educate) organization, or a clientele (children) organization; the forest service as a purpose (forest conservation), process (forest management), clientele (lumbermen and cattlemen utilizing public forests), or area (publicly owned forest lands) organization. When concrete illustrations of this sort are selected, the lines of demarcation between these categories become very hazy and unclear indeed.

"Organization by major purpose," says Gulick, ". . . serves to bring together in a single large department all of those who are at work endeavoring to render a particular service."[6] But what is a particular service? Is fire protection a single purpose, or is it merely a part of the purpose of public safety?—or is it a combination of purposes including fire prevention and fire fighting? It must be concluded that there is no such thing as a purpose, or a unifunctional (single-purpose) organization. What is to be considered a single function depends entirely on language and techniques.[7] If the English language has a comprehensive term which covers both of two subpurposes it is natural to think of the two together as a single purpose. If such a term is lacking, the two subpurposes become purposes in their own right. On the other hand, a single activity may contribute to several objectives, but since they are technically (procedurally) inseparable, the activity is considered a single function or purpose.

The fact, mentioned previously, that purposes form a hierarchy, each subpurpose contributing to some more final and comprehensive end, helps to make clear the relation between purpose and process. "Organization by major process," says Gulick, ". . . tends to bring together in a single department all of those who are at work making use of a given special skill or technology, or are members of a given profession."[8] Consider a simple skill of this kind—typing. Typing is a skill which brings about a means-end coordination of muscular movements, but at a very low level in the means-end hierarchy. The content of the typewritten letter is indifferent to the skill that produces it. The skill consists merely in the ability to hit the letter "*t*" quickly whenever the letter "*t*" is required by the content and to hit the letter "*a*" whenever the letter "a" is required by the content.

There is, then, no essential difference between a "purpose" and a "process," but only a distinction of degree. A "process" is an activity whose immediate purpose is at a low level in the hierarchy of means and ends, while a "purpose" is a collection of activities whose orienting value or aim is at a high level in the means-end hierarchy.

Next consider "clientele" and "place" as bases of organization. These categories are really not separate from purpose, but a part of it. A complete statement of the purpose of a fire department would have to include the area served by it: "to reduce fire losses on property in the city of X." Objectives of an administrative organization are phrased in terms of a service to be provided and an area for which it is provided. Usually, the term "*purpose*" is meant to refer only to the first element, but the second is just as legitimately an aspect of purpose.

Area of service, of course, may be a specified clientele quite as well as a geographical area. In the case of an agency which works on "shifts," time will be a third dimension of purpose—to provide a given service in a given area (or to a given clientele) during a given time period.

With this clarification of terminology, the next task is to reconsider the problem of specializing the work of an organization. It is no longer legitimate to speak of a "purpose" organization, a "process" organization, a "clientele" organization, or an "area" organization. The same unit might fall into any one of these four categories, depending on the nature of the larger organizational unit of which it was a part. A unit providing public health and medical services for school-age children in Multnomah County might be considered (1) an "area" organization if it were part of a unit providing the same service for the state of Oregon; (2) a "clientele" organization if it were part of a unit providing similar services for children of all ages; (3) a "purpose" or a "process" organization (it would be impossible to say which) if it were part of an education department.

It is incorrect to say that Bureau A is a process bureau; the correct statement is that Bureau A is a process bureau *within* Department X.[9] This latter statement would mean that Bureau A incorporates all the processes of a certain kind in Department X, without reference to any special subpurposes, subareas, or subclientele of Department X. Now it is conceivable that a particular unit might incorporate all processes of a certain kind but that these processes might relate to only certain particular subpurposes of the department purpose. In this case, which corresponds to the health unit in an education department mentioned above, the unit would be specialized by both purpose and process. The health unit would be the only one in the education department using the medical art (process) and concerned with health (subpurpose).

Even when the problem is solved of proper usage for the terms "purpose," "process," "clientele," and "area," the principles of administration give no guide as to which of these four competing bases of specialization is applicable in any particular situation. The British Machinery of Government Committee had no doubts about the matter. It considered purpose and clientele as the two possible bases of organization and put its faith entirely in the former. Others have had equal assurance in choosing between purpose and process. The reasoning which leads to these unequivocal conclusions leaves something to be desired. The Machinery of Government Committee gives this sole argument for its choice:

> Now the inevitable outcome of this method of organization [by clientele] is a tendency to Lilliputian administration. It is impossible that the specialized service which each Department has to render to the community can be of as high a standard when its work is at the same time limited to a particular class of persons and extended to every variety of provision for them, as when the Department concentrates itself on the provision of the particular service only by whomsoever required, and looks beyond the interest of comparatively small classes.[10]

The faults in this analysis are obvious. First, there is no attempt to determine how a service is to be recognized. Second, there is a bald assumption, absolutely without proof, that a child health unit, for example, in a department of child welfare could not offer services of "as high a standard" as the same unit if it were located in a department of health. Just how the shifting of the unit from one department to another would improve or damage the quality of its work is not explained. Third, no basis is set forth for adjudicating the competing claims of purpose and process—the two are merged in the ambiguous term "service." It is not necessary here to decide whether the committee was right or wrong in its recommendation; the important point is that the recommendation represented a choice, without any apparent logical or empirical grounds, between contradictory principles of administration.

Even more remarkable illustrations of illogic can be found in most discussions of purpose versus process. They would be too ridiculous to cite if they were not commonly used in serious political and administrative debate.

> For instance, where should agricultural education come: in the Ministry of Education, or of Agriculture? That depends on whether we want to see the best farming taught, though possibly by old methods, or a possibly out-of-date style of farming, taught in the most modern and compelling manner. The question answers itself.[11]

But does the question really answer itself? Suppose a bureau of agricultural education were set up, headed, for example, by a man who had had extensive experience in agricultural research or as administrator of an agricultural school, and staffed by men of similarly appropriate background. What reason is there to believe that if attached to a Ministry of Education they would teach old-fashioned farming by new-fashioned methods, while if attached to a Ministry of Agriculture they would teach new-fashioned farming by old-fashioned methods? The administrative problem of such a bureau would be to teach new-fashioned farming by new-fashioned methods, and it is a little difficult to see how the departmental location of the unit would affect this result. "The question answers itself" only if one has a rather mystical faith in the potency of bureau-shuffling as a means for redirecting the activities of an agency.

These contradictions and competitions have received increasing attention from students of administration during the past few years. For example, Gulick, Wallace, and Benson have stated certain advantages and disadvantages of the several modes of specialization, and have considered the conditions under which one or the other mode might best be adopted.[12] All this analysis has been at a theoretical level—in the sense that data have not been employed to demonstrate the superior effectiveness claimed for the different modes. But though theoretical, the analysis has lacked a theory. Since no comprehensive framework has been constructed within which the discussion could take place, the analysis has tended either to the logical one-sidedness which characterizes the examples quoted above or to inconclusiveness.

The Impasse of Administrative Theory. The four "principles of administration" that were set forth at the beginning of this paper have now been subjected to critical analysis. None of the four survived in very good shape, for in each case there was found, instead of an unequivocal principle, a set of two or more mutually incompatible principles apparently equally applicable to the administrative situation.

Moreover, the reader will see that the very same objections can be urged against the customary discussions of "centralization" versus "decentralization," which usually conclude, in effect, that "on the one hand, centralization of decision-making functions is desirable; on the other hand, there are definite advantages in decentralization."

Can anything be salvaged which will be useful in the construction of an administrative theory? As a matter of fact, almost everything can be salvaged. The difficulty has arisen from treating as "principles of administration" what are really only criteria for describing and diagnosing administrative situations. Closet space is certainly an important item in the design of a successful house; yet a house designed entirely with a view to securing a maximum of closet space—all other considerations being forgotten—would be considered, to say the least, somewhat unbalanced. Similarly, unity of command, specialization by purpose, decentralization are all items to be considered in the design of an efficient administrative organization. No single one of these items is of sufficient importance to suffice as a guiding principle for the administrative analyst. In the design of administrative organization, as in their operation, overall efficiency must be the guiding criterion. Mutually incompatible advantages must be balanced against each other, just as an architect weighs the advantages of additional closet space against the advantages of a larger living room.

This position, if it is a valid one, constitutes an indictment of much current writing about administrative matters. As the examples cited in this chapter amply demonstrate, much administrative analysis proceeds by selecting a single criterion and applying it to an administrative situation to reach a recommendation; while the fact that equally valid, but contradictory, criteria exist which could be applied with equal reason, but with a different result, is conveniently ignored. A valid approach to the study of administration requires that *all* the relevant diagnostic criteria be identified; that each administrative situation be analyzed in terms of the entire set of criteria; and that research be instituted to determine how weights can be assigned to the several criteria when they are, as they usually will be, mutually incompatible.

AN APPROACH TO ADMINISTRATIVE THEORY

This program needs to be considered step by step. First, what is included in the description of administrative situations for purposes of such an analysis? Second, how can weights be assigned to the various criteria to give them their proper place in the total picture?

The Description of Administrative Situations. Before a science can develop principles, it must possess concepts. Before a law of gravitation could be formulated, it was necessary to have the notions of "acceleration" and "weight." The first task of administrative theory is to develop a set of concepts that will permit the description in terms relevant to the theory, of administrative situations. These concepts, to be scientifically useful, must be operational; that is, their meanings must correspond to empirically observable facts or situations. The definition of "authority" given earlier in this paper is an example of an operational definition.

What is a scientifically relevant description of an organization? It is a description that, so far as possible, designates for each person in the organization what decisions that person makes and the influences to which he is subject in making each of these decisions. Current descriptions of administrative organizations fall far short of this standard. For the most part, they confine themselves to the allocation of *functions* and the formal structure of *authority.* They give little attention to the other types of organizational influence or to the system of communication.[13]

What does it mean, for example to say: "The department is made up of three bureaus. The first has the function of

______, the second the function of ______, and the third the function of ______?" What can be learned from such a description about the workability of the organizational arrangement? Very little, indeed. For from the description there is obtained no idea of the degree to which decisions are centralized at the bureau level or at the departmental level. No notion is given as to the extent to which the (presumably unlimited) authority of the department over the bureau is actually exercised or by what mechanisms. There is no indication of the extent to which systems of communication assist the coordination of the three bureaus or, for that matter, to what extent coordination is required by the nature of their work. There is no description of the kinds of training the members of the bureau have undergone or of the extent to which this training permits decentralization at the bureau level. In sum, a description of administrative organizations in terms almost exclusively of functions and lines of authority is completely inadequate for purposes of administrative analysis.

Consider the term "centralization." How is it determined whether the operations of a particular organization are "centralized" or "decentralized"? Does the fact that field offices exist prove anything about decentralization? Might not the same decentralization take place in the bureaus of a centrally located office? A realistic analysis of centralization must include a study of the allocation of decisions in the organization and the methods of influence that are employed by the higher levels to affect the decisions at the lower levels. Such an analysis would reveal a much more complex picture of the decision-making process than any enumeration of the geographical locations of organizational units at the different levels.

Administrative description suffers currently from superficiality, oversimplification, lack of realism. It has confined itself too closely to the mechanism of authority and has failed to bring within its orbit the other, equally important, modes of influence on organizational behavior. It has refused to undertake the tiresome task of studying the actual allocation of decision-making functions. It has been satisfied to speak of "authority," "centralization," "span of control," "function," without seeking operational definitions of these terms. Until administrative description reaches a higher level of sophistication, there is little reason to hope that rapid progress will be made toward the identification and verification of valid administrative principles.

Does this mean that a purely formal description of an administrative organization is impossible—that a relevant description must include an account of the content of the organization's decisions? This is a question that is almost impossible to answer in the present state of knowledge of administrative theory. One thing seems certain: content plays a greater role in the application of administrative principles than is allowed for in the formal administrative theory of the present time. This is a fact that is beginning to be recognized in the literature of administration. If one examines the chain of publications extending from Mooney and Reilley, through Gulick and the President's Committee controversy, to Schuyler Wallace and Benson, he sees a steady shift of emphasis from the "principles of administration" themselves to a study of the *conditions* under which competing principles are respectively applicable. Recent publications seldom say that "organization should be by purpose," but rather that "under such and such conditions purpose organization is desirable." It is to these conditions which underlie the application of the proverbs of administration that administrative theory and analysis must turn in their search for really valid principles to replace the proverbs.

The Diagnosis of Administrative Situations. Before any positive suggestions can be made, it is necessary to digress a bit and to consider more closely the exact nature of the propositions of administrative theory. The theory of administration is concerned with how an organization should be constructed and operated in order to accomplish its work efficiently. A fundamental principle of administration, which follows almost immediately from the rational character of "good" administration, is that among several alternatives involving the same expenditure that one should always be selected which leads to the greatest accomplishment of administrative objectives; and among several alternatives that lead to the same accomplishment that one should be selected which involves the least expenditure. Since this "principle of efficiency" is characteristic of any activity that attempts rationally to maximize the attainment of certain ends with the use of scarce means, it is as characteristic of economic theory as it is of administrative theory. The "administrative man" takes his place alongside the classical "economic man."[14]

Actually, the "principle" of efficiency should be considered a definition rather than a principle: it is a definition of what is meant by "good" or "correct" administrative behavior. It does not tell *how* accomplishments are to be maximized, but merely states that this maximization is the aim of administrative activity, and that administrative theory must disclose under what conditions the maximization takes place.

Now what are the factors that determine the level of efficiency which is achieved by an administrative organization? It is not possible to make an exhaustive list of these but the principal categories can be enumerated. Perhaps the simplest method of approach is to consider the single member of the administrative organization and ask what the limits are to the quantity and quality of his output. These limits include (*a*) limits on his ability to perform and (*b*) limits on his ability to make correct decisions. To the extent that these limits are removed, the administrative organization approaches its goal of high efficiency. Two persons, given the same skills, the same objectives and values, the same knowledge and information, can rationally decide only upon the same course of action. Hence, administrative theory must be interested in the factors that will determine with what skills, values, and knowledge the organization member undertakes his work. These are the "limits" to rationality with which the principles of administration must deal.

On one side, the individual is limited by those skills, habits, and reflexes which are no longer in the realm of the conscious. His performance, for example, may be limited by his manual dexterity or his reaction time or his strength. His decision-making processes may be limited by the speed of his mental processes, his skill in elementary arithmetic, and so forth. In this area, the principles of administration must be concerned with the physiology of the human body and with the laws of skill-training and of habit. This is the field that has been most successfully cultivated by the followers of Taylor and in which has been developed time-and-motion study and the therblig.

On a second side, the individual is limited by his values and those conceptions of purpose which influence him in making his decisions. If his loyalty to the organization is high, his decisions may evidence sincere acceptance of the objectives set for the organization; if that loyalty is lacking, personal motives may interfere with his administrative efficiency. If his loyalties are attached to the bureau by which he is employed, he may sometimes make decisions that are inimical to the larger unit of which the bureau is a part. In this area the principles of administration must be concerned with the determinants of loyalty and morale, with leadership and initiative, and with the influences that determine where the individual's organizational loyalties will be attached.

On a third side, the individual is limited by the extent of his knowledge of things relevant to his job. This applies both to the basic knowledge required in decision making—a bridge designer must know the fundamentals of mechanics—and to the information that is required to make his decisions appropriate to the given situation. In this area, administrative theory is concerned with such fundamental questions as these: What are the limits on the mass of knowledge that human minds can accumulate and apply? How rapidly can knowledge be assimilated? How is specialization in the administrative organization to be related to the specializations of knowledge that are prevalent in the community's occupational structure? How is the system of communication to channel knowledge and information to the appropriate decision-points? What types of knowledge can, and what types cannot, be easily transmitted? How is the need for intercommunication of information affected by the modes of specialization in the organization? This is perhaps the *terra incognita* of administrative theory, and undoubtedly its careful exploration will cast great light on the proper application of the proverbs of administration.

Perhaps this triangle of limits does not completely bound the area of rationality, and other sides need to be added to the figure. In any case, this enumeration will serve to indicate the kinds of considerations that must go into the construction of valid and noncontradictory principles of administration.

An important fact to be kept in mind is that the limits of rationality are variable limits. Most important of all, consciousness of the limits may in itself alter them. Suppose it were discovered in a particular organization, for example, that organizational loyalties attached to small units had frequently led to a harmful degree of intraorganizational competition. Then, a program which trained members of the organization to be conscious of their loyalties, and to subordinate loyalties to the smaller group to those of the large, might lead to a very considerable alteration of the limits in that organization.[15]

A related point is that the term "rational behavior," as employed here, refers to rationality when that behavior is evaluated in terms of the objectives of the larger organization; for, as just pointed out, the difference in direction of the individual's aims from those of the larger organization is just one of those elements of nonrationality with which the theory must deal.

A final observation is that, since administrative theory is concerned with the nonrational limits of the rational, it follows that the larger the area in which rationality has been achieved the less important is the exact form of the administrative organization. For example, the function of plan preparation, or design, if it results in a written plan that can be communicated interpersonally without difficulty, can be located almost anywhere in the organization without affecting results. All that is needed is a procedure whereby the plan can be given authoritative status, and this can be provided in a number of ways. A discussion, then, of the proper location for a planning or designing unit is apt to be highly inconclusive and is apt to hinge on the personalities in the organization and their relative enthusiasm, or lack of it, toward the planning function rather than upon any abstract principles of good administration.[16]

On the other hand, when factors of communication or faiths or loyalty are crucial to the making of a decision, the location of the decision in the organization is of great importance. The method of allocating decisions in the army, for instance, automatically provides (at least in the period prior to the actual battle) that each decision will be made where the knowledge is available for coordinating it with other decisions.

Assigning Weights to the Criteria. A first step, then, in the overhauling of the proverbs of administration is to develop a vocabulary, along the lines just suggested, for the description of administrative organization. A second step, which has also been outlined, is to study the limits of rationality in order to develop a complete and comprehensive enumeration of the criteria that must be weighed in evaluating an administrative organization. The current proverbs represent only a fragmentary and unsystematized portion of these criteria.

When these two tasks have been carried out, it remains to assign weights to the criteria. Since the criteria, or "proverbs," are often mutually competitive or contradictory, it is not sufficient merely to identify them. Merely to know, for example, that a specified change in organization will reduce the span of control is not enough to justify the change. This gain must be balanced against the possible resulting loss of contact between the higher and lower ranks of the hierarchy.

Hence, administrative theory must also be concerned with the question of the weights that are to be applied to these criteria—to the problems of their relative importance in any concrete situation. This question is not one that can be solved in a vacuum. Armchair philosophizing about administration—of which the present paper is an example—has gone about as far as it can profitably go in this particular direction. What is needed now is empirical research and experimentation to determine the relative desirability of alternative administrative arrangements.

The methodological framework for this research is already at hand in the principle of efficiency. If an administrative organization whose activities are susceptible to objective evaluation be subjected to study, then the actual change in accomplishment that results from modifying administrative arrangements in these organizations can be observed and analyzed.

There are two indispensable conditions to successful research along these lines. First, it is necessary that the objectives of the administrative organization under study be defined in concrete terms so that results, expressed in terms of these objectives, can be accurately measured. Second, it is necessary that sufficient experimental control be exercised to make possible the isolation of the particular effect under study from other disturbing factors that might be operating on the organization at the same time.

These two conditions have seldom been even partially fulfilled in so-called "administrative experiments." The mere fact that a legislature passes a law creating an administrative agency, that the agency operates for five years, that the agency is finally abolished, and that a historical study is then made of the agency's operations is not sufficient to make of that agency's history an "administrative experiment." Modern American legislation is full of such "experiments" which furnish orators in neighboring states with abundant ammunition when similar issues arise in their bailiwicks, but which provide the scientific investigator with little or nothing in the way of objective evidence, one way or the other.

In the literature of administration, there are only a handful of research studies that satisfy these fundamental conditions of methodology—and these are, for the most part, on the periphery of the problem of organization. There are, first of all, the studies of the Taylor group which sought to determine the technological conditions of efficiency. Perhaps none of these is a better example of the painstaking methods of science than Taylor's own studies of the cutting of metals.[17]

Studies dealing with the human and social aspects of administration are even rarer than the technological studies. Among the more important are the whole series of studies on fatigue, starting in Great Britain during World War I and culminating in the Westinghouse experiments.[18]

In the field of public administration, almost the sole example of such experimentation is the series of studies that have been conducted in the public welfare field to determine the proper case loads for social workers.[19]

Because, apart from these scattered examples, studies of administrative agencies have been carried out without benefit of control or of objective measurement of results, they have had to depend for their recommendations and conclusions upon *a priori* reasoning proceeding from "principles of administration." The reasons have already been stated why the "principles" derived in this way cannot be more than "proverbs."

Perhaps the program outlined here will appear an ambitious or even a quixotic one. There should certainly be no illusions, in undertaking it, as to the length and deviousness of the path. It is hard to see, however, what alternative remains open. Certainly neither the practitioner of administration nor the theoretician can be satisfied with the poor analytic tools that the proverbs provide him. Nor is there any reason to believe that a less drastic reconversion than that outlined here will rebuild those tools to usefulness.

It may be objected that administration cannot aspire to be a "science"; that by the nature of its subject it cannot be more than an "art." Whether true or false, this objection is irrelevant to the present discussion. The question of how "exact" the principles of administration can be made is one that only experience can answer. But as to whether they should be logical or illogical there can be no debate. Even an "art" cannot be founded on proverbs.

NOTES

1. Lest it be thought that this deficiency is peculiar to the science—or "art"—of administration, it should be pointed out that the same trouble is shared by most Freudian psychological theories, as well as by some sociological theories.

2. Luther Gulick, "Notes on the Theory of Organization," in Luther Gulick and L. Urwick (eds.), *Papers on the Science of Administration* (Institute of Public Administration, Columbia University, 1937), p. 9.

3. This point is discussed in Herbert A. Simon "Decision-Making and Administrative Organization," 4 *Public Administration Review* 20–21 (Winter, 1944).

4. Gulick, "Notes on the Theory of Organization," p. 9; L. D. White, *Introduction to the Study of Public Administration* (Macmillan Co., 1939), p. 45.

5. Frederick W. Taylor, *Shop Management* (Harper & Bros., 1911), p. 99; Macmahon, Millett, and Ogden *The Administration of Federal Work Relief* (Public Administration Service, 1941), pp. 265–68; and L. Urwick, who describes British army practice in "Organization as a Technical Problem," Gulick and Urwick (eds.) *op. cit.*, pp. 67–69.
6. *Op. cit.*, p. 21.
7. If this is correct, then any attempt to prove that certain activities belong in a single department because they relate to a single purpose is doomed to fail. See, for example, John M. Gaus and Leon Wolcott, *Public Administration and the U.S. Department of Agriculture* (Public Administration Service, 1940).
8. *Op. cit.*, p. 23.
9. This distinction is implicit in most of Gulick's analysis of specialization. However, since he cites as examples single departments within a city, and since he usually speaks of "grouping activities" rather than "dividing work," the relative character of these categories is not always apparent in this discussion (*op. cit.*, pp. 15–30).
10. *Report of the Machinery of Government Committee* (H. M. Stationery Office, 1918).
11. Sir Charles Harris, "Decentralization," 3 *Journal of Public Administration* 117–33 (April, 1925).
12. Gulick, "Notes on the Theory of Organization," pp. 21–30; Schuyler Wallace, *Federal Departmentalization* (Columbia University Press, 1941); George C. S. Benson, "International Administrative Organization," 1 *Public Administrative Review* 473–86 (Autumn, 1941).
13. The monograph by MacMahon, Millett, and Ogden, *op. cit.*, perhaps approaches nearer than any other published administrative study to the sophistication required in administrative description. See, for example, the discussion on pp. 233–36 of headquarters-field relationships.
14. For an elaboration of the principle of efficiency and its place in administrative theory see Clarence E. Ridley and Herbert A. Simon, *Measuring Municipal Activities* (International City Managers' Association, 2nd ed., 1943), particularly Chapter I and the preface to the second edition.
15. For an example of the use of such training, see Herbert A. Simon and William Divine, "Controlling Human Factors in an Administrative Experiment," 1 *Public Administration Review* 487–92 (Autumn, 1941).
16. See, for instance, Robert A. Walker, *The Planning Function in Urban Government* (University of Chicago Press, 1941), pp. 166–75. Walker makes out a strong case for attaching the planning agency to the chief executive. But he rests his entire case on the rather slender reed that "as long as the planning agency is outside the governmental structure . . . planning will tend to encounter resistance from public officials as an invasion of their responsibility and jurisdiction." This "resistance" is precisely the type of nonrational loyalty which has been referred to previously, and which is certainly a variable.
17. F. W. Taylor, *On the Art of Cutting Metals* (American Society of Mechanical Engineers, 1907).
18. Great Britain, Ministry of Munitions, Health of Munitions Workers Committee, *Final Report* (H. M. Stationery Office, 1918); F. J. Roethlisberger and William J. Dickson, *Management and the Worker* (Harvard University Press, 1939).
19. Ellery F. Reed, *An Experiment in Reducing the Cost of Relief* (American Public Welfare Administration, 1937); Rebecca Staman, "What Is the Most Economical Case Load in Public Relief Administration?" 4 *Social Work Technique* 117–21 (May-June, 1938); Chicago Relief Administration, *Adequate Staff Brings Economy* (American Public Welfare Association, 1939); Constance Hastings and Saya S. Schwartz, *Size of Visitor's Caseload as a Factor in Efficient Administration of Public Assistance* (Philadelphia County Board of Assistance, 1939); Simon *et al.*, *Determining Work Loads for Professional Staff in a Public Welfare Agency* (Bureau of Public Administration, University of California, 1941).

19 The Science of Public Administration: Three Problems

Robert A. Dahl

The effort to create a science of public administration has often led to the formulation of universal laws or, more commonly, to the assertion that such universal laws *could* be formulated for public administration.[1] In an attempt to make the science of public administration analogous to the natural sciences, the laws or putative laws are stripped of normative values, of the distortions caused by the incorrigible individual psyche, and of the presumably irrelevant effects of the cultural environment. It is often implied that "principles of public administration" have a universal validity independent not only of moral and political ends, but of the frequently nonconformist personality of the individual, and the social and cultural setting as well.

Perhaps the best known expression of this kind is that of W. F. Willoughby. Although he refused to commit himself as to the propriety of designating administration as a science, Willoughby nevertheless asserted that "in administration, there are certain fundamental principles of general application analogous to those characterizing any science. . . ."[2] A more recent statement, and evidently an equally influential one, is L. Urwick's contention that "there are certain principles which govern the association of human beings *for any purpose*, just as there are certain engineering principles which govern the building of a bridge."[3]

Others argue merely that it is possible to discover general principles of wide, although not necessarily of universal validity.[4] Surely this more modest assessment of the role of public administration as a study is not, as an abstract statement, open to controversy. Yet even the discovery of these more limited principles is handicapped by the three basic problems of values, the individual personality, and the social framework.

PUBLIC ADMINISTRATION AND NORMATIVE VALUES

The first difficulty of constructing a science of public administration stems from the frequent impossibility of excluding normative considerations from the problems of public administration. Science as such is not concerned with the discovery or elucidation of normative values; indeed, the doctrine is generally, if not quite universally, accepted that science *cannot* demonstrate moral values, that science cannot construct a bridge across the great gap from "is" to "ought." So long as the naturalistic fallacy is a stumbling block to philosophers, it must likewise impede the progress of social scientists.

Source: From *Public Administration Review,* 7, no. 1 (1947), pp. 1–11.

Much could be gained if the clandestine smuggling of moral values into the social sciences could be converted into open and honest commerce. Writers on public administration often assume that they are snugly insulated from the storms of clashing values; usually, however, they are most concerned with ends at the very moment that they profess to be least concerned with them. The doctrine of efficiency is a case in point; it runs like a half-visible thread through the fabric of public administration literature as a dominant goal of administration. Harvey Walker has stated that "the objective of administration is to secure the maximum beneficial result contemplated by the law with the minimum expenditure of the social resources."[5] The term "social resources" is sufficiently ambiguous to allow for almost any interpretation, but it suggests that the general concept involved is one of maximizing "output" and minimizing "cost." Likewise, many of the promised benefits of administrative reorganization in state governments are presumed to follow from proposed improvements in "efficiency in operation." And yet, as Charles Hyneman has so trenchantly observed, there are in a democratic society other criteria than simple efficiency in operation.[6]

Luther Gulick concedes that the goal of efficiency is limited by other values.

> In the science of administration, whether public or private, the basic "good" is efficiency. The fundamental objective of the science of administration is the accomplishment of the work in hand with the least expenditure of man-power and materials. Efficiency is thus axiom number one in the value scale of administration. This brings administration into apparent conflict with certain elements of the value scale of politics, whether we use that term in its scientific or in its popular sense. But both public administration and politics are branches of political science, so that we are in the end compelled to mitigate the pure concept of efficiency in the light of the value scale of politics and the social order.[7]

He concludes, nevertheless, "that these interferences with efficiency [do not] in any way eliminate efficiency as the fundamental value upon which the science of administration may be erected. They serve to condition and to complicate, but not to change the single ultimate test of value in administration."[8]

It is far from clear what Gulick means to imply in saying that "interferences with efficiency" caused by ultimate political values may "condition" and "complicate" but do not "change" the "single ultimate test" of efficiency as the goal of administration. Is efficiency the supreme goal not only of private administration, but also of public administration, as Gulick contends? If so, how can one say, as Gulick does, that "there are . . . highly inefficient arrangements like citizen boards and small local governments which *may* be necessary in a democracy as educational devices?" Why speak of efficiency as the "single ultimate test of value in administration" if it is not ultimate at all—if, that is to say, in a conflict between efficiency and "the democratic dogma" (to use Gulick's expression) the latter must prevail? Must this dogma prevail only because it has greater political and social force behind it than the dogma of efficiency; or ought it to prevail because it has, in some sense, greater value? How can administrators and students of public administration discriminate between those parts of the democratic dogma that are so strategic they ought to prevail in any conflict with efficiency and those that are essentially subordinate, irrelevant, or even false intrusions into the democratic hypothesis? What *is* efficiency? Belsen and Dachau were "efficient" by one scale of values. And in any case, why is efficiency the ultimate test? According to what and whose scale of values is efficiency placed on the highest pedestal? Is not the worship of efficiency itself a particular expression of a special value judgment? Does it not stem from a mode of thinking and a special moral hypothesis resting on a sharp distinction between means and ends?

The basic problems of *public* administration as a discipline and as a potential science are much wider than the problems of mere *administration.* The necessarily wider preoccupation of a study of *public* administration, as contrasted with *private* administration, inevitably enmeshes the problems of public administration in the toils of ethical considerations. Thus the tangled question of the right of public employees to strike can scarcely be answered without a tacit normative assumption of some kind. A pragmatic answer is satisfactory only so long as no one raises the question of the "rights" involved. And to resolve the question of rights merely by reciting *legal* norms is to beg the whole issue; it is to confess that an answer to this vital problem of public personnel must be sought elsewhere than with students of public administration. Moreover, if one were content to rest one's case on legal rights, it would be impossible to reconcile in a single "science of public administration" the diverse legal and institutional aspects of the right to strike in France, Great Britain, and the United States.

The great question of responsibility, certainly a central one to the study of public administration once it is raised above the level of academic disquisitions on office management, hinges ultimately on some definition of ends, purposes, and values in society. The sharp conflict of views on responsibility expressed several years ago by Carl Friedrich and Herman Finer resulted from basically different interpretations of the nature and purposes of democratic government. Friedrich tacitly assumed certain values in his discussion of the importance of the bureaucrat's "inner check" as an instrument of control. Finer brought Friedrich's unexpressed values into sharp focus and in a warm criticism challenged their compatibility with the democratic faith.[9]

It is difficult, moreover, to escape the conclusion that much of the debate over delegated legislation and administrative adjudication, both in this country and in England, actually arises from a concealed conflict in objectives. Those to whom economic regulation and control are anathema have with considerable consistency opposed the growth of delegated legislation and the expansion of the powers of administrative tribunals—no doubt from a conviction that previously existing economic rights and privileges are safer in the courts than in administrative tribunals; whereas those who support this expansion of administrative power and techniques generally also favor a larger measure of economic regulation and control. Much of the debate that has been phrased in terms of means ought more properly to be evaluated as a conflict over general social goals.

One might justifiably contend that it is the function of a science of public administration, not to determine ends, but to devise the best means to the ends established by those agencies entrusted with the setting of social policy. The science of public administration, it might be argued, would be totally nonnormative, and its doctrines would apply with equal validity to any regime, democratic or totalitarian, once the ends were made clear. "Tell me what you wish to achieve," the public administration scientist might say, "and I will tell you what administrative means are best designed for your purposes." Yet even this view has difficulties, for in most societies, and particularly in democratic ones, ends are often in dispute; rarely are they clearly and unequivocally determined. Nor can ends and means ever be sharply distinguished, since ends determine means and often means ultimately determine ends.[10]

The student of public administration cannot avoid a concern with ends. What he *ought* to avoid is the failure to make explicit the ends or values that form the groundwork of his doctrine. If purposes and normative considerations were consistently made plain, a net gain to the science of public administration would result. But to refuse to recognize that the study of public administration must be founded on some clarification of ends is to perpetuate the gobbledygook of science in the area of moral purposes.

A science of public administration might proceed, then, along these lines:

1. *Establishing a basic hypothesis.* A nonnormative science of public administration might rest on a basic hypothesis that removed ethical problems from the area covered by the science. The *science* of public administration would begin where the *basic hypothesis* leaves off. One could quarrel with the moral or metaphysical assumptions in the basic hypothesis; but all normative argument would have to be carried on at that level, and not at the level of the science. The science, as such, would have no ethical content.

   Can such a basic hypothesis be created? To this writer the problem appears loaded with enormous and perhaps insuperable difficulties; yet it is unlikely that a science of public administration will ever be possible until this initial step is taken.
2. *Stating ends honestly.* Some problems of the public services, like that of responsibility, evidently cannot be divorced from certain ends implied in the society served by the public services. If this is true, there can never be a universal science of public administration so long as societies and states vary in their objectives. In all cases where problems of public administration are inherently related to specific social ends and purposes, the most that can be done is to force all normative assumptions into the open, and not let them lie half concealed in the jungle of fact and inference to slaughter the unwary.

PUBLIC ADMINISTRATION AND HUMAN BEHAVIOR

A second major problem stems from the inescapable fact that a science of public administration must be a study of certain aspects of human behavior. To be sure, there are parts of public administration in which man's behavior can safely be ignored; perhaps it is possible to discuss the question of governmental accounting and auditing without much consideration of the behavior patterns of governmental accountants and auditors. But most problems of public administration revolve around human beings; and the study of public administration is therefore essentially a study of human beings as they have behaved, and as they may be expected or predicted to behave, under certain special circumstances. What marks off the field of public administration from psychology or sociology or political institutions is its concern with *human behavior in the area of services performed by governmental agencies.*[11]

This concern with human behavior greatly limits the immediate potentialities of a science of public administration. First, it diminishes the possibility of using experimental procedures; and experiment, though perhaps not indispensable to the scientific method, is of enormous aid. Second, concern with human behavior seriously limits the uniformity of data, since the datum is the discrete and highly variable man or woman. Third, because the data concerning human behavior constitute an incredibly vast and complex mass, the part played by the preferences of the observer is exaggerated, and possibilities of independent verification are diminished. Fourth, concern with human action weakens the reliability of all "laws of public administration," since too little is known of the mainsprings of human action to insure certitude, or even high probability, in predictions about man's conduct.

All these weaknesses have been pointed out so often in discussing the problems of the social sciences that it should be unnecessary to repeat them here. And yet many of the supposed laws of public administration and much of the claim to a science of public administration derive from assumptions about the nature of man that are scarcely tenable at this late date.

The field of organizational theory serves as an extreme example, for it is there particularly that the nature of man is often lost sight of in the interminable discussions over idealized and abstract organizational forms. In this development, writers on public administration have been heavily influenced by the rational character that capitalism has imposed on the organization of production, and have ignored the irrational qualities of man himself.

Capitalism, especially in its industrial form, was essentially an attempt to organize production along rational lines. In the organization of the productive process, the capitalistic entrepreneur sought to destroy the old restrictive practices and standards of feudalism and mercantilism; to rid the productive process of the inherited cluster of methods and technics that characterized the guilds and medieval craftsmen; in short, to organize production according to rational rather than traditional concepts. Combined with a new acquisitive ideal, this rational approach to production transformed not only the whole economic process but society itself. The rapid growth of mechanization, routine, and specialization of labor further increased the technically rational quality of capitalist production. It was perhaps inevitable that concepts should arise which subordinated individual vagaries and differences to the ordered requirements of the productive process: for it was this very subordination that the replacement of feudal and mercantilist institutions by capitalism had accomplished. The organization (though not the control) of production became the concern of the engineer; and because the restrictive practices authorized by tradition, the protective standards of the guilds, the benevolent regulations of a mercantilist monarchy, and even the nonacquisitive ideals of the individual had all been swept away, it was actually feasible to organize production without much regard for the varying individual personalities of those in the productive process. The productive process, which to the medieval craftsman was both a means and an end in itself, became wholly a means.

Ultimately, of course, men like Taylor provided an imposing theoretical basis for regarding function, based on a logical distribution and specialization of labor, as the true basis of organization. Men like Urwick modified and carried forward Taylor's work, and in the process have tremendously influenced writers on public administration. Urwick, so it must have appeared, provided a basis for a genuine science of administration. "There are principles," he wrote, "*which should govern arrangements for human association of any kind.* These principles can be studied as a technical question, *irrespective of the purpose of the enterprise, the personnel composing it, or any constitutional, political, or social theory underlying its creation.*"[12] And again, "Whatever the motive underlying persistence in bad structure it is always more hurtful to the greatest number than good structure."[13]

Sweeping generalizations such as these give promise of a set of "universal principles": i.e., a science. American students of public administration could not fail to be impressed.

Aside from the fact that Urwick ignored the whole question of ends, it is clear that he also presupposed (though he nowhere stated what sort of human personality he *did* presuppose) an essentially rational, amenable individual; he presupposed, that is to say, individuals who would accept logical organization and would not (for irrelevant and irrational reasons) rebel against it or silently supersede it with an informal organization better suited to their personality needs. Urwick must have supposed this. For if there is a large measure of irrationality in human behavior, then an organizational structure formed on "logical" lines may in practice frustrate, anger, and embitter its personnel. By contrast, an organization not based on the logic of organizational principles may better utilize the peculiar and varying personalities of its members. Is there any evidence to suggest that in such a case the "logical" organization will achieve its purposes in some sense "better" or more efficiently than the organization that adapts personality needs to the purposes of the organization?[14] On what kind of evidence are we compelled to assume that the rationality of organizational structure will prevail over the irrationality of man?

Patently the contention that one system of organization is more rational than another, *and therefore better,* is valid only (a) if individuals are dominated by reason or (b) if they are so thoroughly dominated by the technical process (as on the assembly line, perhaps) that their individual preferences may safely be ignored. However much the latter assumption might apply to industry (a matter of considerable doubt), clearly it has little application to public administration, where technical processes are, on the whole, of quite subordinate importance. As for the first assumption, it has been discredited by all the findings of modern psychology. The science of organization had learned too much from industry and not enough from Freud.

The more that writers on public administration have moved from the classroom to the administrator's office, the more Urwick's universal principles have receded. As early as 1930, in a pioneering work, Harold Lasswell described the irrational and unconscious elements in the successful and unsuccessful administrator.[15] Meanwhile, experiments in the Hawthorne plant of Western Electric Company were indicating beyond doubt that individual personalities and social relationships had great effects even on routinized work in industry. Increased output was the result of "the organization of human relations, rather than the organization of technics."[16] Urwick had said (with little or no supporting evidence): "The idea that organizations should be built up round and adjusted to individual idiosyncracies, rather than that individuals should be adapted to the requirements of sound principles of organization, is . . . foolish. . . ." The Hawthorne experiment demonstrated, on the contrary, that ". . . no study of human situations which fails to take account of the nonlogical social routines can hope for practical success."[17]

In 1939, Leonard White seriously qualified the principle of subordinating individuals to structure by adding the saving phrase of the neoclassical economists: "in the long run." "To what extent," he said, "it is desirable to rearrange structure in preference to replacing personnel is a practical matter to be determined in the light of special cases. In the long run, the demands of sound organization require the fitting of personnel to it, rather than sacrificing normal organizational relationships to the needs or whims of individuals."[18] In the same year, Macmahon and Millett went far beyond the customary deductive principles of public administration theory by making an actual biographical study of a number of federal administrators.[19] In the most recent [1946] text on public administration, the importance of personality is frankly admitted. ". . . administrative research," say the authors, "does not seek its goal in the formulation of mechanical rules or equations, into which human behavior must be molded. Rather, it looks toward the systematic ordering of functions *and human relationships* so that organizational decisions can and will be based upon the certainty that each step taken will actually serve the purpose of the organization as a whole."[20] And one whole chapter of this text is devoted to informal organizations—the shadow relationships that frequently dominate the formal structure of the organization.

Thus by a lengthy and circumspect route, man has been led through the back door and readmitted to respectability. It is convenient to exile man from the science of public administration; it is simpler to forget man and write with "scientific" precision than to remember him and be cursed with his maddening unpredictability. Yet his exclusion is certain to make the study of public administration sterile, unrewarding, and essentially unreal.

If there is ever to be a science of public administration it must derive from an understanding of man's behavior in the area marked off by the boundaries of public administration. This area, to be sure, can never be clearly separated from man's behavior in other fields; all the social sciences are interdependent and all are limited by the basic lack of understanding of man's motivations and responses. Yet the ground of peculiar concern for a prospective science of public administration is that broad region of services administered by the government; until the manifold motivations and actions in this broad region have been explored and rendered predictable, there can be no science of public administration.

It is easier to define this area in space than in depth. One can arbitrarily restrict the prospective science of public administration to a certain region of human activity; but one cannot say with certainty how deeply one must mine this region in order to uncover its secrets. Does concern with human behavior mean that the researcher in public administration must be a psychiatrist and a sociologist? Or does it mean rather that in plumbing human behavior the researcher must be capable of using the investigations of the psychiatrist and sociologist? The need for specialization—a need, incidentally, which science itself seems to impose on human inquiry—suggests that the latter alternative must be the pragmatic answer.

Development of a science of public administration implies the development of a science of man in the area of services administered by the public. No such development can be brought about merely by the constantly reiterated assertion that public administration is already a science. We cannot achieve a science by creating in a mechanized "administrative man" a modern descendant of the eighteenth century's rational man, whose only existence is in books on public administration and whose only activity is strict obedience to "universal laws of the science of administration."

PUBLIC ADMINISTRATION AND THE SOCIAL SETTING

If we know precious little about "administrative man" as an individual, perhaps we know even less about him as a social animal. Yet we cannot afford to ignore the relationship between public administration and its social setting.

No anthropologist would suggest that a social principle drawn from one distinct culture is likely to be transmitted unchanged to another culture; Ruth Benedict's descriptions of the Pueblo Indians of Zuñi, the Melanesians of Dobu, and the Kwakiutl Indians of Vancouver Island leave little doubt that cultures can be integrated on such distinctly different lines as to be almost noncomparable.[21] If the nation-states of western civilization by no means possess such wholly contrasting cultures as the natives of Zuñi, Dobu, and Vancouver Island, nevertheless few political scientists would contend that a principle of political organization drawn from one nation could be adopted with equal success by another; one would scarcely argue that federalism has everywhere the same utility or that the unitary state would be equally viable in Britain and the United States or that the American presidential system would operate unchanged in France or Germany.

There should be no reason for supposing, then, that a principle of public administration has equal validity in every nation-state, or that successful public administration practices in one country will necessarily prove successful in a different social, economic, and political environment. A particular nation-state embodies the results of many historical episodes, traumas, failures, and successes which have in turn created peculiar habits, mores, institutionalized patterns of behaviour, *Weltanschauungen*, and even "national psychologies."[22] One cannot assume that public administration can escape the effects of this conditioning; or that it is somehow independent of and isolated from the culture or social setting in which it develops. At the same time, as value can be gained by a comparative study of government based upon a due respect for differences in the political, social, and economic environment of nation-states, so too the comparative study of public administration ought to be rewarding. Yet the comparative aspects of public administration have largely been ignored; and as long as the study of public administration is not comparative, claims for "a science of public administration" sound rather hollow. Conceivably there might be a science of American public administration and a science of British public administration and a science of French public administration; but can there be "a science of public administration" in the sense of a body of generalized principles independent of their peculiar national setting?

Today we stand in almost total ignorance of the relationship between "principles of public administration" and their general setting. Can it be safely affirmed, on the basis of existing knowledge of comparative public administration, that there are *any* principles independent of their special environment?

The discussion over an administrative class in the civil service furnishes a useful example of the difficulties of any approach that does not rest on a thorough examination of developmental and environmental differences. The manifest benefits and merits of the British administrative class have sometimes led

American students of public administration to suggest the development of an administrative class in the American civil service; but proposals of this kind have rarely depended on a thorough comparison of the historical factors that made the administrative class a successful achievement in Britain, and may or may not be duplicated here. Thus Wilmerding has virtually proposed the transfer to the United States of all the detailed elements in the British civil service; although he does not explicitly base his proposals on British experience except in a few instances, they follow British practices with almost complete fidelity.[23]

White has likewise argued for the creation of an "administrative corps" along the lines of the British administrative class. He has suggested that reform of the civil service in Britain and creation of an administrative class were accomplished in little more than two generations; profiting by British experience, he argues, we ought to be able to accomplish such a reform in even shorter time.[24]

Since the question of an administrative class is perhaps the outstanding case where American writers on public administration have employed the comparative method to the extent of borrowing from foreign experience, it is worthy of a brief analysis to uncover some of the problems of a comparative "science of public administration." For it throws into stark perspective the fundamental difficulties of drawing universal conclusions from the institutions of any one country, and at the same time sharply outlines the correlative problem of comparing the institutions of several nations in order to derive general principles out of the greater range of experiences.

The central difficulty of universal generalizations may be indicated in this way: An administrative class based on merit rests upon four conditions. All of these prerequisites were present coincidentally in Britain in the mid-nineteenth century; and none of them is present in quite the same way here.

First of all, an administrative class of the British type rests upon a general political acceptance of the hierarchical idea. This acceptance in Britain was not the product of forty years; it was the outcome of four centuries. It is not too much to say that it was the four centuries during which the public service was the particular prerogative of the upper classes that made a hierarchical civil service structure feasible in Britain. The Tudor monarchy had rested upon a combination of crown power administered under the King by representatives of the upper middle and professional classes in the towns and newly created members of the gentry in the country; Tudor authority was in effect derived from an alliance of King and upper middle classes against the aristocracy. From the Revolution of 1688 until 1832, public service was the special domain of an increasingly functionless aristocracy whose monopoly of public office was tacitly supported by the upper middle classes of the cities. Whatever the Reform Bill of 1832 accomplished in terms of placing the urban oligarchy overtly in office, no one in Britain had many illusions that a change in the hierarchical structure of politics and public service was entailed. The upper middle classes were no more keen than were the landed gentry of the eighteenth century to throw open the doors of public service and politics to "the rabble."

Out of this long historic background the idea of an administrative class emerged. The unspoken political premises of the dominant groups in the nation reflected an acceptance of hierarchy in the social, economic, and political structure of Britain; the contention, common in the American scene, that an administrative class is "undemocratic" played no real part in mid-nineteenth century Britain. One may well question whether it would be so easy to create an administrative class in any society, like the American, where egalitarianism is so firmly rooted as a political dogma; however desirable such a class may be, and however little it may actually violate the democratic ideal, one is entitled to doubt that the overt creation of an administrative elite is a practical possibility in American politics.[25] In any case, the idea must be fitted into the peculiar mores and the special ethos of the United States, and cannot be lightly transferred from Britain to this country.[26]

Second, the administrative class idea rests upon a scholastic system that creates the educated nonspecialist, and a recruiting system that selects him. Too often, the proposal has been made to recruit persons of general rather than specialized training for an "administrative corps" without solving the prior problem of producing such "generalists" in the universities. The British public school system and the universities have long been dominated by the ideal of the educated gentleman; and for centuries they have succeeded admirably in producing the "generalist" mind, even when that mind is nourished on apparently specialized subjects. It is a peculiarly British paradox that persons of high general ability are recruited into the civil service by means of examinations that heavily weight such specialities as classical languages and mathematics. In so far as this country has an educational ideal (a question on which this writer speaks with considerable trepidation), it appears to be, or to have been, the ideal of the specialist. Much more is involved, too, than a question of education; at base the problem is one of social mores that give the specialist a prestige and a social utility that no person of general education is likely to attain. That the recruiting process has been forced to adapt itself to the educational specialization characteristic of American universities (indeed, one might say of American life) is scarcely astonishing. It would be more astonishing if the Civil Service Commission were able to recruit nonexistent "generalists" to perform unrecognized functions within a corps of practitioners where almost everyone regards himself as a subject-matter specialist.[27]

In the third place, the administrative class idea rests upon the acceptance of merit as the criterion of selection. In Britain this acceptance was no mere accident of an inexplicable twenty-year change in public standards of morality. If patronage disappeared in Britain, it was partly because patronage had ceased to have any real function, whereas efficiency had acquired a new social and political utility. Prior to the nineteenth century, patronage had two vital functions: it provided a place for the sons of the aristocracy who were excluded from inheritance by primogeniture; and it placed in the hands of the King and his ministers a device for guaranteeing, under the limited franchise of the eighteenth century, a favorable House of Commons. Both these factors disappeared during the first decades of the nineteenth century. With the expansion of the electorate after 1832, the monarchy was forced to withdraw from politics, or risk the chance of a serious loss of prestige in an electorate that was now too large to control.[28] Meanwhile, the development of dissolution as a power available to the Prime Minister upon his request from the Crown gave the executive a means of party discipline and control far more effective than the promise of office. Finally, the accession to power of the manufacturing and trading classes by the reforms of 1832 placed a new emphasis on efficiency, both as a means of cutting down public expenses and insuring economies in government, and (especially after 1848) of warding off the revolutionary threat that might develop out of governmental incompetence.[29]

All these conditions made possible, and perhaps inevitable, the substitution of merit for patronage. To talk as if reform arose out of some change in public morality, obscure and mysterious in origin but laudable in character, is to miss the whole significance of British reforms. In the present-day politics of the United States, it is not so clear that the utility of patronage has disappeared; under the American system of separation of powers, patronage remains almost as useful as it was under the British constitution of the eighteenth century. And in any case, it is self-evident that the problem here lies in a distinctly different political and social setting from that of Victorian England.

Last, a successful administrative class rests upon the condition that such a group possesses the prestige of an elite; for unless the class has an elite status, it is in a poor position to compete against any other elite for the brains and abilities of the nation. It is one thing to *offer* a career in a merit service; it is quite another to insure that such a service has enough prestige to acquire the best of the nation's competence. The argument that the mere creation of an administrative class would be sufficient to endow that group with prestige in the United States may or may not be valid; it is certainly invalid to argue that this was the causal sequence in Britain. In assessing the ability of the British civil service to recruit the best products of the universities, one can scarcely overlook the profound significance of the fact that for centuries the public service was one of the few careers into which a member of the aristocracy could enter without loss of prestige. Like the church, the army, and politics, and unlike trade and commerce, public service was a profession in which the aristocracy could engage without violating the mores of the class. Even during the eighteenth century and the first half of the nineteenth, when the burden of incompetence and patronage in the public service was at its heaviest, government was a field into which the social elite could enter without a diminution of prestige, and often enough without even a loss in leisure. Throughout the age of patronage, the British public service succeeded in obtaining some of the best of Britain's abilities.[30] The effect of the reforms after 1853 was to make more attractive a profession that already outranked business and industry in prestige values. In Britain, as in Germany, the psychic income accruing from a career in the civil service more than compensates for the smaller economic income. Contrast this with the United States, where since the Civil War prestige has largely accrued to acquisitive successes. It is small wonder that in the United States the problem of government competition with business for the abilities of the community should be much more acute.

If these remarks about the British administrative class are well founded, then these conclusions suggest themselves:

1. Generalizations derived from the operation of public administration in the environment of one nation-state cannot be universalized and applied to public administration in a different environment. A principle *may* be applicable in a different framework. But its applicability can be determined only after a study of that particular framework.

2. There can be no truly universal generalizations about public administration without a profound study of varying national and social characteristics impinging on public administration, to determine what aspects of public administration, if any, are truly independent of the national and social setting. Are there discoverable principles of *universal* validity, or are all principles valid only in terms of a special environment?
3. It follows that the study of public administration inevitably must become a much more broadly based discipline, resting not on a narrowly defined knowledge of techniques and processes, but rather extending to the varying historical, sociological, economic, and other conditioning factors that give public administration its peculiar stamp in each country.

The relation of public administration to its peculiar environment has not been altogether ignored.[31] Unhappily, however, comparative studies are all too infrequent; and at best they provide only the groundwork. We need many more studies of comparative administration before it will be possible to argue that there are any universal principles of public administration.

IN CONCLUSION

We are a long way from a science of public administration. No science of public administration is possible unless: (1) the place of normative values is made clear; (2) the nature of man in the area of public administration is better understood and his conduct is more predictable; and (3) there is a body of comparative studies from which it may be possible to discover principles and generalities that transcend national boundaries and peculiar historical experiences.

NOTES

1. See, for example, F. Merson, "Public Administration: A Science," 1 *Public Administration* 220 (1923); B. W. Walker Watson, "The Elements of Public Administration, A Dogmatic Introduction," 10 *Public Administration* 397 (1932); L. Gulick, "Science, Values and Public Administration," *Papers on the Science of Administration*, ed. by Gulick & Urwick, (Institute of Public Administration, 1937); Cyril Renwick, "Public Administration: Towards a Science," *The Australian Quarterly* (March 1944), p. 73.
2. *Principles of Public Administration* (The Brookings Institution, 1927), Preface, p. ix.
3. See fn. 12, *infra*, for the full quotation and citation.
4. This I take to be Professor Leonard D. White's position. See his "The Meaning of Principles in Public Administration," in *The Meaning of Principles in Public Administration* (University of Chicago Press, 1936), pp. 13–25.
5. *Public Administration* (Farrar & Rinehart, 1937), p. 8.
6. "Administrative Reorganization," 1 *The Journal of Politics* 62–65 (1939).
7. *Op. cit.*, pp. 192–93.
8. *Op. cit.*, p. 193.
9. C. J. Friedrich, "Public Policy and the Nature of Administrative Responsibility," in *Public Policy* (Harvard University Press, 1940); Herman Finer, "Administrative Responsibility in Democratic Government," 1 *Public Administration Review* 335 (1940–41). See also Friedrich's earlier formulation, which touched off the dispute, "Responsible Government Service under the American Constitution," in *Problems of the American Public Service* (McGraw-Hill Book Co., 1935); and Finer's answer to Friedrich in 51 *Political Science Quarterly* 582 (1936).
10. See Aldous Huxley's discussion in *Ends and Means* (Harper & Row, 1937), and Arthur Koestler, *The Yogi and the Commissar* (Macmillan Co., 1945).
11. See Ernest Barker's excellent and useful distinctions between state, government, and administration, in *The Development of Public Services in Western Europe, 1660–1930* (Oxford University Press, 1944). p. 3. Administration "is the sum of persons and bodies who are engaged, under the direction of government, in discharging the ordinary public services which must be rendered daily if the

system of law and duties and rights is to be duly "served." Every right and duty implies a corresponding "service;" and the more the State multiplies rights and duties, the more it multiplies the necessary services of its ministering officials." See also Leon Duguit, *Law in the Modern State* (B. W. Huebsch, 1919), Ch. II.

12. L. Urwick, "Organization as a Technical Problem," *Papers on the Science of Administration*, p. 49. (Italics added.) See also his "Executive Decentralisation with Functional Coordination," 13 *Public Administration* 344 (1935), in which he sets forth "some axioms of organisation," among others that "there are certain principles which govern the association of human beings *for any purpose*, just as there are certain engineering principles which govern the building of a bridge. Such principles should take priority of *all traditional, personal or political considerations*. If they are not observed, co-operation between those concerned will be less effective than it should be in realising the purpose for which they have decided to co-operate. There will be waste of effort." (Italics added.) See also his criticisms of the "practical man fallacy," p. 346.

13. *Ibid.*, p. 85.

14. See John M. Gaus's excellent definitions: "Organization is the arrangement of personnel for facilitating the accomplishment of some agreed purpose through the allocation of functions and responsibilities. It is the relating of efforts and capacities of individuals and groups engaged upon a common task in such a way as to secure the desired objective with the least friction and the most satisfaction to those for whom the task is done and those engaged in the enterprise. . . . Since organization consists of people brought into a certain relationship because of a humanly evolved purpose, it is clear that it should be flexible rather than rigid. There will be constant readjustments necessary because of personalities and other natural forces and because of the unpredicted and unpredictable situations confronted in its operations." "A Theory of Organization in Public Administration," in *The Frontiers of Public Administration*, pp. 66–67.

15. *Psychopathology and Politics* (University of Chicago Press, 1930), Ch. 8 "Political Administrators."

16. L. J. Henderson, T. N. Whitehead, and Elton Mayo, "The Effects of Social Environment," in *Papers on the Science of Administration, op. cit.*, p. 149. It is worth noting that this essay properly interpreted contradicts the implicit assumptions of virtually every other essay in that volume; and it is, incidentally, the only wholly empirical study in the entire volume.

17. Urwick, *op. cit.*, p. 85, and Henderson, *et al.*, p. 155. Urwick has set up a false dilemma that makes his choice more persuasive. Actually, the choice is not between (a) wholly subordinating organizational structure to individual personalities, which obviously might lead to chaos or (b) forcing all personalities into an abstractly correct organizational structure which might (and often does) lead to waste and friction. There is a third choice, (c) employing organizational structure and personalities to the achievement of a purpose. By excluding purpose, Urwick has, in effect, set up organization as an end in *itself*. An army may be organized more efficiently (according to abstract organizational principles) than the political structure of a democratic state, but no one except an authoritarian is likely to contend that it is a *superior* organization—*except for the purposes it is designed to achieve.* Yet once one admits the element of purpose, easy generalizations about organizational principles become difficult if not impossible; and the admission presupposes, particularly in the case of public organizations, a clear statement of ends and purposes.

18. Leonard White, *Introduction to the Study of Public Administration* (Macmillan Co., 1939), p. 38.

19. A. W. Macmahon and J. D. Millett, *Federal Administrators* (Columbia University Press, 1939).

20. Fritz Morstein Marx, ed., *Elements of Public Administration* (Prentice-Hall, 1946), p. 49. (Italics added.)

21. *Patterns of Culture* (Houghton Mifflin Co., 1934).

22. See the fragmentary but revealing discussion on national differences in *Human Nature and Enduring Peace* (Third Yearbook of the Society for the Psychological Study of Social Issues) Gardner Murphy, ed. (Houghton Mifflin, 1945).

23. Lucius Wilmerding, Jr., *Government by Merit* (McGraw-Hill Book Co., 1935).

24. "The British civil service, which the whole world now admires, went through nearly twenty years of transition before its foundations even were properly laid. It went through another twenty years of gradual adjustment before the modern service as we know it today was fully in operation. . . .

In the light of British experience, and by taking advantage of modern knowledge about large-scale organization, we can easily save the twenty years in which the British were experimenting to find the proper basis for their splendid service. We shall, however, need ten years of steady growth, consciously guided and planned, to put a new administrative corps into operation, and probably another ten years before it is completely installed." *Government Career Service* (University of Chicago Press, 1935), p. 8.

25. Significantly, the most recent study of reform of the American civil service states, "We do not recommend the formation of a specially organized administrative corps for which a special type of selection and training is proposed." *Report of President's Committee on Civil Service Improvement* (Government Printing Office, 1941), p. 57. Instead, the Committee recommends that "all positions whose duties are administrative in nature, in grades CAF-11, P-4, and higher . . . be identified as an occupational group within the existing classification structure." This is a noteworthy step in an attempt to achieve the advantages of an administrative class within the framework of American mores and institutions. It is therefore a great advance over the earlier proposal in the Report of the Commission of Inquiry on Public Service Personnel, *Better Government Personnel* (McGraw-Hill Book Co., 1935), which recommended the outright creation of a distinct administrative class (p. 30).

26. This was the essential point, stated in more specific terms, of Lewis Meriam's criticism of the administrative corps idea. See his excellent *Public Service and Special Training* (University of Chicago Press, 1936).

27. It is noteworthy that the latest U.S. Civil Service Commission announcement for the junior professional assistant examination (November, 1946) follows the subject-matter specialist concept; junior professional assistants will be recruited in terms of specialities unthinkable in the British administrative class examinations for university graduates. See, by comparison, *Specimen Question Papers for the Reconstruction Competition for Recruitment to (1) The Administrative Class of the Home Civil Service, (2) The Senior Branch of the Foreign Service,* (C.S.C. 18) (H. M. Stationery Office 1946).

28. See D. Lindsay Keir, *The Constitutional History of Modern Britain 1485–1937* (A. & C. Black, 1943), p. 405.

29. See J. Donald Kingsley, *Representative Bureaucracy, An Interpretation of the British Civil Service* (Antioch Press, 1944), Ch. III.

30. Hiram Stout, *Public Service in Great Britain* (University of North Carolina Press, 1938), pp. 25–26, 82–83.

31. See, for example, Walter Dorn, "The Prussian Bureaucracy in the Eighteenth Century," 46 *Political Science Quarterly* 403–23 (1931) and 47 *Ibid.*, 75–94, 259–73 (1932); Fritz Morstein Marx, "Civil Service in Germany," in *Civil Service Abroad* (McGraw-Hill Book Co., 1935); John M. Gaus, "American Society and Public Administration," *The Frontiers of Public Administration* (University of Chicago Press, 1936).

20
The Cooptative Mechanism

Philip Selznick

To risk a definition: *cooptation is the process of absorbing new elements into the leadership or policy determining structure of an organization as a means of averting threats to its stability or existence.* With the help of this concept we are enabled more closely and more rigorously to specify the relation between TVA and some important local institutions and thus uncover an important aspect of the real meaning and significance of the Authority's grass-roots policy. At the same time, it is clear that the idea of cooptation plunges us into the field of bureaucratic behavior as that is related to such democratic ideals as "local participation."

Cooptation tells us something about the process by which an institutional environment impinges itself upon an organization and effects changes in its leadership, structure, or policy. Cooptation may be formal or informal, depending upon the specific problem to be solved.

Formal Cooptation. When there is a need for the organization to publicly absorb new elements, we shall speak of formal cooptation. This involves the establishment of openly avowed and formally ordered relationships. Appointments to official posts are made, contracts are signed, new organizations are established—all signifying participation in the process of decision and administration. There are two general conditions which lead an organization to resort to formal cooptation, though they are closely related:

1. When the legitimacy of the authority of a governing group or agency is called into question. Every group or organization which attempts to exercise control must also attempt to win the consent of the governed. Coercion may be utilized at strategic points, but it is not effective as an enduring instrument. One means of winning consent is to coopt into the leadership or organization elements which in some way reflect the sentiment or possess the confidence of the relevant public or mass and which will lend respectability or legitimacy to the organs of control and thus reestablish the stability of formal authority. This device is widely used, and in many different contexts. It is met in colonial countries, where the organs of alien control reaffirm their legitimacy by coopting native leaders into the colonial administration. We find it in the phenomenon of "crisis-patriotism" wherein normally disfranchised groups are temporarily given representation in the councils of government in order to win their solidarity in a time of national stress. Cooptation has been considered by the United States Army in its study of proposals to give enlisted personnel representation in the courts-martial machinery—a clearly adaptive response to stresses

Source: Philip Selznick, *TVA and the Grass Roots* (Berkeley: University of California Press, 1949), pp. 13–16, 219–226. Footnotes renumbered.

made explicit during World War II. The "unity" parties of totalitarian states are another form of cooptation; company unions or some employee representation plans in industry are still another. In each of these examples, the response of formal authority (private or public, in a large organization or a small one) is an attempt to correct a state of imbalance by formal measures. It will be noted, moreover, that what is shared is the responsibility for power rather than power itself.

2. When the need to invite participation is essentially administrative, that is, when the requirements of ordering the activities of a large organization or state make it advisable to establish the forms of self-government. The problem here is not one of decentralizing decision but rather of establishing orderly and reliable mechanisms for reaching a client public or citizenry. This is the "constructive" function of trade unions in great industries where the unions become effective instruments for the elimination of absenteeism or the attainment of other efficiency objectives. This is the function of self-government committees in housing projects or concentration camps, as they become reliable channels for the transmission of managerial directives. Usually, such devices also function to share responsibility and thus to bolster the legitimacy of established authority. Thus any given act of formal cooptation will tend to fulfill both the political function of defending legitimacy and the administrative function of establishing reliable channels for communication and direction.

In general, the use of formal cooptation by a leadership does not envision the transfer of actual power. The forms of participation are emphasized but action is channeled so as to fulfill the administrative functions while preserving the locus of significant decision in the hands of the initiating group. The concept of formal cooptation will be utilized primarily in the analysis of TVA's relation to the voluntary associations established to gain local participation in the administration of the Authority's programs.

Informal Cooptation. Cooptation may be, however, a response to the pressure of specific centers of power within the community. This is not primarily a matter of the sense of legitimacy or of a general and diffuse lack of confidence. Legitimacy and confidence may be well established with relation to the general public, yet organized forces which are able to threaten the formal authority may effectively shape its structure and policy. The organization faced with its institutional environment, or the leadership faced with its ranks, must take into account these outside elements. They may be brought into the leadership or policy-determining structure, may be given a place as a recognition of and concession to the resources they can independently command. The representation of interests through administrative constituencies is a typical example of this process. Or, within an organization, individuals upon whom the group is dependent for funds or other resources may insist upon and receive a share in the determination of policy. This type of cooptation is typically expressed in informal terms, for the problem is not one of responding to a state of imbalance with respect to the "people as a whole" but rather one of meeting the pressure of specific individuals or interest groups which are in a position to enforce demands. The latter are interested in the substance of power and not necessarily in its forms. Moreover, an open acknowledgment of capitulation to specific interests may itself undermine the sense of legitimacy of the formal authority within the community. Consequently, there is a positive pressure to refrain from explicit recognition of the relationship established. This concept will be utilized in analyzing the underlying meaning of certain formal methods of cooperation initiated in line with the TVA's grass-roots policy.

Cooptation reflects a state of tension between formal authority and social power. This authority is always embodied in a particular structure and leadership, but social power itself has to do with subjective and objective factors which control the loyalties and potential manipulability of the community. Where the formal authority or leadership reflects real social power, its stability is assured. On the other hand, when it becomes divorced from the sources of social power its continued existence is threatened. This threat may arise from the sheer alienation of sentiment or because other leaderships control the sources of social power. Where a leadership has been accustomed to the assumption that its constituents respond to it as individuals, there may be a rude awakening when organization of those constituents creates nucleuses of strength which are able to effectively demand a sharing of power.

The significance of cooptation for organizational analysis is not simply that there is a change in or a broadening of leadership, and that this is an adaptive response, but also *that this change is consequential for the character and role of the organization or governing body.* Cooptation results in some constriction of the field of choice available to the organization or leadership in question. The character of the coopted elements will necessarily shape the modes of action available to the group which has won adaptation at the price of commitment to outside elements. In other words, if it is true that the TVA has, whether as a defensive or as an idealistic measure, absorbed local elements into its policy-determining structure, we should expect to find that this process has had an effect upon the evolving character of the Authority itself. From the viewpoint of the initiators of the project, and of its public supporters, the force and direction of this effect may be completely unanticipated.

The important consideration is that the TVA's choice of methods could not be expected to be free of the normal dilemmas of action. If the sentiment of the people (or its organized expression) is conservative, democratic forms may require a blunting of social purpose. A perception of the details of this tendency is all important for the attempt to bind together planning and democracy. Planning is always positive—for the fulfillment of some program,—but democracy may negate its execution. This dilemma requires an understanding of the possible unanticipated consequences which may ensue when positive social policy is coupled with a commitment to democratic procedure. . . . [Pages 17–218 of original have been omitted; text continues with page 219.]

The use of voluntary associations is not new, and is far from unique or peculiar to the program or administration of the Tennessee Valley Authority.[1] Indeed, it is useful to think of the cooptation of citizens into an administrative apparatus as a general response made by governments to what has been called "the fundamental democratization" of society.[2] The rise of the mass man,[3] or at least the increasing need for governments to take into account and attempt to manipulate the sentiments of the common man, has resulted in the development of new methods of control. These new methods center about attempts to organize the mass, to change an undifferentiated and unreliable citizenry into a structured, readily accessible public. Accessibility for administrative purposes seems to lead rather easily to control for the same or broader purposes. Consequently, there seems to be a continuum between the voluntary associations set up by the democratic (mass) state—such as committees of farmers to boost or control agricultural production—and the citizens' associations of the totalitarian (mass) state. Indeed, the devices of corporatism emerge as relatively effective responses to the need to deal with the mass, and in time of war the administrative techniques of avowedly democratic countries and avowedly totalitarian countries tend to converge.

Democracy in administration rests upon the idea of broadening participation. Let the citizen take a hand in the working of his government, give him a chance to help administer the programs of the positive state. At its extreme, this concept of democracy comes to be applied to such structures as conscript armies, which are thought to be democratic if they include all classes of the population on an equal basis. If analysis and appraisal is to be significant, however, it is necessary to inquire into the concrete meaning of such an unanalyzed abstraction as "participation." In doing so, we shall have to distinguish between substantive participation, involving an actual role in the determination of policy, and mere administrative involvement. In the conscript army, we have a broadening involvement of citizens, with a concomitant abdication of power. The same may be said of the Japanese *tonari gumi*, neighborhood associations which helped to administer rationing and other wartime programs. Such organizations, which have had their counterparts in many parts of the world, involve the local citizens, but primarily for the convenience of the administration. It is easy enough for administrative imperatives which call for decentralization to be given a halo; that becomes especially useful in countries which prize the symbols of democracy. But a critical analysis cannot overlook that pattern which simply transforms an unorganized citizenry into a reliable instrument for the achievement of administrative goals, and calls it "democracy."[4]

The tendency for participation to become equivalent to involvement has a strong rationale. In many cases, perhaps in most, the initiation of local citizens' associations comes from the top, and is tied to the pressing problem of administering a program. The need for uniformity in structure; for a channel through which directives, information, and reports will be readily disseminated; for the stimulation of a normally apathetic clientele; and for the swift dispatch of accumulated tasks—these and other imperatives are met with reasonable adequacy when involvement alone has been achieved. Some additional impetus, not provided for in the usual responsibilities of the administrative agency, is normally required if the process is to be pushed beyond the level of involvement. Indeed, it is doubtful that much can be achieved beyond that level. Such associations, voluntary or compulsory,[5] are commonly established *ad hoc*, sponsored by some particular agency.[6] That agency is charged with a set of program responsibilities. These cannot be readily changed, nor can they be effectively delegated. As an administrative organization, the agency cannot abandon the necessity for unity of command and continuity of policy—not only over time but down the hierarchy as well. What, therefore, can be the role of the coopted local association or committee? It cannot become an effective part of the major policy-determining structure of the agency.[7] In practice only a limited sphere of decision is permitted, involving some adaptation of general directives to local conditions, and within that circumscribed sphere the responsible (usually paid) officials of the agency will play an effective part.

With these general considerations in mind, it may be well to mention at least one phase of the historical context within which the TVA's use of voluntary associations has developed. Especially in the field of agricultural administration, the TVA's methods have paralleled an emerging trend in the administration of the federal government. This is not often recognized within the Authority, but there can be little doubt that the United States Department of Agriculture has gone much farther in developing both the theory and the practice of citizen participation than has the TVA. The emergence of this trend accompanied the construction of a vast apparatus to administer an action program reaching virtually every farmer in the nation.

One formulation of the idea of "agricultural democracy" was undertaken in 1940 by M. L. Wilson, Director of Extension Work of the Department of Agriculture.[8] Wilson noted the movement toward a greater group interest on the part of farmers, and the pressure for equality through government intervention, culminating in the enactment of the Agricultural Adjustment Act of 1933 and subsequent New Deal agricultural legislation. The administration of the new government programs was based on the ideal of cooperation and voluntary participation, leading to a set of procedures which, in Wilson's view, can be thought of as the general principles of agricultural democracy:

1. Decentralized administration in varying degrees through community, county, and state farmer committees, elected by cooperating farmers or appointed by the Secretary of Agriculture.
2. The use of referendums in determining certain administrative policies, especially those having to do with quotas, penalties, and marketing agreements.
3. The use of group discussion and other adult education techniques as a means of promoting understanding of the problems and procedures involved in administration of the various programs and referendums.
4. Cooperative planning in program formulation and localization of programs.[9]

This program emphasizes the importance of participation within the democratic pattern of culture. Moreover, in theory, participation includes both policy forming and administrative functions.

The technique of coopting local citizens through voluntary associations and as individuals into the administration of various agricultural programs was widely developed during the nineteen-thirties. In 1940, it was reported that over 890,000 citizens were helping to plan and operate nine rural action programs:[10] community, county, and state committees of the Agricultural Adjustment Administration, operating through over 3,000 county agricultural associations; land-use planning committees organized through the Bureau of Agricultural Economics; farmer associations aiding in the administration of Farm Credit Administration loans; rehabilitation and tenant-purchase committees organized by the Farm Security Administration; local district advisory boards for the Grazing Service; cooperatives dealing with the Rural Electrification Administration; governing boards of soil conservation districts serviced by Soil Conservation Service; these together form an administrative pattern of which the TVA ventures along this line were only a part. . . .

The trend toward cooptation of farmers in the administration of a national agricultural program reached a high point with the organization of the county land-use planning program in 1938. The idea of democratic planning with farmer participation was given considerable attention, and an attempt was made to construct a hierarchy of representative committees which would embody the democratic ideal.[11] At the same time, the achievement of a primary administrative objective was envisioned. The land-use planning organization program received its impetus from a conference of representatives of the Department of Agriculture and the Association of Land-Grant Colleges and Universities held at Mt. Weather, Virginia, in July, 1938. The Mt. Weather Agreement[12] recommended a system of coordinated land-use planning to overcome the confusion created by the existence of a large number of points of contact between governmental agencies and local farmers. By providing that local officials of the national agricultural agencies would be represented on the farmer committees, it was felt that a single point of contact would be established. It is possible that the land-use planning system would have been established without this impetus from a pressing administrative imperative, but it is clear that the latter was the occasion for the new organization. The problems of the officialdom were primary, and logically so, for their responsibilities had to do with the efficient execution of statutory programs—not the creation of new culture patterns. The latter might, time and resources permitting, have become an effective collateral objective, but it would be idle to suppose that the requirements of administration would not assume priority within the system.

The cooptative construction of systems of voluntary associations fulfills important administrative needs. These are general, and include:

1. The achievement of ready accessibility, which requires the establishment of routine and reliable channels through which information, aid, and requests may be brought to segments of the population. The committee device permits the assembling of leading elements on a regular basis, so that top levels of administration may have reason to anticipate that quota assignments will be fulfilled; and the local organization provides an administrative focus in terms of which the various line divisions may be coordinated in the field.
2. As the program increases in intensity it becomes necessary for the lower end of administration to be some sort of group rather than the individual citizen. A group-oriented local official may reach a far larger number of people by working through community and county organizations than by attempting to approach his constituency as individuals. Thus the voluntary association permits the official to make use of untapped administrative resources.
3. Administration may be decentralized so that the execution of a broad policy is adapted to local conditions by utilizing the special knowledge of local citizens; it is not normally anticipated, however, that the policy itself will be placed in jeopardy.
4. The sharing of responsibility, so that local citizens, through the voluntary associations or committees, may become identified with and committed to the program—and, ideally, to the apparatus—of the operating agency.

These needs define the relevance of the voluntary-association device to the organizational problems of those who make use of it. It is only as fulfilling such needs as these that the continuity—in both structure and function—of this type of cooptation under democratic and totalitarian sponsorship can be understood.

From the above it is not surprising that criticisms of the county planning program have stressed deviations from the democratic ideal, particularly in lack of representativeness and the tendency for established organizations such as the Farm Bureau to take control of the local committees.[13] Insofar, however, as this represents criticism of a program developing toward complete fulfillment of the ideal, it is not basic. More significant for this analysis are such criticisms as the following:

> . . . it is the central thesis of this paper that county planning did not succeed because no desire to solve community and county problems was created in the population of the area in which the county planning program was to function. . . . Most administrators of county planning conceive of rural planning as another administrative problem, as a procedure.[14]

The normal pattern—perhaps inevitable because of the rapid creation of a nationally ramified system of committees—established an organization set down from above, oriented toward the administration of the national program. As a consequence, the problems of the local official *qua* official assumed priority. "One needed only to talk with representatives of the several agencies engaged in trying to "enforce" the county planning system to recognize how ubiquitous this condition [of apathy] was."[15] To the extent that the problems of the officialdom are sufficiently pressing to stamp the character of the organization, it may be expected that involvement rather than meaningful participation will prevail. This same point is made in another way by John D. Lewis, in tracing one of the bases for the lack of complete representativeness.

> The pressure to "get things done" has tended to encourage appointment rather than election. The Division in Washington naturally expects its field agents to report results that will justify the high hope with which the program was launched, and the state office in turn pushes the county agents for progress reports with which to appease Washington administrators. Democratic procedure is notoriously slow procedure. Consequently the first thought of an overworked county agent, unless he is genuinely impressed by the importance of finding a truly democratic committee, will be to find a group of industrious and cooperative farmers who can be depended upon to work together harmoniously. With the best of intentions and with no thought of deliberately stacking the committee, he may set up a committee of "outstanding leaders" who have a sincere desire to act in the interest of the whole county, but who have only a second-hand knowledge and indirect concern about the problems of less successful farmers in the county.[16]

In effect, those responsible for organizing the system of committees or associations are under pressure to shape their actions according to exigencies of the moment, and those exigencies have to do primarily with the needs of administration. As the needs of administration become dominant, the tendency for democratic participation to be reduced to mere involvement may be expected to increase. At the extreme, the democratic element drops out and the cooptative character of the organizational devices employed becomes identified with their entire meaning.[17]

NOTES

1. Perhaps as testimony to the effectiveness with which the grass-roots doctrine is circulated within the TVA, there appears to have developed a feeling that the Authority has somehow originated a unique administrative device, binding the agency to its client public in some special way. This is partly referrable to enthusiasm, partly to the prevalent idea that other federal agencies, lacking the halo of regional decentralization, are unlikely to be really interested in democratic administration. It is hardly necessary to enter that controversy here, or to lay undue emphasis upon it. Yet although the grass-roots method is considered one of the major collateral objectives

of the Authority, relatively little attention has been paid to the mechanics of its implementation and certainly the experience of other organizations facing the same problems and using voluntary associations has not been seriously studied inside the Authority.

2. Karl Mannheim, *Man and Society in an Age of Reconstruction* (New York: Harcourt, Brace, 1941), pp. 44 ff.

3. See Jose Ortega y Gasset, *The Revolt of the Masses* (New York: Norton, 1932).

4. This is no necessary reflection on the integrity or the intentions of the responsible leadership. It is normal for programs infused with a moral content to be reduced to those elements of the program which are relevant to action. Thus the moral ideal of socialism has been reduced rather easily to concrete objectives, such as nationalization of industry. Administrative objectives, such as the establishment of a ramified system of citizens' committees, are similar.

5. This distinction tends to melt away as the program administered comes closer to becoming an exclusive means of distributing the necessities of life, or if inducements are such as to eliminate any practical alternatives to participation.

6. This may be the effective situation, even where there is not legal sponsorship. Thus, the local soil conservation districts are creatures of the state legislatures, but serviced by the Department of Agriculture's Soil Conservation Service. It is probably not inappropriately that they have been known in some areas as "SCS" districts.

7. This might happen if the local groups formed an independent central organization, but that is not envisioned by the administrative agency, unless it already has control of a preexisting central organization, as when a national government utilizes a preexisting party structure to aid in the administration of its program.

8. "A Theory of Agricultural Democracy," an address before the American Political Science Association, Chicago, December 28, 1940. Published as Extension Service Circular 355, March, 1941 (mim.). See also M. L. Wilson, *Democracy Has Roots* (New York: Carrick & Evans, 1939), chap. vii. Also, Howard R. Tolley, *The Farmer Citizen at War* (New York: The Macmillan Co., 1943), Pt. V.

9. Wilson, "A Theory of Agricultural Democracy," p. 5. It is interesting to note that Mr. Wilson, Director of Extension Work, considered the AAA program to have represented the practical beginning of agricultural democracy. The TVA agriculturists, loyal essentially to the local extension service organizations, would not have made such a statement.

10. Carleton R. Ball, "Citizens Help Plan and Operate Action Programs," *Land Policy Review* (March-April, 1940), p. 19.

11. See "The Land Use Planning Organization," County Planning Series No. 3, Bureau of Agricultural Economics, May, 1940; also, *Land Use Planning Under Way*, prepared by the BAE in cooperation with the Extension Service, FSA, SCA, AAA, and Forest Service, USDA, Washington, July, 1940; and John M. Gaus and Leon O. Wolcott, *Public Administration and the U.S. Department of Agriculture* (Chicago: Public Administration Service, 1940), pp. 151 ff.

12. Reprinted as an appendix to Gaus and Wolcott, *op. cit.* Russell Lord (*The Agrarian Revival*, p. 193) notes extension service references to this agreement as "The Truce of Mt. Weather." Truce indeed, for by the middle of 1942 the Congress had scuttled the program, with the support of the American Farm Bureau Federation. See Charles M. Hardin, "The Bureau of Agricultural Economics Under Fire: A Study in Valuation Conflicts," *Journal of Farm Economics*, Vol. 28 (August, 1946).

13. See John D. Lewis, "Democratic Planning in Agriculture," *American Political Science Review*, XXXV (April and June, 1941); also Neal C. Gross, "A Post Mortem on County Planning," *Journal of Farm Economics*, XXV (August, 1943); and Bryce Ryan, "Democratic Telesis and County Agricultural Planning," *Journal of Farm Economics*, XXII (November, 1940).

14. Gross, p. 647.

15. *Ibid.*, p. 653. Mr. Gross also points out that the units of planning tended to follow the convenience of the administrators, rather than local interest patterns.

16. Lewis, *op. cit.*, p. 247.

17. Unless "democracy" is reinterpreted, so that it reaches a higher level with the subordination of the mass to the organization. The above account, one sided in its emphasis, in no way deprecates the democratic aims of the initiators of the planning program. We are concerned here only with the explication of underlying trends to which the concept of cooptation lends significance.

21
Power and Administration
Norton E. Long

I

There is no more forlorn spectacle in the administrative world than an agency and a program possessed of statutory life, armed with executive orders, sustained in the courts, yet stricken with paralysis and deprived of power. An object of contempt to its enemies and of despair to its friends.

The lifeblood of administration is power. Its attainment, maintenance, increase, dissipation, and loss are subjects the practitioner and student can ill afford to neglect. Loss of realism and failure are almost certain consequences. This is not to deny that important parts of public administration are so deeply entrenched in the habits of the community, so firmly supported by the public, or so clearly necessary as to be able to take their power base for granted and concentrate on the purely professional side of their problems. But even these islands of the blessed are not immune from the plague of politics, as witness the fate of the hapless Bureau of Labor Statistics and the perennial menace of the blind 5 percent across-the-board budget cut. Perhaps Carlyle's aphorism holds here, "The healthy know not of their health but only the sick." To stay healthy one needs to recognize that health is a fruit, not a birthright. Power is only one of the considerations that must be weighed in administration, but of all it is the most overlooked in theory and the most dangerous to overlook in practice.

The power resources of an administrator of an agency are not disclosed by a legal search of titles and court decisions or by examining appropriations or budgetary allotments. Legal authority and a treasury balance are necessary but politically insufficient bases of administration. Administrative rationality requires a critical evaluation of the whole range of complex and shifting forces on whose support, acquiescence, or temporary impotence the power to act depends.

Analysis of the sources from which power is derived and the limitations they impose is as much a dictate of prudent administration as sound budgetary procedure. The bankruptcy that comes from an unbalanced power budget has consequences far more disastrous than the necessity of seeking a deficiency appropriation. The budgeting of power is a basic subject matter of a realistic science of administration.

It may be urged that for all but the top hierarchy of the administrative structure the question of power is irrelevant. Legislative authority and administrative orders suffice. Power adequate to the function to be performed flows down the chain of command. Neither statute nor executive order, however, confers more than legal authority to act.

Source: From *Public Administration Review* 9 (Autumn 1949), pp. 257–264.

Whether Congress or President can impart the substance of power as well as the form depends upon the lineup of forces in the particular case. A price control law wrung from a reluctant Congress by an amorphous and unstable combination of consumer and labor groups is formally the same as a law enacting a support price program for agriculture backed by the disciplined organizations of farmers and their congressmen. The differences for the scope and effectiveness of administration are obvious. The Presidency, like Congress, responds to and translates the pressures that play upon it. The real mandate contained in an Executive order varies with the political strength of the group demand embodied in it, and in the context of other group demands.

Both Congress and President do focus the general political energies of the community and so are considerably more than mere means for transmitting organized pressures. Yet power is not concentrated by the structure of government or politics into the hands of a leadership with a capacity to budget it among a diverse set of administrative activities. A picture of the Presidency as a reservoir of authority from which the lower echelons of administration draw life and vigor is an idealized distortion of reality.

A similar criticism applies to any like claim for an agency head in his agency. Only in varying degrees can the powers of subordinate officials be explained as resulting from the chain of command. Rarely is such an explanation a satisfactory account of the sources of power.

To deny that power is derived exclusively from superiors in the hierarchy is to assert that subordinates stand in a feudal relation in which to a degree they fend for themselves and acquire support peculiarly their own. A structure of interests friendly or hostile, vague and general or compact and well defined, encloses each significant center of administrative discretion. This structure is an important determinant of the scope of possible action. As a source of power and authority it is a competitor of the formal hierarchy.

Not only does political power flow in from the sides of an organization, as it were; it also flows up the organization to the center from the constituent parts. When the staff of the Office of War Mobilization and Reconversion advised a hard-pressed agency to go out and get itself some popular support so that the President could afford to support it, their action reflected the realities of power rather than political cynicism.

It is clear that the American system of politics does not generate enough power at any focal point of leadership to provide the conditions for an even partially successful divorce of politics from administration. Subordinates cannot depend on the formal chain of command to deliver enough political power to permit them to do their jobs. Accordingly they must supplement the resources available through the hierarchy with those they can muster on their own, or accept the consequences in frustration—a course itself not without danger. Administrative rationality demands that objectives be determined and sights set in conformity with a realistic appraisal of power position and potential.

II

The theory of administration has neglected the problem of the sources and adequacy of power, in all probability because of a distaste for the disorderliness of American political life and a belief that this disorderliness is transitory. An idealized picture of the British parliamentary system as a Platonic form to be realized or approximated has exerted a baneful fascination in the field. The majority party with a mandate at the polls and a firmly seated leadership in the Cabinet seems to solve adequately the problem of the supply of power necessary to permit administration to concentrate on the fulfillment of accepted objectives. It is a commonplace that the American party system provides neither a mandate for a platform nor a mandate for a leadership.

Accordingly, the election over, its political meaning must be explored by the diverse leaders in the executive and legislative branches. Since the parties have failed to discuss issues, mobilize majorities in their terms, and create a working political consensus on measures to be carried out, the task is left for others—most prominently the agencies concerned. Legislation passed and powers granted are frequently politically premature. Thus the Council of Economic Advisers was given legislative birth before political acceptance of its functions existed. The agencies to which tasks are assigned must devote themselves to the creation of an adequate consensus to permit administration. The mandate that the parties do not supply must be attained through public relations and the mobilization of group support. Pendleton Herring and others have shown just how vital this support is for agency action.

The theory that agencies should confine themselves to communicating policy suggestions to executive and legislature, and refrain from appealing to their clientele and the public, neglects the failure of the parties to provide either a clear-cut decision as to what they should do or an adequately mobilized political support for a course of action. The bureaucracy under the American political system has a large share of responsibility for the public promotion of policy and even more in organizing the political basis for its survival and growth. It is generally recognized that the agencies have a special competence in the technical aspects of their fields which of necessity gives them a rightful policy initiative. In addition, they have or develop a shrewd understanding of the politically feasible in the group structure within which they work. Above all, in the eyes of their supporters and their enemies they represent the institutionalized embodiment of policy, an enduring organization actually or potentially capable of mobilizing power behind policy. The survival interests and creative drives of administrative organizations combine with clientele pressures to compel such mobilization. The party system provides no enduring institutional representation for group interest at all comparable to that of the bureaus of the Department of Agriculture. Even the subject matter committees of Congress function in the shadow of agency permanency.

The bureaucracy is recognized by all interested groups as a major channel of representation to such an extent that Congress rightly feels the competition of a rival. The weakness in party structure both permits and makes necessary the present dimensions of the political activities of the administrative branch—permits because it fails to protect administration from pressures and fails to provide adequate direction and support, makes necessary because it fails to develop a consensus on a leadership and a program that makes possible administration on the basis of accepted decisional premises.

Agencies and bureaus more or less perforce are in the business of building, maintaining, and increasing their political support. They lead and in large part are led by the diverse groups whose influence sustains them. Frequently they lead and are themselves led in conflicting directions. This is not due to a dull-witted incapacity to see the contradictions in their behavior but is an almost inevitable result of the contradictory nature of their support.

Herbert Simon has shown that administrative rationality depends on the establishment of uniform value premises in the decisional centers of organization. Unfortunately, the value premises of those forming vital elements of political support are often far from uniform. These elements are in Barnard's and Simon's sense "customers" of the organization and therefore parts of the organization whose wishes are clothed with a very real authority. A major and most time-consuming aspect of administration consists of the wide range of activities designed to secure enough "customer" acceptance to survive and, if fortunate, develop a consensus adequate to program formulation and execution.

To varying degrees, dependent on the breadth of acceptance of their programs, officials at every level of significant discretion must make their estimates of the situation, take stock of their resources, and plan accordingly. A keen appreciation of the real components of their organization is the beginning of wisdom. These components will be found to stretch far beyond the government payroll. Within the government they will encompass Congress, congressmen, committees, courts, other agencies, presidential advisers, and the President. The Aristotelian analysis of constitutions is equally applicable and equally necessary to an understanding of administrative organization.

The broad alliance of conflicting groups that makes up presidential majorities scarcely coheres about any definite pattern of objectives, nor has it by the alchemy of the party system had its collective power concentrated in an accepted leadership with a personal mandate. The conciliation and maintenance of this support is a necessary condition of the attainment and retention of office involving, as Madison so well saw, "the spirit of party and faction in the necessary and ordinary operations of government." The President must in large part be, if not all things to all men, at least many things to many men. As a consequence, the contradictions in his power base invade administration. The often criticized apparent cross-purposes of the Roosevelt regime cannot be put down to inept administration until the political facts are weighed. Were these apparently self-defeating measures reasonably related to the general maintenance of the composite majority of the Administration? The first objective—ultimate patriotism apart—of the administrator is the attainment and retention of the power on which his tenure of office depends. This is the necessary precondition for the accomplishment of all other objectives.

The same ambiguities that arouse the scorn of the naive in the electoral campaigns of the parties are equally inevitable in administration and for the same reasons. Victory at the polls does not yield either a clear-cut grant of power or a unified majority support for a coherent program. The task of the Presidency lies in feeling out the alternatives of policy which are consistent with the retention and increase of the group support on which the Administration rests. The lack of a budgetary theory (so frequently deplored) is not due to any incapacity to apply rational analysis to the comparative contribution of the various activities of government to a determinate hierarchy of purposes. It more probably stems from a fastidious distaste for the frank recognition of the budget as a politically expedient allocation of resources. Appraisal in terms of their political contribution to the Administration provides almost a sole common denominator between the Forest Service and the Bureau of Engraving.

Integration of the administrative structure through an overall purpose in terms of which tasks and priorities can be established is an emergency phenomenon. Its realization, only partial at best, has been limited to war and the extremity of depression. Even in wartime the Farm Bureau Federation, the American Federation of Labor, the Congress of Industrial Organizations, the National Association of Manufacturers, the Chamber of Commerce, and a host of lesser interests resisted coordination of themselves and the agencies concerned with their interests. A Presidency temporarily empowered by intense mass popular support acting in behalf of a generally accepted and simplified purpose can, with great difficulty, bribe, cajole, and coerce a real measure of joint action. The long-drawn-out battle for conversion and the debacle of orderly reconversion underline the difficulty of attaining, and the transitory nature of, popularly based emergency power. Only in crises are the powers of the Executive nearly adequate to impose a common plan of action on the executive branch, let alone the economy.

In ordinary times the manifold pressures of our pluralistic society work themselves out in accordance with the balance of forces prevailing in Congress and the agencies. Only to a limited degree is the process subject to responsible direction or review by President or party leadership.

The program of the President cannot be a Gosplan for the government precisely because the nature of his institutional and group support gives him insufficient power. The personal unity of the presidency cannot perform the function of Hobbes' sovereign since his office lacks the authority of Hobbes' contract. Single headedness in the executive gives no assurance of singleness of purpose. It only insures that the significant pressures in a society will be brought to bear on one office. Monarchy solves the problem of giving one plan to a multitude only when the plenitude of its authority approaches dictatorship. Impatient social theorists in all ages have turned to the philosopher king as a substitute for consensus. Whatever else he may become, it is difficult to conceive of the American president ruling as a philosopher king, even with the advice of the Executive Office. The monarchical solution to the administrative problems posed by the lack of a disciplined party system capable of giving firm leadership and a program to the legislature is a modern variant of the dreams of the eighteenth-century savants and well nigh equally divorced from a realistic appraisal of social realities.

Much of administrative thought, when it does not assume the value of coordination for coordination's sake, operates on the assumption that there must be something akin to Rousseau's *volonté générale* in administration to which the errant *volonté de tous* of the bureaus can and should be made to conform. This will-o'-the-wisp was made the object of an illuminating search by Pendleton Herring in his *Public Administration and the Public Interest.* The answer for Rousseau was enlightened dictatorship or counting the votes. The administrative equivalent to the latter is the resultant of the relevant pressures, as Herring shows. The first alternative seems to require at least the potency of the British Labour party and elsewhere has needed the disciplined organization of a fascist, nazi, or communist party to provide the power and consensus necessary to coordinate the manifold activities of government to a common plan.

Dictatorship, as Sigmund Neumann has observed, is a substitute for institutions which is required to fill the vacuum when traditional institutions break down. Force supplies the compulsion and guide to action in place of the normal routines of unconscious habit. Administrative organizations, however much they may appear the creations of art, are institutions produced in history and woven in the web of social relationships that gives them life and being. They present the same refractory material to the hand of the political artist as the rest of society of which they form a part.

Just as the economists have attempted to escape the complexities of institutional reality by taking refuge in the frictionless realm of theory, so some students of administration, following their lead, have seen in the application of the doctrine of opportunity costs a clue to a science of administration. Valuable as this may be in a restricted way, Marx has more light to throw on the study of institutions. It is in the dynamics and interrelations of institutions that we have most hope of describing and therefore learning to control administrative behavior.

III

The difficulty of coordinating government agencies lies not only in the fact that bureaucratic organizations are institutions having survival interests which may conflict with their rational adaptation to over-all purpose, but even more in their having roots in society. Coordination of the varied activities of a modern government almost of necessity involves a substantial degree of coordination of the economy. Coordination of government agencies involves far more than changing the behavior and offices of officials in Washington and the field. It involves the publics that are implicated in their normal functioning. To coordinate fiscal policy, agricultural policy, labor policy, foreign policy, and military policy, to name a few major areas, moves beyond the range of government charts and the habitat of the bureaucrats to the market place and to where the people live and work. This suggests that the reason why government reorganization is so difficult is that far more than government in the formal sense is involved in reorganization. One could overlook this in the limited government of the nineteenth century but the multibillion dollar government of the mid-twentieth permits no facile dichotomy between government and economy. Economy and efficiency are the two objectives a laissez faire society can prescribe in peacetime as over-all government objectives. Their inadequacy either as motivation or standards has long been obvious. A planned economy clearly requires a planned government. But, if one can afford an unplanned economy, apart from gross extravagance, there seems no compelling and therefore, perhaps, no sufficiently powerful reason for a planned government.

Basic to the problem of administrative rationality is that of organizational identification and point of view. To whom is one loyal—unit, section, branch, division, bureau, department, administration, government, country, people, world history, or what? Administrative analysis frequently assumes that organizational identification should occur in such a way as to merge primary organization loyalty in a larger synthesis. The good of the part is to give way to the reasoned good of the whole. This is most frequently illustrated in the rationalizations used to counter self-centered demands of primary groups for funds and personnel. Actually the competition between governmental power centers, rather than the rationalizations, is the effective instrument of coordination.

Where there is a clear common product on whose successful production the subgroups depend for the attainment of their own satisfaction, it is possible to demonstrate to almost all participants the desirability of cooperation. The shoe factory produces shoes, or else, for all concerned. But the government as a whole and many of its component parts have no such identifiable common product on which they all depend. Like the proverbial Heinz, there are fifty-seven or more varieties unified, if at all, by a common political profit and loss account.

Administration is faced by somewhat the same dilemma as economics. There are propositions about the behavior patterns conducive to full employment—welfare economics. On the other hand, there are propositions about the economics of the individual firm—the counsel of the business schools. It is possible to show with considerable persuasiveness that sound considerations for the individual firm may lead to a depression if generally adopted, a result desired by none of the participants. However, no single firm can afford by itself to adopt the course of collective wisdom; in the absence of a common power capable of enforcing decisions premised on the supremacy of the collective interest, *sauve qui peut* is common sense.

The position of administrative organizations is not unlike the position of particular firms. Just as the decisions of the firms could be coordinated by the imposition of a planned economy so could those of the component parts of the government. But just as it is possible to operate a formally unplanned economy by the loose coordination of the market, in the same fashion it is possible to operate a government by the loose coordination of the play of political forces through its institutions.

The unseen hand of Adam Smith may be little in evidence in either case. One need not believe in a doctrine of social or administrative harmony to believe that formal centralized planning—while perhaps desirable and in some cases necessary—is not a must. The complicated logistics of supplying the city of New York runs smoothly down the grooves of millions of well adapted habits projected from a distant past. It seems naive on the one hand to believe in the possibility of a vast, intricate, and delicate economy operating with a minimum of formal over-all direction, and on the other to doubt that a relatively simple mechanism such as the government can be controlled largely by the same play of forces.

Doubtless the real reasons for seeking coordination in the government are the same that prompt a desire for economic planning. In fact, apart from waging war with its demand for rapid change, economic planning would seem to be the only objective sufficiently compelling and extensive to require a drastic change in our system of political laissez faire. Harold Smith, testifying before the Senate Banking and Currency Committee on the Employment Act of 1946, showed how extensive a range of hitherto unrelated activities could be brought to bear on a common purpose—the maintenance of maximum employment and purchasing power. In the flush of the war experience and with prophecies of reconversion unemployment, a reluctant Congress passed a pious declaration of policy. Senator Flanders has recorded the meager showing to date.

Nevertheless, war and depression apart, the Employment Act of 1946 for the first time provides an inclusive common purpose in terms of which administrative activities can be evaluated and integrated. While still deficient in depth and content, it provides at least a partial basis for the rational budgeting of government activities. The older concept of economy and efficiency as autonomous standards still lingers in Congress, but elsewhere their validity as ends in themselves is treated with skepticism.

If the advent of Keynesian economics and the erosion of laissez faire have created the intellectual conditions requisite for the formulation of overall government policy, they do not by any means guarantee the political conditions necessary for its implementation. We can see quite clearly that the development of an integrated administration requires an integrating purpose. The ideals of Locke, Smith, Spencer, and their American disciples deny the need for such a purpose save for economy and efficiency's sake. Marx, Keynes, and their followers by denying the validity of the self-regulating economy have endowed the state with an over-arching responsibility in terms of which broad coordination of activities is not only intellectually possible but theoretically, at least, necessary. Intellectual perception of the need for this coordination, however, has run well ahead of the public's perception of it and of the development of a political channeling of power adequate to its administrative implementation.

Most students of administration are planners of some sort. Most congressmen would fly the label like the plague. Most bureaucrats, whatever their private faith, live under two jealous gods, their particular clientele and the loyalty check. Such a condition might, if it exists as described, cast doubt on whether even the intellectual conditions for rational administrative coordination exist. Be that as it may, the transition from a government organized in clientele departments and bureaus, each responding to the massive feudal power of organized business, organized agriculture, and organized labor, to a government integrated about a paramount national purpose will require a political power at least as great as that which tamed the earlier feudalism. It takes a sharp eye or a tinted glass to see such an organized power on the American scene. Without it, administrative organization for over-all coordination has the academic air of South American constitution making. One is reminded of the remark attributed to the Austrian economist Mises; on being told that the facts did not agree with his theory, he replied "*desto schlechter für die Tatsache.*"

IV

It is highly appropriate to consider how administrators should behave to meet the test of efficiency in a planned polity; but in the absence of such a polity and while, if we like, struggling to get it, a realistic science of administration will teach administrative behavior appropriate to the existing political system.

A close examination of the presidential system may well bring one to conclude that administrative rationality in it is a different matter from that applicable to the British ideal. The American Presidency is an office that has significant monarchical characteristics despite its limited term and elective nature. The literature on court and palace has many an insight applicable to the White House. Access to the President, reigning favorites, even the court jester, are topics that show the continuity of institutions. The maxims of LaRochefoucauld and the memoirs of the Duc de Saint Simon have a refreshing realism for the operator on the Potomac.

The problem of rival factions in the President's family is as old as the famous struggle between Jefferson and Hamilton, as fresh and modern as the latest cabal against John Snyder. Experience seems to show that this personal and factional struggle for the President's favor is a vital part of the process of representation. The vanity, personal ambition, or patriotism of the contestants soon clothes itself in the generalities of principle and the clique aligns itself with groups beyond the capital. Subordinate rivalry is tolerated if not encouraged by so many able executives that it can scarcely be attributed to administrative ineptitude. The wrangling tests opinion, uncovers information that would otherwise never rise to the top, and provides effective opportunity for decision rather than mere ratification of prearranged plans. Like most judges, the executive needs to hear argument for his own instruction. The alternatives presented by subordinates in large part determine the freedom and the creative opportunity of their superiors. The danger of becoming a Merovingian is a powerful incentive to the maintenance of fluidity in the structure of power.

The fixed character of presidential tenure makes it necessary that subordinates be politically expendable. The President's men must be willing to accept the blame for failures not their own. Machiavelli's teaching on how princes must keep the faith bears rereading. Collective responsibility is incompatible with a fixed term of office. As it tests the currents of public opinion, the situation on the Hill, and the varying strength of the organized pressures, the White House alters and adapts the complexion of the Administration. Loyalties to programs or to groups and personal pride and interest frequently conflict with whole-souled devotion to the Presidency. In fact, since such devotion is not made mandatory by custom, institutions, or the facts of power, the problem is perpetually perplexing to those who must choose.

The balance of power between executive and legislature is constantly subject to the shifts of public and group support. The latent tendency of the American Congress is to follow the age-old parliamentary precedents and to try to reduce the President to the role of constitutional monarch. Against this threat and to secure his own initiative, the President's resources are primarily demagogic, with the weaknesses and strengths that dependence on mass popular appeal implies. The unanswered question of American government—"who is boss?"—constantly plagues administration. The disruption of unity of command is not just the problem of Taylor's functional foreman, but goes to the stability and uniformity of basic decisional premises essential to consequent administration.

It is interesting to speculate on the consequences for administration of the full development of congressional or presidential government. A leadership in Congress that could control the timetable of the House and Senate would scarcely content itself short of reducing the President's Cabinet to what in all probability it was first intended to be, a modified version of the present Swiss executive. Such leadership could scarcely arise without centrally organized, disciplined, national parties far different from our present shambling alliances of state and local machines.

A Presidency backed by a disciplined party controlling a majority in Congress would probably assimilate itself to a premiership by association of legislative leadership in the formulation of policy and administration. In either line of development the crucial matter is party organization. For the spirit of the party system determines the character of the government.

That the American party system will develop toward the British ideal is by no means a foregone conclusion. The present oscillation between a strong demagogic Presidency and a defensively powerful congressional oligarchy may well prove a continuing pattern of American politics, as it was of Roman. In the absence of a party system providing an institutionalized centripetal force in our affairs, it is natural to look to the Presidency as Goldsmith's weary traveler looked to the throne.

The Presidency of the United States, however, is no such throne as the pre-World War I *Kaiserreich* that provided the moral and political basis for the Prussian bureaucracy. Lacking neutrality and mystique, it does not even perform the function of the British monarchy in providing a psychological foundation for the permanent civil service. A leaderless and irresponsible Congress frequently makes it appear the strong point of the republic. The Bonapartist experience in France, the Weimar Republic, and South American examples nearer home, despite important social differences, are relevant to any thoughtful consideration of building a solution to legislative anarchy on the unity of the executive.

The present course of American party development gives little ground for optimism that a responsible two party system capable of uniting Congress and Executive in a coherent program will emerge. The increasingly critical importance of the federal budget for the national economy and the inevitable impact of world power status on the conduct of foreign affairs make inescapable the problem of stable leadership in the American system. Unfortunately they by no means insure a happy or indeed any solution.

Attempts to solve administrative problems in isolation from the structure of power and purpose in the polity are bound to prove illusory. The reorganization of Congress to create responsibility in advance of the development of party responsibility was an act of piety to principle, of educational value; but as a practical matter it raised a structure without foundation. In the same way, reorganization of the executive branch to centralize administrative power in the Presidency while political power remains dispersed and divided may effect improvement, but in a large sense it must fail. The basic prerequisite to the administration of the textbooks is a responsible two-party system. The means to its attainment are a number one problem for students of administration. What Schattschneider calls the struggle for party government may sometime yield us the responsible parliamentary two-party system needed to underpin our present administrative theory. Until that happy time, exploration of the needs and necessities of our present system is a high priority task of responsible scholarship.

22
Toward a Theory of Budgeting

Verne B. Lewis

The $64.00 question on the expenditure side of public budgeting is: On what basis shall it be decided to allocate X dollars to Activity A instead of allocating them to Activity B, or instead of allowing the taxpayer to use the money for his individual purposes? Over a decade ago V. O. Key called attention to the lack of a budgetary theory which would assist in arriving at an answer to this question.[1] Pointing out that budgeting is essentially a form of applied economics, since it requires the allocation of scarce resources among competing demands, Professor Key urged that this question be explored from the point of view of economic theory.

The purpose of this article is to analyze three propositions that are derived from economic theory[2] and appear to be applicable to public budgeting and to be appropriate building blocks for construction of an economic theory of budgeting. In brief, the three principles are:

1. Since resources are scarce in relation to demands, the basic economic test which must be applied is that the return from every expenditure must be worth its cost in terms of sacrificed alternatives. Budget analysis, therefore, is basically a comparison of the relative merits of alternative uses of funds.
2. Incremental analysis (that is, analysis of the additional values to be derived from an additional expenditure) is necessary because of the phenomenon of diminishing utility. Analysis of the increments is necessary and useful only at or near the margin; this is the point of balance at which an additional expenditure for any purpose would yield the same return.
3. Comparison of relative merits can be made only in terms of relative effectiveness in achieving a common objective.

Part I of this article will be devoted to consideration of these principles. In Part II a proposal, which will be called the alternative budget procedure, will be outlined and analyzed in terms of the three principles. Primary emphasis throughout will be placed on the applicability of concepts developed by the economists to methods of analyzing budget estimates. The discussion is pointed specifically at problems of the federal government; the general ideas, however, should be equally applicable to state and local governmental units.

I

Relative Value

Budget decisions must be made on the basis of relative values. There is no absolute standard of value. It is not enough to say that an expenditure for a particular purpose is desirable or worth while. The results must be more valuable than

Source: From *Public Administration Review* (Winter 1952), pp. 42–54.

they would be if the money were used for any other purpose.

Comparison of relative values to be obtained from alternative uses of funds is necessary because our resources are inadequate to do all the things we consider desirable and necessary. In fact, public budgeting is necessary only because our desires exceed our means. The desires of human beings are virtually unlimited. Although the supply of resources has been greatly expanded in recent decades, the supply is still short in relation to demands. It would be nice if we had enough to go around, but we do not. Some demands can be met only in part, some not at all.

Scarcity of resources in relation to demands confronts us at every level of public budgeting. Public services consume scarce materials and manpower which have alternative uses. If used for governmental activities, they cannot be used for private purposes. If used for Activity A of the government, they cannot be used for Activity B. Expressed in terms of money, the problem of scarcity arises in connection with appropriations. As individual taxpayers, we put pressures on Congress to hold down federal taxes so that a larger proportion of our already inadequate personal incomes will be available to satisfy our individual desires. In view of these pressures, Congress usually appropriates less than is requested by the President and interest groups. The President in turn usually requests the Congress to appropriate less than the total of the estimates submitted to him by agency heads. Rarely does an agency have sufficient funds to do all the things it would like to do or that it is requested to do by citizen groups.

Confronted with limited resources, congressmen and administrative officials must make choices. The available money will buy this *or* that, but not *both.* On what basis should the choice be made?

The economists, who specialize in problems of scarcity, have a general answer to this question. It is found in the doctrine of marginal utility. This doctrine, as applied to public budgeting, has been formulated by Professor Pigou as follows:

> As regards the distribution, as distinct from the aggregate cost, of optional government expenditure, it is clear that, just as an individual will get more satisfaction out of his income by maintaining a certain balance between different sorts of expenditure, so also will a community through its government. The principle of balance in both cases is provided by the postulate that resources should be so distributed among different uses that the marginal return of satisfaction is the same for all of them. . . . Expenditure should be distributed between battleships and poor relief in such wise that the last shilling devoted to each of them yields the same real return. We have here, so far as theory goes, a test by means of which the distribution of expenditure along different lines can be settled.[3]

Other aspects of the marginal utility concept will be considered in later sections; here we want to note that this concept poses the problem in terms of relative values rather than absolutes. To determine the distribution of funds between battleships and poor relief we must weigh the relative value of the results to be obtained from these alternative uses. Is it worth while to spend an additional $1,000,000 for battleships? We can answer "yes" only if we think we would get more valuable results than would be obtained by using that $1,000,000 for poor relief.

When the economists approach the problem in terms of costs rather than results they arrive at the same conclusion. Fundamentally, as the economists indicate in their "opportunity" or "displacement" concept of costs, "the cost of a thing is simply the amount of other things which has to be given up for its sake."[4] If Robinson Crusoe finds he has time to build a house *or* catch some fish, but not *both,* the cost of the house is the fish he does not catch or vice versa. The cost of anything is therefore the result that would have been realized had the resources been used for an alternative purpose.

Of what significance from the point of view of budget analysis are these concepts of relative value and displacement costs? They indicate that the basic objective of budget analysis is the comparison of the relative value of results to be obtained from alternative uses of funds. If an analyst is convinced after reading the usual argument supporting a budget request that the activity in question is desirable and necessary, his task has just begun. To be justifiable in terms of making the most advantageous use of resources, the returns from an expenditure for any activity must be more desirable and more necessary for any alternative use of the funds. On the other hand, a budget request for an activity cannot legitimately be turned down solely on the basis that the activity costs too much. Costs and results must be considered together. The costs must be judged in relation to the results and the results must be worth their costs in terms of alternative results that are foregone or displaced.

Incremental Analysis

If the basic guide for budget analysis is that results must be worth their costs, budget analysis must include a comparison of relative values. How can such a comparison of values be made?

The marginal utility concept suggests a way of approaching the problem. The method, briefly, is to divide available resources into increments and consider which of the alternative uses of each increment would yield the greatest return. Analysis of increments is necessary because of the phenomenon of diminishing utility. This means, roughly, that as we acquire more and more units of anything, the additional units have less and less use value. If enough units are acquired, an added unit may be of no value at all and may even be objectionable. To illustrate, four tires on a car are essential, a fifth tire is less essential but is handy to have, whereas a sixth tire just gets in the way. Although a sixth tire will cost as much as any of the first five, it has considerably less use value. In deciding how many tires to buy, we must therefore consider the use value to be derived from each *additional* tire.

Because of the phenomenon of diminishing utility, there is no point in trying to determine the *total* or *average* benefits to be obtained from total expenditures for a particular commodity or function. We must analyze the benefits by increments. If one million bazookas make a valuable contribution toward winning a war, we cannot assume that the contribution would be doubled if we had two million. Perhaps there are not enough soldiers to use that many. No matter how valuable bazookas might be in winning a war, a point would be reached sometime on the diminishing scale of utility where additional expenditures for bazookas would be completely wasted. Since we do not have enough resources to do all the things we would like to do, we certainly should not produce anything that will not or cannot be used.

But we cannot assume that we would make the best use of resources even if we produced no more bazookas than could be used. Perhaps the manpower and materials consumed in producing the last thousand bazookas would serve a more valuable purpose if they were used for producing additional hand grenades or some other item. This reasoning leads us back to the basic criterion for deciding how much should be spent for each activity. We should allocate enough money for bazookas so that the last dollar spent for bazookas will serve as valuable a purpose as the last dollar for hand grenades or any other purpose. If more than this amount is spent for bazookas, we sacrifice a more valuable alternative use. Thus, as is suggested by the marginal utility theory, maximum returns can be obtained only if expenditures are distributed among different purposes in such a way that the last dollar spent for each yields the same real return.

The marginal utility concept also indicates that a comparison of incremental values is meaningful and necessary only at or near the margins. When analyzing the value of the returns by increments of expenditure near the margins we would ask: How much will be sacrificed if proposed expenditures for Function A are reduced by $1,000? Can efficiency be increased so that output will not have to be reduced? What would be the consequences of lowering standards of quality? Of reducing quantities? Of postponing some portion of the work?

When these issues are explored, the payoff question can be tackled. Would the sacrifices be greater or less if the $1,000 cut is applied to Function B rather than to Function A? This question brings up the most difficult and most critical problem. How can the values of unlike functions be compared? How can the value of an atom bomb and cancer research be compared? Or public roads and public schools? So far we have not indicated how this question can be answered. We have only narrowed the field by indicating that the value of functions must be compared by increments rather than in total and that the value of increments need only be compared near the marginal point of balance. Incremental analysis at the margins is just a tool, though a useful one, we believe. It does not supply the answers, but it helps to focus attention on the real points at issue.

Relative Effectiveness

The relative value of different things cannot be compared unless they have a common denominator. The common aspect of an atom bomb and cancer research, of public roads and public schools, is the broad purpose each is designed to serve. These items, as well as all other public and private activities, are undertaken to serve human needs and desires. We can only compare their values by evaluating their relative effectiveness in serving a common objective.

To revert to a previously used example, we do not make bazookas just for the sake of making bazookas. We make them because they help win wars. Although bazookas, hand grenades, and K-rations are unlike things, they serve a common military purpose. The relative values of these items can be weighed in terms of their relative effectiveness in fighting a war. We do not fight wars for their own sake either. They are fought for a larger purpose of national security. Economic aid to foreign countries also serves this purpose. Since they share a common objective, the relative value of military activities and economic aid can also be compared in terms of their effectiveness in achieving this objective.

Let us take a different type of case which is less general and more tangible than national security. Purchasing officers and engineers perform quite different functions. Yet if they are working in an organization which does construction work, for example, they share the common objective of that organization. Operating within a ceiling on total expenditures, the head of the agency might be faced with this question: Would a part of the money allocated to the procurement section yield greater returns if transferred to the engineering section? This question involves value comparisons of unlike things, whether for a private firm or for a government agency. Moreover, the firm or the agency usually cannot express the contributions of procurement officers and engineers in terms of precise numbers. Nevertheless, reasonable men who are reasonably well informed arrive at substantially the same answer to such questions, provided the basic objective has been decided in advance. If the objective is to build a structure according to prescribed specifications in X months and at not to exceed Y dollars, this objective provides a common basis for evaluation. The answer will depend upon forecasts of facts and will also be influenced by relative need. For example, if design is on schedule but construction is being delayed because purchase orders are not being issued on schedule, additions to the procurement staff would probably yield greater returns than additions to the design staff. On the other hand, if design is behind schedule and, as a consequence, the procurement staff has no material requisitions to process, more design engineers would yield the greater return.

Evaluation in terms of relative effectiveness in achieving a common objective is, therefore, a second fundamental method of budget analysis.[5]

Evaluation in terms of common purposes is another way of saying that alternative means can be evaluated in terms of the end they are designed to achieve. That end can be considered, in turn, as a means of achieving a broader end. This process requires, of course, that the ultimate ends be somehow established. How can these fundamental decisions be made? In a democracy we are not so much concerned with how they are made as by whom they are made. The ideal of democracy is that the desires of the people, no matter how they are arrived at or how unwise they may be, should control the actions of the government. The representatives of the people in Congress make the fundamental decisions as to the ultimate aims of governmental services. These decisions, in the form of laws and appropriation acts, provide the basis for economic calculation by administrative agencies in the same way as consumer action in the marketplace provides the basis for decisions in the private economy.

We now have some basic elements of an economic theory of budgeting. The economic aim of budgeting is to achieve the best use of our resources. To meet this test, the benefits derived from any expenditure must be worth their cost in terms of sacrificed or displaced alternatives. As a first step in applying that test, we can use incremental analysis at the margins as a means of concentrating attention at the areas where comparison of values is necessary and meaningful. These values can be compared by determining their relative effectiveness in achieving a common purpose. Analysis in terms of common purposes requires a set of basic premises which are found in the ultimate ends or purposes established by Congress, acting for the people. This means that Congress is charged by the people with the basic responsibility for deciding what constitutes the "best use of resources," so far as the federal government is concerned.

Practical Limitations

Although the propositions outlined above concerning relative value, incremental analysis, and relative effectiveness constitute, in a sense, a formula for budget analysis which appears to be theoretically sound, the formula is not always easy to apply. Precise numbers to use in the equations are frequently unavailable. Although the formula will work in a theoretically valid manner, even if one has to guess the numbers to put into the equation, the practical usefulness of the answers will depend upon the accuracy of the numbers.

One area where firm numbers are hard to get involves forecasts of future needs and conditions. As we have noted, value is a function of need and need changes from time to time. In comparing the relative value of guns and butter, for example, we will strike a balance between them at different points at different times depending upon whether we are engaged in a hot war, a cold war, or no war at all. The balance between public health and police will be struck at one point if communicable diseases are rampant at a time when the traffic accident rate is low. The balance will be struck at a different point if the state of public health is good but the accident rate is alarming.

Budgetary decisions have to be based not only on relative needs as they are today but also on forecasts of what the needs will be tomorrow, next year, or in the next decade. The point is illustrated most dramatically by the decision made by the federal government during World War II to try to develop an atomic bomb. At the time, no one knew whether a bomb could be made, or if it could be made in time to help win the war. Hence, the government in deciding to divert tremendous quantities of scarce resources to this purpose had to take a calculated risk. Its decision was based not on firm facts but on forecasts and hopes as to the values to be realized.

There are probably as many budget arguments over forecasts of needs as there are over the relative merits of the expenditures which are proposed to meet those needs.

Not only must budget decisions be based, in some cases, on sheer guesses as to future needs and future accomplishments, but often the nature of governmental activities is such that accomplishments in relation to costs cannot be precisely measured even after the fact. How can one tell, for example, how much fire damage was prevented for each $1,000 spent by the fire department for fire prevention?

Perhaps it was the frequent difficulty in obtaining precise numbers that led Professor Key to question the applicability of the marginal utility theory to public budgeting. He concluded:

> The doctrine of marginal utility, developed most finely in the analysis of the market economy, has a ring of unreality when applied to public expenditures. The most advantageous utilization of public funds resolves itself into a matter of value preferences between ends lacking a common denominator. As such, the question is a problem of political philosophy.[6]

Whether firm numbers are available or not, judgments and decisions have to be made. The lack of precise numbers does not invalidate the basic principles or methods of calculation which we have outlined. The methods have to be judged on the basis of whether or not they lead to proper conclusions *if* it is assumed that the numbers used in the equations are the right ones. Obtaining the right numbers, though a fundamental and difficult problem, is separate and distinct from the problem of developing methods of calculation.

On the other hand, Professor Key may have been questioning the basic principle. It is perfectly true, as Key points out, that budgeting involves questions of value preferences which must be based on philosophy rather than science or logic. We agree that it is a problem for philosophers, but not exclusively, since the methods of the economists can also be applied. The problem of value has long been one of the central topics on the agenda of the economists. They do not approach the problem from the point of view of trying to develop an absolute standard of value or from the point of view of trying to prescribe which ends, goals, or objectives men should strive for. Rather they concentrate on methods to be used to achieve the most valuable use of scarce resources as judged by whatever standard of value men embrace. While the philosopher helps us to decide which goals we should strive for, the economist helps us achieve those goals most efficiently. Thus, I believe, the economists' approach to the problem of value as expressed in the marginal utility theory can be accepted as a useful approach to public budgeting.

The views outlined in this article concerning the applicability of the methods of the economists to public budgeting run sharply counter to the views of some economists. Ludwig von Mises, for example, contends, in his book, *Bureaucracy*,[7] that there is no method of economic calculation which can be applied to government. It can be shown, I think, that the problem in government, so far as it exists, arises out of the lack of firm numbers rather than out of the lack of a method.

Dr. Mises' central argument is that bureaucrats have no means of calculating the relative usefulness of governmental activities because these activities have no price in the marketplace. Therefore, he contends, government agencies have no criterion of value to apply. In private business, he points out (p. 26), "the ultimate basis of economic calculation is the valuation of all consumers' goods on the part of all the people" in the marketplace. Further, "economic calculation makes it possible for business to adjust production to the demands of the consumers" (p. 27). On the other hand, he argues, "if a public enterprise is to be operated without regard to profits, the behavior of the public no longer provides a criterion of its usefulness" (p. 61). Therefore, he concludes, "the problem of bureaucratic management is precisely the absence of such a method of calculation" (p. 49).

We can agree with the part of his argument that says market prices provide a criterion of value which serves as a basis for economic calculation in private business; but we cannot agree that government agencies are completely lacking in such a criterion. As has been noted, appropriations, like market prices, indicate in quantitative terms how much the representatives of the people are willing to pay for goods and services rendered by the government. In appropriating funds, congressmen express their attitudes concerning the usefulness of governmental activities as definitely as individuals do when they buy bread at the corner bakery. Congressmen, in effect, are serving as purchasing agents for the American people.

What function does the market price criterion serve in determining whether an activity is worth its cost? One function is to provide the numbers necessary for determining how the cost of doing a particular job can be reduced to a minimum. Nothing, of course, is worth its cost if the same result can somehow be achieved at a lower cost. Market prices are as useful in government as they are in business in this regard. In constructing a road, a building, or a dam—even in running an office—the government has to pay market prices for the raw material and manpower it uses just as a private businessman does. If the guide to economic calculations is the market price, the government engineer has numbers to put into his equations just as his engineering brother in private industry has. Market prices provide the data he needs to calculate which combination of available materials, men, and machines will be least costly.

After all corners have been cut and the cost of doing a job has been reduced to the minimum, we face a broader question. Is the job worth doing? Dr. Mises undoubtedly would answer that a job is worth doing in private business if it yields a profit. In attempting to calculate whether a given activity will yield a profit, a businessman, however, faces some of the problems faced by government. He has to forecast market conditions. The numbers he forecasts may or may not be right. Likewise, a businessman cannot always determine even after the fact whether an individual activity has been profitable or not. No method has yet been found, for example, of measuring precisely how much of a company's profit or loss results from such activities as advertising, research and employee welfare programs. Moreover, a businessman, if he wants to maximize profits, cannot engage in an activity just because it is profitable. It must be more profitable than alternative activities open to him. Thus, he is faced with the same problem of relative value as is the government official. Suppose it costs $1.00 a pound to recover scrap materials in a private factory and that the scrap can be sold on the market for $1.10 a pound, thereby yielding a profit of 10 percent. Does it automatically follow that the scrap should be recovered? Not at all, since the firm might make a profit of 20 percent if the men and materials were used instead for making new products.

The method of calculation by a government agency for a similar situation would be exactly the same. In fact, if government appropriations specified precisely the quantities, quality, standards, and maximum permissible unit prices for each government service, the problem of economic calculation would not only be exactly the same but the answer could be expressed in terms of a profit equivalent. If the agency could produce at a lower unit cost than specified by Congress, the funds saved would be comparable to profit and would be returned to the Treasury as a dividend to the taxpayers.

In many cases, however, government services are of such a nature that Congress cannot enact precise specifications. For example, the production of plutonium by the Atomic Energy Commission has not yet reached the stage where such specifications can be written. Congress, in effect, tells the commission to produce as much plutonium as it can, according to specifications deemed most suitable by the commission, with a total expenditure not to exceed X million dollars. The commission then has no basis for knowing exactly what dollar value is placed on a pound of plutonium by the Congress. Nevertheless, the commission is not without means of making economic decisions. The problem might be to decide whether it is worth spending Y dollars to recover scrap plutonium which accumulates during the manufacturing process. The decision can be made on the basis of comparison of alternative means of accomplishing a common objective. This objective is to produce the maximum amount of usable plutonium during a specified period within the limits of available funds and other resources. In the light of this objective the commission can afford to spend as much per pound for recovery as it has to spend to produce a pound of new plutonium. If it spent either more or less than this amount, the total usable quantity of plutonium produced during a period would be less than the potential maximum. Faced with this kind of problem, a private business would calculate in precisely the same way. The common objective of new production and recovery operations might be expressed in terms of dollars of profit rather than pounds of product, but the answer would be the same.

When the problem facing the government involves activities such as education, foreign relations, and public recreation where the goals are less tangible, where the results are less subject to measurement, and where the amount of results arising from an increment of expenditures is more difficult to determine, the numbers used in the equations will be less firm. Even so, we conclude, Dr. Mises' arguments notwithstanding, that the differences between business and government in economic calculation lie not so much in the methods of calculation as in the availability of precise numbers with which to calculate.

II

In the foregoing analysis of economic ideas in relation to public budgeting, we have stressed the importance of looking upon budgeting as a problem of relative values and have examined the applicability of two methods—incremental analysis and evaluation of relative effectiveness—in achieving a common objective to budget analysis.

On the administrative implications of these ideas, Professor Key has said, "Perhaps the approach toward the practical working out of the issue lies in canalizing of decisions through the governmental machinery so as to place alternatives in juxtaposition and compel consideration of relative values."[8]

The budget machinery of the federal government does accomplish this purpose. The federal budget forces a simultaneous, or nearly simultaneous, consideration of all the competing claims by the President and the Congress. Moreover, at each level in the administrative hierarchy, the budget forces consideration of the relative merits of competing claims within each jurisdiction.[9]

Budget estimates and justifications are rarely prepared in a manner, however, which makes it easy to compare relative merits. We shall, therefore, now outline a budget system designed to facilitate such comparisons and to apply other ideas derived from the preceding economic analysis. After outlining this system, we shall compare it with other budget methods now being used.

The system to be described will be called the alternative budget system. Under this procedure, each administrative official who prepares a budget estimate, either as a basis for an appropriation request or an allotment request after the appropriation is made, would be required to prepare a basic budget estimate supplemented by skeleton plans for alternative amounts. If the amount of the basic estimate equals 100, the alternatives might represent, respectively, 80, 90, 110, and 120 percent of that amount. The number of alternatives might vary with the situation. Ordinarily, three alternatives would seem to secure a sufficient range of possibilities. In the interest of providing a safety valve, each subordinate might be permitted to prepare one or more additional alternative budgets totaling more than the top figure prescribed by his superior. In order to focus attention on problems near the margins, the amounts of the alternative budgets should range from a little less than the lowest amount that is likely to be approved to a little more than the recommended amount. Increments of 10 percent might be appropriate in some cases; larger or smaller increments might be required in others.

The establishment of the alternative levels would have to start with the President. He would select alternative levels of overall governmental expenditure, and he would establish corresponding alternative levels for each department or agency. The head of each department or agency would, in turn, establish alternative levels for each of his subordinates which would be consistent with the prescribed departmental levels.

In preparing the alternative budgets, the subordinate official would first indicate, as he does under present procedures, the nature, quantity, and quality of services his agency could render the taxpayers if the amount of the basic budget were approved. In addition, he would indicate the recommended revisions in the plan of service for each of the alternative amounts and the benefits or sacrifices which would result.

At each superior level the responsible official would review the alternative proposals submitted by his several subordinates and select from them the features that would be, in his opinion, the most advantageous to the taxpayers for each alternative amount set for him by the next highest organization level. Finally, the President would submit alternative budgets to the Congress. At this level the alternatives would reflect the major issues involved in determining the work program for the entire government.

The advantages of the alternative budget procedure will be brought out by comparing it with other budget methods and techniques now in use. For convenience, the other techniques will be labeled (a) open-end budgeting, (b) fixed-ceiling budgeting, (c) work measurement and unit costing, (d) increase-decrease analysis, (e) priority listings and (f) item-by-item control. These methods are not mutually exclusive; some of them could very well be incorporated as features of the alternative budget plan. Some are used primarily in budget estimating, others in budget control.

Open-End Budgeting

Some agencies of the federal government (and in some years the Bureau of the Budget) permit subordinate officials to submit a single budget estimate for whatever amount the subordinate decides to recommend. This method has been used not only for preparing requests for appropriations but also for submission of allotment requests to agency heads after the appropriations have been made. This single estimate represents, by and large, the official's judgment as to optimum program for his agency for the ensuing year, tempered perhaps by his judgment as to what the traffic will bear in view of the general political and economic climate existing at the time. No restrictions are placed on him; the sky is the limit so far as the amount he can request is concerned. For this reason, we have selected the short title "open-end budgeting" as being descriptive of this method.

In justification for such a budget estimate, the official, in effect, says, "I think it is desirable (or important, or essential) that the taxpayers be given the services outlined in this budget. Such a program will cost X dollars. Any reductions in the amount requested will deprive the public of exceedingly valuable services." While such general statements are, of course, backed up by more or less specific facts and figures, the information provided leaves many gaps from the point of view of what the superior official needs in order to weigh the importance of each dollar requested by one subordinate against each dollar requested by other subordinates.

Statements which merely prove that a program is desirable do not fulfill the needs of a superior who is faced with the necessity of reducing the total amount requested by the subordinates, not because he thinks the requests are for undesirable or unnecessary purposes, but simply because the pattern is too big for the cloth. The subordinate's budget estimates and justifications, submitted to him under the open-end procedure, are deficient because they do not indicate specifically how plans would be changed if a smaller amount were available or specifically the subordinate's judgment as to the consequences of such a change in plans. Almost the entire burden, then, of ascertaining where the reductions can be made with the least harmful consequences is placed on the superior official, who naturally is less well informed on the details than are his subordinates.

In what way would the assistance rendered by the subordinate to his superior be enhanced if the alternative budget method were used? Under any circumstances the contribution of a subordinate official is limited by the fact that he is concerned with a segment rather than with the whole. His advice as to how much should be appropriated for his particular sphere of activities obviously cannot be accepted without careful scrutiny. He lacks information about other activities which would be necessary to make a comparison of relative importance. Even if he had complete information, he would be quite unique if he did not place a higher valuation on his own activities than others do. This generalization is borne out by the fact that the aggregate of requests from subordinate officials is invariably more than the public, acting through Congress, is willing to devote to public services.

The subordinate administrative official can be expected, however, to make a substantial contribution in advising the Congress and the President on the relative merits of competing demands within his own jurisdiction, even though he cannot be expected to weigh those demands against demands in other jurisdictions. The subordinate official can perform an indispensable service by comparing the relative effectiveness of each activity in achieving the goals of his agency and by indicating how he thinks any specified amount of money can best be distributed among the programs of his agency. His service in this respect is valuable not only because considerable technical knowledge and experience usually is required as a basis for arriving at such judgments, but also because the pressure of time may force the President and the Congress to rely greatly on his judgment.

This phase of the contribution of the subordinate official to budget-making is comparable to services I can get from an architect if I should decide to build a house. The architect's advice as to whether I should spend eight, twelve, or sixteen thousand dollars for a house is not very helpful. On the other hand, the architect can be very helpful in advising me as to how I can get the most of what I want in a house for any given sum I choose to spend.

Another way in which a subordinate can be of service is in advising his superiors on probable gains or losses from appropriating more or less for his portion of the government's work. This kind of contribution is comparable to the assistance an architect can render by analyzing the additional features in a house which can be obtained for each increment of cost, and by indicating the features that would have to be sacrificed if costs were reduced by specified amounts.

Alternative budgets prepared by subordinates would take advantage of both of these types of assistance. The subordinate would indicate his judgment as to the best way of using several alternative amounts and in addition he would analyze the benefits to be gained by each increment of funds.

Fixed-Ceiling Budgeting

If the open-end procedure is one extreme, the fixed-ceiling method represents the opposite pole. Under this plan, a fixed ceiling is established in advance which the subordinate's budget estimate cannot exceed. Such a ceiling creates for the subordinate a situation similar to that facing the President if he should decide to recommend a balanced budget. Then the amount of anticipated revenues constitutes the ceiling on the amount of expenditures he can recommend.

Whatever the merits, or lack thereof, of allowing revenues to determine the total amount to be spent by the government, working to a set ceiling does have the advantage of forcing consideration, at the presidential level, of relative merits to a greater extent than is likely to prevail under open-end budgeting. In open-end budgeting, it is easy to keep adding items that appear to be desirable and thereby pass the buck to the next level of review in the event the total cost of the "desirable" items exceeds an acceptable figure. But prescribing a single fixed ceiling in advance for subordinate levels of the executive branch involves the danger of judging a case before the evidence is heard. The basic reason for requiring estimates from subordinate officials is that higher officials do not have enough detailed information, time, or specialized skill to prepare the plans themselves. How can these officials judge the merits of the experts' plans before they are submitted? In setting the ceiling figures in advance, how can one be sure that the ceiling for one function is not set too high and the ceiling for another too low?

The alternative budget plan, like the fixed-ceiling practice, forces consideration of relative merits within a given amount at each organization level, but the final decision as to amount does not have to be made by the superior until the evidence is in.

WORK LOAD MEASUREMENT AND UNIT COSTING

Increasing emphasis has been placed in recent years on work load measurement and unit costing for budgetary purposes. The ultimate goal is to devise units of work and to determine unit costs wherever possible so that budget requests can be stated in this fashion: "It costs X dollars to perform each unit of this type of work. If you want us to perform 100 units, the cost will be 100 times X dollars. If you want only fifty units the cost will be fifty times X dollars."

This approach is useful for budgeting in many situations. It supplies some of the numbers needed for the economic calculation discussed in Part I. Precise, quantitative measures, if pertinent and feasible, are better than vague generalities. Some budget questions cannot be answered, however, in terms of work load and unit cost data. These data will show how many units are being done, but not how many should be done. They show what unit costs are, but not what they should be. They may or may not give an indication of the quality of the work, but they leave unanswered the question of the proper quality standards.

A further limitation on use of work load measurement is that the end product of many agencies is not measurable by any means yet devised. In other cases, the amount of work performed is not a measure of its significance or value. Some work is standby in character. Some facilities, for example, are maintained to meet emergencies if and when they arise. In such cases the less work there is to be done the better. Much of the work of military agencies and fire fighters is of this type. In other cases, too, the amount of work performed is inadequate as an index of results. This is true with respect to many research projects and enforcement activities. In the case of research, it is the final result that counts, not the amount of work required to achieve the result. In enforcement work, the number of infractions dealt with is not an adequate measure since the ideal would be to have no infractions at all.

Lacking an adequate way of measuring or even identifying the end product in precise terms, it is still possible in many cases to develop significant measures of work load of subsidiary activities that contribute to the end product. Examples are number of letters typed, miles patrolled, or purchase orders processed. Detailed data of this type are useful in budgeting but their use is largely confined to the lower organization levels. The sheer mass of such data precludes their extensive use at higher levels.

The alternative budget proposal would permit use of work load and unit cost data to the extent feasible in each case. Under each alternative total figure, the number of units of work that could be performed, the quality standards, and unit costs could be shown. Thus the benefits to be derived from work load measurement would be fully utilized under the alternative budget procedure. In addition, the judgment of subordinates would be obtained on questions which cannot be answered by work load data alone. Such questions involve, for example, the gains or losses of performing alternative amounts of work, the achievement of alternative quality standards, and the effects of spending more or less per unit of work.

Increase-Decrease Analysis

A common technique in the federal government is to require in budget estimates identification of the items representing increases and decreases as compared with the prior year's budget. Special explanations are required for the increases. Budget reviewers are frequently criticized for concentrating on the increases and giving too little attention to items in the base amount. This criticism is justified in part because the amount appropriated last year is not necessarily appropriate for this year and the activities carried on last year are not necessarily appropriate for this year. However, the sheer mass of work involved in reviewing budget estimates precludes examination of every detail every year. Even if it were possible, it would not be necessary, for conditions do not change so fast that every issue has to be rehashed every year.

The basic fault of the increase-decrease method is the fact that it does not require comparison of the relative values of the old and the new. While the proposed increase may be for an eminently desirable purpose, it does not necessarily follow that the appropriation of the agency should be increased. Perhaps other programs of the agency should be cut back enough, or more, to make room for the new. The alternative budget approach has all the advantages of the increase-decrease method without having this basic fault. It would require agencies to weigh the relative merits of all proposals, whether old or new, and thus would reflect the agency's evaluation of the importance of the proposed additions to the spending program in relation to the items composing the base.

Priority Listings

Subordinates are required, in some cases, to indicate priorities of items included in their budget estimates or allotment requests to assist reviewers in determining where cutbacks should be made. Budgets for construction of physical facilities, for example, might contain a listing in priority order of the facilities proposed. The assumption underlying this method is that a budget reduction would be met by eliminating enough projects at the lower end of the list to bring the estimates down to the desired level. When that is the case priority listings are useful. Elimination of the lowest priority items, however, is only one of several means of reducing estimates. Some of the other types of adjustments are as follows: cheaper materials may be used in some or all of the facilities; the size, strength, or durability of the facilities may be decreased; or certain features may be eliminated or postponed until a later date. All of these types of adjustments can be reflected in alternative budgets since they all affect dollar requirements. The priority approach reflects only the one kind of adjustment.

Item-by-Item Control

Approval of individual items of expenditure by higher authority is a common budgetary control technique. Equipment purchases, additions to staff, travel, expensive types of communications as well as entire projects, are frequently subjected to this type of control. An actual case will illustrate the problems involved. During World War II, the Secretary of the Navy was concerned about the expansion of the physical plant of the Navy in the continental United States. In an effort to assure that no facilities would be built unless vitally needed for war purposes and that costs and use of scarce materials would be minimized, the Secretary of the Navy required that all proposed construction projects should be subject to his approval. Prior to this approval they had to be screened at several different levels in the Navy Department. The projects were reviewed by officials in the sponsoring bureau, by the Bureau of Yards and Docks (to insure conformity to wartime engineering standards), by the Chief of Naval Operations (to determine their military necessity), and by a special committee in the Secretary's office composed mainly of civilian businessmen (to determine their overall justification). Even with this series of reviews, the Secretary apparently was not convinced that outlays for facilities were being held down as much as they should be. The process was something less than satisfactory to subordinate officials, too, but for different reasons. They complained of the delays involved in getting a decision and of the amount of time and effort required to justify and rejustify each proposal at the several screening points.

The root of the difficulty, if the thesis of this article is sound, is that controls of individual items do not require or facilitate systematic consideration of relative desirability. Item-by-item control poses the problem at each level of review in these terms: Is the proposal desirable, or essential, or justified? A more pertinent question is: Is the proposal more essential than any alternative use of the funds?

The alternative budget procedure could be applied to this situation in the following manner: bureau chiefs, as well as officials at lower levels, if desired, would be asked to prepare alternative programs for construction of facilities for the period in question. The bureau chiefs in presenting these alternatives would, in effect, tell the Chief of Naval Operations and the Secretary, "If only X dollars are available, I recommend using the money this way . . .; if two X dollars are available, I think the money should be used this way. . . . The advantages and disadvantages of each plan are as follows: . . ." Having an opportunity to see the picture as a whole, having before him alternatives from which to choose, and having the judgment of his subordinates as to gains and losses resulting from each alternative, the Secretary, it would seem, would be able to make his decision fairly readily and with assurance. It is unlikely that he would have to spend as much time reviewing details as is necessary under the item-by-item approach. He would be in a better position to exercise his responsibilities while the subordinates would be freed from the delays, burdens, and irritation invariably involved in piece-by-piece screening processes.

In addition to the specific points discussed above, the alternative budget plan appears to have certain general advantages. It would, we believe, make budgeting a little more palatable to the technically minded operating official who must prepare and justify budgets. His role will be less that of a special pleader for *the* plan he thinks should be accepted and more that of an expert adviser. He will be less like an architect who tries to sell a client on a single plan costing a certain sum and more like an architect advising the client on the relative merits of several house plans and suggesting how the client can get the most for his money regardless of the amount he decides to spend.

Budget analysts under this plan would have a frame of reference which would enable them to operate more effectively. At present, much of their effort is directed toward determining desirability or necessity and not enough attention is given to issues of relative desirability. Under the plan suggested here, the primary job of the budget analyst would be to assist his superior in weighing the relative value of alternative uses of each increment of funds as a step in developing the alternatives to be submitted to the next higher level in the organization. Another aspect of his work would be to explore some of the many possible variations and combinations of features that could not be reflected in the limited number of alternatives formally submitted by the lower officials. Moreover, the analyst would have to check for accuracy, objectivity, and general adequacy the subordinate official's statements of the advantages and disadvantages of the alternatives submitted.

Another significant advantage of the alternative budget proposal is that it would make budgeting somewhat less authoritarian. It would make the budget recommendations of administrative officials less final without weakening in any way their usefulness.

At present, an item screened out of a budget by any administrative official even though it is of major importance is not considered at later stages unless it is brought to the attention of higher executive officials or the Congress by some method which is prohibited by the prevailing rules. To put it mildly, quite definite steps are taken to discourage later consideration. A bureau chief, for example, would be considered out of bounds if he appealed to the President for consideration of an item screened out of his budget by his departmental head. Any administrative officer is prohibited from recommending congressional consideration of any alternatives to the single proposal contained in the President's budget unless specifically requested to do so by a member of Congress. Publication of requests submitted by the departments to the President is also banned.

It is not at all unlikely that superior administrative officials or the Congress would want to adopt some of these screened-out items if they had an opportunity to consider them. Since Congress, in our form of government, is largely responsible for deciding what shall or shall not be done by the executive agencies, the wisdom of such strict censoring of proposals submitted for consideration by Congress seems questionable. Since the President's budget estimates are only recommendations, there would seem to be no disadvantage in his outlining the major alternatives from which he made his selection. In this way the views of subordinates who may have an honest difference of opinion with the

President could be submitted to Congress for consideration openly and without subterfuge. After considering the evidence pertaining to each alternative, Congress could then take its choice. Since the making of such choices is involved in exercising congressional control over the purse strings—a control which historically and currently is a basic cornerstone of democratic government—the provision of information which will assist Congress in evaluating the major alternative courses is of vital importance.[10]

In general, the alternative budget plan is designed to emphasize throughout the budget process the economic ideas discussed in Part I of this article. Its purpose is to pose budget questions at every level in terms of relative value. It also is designed to make maximum use of the expert knowledge and judgment of officials at the lower organization levels by having them analyze, incrementally, the estimates of their agencies and evaluate the relative effectiveness of their several activities in achieving the goals of their organizations.

In proposing this system, I am not particularly concerned with detailed mechanics. There are undoubtedly other ways of accomplishing substantially the same results as this plan is designed to achieve. More important than the precise mechanics is the way of looking at budget problems, the approach to budget analysis and control which this plan reflects.

How practical is the alternative budget plan? How well will it work in practice? The answers to these questions depend in large measure on the relationships between superior and subordinate and between the administration and the Congress. Neither this system nor any other can work satisfactorily if the relations are strained, if the reviewer lacks confidence in the integrity or judgment of the official who is submitting the estimate, or if those who prepare the estimates are not sincerely interested in providing information which the reviewers need to form an intelligent judgment on the merits of the issues.

Perhaps undue faith in the rationality of man underlies the approach to budgeting outlined in this article. In real life, budget decisions are undoubtedly influenced to a greater or lesser extent by such noneconomic and non-rational factors as pride and prejudice, provincialism and politics. These aspects deserve consideration, but they lie beyond the scope of this article. My primary purpose herein has been to stimulate further consideration of the economic aspects of budgeting.[11]

NOTES

1. V. O. Key, Jr., "The Lack of a Budgetary Theory," *American Political Science Review* 34 (December, 1940): 1137–44.
2. Ideas derived from Herbert A. Simon's works concerning the applicability of economic concepts to administration have been particularly useful for this purpose. See his *Administrative Behavior* (New York: Macmillan, 1947).
3. As quoted by Key, *op. cit.*, p. 1139.
4. L. M. Fraser, *Economic Thought and Language* (A. and C. Black Ltd., 1937), p. 103.
5. This method, as it applies to public administration in general, has been extensively analyzed by Herbert A. Simon under the heading of the "criterion of efficiency," *op. cit.*, pp. 172–97.
6. Key, *op. cit.*, p. 1143.
7. Ludwig von Mises, *Bureaucracy* (New Haven, Conn.: Yale University Press, 1944), p. 47.
8. *Op. cit.*, p. 1142.
9. See also, Simon, *op. cit.*, p. 214.
10. Simon also has recommended submission of alternative budget plans to legislatures for substantially the same reason. *Op. cit.*, p. 195.
11. Note on relation to a performance budget. A performance budget, as proposed by the Hoover Commission, would give primary emphasis to the result or end product to be obtained

with the money spent by the government. The commission wisely criticized budget presentations that deal only with the ingredients that are required to produce the end product. Certainly first attention should be given to what is to be accomplished rather than to the people who have to be employed, or the materials which have to be bought, in order to accomplish the basic purpose. Emphasizing performance or end results does not require us to ignore the ingredients or the means to the ends. It should not lead to that result. Important budget issues often involve only the means. While there may be agreement about purpose, the methods may be in dispute. For example, a conservation agency may be responsible for inducing producer-conservation of some natural resource. Should the objective be accomplished by an educational program, by regulatory action, or by subsidy? The alternative budget plan is flexible enough to be adapted to the situation. Alternative purposes as well as alternative methods could and should be reflected in the alternative budget estimates. Whether greater emphasis would be placed on purposes than on methods would depend upon the nature of the problem.

23
What Is Public Administration?

Dwight Waldo

When announcement of the first atomic explosions was made there was a deep sense of awe at the power unleashed. Imagination and reason strained to comprehend what had happened and how it had been brought to pass. The sense of awe was extended to the physical science and engineering which had made this stupendous phenomenon possible.

Along with an account of the general principles of physics involved and how they had been conceived and brought to successful test by the various physicists, the government of the United States gave also an account of the human science and engineering that lay behind the achievement. In brief, a special administrative system named the Manhattan Engineer District had been set up as a subdivision of the government of the United States. The Manhattan Engineer District spent two billion dollars, under conditions of such great secrecy that comparatively few Americans knew it existed and many of its own employees did not know its purpose. It brought together thousands of variously and highly trained men, and many and rare materials and objects, from all over the earth. It built extensive facilities and created specialized subadministrative systems across the continent, tying them together in intricate ways with the administrative systems we know as business enterprises and universities. The success of the Manhattan Engineer District lies before all: its purpose was the achievement of militarily usable explosions based on nuclear fission.

Now it is a reasonable conclusion, based upon evidence, that most people regarded the atomic bomb as an achievement of physical science alone, and that the account of the Manhattan Engineer

Source: From *The Study of Public Administration,* by Dwight Waldo. Copyright © 1955 by Random House, Inc. Reprinted by permission of the publisher.

District did not make much of an impression—and has been generally forgotten. *But might we not seriously entertain another point of view: that the atomic bomb was as much an achievement on the human side as on the side of physical science?*

Not that the atomic bomb was a triumph of human morality. Perhaps the reverse was true, though judgment upon the atomic bomb cannot be dissociated from judgment upon war itself and all its modern machinery. What should be noticed is that in the perspective of history the human technology in achieving the bomb was a remarkable thing—perhaps as far removed from the social experience and imagination of any primitive people as the bomb itself from their physical experience and imagination.

To be sure, the all-but-universal judgment of the day is that our physical science is progressive or mature, while our social science is backward, infantile, or adolescent. This may be true. Certainly it is true by definition if the criteria commonly used in making this judgment are accepted as the proper ones: these criteria (for example, mathematical sophistication) are the distinguishing marks of the physical sciences! But though it may be true, this judgment tends to obscure and to depreciate what we have achieved in the area of human "technology," to use a word not as hard and argumentative as science.

Because we have lived from birth in a society with an advanced technology of cooperation and have learned so much of this technology without awareness, we accept the miracles of human cooperation all about us as though they were natural or indeed inevitable. But they are not. Far from it. This technology was achieved through incalculable human industry, much systematic thought, and the flashes of inspiration of occasional geniuses. The technology of human cooperation must be learned afresh with each generation. Still fuller achievement of human purposes depends upon its extension by study and invention.

This essay is intended as an introduction to the study of one phase or aspect of human cooperation, namely, public administration. Public administration is much less than the whole process or concept of human cooperation. Those who study law, or anthropology, or economics, for example, are also studying human cooperation. There are specialized technologies within the technology of human cooperation; and there are also varying conceptual apparatuses by which study *in* or the study *of* these technologies may be approached. Public administration in our society is one of the technologies within the technology, and has its own special conceptual apparatuses in its practice and in its study.

THE PROBLEM OF DEFINITION

Logic and convention both require that we now deal more carefully with the problem of definition: What is public administration? But in truth there is no good definition of public administration. Or perhaps there are good short definitions, but no good short explanation. The immediate effect of all one-sentence or one-paragraph definitions of public administration is mental paralysis rather than enlightenment and stimulation. This is because a serious definition of the term—as against an epigrammatical definition, however witty—inevitably contains several abstract words or phrases. In short compass these abstract words and phrases can be explained only by other abstract words and phrases, and in the process the reality and importance of "it" become fogged and lost. With this warning let us consider two typical definitions:

1. Public administration is the organization and management of men and materials to achieve the purposes of government.
2. Public administration is the art and science of management as applied to affairs of state.

These are the ways public administration is usually defined. There is nothing wrong with such definitions—except that in themselves they do not help much in advancing understanding. Perhaps these definitions do evoke sharp concepts and vivid images in the reader's mind. But if they do not, it is better to proceed, rather than puzzle over each word, in the hope that the following explanations, descriptions, and comments will bring understanding in their train.

Administration: Art or Science?

Let us give a moment's attention to a traditional dispute in the definition of public administration, and a related source of frequent confusion in the use of the term. The conflict has concerned whether public administration is an art or science. Some students and administrators, impressed with the achievements of the natural and physical sciences, have been insistent that public administration can and should become a science in the same sense. Other students and administrators, impressed with a fluid, creative quality in actual administration, with such intangibles as judgment and leadership, have been equally insistent that public administration cannot become a science, that it is an art.

Much nonsense has resulted from the debates of the science-art controversy, but also considerable clarification of concepts and agreement on usage. It is fashionable nowadays to refer to the "art *and* science" of public administration, in the manner of the second definition above. This usage reflects a general conclusion that public administration has important aspects of *both* science and art. It reflects also, however, a desire to bypass the definitional problems, to compromise the issues by yielding to both sides, to get on with the study and practice of public administration, whatever it is. This disposition to get on is no doubt healthy, and diminishes a picayune and wasteful squabbling over words alone. But it must not be forgotten that definitions are important to fruitful study and effective action. The problem of how people are to be educated or trained for participating in public administration, for example, is one that can be solved only after a decision as to what, after all, is meant by public administration.[1]

Dual Usage of the Words Public Administration

A fertile source of confusion and error, closely related to the science-art controversy, is the fact that the words "public administration" have two usages. They are used to designate and delineate both (1) an area of intellectual inquiry, a discipline or study, and (2) a process or activity—that of administering public affairs. While the two meanings are of course closely related, they are nevertheless different; it is a difference similar to that between biology as the study of organisms and the organisms themselves.

Now if this distinction seems so obvious as not to warrant the making, the excuse must be that it is nevertheless a distinction often missed. It is obvious, in retrospect, that a great deal (but not all) of the controversy over whether public administration is a science or an art stemmed from failure to agree on which public administration was being discussed, the discipline or the activity. It is quickly apparent that it is easier to make the case for science on the *systematic study*, and the case for art on the *practice*, of public administration.

A student of public administration must cultivate a sharp eye for the two usages of the term. Sometimes the meaning will be clear from definition or context, but often there is simply ambiguity and confusion. Sometimes this is true because a writer begins with a definition of public administration as a process or activity, and then proceeds, abruptly or gradually, to use the term also to refer to the systematic study of public administration. Sometimes too the attempt is made to embrace both meanings within the same definition, which opens great opportunity for confusion. (Turn back now and scrutinize the two definitions given on an earlier page. In terms of the distinction made, is their intent clear?)

Let us confess that in attempting to clarify a distinction which is important we have made it sharper than it is in fact. To explain, recall the analogy drawn above between biology as the study of organisms and the organisms themselves. In this case the distinction is sharp, because while biology includes the study of man as an organism, this is but a small part of the whole; and on the other hand, no organism except man makes much of a study of other organisms. In the case of public administration, however, the central concern of the study is man himself, in certain aspects and sets of relationships; and on the other hand, much studying of public administration is carried on by men while engaged in the activities and process of public administration. The file clerk meditating on a better filing system for his needs, the supervisor deciding upon a new distribution of work among his staff, the group of publicly employed social scientists making an elaborate study of how employee morale can be maintained, are all studying public administration in some sense or aspect.

THE CONCEPT OF RATIONAL ACTION

The point will be made clearer by the introduction of the concept of *rational action*, defined here as action correctly[2] calculated to realize given desired goals with minimum loss to the realization of other desired goals. We will use the concept somewhat crudely, and not pause here to consider such interesting and important questions as whether man does wish or should wish that all his actions be rational. We will be content for the moment with the general observation or belief that man can and does maximize his goal achievement by taking thought, by correctly relating means to ends.

Now public administration in *both* senses is rational action as just defined. It is action designed to maximize the realization of goals that are public by definition. In public administration *as an activity* there is continuous calculation of the means to maximize public goals, although there is great variation in the goal awareness, knowledge, and level of abstraction of those engaged in the activity. A top leader may be highly trained and spend his time and energy in a conscious and careful calculation of means to realize given public goals. A machine-operator, on the other hand, may not know or care about the "public" goals of the agency for which he works. Still, the work of the machine-operator will be rational, in the sense that it is a joining of means to ends—say, the operation of a calculating machine for the solving of arithmetical problems. Rationality may be built into a mechanical operation or even a profession. The task of a leader or administrator is then to relate such built-in rationality to goals which *he* seeks in such a way that these goals are maximized.

In public administration *as a study* there is also continuous calculation of the means by which public goals may be maximized. In fact this is not only a central concern of the discipline but, many would say, its sole legitimate concern. In this case too, however, there is great variation—in types of approach, in level of abstraction, in size of problem, in the generality or particularity of goals to be maximized, and so forth. Time-and-motion studies of mechanical operations, leadership decision-making, community value-structures affecting administration, auditing procedures, trade-union characteristics in public administration—these are random examples suggesting the range and variation of studies.

To visualize how study and action can blend together in the concept of rational action, let us imagine a case. Suppose that a firm of management consultants is hired on contract by a state department of public works, with the specific task of determining whether use of mechanical equipment might be made more rational. The persons assigned to the study would observe and gather data and enlist the interest and support of those employees in the department who are concerned with mechanical equipment. Eventually they would present recommendations, and these recommendations might be accepted and put into effect immediately, by the consultants working together with those in the department. In such a case, study and action are so blended that the distinction does not make much sense; and of course study is also a form of action, in the final analysis. Still, at the extreme instead of at the mean, the distinction is a very useful one. A helpful analogy is the familiar range of the spectrum: between the extreme bands are many variations and gradations.

THE MEANING OF ADMINISTRATION: COOPERATIVE RATIONAL ACTION

Up to this point we have invariably dealt with the expression *public administration* and at no time with the noun *administration* alone. An appropriate next step is to examine into the meaning of the noun alone, and then into that of the adjective.

We may proceed by analogy: Public administration is a species belonging to the genus administration, which genus in turn belongs to a family which we may call *cooperative human action*. The word *cooperative* is here defined in terms of results: human activity is cooperative if it has effects that would be absent if the cooperation did not take place. Thus—to take a frequently used illustration—when two men roll a stone which neither could roll alone, they have cooperated. The result, the rolled stone, is the test. But what if one of the two men has lent his effort unwillingly, perhaps under threat of bodily harm from the other: Is this cooperation? It is, in the meaning here assigned. Cooperation as ordinarily used suggests willingness, even perhaps enthusiasm; so we are straining the customary meaning. But the English language seems to have no word better adapted to the meaning here desired. The expression *antagonistic cooperation*, incidentally, is sometimes used in the social sciences to distinguish unwilling from willing cooperation.

We are now in a position to describe administration. Administration is a type of cooperative human effort that has a high degree of rationality. This description in turn needs some qualification.

First, administration is not necessarily the only type of human cooperation that is rational. For example, the American economic system utilizes competition between companies—antagonistic cooperation—as well as administration within them to achieve rational action in the production and distribution of economic goods.[3]

Second, there is an important question implicit in the phrase "high degree of rationality." It is well to note this question, though it cannot be discussed fully here. Whose goals or ends shall be used in assessing rationality? A little reflection will suggest that the *personal* goals of many if not all of the people in a particular administrative system are different from the formally stated goals of that system; sometimes, indeed, a product (for example, a military item) may be secret, its use unknown to many of those engaged in its manufacture. The idea of purpose or goal is essential to the definition of administration. But like quicksilver it is hard to grasp; it eludes and scatters. What shall we say is the purpose or goal of the Chevrolet Division of General Motors? In one sense certainly to make automobiles; and in another sense certainly to make profits for the stockholders. But the personal goals of all officers and employees are certainly in some senses neither of these, or at least not wholly these.[4]

Administration was described as a type of cooperative human endeavor with a high degree of rationality. What distinguishes it as a *type?* The answer depends in part upon the perspective. In one perspective the sociologist views the distinguishing characteristics as those he subsumes under the concept of *bureaucracy* (this is discussed in Chapter Five). In the conventional perspective of the student of administration these characteristics are best subsumed under the two terms *organization* and *management.*

The Nature of Organization

The terms *organization* and *management* require explanation in turn. We may begin with another analogy: organization is the anatomy, management the physiology, of administration. Organization is structure; management is functioning. But each is dependent upon and inconceivable without the other in any existing administrative system, just as anatomy and physiology are intertwined and mutually dependent in any living organism.[5] We are close to the truth, in fact, when we assert that organization and management are merely convenient categories of analysis, two different ways of viewing the same phenomena. One is static and seeks for pattern; the other is dynamic and follows movement.

More precisely, organization may be defined as *the structure of authoritative and habitual personal interrelations in an administrative system.* In any administrative system some persons give orders to others, for certain activities if not for all, and these orders or instructions are habitually followed by other persons; that is to say, some have more power than others, as evidenced by habitual command-obedience or instruction-response relationships. Usually there is an official theory or statement of what the authoritative interrelationships should be in a given administrative system. In an army unit, for example, authority is officially exercised according to the ranks (lieutenant, major, etc.) in the chain of command.

There may be considerable discrepancy, however, between the official theory or statement of authoritative interrelations and the actual, habitual exercise of authority, as evidenced by the actual giving and following of orders or directions. In truth, in any actual administrative system there is usually some discrepancy between the official theory or statement and the facts of authority as evidenced by customary action; and in some cases the official theory or statement may even be no more than a polite fiction, so far do the facts depart from it. Moreover, all or nearly all so-called subordinates, those we think of as docilely taking orders, have means or techniques for changing the behavior of their superiors—for example, the workers' slowdown, or the secretary's smile or frown. A pure one-way power relationship in human affairs is very rare, if indeed it exists. In short, the word *authoritative* in the above definition is ambiguous, since the test of authority may be either the official theory or habitual response. The definition was framed in the knowledge of this ambiguity, which is important but cannot be explored further here. In any case—this is our present point—there are more or less firm structures of personal interrelationships in an administrative system, and these we designate *organization.*

The Nature of Management

Turning to *management,* we may define it as *action intended to achieve rational cooperation in an administrative system.* An administrative system is what we are seeking to explain, and rational cooperation has already been defined. Our attention focuses, then, upon the phrase *action intended to achieve.*

Action is to be construed very broadly: *any change intended to achieve rational cooperation.* It includes self-change or activity, all effects of man upon man, and all effects of man upon nonhuman things. In the postal system, for example, action includes the deliberations of the Postmaster General on such a matter as the desirability of a system of regional postal centers, the instructions of a city postmaster in supervising his staff, and the activities of a deliverer in sorting his daily batch of mail. There is an authoritative quality involved in many of these actions: some men habitually give more instructions (which are followed) than others. Hence some writers define management in terms of direction or control. But this definition is likely to lead to an undesirable narrowing of attention.

The word *intended* in the definition has this significance: there may be a distinction between actions intended to achieve rational cooperation and actions which in fact do so. The reason for this is that in terms of given goals, actions intended to be rational may fail because not all the relevant facts and conditions are known or properly included in judgments and decisions—something which occurs in private life as well as in group activity. On the other hand, actions which are not part of any conscious rational calculation may nevertheless contribute to rational cooperation. Such actions may be sheerly accidental, or they may be actions we associate with emotions, personality, and so forth—areas beyond full scientific statement and calculation, for the present at least. *Management* is customarily used of actions *intended* to achieve rationality (and carries the presumption that the intention is usually realized), but of course an astute practitioner or student will be aware of the difference between intention and actuality and will never forget the large area still unmanageable. Incidentally, a great deal of political theory, especially in modern centuries, has concerned itself with the question of the general scope and the particular areas of human manageability. Students of administration can profit from the literature of this debate. And their findings and experience are in turn an important contribution to it.

THE MEANING OF PUBLIC

After this attempt at a formal definition of administration we return to the question, What is *public* administration? What qualities are signified by the adjective? How is public administration distinguished from administration in general, the species differentiated from the genus?

This is a difficult question. We might begin by defining *public* in terms of such words as *government* and *state*, as is often done. An attempt to understand these words in turn leads to an inquiry into such legal and philosophical concepts as sovereignty, legitimacy, and general welfare. These are important matters, and a student or practitioner of public administration ought to have made serious inquiry into general political theory. Such inquiry helps in understanding various phenomena, such as the coercions sometimes exercised in public administration.

Or we might take a quite different, empirical tack and attempt to define *public* simply by the test of opinion: In a particular society what functions or activities are believed to be public? This proposal has a certain crude truth or usefulness. In the United States, for example, there is certainly a general opinion that, say, the administration of military affairs is public, whereas the administration of automobile sales is private. But complications arise quickly in following this approach. People's opinions differ and are extremely hard to determine and assess (and to suggest another type of complication, the administration of automobile sales is subject to much public control, even in peacetime).

Or we might take the common-sense approach and ask simply, Does the government carry on the function or activity? For many common-sense purposes this approach is quite adequate. It will satisfy most of the purposes of the citizen, and many of those of the student and practitioner of administration. But for many purposes of study, analysis, and informed action it is quite inadequate. Even at the level of common sense it is not completely adequate. For example, there are unstable political situations in which it is difficult to identify "the government" and what is "legal." And there are borderline activities of which one is hard put to it to say whether the government carries them on or not, such are the subtleties of law and circumstances. For example, the development of atomic energy is public in the sense that the government of the United States is in charge. Indeed, there is much secrecy, and tight controls; the situation is sometimes referred to as a monopoly. Yet this program involves an intricate network of contractual relationships, not only with state and local authorities, but with private corporations and individuals. Shall we call developmental programs carried on under contract by Union Carbide and Carbon Corporation public administration?

The most fruitful approach to the meaning and significance of *public* for the student of administration is through use of certain concepts which have been developed most fully in such disciplines as sociology and anthropology. The ones suggested as being particularly useful are associated with the expressions *structural-functional analysis* and *culture.* The concepts involved in these terms are by no means completely clear and precise. About them highly technical and intense professional debates are carried on. Nevertheless they are very useful to the student of administration even if used crudely. They provide needed insight, if not firm scientific generalizations.

Clarification through Structural-Functional Analysis

Structural-functional analysis seeks the basic or enduring patterns of human needs, wants, dispositions, and expressions in *any* society. Recognizing the great diversity in human societies, it yet seeks for common denominators, for the universal grammar and syntax of collective living.

Such studies provide the basis for a meaning of *public* which one could designate universal or inherent. What is indicated—if not precisely concluded—is that institutions and activities that are associated with the identity of a group, with group life as a whole, have special coercive, symbolic, and ceremonial aspects. There is inevitably a sacred aura surrounding some aspects of government. In some societies, of course, Church and State are one, or closely joined. But even where they are officially separated, and even indeed when religion, as such, is officially proscribed by the government, the government—if it is "legitimate"—has this sacred quality. (Nationalism is, of course, often described as a secular religion.)

This approach helps us to understand the special public quality of certain functions of government, for example, the apprehension and trial at law of persons accused of crimes, and the punishment or incarceration of the convicted; the manufacture and control of money; the conduct of foreign relations; or the recruitment, training, and control of armed forces. There is about such activities a monopoly aspect, and they are heavily vested with special coercions, symbolisms, and ceremonies. It is especially in such areas of activity that when a private citizen becomes a public official we expect him to play a new role, one which gives him special powers and prestige, but also requires of him observance of certain proprieties and ceremonies.

Incidentally, though the concept of rational action seems the most useful one in defining administration, we could also use the ideas and findings of structural-functional analysis for this purpose. We could, that is to say, construct a model of what an administrative system is like as a general type, using the concepts and idiom of structural-functional analysis.

Clarification through the Concept of Culture

The concept of culture is used in the social sciences—especially anthropology and sociology—to denote the entire complex of beliefs and ways of doing things of a society. We may analyze it as follows for our purposes: By *beliefs* is meant the systems of ideas held with respect to such matters as religion, government, economics, philosophy, art, and personal interrelations. By *ways of doing things* is meant patterns of activity with respect to food, clothing, shelter, courtship and marriage, child-rearing, entertainment, aesthetic expression, and so forth. The concept implies or asserts that there is a close connection between beliefs and ways of doing things—for example, between ideas concerning art, and modes of aesthetic expression. It further implies or asserts that the various beliefs and ways of doing things in a particular culture are a system in the sense that they are dependent one upon the other, in such a way that a change in one sets off a complicated (and given the present state of our knowledge, at least, often unanticipated and uncontrollable) train of results in others. For example, the introduction of firearms or of the horse into the culture of a primitive people is likely ultimately to affect such matters as artistic expression and marriage customs.

Now the concept of culture tends somewhat to turn attention in the opposite direction from structural-functional analysis. It emphasizes the variety of human experience in society rather than the recurrent patterns. Indeed, the concept has been used in arguing the almost complete plasticity of human beings and of society—and this is the source of one of the professional controversies referred to above. The professional controversies as to the *limits* of the truth or usefulness of concepts should not mislead us, however. The two concepts or sets of concepts we are dealing with here are not necessarily antithetical, but rather are customarily supplementary over a large area of social analysis.

As structural-functional analysis provides tools for dealing with recurrent phenomena, the concept of culture provides tools for dealing with *variety.* The feeling or intuition that administration is administration wherever it is comes very quickly to the student of administration; and this theme is heavily emphasized in the American literature dealing with administration. Yet the student will also become aware, as he advances, that there are important *differences* between administrative systems, depending upon the location, the tasks, the environment, and the inhabitants of the system. And he needs handles by which he can grasp and deal with the differences.

Our present concern is with the differences between private and public administration. The thesis here is that unless we take the broad view provided by intercultural comparison, we are likely to fall into error, designating a distinction as universal when it is a true or important distinction only in our own country or cultural tradition. There come to mind here the common generalizations of writers in the United States which are true of a significant part or aspect of public administration in liberal democratic societies, but are by no means true of public administration by definition, as is implied or suggested. Precisely, consider the generalization that public administration is distinguished by special care for equality of treatment, legal authorization of and responsibility for action, public justification or justifiability of decisions, financial probity and meticulousness, and so forth. It does not take much knowledge of comparative administration to appreciate the very limited applicability of these characteristics to some "public" administration.

The concept of culture—plus knowledge about the actual culture—enables us to see administration in any particular society in relation to all factors which surround and condition it: political theories, educational system, class and caste distinctions, economic technology, and so forth. And enabling us to see administration in terms of its environment, it enables us to understand differences in administration between different societies which would be inexplicable if we were limited to viewing administration analytically in terms of the universals of administration itself. *For as the constituent parts of culture vary within a society, or between societies, so does administration vary as a system of rational cooperative action in that society,* or *between societies.*

Administration is a part of the cultural complex; and it not only is acted upon, it acts. Indeed, by definition a system of rational cooperative action, it inaugurates and controls much change. Administration may be thought of as the major invention and device by which civilized men in complex societies try to control their culture, by which they seek simultaneously to achieve—within the limitations of their wit and knowledge—the goals of stability and the goals of change.

WHAT IS PUBLIC ADMINISTRATION? A SUMMARY EXPLANATION

Let us return again to the question: What is *public* administration? The ideas associated with structural-functional analysis and culture will not enable us to *define* public with precision, but they help us in understanding the significance and implications of the term. They help us to understand why public administration has some general or generic aspects but also why the line between public and private is drawn in different places and with differing results—why "public" doesn't have precisely the same meaning in any two different cultural contexts. They help make some sense of the undoubted facts of similarity in diversity and diversity in similarity that characterize the Universe of Administration.

Whether public administration is an art or a science depends upon the meaning and emphasis one assigns these terms. The answer is affected too by the kind of public administration referred to—the study or discipline on the one hand, the activity or process on the other.

The central idea of public administration is rational action, defined as action correctly calculated to realize given desired goals. Public administration both as a *study* and as an *activity* is intended to maximize the realization of goals; and often the two blend into each other, since in the last analysis study is also a form of action.

Administration is cooperative human action with a high degree of rationality. Human action is *cooperative* if it has effects that would be absent if the cooperation did not take place. The significance of *high degree* of rationality lies in the fact that human cooperation varies in effectiveness of goal attainment, whether we think in terms of formal goals, the goals of leaders, or the goals of all who cooperate.

The distinguishing characteristics of an administrative system, seen in the customary perspective of administrative students, are best subsumed under two concepts, organization and management, thought of as analogous to anatomy and physiology in a biological system. *Organization* is the structure of authoritative *and* habitual personal interrelations in an administrative system. *Management* is action intended to achieve rational cooperation in an administrative system.

The significance of *public* can be sought in varying ways, each having some utility. For some purposes, for example, a simple determination of the legal status of an administrative system will suffice. For some important purposes, however, it is desirable to go beyond the boundaries of public administration as it has conventionally been studied and to adopt some of the concepts and tools of sociology and anthropology. *Structural-functional analysis* helps to identify the generic meaning or enduring significance of *public* in all societies. The concept of culture, on the other hand, helps in identifying and dealing with the varying aspects of *public* between societies, as well as with various relations of administration within a society.

THE IMPORTANCE OF NONRATIONAL ACTION

In this attempt to define and explain public administration in brief compass we have constructed a simple model. Of necessity many concepts of importance in the study of public administration have been omitted, and some of the concepts included have been dealt with rather summarily. Some of the omitted concepts are introduced, and perhaps some of the inadequacies repaired, in the following chapters. This is the appropriate place, however, to deal with what is perhaps a bias or distortion in our model, since the basis or source of the distortion largely lies outside of the later discussions.

The point is this: perhaps the model, by stressing rational action, creates a false impression of the amount of rationality (as defined) existing or possible in human affairs.

Now we may properly hold that the concept of rational action is placed at the center of administrative study and action. This is what it is about, so to speak. But the emphasis needs to be qualified—mellowed—by knowledge and appreciation of the nonrational. It is now generally agreed that earlier students of administration had a rationalist bias that led them to overestimate the potentialities of man (at least in the foreseeable future) for rational action.

Most of the streams of modern psychology emphasize—indeed perhaps overemphasize—the irrational component in human psychology: the role of the conditioned response, the emotive, the subconscious. Much of anthropology and sociology stresses complementary themes: the large amount of adaptive social behavior that is below the level of individual—and even group—conscious choice of goals and means to realize the goals. (The fact that goals are not chosen consciously does not mean that there are no goals in this behavior, nor that the goals are necessarily unimportant, nor even that they are any less true or meaningful than those consciously chosen. A baby responding to food stimuli, for example, is not choosing the goal of survival—but survival is usually thought a highly important goal. Actually, though such words as *conscious* and *unconscious* or *deliberate* and *adaptive* suggest two different realms of behavior, there is probably no sharp break, but rather varying levels of awareness of ends and means.)

The general picture that the nonrationalist conclusion of the psychologists, anthropologists, and sociologists (and others—the sources and manifestations of this mode of thought are many) present for the student of administration is this: An administrative organization has an internal environment and an external environment that are largely nonrational, at least so far as the formal goals of the administrative organization are concerned. People do not come into administrative organizations as pieces of putty, as units of abstract energy, nor as mere tools sharpened to some technical or professional purpose. They bring with them their whole cultural conditioning and their personal idiosyncrasies. Each is genetically unique, and all are members of institutions—families, churches, clubs, unions, and so forth—outside the administrative organization; and within the administrative organization they form into natural or adaptive groups of various kinds—friendships, cliques, car pools, and so forth—that flow across the lines of formal administrative organization, sometimes darkening, sometimes lightening, and sometimes erasing these lines.

Students of administration have become increasingly aware of the nonrational factors that surround and condition administration. They have broadened the base of their study to include much information that was formerly either unavailable or ignored. The goal of rationality has not been abandoned. Rather, it has been put in a new perspective: to achieve rationality demands a respect for the large area of the nonrational and much knowledge of it. Partly this new perspective is but a more serious heeding of Bacon's maxim: "Nature to be commanded must be obeyed." (These nonrational factors are not to be understood as, by definition, working against formal organization goals, but rather, paradoxically, as phenomena which, properly understood, can often be directed toward the realization of organization goals. They are resources as well as liabilities. Thus personal rivalries can be channeled—as by an official contest—to help rather than hinder goal achievement.) Partly the new perspective is a philosophical or psychological reorientation, as implied in the word *respect.* Students of administration now know that they are not going to take heaven by storm, that is to say, quickly reduce human affairs to rule and chart. Some of them, even, without ceasing to desire and strive for more rationality than we have now achieved, are heard to say that complete rationality in human affairs is not the proper goal; that a world in which *all* is orderly and predictable, with no room for spontaneity, surprise, and emotional play, is an undesirable world.

NOTES

1. Another distinction, related and similar to the distinction between science and art, is that between pure and applied, or theoretical and practical, science. This distinction, which has important uses, is discussed below in connection with logical positivism. For a statement of it see Herbert A. Simon: *Administrative Behavior: A Study of Decision-Making Processes in Administrative Organization* (New York, Macmillan, 1947), Appendix.
2. This is an important—and difficult—word. One source of difficulty lies in the fact that given actions may produce desired results for the wrong reasons. Thus actions enjoined by superstition are found sometimes to be correct (i.e., goal-maximizing) by science, but the explanations in the two systems of interpretation are quite different. Another source of difficulty or ambiguity is discussed under The Meaning of Management.
3. See *Politics, Economics and Welfare* (New York, Harper & Row, 1953) by Robert A. Dahl and Charles E. Lindblom for a discussion of different forms of rational cooperation.
4. Sometimes a distinction is made between *purpose* and *function* in an attempt to deal with this problem. Dahl and Lindblom (p. 38) apply the idea of *net* goal achievement to the problem of multiple goals. "What do we mean by 'rationality'? And how can one test whether one action is more rational than another? The first question is easier to answer than the second. An action is rational to the extent that it is 'correctly' designed to maximize goal achievement, given the goal in question and the real world as it exists. Given more than one goal (the usual human situation), an action is rational to the extent that it is correctly designed to maximize *net* goal achievement."
5. This analogy is for introductory and explanatory purposes, and is to be viewed in this light. The definitions of organization and management that follow in the text admittedly comprehend less than the whole of societal anatomy and physiology respectively. And we are not here concerned with the familiar sociological distinction between patterns and consequences, or with distinguishing between static and dynamic models.

24
Basic Concepts in the Study of Public Management

Catheryn Seckler-Hudson

Sit down before facts as a little child; be prepared to give up any preconceived notion; follow humbly wherein and to whatever abysses nature leads, or you shall learn nothing.

THOMAS HUXLEY

Less than one hundred years ago it was considered quite adequate for the political science student or even the political science professor to study American government as consisting of the legislative, the executive, and the judicial branches. Emphasis was placed on *structure.* Functions of government were relatively few and simple. The philosophy of "that government is best which governs least" was still quite palatable. Such phrases as "the welfare state," "the administrative state," and "the service state" were not used in speaking or thinking of the American system of government. George Washington appointed only four cabinet members at the beginning of his first term as President, and there were no regulatory agencies or commissions until the latter part of the nineteenth century. Indeed it was not until 1889 that the Department of Agriculture was established and not until after 1900 that the Departments of Commerce, of Labor, and of Health, Education, and Welfare were created by Congress.

Today one need only consult the current Federal Budget of the United States for a panoramic view of the multifarious programs and multitudinous organizations that comprise our Federal system of government. Or one need only review the Annual reports of the dozens of major departments and agencies of the Federal Government to realize the scope and range of services tendered our citizens through the instrumentality of public administration, that is, those governmental operations which have as their end goal the implementation and execution of public policy.

Raymond B. Fosdick in writing of our environment which has become ". . . so baffling, that few individuals can understand it all and fewer still can control it. . . ." gives the following illustration of changing government in the United States:

> ". . . Government a hundred years ago was a comparatively simple affair. It dealt with matters that were easily within the scope of the average man's intelligence. In its practical aspects there was little that was technical about it. . . . Even in its national aspect government was not complex. There were few technical bureaus and those that existed did not affect the daily lives of the citizens. . . .
>
> "But those days are gone. . . . Government has become infinitely complex and

Source: Permission to reprint granted by Lomond Publications, Inc. (Mt. Airy, Maryland), distributor of *Organization and Management: Theory and Practice* by Catheryn Seckler-Hudson, originally published by The American University Press, Copyright 1955.

> technical. It has to do for the most part with matters which are far beyond the intelligence of the average citizen. . . . Consequently, the breach between the citizenship and its government is widening as science increases the intricacy of its operations. Our elections, many of them, are fought out on the basis of issues about which the voters have no intelligent conception whatsoever, nor could a majority of them acquire such a conception even if there were time and machinery for their education. . . . Government is getting out of the hands of the people, not in the sense that anybody is taking it away from them, but in the sense that with the rapid extension of its technical aspects it is becoming more and more difficult to comprehend and control."[1]

It is the conscious awareness of the bigness and complexity of our government that has given rise to the study of public management—the attempt to systematically arrange and order our governmental affairs so as to achieve the desired ends of government insofar as this goal is humanly possible to reach. This attempt at systematic management through intelligent leadership is in accordance with the philosophy of Mary Parker Follett, which was in essence ". . . that the democratic way of life, implemented by intelligent organization and administration of government and of industry, is to work toward an honest integration of all points of view, to the end that every individuality may be mobilized and made to count both as a person and as an effective part of his group and of society as a whole."[2]

This dynamic philosophy is as appealing and basic today, in a world disturbed by complex tragedies and catastrophic technological advances, as it was in the simpler civilization before the First World War. The human desire for the realization of this philosophy remains very strong although its achievement may have become more difficult. The question arises as to whether we have passed the day when this democratic way of administration can be guaranteed. In order to approach that question, one needs to understand the principal factors of modern administration in a democratic society. These factors permeate and underlie the day-to-day attempts of men to work together systematically to get tasks done, and they provide a setting in which the individual and groups of individuals operate toward goals. What are these prevailing factors?

1. Specialization in Most Aspects of Modern Administration Is Increasing and Deepening. More and more frequently man is dividing labor and effort into smaller and smaller parts. The modern advances in technology call for more specific expertness. Size and complexity of modern organizations call for greater subdivision so as to provide manageable parts. No one person can hope to know more than a particle of the knowledge that exists. Therefore, men and women find themselves working on minute tasks which, in and of themselves, are relatively unimportant, but which, when properly assembled and combined with hundreds of other tasks, create new combinations and discoveries.

The benefits of specialization are well known. But these benefits may be lost unless we can avoid the dangers of specialization. One danger of specialization is that in his specialized effort *the individual himself will get lost.* He may become so intent on his work, which may deepen day by day, that he will, figuratively speaking, sink into a rut that will gradually engulf him. He may see no relationship between his own efforts and those of others, and hence he will feel no responsibility for anything beyond the immediate limits of his own performance. Indeed, he may penetrate deeper and deeper into his own specialization but understand less and less the social implications of what he is doing. At this point it becomes a real question as to whether the efforts of the specialist are of benefit either to the individual or to society. For the true specialist recognizes relationships between his own work and that of others—between his own contribution and that of the whole. He recognizes that it is the interweaving of his ideas and his contribution with those of many others that makes for dynamic, yet orderly, effort.

A second danger of specialization is that the fruits of specialized effort will be lost to society. As the specialist isolates himself more from the world of relationships, his efforts, though in and of themselves good, may be unused. What social value has an invention if it is never put to use? What meaning has a first-class technical report if it is never read? What social worth has a magnificent painting if it is never seen? What basic value has any given line of research unless it is meaningful in terms of some larger whole?

One of the grave dangers we face in administrative management in the Federal Government is that we have too many specialists who are isolated with "atom assignments" of which no one in particular knows, and the results of which no one cares. Even the specialists who are told to write "scientific" reports, too frequently write reports which may be scholarly and reliable in the highest sense of the word, but which no one reads or studies. The *completed report* seems more important than the use that is made of it, and altogether too often the completed assignment is considered an end in itself. Figure 1 depicts the dangers of specialization in this type of setting. Specialized effort is shown as an end in itself—represented by *parallel lines that never meet.*

2. Coordination of Specialized Effort Is Imperative, If Administration Is To Be Effective. If the fruits of the specialists are to be preserved, then at some points in the organization there must be a careful collecting and combining of these particles in order to give them meaning and pattern. Consider any great musical orchestration. There are dozens of specialized artists—each with his own instrument. Suppose each artist, at any one time, played his individual part on his individual instrument without regard for any of the other artists. You might witness individual perfection. But the net result would be chaos and confusion.

FIGURE 1 • THE DANGER OF SPECIALIZATION IN AN ORGANIZATION

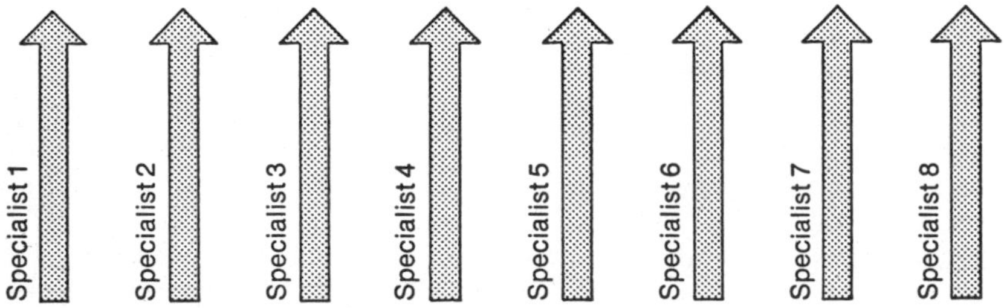

Result: Most, if not all, of the specialized effort is wasted because of lack of coordination.

It is only when the director of the orchestra coordinates the performance of each artist with that of each of the other artists that every individual has become an effective part of a great contribution. The coordinator has effected a sense of relationships among many specialists wherein the efforts of each has been made to count. The coordinator has prevented each artist from sinking into his rut of specialization to the point where many individual ruts would run parallel to each other, but never meet to form a pattern.

Tens of thousands of such illustrations showing the necessity for the coordinative function could be given. For example, the football players, each with special talent knit together by a coach, to make an effective team; a technical laboratory staffed with experts each with special talent needing at some point the services of a generalist who knows how to relate the productions of the technicians so as to make them worthwhile; or the beautiful mosaic which is merely a heap of small colored stones until some genius properly relates and combines the many tiny stones into a magnificent pattern.

One of the great needs of modern public administration is for the generalist—the coordinator—who has the genius to build something worth-while out of the special efforts of individual performers.[3]

If such genius cannot be discovered or trained, then the work of thousands will remain meaningless, and thousands of personalities will never experience the development and growth that come from knowing that one's efforts are an integral part of a worth-while pattern. Indeed, as Luther Gulick has written, "If subdivision of work is inescapable, coordination becomes mandatory."[4] Nor can we assume that coordination is something that will automatically occur. "It must be won by intelligent, vigorous, persistent and organized effort."[5] Figure 2 depicts the coordination of specialized efforts in an organization, providing for parallel lines of effort to meet in terms of a known end purpose or objective. The coordinative function is shown as the continuous combining and relating of the many parts and functions in order to achieve the objective. The figure also indicates the importance of communication and interrelationship among specialists so that each can appreciate and supplement the work of each, and in turn complement each other in helping achieve the objective of the total organization of which he is a part.

3. *There Should Exist a Central Policy toward Which Specialization and Coordination Can Be Directed.* Coordination represents but a method, the true value of which lies in directing individual efforts toward some goal. Or, as Russell Robb says: "Organization is but a means to an end; it provides a method."[6] Without a goal or a policy, organization and administration would indeed be meaningless. Lyndall Urwick writes:

> "There must be an objective. That sounds obvious. But if situations are analyzed in detail it is quite extraordinary how many undertakings and parts of undertakings are discovered which are just going along by their own momentum, with only the very vaguest and most hazy idea of where they're trying to go or why."[7]

The purpose of a policy is to provide a framework for effort. Without a policy, or with an unclear policy, even the coordinator has no standard against which to measure results. For administration does not operate in a vacuum—it operates *for* something and *toward* something and that "something" must be made clear in terms of a policy that gives meaning to the systemized effort. Figure 2 depicts the importance of the over-all objective or policy in an organization.

Perhaps it is in the field of policy formation that governmental administration is deficient. Since the Congress of the United States is the law-making body in our governmental system, and since public laws are piecemeal affairs, it is difficult, if not impossible, to express at a given time the clear-cut policy of the federal government. Public laws are at best a matter of compromise and frequently the law is general and vague. Thus it becomes necessary for the administrator of the law to interpret its meaning to the best of his ability. Since the administrator is usually somewhat of a specialist himself, at least in program interest, it is natural that the administration of the law often takes on the color of the specialist. Furthermore, when it is considered that hundreds of major laws are enacted by each Congress and that, in turn,

FIGURE 2 • COORDINATION OF SPECIALIZED EFFORTS IN AN ORGANIZATION

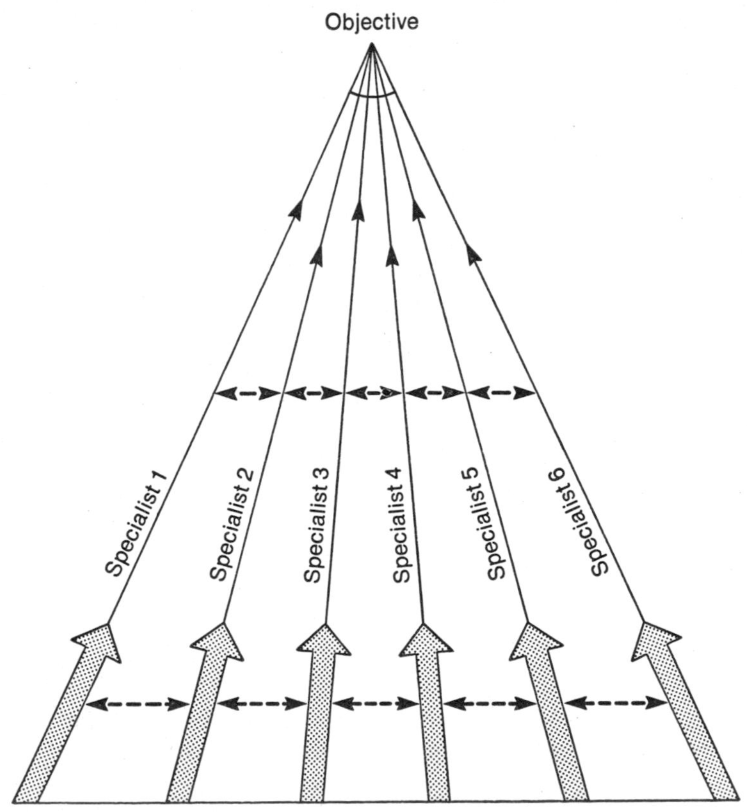

Note: Communication is provided upward and across the lines of specialization.

Result: The efforts of each specialist are combined and related so that each can make a contribution to the end purpose of the organization. This is the coordinative function.

hundreds of administrators are interpreting and administering these laws, it is small wonder that the national policy is difficult, if not impossible, to state in concise terms. Despite these handicaps and difficulties, the principle remains sound: that to be meaningful, specialization and coordination of effort must be carried on in terms of stated policy or goal. For where there is no goal, there is no destination point; and where there is no destination point we become wanderers—perhaps busy about many things—but lacking either purpose or vision.

4. *Appropriate Methods and Procedures Which Will Achieve the Policy Should Be Developed and Utilized.* By and large, the selection of methods of operating is regarded as a highly individualistic undertaking. Leaders are prone to regard methodology as a private reserve and to tolerate little interference thereon. While it is true that a leader should exercise a good deal of authority in determining the major methods and procedures by which he operates, it is likewise true that disunity can occur easily with respect to method or procedure as well as with respect to policy and objective. With the growth of democratic administration, it is doubtful whether methodology and procedure can be isolated to the sole jurisdiction of the executive. If followership within an organization is to be effective, not only the policy but the methods and procedures as well must be acceptable to those affected by them.

The selection and utilization of methods and procedures often influence and condition policy. A clever administrator with policy legislation to guide him, can, through the simple technique of delay, or of careful timing, frequently bend the implementation of policy to his own liking. Or a particular method of scheduling projects and tasks or the failure to delegate work effectively may serve to defeat what was intended. And in our governmental system especially, the use of liberal, as opposed to strict, administrative interpretation of public laws, conditions and reconditions policy results.

In any effective endeavor there is needed a systematic, orderly, and reliable way of working. The purposes of such are manifold. Systematic methods and procedures should help reduce lost time and eliminate errors, undue duplication, and waste. They should provide for effective utilization of individuals, funds, and equipment. They should command the respect of the employees, and of others with whom the organization works. More importantly, the methods and procedures should be such as to promote and achieve the policy of the organization rather than to in any degree impair it. And this should be done without any serious violation of other principles of administration.

Obviously there is no single correct way of operating. The nature of the situation, the factors of size and complexity, the importance of the time element, the availability of resources, the urgency of the purpose to be served, and the nature and force of public opinion, are major conditioning matters in the choice of method and procedure. The important concept to keep in mind is that the procedures and methods within a given unit are the warp and the woof which hold the organization together, and keep it in movement. They are selected work ways to achieve policy goals, and like specialization and coordination are but means toward ends. The system of methods and procedures is shown in Figure 3 as the route which leads from a felt need or purpose to the satisfaction of that purpose. Little wonder that the development of valid and acceptable methods in operating organizations is becoming one of the basic and most studied threads of administration. Man's quest for better ways of doing things is ever an ongoing process.

5. *Administration Takes Place in a Dynamic Setting.* The basic operational unit in organization and administration is the human being. The human being is not an automaton. He is a vibrant, changing personality with a culture of his own. His personality and its effect on other personalities and the interplay of many personalities condition organization and administration. Wherever there is an administrative situation—that is, wherever there are individuals working together toward some goal—one can witness the influence of *human dynamics.* This fact is the basis of the statement that "administration does not operate in a vacuum; it operates in terms of its cultural setting." To understand the importance of personalities in administration, one need only note any office or bureau of government in operation. Notice the influence of particular persons on the "work-ways" of the group, or the spirit of teamwork or lack of it. And if the office under study is a highly integrated one, note the skepticism and real concern with which newcomers are regarded, even at the secretarial level. If the principal function of the office is that of research, in all likelihood the selection of new or additional personnel will be regarded as a matter of major concern to all those who work therein. For the injection of a single new personality in a highly sensitive research organization could affect the efforts and results of the efforts of every other researcher in the unit.

In addition to human dynamics, administration is conditioned by the dynamics of *politics* and *public opinion.* Evidences of this are everywhere. A national election and its effect on the passage of public laws; a new State Governor and his influence on state administration; a Democratic President and a Republican Congress and the resultant administrative adjustments; an economy-minded House of Representatives and its effect on the budgets of administrative agencies; a public opinion resistant to higher prices or higher taxes and the resulting restraints placed on the National Government. Towering over and above such examples is the entire field of international politics and the complex environment created by it. Yet it is precisely this complex environment in which administration must operate—conditioned by international politics, and conditioning such politics in turn. Administration is indeed a moving drama of processes, problems, politics, and personalities!

A third category of dynamics which helps to set the stage for organization and administration consists of *changing*

FIGURE 3 • THE ROUTE FROM A KNOWN PURPOSE TO THE ACHIEVEMENT OF IT

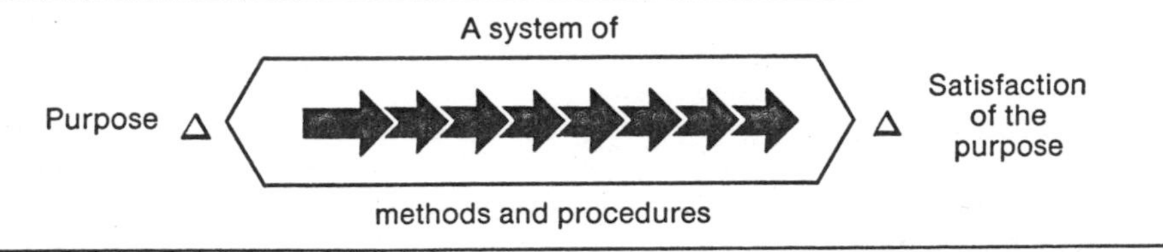

social situations. Administration must respond to such cataclysmic changes as those provoked by world wars, abrupt reconversions to peace, economic depressions, floods, fires, droughts, or excessive inflation. We are witnessing today the adjustment of our entire governmental administration to such matters as changing needs of underdeveloped parts of the earth, the establishment of cultural and educational centers in cities whose names were scarcely known a decade ago, and to the significant attempts to improve our part in international administrative organizations because our role has become so clearly one of leadership instead of isolation.

All of these and many other social changes have influenced not only the structure of our public administration, but its philosophy as well. They have influenced not only the public service personnel, but the very purposes of government. They have conditioned not only a domestic policy but have created a new international outlook.

Equally important as a part of the dynamic setting for administration is our *changing technology.* Such technical advances as the creation of new submarines, atomic and hydrogen bombs and the practical release of nuclear energy, the discovery of radar and the proximity fuse of the Army and Navy, the invention of radio and television and long-range cameras, and hundreds of other advances which defy understanding by the ordinary mind continuously condition administration. One specific example of such conditioning is the attempt to coordinate the military establishments in the United States and all of the research pertaining to national defense toward the goal of *Survival in the Air Age.*[8] Of our changing technology Raymond B. Fosdick has written:

> ". . . Modern science has revolutionized, not man, but his world. It has made his old ideas infinitely more dangerous. It has taken away his flintlock musket and his firebrand and given him instead machine guns and poison gas. It has brought him into intimate contact with his neighbours, and exposed him to all the irritations that arise from propinquity. It has extended his field of self-interest so that in the pursuit of happiness and even of life he collides with his fellows on the other side of the globe."[9]

This, then, is the setting for organized administration in a modern democracy. A setting wherein the dynamics of politics and public opinion, personalities, situational factors, and technological change condition and recondition administration. A setting in which administrators must be able to adjust to change. It is a setting in which "all advancement in intelligence and insight depends upon our ability to call in question and reconsider what we have hitherto taken for granted."[10] Somehow, if we are to survive within this turbulent laboratory of social living, administration must (1) provide for the gains of special knowledge and effort; (2) combine and relate the efforts of the specialists into a coordinated pattern; (3) identify a worth-while and clear policy or goal; and (4) develop and utilize reliable methods in the systematic pursuit of such policies and goals. On the one hand, the task seems impossible; on the other it is challenging and inescapable.

Summary

In this volume organization will be regarded as the division and unification of effort toward some goal or policy. Management will be regarded as the effective utilization of human resources and material in an effort to reach the known goal. Organization and management pervade all levels, areas, and kinds of activities—from personal affairs to world-wide matters. Herein, however, emphasis is placed on *public* organization and management—that is the area which has to do with the administration of public or governmental policies.

These concepts of organization and management when applied to governmental administration rest upon certain postulates which may be summarized briefly as follows:

1. If public administration is to be effective, there must exist an identifiable national POLICY in which the objectives and goals of our people are the controlling factors.
2. There should be in our system of public management, including its many subdivisions, a CENTER OF DIRECTION—a responsible general manager (president, governor, mayor, etc.) with clear and adequate authority and corresponding responsibility and accountability to the electorate.
3. As a framework for effective operation, there should be established a clear-cut, structural ORGANIZATION in which there is (a) clear definition of tasks and functions, (b) equitable allocation of resources to the defined tasks, (c) structural relationships through which to operate, and (d) adequate leadership and internal coordination.
4. There should be established and developed appropriate METHODS OF OPERATION in order to achieve the policies. The methods and procedures should be subjected to continuous reexamination in the light of experience, change, need, and scientific data.
5. There should be provided a COMPREHENSIVE MEANS OF INTERACTION—that is, channels of communication which will facilitate understanding and coordination of work.
6. There should be recognized at all points that every aspect of administration works in, and must respond to, a DYNAMIC SETTING. Provision, therefore, must be made for continuous adaptation and growth.

NOTES

1. Raymond B. Fosdick, *The Old Savage in the New Civilization* (Doubleday, Garden City, N.Y., 1928), pp. 15–17.
2. Henry C. Metcalf and Lyndall Urwick, eds., *Dynamic Administration: The Collected Papers of Mary Parker Follett* (New York: Harper & Row, 1940), p. 9. This book should be read carefully by every serious student of public affairs.
3. Leonard D. White, in *Introduction to the Study of Public Administration,* 3rd ed. (New York: Macmillan, 1948), p. 36, defines coordination as ". . . the adjustment of the functions of the parts to each other, and of the movement and operation of parts in time so that each can make its maximum contribution to the product of the whole."
4. See Luther Gulick and Lyndall Urwick, eds., *Papers on the Science of Administration* (New York: Institute of Public Administration, 1937), p. 6.
5. *Ibid.*
6. Russell Robb, *Lectures on Organization,* privately printed, 1910, p. 45.
7. Lyndall Urwick, *The Elements of Administration* (New York: Harper & Row, 1943), p. 26.
8. A Report by the President's Air Policy Commission, *Survival in the Air Age* (Washington, D.C.: United States Government Printing Office, 1948). The entire report is pertinent to technological dynamics.
9. Fosdick, *The Old Savage in the New Civilization, op. cit.,* p. 232.
10. James Harvey Robinson, *The Human Comedy,* (New York: Harper & Row, 1937), p. 5.

25
Parkinson's Law or the Rising Pyramid
C. Northcote Parkinson

Work expands so as to fill the time available for its completion. General recognition of this fact is shown in the proverbial phrase "It is the busiest man who has time to spare." Thus, an elderly lady of leisure can spend the entire day in writing and dispatching a postcard to her niece at Bognor Regis. An hour will be spent in finding the postcard, another in hunting for spectacles, half an hour in a search for the address, an hour and a quarter in composition, and twenty minutes in deciding whether or not to take an umbrella when going to the mailbox in the next street. The total effort that would occupy a busy man for three minutes all told may in this fashion leave another person prostrate after a day of doubt, anxiety, and toil.

Granted that work (and especially paperwork) is thus elastic in its demands on time, it is manifest that there need be little or no relationship between the work to be done and the size of the staff to which it may be assigned. A lack of real activity does not, of necessity, result in leisure. A lack of occupation is not necessarily revealed by a manifest idleness. The thing to be done swells in importance and complexity in a direct ratio with the time to be spent. This fact is widely recognized, but less attention has been paid to its wider implications, more especially in the field of public administration. Politicians and taxpayers have assumed (with occasional phases of doubt) that a rising total in the number of civil servants must reflect a growing volume of work to be done. Cynics, in questioning this belief, have imagined that the multiplication of officials must have left some of them idle or all of them able to work for shorter hours. But this is a matter in which faith and doubt seem equally misplaced. The fact is that the number of the officials and the quantity of the work are not related to each other at all. The rise in the total of those employed is governed by Parkinson's Law and would be much the same whether the volume of the work were to increase, diminish, or even disappear. The importance of Parkinson's Law lies in the fact that it is a law of growth based upon an analysis of the factors by which that growth is controlled.

The validity of this recently discovered law must rest mainly on statistical proofs, which will follow. Of more interest to the general reader is the explanation of the factors underlying the general tendency to which this law gives definition. Omitting technicalities (which are numerous) we may distinguish at the outset two motive forces. They can be represented for the present purpose by two almost axiomatic statements, thus: (1) "An official wants to multiply subordinates, not rivals" and (2) "Officials make work for each other."

Source: C. Northcote Parkinson, *Parkinson's Law and Other Studies in Administration* (Boston: Houghton Mifflin, 1957), pp. 1–8, 10–13.

To comprehend Factor 1, we must picture a civil servant, called A, who finds himself overworked. Whether this overwork is real or imaginary is immaterial, but we should observe, in passing, that A's sensation (or illusion) might easily result from his own decreasing energy: a normal symptom of middle age. For this real or imagined overwork there are, broadly speaking, three possible remedies. He may resign; he may ask to halve the work with a colleague called B; he may demand the assistance of two subordinates, to be called C and D. There is probably no instance in history, however, of A choosing any but the third alternative. By resignation he would lose his pension rights. By having B appointed, on his own level in the hierarchy, he would merely bring in a rival for promotion to W's vacancy when W (at long last) retires. So A would rather have C and D, junior men, below him. They will add to his consequence and, by dividing the work into two categories, as between C and D, he will have the merit of being the only man who comprehends them both. It is essential to realize at this point that C and D are, as it were, inseparable. To appoint C alone would have been impossible. Why? Because C, if by himself, would divide the work with A and so assume almost the equal status that has been refused in the first instance to B; a status the more emphasized if C is A's only possible successor. Subordinates must thus number two or more, each being thus kept in order by fear of the other's promotion. When C complains in turn of being overworked (as he certainly will) A will, with the concurrence of C, advise the appointment of two assistants to help C. But he can then avert internal friction only by advising the appointment of two more assistants to help D, whose position is much the same. With this recruitment of E, F, G, and H the promotion of A is now practically certain.

Seven officials are now doing what one did before. This is where Factor 2 comes into operation. For these seven make so much work for each other that all are fully occupied and A is actually working harder than ever. An incoming document may well come before each of them in turn. Official E decides that it falls within the province of F, who places a draft reply before C, who amends it drastically before consulting D, who asks G to deal with it. But G goes on leave at this point, handing the file over to H, who drafts a minute that is signed by D and returned to C, who revises his draft accordingly and lays the new version before A.

What does A do? He would have every excuse for signing the thing unread, for he has many other matters on his mind. Knowing now that he is to succeed W next year, he has to decide whether C or D should succeed to his own office. He had to agree to G's going on leave even if not yet strictly entitled to it. He is worried whether H should not have gone instead, for reasons of health. He has looked pale recently—partly but not solely because of his domestic troubles. Then there is the business of F's special increment of salary for the period of the conference and E's application for transfer to the Ministry of Pensions. A has heard that D is in love with a married typist and that G and F are no longer on speaking terms—no one seems to know why. So A might be tempted to sign C's draft and have done with it. But A is a conscientious man. Beset as he is with problems created by his colleagues for themselves and for him—created by the mere fact of these officials' existence—he is not the man to shirk his duty. He reads through the draft with care, deletes the fussy paragraphs added by C and H, and restores the thing back to the form preferred in the first instance by the able (if quarrelsome) F. He corrects the English—none of these young men can write grammatically—and finally produces the same reply he would have written if officials C to H had never been born. Far more people have taken far longer to produce the same result. No one has been idle. All have done their best. And it is late in the evening before A finally quits his office and begins the return journey to Ealing. The last of the office lights are being turned off in the gathering dusk that marks the end of another day's administrative toil. Among the last to leave, A reflects with bowed shoulders and a wry smile that late hours, like gray hairs, are among the penalties of success.

From this description of the factors at work the student of political science will recognize that administrators are more or less bound to multiply. Nothing has yet been said, however, about the period of time likely to elapse between the date of A's appointment and the date from which we can calculate the pensionable service of H. Vast masses of statistical evidence have been collected and it is from a study of this data that Parkinson's Law has been deduced. Space will not allow of detailed analysis but the reader will be interested to know that research began in the British Navy Estimates. These were chosen because the Admiralty's responsibilities are more easily measurable than those of, say, the Board of Trade. The question is merely one of numbers and tonnage. Here are some typical figures. The strength of the Navy in 1914 could be shown as 146,000 officers and men, 3249 dockyard officials and clerks, and 57,000 dockyard workmen. By 1928 there were only 100,000 officers and men and only 62,439 workmen, but the dockyard officials and clerks by then numbered 4558. As for warships, the strength in 1928 was a mere fraction of what it had been in 1914—fewer than 20 capital ships in commission as compared with 62. Over the same period the Admiralty officials had increased in number from 2000 to 3569, providing (as was remarked) "a magnificent navy on land." These figures are more clearly set forth in tabular form. (See Table 1.)

The criticism voiced at the time centered on the ratio between the numbers of those available for fighting and those available only for administration. But that comparison is not to the present purpose. What we have to note is that the 2000 officials of 1914 had become the 3569 of 1928; and that this growth was unrelated to any possible increase in their work. The Navy during that period had diminished, in point of fact, by a third in men and two-thirds in ships. Nor, from 1922 onward, was its strength even expected to increase; for its total of ships (unlike its total of officials) was limited by the Washington Naval Agreement of that year. Here we have then a 78 percent increase over a period of fourteen years; an average of 5.6 percent increase a year on the earlier total. In fact, as we shall see, the rate of increase was not as regular as that. All we have to consider, at this stage, is the percentage rise over a given period.

Can this rise in the total number of civil servants be accounted for except on the assumption that such a total must always rise by a law governing its growth? It might be urged at this point that the period under discussion was one of rapid development in naval technique. The use of the flying machine was no longer confined to the eccentric. Electrical devices were being multiplied and elaborated. Submarines were tolerated if not approved. Engineer officers were beginning to be regarded as almost human. In so revolutionary an age we might expect that storekeepers would have more elaborate inventories to compile. We might not wonder to see more draughtsmen on the payroll, more designers, more technicians and scientists. But these, the dockyard officials, increased only by 40 percent in number when the men of Whitehall increased their total by nearly 80 percent. For every new foreman or electrical engineer at Portsmouth there had to be two more clerks at Charing Cross. From this we might be tempted to conclude, provisionally, that the rate of increase in administrative staff is likely to be double that of the technical staff at a time when the actually useful strength (in this case, of seamen) is being reduced by 31.5 percent. It has been proved statistically, however, that this last percentage is irrelevant. The officials would have multiplied at the same rate had there been no actual seamen at all.

It would be interesting to follow the further progress by which the 8118 Admiralty staff of 1935 came to number 33,788 by 1954. But the staff of the Colonial Office affords a better field of study during a period of imperial decline. Admiralty statistics are complicated by factors (like the Fleet Air Arm) that make comparison difficult as between one year and the next. The Colonial Office growth is more significant in that it is more purely administrative. Here the relevant statistics are as follows:

1935	1939	1943	1947	1954
372	450	817	1139	1661

Before showing what the rate of increase is, we must observe that the extent of this department's responsibilities was far from constant during these twenty years. The colonial territories were not much altered in area or population between 1935 and 1939. They were considerably diminished by 1943, certain areas being in enemy hands. They were increased again in 1947, but have since then shrunk steadily from year to year as successive colonies achieve self-government. It would be rational to suppose that these changes in the scope of Empire would be reflected in the size of its central administration. But a glance at the figures is enough to convince us that the staff totals represent nothing but so many stages in an inevitable increase. And this increase, although related to that observed in other departments, has nothing to do with the size—or even the existence—of the Empire. What are the percentages of increase? We must ignore, for this purpose, the rapid increase in staff which accompanied the diminution of responsibility during World

TABLE 1 • ADMIRALTY STATISTICS

Year	Capital Ships in Commission	Officers and Men in R.N.	Dockyard Workers	Dockyard Officials and Clerks	Admiralty Officials
1914	62	146,000	57,000	3249	2000
1928	20	100,000	62,439	4558	3569
Increase or Decrease	−67.74%	−31.5%	+9.54%	+40.28%	+78.45%

War II. We should note rather, the peacetime rates of increase: over 5.24 percent between 1935 and 1939, and 6.55 percent between 1947 and 1954. This gives an average increase of 5.89 percent each year, a percentage markedly similar to that already found in the Admiralty staff increase between 1914 and 1928.

Further and detailed statistical analysis of departmental staffs would be inappropriate in such a work as this. It is hoped, however, to reach a tentative conclusion regarding the time likely to elapse between a given official's first appointment and the later appointment of his two or more assistants.

Dealing with the problem of pure staff accumulation, all our researches so far completed point to an average increase of 5.75 percent per year. This fact established, it now becomes possible to state Parkinson's Law in mathematical form: In any public administrative department not actually at war, the staff increase may be expected to follow this formula—

$$x = \frac{2k^m + l}{n}$$

k is the number of staff seeking promotion through the appointment of subordinates; *l* represents the difference between the ages of appointment and retirement; *m* is the number of man-hours devoted to answering minutes within the department; and *n* is the number of effective units being administered. *x* will be the number of new staff required each year. Mathematicians will realize, of course, that to find the percentage increase they must multiply *x* by 100 and divide by the total of the previous year, thus:

$$\frac{100\,(2k^m + l)}{yn}\%$$

where *y* represents the total original staff. This figure will invariably prove to be between 5.17 percent and 6.56 percent, irrespective of any variation in the amount of work (if any) to be done.

The discovery of this formula and of the general principles upon which it is based has, of course, no political value. No attempt has been made to inquire whether departments *ought* to grow in size. Those who hold that this growth is essential to gain full employment are fully entitled to their opinion. Those who doubt the stability of an economy based upon reading each other's minutes are equally entitled to theirs. It would probably be premature to attempt at this stage any inquiry into the quantitative ratio that should exist between the administrators and the administered. Granted, however, that a maximum ratio exists, it should soon be possible to ascertain by formula how many years will elapse before that ratio, in any given community, will be reached. The forecasting of such a result will again have no political value. Nor can it be sufficiently emphasized that Parkinson's Law is a purely scientific discovery, inapplicable except in theory to the politics of the day. It is not the business of the botanist to eradicate the weeds. Enough for him if he can tell us just how fast they grow.

26
The Human Side of Enterprise
Douglas Murray McGregor

It has become trite to say that industry has the fundamental know-how to utilize physical science and technology for the material benefit of mankind, and that we must now learn how to utilize the social sciences to make our human organizations truly effective.

To a degree, the social sciences today are in a position like that of the physical sciences with respect to atomic energy in the thirties. We know that past conceptions of the nature of man are inadequate and, in many ways, incorrect. We are becoming quite certain that, under proper conditions, unimagined resources of creative human energy could become available within the organizational setting.

We cannot tell industrial management how to apply this new knowledge in simple, economic ways. We know it will require years of exploration, much costly development research, and a substantial amount of creative imagination on the part of management to discover how to apply this growing knowledge to the organization of human effort in industry.

MANAGEMENT'S TASK: THE CONVENTIONAL VIEW

The conventional conception of management's task in harnessing human energy to organizational requirements can be stated broadly in terms of three propositions. In order to avoid the complications introduced by a label, let us call this set of propositions "Theory X":

1. Management is responsible for organizing the elements of productive enterprise—money, materials, equipment, people—in the interest of economic ends.
2. With respect to people, this is a process of directing their efforts, motivating them, controlling their actions, modifying their behavior to fit the needs of the organization.
3. Without this active intervention by management, people would be passive—even resistant—to organizational needs. They must therefore be persuaded, rewarded, punished, controlled—their activities must be directed. This is management's task. We often sum it up by saying that management consists of getting things done through other people.

Behind this conventional theory there are several additional beliefs—less explicit, but widespread:

4. The average man is by nature indolent—he works as little as possible.
5. He lacks ambition, dislikes responsibility, prefers to be led.
6. He is inherently self-centered, indifferent to organizational needs.
7. He is by nature resistant to change.
8. He is gullible, not very bright, the ready dupe of the charlatan and the demagogue.

Source: Reprinted by permission of the publisher from *Management Review,* November 1957,

The human side of economic enterprise today is fashioned from propositions and beliefs such as these. Conventional organization structures and managerial policies, practices, and programs reflect these assumptions.

In accomplishing its task—with these assumptions as guides—management has conceived of a range of possibilities.

At one extreme, management can be "hard" or "strong." The methods for directing behavior involve coercion and threat (usually disguised), close supervision, tight controls over behavior. At the other extreme, management can be "soft" or "weak." The methods for directing behavior involve being permissive, satisfying people's demands, achieving harmony. Then they will be tractable, accept direction.

This range has been fairly completely explored during the past half century, and management has learned some things from the exploration. There are difficulties in the "hard" approach. Force breeds counter-forces: Restriction of output, antagonism, militant unionism, subtle but effective sabotage of management objectives. This "hard" approach is especially difficult during times of full employment.

There are also difficulties in the "soft" approach. It leads frequently to the abdication of management—to harmony, perhaps, but to indifferent performance. People take advantage of the soft approach. They continually expect more, but they give less and less.

Currently, the popular theme is "firm but fair." This is an attempt to gain the advantages of both the hard and the soft approaches. It is reminiscent of Teddy Roosevelt's "speak softly and carry a big stick."

IS THE CONVENTIONAL VIEW CORRECT?

The findings which are beginning to emerge from the social sciences challenge this whole set of beliefs about man and human nature and about the task of management. The evidence is far from conclusive, certainly, but it is suggestive. It comes from the laboratory, the clinic, the schoolroom, the home, and even to a limited extent from industry itself.

The social scientist does not deny that human behavior in industrial organization today is approximately what management perceives it to be. He has, in fact, observed it and studied it fairly extensively. But he is pretty sure that this behavior is *not* a consequence of man's inherent nature. It is a consequence rather of the nature of industrial organizations, of management philosophy, policy, and practice. The conventional approach of Theory X is based on mistaken notions of what is cause and what is effect.

Perhaps the best way to indicate why the conventional approach of management is inadequate is to consider the subject of motivation.

PHYSIOLOGICAL NEEDS

Man is a wanting animal—as soon as one of his needs is satisfied, another appears in its place. This process is unending. It continues from birth to death.

Man's needs are organized in a series of levels—a hierarchy of importance. At the lowest level, but pre-eminent in importance when they are thwarted, are his *physiological needs.* Man lives for bread alone, when there is no bread. Unless the circumstances are unusual, his needs for love, for status, for recognition are inoperative when his stomach has been empty for a while. But when he eats regularly and adequately, hunger ceases to be an important motivation. The same is true of the other physiological needs of man—for rest, exercise, shelter, protection from the elements.

A *satisfied need is not a motivator of behavior!* This is a fact of profound significance that is regularly ignored in the conventional approach to the management of people. Consider your own need for air. Except as you are deprived of it, it has no appreciable motivating effect upon your behavior.

SAFETY NEEDS

When the physiological needs are reasonably satisfied, needs at the next higher level begin to dominate man's behavior—to motivate him. These are called *safety needs.* They are needs for protection against danger, threat, deprivation. Some people mistakenly refer to these as needs for security. However, unless man is in a dependent relationship where he fears arbitrary deprivation, he does not demand security. The need is for the "fairest possible break." When he is confident of this, he is more than willing to take risks. But when he feels threatened or dependent, his greatest need is for guarantees, for protection, for security.

The fact needs little emphasis that, since every industrial employee is in a dependent relationship, safety needs may assume considerable importance. Arbitrary management actions, behavior which arouses uncertainty with respect to continued employment or which reflects favoritism or discrimination, unpredictable administration of policy—these can be powerful motivators of the safety needs in the employment relationship *at every level,* from worker to vice president.

SOCIAL NEEDS

When man's physiological needs are satisfied and he is no longer fearful about his physical welfare, his *social needs* become important motivators of his behavior—needs for belonging, for association, for acceptance by his fellows, for giving and receiving friendship and love.

Management knows today of the existence of these needs, but it often assumes quite wrongly that they represent a threat to the organization. Many studies have demonstrated that the tightly knit, cohesive work group may, under proper conditions, be far more effective than an equal number of separate individuals in achieving organizational goals.

Yet management, fearing group hostility to its own objectives, often goes to considerable lengths to control and direct human efforts in ways that are inimical to the natural "groupiness" of human beings. When man's social needs—and perhaps his safety needs, too—are thus thwarted, he behaves in ways which tend to defeat organizational objectives. He becomes resistant, antagonistic, uncooperative. But this behavior is a consequence, not a cause.

EGO NEEDS

Above the social needs—in the sense that they do not become motivators until lower needs are reasonably satisfied—are the needs of greatest significance to management and to man himself. They are the *egoistic needs,* and they are of two kinds:

1. Those needs that relate to one's self-esteem—needs for self-confidence, for independence, for achievement, for competence, for knowledge.
2. Those needs that relate to one's reputation—needs for status, for recognition, for appreciation, for the deserved respect of one's fellows.

Unlike the lower needs, these are rarely satisfied; man seeks indefinitely for more satisfaction of these needs once they have become important to him, but they do not appear in any significant way until physiological, safety, and social needs are all reasonably satisfied.

The typical industrial organization offers few opportunities for the satisfaction of these egoistic needs to people at lower levels in the hierarchy. The conventional methods of organizing work, particularly in mass-production industries, give little heed to these aspects of human motivation. If the practices of scientific management were deliberately calculated to thwart these needs, they could hardly accomplish this purpose better than they do.

SELF-FULFILLMENT NEEDS

Finally—a capstone, as it were, on the hierarchy of man's needs—there are what we may call the *needs for self-fulfillment.* These are the needs for realizing one's own potentialities, for continued self-development, for being creative in the broadest sense of that term.

It is clear that the conditions of modern life give only limited opportunity for these relatively weak needs to obtain expression. The deprivation most people experience with respect to other lower-level needs diverts their energies into the struggle to satisfy *those* needs, and the needs for self-fulfillment remain dormant.

MANAGEMENT AND MOTIVATION

We recognize readily enough that a man suffering from a severe dietary deficiency is sick. The deprivation of physiological needs has behavioral consequences. The same is true—although less well recognized—of deprivation of higher-level needs. The man whose needs for safety, association, independence, or status are thwarted is sick just as surely as the man who has rickets. And his sickness will have behavioral consequences. We will be mistaken if we attribute his resultant passivity, his hostility, his refusal to accept responsibility to his inherent "human nature." These forms of behavior are *symptoms* of illness—of deprivation of his social and egoistic needs.

The man whose lower-level needs are satisfied is not motivated to satisfy those needs any longer. For practical purposes they exist no longer. Management often asks, "Why aren't people more productive? We pay good wages, provide good working conditions, have excellent fringe benefits and steady employment. Yet people do not seem to be willing to put forth more than minimum effort."

The fact that management has provided for these physiological and safety needs has shifted the motivational emphasis to the social and perhaps to the egoistic needs. Unless there are opportunities *at work* to satisfy these higher-level needs, people will be deprived; and their behavior will reflect this deprivation. Under such conditions, if management continues to focus its attention on physiological needs, its efforts are bound to be ineffective.

People *will* make insistent demands for more money under these conditions. It becomes more important than ever to buy the material goods and services which can provide limited satisfaction of the thwarted needs. Although money has only limited value in satisfying many higher-level needs, it can become the focus of interest if it is the *only* means available.

THE CARROT-AND-STICK APPROACH

The carrot-and-stick theory of motivation (like Newtonian physical theory) works reasonably well under certain circumstances. The *means* for satisfying man's physiological and (within limits) his safety needs can be provided or withheld by management. Employment itself is such a means, and so are wages, working conditions, and benefits. By these means the individual can be controlled so long as he is struggling for subsistence.

But the carrot-and-stick theory does not work at all once man has reached an adequate subsistence level and is motivated primarily by higher needs. Management cannot provide a man with self-respect, or with the respect of his fellows, or with the satisfaction of needs for self-fulfillment. It can create such conditions that he is encouraged and enabled to seek such satisfactions for *himself,* or it can thwart him by failing to create those conditions.

But this creation of conditions is not "control." It is not a good device for directing behavior. And so management finds itself in an odd position. The high standard of living created by our modern technological know-how provides quite adequately for the satisfaction of physiological and safety needs. The only significant exception is where management practices have not created confidence in a "fair break"—and thus where safety needs are thwarted. But by making possible the satisfaction of low-level needs, management has deprived itself of the ability to use as motivators the devices on which conventional theory has taught it to rely—rewards, promises, incentives, or threats and other coercive devices.

The philosophy of management by direction and control—*regardless of whether it is hard or soft*—is inadequate to motivate because the human needs on which this approach relies are today unimportant motivators of behavior. Direction and control are essentially useless in motivating people whose important needs are social and egoistic. Both the hard and the soft approach fail today because they are simply irrelevant to the situation.

People, deprived of opportunities to satisfy at work the needs which are now important to them, behave exactly as we might predict—with indolence, passivity, resistance to change, lack of responsibility, willingness to follow the demagogue, unreasonable demands for economic benefits. It would seem that we are caught in a web of our own weaving.

A NEW THEORY OF MANAGEMENT

For these and many other reasons, we require a different theory of the task of managing people based on more adequate assumptions about human nature and human motivation. I am going to be so bold as to suggest the broad dimensions of such a theory. Call it "Theory Y," if you will.

1. Management is responsible for organizing the elements of productive enterprise—money, materials, equipment, people—in the interest of economic ends.
2. People are *not* by nature passive or resistant to organizational needs. They have become so as a result of experience in organizations.
3. The motivation, the potential for development, the capacity for assuming responsibility, the readiness to direct behavior toward organizational goals are all present in people. Management does not put them there. It is a responsibility of management to make it possible for people to recognize and develop these human characteristics for themselves.
4. The essential task of management is to arrange organizational conditions and methods of operation so that people can achieve their own goals *best* by directing *their own* efforts toward organizational objectives.

This is a process primarily of creating opportunities, releasing potential, removing obstacles, encouraging growth, providing guidance. It is what Peter Drucker has called "management by objectives" in contrast to "management by control." It does *not* involve the abdication of management, the absence of leadership, the lowering of standards, or the other characteristics usually associated with the "soft" approach under Theory X.

SOME DIFFICULTIES

It is no more possible to create an organization today which will be a full, effective application of this theory than it was to build an atomic power plant in 1945. There are many formidable obstacles to overcome.

The conditions imposed by conventional organization theory and by the approach of scientific management for the past half century have tied men to limited jobs which do not utilize their capabilities, have discouraged the acceptance of responsibility, have encouraged passivity, have eliminated meaning from work. Man's habits, attitudes, expectations—his whole conception of membership in an industrial organization—have been conditioned by his experience under these circumstances.

People today are accustomed to being directed, manipulated, controlled in industrial organizations and to finding satisfaction for their social, egoistic, and self-fulfillment needs away from the job. This is true of much of management as well as of workers. Genuine "industrial citizenship"—to borrow again a term from Drucker—is a remote and unrealistic idea, the meaning of which has not even been considered by most members of industrial organizations.

Another way of saying this is that Theory X places exclusive reliance upon external control of human behavior, while Theory Y relies heavily on self-control and self-direction. It is worth noting that this difference is the difference between treating people as children and treating them as mature adults. After generations of the former, we cannot expect to shift to the latter overnight.

STEPS IN THE RIGHT DIRECTION

Before we are overwhelmed by the obstacles, let us remember that the application of theory is always slow. Progress is usually achieved in small steps. Some innovative ideas which are entirely consistent with Theory Y are today being applied with some success.

Decentralization and Delegation

These are ways of freeing people from the too-close control of conventional organization, giving them a degree of freedom to direct their own activities, to assume responsibility, and, importantly, to satisfy their egoistic needs. In this connection, the flat organization of Sears Roebuck & Co. provides an interesting example. It forces "management by objectives," since it enlarges the number of people reporting to a manager until he cannot direct and control them in the conventional manner.

Job Enlargement

This concept, pioneered by IBM and Detroit Edison, is quite consistent with Theory Y. It encourages the acceptance of responsibility at the bottom of the organization; it provides opportunities for satisfying social and egoistic needs. In fact, the reorganization of work at the factory level offers one of the more challenging opportunities for innovation consistent with Theory Y.

Participation and Consultative Management

Under proper conditions, participation and consultative management provide encouragement to people to direct their creative energies toward organizational objectives, give them some voice in decisions that affect them, provide significant opportunities for the satisfaction of social and egoistic needs. The Scanlon Plan is the outstanding embodiment of these ideas in practice.

Performance Appraisal

Even a cursory examination of conventional programs of performance appraisal within the ranks of management will reveal how completely consistent they are with Theory X. In fact, most such programs tend to treat the individual as though he were a product under inspection on the assembly line.

A few companies—among them General Mills, Inc., Ansul Chemical, and General Electric Company—have been experimenting with approaches which involve the individual in setting "targets" or objectives *for himself* and in a *self*-evaluation of performance semiannually or annually. Of course, the superior plays an important leadership role in this process—one, in fact, which demands substantially more competence than the conventional approach. The role is, however, considerably more congenial to many managers than the role of "judge" or "inspector" which is usually forced upon them. Above all, the individual is encouraged to take a greater responsibility for planning and appraising his own contribution to organizational objectives; and the accompanying effects on egoistic and self-fulfillment needs are substantial.

APPLYING THE IDEAS

The not infrequent failure of such ideas as these to work as well as expected is often attributable to the fact that a management has "bought the idea" but applied it within the framework of Theory X and its assumptions.

Delegation is not an effective way of exercising management by control. Participation becomes a farce when it is applied as a sales gimmick or a device for kidding people into thinking they are important. Only the management that has confidence in human capacities and is itself directed toward organizational objectives rather than toward the preservation of personal power can grasp the implications of this emerging theory. Such management will find and apply successfully other innovative ideas as we move slowly toward the full implementation of a theory like Y.

THE HUMAN SIDE OF ENTERPRISE

It is quite possible for us to realize substantial improvements in the effectiveness of industrial organizations during the next decade or two. The social sciences can contribute much to such developments; we are only beginning to grasp the indications of the growing body of knowledge in these fields. But if this conviction is to become a reality instead of a pious hope, we will need to view the process much as we view the process of releasing the energy of the atom for constructive human ends—as a slow, costly, sometimes discouraging approach toward a goal which would seem to many to be quite unrealistic.

The ingenuity and the perseverance of industrial management in the pursuit of economic ends have changed many scientific and technological dreams into commonplace realities. It is now becoming clear that the application of these same talents to the human side of enterprise will not only enhance substantially these materialistic achievements, but will bring us one step closer to "the good society."

27
The Science of "Muddling Through"

Charles E. Lindblom

Suppose an administrator is given responsibility for formulating policy with respect to inflation. He might start by trying to list all related values in order of importance, e.g., full employment, reasonable business profit, protection of small savings, prevention of a stock market crash. Then all possible policy outcomes could be rated as more or less efficient in attaining a maximum of these values. This would of course require a prodigious inquiry into values held by members of society and an equally prodigious set of calculations on how much of each value is equal to how much of each other value. He could then proceed to outline all possible policy alternatives. In a third step, he would undertake systematic comparison of his multitude of alternatives to determine which attains the greatest amount of values.

In comparing policies, he would take advantage of any theory available that generalized about classes of policies. In considering inflation, for example, he would compare all policies in the light of the theory of prices. Since no alternatives are beyond his investigation, he would consider strict central control and the abolition of all prices and markets on the one hand and elimination of all public controls with reliance completely on the free market on the other, both in the light of whatever theoretical generalizations he could find on such hypothetical economies.

Finally, he would try to make the choice that would in fact maximize his values.

An alternative line of attack would be to set as his principal objective, either explicitly or without conscious thought, the relatively simple goal of keeping prices level. This objective might be compromised or complicated by only a few other goals, such as full employment. He would in fact disregard most other social values as beyond his present interest, and he would for the moment not even attempt to rank the few values that he regarded as immediately relevant. Were he pressed, he would quickly admit that he was ignoring many related values and many possible important consequences of his policies.

As a second step, he would outline those relatively few policy alternatives that occurred to him. He would then compare them. In comparing his limited number of alternatives, most of them familiar from past controversies, he would not ordinarily find a body of theory precise enough to carry him through a comparison of their respective consequences. Instead he would rely heavily on the record of past experience with

Source: From *Public Administration Review* 19 (Spring 1959), pp. 79–88.

small policy steps to predict the consequences of similar steps extended into the future.

Moreover, he would find that the policy alternatives combined objectives or values in different ways. For example, one policy might offer price level stability at the cost of some risk of unemployment; another might offer less price stability but also less risk of unemployment. Hence, the next step in his approach—the final selection—would combine into one the choice among values and the choice among instruments for reaching values. It would not, as in the first method of policy-making, approximate a more mechanical process of choosing the means that best satisfied goals that were previously clarified and ranked. Because practitioners of the second approach expect to achieve their goals only partially, they would expect to repeat endlessly the sequence just described, as conditions and aspirations changed and as accuracy of prediction improved.

BY ROOT OR BY BRANCH

For complex problems, the first of these two approaches is of course impossible. Although such an approach can be described, it cannot be practiced except for relatively simple problems and even then only in a somewhat modified form. It assumes intellectual capacities and sources of information that men simply do not possess, and it is even more absurd as an approach to policy when the time and money that can be allocated to a policy problem is limited, as is always the case. Of particular importance to public administrators is the fact that public agencies are in effect usually instructed not to practice the first method. That is to say, their prescribed functions and constraints—the politically or legally possible—restrict their attention to relatively few values and relatively few alternative policies among the countless alternatives that might be imagined. It is the second method that is practiced.

Curiously, however, the literatures of decision-making, policy formulation, planning, and public administration formalize the first approach rather than the second, leaving public administrators who handle complex decisions in the position of practicing what few preach. For emphasis I run some risk of overstatement. True enough, the literature is well aware of limits on man's capacities and of the inevitability that policies will be approached in some such style as the second. But attempts to formalize rational policy formulation—to lay out explicitly the necessary steps in the process—usually describe the first approach and not the second.[1]

The common tendency to describe policy formulation even for complex problems as though it followed the first approach has been strengthened by the attention given to, and successes enjoyed by, operations research, statistical decision theory, and systems analysis. The hallmarks of these procedures, typical of the first approach, are clarity of objective, explicitness of evaluation, a high degree of comprehensiveness of overview, and, wherever possible, quantification of values for mathematical analysis. But these advanced procedures remain largely the appropriate techniques of relatively small-scale problem-solving where the total number of variables to be considered is small and value problems restricted. Charles Hitch, head of the Economics Division of RAND Corporation, one of the leading centers for application of these techniques, has written:

> I would make the empirical generalization from my experience at RAND and elsewhere that operations research is the art

> of sub-optimizing, i.e., of solving some lower-level problems, and that difficulties increase and our special competence diminishes by an order of magnitude with every level of decision making we attempt to ascend. The sort of simple explicit model which operations researchers are so proficient in using can certainly reflect most of the significant factors influencing traffic control on the George Washington Bridge, but the proportion of the relevant reality which we can represent by any such model or models in studying, say, a major foreign-policy decision, appears to be almost trivial.[2]

Accordingly, I propose in this paper to clarify and formalize the second method, much neglected in the literature. This might be described as the method of *successive limited comparisons.* I will contrast it with the first approach, which might be called the rational-comprehensive method.[3] More impressionistically and briefly—and therefore generally used in this article—they could be characterized as the branch method and root method, the former continually building out from the current situation, step-by-step and by small degrees; the latter starting from fundamentals anew each time, building on the past only as experience is embodied in a theory, and always prepared to start completely from the ground up.

Let us put the characteristics of the two methods side by side in simplest terms. (See Figure 1.)

Assuming that the root method is familiar and understandable, we proceed directly to clarification of its alternative by contrast. In explaining the second, we shall be describing how most administrators do in fact approach complex questions, for the root method, the "best" way as a blueprint or model, is in fact not workable for complex policy questions, and administrators are forced to use the method of successive limited comparisons.

INTERTWINING EVALUATION AND EMPIRICAL ANALYSIS (1b)

The quickest way to understand how values are handled in the method of successive limited comparisons is to see how the root method often breaks down in *its* handling of values or objectives. The idea that values should be clarified, and in advance of the examination of alternative policies, is appealing. But what happens when we attempt it for complex social problems? The first difficulty is that on many critical values or objectives, citizens disagree, congressmen disagree, and public administrators disagree. Even where a fairly specific objective is prescribed for the administrator, there remains considerable room for disagreement on subobjectives. Consider, for example, the conflict with respect to locating public housing, described in Meyerson and Banfield's study of the Chicago Housing Authority[4]—disagreement which occurred despite the clear objective of providing a certain number of public housing units in the city. Similarly conflicting are objectives in highway location, traffic control, minimum wage administration, development of tourist facilities in national parks, or insect control.

Administrators cannot escape these conflicts by ascertaining the majority's preference, for preferences have not been registered on most issues; indeed, there often *are* no preferences in the absence of public discussion sufficient to bring an issue to the attention of the electorate. Furthermore, there is a question of whether intensity of feeling should be considered as well as the number of persons preferring each alternative. By the impossibility of doing otherwise, administrators often are reduced to deciding policy without clarifying objectives first.

Even when an administrator resolves to follow his own values as a criterion for decisions, he often will not know how to rank them when they conflict with one another, as they usually do. Suppose, for example, that an administrator must relocate tenants living in tenements scheduled for destruction. One objective is to empty the buildings fairly promptly, another is to find suitable accommodation for persons displaced, another is to avoid friction with residents in other areas in which a large influx would be unwelcome, another is to deal with all concerned through persuasion if possible, and so on.

How does one state even to himself the relative importance of these partially conflicting values? A simple ranking of them is not enough; one needs ideally to know how much of one value is worth sacrificing for some of another value. The answer is that typically the administrator chooses—and must choose—directly among policies in which these values are combined in different ways. He cannot first clarify his values and then choose among policies.

A more subtle third point underlies both the first two. Social objectives do not always have the same relative values. One objective may be highly prized in one circumstance, another in another circumstance. If, for example, an administrator values highly both the dispatch with which his agency can carry through its projects *and* good public relations, it matters little which of the two possibly conflicting values he favors in some abstract or general sense. Policy questions arise in forms which put to administrators such a question as: Given

FIGURE 1

Rational-Comprehensive (Root)	Successive Limited Comparisons (Branch)
1a. Clarification of values or objectives distinct from and usually prerequisite to empirical analysis of alternative policies.	1b. Selection of value goals and empirical analysis of the needed action are not distinct from one another but are closely intertwined.
2a. Policy-formulation is therefore approached through means-end analysis: First the ends are isolated, then the means to achieve them are sought.	2b. Since means and ends are not distinct, means-end analysis is often inappropriate or limited.
3a. The test of a "good" policy is that it can be shown to be the most appropriate means to desired ends.	3b. The test of a "good" policy is typically that various analysts find themselves directly agreeing on a policy (without their agreeing that it is the most appropriate means to an agreed objective).
4a. Analysis is comprehensive; every important relevant factor is taken into account.	4b. Analysis is drastically limited: i) Important possible outcomes are neglected. ii) Important alternative potential policies are neglected. iii) Important affected values are neglected.
5a. Theory is often heavily relied upon.	5b. A succession of comparisons greatly reduces or eliminates reliance on theory.

the degree to which we are or are not already achieving the values of dispatch and the values of good public relations, is it worth sacrificing a little speed for a happier clientele, or is it better to risk offending the clientele so that we can get on with our work? The answer to such a question varies with circumstances.

The value problem is, as the example shows, always a problem of adjustments at a margin. But there is no practicable way to state marginal objectives or values except in terms of particular policies. That one value is preferred to another in one decision situation does not mean that it will be preferred in another decision situation in which it can be had only at great sacrifice of another value. Attempts to rank or order values in general and abstract terms so that they do not shift from decision to decision end up by ignoring the relevant marginal preferences. The significance of this third point thus goes very far. Even if all administrators had at hand an agreed set of values, objectives, and constraints, and an agreed ranking of these values, objectives, and constraints, their marginal values in actual choice situations would be impossible to formulate.

Unable consequently to formulate the relevant values first and then choose among policies to achieve them, administrators must choose directly among alternative policies that offer different marginal combinations of values. Somewhat paradoxically, the only practicable way to disclose one's relevant marginal values even to oneself is to describe the policy one chooses to achieve them. Except roughly and vaguely, I know of no way to describe—or even to understand—what my relative evaluations are for, say, freedom and security, speed and accuracy in governmental decisions, or low taxes and better schools than to describe my preferences among specific policy choices that might be made between the alternatives in each of the pairs.

In summary, two aspects of the process by which values are actually handled can be distinguished. The first is clear: evaluation and empirical analysis are intertwined; that is, one chooses among values and among policies at one and the same time. Put a little more elaborately, one simultaneously chooses a policy to attain certain objectives and chooses the objectives themselves. The second aspect is related but distinct: the administrator focuses his attention on marginal or incremental values. Whether he is aware of it or not, he does not find general formulations of objectives very helpful and in fact makes specific marginal or incremental comparisons. Two policies, X and Y, confront him. Both promise the same degree of attainment of objectives *a, b, c, d,* and *e.* But X promises him somewhat more of *f* than does Y, while Y promises him somewhat more of *g* than does X. In choosing between them, he is in fact offered the alternative of a marginal or incremental amount of *f* at the expense of a marginal or incremental amount of *g.* The only values that are relevant to his choice are these increments by which the two policies differ; and, when he finally chooses between the two marginal values, he does so by making a choice between policies.[5]

As to whether the attempt to clarify objectives in advance of policy selection is more or less rational than the close intertwining of marginal evaluation and empirical analysis, the principal difference established is that for complex problems the first is impossible and irrelevant, and the second is both possible and relevant. The second is possible because the administrator need not try to analyze any values except the values by which alternative policies differ and need not be concerned with them except as they differ marginally. His need for information on values or objectives is drastically reduced as compared with the root method; and his capacity for grasping, comprehending, and relating values to one another is not strained beyond the breaking point.

RELATIONS BETWEEN MEANS AND ENDS (2b)

Decision-making is ordinarily formalized as a means-ends relationship: means are conceived to be evaluated and chosen in the light of ends finally selected independently of and prior to the choice of means. This is the means-ends relationship of the root method. But it follows from all that has just been said that such a means-ends relationship is possible only to the extent that values are agreed upon, are reconcilable, and are stable at the margin. Typically, therefore, such a means-ends relationship is absent from the branch method, where means and ends are simultaneously chosen.

Yet any departure from the means-ends relationship of the root method will strike some readers as inconceivable. For it will appear to them that only in such a relationship is it possible to determine whether one policy choice is better or worse than another. How can an administrator know whether he has made a wise or foolish decision if he is without prior values or objectives by which to judge his decisions? The answer to this question calls up the third distinctive difference between root and branch methods: how to decide the best policy.

THE TEST OF "GOOD" POLICY (3b)

In the root method, a decision is "correct," "good," or "rational" if it can be shown to attain some specified objective, where the objective can be specified without simply describing the decision itself. Where objectives are defined only through the marginal or incremental approach to values described above, it is still sometimes possible to test whether a policy does in fact attain the desired objectives; but a precise statement of the objectives takes the form of a description of the policy chosen or some alternative to it. To show that a policy is mistaken one cannot offer an abstract argument that important objectives are not achieved; one must instead argue that another policy is more to be preferred.

So far, the departure from customary ways of looking at problem-solving is not troublesome, for many administrators will be quick to agree that the most effective discussion of the correctness of policy does take the form of comparison with other policies that might have been chosen. But what of the situation in which administrators cannot agree on values or objectives, either abstractly or in marginal terms? What then is the test of "good" policy? For the root method, there is no test. Agreement on objectives failing, there is no standard of "correctness." For the method of successive limited comparisons, the test is agreement on policy itself, which remains possible even when agreement on values is not.

It has been suggested that continuing agreement in Congress on the desirability of extending old age insurance stems from liberal desires to strengthen the welfare programs of the federal government and from conservative desires to reduce union demands for private pension plans. If so, this is an excellent demonstration of the ease with which individuals of different ideologies often can agree on concrete policy. Labor mediators report a similar phenomenon: the contestants cannot agree on criteria for settling their disputes but can agree on specific proposals. Similarly, when one administrator's objective turns out to be another's means, they often can agree on policy.

Agreement on policy thus becomes the only practicable test of the policy's correctness. And for one administrator to seek to win the other over to agreement on ends as well would accomplish nothing and create quite unnecessary controversy.

If agreement directly on policy as a test for "best" policy seems a poor substitute for testing the policy against its objectives, it ought to be remembered that objectives themselves have no ultimate validity other than they are agreed upon. Hence agreement is the test of "best" policy in both methods. But where the root method requires agreement on what elements in the decision constitute objectives and on which of these objectives should be sought, the branch method falls back on agreement wherever it can be found.

In an important sense, therefore, it is not irrational for an administrator to defend a policy as good without being able to specify what it is good for.

NONCOMPREHENSIVE ANALYSIS (4b)

Ideally, rational-comprehensive analysis leaves out nothing important. But it is impossible to take everything important into consideration unless "important" is so narrowly defined that analysis is in fact quite limited. Limits on human intellectual capacities and on available information set definite limits to man's capacity to be comprehensive. In actual fact, therefore, no one can practice the rational-comprehensive method for really complex problems, and every administrator faced with a sufficiently complex problem must find ways drastically to simplify.

An administrator assisting in the formulation of agricultural economic policy cannot in the first place be competent on all possible policies. He cannot even comprehend one policy entirely. In planning a soil bank program, he cannot successfully anticipate the impact of higher or lower farm income on, say, urbanization—the possible consequent loosening of family ties, possible consequent eventual need for revisions in social security and further implications for tax problems arising out of new federal responsibilities for social security and municipal responsibilities for urban services. Nor, to follow another line of repercussions, can he work through the soil bank program's effects on prices for agricultural products in foreign markets and consequent implications for foreign relations, including those arising out of economic rivalry between the United States and the U.S.S.R.

In the method of successive, limited comparisons, simplification is systematically achieved in two principal ways. First, it is achieved through limitation of policy comparisons to those policies that differ in relatively small degree from policies presently in effect. Such a limitation immediately reduces the number of alternatives to be investigated and also drastically simplifies the character of the investigation of each. For it is not necessary to undertake fundamental inquiry into an alternative and its consequences; it is necessary only to study those respects in which the proposed alternative and its consequences differ from the status quo. The empirical comparison of marginal differences among alternative policies that differ only marginally is, of course, a counterpart to the incremental or marginal comparison of values discussed above.[6]

Relevance as Well as Realism

It is a matter of common observation that in Western democracies public administrators and policy analysts in general do largely limit their analyses to incremental or marginal differences in policies that are chosen to differ only incrementally. They do not do so, however, solely because they desperately need some way to simplify their problems; they also do so in order to be relevant. Democracies change their policies almost entirely through incremental adjustments. Policy does not move in leaps and bounds.

The incremental character of political change in the United States has often been remarked. The two major political parties agree on fundamentals; they offer alternative policies to the voters only on relatively small points of difference. Both parties favor full employment, but they define it somewhat differently; both favor the development of water power resources, but in slightly different ways; and both favor unemployment compensation, but not the same level of benefits. Similarly, shifts of policy within a party take place largely through a series of relatively small changes, as can be seen in their only gradual acceptance of the idea of governmental responsibility for support of the unemployed, a change in party positions beginning in the early 1930s and culminating in a sense in the Employment Act of 1946.

Party behavior is in turn rooted in public attitudes, and political theorists cannot conceive of democracy's surviving in the United States in the absence of fundamental agreement on potentially disruptive issues, with consequent limitation of policy debates to relatively small differences in policy.

Since the policies ignored by the administrator are politically impossible and so irrelevant, the simplification of analysis achieved by concentrating on policies that differ only incrementally is not a capricious kind of simplification. In addition, it can be argued that, given the limits on knowledge within which policy-makers are confined, simplifying by limiting the focus to small variations from present policy makes the most of available knowledge. Because policies being considered are like present and past policies, the administrator can obtain information and claim some insight. Nonincremental policy proposals are therefore typically not only politically irrelevant but also unpredictable in their consequences.

The second method of simplification of analysis is the practice of ignoring important possible consequences of possible policies, as well as the values attached to the neglected consequences. If this appears to disclose a shocking shortcoming of successive limited comparisons, it can be replied that, even if the exclusions are random, policies may nevertheless be more intelligently formulated than through futile attempts to achieve a comprehensiveness beyond human capacity. Actually, however, the exclusions, seeming arbitrary or random from one point of view, need be neither.

Achieving a Degree of Comprehensiveness

Suppose that each value neglected by one policy-making agency were a major concern of at least one other agency. In that case, a helpful division of labor would be achieved, and no agency need find its task beyond its capacities. The shortcomings of such a system would be that one agency might destroy a value either before another agency could be activated to safeguard it or in spite of another agency's efforts. But the possibility that important values may be lost is present in any form of organization, even where agencies attempt to comprehend in planning more than is humanly possible.

The virtue of such a hypothetical division of labor is that every important interest or value has its watchdog. And these watchdogs can protect the interests in their jurisdiction in two quite different ways: first, by redressing damages done by other agencies; and, second, by anticipating and heading off injury before it occurs.

In a society like that of the United States in which individuals are free to combine to pursue almost any possible common interest they might have and in which government agencies are sensitive to the pressures of these groups, the system described is approximated. Almost every interest has its watchdog. Without claiming that every interest has a sufficiently powerful watchdog, it can be argued that our system often can assure a more comprehensive regard for the values of the whole society than any attempt at intellectual comprehensiveness.

In the United States, for example, no part of government attempts a comprehensive overview of policy on income distribution. A policy nevertheless evolves, and one responding to a wide variety of interests. A process of mutual adjustment among farm groups, labor unions, municipalities and school boards, tax authorities, and government agencies with responsibilities in the fields of housing, health, highways, national parks, fire, and police accomplishes a distribution of income in which particular income problems neglected at one point in the decision processes become central at another point.

Mutual adjustment is more pervasive than the explicit forms it takes in negotiation between groups; it persists through the mutual impacts of groups upon each other even where they are not in communication. For all the imperfections and latent dangers in this ubiquitous process of mutual adjustment, it will often accomplish an adaptation of policies to a wider range of interests than could be done by one group centrally.

Note, too, how the incremental pattern of policy-making fits with the multiple pressure pattern. For when decisions are only incremental—closely related to known policies, it is easier for one group to anticipate the kind of moves another might make and easier too for it to make correction for injury already accomplished.[7]

Even partisanship and narrowness, to use pejorative terms, will sometimes be assets to rational decision-making, for they can doubly insure that what one agency neglects, another will not; they specialize personnel to distinct points of view. The claim is valid that effective rational coordination of the federal administration, if possible to achieve at all, would require an agreed set of values[8]—if "rational" is defined as the practice of the root method of decision-making. But a high degree of administrative coordination occurs as each agency adjusts its policies to the concerns of the other agencies in the process of fragmented decision-making I have just described.

For all the apparent shortcomings of the incremental approach to policy alternatives with its arbitrary exclusion coupled with fragmentation, when compared to the root method, the branch method often looks far superior. In the root method, the inevitable exclusion of factors is accidental, unsystematic, and not defensible by any argument so far developed, while in the branch method the exclusions are deliberate, systematic, and defensible. Ideally, of course, the root method does not exclude; in practice it must.

Nor does the branch method necessarily neglect long-run considerations and objectives. It is clear that important values must be omitted in considering policy, and sometimes the only way long-run objectives can be given adequate attention is through the neglect of short-run considerations. But the values omitted can be either long-run or short-run.

SUCCESSION OF COMPARISONS (5b)

The final distinctive element in the branch method is that the comparisons, together with the policy choice, proceed in a chronological series. Policy is not made once and for all; it is made and re-made endlessly. Policy-making is a process of successive approximation to some desired objectives in which what is desired itself continues to change under reconsideration.

Making policy is at best a very rough process. Neither social scientists, nor politicians, nor public administrators yet know enough about the social world to avoid repeated error in predicting the consequences of policy moves. A wise policy-maker consequently expects that his policies will achieve only part of what he hopes and at the same time will produce unanticipated consequences he would have preferred to avoid. If he proceeds through a *succession* of incremental changes, he avoids serious lasting mistakes in several ways.

In the first place, past sequences of policy steps have given him knowledge about the probable consequences of further similar steps. Second, he need not attempt big jumps toward his goals that would require predictions beyond his or anyone else's knowledge, because he never expects his policy to be a final resolution of a problem. His decision is only one step, one that if successful can quickly be followed by another. Third, he is in effect able to test his previous predictions as he moves on to each further step. Lastly, he often can remedy a past error fairly quickly—more quickly than if policy proceeded through more distinct steps widely spaced in time.

Compare this comparative analysis of incremental changes with the aspiration to employ theory in the root method. Man cannot think without classifying, without subsuming one experience under a more general category of experiences. The attempt to push categorization as far as possible and to find general propositions which can be applied to specific situations is what I refer to with the word "theory." Where root analysis often leans heavily on theory in this sense, the branch method does not.

The assumption of root analysts is that theory is the most systematic and economical way to bring relevant knowledge to bear on a specific problem. Granting the assumption, an unhappy fact is that we do not have adequate theory to apply to problems in any policy area, although theory is more adequate in some areas—monetary policy, for example—than in others. Comparative analysis, as in the branch method, is sometimes a systematic alternative to theory.

Suppose an administrator must choose among a small group of policies that differ only incrementally from each other and from present policy. He might aspire to "understand" each of the alternatives—for example, to know all the consequences of each aspect of each policy. If so, he would indeed require theory. In fact, however, he would usually decide that, *for policy-making purposes,* he need know, as explained above, only the consequences of each of those aspects of the policies in which they differed from one another. For this much more modest aspiration, he requires no theory (although it might be helpful, if available), for he can proceed to isolate probable differences by examining the differences in consequences associated with past differences in policies, a feasible program because he can take his observations from a long sequence of incremental changes.

For example, without a more comprehensive social theory about juvenile delinquency than scholars have yet produced, one cannot possibly understand the ways in which a variety of public policies—say on education, housing, recreation, employment, race relations, and policing—might encourage or discourage delinquency. And one needs such an understanding if he undertakes the comprehensive overview of the problem prescribed in the models of the root method. If, however, one merely wants to mobilize knowledge sufficient to assist in a choice among a small group of similar policies—alternative policies on juvenile court procedures, for example—he can do so by comparative analysis of the results of similar past policy moves.

THEORISTS AND PRACTITIONERS

This difference explains—in some cases at least—why the administrator often feels that the outside expert or academic problem-solver is sometimes not helpful and why they in turn often urge more theory on him. And it explains why an administrator often feels more confident when "flying by the seat of his pants" than when following the advice of theorists. Theorists often ask the administrator to go the long way round to the solution of his problems, in effect ask him to follow the best canons of the scientific method, when the administrator knows that the best available theory will work less well than more modest incremental comparisons. Theorists do not realize that the administrator is often in fact practicing a systematic method. It would be foolish to push this explanation too far, for sometimes practical decision-makers are pursuing neither a theoretical approach nor successive comparisons, not any other systematic method.

It may be worth emphasizing that theory is sometimes of extremely limited helpfulness in policy-making for at least two rather different reasons. It is greedy for facts; it can be constructed only through a great collection of observations. And it is typically insufficiently precise for application to a policy process that moves through small changes. In contrast, the comparative method both economizes on the need for facts and directs the analyst's attention to just those facts that are relevant to the fine choices faced by the decision-maker.

With respect to precision of theory, economic theory serves as an example. It predicts that an economy without money or prices would in certain specified ways misallocate resources, but this finding pertains to an alternative far removed from the kind of policies on which administrators need help. On the other hand, it is not precise enough to predict the consequences of policies restricting business mergers, and this is the kind of issue on which the administrators need help. Only in relatively restricted areas does economic theory achieve sufficient precision to go far in resolving policy questions; its helpfulness in policy-making is always so limited that it requires supplementation through comparative analysis.

SUCCESSIVE COMPARISON AS A SYSTEM

Successive limited comparisons is, then, indeed a method or system; it is not a failure of method for which administrators ought to apologize. None the less, its imperfections, which have not been explored in this paper, are many. For example, the method is without a built-in safeguard for all relevant values, and it also may lead the decision maker to overlook excellent policies for no other reason than that they are not suggested by the chain of successive policy steps leading up to the present. Hence, it ought to be said that under this method, as well as under some of the most sophisticated variants of the root method—operations research, for example—policies will continue to be as foolish as they are wise.

Why then bother to describe the method in all the above detail? Because it is in fact a common method of policy formulation, and is, for complex problems, the principal reliance of administrators as well as of other policy analysts.[9] And because it will be superior to any other decision-making method available for complex problems in many circumstances, certainly superior to a futile attempt at superhuman comprehensiveness. The reaction of the public administrator to the exposition of method doubtless will be less a discovery of a new method than a better acquaintance with an old. But by becoming more conscious of their practice of this method, administrators might practice it with more skill and know when to extend or constrict its use. (That they sometimes practice it effectively and sometimes not may explain the extremes of opinion on "muddling through," which is both praised as a highly sophisticated form of problem-solving and denounced as no method at all. For I suspect that in so far as there is a system in what is known as "muddling through," this method is it.)

One of the noteworthy incidental consequences of clarification of the method is the light it throws on the suspicion an administrator sometimes entertains that a consultant or adviser is not speaking relevantly and responsibly when in fact by all ordinary objective evidence he is. The trouble lies in the fact that most of us approach policy problems within a framework given by our view of a chain of successive policy choices made up to the present. One's thinking about appropriate policies with respect, say, to urban traffic control is greatly influenced by one's knowledge of the incremental steps taken up to the present. An administrator enjoys an intimate knowledge of his past sequences that "outsiders" do not share, and his thinking and that of the "outsider" will consequently be different in ways that may puzzle both. Both may appear to be talking intelligently, yet each may find the other unsatisfactory. The relevance of the policy chain of succession is even more clear when an American tries to discuss, say, antitrust policy with a Swiss, for the chains of policy in the two countries are strikingly different and the two individuals consequently have organized their knowledge in quite different ways.

If this phenomenon is a barrier to communication, an understanding of it promises an enrichment of intellectual interaction in policy formulation. Once the source of difference is understood, it will sometimes be stimulating for an administrator to seek out a policy analyst whose recent experience is with a policy chain different from his own.

This raises again a question only briefly discussed above on the merits of like-mindedness among government administrators. While much of organization theory argues the virtues of common values and agreed organizational objectives, for complex problems in which the root method is inapplicable, agencies will want among their own personnel two types of diversification: administrators whose thinking is organized by reference to policy chains other than those familiar to most members of the organization and, even more commonly, administrators whose professional or personal values or interests create diversity of view (perhaps coming from different specialties, social classes, geographical areas) so that, even within a single agency, decision-making can be fragmented and parts of the agency can serve as watchdogs for other parts.

NOTES

1. James G. March and Herbert A. Simon similarly characterize the literature. They also take some important steps, as have Simon's recent articles, to describe a less heroic model of policy-making. See *Organizations* (John Wiley and Sons, 1958), p. 137.
2. "Operations Research and National Planning—A Dissent," 5 *Operations Research* 718 (October, 1957). Hitch's dissent is from particular points made in the article to which his paper is a reply: his claim that operations research is for low-level problems is widely accepted.

   For examples of the kind of problems to which operations research is applied, see C. W. Churchman, R. L. Ackoff and E. L. Arnoff, *Introduction to Operations Research* (John Wiley and Sons, 1957); and J. F. McCloskey and J. M. Coppinger (eds.), *Operations Research for Management,* Vol. II (The Johns Hopkins Press, 1956).
3. I am assuming that administrators often make policy and advise in the making of policy and am treating decision making and policy-making as synonymous for purposes of this paper.
4. Martin Meyerson and Edward C. Banfield, *Politics, Planning and the Public Interest* (The Free Press, 1955).
5. The line of argument is, of course, an extension of the theory of market choice, especially the theory of consumer choice, to public policy choices.
6. A more precise definition of incremental policies and a discussion of whether a change that appears "small" to one observer might be seen differently by another is to be found in my "Policy Analysis," 48 *American Economic Review* 298 (June, 1958).
7. The link between the practice of the method of successive limited comparisons and mutual adjustment of interests in a highly fragmented decision-making process adds a new facet to pluralist theories of government and administration.
8. Herbert Simon, Donald W. Smithburg, and Victor A. Thompson, *Public Administration* (Alfred A. Knopf, 1950), p. 434.
9. Elsewhere I have explored this same method of policy formulation as practiced by academic analysts of policy ("Policy Analysis," 48 *American Economic Review* 298 [June, 1958]). Although it has been here presented as a method for public administrators, it is no less necessary to analysts more removed from immediate policy questions, despite their tendencies to describe their own analytical efforts as though they were the rational-comprehensive method with an especially heavy use of theory. Similarly, this same method is inevitably resorted to in personal problem-solving, where means and ends are sometimes impossible to separate, where aspirations or objectives undergo constant development, and where drastic simplification of the complexity of the real world is urgent if problems are to be solved in the time that can be given to them. To an economist accustomed to dealing with the marginal or incremental concept in market processes, the central idea in the method is that both evaluation and empirical analysis are incremental. Accordingly I have referred to the method elsewhere as "the incremental method."

CHAPTER IV

The 1960s

Perhaps no other single decade has had the impact of the 1960s on public administration. Dominated by the systems approach, modern public administration was confident, both of its mandate for change and of its capacity and expertise to foster change. Dwight Waldo, writing in retrospect about this decade recognized it as the apex of the "scientific-technical" era.[1] A newly inaugurated president, John F. Kennedy, would in 1961 set a national objective to land American astronauts on the moon by the end of the decade. The National Aeronautics and Space Administration (NASA) would achieve this feat of public administration in 1969. A larger set of goals was embodied in the Great Society programs of the Johnson administration, which were to bring an unprecedented degree of social intervention and change. The range of social programs initiated was rivaled only by the New Deal. Similar confidence was exuded in the economic arena where a major tax cut revived a faltering and slow economy and heralded the triumph of Keynesian[2] economics whereby government could "manage" the nation's economy through the use of various fiscal and monetary techniques. Intergovernmental revenue transfer programs were considered[3] that would subsequently alter the whole scale of governmental budgeting at federal, state, and local levels. There were seemingly few obstacles that could not be overcome by the modern administrative state. It only required good policy analysis and planning, appropriately developed management systems, and the new professional-technical expertise of the art, science, and practice of public administration.

By the 1960s the social sciences were strongly influenced by the systems approach to analyzing societal phenomena. Chester I. Barnard's theories about organizations being cooperative systems had been consistently validated. Daniel Katz (1903–) and Robert L. Kahn (1918–) in their 1966 book, *The Social Psychology of Organizations,* sought to apply existing knowledge on social systems in general to organizations in particular. Reprinted here from their book is a chapter, "Organizations and the System Concept," which provides a systems framework for understanding how organizations operate.

Katz and Kahn provide succinct definitions of the characteristics of open systems of organizations that reflected, in their view, the general state of modern organizational environments. Closed systems, or traditional fixed bureaucratic structures, were fine if the environment was stable and controllable. They saw accurately that organizational environments were increasingly dynamic and unstable, and that environments could differ dramatically for various organizations. Katz and Kahn concluded that the traditional closed system view of organizations led to a failure to fully appreciate the interdependence and interactions between organizations and their environments. Their work, applying systems theories to organizational theory, would mark the beginning of the realization that the old debate between human relations and scientific management, the debate between open and closed models of organizations, was over. Future efforts would be primarily directed towards understanding the interactions of organizations and their environments as open dynamic systems.

Budgeting during the 1960s was dominated by PPBS—planning programming budgeting systems. First installed in the Defense Department during the Kennedy administration, it seemed to represent the height of rationality for the budget process. Allen Schick (1934–), in his 1966 *Public Administration Review* article, "The Road to PPB: The Stages of Budget Reform," reprinted here, chronicled the development of budgetary theory from the concerns for accountability and control, which were the hallmark of the line-item budget, to performance budgeting with its emphasis on managerial efficiency, to PPBS, which stressed objectives, planning, and program effectiveness.

In 1965 Lyndon Johnson mandated the use of PPBS for all federal agencies. The application of PPBS, which required among other things that agencies detail program objectives and indicators for evaluation, make five-year expenditure forecasts, and generate numerous special cost-benefit analyses and zero-base reviews of program activities, marked perhaps the zenith of the management systems approach to public administration. PPBS, initially developed by David Novick (1906–) at the Rand Corporation,[4] had achieved remarkable success in the Defense Department. (Indeed, it is still in use there.) But its effectiveness was considerably less in the domestic agencies. Numerous state governments had also adopted the PPBS approach to budgeting as the systems approach to budgeting swept over public administration's most critical subfield. Allen Schick's article, exploring both the concepts and rationale embodied in PPBS, and how budgetary reform had developed historically remains one of the landmark essays in public budgeting. Schick, for many years with the Congressional Research Service staff and now at the University of Maryland, would continue to write significant works on budgeting and become the generally recognized informal leader of the management systems approach to public budgeting.

While the mandates and indeed much of the energy for social change in the 1960s certainly emanated from the federal government, implementation of actual program results usually had to come about at the state and local government levels. Public administration as it wrestled with social intervention rediscovered, so to speak, its other half in a renewed interest in the American "federal" system of government. The Johnson administration's approach to intergovernmental relations was called "creative federalism," which implied that there would be joint planning and decision making among all levels of government (as well as the private sector) in the management of intergovernmental programs. Morton Grodzins

(1917–1964) of the University of Chicago had long noted that this was the case. He developed the concept of "marble-cake" federalism to describe the cooperative relationships among the varying levels of government that result in an intermingling of activities. This was in contrast to the more traditional view of "layer-cake" federalism that held that the three levels of government were totally separate. In his *The American System: A New View Of Government in the United States*,[5] Grodzins, in the first chapter of his book reprinted here, observed that with tens of thousands of tax-levying governmental units, nearly half of which were school districts, the process of "federal governance" was immensely complex. He saw little correspondence between areas of governance and problems of government. "Government by chaos and cooperation," as he termed it, required a special understanding to perform adequate policy and program analyses. Remarkably, his overall assessment is quite positive; shared functions could and did work; intergovernmental grant and transfer programs could be designed and implemented effectively.

Accompanying the systems approach that dominated so much of public administration in the 1960s was the advance of policy analysis. A direct and practical consideration of policy analysis in public administration is provided by Yehezkel Dror (1928–) in his 1967 *Public Administration Review* article, "Policy Analysts: A New Professional Role in Government Service." Dror's article, which is reprinted here, was one of the first to identify and define this old function but new occupational specialty. Policy analysis would encompass both the policy formulation process (i.e., understanding the politics and participation aspects) and policy content (i.e., consideration of alternative policy outcomes by analyzing costs, benefits, distribution of benefits, etc.) Economic analysis played a pivotal role in the policy analyst's trade, but Dror recognized the limitations of what he termed a "one-sided invasion of public decision making by economics." Dror, a major critic of the incremental approach to policymaking, was one of the first to call for constructing a "policy sciences" approach that would balance economic and political roles in policy analysis.[6]

Anthony Downs' (1930–)[7] 1967 Rand Corporation study, *Inside Bureaucracy*, was an exhaustive analysis of American bureaucracy, which, while derivative of the systems approach, sought to develop laws and propositions that would aid in predicting the behavior of bureaus and bureaucrats. It was here that Downs sought to expand upon Weber's "ideal-type" by suggesting that two new elements be added to Weber's definition. First, the organization must be large; "any organization in which the highest ranking members know less than half of the other members can be considered large." Second, most of the organization's output cannot be "directly or indirectly evaluated in any markets external to the organization by means of voluntary *quid pro quo* transactions."

Downs' chapter on the "Life Cycles of Bureaus," reprinted here, recognizes stages of bureaucratic growth and stagnation as well as associated repercussions on administrative performance. Downs was bold, considering the times, in articulating his case for organizational behavior in pursuit of survival. After all, bureaucracies had been accused of being autocratic, inhumane, and insensitive to both their constituents and to their own organizational members. Now Downs was examining them for behavior designed to ensure their own preservation. It is interesting to note in this context that Downs builds upon the work of Parkinson.

Downs' last section examines the concept of death in bureaucracy and suggests that greater attention be given to understanding the policy and administrative implications for this stage of bureaucratic development.[8] Still, it is his concept of life cycle that has had the most influence on subsequent organization theorists. Not only would organizational environments differ but organizational responses would be predicated upon their own stages of development at different times in their life cycle.

However, just when society seemed to be coming to terms with bureaucratic institutions, Warren Bennis (1925–) was sounding their death knell. Bennis indicted present organizational formats as inadequate for a future that would demand rapid organizational and technological changes, participatory management, and the growth of a more professionalized workforce. He predicted in his 1967 *Personnel Administration* article "Organizations of the Future," reprinted here, that organization would have to be, of necessity, more responsive and flexible to these needs and in consequence, decidedly less bureaucratic, less structured, and less rigid.[9]

Bennis was one of the first to put together the concept that organizations in the future would rely on totally different ideas of the nature of human behavior and worth, power, and organizational form. His article provides a summary of the lessons of behavioral science and open systems theory and then constructs a number of predictions about the effects of these new organizational templates on society. His case is largely an external one; that is, the first consideration must be the interactions and impacts of organizations on society. Inherent in his work is a concern for democratic organizational leadership,[10] a theme to which he will return in the 1980s with his development of the idea of "transformational leadership."[11]

The 1960s was a period of great expansion and great change for public administration in government as well as in the academic world. The Great Society programs of the Johnson administration fueled a corresponding explosion in state and local government employment, which in turn helped support and justify growing academic efforts. However, the decade ended on a questionable note because of a number of factors—the Vietnam War, the new-found militancy of public employees and students, the emergence of more sophisticated client groups, and the yet-to-be implemented commitment to equal employment opportunity and the concept of a representative bureaucracy. Perhaps the best analysis of the effects of these issues on public administration was provided by Dwight Waldo, when he examined the implications of these trends in his 1968 *Public Administration Review* article, "Public Administration in a Time of Revolution."

Waldo would subsequently use the word *turbulence* instead of *revolution* to refer to these times.[12] In fact, in his article, reprinted here, he questions whether the 1960s represents a true revolution. Instead, he waters down the idea of revolution by referring to them as "contemporary revolutions." But the reactions to technology and science, bureaucracy and big government, and the rising expectations of society were quite real and demanded serious and comprehensive responsives by public administration. Waldo, then editor of *Public Administration Review,* had one of the major leadership roles in public administration. His writing on the impacts of a time of revolution provided great impetus for self-examination. While the themes in his article are clear—greater social equity, increased citizen participation, more organizational humanism—the outcomes were not. In the next decade, the issues raised in Waldo's provocative analysis would be a major part of an attempt to review and reform public administration.

The end of the decade was characterized by more than social unrest and public discontent over Vietnam. It was apparent that some of the management systems and programs developed during the period were not living up to expectations. PPBS, Planning Programming Budgeting Systems, perhaps the trademark of the systems approach, was a case in point. PPBS was never without its critics. In 1964, Aaron Wildavsky (1930–) published *The Politics of the Budgetary Process,*[13] the immensely well-received critique of how budgeting was, in reality, an incremental process sharply influenced by political considerations. In 1969, he wrote a devastating critique of PPBS in his *Public Administration Review* article, "Rescuing Policy Analysis From PPBS," reprinted here. Aside from stating flatly that he thought PPBS was unworkable, Wildavsky demonstrated how the planning and analytical functions of PPBS were contradictory to the essential nature of budgeting.

What was once mandatory for all federal agencies and widely adopted by state and local jurisdictions, by the end of the decade was officially *un*adopted by the federal government and was widely considered to be unusable in its original format. Nevertheless, PPBS' influence as a major budgeting process remains. Where it is still in use, however, it tends to exist in a hybird instead of a pure form.

Wildavsky, who would later form and be the first dean of the University of California at Berkeley's Graduate School of Public Policy,[14] was greatly influenced by Charles Lindblom under whom he studied while a doctoral student at Yale. Incremental approaches to budgeting or what would later be called "traditional budgeting" was the counter school of thought to the management systems emphasis. The principle contention was that budgets are inherently political and that studying budgeting and budgets is useful because it explains how and what choices (political compromises) have been made. Wildavsky even rebutted V. O. Key's classic question: "On what basis shall it be decided to allocate X dollars to activity A instead of activity B?" as unanswerable and irrelevant. What mattered was that the process of budgeting should facilitate decision making and assist in obtaining consensus about policy goals and program objectives.

Following in the tradition of C. Northcote Parkinson, Laurence J. Peter (1919–) and Raymond Hull (1919–) offered "The Peter Principle." They postulated that so many things went wrong in the world because hierarchical organizations were constantly promoting people to work at their level of incompetence. In answer to the logical question of who then does the work that has to be done, Peter asserts that "work is accomplished by those employees who have not yet reached their level of incompetence." The world cheered, made the book of the same title a best-seller (the first chapter of which is reprinted here), and waited with indifference for the spate of scholarly challenges and analyses that followed in the wake of the principle's promulgation.[15]

One of the major rallying cries of the political activists of the 1960s was "power to the people," which in administrative terms is a call for decentralization of public services, the ultimate decentralization being, of course, anarchy. Herbert Kaufman (1922–)[16] assessed its intertwined implications in his 1969 *Public Administration Review* article, "Administration Decentralization and Political Power," reprinted here. Central to his concerns about decentralization were the issues of leadership, bureaucratic representativeness, and the idea of "neutral competence."[17]

Kaufman correctly saw that a modern, highly complex society needed new modes of representation to involve the public and insure responsive administration. But the implications of this might be considerably beyond the capacities of public administration in the 1960s. Kaufman accepted the notion that administrative decentralization could provide for greater local influence in public policy-making. But it could also generate a number of other problems and conflicts, including possible interference with the pursuit of national mandates for economic and social equity, competition between local governments and programs, and decreased economies of scale leading to inefficiencies in government operations.

The final voice excerpted from the tremendous period of change that was the 1960s is that of Theodore J. Lowi (1931–).[18] His *The End of Liberalism: Ideology, Policy and the Crisis of Public Authority*[19] provided a massive critique of the modern democratic government and a condemnation of the paralyzing effects of interest-group pluralism. Lowi asserts that public authority is parceled out to private interest groups resulting in a weak, decentralized government incapable of long-range planning. These powerful interest groups operate to promote private goals; they do not compete to promote the public interest. Government then becomes not an institution capable of making hard choices among conflicting values, but a holding company for interests. The various interests are promoted by alliances of interest groups, relevant government agencies, and the appropriate legislative committees. Lowi denied the very virtues that E. Pendleton Herring and other group theorists saw in their promotion of interest-group pluralism. Overall, Lowi presents a scathing indictment of the administrative process in which agencies charged with regulation are seen as basically protectors of those being regulated.

Lowi's critical analysis, a chapter of which is reprinted here, was widely received as accurate and penetrating, but his remedy, a return to legal or constitutional democracy, what he calls "juridical democracy," was seen as unworkable. Despite its apparent flaws, there seems to be no immediately available alternative to interest group pluralism and its often paralyzing effects on modern government. Still Lowi's work is a very fitting epitaph for the 1960s. In this decade of great promise and great change, public administration encountered a whole new set of obstacles and limitations, both external and internal. An agenda for self-examination and reform was being formed that would become a high priority in the decade that followed.

NOTES

1. Dwight Waldo, *The Administrative State: A Study of the Political Theory of American Public Administration,* 2nd ed. (New York: Holmes & Meier Publishers, 1984), p. xiii.
2. John Maynard Keynes (1883–1946) is the English economist who wrote this century's most influential book on economics, *The General Theory of Employment, Interest and Money* (London: Macmillan, 1936), which called for using a government's fiscal and monetary policies to positively affect a capitalistic economy.
3. Revenue sharing was first seriously recommended by Walter Heller when he served as chairman of President Kennedy's Council of Economic Advisors. It would not become a reality until the State and Local Fiscal Assistance Act of 1972.
4. David Novick, "The Origin and History of Program Budgeting," *California Management Review* 11 No. 1 (1968).
5. (Chicago: Rand McNally, 1966). This book was essentially completed before the author's death; then it was edited and prepared for publication by Daniel J. Elazar of Temple University, a former student of Grodzins, and now a major voice on federalism in his own right.
6. See his: "Prolegomena to the Policy Sciences," *Policy Sciences* 1 (September 1970); *Design for Policy Sciences* (New York: American Elsevier, 1971); *Ventures in Policy Sciences* (New York: American Elsevier, 1971).
7. Downs is the economist generally credited with establishing the intellectual framework for "public choice" economics in his *An Economic Theory of Democracy* (New York: Harper & Row, 1957).
8. There has since emerged a significant body of literature on policy termination. See, for example: Robert P. Biller, "On Tolerating Policy and Organizational Termination: Some Design Considerations," *Policy Sciences* 16 (June 1976); Carol L. Ellis, "Program Termination: A Word To the Wise," *Public Administration Review* 43 (July–August 1983).
9. For expansions of these themes, see his: *Changing Organizations* (New York: McGraw-Hill, 1966) and with Philip E. Slater, *The Temporary Society,* (New York: Harper & Row, 1968).
10. See his and Philip E. Slater's "Democracy is Inevitable," *Harvard Business Review* (March–April 1964).
11. Warren Bennis, "Transformative Power and Leadership," in *Leadership and Organizational Culture,* ed. Thomas J. Sergiovanni and John E. Corbally (Urbana: University of Illinois Press, 1984).
12. He used it in the title of a book he later edited that dealt with these same themes: *Public Administration in a Time of Turbulence* (Scranton: Pa.: Chandler Publishing Co., 1971).
13. (Boston: Little, Brown, 1964; 4th edition, 1984).
14. For Wildavsky's advice on how to create and manage a graduate school of public policy, see the Appendix, "Principles for a Graduate School of Public Policy," to his *Speaking Truth To Power: The Art and Craft of Policy Analysis* (Boston, Little, Brown 1979).
15. See, for example: Joe D. Batten, "The Peter What? A Challenge to the Peter Principle," *Training and Development Journal* 25 (April 1971); Paul W. Cummings, "Incompetencies of the Peter Principle," *Training and Development Journal* 25 (September 1971); Kenneth T. Cann and Joseph P. Cangemi, "Peter's Peter Principle," *Personnel Journal* 50 (November 1971).
16. Kaufman, a former Yale professor and Brookings Institution scholar, is the author of many landmark works in public administration including: *The Forest Ranger: A Study in Administrative Behavior* (Baltimore: The Johns Hopkins Press, 1960); with Wallace S. Sayre, *Governing New York City* (New York: W. W. Norton, 1960); *Administrative Feedback: Monitoring Subordinates' Behavior* (Washington, D.C.: Brookings Institution, 1973); *Are Government Organizations Immortal?* (Washington, D.C.: Brookings Institution, 1976); *Red Tape: Its Origins, Uses, and Abuses* (Washington, D.C.: Brookings Institution, 1977); *The Administrative Behavior of Federal Bureau Chiefs* (Washington, D.C.: Brookings Institution, 1981).
17. The concept of "neutral competence" envisions a continuous, politically uncommitted cadre of bureaucrats at the disposal of elected or appointed political executives. For discussions, see: Herbert Kaufman, "Emerging Conflicts in the Doctrines of Public Administration," *American Political Science*

Review 50 (December 1956); Hugh Heclo, "OMB and the Presidency—The problem of 'Neutral Competence,' " *The Public Interest*, No. 38 (Winter 1975).

18. Lowi, a political scientist at Cornell University, is also the author of: *At the Pleasure of the Mayor: Patronage and Power in New York City, 1898–1958* (New York: Free Press, 1964); *American Government: Incomplete Conquest* (Hinsdale, Ill.: Dryden Press, 1976).

19. (New York: W. W. Norton, 1969; 2nd edition, 1979).

A CHRONOLOGY OF PUBLIC ADMINISTRATION: 1960–1969

1960 Richard Neustadt's *Presidential Power* asserts that the president's (or any executive's) essential power is that of persuasion.

Herbert Kaufman's *The Forest Ranger* shows how organizational and professional socialization can develop in employees the will and capacity to conform.

1961 Victor A. Thompson's *Modern Organization* finds that there is "an imbalance between ability and authority" causing bureaucratic dysfunctions all over the place.

Who Governs? is published; Robert A. Dahl's description of community power in New Haven, Connecticut, would become one of the most famous descriptions of American pluralism at the local level.

Burns and Stalker's *The Management of Innovation* articulates the need for different types of management systems (organic or mechanistic) under differing circumstances.

Rensis Likert's *New Patterns of Management* offers an empirically based defense of participatory management and organization development techniques.

President Dwight D. Eisenhower in his farewell address warns the nation that "in the councils of government we must guard against the acquisition of unwarranted influence, whether sought or unsought, by the military-industrial complex."

President John F. Kennedy's Executive Order 10925 for the first time requires that "affirmative action" be used to implement the policy of nondiscrimination in employment by the federal government and its contractors.

The Peace Corps is established.

Alan B. Shepard becomes the first American astronaut to fly in space.

President Kennedy calls for the landing of American astronauts on the moon by the end of the decade.

David Novick and the Rand Corporation help the Department of Defense install PPBS.

1962 President John F. Kennedy issues Executive Order 10988, which encourages the unionization of federal workers.

Robert Presthus' *The Organizational Society* presents his threefold classification of patterns of organizational accommodation: "upward-mobiles" who identify and accept the values of the organization, "indifferents" who reject such values and find personal satisfaction off the job, and "ambivalents" who want the rewards of organizational life but can't cope with the demands.

1963 The "March on Washington" for civil rights takes place on August 28; Martin Luther King, Jr., delivers his "I have a dream" speech.

President John F. Kennedy is assassinated on November 22 in Dallas, Texas; Vice President Lyndon B. Johnson becomes president.

1964 The Civil Rights Act prohibits discrimination on the basis of race, color, religion, sex, or national origin in most private-sector employment; creates the Equal Employment Opportunity Commission for enforcement.

Aaron Wildavsky publishes *The Politics of the Budgetary Process,* which becomes the definitive analysis of the tactics public managers use to get budgets passed.

The Economic Opportunity Act becomes the anchor of President Lyndon B. Johnson's "war on poverty" and other major initiatives in his Great Society domestic programs.

Blake and Mouton's *The Managerial Grid* explains how a graphic gridiron can facilitate an organization development program.

Michel Crozier in *The Bureaucratic Phenomenon* defines a bureaucracy as "an organization which cannot correct its behavior by learning from its errors."

1965 PPBS made mandatory for all federal agencies by the Johnson administration.

Don K. Price publishes *The Scientific Estate* in which he posits that decisional authority is inexorably flowing from the executive suite to the technical office.

Robert L. Kahn's *Organizational Stress* is the first major study of the mental health consequences of organizational role conflict and ambiguity.

James G. March edits the huge *Handbook of Organizations* which sought to summarize all existing knowledge on organization theory and behavior.

The Department of Housing and Urban Development is established.

Medicare is created through amendments to the Social Security Act.

1966 The Freedom of Information Act allows greater access to federal agency files.

Morton Grodzins claims in *The American System* that the federal system is a marble, not a layer, cake because "no important activity of government in the United States is the exclusive province of one of the levels."

Katz and Kahn in *The Social Psychology of Organizations* seek to develop open systems theory to unify the findings of behavioral science on organizational behavior.

Warren Bennis in *Changing Organizations* sounds the death knell for bureaucratic institutions because they are inadequate for a future that will demand rapid organizational change, participatory management, and the growth of a more professionalized workforce.

1967 Age Discrimination in Employment Act passed; it will be amended to raise to seventy the minimum mandatory retirement age for all employees except federal employees who have no mandatory retirement age.

The National Academy of Public Administration is organized; its first members will be all of the living past presidents of the American Society for Public Administration.

Edward A. Suchman's *Evaluative Research* puts forth the concept that evaluation is a generic field of study; that evaluative research and practice can and must be studied in a general context outside of evaluation applications in the various specialty fields.

The National Advisory Commission on Civil Disorders, the Kerner Commission, established to study the causes of urban riots, reports that the "nation is rapidly moving toward two increasingly separate Americas," one black and one white.

James D. Thompson's *Organizations in Action* sought to close the gap between open and closed systems theory by suggesting that organizations deal with the uncertainty of their environments by creating specific elements designed to cope with the outside world while other elements are able to focus on the rational nature of technical operations.

Terry Sanford in *Storm Over the States* develops the concept of "picket-fence federalism," which holds that bureaucratic specialists at the various governmental level exercise considerable power over the nature of intergovernmental programs.

Anthony Downs' *Inside Bureaucracy* seeks to develop laws and propositions that would aid in predicting the behavior of bureaus and bureaucrats.

Yehezkel Dror identifies an old function but new occupational speciality, that of policy analyst.

Antony Jay in *Management and Machiavelli* applies Machiavelli's political principles (from *The Prince*) to modern organizational management.

1968 "Younger" public administration scholars meeting at Syracuse University's Minnowbrook conference site call for a "new public administration" that would emphasize social equity concerns.

Harold Wilensky's *Organizational Intelligence* presents the pioneering study of the flow and perception of information in organizations.

The Federal Executive Institute in Charlottesville, Virginia, is established as an in-residence training facility for executive development.

James H. Boren founds the International Association of Professional Bureaucrats, which is dedicated to bureaucratic reform and the status quo: Its motto is "When in charge, ponder. When in trouble, delegate. When in doubt, mumble."

Frederick C. Mosher's *Democracy and the Public Service* traces the evolution of the American civil service and confronts the problem of professionalism.

Martin Luther King, Jr., is assassinated.

Robert F. Kennedy is assassinated.

Richard M. Nixon is elected president.

Dwight Waldo asserts that public administration is in a time of revolution.

1969 The "rape of the merit system" is encouraged by the *Federal Political Personnel Manual,* popularly known as the Malek Manual after Fred Malek, chief of the Nixon administration's White House personnel office.

Aaron Wildavsky explains in "Rescuing Policy Analysis From PPBS" how the planning and analytical functions of PPBS were contradictory to the essential nature of budgeting.

Herbert Kaufman addresses the administrative implications of the 1960s cry of "power to the people" in "Administrative Decentralization and Political Power."

Laurence J. Peter promulgates his principle that "in a hierarchy every employee tends to rise to his level of incompetence."

Theodore Lowi's *The End of Liberalism* attacks interest group pluralism for paralyzing the policy-making process.

President Richard M. Nixon's Executive Order 11491 expands the scope of collective bargaining for federal employees.

Neil Armstrong, an American astronaut, becomes the first man to walk on the moon.

---

28 Organizations and the System Concept

Daniel Katz & Robert L. Kahn

The aims of social science with respect to human organizations are like those of any other science with respect to the events and phenomena of its domain. The social scientist wishes to understand human organizations, to describe what is essential in their form, aspects, and functions. He wishes to explain their cycles of growth and decline, to predict their effects and effectiveness. Perhaps he wishes as well to test and apply such knowledge by introducing purposeful changes into organizations—by making them, for example, more benign, more responsive to human needs.

Such efforts are not solely the prerogative of social science, however; common sense approaches to understanding and altering organizations are ancient and perpetual. They tend, on the whole, to rely heavily on two assumptions: that the location and nature of an organization are given by its name; and that an organization is possessed of built-in goals—because such goals were implanted by its founders, decreed by its present leaders, or because they emerged mysteriously as the purposes of the organizational system itself. These assumptions scarcely provide an adequate basis for the study of organizations and at times can be misleading and even fallacious. We propose, however, to make use of the information to which they point.

The first problem in understanding an organization or a social system is its location and identification. How do we

Source: Daniel Katz and Robert L. Kahn, *The Social Psychology of Organizations*, pp. 14–29. Footnotes renumbered.

know that we are dealing with an organization? What are its boundaries? What behavior belongs to the organization and what behavior lies outside it? Who are the individuals whose actions are to be studied and what segments of their behavior are to be included?

The fact that popular names exist to label social organizations is both a help and a hindrance. These popular labels represent the socially accepted stereotypes about organizations and do not specify their role structure, their psychological nature, or their boundaries. On the other hand, these names help in locating the area of behavior in which we are interested. Moreover, the fact that people both within and without an organization accept stereotypes about its nature and functioning is one determinant of its character.

The second key characteristic of the common sense approach to understanding an organization is to regard it simply as the epitome of the purposes of its designer, its leaders, or its key members. The teleology of this approach is again both a help and a hindrance. Since human purpose is deliberately built into organizations and is specifically recorded in the social compact, the by-laws, or other formal protocol of the undertaking, it would be inefficient not to utilize these sources of information. In the early development of a group, many processes are generated which have little to do with its rational purpose, but over time there is a cumulative recognition of the devices for ordering group life and a deliberate use of these devices.

Apart from formal protocol, the primary mission of an organization as perceived by its leaders furnishes a highly informative set of clues for the researcher seeking to study organizational functioning. Nevertheless, the stated purposes of an organization as given by its by-laws or in the reports of its leaders can be misleading. Such statements of objectives may idealize, rationalize, distort, omit, or even conceal some essential aspects of the functioning of the organization. Nor is there always agreement about the mission of the organization among its leaders and members. The university president may describe the purpose of his institution as one of turning out national leaders; the academic dean sees it as imparting the cultural heritage of the past, the academic vice president as enabling students to move toward self-actualization and development, the graduate dean as creating new knowledge, the dean of men as training youngsters in technical and professional skills which will enable them to earn their living, and the editor of the student newspaper as inculcating the conservative values which will preserve the status quo of an outmoded capitalistic society.

The fallacy here is one of equating the purposes or goals of organizations with the purposes and goals of individual members. The organization as a system has an output, a produce or an outcome, but this is not necessarily identical with the individual purposes of group members. Though the founders of the organization and its key members do think in teleological terms about organization objectives, we should not accept such practical thinking, useful as it may be, in place of a theoretical set of constructs for purposes of scientific analysis. Social science, too frequently in the past, has been misled by such short-cuts and has equated popular phenomenology with scientific explanation.

In fact, the classic body of theory and thinking about organizations has assumed a teleology of this sort as the easiest way of identifying organizational structures and their functions. From this point of view an organization is a social device for efficiently accomplishing through group means some stated purpose; it is the equivalent of the blueprint for the design of the machine which is to be created for some practical objective. The essential difficulty with this purposive or design approach is that an organization characteristically includes more and less than is indicated by the design of its founder or the purpose of its leader. Some of the factors assumed in the design may be lacking or so distorted in operational practice as to be meaningless, while unforeseen embellishments dominate the organizational structure. Moreover, it is not always possible to ferret out the designer of the organization or to discover the intricacies of the design which he carried in his head. The attempt by Merton to deal with the latent function of the organization in contrast with its manifest function is one way of dealing with this problem.[1] The study of unanticipated consequences as well as anticipated consequences of organizational functioning is a similar way of handling the matter. Again, however, we are back to the purposes of the creator or leader, dealing with unanticipated consequences on the assumption that we can discover the consequences anticipated by him and can lump all other outcomes together as a kind of error variance.

It would be much better theoretically, however, to start with concepts which do not call for identifying the purposes of the designers and then correcting for them when they do not seem to be fulfilled. The theoretical concepts should begin with the input, output, and functioning of the organization as a system and not with the rational purposes of its leaders. We may want to utilize such purposive notions to lead us to sources of data or as subjects of special study, but not as our basic theoretical constructs for understanding organizations.

Our theoretical model for the understanding of organizations is that of an energic input-output system in which the energic return from the output reactivates the system. Social organizations are flagrantly open systems in that the input of energies and the conversion of output into further energic input consist of transactions between the organization and its environment.

All social systems, including organizations, consist of the patterned activities of a number of individuals. Moreover, these patterned activities are complementary or interdependent with respect to some common output or outcome; they are repeated, relatively enduring, and bounded in space and time. If the activity pattern occurs only once or at unpredictable intervals, we could not speak of an organization. The stability or recurrence of activities can be examined in relation to the *energic input* into the system, the *transformation of energies within the system,* and the *resulting product or energic output.* In a factory the raw materials and the human labor are the energic input, the patterned activities of production the transformation of energy, and the finished product the output. To maintain this patterned activity requires a continued renewal of the inflow of energy. This is guaranteed in social systems by the energic return from the product or outcome. Thus the outcome of the cycle of activities furnishes new energy for the initiation of a renewed cycle. The company which produces automobiles sells them and by doing so obtains the means of securing new raw materials, compensating its labor force, and continuing the activity pattern.

In many organizations outcomes are converted into money and new energy is furnished through this mechanism. Money is a convenient way of handling energy units both on the output and input sides, and buying and selling represent one set of social rules for regulating the exchange of money. Indeed, these rules are so effective and so widespread that there is some danger of mistaking the business of buying and selling for the defining cycles of organization. It is a commonplace executive observation that businesses exist to make money, and the observation is usually allowed to go unchallenged. It is, however, a very limited statement about the purposes of business.

Some human organizations do not depend on the cycle of selling and buying to maintain themselves. Universities and public agencies depend rather on bequests and legislative appropriations, and in so-called voluntary organizations the output reenergizes the activity of organization members in a more direct fashion. Member activities and accomplishments are rewarding in themselves and tend therefore to be continued, without the mediation of the outside environment. A society of bird watchers can wander into the hills and engage in the rewarding activities of identifying birds for their mutual edification and enjoyment. Organizations thus differ on this important dimension of the source of energy renewal, with the great majority utilizing both intrinsic and extrinsic sources in varying degree. Most large-scale organizations are not as self-contained as small voluntary groups and are very dependent upon the social effects of their output for energy renewal.

Our two basic criteria for identifying social systems and determining their functions are (1) tracing the pattern of energy exchange or activity of people as it results in some output and (2) ascertaining how the output is translated into energy which reactivates the pattern. We shall refer to organizational functions or objectives not as the conscious purposes of group leaders or group members but as the outcomes which are the energic source for a maintenance of the same type of output.

This model of an energic input-output system is taken from the open system theory as promulgated by von Bertalanffy.[2] Theorists have pointed out the applicability of the system concepts of the natural sciences to the problems of social science. It is important, therefore, to examine in more detail the constructs of system theory and the characteristics of open systems.

System theory is basically concerned with problems of relationships, of structure, and of interdependence rather than with the constant attributes of objects. In general approach it resembles field theory except that its dynamics deal with temporal as well as spatial patterns. Older formulations of system constructs dealt with the closed systems of the physical sciences, in which relatively self-contained structures could be treated successfully as if they were independent of external forces. But living systems, whether biological organisms or social organizations, are acutely dependent upon their external environment and so must be conceived of as open systems.

Before the advent of open-system thinking, social scientists tended to take one of two approaches in dealing with social structures; they tended either (1) to regard them as closed systems to which the laws of physics applied or (2) to endow them with some vitalistic concept like entelechy. In the former case they ignored the environmental forces affecting the organization and in the latter case they fell back upon some magical purposiveness to account for organizational functioning. Biological theorists, however, have rescued us from this trap by pointing out that the concept of the open system means that we neither have to follow the laws of traditional physics, nor in deserting them do we have to abandon science. The laws of Newtonian physics are correct generalizations but they are limited to closed systems. They do not apply in the same fashion to open systems which maintain themselves through constant commerce with their environment, i.e., a continuous inflow and outflow of energy through permeable boundaries.

One example of the operation of closed versus open systems can be seen in the concept of entropy and the second law of thermodynamics. According to the second law of thermodynamics a system moves toward equilibrium; it tends to run down, that is, its differentiated structures tend to move toward dissolution as the elements composing them become arranged in random disorder. For example, suppose that a bar of iron has been heated by the application of a blowtorch on one side. The arrangement of all the fast (heated) molecules on one side and all the slow molecules on the other is an unstable state, and over time the distribution of molecules becomes in effect random, with the resultant cooling of one side and heating of the other, so that all surfaces of the iron approach the same temperature. A similar process of heat exchange will also be going on between the iron bar and its environment, so that the bar will gradually approach the temperature of the room in which it is located, and in so doing will elevate somewhat the previous temperature of the room. More technically, entropy increases toward a maximum and equilibrium occurs as the physical system attains the state of the most probable distribution of its elements. In social systems, however, structures tend to become more elaborated rather than less differentiated. The rich may grow richer and the poor may grow poorer. The open system does not run down, because it can import energy from the world around it. Thus the operation of entropy is counteracted by the importation of energy and the living system is characterized by negative rather than positive entropy.

COMMON CHARACTERISTICS OF OPEN SYSTEMS

Though the various types of open systems have common characteristics by virtue of being open systems, they differ in other characteristics. If this were not the case, we would be able to obtain all our basic knowledge about social organizations through the study of a single cell.

The following nine characteristics seem to define all open systems.

1. Importation of Energy

Open systems import some form of energy from the external environment. The cell receives oxygen from the bloodstream; the body similarly takes in oxygen from the air and food from the external world. The personality is dependent upon the external world for stimulation. Studies of sensory deprivation show that when a person is placed in a darkened soundproof room, where he has a minimal amount of visual and auditory stimulation, he develops hallucinations and other signs of mental stress.[3] Deprivation of social stimulation also can lead to mental disorganization.[4] Köhler's studies of the figural after-effects of continued stimulation show the dependence of perception upon its energic support from the external world.[5] Animals deprived of visual experience from birth for a prolonged period never fully recover their visual capacities.[6] In other words, the functioning personality is heavily dependent upon the continuous inflow of stimulation from the external environment. Similarly, social organizations must also draw renewed supplies of energy from other institutions, or people, or the material environment. No social structure is self-sufficient or self-contained.

2. The Through-Put

Open systems transform the energy available to them. The body converts starch and sugar into heat and action. The personality converts chemical and electrical forms of stimulation into sensory qualities, and information into thought patterns. The organization creates a new product, or processes materials, or trains people, or provides a service. These activities entail some reorganization of input. Some work gets done in the system.

3. The Output

Open systems export some product into the environment, whether it be the invention of an inquiring mind or a bridge constructed by an engineering firm. Even the biological organism exports physiological products such as carbon dioxide from the lungs which helps to maintain plants in the immediate environment.

4. Systems as Cycles of Events

The pattern of activities of the energy exchange has a cyclic character. The product exported into the environment furnishes the sources of energy for the repetition of the cycle of activities. The energy reinforcing the cycle of activities can derive from some exchange of the product in the external world or from the activity itself. In the former instance, the industrial concern utilizes raw materials and human labor to turn out a product which is marketed, and the monetary return is used to obtain more raw materials and labor to perpetuate the cycle of activities. In the latter instance, the voluntary organization can provide expressive satisfactions to its members so that the energy renewal comes directly from the organizational activity itself.

The problem of structure, or the relatedness of parts, can be observed directly in some physical arrangement of things where the larger unit is physically bounded and its subparts are also bounded within the larger structure. But how do we deal with social structures, where physical boundaries in this sense do not exist? It was the genius of F. H. Allport which contributed the answer, namely that the structure is to be found in an interrelated set of events which return upon themselves to complete and renew a cycle of activities.[7] It is events rather than things which are structured, so that social structure is a dynamic rather than a static concept. Activities are structured so that they comprise a unity in their completion or closure. A simple linear stimulus-response exchange between two people would not constitute social structure. To create structure, the responses of A would have to elicit B's reactions in such a manner that the responses of the latter would stimulate A to further responses. Of course the chain of events may involve many people, but their behavior can be characterized as showing structure only when there is some closure to the chain by a return to its point of origin with the probability that the chain of events will then be repeated. The repetition of the cycle does not have to involve the same set of phenotypical happenings. It may expand to include more sub-events of exactly the same kind or it may involve similar activities directed toward the same outcomes. In the individual organism the eye may move in such a way as to have the point of light fall upon the center of the retina. As the point of light moves, the movements of the eye may also change but to complete the same cycle of activity, i.e., to focus upon the point of light.

A single cycle of events of a self-closing character gives us a simple form of structure. But such single cycles can also combine to give a larger structure of events or an event system. An event system may consist of a circle of smaller cycles or hoops, each one of which makes contact with several others. Cycles may also be tangential to one another from other types of subsystems. The basic method for the identification of social structures is to follow the energic chain of events from the input of energy through its transformation to the point of closure of the cycle.

5. Negative Entropy

To survive, open systems must move to arrest the entropic process; they must acquire negative entropy. The entropic process is a universal law of nature in which all forms of organization move toward disorganization or death. Complex physical systems move toward simple random distribution of their elements and biological organisms also run down and perish. The open system, however, by importing more energy from its environment than it expends, can store energy and can acquire negative entropy. There is then a general trend in an open system to maximize its ratio of imported to expended energy, to survive and even during periods of crisis to live on borrowed time. Prisoners in concentration camps on a starvation diet will carefully conserve any form of energy expenditure to make the limited food intake go as far as possible.[8] Social organizations will seek to improve their survival position and to acquire in their reserves a comfortable margin of operation.

The entropic process asserts itself in all biological systems as well as in closed physical systems. The energy replenishment of the biological organism is not of a qualitative character which can maintain indefinitely the complex organizational structure of living tissue. Social systems, however, are not anchored in the same physical constancies as biological organisms and so are capable of almost indefinite arresting of the entropic process. Nevertheless the number of organizations which go out of existence every year is large.

6. Information Input, Negative Feedback, and the Coding Process

The inputs into living systems consist not only of energic materials which become transformed or altered in the work that gets done. Inputs are also informative in character and furnish signals to the structure about the environment and about its own functioning in relation to the environment. Just as we recognize the distinction between cues and drives in individual psychology, so must we take account of information and energic inputs for all living systems.

The simplest type of information input found in all systems is negative feedback. Information feedback of a negative kind enables the system to correct its deviations from course. The working parts of the machine feed back information about the effects of their operation to some central mechanism or subsystem which acts on such information to keep the system on target. The thermostat which controls the temperature of the room is a simple example of a regulatory device which operates on the basis of negative feedback. The automated power plant would furnish more complex examples. Miller emphasizes the critical nature of negative feedback in his proposition: "*When a system's negative feedback discontinues, its steady state vanishes, and at the same time its boundary disappears and the system terminates.*"[9] If there is no corrective device to get the system back on its course, it will expend too much energy or it will ingest too much energic input and no longer continue as a system.

The reception of inputs into a system is selective. Not all energic inputs are capable of being absorbed into every system. The digestive system of living creatures assimilates only those inputs to which it is adapted. Similarly, systems can react only to those information signals to which they are attuned. The general term for the selective mechanisms of a system by which incoming materials are rejected or accepted and translated for the structure is coding. Through the coding process the "blooming, buzzing confusion" of the world is simplified into a few meaningful and simplified categories for a given system. The nature of the functions performed by the system determines its coding mechanisms, which in turn perpetuate this type of functioning.

7. The Steady State and Dynamic Homeostasis

The importation of energy to arrest entropy operates to maintain some constancy in energy exchange, so that open systems which survive are characterized by a steady state. A steady state is not motionless or a true equilibrium. There is a continuous inflow of energy from the external environment and a continuous export of the products of the system, but the character of the system, the ratio of the energy exchanges and the relations between parts, remains the same. The catabolic and anabolic processes of tissue breakdown and restoration within the body preserve a steady state so that the organism from time to time is not the identical organism it was but a highly similar organism. The steady state is seen in clear form in the homeostatic processes for the regulation of body temperature; external conditions of humidity and temperature may vary, but the temperature of the body remains the same. The endocrine glands are a regulatory mechanism for preserving an evenness of physiological functioning. The general principle here is that of Le Châtelier who maintains that any internal or external factor making for disruption of the system is countered by forces which restore the system as closely as possible to its previous state.[10] Krech and Crutchfield similarly hold, with respect to psychological organization, that cognitive structures will react to influences in such a way as to absorb them with minimal change to existing cognitive integration.[11]

The homeostatic principle does not apply literally to the functioning of all complex living systems, in that in counteracting entropy they move toward growth and expansion. This apparent contradiction can be resolved, however, if we recognize the complexity of the subsystems and their interaction in anticipating changes necessary for the maintenance of an overall steady state. Stagner has pointed out that the initial disturbance of a given tissue constancy within the biological organism will result in mobilization of energy to restore the balance, but that recurrent upsets will lead to actions to anticipate the disturbance:

> We eat before we experience intense hunger pangs. . . . energy mobilization for forestalling tactics must be explained in terms of a *cortical tension* which reflects the visceral-proprioceptive pattern of the original biological disequilibration . . . . *Dynamic homeostasis* involves the maintenance of tissue constancies by establishing a constant physical environment—by

> reducing the variability and disturbing effects of external stimulation. Thus the organism does not simply restore the prior equilibrium. A new, more complex and more comprehensive equilibrium is established.[12]

Though the tendency toward a steady state in its simplest form is homeostatic, as in the preservation of a constant body temperature, the basic principle is *the preservation of the character of the system.* The equilibrium which complex systems approach is often that of a quasi-stationary equilibrium, to use Lewin's concept.[13] An adjustment in one direction is countered by a movement in the opposite direction and both movements are approximate rather than precise in their compensatory nature. Thus a temporal chart of activity will show a series of ups and downs rather than a smooth curve.

In preserving the character of the system, moreover, the structure will tend to import more energy than is required for its output, as we have already noted in discussing negative entropy. To insure survival, systems will operate to acquire some margin of safety beyond the immediate level of existence. The body will store fat, the social organization will build up reserves, the society will increase its technological and cultural base. Miller has formulated the proposition that the rate of growth of a system—within certain ranges—is exponential if it exists in a medium which makes available unrestricted amounts of energy for input.[14]

In adapting to their environment, systems will attempt to cope with external forces by ingesting them or acquiring control over them. The physical boundedness of the single organism means that such attempts at control over the environment affect the behavioral system rather than the biological system of the individual. Social systems will move, however, towards incorporating within their boundaries the external resources essential to survival. Again the result is an expansion of the original system.

Thus, the steady state which at the simple level is one of homeostasis over time, at more complex levels becomes one of preserving the character of the system through growth and expansion. The basic type of system does not change directly as a consequence of expansion. The most common type of growth is a multiplication of the same type of cycles or subsystems—a change in quantity rather than in quality. Animals and plant species grow by multiplication. A social system adds more units of the same essential type as it already has. Haire has studied the ratio between the sizes of different subsystems in growing business organizations.[15] He found that though the number of people increased in both the production subsystem and the subsystem concerned with the external world, the ratio of the two groups remained constant. Qualitative change does occur, however, in two ways. In the first place, quantitative growth calls for supportive subsystems of a specialized character not necessary when the system was smaller. In the second place, there is a point where quantitative changes produce a qualitative difference in the functioning of a system. A small college which triples its size is no longer the same institution in terms of the relation between its administration and faculty, relations among the various academic departments, or the nature of its instruction.

In short, living systems exhibit a growth or expansion dynamic in which they maximize their basic character. They react to change or they anticipate change through growth which assimilates the new energic inputs to the nature of their structure. In terms of Lewin's quasistationary equilibrium the ups and downs of the adjustive process do not always result in a return to the old level. Under certain circumstances a solidification or freezing occurs during one of the adjustive cycles. A new base line level is thus established and successive movements fluctuate around this plateau which may be either above or below the previous plateau of operation.

8. Differentiation

Open systems move in the direction of differentiation and elaboration. Diffuse global patterns are replaced by more specialized functions. The sense organs and the nervous system evolved as highly differentiated structures from the primitive nervous tissues. The growth of the personality proceeds from primitive, crude organizations of mental functions to hierarchically structured and well-differentiated systems of beliefs and feelings. Social organizations move toward the multiplication and elaboration of roles with greater specialization of function. In the United States today medical specialists now outnumber the general practitioners.

One type of differentiated growth in systems is what von Bertalanffy terms progressive mechanization. It finds expression in the way in which a system achieves a steady state. The early method is a process which involves an interaction of various dynamic forces, whereas the later development entails the use of a regulatory feedback mechanism. He writes:

> It can be shown that the *primary* regulations in organic systems, that is, those which are most fundamental and primitive in embryonic development as well as in evolution, are of such nature of dynamic interaction. . . . Superimposed are those regulations which we may call *secondary*, and which are controlled by fixed arrangements, especially of the feedback type. This state of affairs is a consequence of a general principle of organization which may be called progressive mechanization. At first, systems—biological, neurological, psychological or social—are governed by dynamic interaction of their components; later on, fixed arrangements and conditions of constraint are established which render the system and its parts more efficient, but also gradually diminish and eventually abolish its equipotentiality.[16]

9. Equifinality

Open systems are further characterized by the principle of equifinality, a principle suggested by von Bertalanffy in 1940.[17] According to this principle, a system can reach the same final state from differing initial conditions and by a variety of paths. The well-known biological experiments on the sea urchin show that a normal creature of that species can develop from a complete ovum, from each half of a divided ovum, or from the fusion product of two whole ova. As open systems move toward regulatory mechanisms to control their operations, the amount of equifinality may be reduced.

SOME CONSEQUENCES OF VIEWING ORGANIZATIONS AS OPEN SYSTEMS

In the following chapter we shall inquire into the specific implications of considering organizations as open systems and into the ways in which social organizations differ from other types of living systems. At this point, however, we should call attention to some of the misconceptions which arise both in theory and practice when social organizations are regarded as closed rather than open systems.

The major misconception is the failure to recognize fully that the organization is continually dependent upon inputs from the environment and that the inflow of materials and human energy is not a constant. The fact that organizations have built-in protective devices to maintain stability and that they are notoriously difficult to change in the direction of some reformer's desires should not obscure the realities of the dynamic interrelationships of any social structure with its social and natural environment. The very efforts of the organization to maintain a constant external environment produce changes in organizational structure. The reaction to changed inputs to mute their possible revolutionary implications also results in changes.

The typical models in organizational theorizing concentrate upon principles of internal functioning as if these problems were independent of changes in the environment and as if they did not affect the maintenance inputs of motivation and morale. Moves toward tighter integration and coordination are made to insure stability, when flexibility may be the more important requirement. Moreover, coordination and control become ends in themselves rather than means to an end. They are not seen in full perspective as adjusting the system to its environment but as desirable goals within a closed system. In fact, however, every attempt at coordination which is not functionally required may produce a host of new organizational problems.

One error which stems from this kind of misconception is the failure to recognize the equifinality of the open system, namely that there are more ways than one of producing a given outcome. In a closed physical system the same initial conditions must lead to the same final result. In open systems this is not true even at the biological level. It is much less true at the social level. Yet in practice we insist that there is one best way of assembling a gun for all recruits, one best way for the baseball player to hurl the ball in from the outfield and that we standardize and teach these best methods. Now it is true under certain conditions that there is one best way, but these conditions must first be established. The general principle, which characterizes all open systems, is that there does not have to be a single method for achieving an objective.

A second error lies in the notion that irregularities in the functioning of a system due to environmental influences are error variances and should be treated accordingly. According to this conception, they should be controlled out of studies of organizations. From the organization's own operations they should be excluded as irrelevant and should be guarded against. The decisions of officers to omit a consideration of external factors or to guard against such influences in a defensive fashion, as if they would go away if ignored, is an instance of this type of thinking. So is the now outmoded "public be damned" attitude of businessmen toward the clientele upon whose support they depend. Open system theory, on the other hand, would maintain that environmental influences are not sources of error variance but are integrally related to the functioning of a social system, and that we cannot understand a system without a constant study of the forces that impinge upon it.

Thinking of the organization as a closed system, moreover, results in a failure to develop the intelligence or feedback function of obtaining adequate information about the changes in environmental forces. It is remarkable how weak many industrial companies are in their market research departments when they are so dependent upon the market. The prediction can be hazarded that organizations in our society will increasingly move toward the improvements of the facilities for research in assessing environmental forces. The reason is that we are in the process of correcting our misconception of the organization as a closed system.

Emery and Trist have pointed out how current theorizing on organizations still reflects the older closed system conceptions. They write:

> In the realm of social theory, however, there has been something of a tendency to continue thinking in terms of a "closed" system, that is, to regard the enterprise as sufficiently independent to allow most of its problems to be analyzed with reference to its internal structure and without reference to its external environment. . . . In practice the system theorists in social science . . . did "tend to focus on the statics of social structure and to neglect the study of structural change." In an attempt to overcome this bias, Merton suggested that "the concept of dysfunction, which implied the concept of strain, stress and tension on the structural level, provides an analytical approach to the study of dynamics and change." This concept has been widely accepted by system theorists but while it draws attention to sources of imbalance within an organization it does not conceptually reflect the mutual permeation of an organization and its environment that is the cause of such imbalance. It still retains the limiting perspectives of "closed system" theorizing. In the administrative field the same limitations may be seen in the otherwise invaluable contributions of Barnard and related writers.[18]

SUMMARY

The open-system approach to organizations is contrasted with common-sense approaches, which tend to accept popular names and stereotypes as basic organizational properties and to identify the purpose of an organization in terms of the goals of its founders and leaders.

The open-system approach, on the other hand, begins by identifying and mapping the repeated cycles of input, transformation, output, and renewed input which comprise the organizational pattern. This approach to organizations represents the adaptation of work in biology and in the physical sciences by von Bertalanffy and others.

Organizations as a special class of open systems have properties of their own, but they share other properties in common with all open systems. These include the importation of energy from the environment, the through-put or transformation of the imported energy into some product form which is characteristic of the system, the exporting of that product into the environment, and the reenergizing of the system from sources in the environment.

Open systems also share the characteristics of negative entropy, feedback, homeostasis, differentiation, and equifinality. The law of negative entropy states that systems survive and maintain their characteristic internal order only so long as they import from the environment more energy than they expend in the process of transformation and exportation. The feedback principle has to do with information input, which is a special kind of energic importation, a kind of signal to the system about environmental conditions and about the functioning of the system in relation to its environment. The feedback of such information enables the system to correct for its own malfunctioning or for changes in the environment, and thus to maintain a steady state or homeostasis. This is a dynamic rather than a static balance, however. Open systems are not at rest but tend toward differentiation and elaboration, both because of subsystem dynamics and because of the relationship between growth and survival. Finally, open systems are characterized by the principle of equifinality, which asserts that systems can reach the same final state from different initial conditions and by different paths of development.

Traditional organizational theories have tended to view the human organization as a closed system. This tendency had led to a disregard of differing organizational environments and the nature of organizational dependency on environment. It has led also to an overconcentration on principles of internal organizational functioning, with consequent failure to develop and understand the processes of feedback which are essential to survival.

NOTES

1. Merton, R. K. 1957. *Social theory and social structure*, rev. ed. New York: Free Press.
2. von Bertalanffy, L. 1956. General System theory. *General Systems.* Yearbook of the Society for the Advancement of General System Theory, **1**, 1–10.
3. Solomon, P., *et. al.* (Eds.) 1961. *Sensory deprivation.* Cambridge, Mass: Harvard University Press.
4. Spitz, R. A. 1945. Hospitalism: an inquiry into the genesis of psychiatric conditions in early childhood. *Psychoanalytic Study of the Child,* **1**, 53–74.
5. Kohler, W., and H. Wallach. 1944. Figural after-effects: an investigation of visual processes. *Proceedings of the American Philosophical Society,* **88**, 269–357. Also, Kohler, W., and D. Emery. 1947. Figural after-effects in the third dimension of visual space. *American Journal of Psychology,* **60**, 159–201.
6. Melzack, R., and W. Thompson. 1956. Effects of early experience on social behavior. *Canadian Journal of Psychology,* **10**, 82–90.
7. Allport, F. H. 1962. A structuronomic conception of behavior: individual and collective. I. Structural theory and the master problem of social psychology. *Journal of Abnormal and Social Psychology,* **64**, 3–30.
8. Cohen, E. 1954. *Human behavior in the concentration camp.* London: Jonathan Cape.
9. Miller, J. G. 1955. Toward a general theory for the behavioral sciences. *American Psychologist,* **10**, 513–531; quote from p. 529.
10. See, Bradley, D. F., and M. Calvin. 1956. Behavior: imbalance in a network of chemical transformations. *General Systems.* Yearbook of the Society for the Advancement of General System Theory, **1**, 56–65.
11. Krech, D., and R. Crutchfield. 1948. *Theory and problems of social psychology.* New York: McGraw-Hill.
12. Stagner, R. 1951. Homeostasis as a unifying concept in personality theory. *Psychological Review,* **58**, 5–17; quote from p. 5.
13. Lewin, K. 1947. Frontiers in group dynamics. *Human Relations,* **1**, 5–41.
14. Miller, *op cit.*
15. Haire, M. 1959. Biological models and empirical histories of the growth of organizations. In M. Haire (Ed.) *Modern organization theory,* New York: Wiley, 272–306.
16. von Bertalanffy. 1956, *op cit,* p. 6.
17. von Bertalanffy, L. 1940. Der organismus als physikalisches system betrachtet. *Naturwissenschaften,* **28**, 521 ff.
18. Emery, F. E., and E. L. Trist. 1960. Sociotechnical systems. In *Management sciences models and techniques.* Vol. 2, London: Pergamon Press; quote from p. 84.

29

The Road to PPB: The Stages of Budget Reform

Allen Schick

Among the new men in the nascent PPB staffs and the fellow travellers who have joined the bandwagon, the mood is of "a revolutionary development in the history of government management." There is excited talk about the differences between what has been and what will be; of the benefits that will accrue from an explicit and "hard" appraisal of objectives and alternatives; of the merits of multiyear budget forecasts and plans; of the great divergence between the skills and role of the analyst and the job of the examiner; of the realignments in government structure that might result from changes in the budget process.

This is not the only version, however. The closer one gets to the nerve centers of budget life—the Divisions in the Bureau of the Budget and the budget offices in the departments and agencies—the more one is likely to hear that "there's nothing very new in PPB; it's hardly different from what we've been doing until now." Some old-timers interpret PPB as a revival of the performance budgeting venture of the early 1950s. Others belittle the claim that—before PPB—decisions on how much to spend for personnel or supplies were made without real consideration of the purposes for which these inputs were to be invested. They point to previous changes that have been in line with PPB, albeit without PPB's distinctive package of techniques and nomenclature. Such things as the waning role of the "green sheets" in the central budget process, the redesign of the appropriation structure and the development of activity classifications, refinements in work measurement, productivity analysis, and other types of output measurement, and the utilization of the Spring Preview for a broad look at programs and major issues.

Between the uncertain protests of the traditional budgeteer and the uncertain expectations of the *avant garde*, there is a third version. The PPB system that is being developed portends a radical change in the central function of budgeting, but it is anchored to half a century of tradition and evolution. The budget system of the future will be a product of past and emerging developments; that is, it will embrace both the budgetary functions introduced during earlier stages of reform as well as the planning function which is highlighted by PPB. PPB is the first budget system *designed* to accommodate the multiple functions of budgeting.

THE FUNCTIONS OF BUDGETING

Budgeting always has been conceived as a process for systematically relating the

Source: From *Public Administration Review* 26 (December 1966), pp. 243–258.

expenditure of funds to the accomplishment of planned objectives. In this important sense, there is a bit of PPB in every budget system. Even in the initial stirrings of budget reform more than 50 years ago, there were cogent statements on the need for a budget system to plan the objectives and activities of government and to furnish reliable data on what was to be accomplished with public funds. In 1907, for example, the New York Bureau of Municipal Research published a sample "program memorandum" that contained some 125 pages of functional accounts and data for the New York City Health Department.[1]

However, this orientation was not *explicitly* reflected in the budget systems—national, state, or local—that were introduced during the first decades of this century, nor is it *explicitly* reflected in the budget systems that exist today. The plain fact is that planning is not the only function that must be served by a budget system. The *management* of ongoing activities and the *control* of spending are two functions which, in the past, have been given priority over the planning function. (See Figure 1.) Robert Anthony identifies three distinct administrative processes, strategic planning, management control, and operational control.

> **Strategic planning** is the process of deciding on objectives of the organization, on changes in these objectives, on the resources used to attain these objectives, and on the policies that are to govern the acquisition, use, and disposition of these resources.
>
> **Management control** is the process by which managers assure that resources are obtained and used effectively and efficiently in the accomplishment of the organization's objectives.
>
> **Operational control** is the process of assuring that specific tasks are carried out effectively and efficiently.[2]

Every budget system, even rudimentary ones, comprises planning, management, and control processes. Operationally, these processes often are indivisible, but for analytic purposes they are distinguished here. In the context of budgeting, *planning* involves the determination of objectives, the evaluation of alternative courses of action, and the authorization of select programs. Planning is linked most closely to budget preparation, but it would be a mistake to disregard the management and control elements in budget preparation or the possibilities for planning during other phases of the budget year. Clearly, one of the major aims of PPB is to convert the annual routine of preparing a budget into a conscious appraisal and formulation of future goals and policies. Management involves the programming of approved goals into specific projects and activities, the design of organizational units to carry out approved programs, and the staffing of these units and the procurement of necessary resources. The management process is spread over the entire budget cycle; ideally, it is the link between goals made and activities undertaken. *Control* refers to the process of binding operating officials to the policies and plans set by their superiors. Control is predominant during the execution and audit stages, although the form of budget estimates and appropriations often is determined by control considerations. The assorted controls and reporting procedures that are associated with budget execution—position controls, restrictions on transfers, requisition procedures, and travel regulations, to mention the more prominent ones—have the purpose of securing compliance with policies made by central authorities.

Very rarely are planning, management, and control given equal attention in the operation of budget systems. As a practical matter, planning, management, and control have tended to be competing processes in budgeting with no neat division of functions among the various participants. Because time is scarce, central authorities must be selective in the things they do. Although this scarcity counsels the devolution of control responsibilities to operating levels, the lack of reliable and relied-on internal control systems has loaded central authorities with control functions at the expense of the planning function. Moreover, these processes often require different skills and generate different ways of handling the budget mission, so that one type of perspective tends to predominate over the others. Thus, in the staffing of the budget offices, there has been a shift from accountants to administrators as budgeting has moved from a control to a management posture. The initial experience with PPB suggests that the next transition might be from administrators to economists as budgeting takes on more of the planning function.

Most important, perhaps, are the differential informational requirements of planning, control, and management processes. Informational needs differ in terms of time spans, levels of aggregation, linkages with organizational and operating units, and input-output foci. The apparent solution is to design a system that serves the multiple needs of budgeting. Historically, however, there has been a strong tendency to homogenize informational structures and to rely on a single classification scheme to serve all budgetary purposes. For the most part, the informational system has been structured to meet the purposes of control. As a result, the type of multiple-purpose budget system envisioned by PPB has been avoided.

An examination of budget systems should reveal whether greater emphasis is placed *at the central levels* on planning, management, or control. A *planning orientation* focuses on the broadest range of issues: What are the long-range goals and policies of the government and how

FIGURE 1 • SOME BASIC DIFFERENCES BETWEEN BUDGET ORIENTATIONS

Characteristic	Control	Management	Planning
Personnel Skill	Accounting	Administration	Economics
Information Focus	Objects	Activities	Purposes
Key Budget Stage (central)	Execution	Preparation	Prepreparation
Breadth of Measurement	Discrete	Discrete/activities	Comprehensive
Role of Budget Agency	Fiduciary	Efficiency	Policy
Decisional-Flow	Upward-aggregative	Upward-aggregative	Downward-disaggregative
Type of Choice	Incremental	Incremental	Teletic
Control Responsibility	Central	Operating	Operating
Management Responsibility	Dispersed	Central	Supervisory
Planning Responsibility	Dispersed	Dispersed	Central
Budget-Appropriations Classifications	Same	Same	Different
Appropriations-Organizational Link	Direct	Direct	Crosswalk

are these related to particular expenditure choices? What criteria should be used in appraising the requests of the agencies? Which programs should be initiated or terminated, and which expanded or curtailed? A *management orientation* deals with less fundamental issues: What is the best way to organize for the accomplishment of a prescribed task? Which of several staffing alternatives achieves the most effective relationship between the central and field offices? Of the various grants and projects proposed, which should be approved? A *control orientation* deals with a relatively narrow range of concerns: How can agencies be held to the expenditure ceilings established by the legislature and chief executive? What reporting procedures should be used to enforce propriety in expenditures? What limits should be placed on agency spending for personnel and equipment?

It should be clear that every budget system contains planning, management, and control features. A control orientation means the subordination, not the absence, of planning and management functions. In the matter of orientations, we are dealing with relative emphases, not with pure dichotomies. The germane issue is the balance among these vital functions at the central level. Viewed centrally, what weight does each have in the design and operation of the budget system?

THE STAGES OF BUDGET REFORM

The framework outlined above suggests a useful approach to the study of budget reform. Every reform alters the planning-management-control balance, sometimes inadvertently, usually deliberately. Accordingly, it is possible to identify three successive stages of reform. In the first stage, dating roughly from 1920 to 1935, the dominant emphasis was on developing an adequate system of expenditure control. Although planning and management considerations were not altogether absent (and indeed occupied a prominent role in the debates leading to the Budget and Accounting Act of 1921), they were pushed to the side by what was regarded as the first priority, a reliable system of expenditure accounts. The second stage came into the open during the New Deal and reached its zenith more than a decade later in the movement for performance budgeting. The management orientation, paramount during this period, made its mark in the reform of the appropriation structure, development of management improvement and work measurement programs, and the focusing of budget preparation on the work and activities of the agencies. The third stage, the full emergence of which must await the institutionalization of PPB, can be traced to earlier efforts to link planning and budgeting as well as to the analytic criteria of welfare economics, but its recent development is a product of modern informational and decisional technologies such as those pioneered in the Department of Defense.

PPB is predicated on the primacy of the planning function; yet it strives for a multipurpose budget system that gives adequate and necessary attention to the control and management areas. Even in embryonic stage, PPB envisions the development of crosswalk grids for the conversion of data from a planning to a management and control framework, and back again. PPB treats the three basic functions as compatible and complementary elements of a budget system, though not as coequal aspects of central budgeting. In ideal form, PPB would centralize the planning function and delegate *primary* managerial and control responsibilities to the supervisory and operating levels respectively.

In the modern genesis of budgeting, efforts to improve planning, management, and control made common cause under the popular banner of the executive-budget concept. In the goals and lexicon of the first reformers, budgeting meant executive budgeting. The two were inseparable. There was virtually no dissent from Cleveland's dictum that "to be a budget it must be prepared and submitted by a responsible executive . . ."[3] Whether from the standpoint of planning, management or control, the executive was deemed in the best position to prepare and execute the budget. As Cleveland argued in 1915, only the executive "could think in terms of the institution as a whole," and therefore, he "is the only one who can be made responsible for leadership."[4]

The executive budget idea also took root in the administrative integration movement, and here was allied with such reforms as functional consolidation of agencies, elimination of independent boards and commissions, the short ballot, and strengthening the chief executive's appointive and removal powers. The chief executive often was likened to the general manager of a corporation, the budget bureau serving as his general staff.

Finally, the executive budget was intended to strengthen honesty and efficiency by restricting the discretion of administrators in this role. It was associated with such innovations as centralized purchasing and competitive bidding, civil service reform, uniform accounting procedures, and expenditure audits.

THE CONTROL ORIENTATION

In the drive for executive budgeting, the various goals converged. There was a radical parting of the ways, however, in the conversion of the budget idea into an operational reality. Hard choices had to be made in the design of expenditure accounts and in the orientation of the budget office. On both counts, the control orientation was predominant.

In varying degrees of itemization, the expenditure classifications established during the first wave of reform were based on objects-of-expenditure, with detailed tabulations of the myriad items required to operate an administrative unit—personnel, fuel, rent, office supplies, and other inputs. On these "line-itemizations" were built technical routines for the compilation and review of estimates and the disbursement of funds. The leaders in the movement for executive budgeting, however, envisioned a system of functional classifications focusing on the work to be accomplished. They regarded objects-of-expenditure as subsidiary data to be included for informational purposes. Their preference for functional accounts derived from their conception of the budget as a planning instrument, their disdain for objects from the contemporary division between politics and administration.[5] The Taft Commission vigorously opposed object-of-expenditure appropriations and recommended that expenditures be classified by class of work, organizational unit, character of expense, and method of financing. In its model budget, the Commission included several functional classifications.[6]

In the establishment of a budget system for New York City by the Bureau of Municipal Research, there was an historic confrontation between diverse conceptions of budgeting.

In evolving suitable techniques, the Bureau soon faced a conflict between functional and object budgeting. Unlike almost all other budget systems which began on a control footing with object classifications, the Bureau turned to control (and the itemization of objects) only after trial-and-error experimentation with program methods.

When confronted with an urgent need for effective control over administration, the Bureau was compelled to conclude that this need was more critical than the need for a planning-functional emphasis. "Budget reform," Charles Beard once wrote, "bears the imprint of the age in which it originated."[7] In an age when personnel and purchasing controls were unreliable, the first consideration was how to prevent administrative improprieties.

> In the opinion of those who were in charge of the development of a budget procedure, the most important service to be rendered was the establishing of central controls so that responsibility could be located and enforced through elected executives. . . . The view was, therefore, accepted, that questions of administration and niceties of adjustment must be left in abeyance until central control has been effectively established and the basis has been laid for careful scrutiny of departmental contracts and purchases as well as departmental work.[8]

Functional accounts had been designed to facilitate rational program decisions, not to deter officials from misfeasance. "The classification by "functions" affords no protection; it only operates as a restriction on the use which may be made of the services."[9] The detailed itemization of objects was regarded as desirable not only "because it provides for the utilization of all the machinery of control which has been provided, but it also admits to a much higher degree of perfection than it has at present attained."[10]

With the introduction of object accounts, New York City had a threefold classification of expenditures: (1) by organizational units; (2) by functions; and (3) by objects. In a sense, the Bureau of Municipal Research was striving to develop a budget system that would serve the multiple purposes of budgeting simultaneously. To the Bureau, the inclusion of more varied and detailed data in the budget was a salutory trend; all purposes would be served and the public would have a more complete picture of government spending. Thus the Bureau "urged from the beginning a classification of costs in as many different ways as there are stories to be told."[11] But the Bureau did not anticipate the practical difficulties which would ensue from the multiple classification scheme. In the 1913 appropriations act

> there were 3992 distinct items of appropriation. . . . Each constituted a distinct appropriation, besides which there was a further itemization of positions and salaries of personnel that multiplied this number several times, each of which operated as limitations on administrative discretion.[12]

This predicament confronted the Bureau with a direct choice between the itemization of objects and a functional classification. As a solution, the Bureau recommended retention of object accounts and the total "defunctionalization" of the budget; in other words, it gave priority to the objects and the control orientation they manifested. Once installed, object controls rapidly gained stature as an indispensable deterrent to administrative misbehavior. Amelioration of the adverse effects of multiple classifications was to be accomplished in a different manner, one which would strengthen the planning and management processes. The Bureau postulated a fundamental distinction between the purposes of budgets and appropriations, and between the types of classification suitable for each.

> . . . an act of appropriation has a single purpose—that of putting a limitation on the amount of obligations which may be incurred and the amount of vouchers which may be drawn to pay for personal services, supplies, etc. The only significant classification of appropriation items, therefore, is according to persons to whom drawing accounts are given and the classes of things to be bought.[13]

Appropriations, in sum, were to be used as statutory controls on spending. In its "Next Steps" proposals, the Bureau recommended that appropriations retain "exactly the same itemization so far as specifications of positions and compensations are concerned and therefore, the same protection."[14]

Budgets, on the other hand, were regarded as instruments of planning and publicity. They should include "all the details of the work plans and specifications of cost of work."[15] In addition to the regular object and organization classifications, the budget would report the "total cost incurred, classified by *functions*—for determining questions of policy having to do with service rendered as well as to be rendered, and laying a foundation for appraisal of results."[16] The Bureau also recommended a new instrument, a *work program,* which would furnish "a detailed schedule or analysis of each function, activity, or process within each organization unit. This analysis would give the total cost and the unit cost wherever standards were established."[17]

Truly a far-sighted conception of budgeting! There would be three documents for the three basic functions of budgeting. Although the Bureau did not use the analytic framework suggested above, it seems that the appropriations were intended for control purposes, the budget for planning purposes, and the work program for management purposes. Each of the three documents would have its specialized information scheme, but jointly they would comprise a multipurpose budget system not very different from PPB, even though the language of crosswalking or systems analysis was not used.

Yet the plan failed, for in the end the Bureau was left with object accounts pegged to a control orientation. The Bureau's distinction between budgets and appropriations was not well understood, and the work-program idea was rejected by New York City on the ground that adequate accounting backup was lacking. The Bureau had failed to recognize that the conceptual distinction between budgets and appropriations tends to break down under the stress of informational demands. If the legislature appropriates by objects, the budget very likely will be classified by objects. Conversely, if there are no functional accounts, the prospects for including such data in the budget are diminished substantially. As has almost always been the case, the budget came to mirror the appropriations act; in each, objects were paramount. It remains to be seen whether PPB will be able to break this interlocking informational pattern.

By the early 1920s the basic functions of planning and management were overlooked by those who carried the gospel of budget reform across the nation. First generation budget workers concentrated on perfecting and spreading the widely approved object-of-expenditure approach, and budget writers settled into a nearly complete preoccupation with forms and with factual descriptions of actual and recommended procedures. Although ideas about the use of the budget for planning and management purposes were retained in Buck's catalogs of "approved" practices,[18] they did not have sufficient priority to challenge tradition.

From the start, federal budgeting was placed on a control, object-of-expenditure footing, the full flavor of which can be perceived in reading Charles G. Dawes' documentary on *The First Year of the Budget of The United States.* According to Dawes,

> the Bureau of the Budget is concerned only with the humbler and routine business of Government. Unlike cabinet officers, it is concerned with no question of policy, save that of economy and efficiency.[19]

This distinction fitted neatly with object classifications that provided a firm accounting base for the routine conduct of government business, but no information on policy implications of public expenditures. Furthermore, in its first decade, the Bureau's tiny staff (40 or fewer) had to coordinate a multitude of well-advertised economy drives which shaped the job of the examiner as being that of reviewing itemized estimates to pare them down. Although Section 209 of the Budget and Accounting Act had authorized the Bureau to study and recommend improvements in the organization and administrative practices of Federal agencies, the Bureau was overwhelmingly preoccupied with the business of control.

THE MANAGEMENT ORIENTATION

Although no single action represents the shift from a control to a management orientation, the turning point in this evolution probably came with the New Deal's broadening perspective of government responsibilities.

During the 1920s and 1930s, occasional voices urged a return to the conceptions of budgeting advocated by the early reformers. In a notable 1924 article, Lent D. Upson argued vigorously that "budget procedure had stopped halfway in its development," and he proposed six modifications in the form of the budget, the net effect being a shift in emphasis from accounting control to functional accounting.[20] A similar position was taken a decade later by Wylie Kilpatrick who insisted that "the one fundamental basis of expenditure is functional, an accounting of payments for the services performed by government."[21]

Meanwhile, gradual changes were preparing the way for a reorientation of budgeting to a management mission. Many of the administrative abuses that had given rise to object controls were curbed by statutes and regulations and by a general upgrading of the public service. Reliable accounting systems were installed and personnel and purchasing reforms introduced, thereby freeing budgeting from some of its watchdog chores. The rapid growth of government activities and expenditures made it more difficult and costly for central officials to keep track of the myriad objects in the budget. With expansion, the bits and pieces into which the objects were itemized became less and less significant, while the aggregate of activities performed became more significant. With expansion, there was heightened need for central management of the incohesive sprawl of administrative agencies.

The climb in activities and expenditures also signaled radical changes in the role of the budget system. As long as government was considered a "necessary evil," and there was little recognition of the social value of public expenditures, the main function of budgeting was to keep spending in check. Because the outputs were deemed to be of limited and fixed value, it made sense to use the budget for central control over inputs. However, as the work and accomplishments of public agencies came to be regarded as benefits, the task of budgeting was redefined as the effective marshalling of fiscal and organizational resources for the attainment of benefits. This new posture focused attention on the problems of managing large programs and organizations, and on the opportunities for using the budget to extend executive hegemony over the dispersed administrative structure.

All these factors converged in the New Deal years. Federal expenditures rose rapidly from $4.2 billion in 1932 to $10 billion in 1940. Keynesian economics (the full budgetary implications of which are emerging only now in PPB) stressed the relationship between public spending and the condition of the economy. The President's Committee on Administrative Management (1937) castigated the routinized, control-minded approach of the Bureau of the Budget and urged that budgeting be used to coordinate Federal activities under presidential leadership. With its transfer in 1939 from the Treasury to the newly-created Executive Office of the President, the Bureau was on its way to becoming the leading management arm of the Federal Government. The Bureau's own staff was increased tenfold; it developed the administrative management and statistical coordination functions that it still possesses; and it installed apportionment procedures for budget execution. More and more, the Bureau was staffed from the ranks of public administration rather than from accounting, and it was during the Directorship of Harold D. Smith (1939–46) that the Bureau substantially embraced the management orientation.[22] Executive Order 8248 placed the President's imprimatur on the management philosophy. It directed the Bureau:

> to keep the President informed of the progress of activities by agencies of the Government with respect to work proposed, work actually initiated, and work completed, together with the relative timing of work between the several agencies of the Government; all to the end that the work programs of the several agencies of the executive branch of the Government may be coordinated and that the monies appropriated by the Congress may be expended in the most economical manner possible to prevent overlapping and duplication of effort.

Accompanying the growing management use of the budget process for the appraisal and improvement of administrative performance and the scientific management movement with its historical linkage to public administration were far more relevant applications of managerial cost accounting to governmental operations. Government agencies sought to devise performance standards and the rudimentary techniques of work measurement were introduced in several agencies including the Forest Service, the Census Bureau, and the Bureau of Reclamation.[23] Various professional associations developed grading systems to assess administrative performance as well as the need for public services. These crude and unscientific methods were the forerunners of more sophisticated and objective techniques. At the apogee of these efforts, Clarence Ridley and Herbert Simon published *Measuring Municipal Activities: A Survey of Suggested Criteria for Appraising Administration*, in which they identified five kinds of measurement—(1) needs, (2) results, (3) costs, (4) effort, and (5) performance—and surveyed the obstacles to the measurement of needs and results. The latter three categories they combined into a measure of administrative efficiency. This study provides an excellent inventory of the state of the technology prior to the breakthrough made by cost-benefit and systems analysis.

At the close of World War II, the management orientation was entrenched in all but one aspect of Federal budgeting—the classification of expenditures. Except for isolated cases (such as TVA's activity accounts and the project structure in the Department of Agriculture), the traditional object accounts were retained though the control function had receded in importance. In 1949 the Hoover Commission called for alterations in budget classifications consonant with the management orientation. It recommended "that the whole budgetary concept of the Federal Government should be refashioned by the adoption of a budget based upon functions, activities, and projects."[24] To create a sense of novelty, the Commission gave a new label—performance budgeting—to what had long been known as functional or activity budgeting. Because its task force had used still another term—program budgeting—there were two new terms to denote the budget innovations of that period. Among writers there was no uniformity in usage, some preferring the "program budgeting" label, others "performance budgeting," to describe the same things. The level of confusion has been increased recently by the association of the term "program budgeting" (also the title of the Rand publication edited by David Novick) with the PPB movement.

Although a variety of factors and expectations influenced the Hoover Commission, and the Commission's proposals have been interpreted in many ways, including some that closely approximate the PPB concept, for purposes of clarity, and in accord with the control-management-planning framework, performance budgeting *as it was generally-understood and applied* must be distinguished from the emergent PPB idea. The term "performance budgeting" is hereafter used in reference to reforms set in motion by the Hoover Commission and the term "program budgeting" is used in conjunction with PPB.

Performance budgeting is management-oriented; its principal thrust is to help administrators to assess the work-efficiency of operating units by (1) casting budget categories in functional terms, and (2) providing work-cost measurements to facilitate the efficient performance of prescribed activities. Generally, its method is particularistic, the reduction of work-cost data unto discrete, measurable units. Program budgeting (PPB) is planning-oriented; its main goal is to rationalize policy making by providing (1) data on the costs and benefits of alternative ways of attaining proposed public objectives, and (2) output measurements to facilitate the effective attainment of chosen objectives. As a policy device, program budgeting departs from simple engineering models of efficiency in which the objective is fixed and the quantity of inputs and outputs is adjusted to an optimal relationship. In PPB, the objective itself is variable; analysis may lead to a new statement of objectives. In order to enable budget makers to evaluate the costs and benefits of alternative expenditure options, program budgeting focuses on expenditure aggregates; the details come into play only as they contribute to an analysis of the total (the system) or of marginal trade-offs among competing proposals. Thus, in this macroanalytic approach, the accent is on comprehensiveness and on grouping data into categories that allow comparisons among alternative expenditure mixes.

Performance budgeting derived its ethos and much of its technique from cost accounting and scientific management; program budgeting has drawn its core ideas from economics and systems analysis. In the performance budgeting literature, budgeting is described as a "tool of management" and the budget as a "work program." In PPB, budgeting is an allocative process among competing claims, and the budget is a statement of policy. Chronologically, there was a gap of several years between the bloom of performance budgeting and the first articulated conceptions of program budgeting. In the aftermath of the first Hoover report, and especially during the early 1950s, there was a plethora of writings on the administrative advantages of the performance budget. Substantial interest in program budgeting did not emerge until the mid-1950s when a number of economists (including Smithies, Novick, and McKean) began to urge reform of the Federal budget system. What the economists had in mind was not the same thing as the Hoover Commission.

In line with its management perspective, the commission averred that "the all-important thing in budgeting is the work of service to be accomplished, and what that work or service will cost."[25] Mosher followed this view closely in writing that "the central idea of the performance budget . . . is that the budget process be focused upon programs and functions—that is, accomplishments to be achieved, work to be done."[26] But from the planning perspective, the all-important thing surely is not the work or service to be accomplished but the objectives or purposes to be fulfilled by the investment of public funds. Whereas in performance budgeting, work and activities are treated virtually as ends in themselves, in program budgeting work and services are regarded as intermediate aspects, the process of converting resources into outputs. Thus, in a 1954 Rand paper, Novick defined a program as "the sum of the steps or interdependent activities which enter into the attainment of a specified objective. The program, therefore, is the end objective and is developed or budgeted in terms of all the elements necessary to its execution."[27] Novick goes on to add, "this is not the sense in which the government budget now uses the term."

Because the evaluation of performance and the evaluation of program are distinct budget functions, they call for different methods of classification which serves as an intermediate layer between objects and organizations. The activities relate to the functions and work of a distinct operating unit; hence their classification ordinarily conforms to organizational lines. This is the type of classification most useful for an administrator who has to schedule the procurement and utilization of resources for the production of goods and services. Activity classifications gather under a single rubric all the expenditure data needed by a manager to run his unit. The evaluation of programs, however, requires an end-product classification that is oriented to the mission and purposes of government. This type of classification may not be very useful for the manager, but it is of great value to the budget maker who has to decide how to allocate scarce funds among competing claims. Some of the difference between end-product and activity classifications can be gleaned by comparing the Coast Guard's existing activity schedule with the proposed program structure on the last page of Bulletin 66–3. The activity structure which was developed under the aegis of performance budgeting is geared to the operating responsibilities of the Coast Guard: Vessel Operations, Aviation Operations, Repair and Supply Facilities, and others. The proposed program structure is hinged to the large purposes sought through Coast Guard operations: Search and Rescue, Aids to

Navigation, Law Enforcement, and so on.

It would be a mistake to assume that performance techniques presuppose program budgeting or that it is not possible to collect performance data without program classifications. Nevertheless, the view has gained hold that a program budget is "a transitional type of budget between the orthodox (traditional) character and object budget on the one hand and performance budget on the other."[28] Kammerer and Shadoan stress a similar connection. The former writes that "a *performance* budget carries the program budget one step further: into *unit costs.*"[29] Shadoan "envisions "performance budgeting" as an extension of . . . the program budget concept to which the element of unit work measurement has been added."[30] These writers ignore the divergent functions served by performance and program budgets. It is possible to devise and apply performance techniques without relating them to, or having the use of, larger program aggregates. A cost accountant or work measurement specialist can measure the cost or effort required to perform a repetitive task without probing into the purpose of the work or its relationship to the mission of the organization. Work measurement—"a method of establishing an equitable relationship between the volume of work performed and manpower utilized"—[31] is only distantly and indirectly related to the process of determining governmental policy at the higher levels. Program classifications are vitally linked to the making and implementation of policy through the allocation of public resources. As a general rule, performance budgeting is concerned with the *process of work* (what methods should be used) while program budgeting is concerned with the *purpose of work* (what activities should be authorized).

Perhaps the most reliable way to describe this difference is to show what was tried and accomplished under performance budgeting. First of all, performance budgeting led to the introduction of activity classifications, the management-orientation of which has already been discussed. Second, narrative descriptions of program and performance were added to the budget document. These statements give the budget-reader a general picture of the work that will be done by the organizational unit requesting funds. But unlike the analytic documents currently being developed under PPB, the narratives have a descriptive and justificatory function; they do not provide an objective basis for evaluating the cost-utility of an expenditure. Indeed, there hardly is any evidence that the narratives have been used for decision making; rather they seem best suited for giving the uninformed outsider some glimpses of what is going on inside.

Third, performance budgeting spawned a multitude of work-cost measurement explorations. Most used, but least useful, were the detailed workload statistics assembled by administrators to justify their requests for additional funds. On a higher level of sophistication were attempts to apply the techniques of scientific management and cost accounting to the development of work and productivity standards. In these efforts, the Bureau of the Budget had a long involvement, beginning with the issuance of the trilogy of work measurement handbooks in 1950 and reaching its highest development in the productivity-measurement studies that were published in 1964. All these applications were at a level of detail useful for managers with operating or supervisory responsibilities, but of scant usefulness for top-level officials who have to determine organizational objectives and goals. Does it really help top officials if they know that it cost $0.07 to wash a pound of laundry or that the average postal employee processes 289 items of mail per hour? These are the main fruits of performance measurements, and they have an important place in the management of an organization. They are of great value to the operating official who has the limited function of getting a job done, but they would put a crushing burden on the policymaker whose function is to map the future course of action.

Finally, the management viewpoint led to significant departures from PPB's principle that the expenditure accounts should show total systems cost. The 1949 National Security Act (possibly the first concrete result of the Hoover report) directed the segregation of capital and operating costs in the defense budget. New York State's performance—budgeting experiment for TB hospitals separated expenditures into cost centers (a concept derived from managerial cost accounting) and within each center into fixed and variable costs. In most manpower and work measurements, labor has been isolated from other inputs. Most important, in many states and localities (and implicitly in Federal budgeting) the cost of continuing existing programs has been separated from the cost of new or expanded programs. This separation is useful for managers who build up a budget in terms of increments and decrements from the base, but it is a violation of program budgeting's working assumption that all claims must be pitted against one another in the competition for funds. Likewise, the forms of separation previously mentioned make sense from the standpoint of the manager, but impair the planner's capability to compare expenditure alternatives.

THE PLANNING ORIENTATION

The foregoing has revealed some of the factors leading to the emergence of the planning orientation. Three important developments influenced the evolution from a management to a planning orientation.

1. Economic analysis—macro and micro—has had an increasing part in the shaping of fiscal and budgetary policy.
2. The development of new informational and decisional technologies has enlarged the applicability of objective analysis to policy making. And,
3. There has been a gradual convergence of planning and budgetary processes.

Keynesian economics with its macroanalytic focus on the impact of governmental action on the private sector had its genesis in the underemployment economy of the Great Depression. In calling attention to the opportunities for attaining full employment by means of fiscal policy, the Keynesians set into motion a major restatement of the central budget function. From the utilization of fiscal policy to achieve economic objectives, it was but a few steps to the utilization of the budget process to achieve fiscal objectives. Nevertheless, between the emergence and the victory of the new economics, there was a lapse of a full generation, a delay due primarily to the entrenched balanced-budget ideology. But the full realization of the budget's economic potential was stymied on the revenue side by static tax policies and on the expenditure side by status spending policies.

If the recent tax policy of the Federal Government is evidence that the new economics has come of age, it also offers evidence of the long-standing failure of public officials to use the taxing power as a variable constraint on the economy. Previously, during normal times, the tax structure was accepted as given, and the task of fiscal analysis was to forecast future tax yields so as to ascertain how much would be available for expenditure. The new approach treats taxes as variable, to be altered periodically in accord with national policy and economic conditions. Changes in tax rates are not to be determined (as they still are in virtually all states and localities) by how much is needed to cover expenditures but by the projected impact of alternative tax structures on the economy.

It is more than coincidental that the advent of PPB has followed on the heels of the explicit utilization of tax policy to guide the economy. In macroeconomics, taxes and expenditures are mirror images of one another; a tax cut and an expenditure increase have comparable impacts. Hence, the hinging of tax policy to economic considerations inevitably led to the similar treatment of expenditures. But there were (and remain) a number of obstacles to the utilization of the budget as a fiscal tool. For one thing, the conversion of the budget process to an economic orientation probably was slowed by the Full Employment Act of 1946 which established the Council of Economic Advisers and transferred the Budget Bureau's fiscal analysis function to the council. The institutional separation between the CEA and the BOB and between fiscal policy and budget making was not compensated by cooperative work relationships. Economic analysis had only a slight impact on expenditure policy. It offered a few guidelines (for example, that spending should be increased during recessions) and a few ideas (such as a shelf of public works projects), but it did not feed into the regular channels of budgeting. The business of preparing the budget was foremost a matter of responding to agency spending pressures, not of responding to economic conditions.

Moreover, expenditures (like taxes) have been treated virtually as givens, to be determined by the unconstrained claims of the spending units. In the absence of central policy instructions, the agencies have been allowed to vent their demands without prior restraints by central authorities and without an operational set of planning guidelines. By the time the Bureau gets into the act, it is faced with the overriding task of bringing estimates into line with projected resources. In other words, the Bureau has had a budget-cutting function, to reduce claims to an acceptable level. The President's role has been similarly restricted. He is the *gatekeeper* of Federal budgeting. He directs the pace of spending increases by deciding which of the various expansions proposed by the agencies shall be included in the budget. But, as the gatekeeper, the President rarely has been able to look back at the items that have previously passed through the gate; his attention is riveted to those programs that are departures from the established base. In their limited roles, neither the Bureau nor the President has been able to inject fiscal and policy objectives into the forefront of budget preparation.

It will not be easy to wean budgeting from its utilization as an administrative procedure for financing ongoing programs to a decisional process for determining the range and direction of public objectives and the government's involvement in the economy. In the transition to a planning emphasis, an important step was the 1963 hearings of the Joint Economic Committee on *The Federal Budget as an Economic Document.* These hearings and the pursuant report of the JEC explored the latent policy opportunities in budget making. Another development was the expanded time horizons manifested by the multiyear expenditure projections introduced in the early 1960s. Something of a breakthrough was achieved via the revelation that the existing tax structure would yield cumulatively larger increments of uncommitted funds— estimated as much as $50 billion by 1970—which could be applied to a number of alternative uses. How much of the funds should be "returned" to the private sector through tax reductions and how much through expenditure increases? How much should go to the States and localities under a broadened system of Federal grants? How much should be allocated to the rebuilding of cities, to the improvement of education, or to the eradication of racial injustices. The traditional budget system lacked the analytic tools to cope with these questions, though decisions ultimately would be made one way or another. The expansion of the time horizon from the single year to a multiyear frame enhances the opportunity for planning and analysis to have an impact on future expenditure decisions. With a one-year perspective, almost all options have been foreclosed by previous commitments; analysis is effective only for the increments provided by self-generating revenue increases or to the extent that it is feasible to convert funds from one use to another. With a longer time span, however, many more options are open, and economic analysis can have a prominent part in determining which course of action to pursue.

So much for the macroeconomic trends in budget reform. On the microeconomic side, PPB traces its lineage to the attempts of welfare economists to construct a science of finance predicted on the principle of marginal utility. Such a science, it was hoped, would furnish objective criteria for determining the optimal allocation of public funds among competing uses. By appraising the marginal costs and benefits of alternatives (poor relief versus battleships in Pigou's classic example), it would be possible to determine which combination of expenditures afforded maximum utility. The quest for a welfare function provided the conceptual underpinning for a 1940 article on "The Lack of a Budgetary Theory" in which V. O. Key noted the absence of a theory which would determine whether "to allocate x dollars to activity A instead of activity B."[32] In terms of its direct contribution to budgetary practice, welfare economics has been a failure. It has not been possible to distill the conflicts and complexities of political life into a welfare criterion or homogeneous distribution formula. But stripped of its normative and formal overtones, its principles have been applied to budgeting by economists such as Arthur Smithies. Smithies has formulated a budget rule that "expenditure proposals should be considered in the light of the objectives they are intended to further, and in general final expenditure decisions should not be made until all claims on the budget can be considered."[33] PPB is the application of this rule to budget practice. By structuring expenditures so as to juxtapose substitutive elements within program categories, and by analyzing the cost and benefits of the various substitutes, PPB has opened the door to the use of marginal analysis in budgeting.

Actually, the door was opened somewhat by the development of new decisional and information technologies, the second item on the list of influences in the evolution of the planning orientation. Without the availability of the decisional-informational capability provided by cost-benefit and systems analysis, it is doubtful that PPB would be part of the budgetary apparatus today. The new technologies make it possible to cope with the enormous informational and analytic burdens imposed by PPB. As aids to calculation, they furnish a methodology for the analysis of alternatives, thereby expanding the range of decision-making in budgeting.

Operations research, the oldest of these technologies, grew out of complex World War II conditions that required the optimal coordination of manpower, material, and equipment to achieve defense objectives. Operations research is most applicable to those repetitive operations where the opportunity for quantification is highest. Another technology, cost-benefit analysis, was intensively adapted during the 1950s to large-scale water resource investments, and subsequently to many other governmental functions. Systems analysis is the most global of these technologies. It involves the skillful analysis of the major factors that go into the attainment of an interconnected set of objectives. Systems analysis has been applied in DOD to the choice of weapons systems, the location of military bases, and the determination of sealift-airlift requirements. Although the extension of these technologies across-the-board to government was urged repeatedly by members of the Rand Corporation during the 1950s, it was DOD's experience that set the stage for the current ferment. It cannot be doubted that the coming of PPB has been pushed ahead several years or more by the "success story" in DOD.

The third stream of influence in the transformation of the budget function has been a closing of the gap between planning and budgeting. Institutionally and operationally, planning and budgeting have run along separate tracks. The national government has been reluctant to embrace central planning of any sort because of identification with socialist management of the economy. The closest thing we have had to a central planning agency was the National Resources Planning Board in the 1939–1943 period. Currently, the National Security Council and the Council of Economic Advisors have planning responsibilities in the defense and fiscal areas. As far as the Bureau of the Budget is concerned, it has eschewed the planning units: in the States, because limitations on debt financing have encouraged the separation of the capital and operating budgets; in the cities, because the professional autonomy and land-use preoccupations of the planners have set them apart from the budgeteers.

In all governments, the appropriations cycle, rather than the anticipation of future objectives, tends to dictate the pace and posture of budgeting. Into the repetitive, one-year span of the budget is wedged all financial decisions, including those that have multiyear implications. As a result, planning, if it is done at all, "occurs independently of budgeting and with little relation to it."[34] Budgeting and planning, moreover, invite disparate perspectives: the one is conservative and negativistic; the other, innovative and expansionist. As Mosher has noted, "budgeting and planning are apposite, if not opposite. In extreme form, the one means saving; the other, spending."[35]

Nevertheless, there has been some *rapprochement* of planning and budgeting. One factor is the long lead-time in the development and procurement of hardware and capital investments. The multiyear projections inaugurated several years ago were a partial response to this problem. Another factor has been the diversity of government agencies involved in related functions. This has given rise to various *ad hoc* coordinating devices, but it also has pointed to the need for permanent machinery to integrate dispersed activities. Still another factor has been the sheer growth of Federal activities and expenditures and the need for a rational system of allocation. The operational code of planners contains three tenets relevant to these budgetary needs: (1) planning is future-oriented; it connects present decisions to the attainment of a desired future state of affairs; (2) planning, ideally, encompasses all resources involved in the attainment of future objectives. It strives for comprehensiveness. The *massive plan* is the one that brings within its scope all relevant factors; (3) planning is means-ends oriented. The allocation of resources is strictly dictated by the ends that are to be accomplished. All this is to say that planning is an economizing process, though planners are more oriented to the future than economists. It is not surprising that planners have found the traditional budget system deficient,[36] nor is it surprising that the major reforms entailed by PPB emphasize the planning function.

Having outlined the several trends in the emerging transition to a planning orientation, it remains to mention several qualifications. First, the planning emphasis is not predominant in federal budgeting at this time. Although PPB asserts the paramountcy of planning, PPB itself is not yet a truly operational part of the budget machinery. We are now at the dawn of a new era in budgeting; high noon is still a long way off. Second, this transition has not been preceded by a reorientation of the Bureau of the Budget. Unlike the earlier change-over from control to management in which the alteration of budgetary techniques *followed* the revision of the Bureau's role, the conversion from management to planning is taking a different course—first, the installation of new techniques; afterwards, a reformulation of the Bureau's mission. Whether this sequence will hinder reform efforts is a matter that cannot be predicted, but it should be noted that in the present instance the Bureau cannot convert to a new mission by bringing in a wholly new staff, as was the case in the late 1930's and early 1940's.

WHAT DIFFERENCE DOES IT MAKE?

The starting point for the author was distinguishing the old from the new in budgeting. The interpretation has been framed in analytic terms, and budgeting has been viewed historically in three stages corresponding to the three basic functions of budgeting. In this analysis, an attempt has been made to identify the difference between the existing and the emerging as a difference between management and planning orientations.

In an operational sense, however, what difference does it make whether the central budget process is oriented toward planning rather than management? Does the change merely mean a new way of making decisions, or does it mean different decisions as well? These are not easy questions to answer, particularly since the budget system of the future will be a compound of all three functions. The case for PPB rests on the assumption that the form in which information is classified and used governs the actions of budget makers, and, conversely, that alterations in form will produce desired changes in behavior. Take away the assumption that behavior follows form, and the movement for PPB is reduced to a trivial manipulation of techniques—form for form's sake without any significant bearing on the conduct of budgetary affairs.

Yet this assumed connection between roles and information is a relatively uncharted facet of the PPB literature. The behavioral side of the equation has been neglected. PPB implies that each participant will behave as a sort of Budgetary Man, a counterpart of the classical Economic Man and Simon's Administrative Man.[37] Budgetary Man, whatever his station or role in the budget process, is assumed to be guided by an unwavering commitment to the rule of efficiency; in every instance he chooses that alternative that optimizes the allocation of public resources.

PPB probably takes an overly mechanistic view of the impact of form on behavior and underestimates the strategic and volitional aspects of budget making. In the political arena, data are used to influence the "who gets what" in budgets and appropriations. If information influences behavior, the reverse also is true. Indeed, data are more tractable than roles; participants are more likely to seek and use data which suit their preferences than to alter their behavior automatically in response to formal changes.

All this constrains, rather than negates, the impact of budget form. The advocates of PPB, probably in awareness of the above limitations, have imported into budgeting men with professional commitments to the types of analysis and norms required by the new techniques, men with a background in economics and systems analysis, rather than with general administrative training.

PPB aspires to create a different environment for choice. Traditionally, budgeting has defined its mission in terms of identifying the existing base and proposed departures from it—"This is where we are; where do we go from here?" PPB defines its mission in terms of budgetary objectives and purposes—"Where do we want to go? What do we do to get there?" The environment of choice under traditional circumstances is *incremental;* in PPB it is *teletic.* Presumably, these different processes will lead to different budgetary outcomes.

A budgeting process which accepts the base and examines only the increments will produce decisions to transfer the present into the future with a few small variations. The curve of government activities will be continuous, with few zigzags or breaks. A budget-making process which begins with objectives will require the base to compete on an equal footing with new proposals. The decisions will be more radical than those made under incremental conditions. This does not mean that each year's budget will lack continuity with the past. There are sunk costs that have to be reckoned, and the benefits of radical changes will have to outweigh the cost of terminating prior commitments. Furthermore, the extended time span of PPB will mean that big investment decisions will be made for a number of years, with each year being a partial installment of the plan. Most important, the political manifestations of sunk costs—vested interests—will bias decisions away from radical departures. The conservatism of the political system, therefore, will tend to minimize the decisional differences between traditional and PPB approaches. However, the very availability of analytic data will cause a shift in the balance of economic and political forces that go into the making of a budget.

Teletic and incremental conditions of choice lead to still another distinction. In budgeting, which is committed to the established base, the flow of budgetary decisions is upward and aggregative. Traditionally, the first step in budgeting, in anticipation of the call for estimates, is for each department to issue its own call to prepare and to submit a set of estimates. This call reaches to the lowest level capable of assembling its own estimates. Lowest level estimates form the building blocks for the next level where they are aggregated and reviewed and transmitted upward until the highest level is reached and the totality constitutes a department-wide budget. Since budgeting is tied to a base, the building-up-from-below approach is sensible; each building block estimates the cost of what it is already doing plus the cost of the increments it wants. (The building blocks, then, are decisional elements, not simply informational elements as is often assumed.)

PPB reverses the informational and decisional flow. Before the call for estimates is issued, top policy has to be made, and this policy constrains the estimates prepared below. For each lower level, the relevant policy instructions are issued by the superior level prior to the preparation of estimates. Accordingly, the critical decisional process—that of deciding on purposes and plans—has a downward and disaggregative flow.

If the making of policy is to be antecedent to the costing of estimates, there will have to be a shift in the distribution of budget responsibilities. The main energies of the Bureau of the Budget are now devoted to budget preparation; under PPB these energies will be centered on what we may term *prepreparation*—the stage of budget making that deals with policy and is prior to the preparation of the budget. One of the steps marking the advent of the planning orientation was the inauguration of the Spring Preview several years ago for the purpose of affording an advance look at departmental programs.

If budget-making is to be oriented to the planning function, there probably will be a centralization of policy-making, both within and among departments. The DOD experience offers some precedent for predicting that greater budgetary authority will be vested in department heads than heretofore, but there is no firm basis for predicting the degree of centralization that may derive from the relatedness of objectives pursued by many departments. It is possible that the mantle of central budgetary policy will be assumed by the Bureau; indeed, this is the expectation in many agencies. On the other hand, the bureau gives little indication at this time that it is willing or prepared to take this comprehensive role.

CONCLUSION

The various differences between the budgetary orientations are charted in the table presented here. All the differences may be summed up in the statement that the ethos of budgeting will shift from justification to analysis. To far greater extent than heretofore, budget decisions will be influenced by explicit statements of objectives and by a formal weighing of the costs and benefits of alternatives.

NOTES

1. New York Bureau of Municipal Research, *Making a Municipal Budget* (New York: 1907), pp. 9–10.
2. Robert N. Anthony, *Planning and Control Systems: A Framework for Analysis* (Boston: 1965), pp. 16–18.
3. Frederick A. Cleveland, "Evolution of the Budget Idea in the United States," *Annals of the American Academy of Political and Social Science* 62 (1915), 16.
4. *Ibid.*, p. 17.
5. See Frank J. Goodnow, "The Limit of Budgetary Control," *Proceedings of the American Political Science Association* (Baltimore: 1913),

p. 72; also William F. Willoughby, "Allotment of Funds by Executive Officials, An Essential Feature of Any Correct Budgetary System," *ibid.*, pp. 78–87.

6. U.S., President's Commission on Economy and Efficiency, *The Need for a National Budget* (Washington: 1912), pp. 210–213.
7. Charles A. Beard, "Prefatory Note," *ibid.*, p. vii.
8. New York Bureau of Municipal Research, "Some Results and Limitations of Central Financial Control in New York City," *Municipal Research* 81 (1917), 10.
9. "Next Steps . . .," *op. cit.*, p. 39.
10. "Next Steps . . .," *op. cit.*, p. 39.
11. "Some Results and Limitations . . .," *op. cit.*, p. 9.
12. "Next Steps . . .," *op. cit.*, p. 35.
13. *Ibid.*, p. 7.
14. "Next Steps . . .," p. 39.
15. "Some Results and Limitations . . .," *op. cit.*, p. 7.
16. *Ibid.*, p. 9.
17. "Next Steps . . .," *op. cit.*, p. 30.
18. See A. E. Buck, *Public Budgeting* (New York: 1929), pp. 181–88.
19. Charles G. Dawes, *The First Year of the Budget of the United States* (New York: 1923), preface, p. ii.
20. Lent D. Upson, "Half-time Budget Methods," *The Annals of the American Academy of Political and Social Science* 113 (1924), 72.
21. Wylie Kilpatrick, "Classification and Measurement of Public Expenditure," *The Annals of the American Academy of Political and Social Science* 133 (1936), 20.
22. See Harold D. Smith, *The Management of Your Government* (New York: 1945).
23. Public Administration Service, *The Work Unit in Federal Administration* (Chicago: 1937).
24. U.S. Commission on Organization of the Executive Branch of the Government, *Budgeting and Accounting* (Washington: 1949), 8.
25. *Ibid.*
26. Frederick C. Mosher, *Program Budgeting: Theory and Practice* (Chicago: 1954), p. 79.
27. David Novick, *Which Program Do We Mean in "Program Budgeting?"* (Santa Monica: 1954), p. 17.
28. Lennex L. Meak and Kathryn W. Killian, *A Manual of Techniques for the Preparation, Consideration, Adoption, and Administration of Operating Budgets* (Chicago: 1963), p. 11.
29. Gladys M. Kammerer, *Program Budgeting: An Aid to Understanding* (Gainesville: 1959), p. 6.
30. Arlene Theuer Shadean, *Preparation, Review, and Execution of the State Operating Budget* (Lexington: 1963), p. 13.
31. U.S. Bureau of the Budget, *A Work Measurement System* (Washington: 1950), p. 2.
32. V. O. Key, "The Lack of a Budgetary Theory," *The American Political Science Review* 34 (1940), 1,138.
33. Arthur Smithies, *The Budgetary Process in the United States* (New York: 1955), p. 16.
34. Mosher, *op. cit.*, p. 47–48.
35. *Ibid.*, p. 48.
36. See Edward C. Banfield, "Congress and the Budget: A Planner's Criticism," *The American Political Science Review,* 43 (1949), 1,217–1,227.
37. Herbert A. Simon, *Administrative Behavior* New York: 1957).

30
The American System
Morton Grodzins

THE AMERICAN SYSTEM AS A SINGLE MECHANISM

I. The Chaos of American Governments

Democratic government, in the abstract at least, should be simple government, if not simple in process at least structured simply enough to be easily comprehended by the citizenry. For simplicity maximizes fulfillment of an important democratic ideal: that citizens understand public institutions. Without this understanding the public cannot make intelligent judgments, especially cannot know how to reward at the polls those who have done well and penalize those who have done poorly. But government in the United States is not simple, either in structure or process.

The structure of the United States government is chaotic. In addition to the federal government and the 50 states, there are something like 18,000 general-purpose municipalities, slightly fewer general-purpose townships, more than 3,000 counties, and so many special-purpose governments that no one can claim even to have counted them accurately. At an educated guess, there are at present some 92,000 tax-levying governments in the country. A given citizen may be buried under a whole pyramid of governments. A resident of Park Forest, Illinois, for example, though he may know very little else about them, knows that he pays taxes to the following governments:

The United States of America
The State of Illinois
Cook (or Will) County
Cook County Forest Preserve District
Suburban Tuberculosis Sanitary District
Rich (or Bloom) Township
Bloom Township Sanitary District
Non–High School District 216 (or 213)
Rich Township High School District
Elementary School District, 163
South Cook County Mosquito Abatement District

The Park Forest citizen enjoys more governments than most people in the United States. But he is by no means unique, and although no one has made the exact calculation, it is not unlikely that a majority of citizens are within the jurisdiction of four or more governments, not counting the state and national ones.

The multitude of governments does not mask any simplicity of activity. There is no neat division of functions among them. If one looks closely, it appears that virtually all governments are involved in virtually all functions. More precisely, there is hardly an activity that does not involve the federal, state, and some local government in important

Source: Morton Grodzins, *The American System: A New View of Government in the United States,* ed. Daniel J. Elazar (Chicago, Ill.: Rand McNally 1966), pp. 3–10. Reprinted with the permission of Mrs. Morton Grodzins.

responsibilities. Functions of the American governments are shared functions. Consider a case that seems least likely to demonstrate this point: the function of providing education. It is widely believed that education is uniquely, even exclusively, a local responsibility. Almost half of all governments in the United States are school districts. Is this a great simplifying fact? Does it indicate a focussing of educational responsibilities in the hands of single-purpose local governments?

The answer to both questions is a clear "no." That there exist something like 37,000 school districts in the United States does not indicate that the educational function, even in the grade and high schools, is in any sense an exclusive function of those districts. In several states local districts are largely administrative arms of state departments of education, and the educational function is principally a state responsibility. In all states, to a greater or lesser degree—and the degree tends to be greater not lesser—local districts are dependent upon state financial aid, state teacher certification, state prescription of textbooks, and state inspection of performance in areas as diverse as building maintenance and the caliber of Latin instruction. School districts also have intricate and diverse relationships with county and city governments: the latter, for example, often act as tax-levying and tax-collecting agencies for the districts; they are responsible for certifying that standards of health and safety are maintained on school property; they must provide special police protection to students.

Nor is the federal government's finger out of the pie. The United States Office of Education provides technical aids of all sorts. Throughout the 1950s a federal milk and school lunch program contributed more than $250 million annually in cash and produce to supply food and milk at low cost to 11 million children in all 50 states. Federal surplus property supplies many essentials of school equipment. Federal aid to vocational education programs makes possible the employment of special teachers. In many areas "affected by" national government installations, federal funds build and maintain school buildings and contribute to general school support. Federal aid trains high school teachers of science, mathematics, and foreign languages; contributes equipment and books for instruction in these fields; makes possible testing and guidance programs for the identification of superior students; and may be used generally to strengthen state departments of education. All of these were initiated before the passage of recent legislation to enlarge further the national government's participation in education.

All this barely hints at the diverse ways in which all planes of governments in the United States participate in the function of education. It does not consider the political relationships among leaders of city, county, state, nation, and school district that basically establish the level of support that schools receive. Nor does it take into account the informal professional ties among teachers, administrators, and other specialists, ties that criss-cross governmental boundaries and from which a good fraction of new ideas and new programs emerge. A complete description of intergovernmental sharing in education would also have to consider how the school district's job is affected by the *mélange* of private, quasi-private, municipal, state, and federally financed programs and institutions that provide education beyond the high school in the United States. Nevertheless, the larger point is clear: grade and high school education is not simply a function of local school districts. It is not neatly a responsibility of one sort or one "level" of government. Rather, education is provided through the joint efforts of many governments. What is true of the "hard case" of education is also true of virtually all functions performed by the governments of the United States.

Many overlapping governments involved in many overlapping functions produce other attributes of the chaotic American system. Areas of government do not often correspond with problems of government. In order to provide adequate facilities for, and control of, automobile transportation, a given large city will have to deal with literally hundreds of other governments. This lack of congruence between area and function complicates the official's problem; it complicates the citizen's even more so. Where does he go and whom does he blame if super-highways become clogged with cars and the air polluted with their exhaust? What does he do if his water tastes foul? It is purchased from one city, runs in open lines through six others, is filtered and chlorinated by his own municipality, and is affected by the drainage systems of several dozen governments as well as by the septic tanks of several thousand homes in unincorporated areas. How does the citizen begin if he wishes to do something about his deteriorating neighborhood? Slum clearance involves three sets of law—local, state, and federal—and perhaps half a dozen separate administrative agencies, each with its own body of regulations. Points of influence and centers of decision are diffuse and obscure. More often than not the citizen cannot name most of the officers he elects, or describe the responsibilities of the governments that serve him. How can he hope to make them responsive to his wishes?

The chaos of structure and function is matched by a chaos of political process. The political parties play a key role, as later discussion will show, but it is a role different in almost every respect from what political parties are classically supposed to perform. Nominating procedures more often than not deprive the voter of genuine choices. Party platforms are election slogans, not statements of program. Legislative procedures are complex and unpublicized. If it is difficult on the administrative plane to discover what government does what, it is frequently impossible in the legislative halls—of locality, state, and nation—to discover who initiates, who obstructs, who is for or against what. Leadership functions, even in the national government, are typically splintered. Legislation and administration proceed through a system of pushing, hauling, bargaining, and cajoling. Legislative committee and economic interest group compete for influence with the administration, which often speaks through several opposing voices, with party leaders in and out of office, with local and state political chiefs, and with professional associations of all varieties. The two houses of the Congress, unlike any other major legislature in the world, vie with each other for power, the leaders of those houses, even when of the same party, often taking opposite sides on a given issue.

To penetrate this jungle and to bring his influence to bear, the citizen votes, writes to his congressman, joins forces with others in order to promote what he wishes to promote and, more typically, oppose what he wishes to oppose. As a businessman he pays dues to the National Association of Manufacturers; as a father of school-age children he contributes to the National Citizen's Council for Better Schools; as a churchgoer he supports the National Association of Churches of Christ. Frequently when these organizations speak, they express the citizen's own views. But not always. He is enraged, because he is a humanitarian, when "his" manufacturer's group opposes a bill before Congress to extend social security. He feels betrayed, because he believes in the local control of education, when "his" committee on education favors federal aid for school construction. He is frightened, because he is opposed to all totalitarian government, when a high officer of "his" church group is accused by a senator of being tinged with communism. The citizen's interest groups may not represent his interests just as his congressman may seem to represent no interest at all except that of his own reelection.

This view of chaos in government is not one of despair. The system of American government flaunts virtually all tenets of legislative responsibility and administrative effectiveness. It appears always to be wasteful of manpower and money. At times it threatens the very democracy it is established to maintain. But it works, it works—and sometimes with beauty.

II. Government by Chaos and Cooperation

Lord Bryce commented on the "working relations" of the national and state governments in the following words:

> The characteristic feature and special interest of the American Union is that it shows us two governments covering the same ground, yet distinct and separate in their action. It is like a great factory wherein two sets of machinery are at work, their revolving wheels apparently intermixed, their bands crossing one another, yet each set doing its own work without touching or hampering the other.[1]

Classic works are sometimes responsible for classic errors. We will see in Chapter Two that Lord Bryce was wrong, even for the period of his own observations, in describing the federal government and the states as "each . . . doing its own work without touching or hampering the other." Subsequent chapters will demonstrate how fallacious this description is for the contemporary American scene. Yet it cannot be said that the error has been, or is, widely recognized. During the very years that Bryce was in the United States the Supreme Court announced:

> There are within the territorial limits of each state two governments, restricted in their sphere of action, but independent of each other, and supreme within their respective spheres. Each has its separate departments, each has its distinct laws, and each has its own tribunals for their enforcement. Neither government can intrude within the jurisdiction of the other or authorize any interference therein by its judicial officers with the action of the other.[2]

The misunderstanding persists today. Lip service is frequently paid to the high degree of collaboration between the units of government in the American system. And there are a few scholars who have explicated some aspects of the collaborative pattern.[3] But the general view is the view of the three-layer cake of government, the institutions and functions of each "level" being considered separately.

In fact, the American system of government as it operates is not a layer cake at all. It is not three layers of government, separated by a sticky substance or anything else. Operationally, it is a marble cake, or what the British call a rainbow cake. No important activity of government in the United States is the exclusive province of one of the levels, not even what may be regarded as the most national of national functions, such as foreign relations; not even the most local of local functions, such as police protection and park maintenance.

If you ask the question "Who does what?" the answer is in two parts. One is that officials of all "levels" do everything together. The second is that where one level is preponderant in a given activity, the other makes its influence felt *politically* (here the voice of the peripheral power units are heard most strongly) or through *money* (here the central view is most influential) or through *professional associations.*

The actual joint sharing of functions is easily illustrated in the field of public welfare. Here the national, state and local governments together administer public assistance programs; the national government alone administers the old age insurance program commonly known as "social security"; the national government and the states (without the local governments but with the assistance of local business groups) administer employment security; the states and the local governments (without the national government) handle general assistance; and, to complete the circle of possible combinations, all three branches of government together administer child welfare services.

This is only the formal view. The informal aspects of welfare administration illustrate the second part of the answer. Even in general assistance programs, where the states and localities formally have exclusive jurisdiction, the national government's standards of professional conduct are greatly influential and becoming more so all the time. Even in a welfare field of so-called exclusive federal concern—hospital care for military veterans, for example—the states and localities exercise controlling power over many fundamental decisions. They can, for example, make it difficult, in some cases impossible, for the national government to close a hospital or to move it from one site to another.

That one set of officials is paid out of the national treasury, one out of state funds, and a third from local budgets is the least important aspect of the matter. If one looks closely at the route of payments, the fact of common concern becomes clear again. All levels collect taxes from the same people. And the government that collects the tax frequently does not pay the officer; intergovernmental transfers, for example, account for a very large fraction of both state and local welfare expenditures. Consider the health officer, styled "sanitarian," of a rural county in a border state. He embodies the whole idea of the marble cake of government. The sanitarian is appointed by the state under merit standards established by the federal government. His base salary comes jointly from state and federal funds, the county provides him with an office and office amenities and pays a portion of his expenses, and the largest city in the county also contributes to his salary and office by virtue of his appointment as a city plumbing inspector. It is impossible from moment to moment to tell under which governmental hat the sanitarian operates. His work of inspecting the purity of food is carried out under federal standards; but he is enforcing state laws when inspecting commodities that have not been in interstate commerce; and somewhat perversely, he also acts under state authority when inspecting milk coming into the county from producing areas across the state border. He is a federal officer when impounding impure drugs shipped from a neighboring state; a federal-state officer when distributing typhoid immunization serum; a state officer when enforcing standards of industrial hygiene; a state-local officer when inspecting the city's water supply; and (to complete the circle) a local officer when insisting that the city butchers adopt more hygienic methods of handling their garbage. But he cannot and does not think of himself as acting in these separate capacities. All business in the county that concerns public health and sanitation he considers his business. Paid largely from federal funds, he does not find it strange to attend meetings of the city council to give expert advice on matters ranging from rotten apples to rabies control. He is even deputized as a member of both the city and county police forces.

The sanitarian is an extreme case, but he accurately represents an important aspect of the whole range of governmental activities in the United States. Functions are not neatly parceled out among the many governments. They are shared functions. It is difficult to find any governmental activity which does not involve all three of the so-called "levels" of the federal system. In the most local of local functions—law enforcement or education, for example—the federal and state governments play important roles. In what, *a priori*, may be considered the purest central government activities—the conduct of foreign affairs, for example—the state and local governments have considerable responsibilities, directly and indirectly.

The federal grant programs are only the most obvious example of shared functions. They also most clearly exhibit how sharing serves to disperse governmental powers. The grants utilize the greater wealth-gathering abilities of the central government and establish nationwide standards, yet they are "in aid" of functions carried out under state law, with considerable state and local discretion. The national supervision of such programs is largely a process of mutual accommodation. Leading state and local officials, acting through their professional organizations, are in considerable part responsible for the very standards that national officers try to persuade all state and local officers to accept.

Even in the absence of joint financing, federal-state-local collaboration is the characteristic mode of action. Federal expertise is available to aid in the building of a local jail (which may later be used to house federal prisoners), to improve a local water purification system, to step up building inspections, to provide standards for state and local personnel in protecting housewives against dishonest butchers' scales, to prevent gas explosions, or to produce a land use plan. States and localities, on the other hand, take important formal responsibilities in the development of national programs for atomic energy, civil defense, the regulation of commerce, and the protection of purity in food and drugs; local political weight is always a factor in the operation of even a post office or a military establishment. From abattoirs and accounting through zoning and zoo administration, any governmental activity is almost certain to involve the influence, if not the formal administration, of all three planes of the federal system.

So the functions of government are not in neat layers. Rather, they are all mixed up: marbled, to use the baker's term. And in no neat order: chaotic, to use the reformer's term. Unless one sees the American federal system from this perspective, he misses the most important fact of all: the system is, in effect, one government serving a common people for a common end.

NOTES

1. James Bryce, *The American Commonwealth*, Vol. I (New York: Macmillan, 1916), p. 318.
2. *Tarble's Case*, 13 Wall. 397 (1871).
3. For example, William Anderson, *The Nation and the States, Rivals or Partners?* (Minneapolis: University of Minnesota Press, 1955); the series of monographs, *Intergovernmental Relations in the United States as Observed in Minnesota*, edited by William Anderson and Edward W. Weidner and published by the University of

Minnesota Press; Henry M. Hart, Jr., and Herbert Wechsler, *The Federal Courts and the Federal System* (Brooklyn: Foundation Press, 1953). An important early work, limited to describing "some of the ways in which the federal and state governments have cooperated and how effective their joint activity has been," is Jane Perry Clark, *The Rise of a New Federalism* (New York: Columbia University Press, 1938).

31
Organizations of the Future
Warren Bennis

Recently, I predicted that in the next 25 to 50 years we will participate in the end of bureaucracy as we know it and the rise of new social systems better suited to 20th-Century demands of industrialization.[1] This forecast was based on the evolutionary principle that every age develops an organizational form appropriate to its genius and that the prevailing form of pyramidal-hierarchal organization, known by sociologists as "bureaucracy" and most businessmen as "that damn bureaucracy," was out of joint with contemporary realities.

I realize now that my prediction is already a distinct reality so that prediction is foreshadowed by practice.

I should like to make clear that by "bureaucracy" I mean the typical organizational structure that coordinates the business of most human organization we know of: industry, government, university, R & D labs, military, religious, voluntary, and so forth.

Bureaucracy, as I refer to it here, is a useful social invention, perfected during the Industrial Revolution to organize and direct the activities of the business firm. Max Weber, the German sociologist who developed the theory of bureaucracy around the turn of the century, once described bureaucracy as a social machine.

The bureaucratic "machine model" was developed as a reaction against the personal subjugation, nepotism, cruelty, and capricious and subjective judgments that often passed for managerial practices during the early days of the Industrial Revolution. Bureaucracy emerged out of the need for more predictability, order, and precision. It was an organization ideally suited to the values and the demands of Victorian Empire. And just as bureaucracy emerged as a creative response to a radically new age, so today new organizational shapes and forms are surfacing before our eyes.

I shall try first to show why the conditions of our modern industrialized world will bring about the decline of bureaucracy and force a reconsideration of new organizational structures. Then, I will suggest a rough model of the organization of the future. Finally, I shall set forth the new tasks and challenges for the training and development manager.

Source: From *Personnel Administration* (September-October 1967). Reprinted by permission of the International Personnel Management Association, 1850 K Street, N.W., Washington, DC 20006.

WHY IS BUREAUCRACY VULNERABLE?

There are at least four relevant threats to bureaucracy. The first is a human, basically psychological one, which I shall return to later on, while the other three spring from extraordinary changes in our environment. The latter three are (1) rapid and unexpected change, (2) growth in size where volume of organization's traditional activities is not enough to sustain growth, and (3) complexity of modern technology where integration of activities and persons of very diverse, highly specialized competence is required.[2]

It might be useful to examine the extent to which these conditions exist *right now.*

Rapid and Unexpected Change

It may be enough simply to cite the knowledge and population explosion. More revealing, however, are the statistics that demonstrate these events:

- Our productivity per man hour now doubles almost every 20 years rather than every 40 years, which was true before World War II.
- The federal government alone spent 16 billion in R&D activities in 1965 and will spend 35 billion by 1980.
- The time lag between a technical discovery and recognition of its commercial uses was 30 years before World War I, 16 years between the wars, and only 9 years since World War II.
- In 1946 only 30 cities in the world had populations of more than one million. Today there are 80. In 1930 there were 40 people for each square mile of the earth's land surface. Today, there are 63. By the year 2,000, there are expected to be 142.

Growth in Size

Not only have more organizations grown larger, but they have become more complex and more international. Firms like Standard Oil of New Jersey (with 57 foreign affiliates), Socony Mobil, National Cash Register, Singer, Burroughs, and Colgate-Palmolive derive more than half their income or earnings from foreign sales. A long list of others, such as Eastman Kodak, Pfizer, Caterpillar Tractor, International Harvester, Corn Products, and Minnesota Mining and Manufacturing make from 30 to 50 percent of their sales abroad.[3] General Motors' sales are not only nine times those of Volkswagen, they are also bigger than the gross national product of The Netherlands and well over those of a hundred other countries. If we have seen the sun set on the British empire, it will be a long time before it sets on the empires of General Motors, ITT, Royal Dutch/Shell and Unilever.

Today's Activities Require Persons of Very Diverse, Highly Specialized Competence

Numerous dramatic examples can be drawn from studies of labor markets and job mobility. At some point during the past decade, the U.S. became the first nation in the world ever to employ more people in *service occupations* than in the production of tangible goods. Examples of this trend are:

- In the field of education, the *increase* in employment between 1950 and 1960 was greater than the total number employed in the steel, copper, and aluminum industries.
- In the field of health, the *increase* in employment between 1950 and 1960 was greater than the total number employed in automobile manufacturing in either year.
- In financial firms, the *increase* in employment between 1950 and 1960 was greater than total employment in mining in 1960.[4]

Rapid change, hurried growth, and increase in specialists: with these three logistical conditions we should expect bureaucracy to decline.

CHANGE IN MANAGERIAL BEHAVIOR

Earlier I mentioned a fourth factor which seemed to follow along with the others, though its exact magnitude, nature, and antecedents appear more obscure and shadowy due to the relative difficulty of assigning numbers to it. This factor stems from the personal observation that over the past decade there has been a fundamental change in the basic philosophy that underlies managerial behavior. The change in philosophy is reflected most of all in:

- A new concept of *Man,* based on increased knowledge of his complex and shifting needs, which replaces an oversimplified, innocent push-button idea of man.
- A new concept of *power,* based on collaboration and reason, which replaces a model of power based on coercion and threat.
- A new concept of *organization values,* based on humanistic-democratic ideals, which replaces the depersonalized mechanistic value system of bureaucracy.

These transformations of Man, power, and values have gained wide intellectual acceptance in management quarters. They have caused a terrific amount of rethinking on the part of many organizations. They have been used as a basis for policy formulation by many large-scale organizations. This philosophy is clearly not compatible with bureaucratic practices.

The primary cause of this shift in management philosophy stems not from the bookshelf but from the manager himself. Many of the behavioral scientists, like McGregor or Likert, have clarified and articulated—even legitimized—what managers have only half registered to themselves. I am convinced that the success of McGregor's *The Human Side of Enterprise* was based on a rare empathy for a vast audience of managers who were wistful for an alternative to a mechanistic conception of authority. (See Figure 1.) It foresaw a vivid utopia of more authentic human relationships than most organizational practices allow. Furthermore, I suspect that the desire for relationships has little to do with a profit motive *per se,* though it is often rationalized as doing so.[5] The real push for these changes stems from some powerful needs, not only to humanize the organization, but to use the organization as a crucible of personal growth and development, for self-realization.[6]

CORE ORGANIZATION PROBLEMS

As a result of these changes affecting organizations of the future, new problems and tasks are emerging. They fall, I believe, into five major categories, which I visualize as the core tasks confronting organizations of the future.

1. *Integration* encompasses the entire range of issues having to do with the incentives, rewards, and motivation of the individual and how the organization succeeds or fails in adjusting to these needs. In other words, it is the ratio between individual needs and organizational demands that creates the transaction most satisfactory to both. The problem of *integration* grows out of our "*consensual society,*" where personal attachments play a great part, where the individual is appreciated, in which there is concern for his well-being, not just in a veterinary-hygiene sense, but as a moral, integrated personality.

2. The problem of *social influence* is essentially the problem of power and how power is distributed. It is a complex issue and alive with controversy, partly because of an ethical component and partly because studies of leadership and power distribution can be interpreted in many

FIGURE 1 • HUMAN PROBLEMS CONFRONTING CONTEMPORARY ORGANIZATIONS

Problem	Bureaucratic Solutions	New 20th-Century Conditions
Integration. The problem of how to integrate individual needs and organizational goals.	No solution because of no problem. Individual vastly oversimplified, regarded as passive instrument. Tension between "personality" and role disregarded.	Emergence of human sciences and understanding of man's complexity. Rising aspirations. Humanistic-democratic ethos.
Social Influence. The problem of the distribution of power and sources of power and authority.	An explicit reliance on legal-rational power, but an implicit usage of coercive power. In any case, a confused, ambiguous shifting complex of competence, coercion, and legal code.	Separation of management from ownership. Rise of trade unions and general education. Negative and unintended effects of authoritarian rule.
Collaboration. The problem of producing mechanisms for the control of conflict.	The "rule of hierarchy" to resolve conflicts between ranks and the "rule of coordination" to resolve conflict between horizontal groups. "Loyalty."	Specialization and professionalization and increased need for interdependence. Leadership too complex for one-man rule or omniscience.
Adaptation. The problem of responding appropriately to changes induced by the environment.	Environment stable, simple, and predictable; tasks routine. Adapting to change occurs in haphazard and adventitious ways. Unanticipated consequences abound.	External environment of firm more "turbulent," less predictable. Unprecedented rate of technological change.
"*Revitalization.*" The problem of growth and decay.	Underlying assumption that the future will be certain and basically similar, if not more so, to the past.	Rapid changes in technologies, tasks, manpower, raw materials, norms and values of society, goals of enterprise and society all make constant attention to the process of revision imperative.

ways, and almost always in ways which coincide with one's biases (including a cultural leaning toward democracy).

The problem of power has to be seriously reconsidered because of dramatic situational changes that make the possibility of one-man rule or the "Great Man" not necessarily "bad" but impractical. I am referring to changes in the role of top management. Peter Drucker, over 12 years ago, listed 41 major responsibilities of the chief executive and declared that "90 percent of the trouble we are having with the chief executive's job is rooted in our superstition of the one-man chief."[7] The broadening product base of industry, impact of new technology, the scope of international operations, make one-man control quaint, if not obsolete.

3. The problem of *collaboration* grows out of the very same social processes of conflict and stereotyping, and centrifugal forces that divide nations and communities. They also employ furtive, often fruitless, always crippling mechanisms of conflict resolution: avoidance or suppression, annihilation of the weaker party by the stronger, sterile compromises, and unstable collusions and coalitions. Particularly as organizations become more complex they fragment and divide, building tribal patterns and symbolic codes which often work to exclude others (secrets and noxious jargon, for example) and on occasion to exploit differences for inward (and always fragile) harmony. Some large organizations, in fact, can be understood only through an analysis of their cabals, cliques, and satellites, where a venture into adjacent spheres of interest is taken under cover of darkness and fear of ambush. Dysfunctional intergroup conflict is so easily stimulated, that one wonders if it is rooted in our archaic heritage when man struggled, with an imperfect symbolic code and early consciousness, for his territory. Robert R. Blake in his experiments has shown how simple it is to induce conflict, how difficult to arrest it.[8] Take two groups of people who have never been together before, and give them a task that will be judged by an impartial jury. In less than one hour, each group devolves into a tightly-knit band with all the symptoms of an "in-group." They regard their product as a "masterwork" and the other group's as "commonplace" at best. "Other" becomes "enemy;" "We are good; they are bad. We are right; they are wrong."[9]

Jaap Rabbie, conducting experiments on the antecedents of intergroup conflict at the University of Utrecht, has been amazed by the ease with which conflict and stereotype develop.[10] He brings into the experimental room two groups and distributes green name tags and green pens to one group and refers to it as the "green group." He distributes red pens and red name tags to the other group and refers to it as the "red group." The groups do not compete; they do not even interact. They are in sight of each other for only minutes while they silently complete a questionnaire. Only 10 minutes is needed to activate defensiveness and fear.

In a recent essay on animal behavior, Erikson develops the idea of "pseudo-species."[11] Pseudo-species act as if they were separate species created at the beginning of time by supernatural intent. He argues:

> Man has evolved (by whatever kind of evolution and for whatever adaptive reasons) in pseudo-species, i.e., tribes, clans, classes, etc. Thus, each develops not only a *distinct sense of identity* but also a conviction of harboring *the* human identity, fortified against other pseudo-species by prejudices which mark them as extra-specific and inimical to "genuine" human endeavor. Paradoxically, however, newly born man is (to use Ernst Mayr's term) a generalist creature who could be made to fit

> into any number of pseudo-species and must, therefore, become "specialized" during a prolonged childhood. . . .

Modern organizations abound with pseudo-species, bands of specialists held together by the illusion of a unique identity and with a tendency to view other pseudo-species with suspicion and mistrust. Ways must be discovered to produce generalists and diplomats, and we must find more effective means of managing inevitable conflict and minimizing the pseudo-conflict. This is not to say that conflict is always avoidable and dysfunctional. Some types of conflict may lead to productive and creative ends.

4. The problem of *adaptation* is caused by our turbulent environment. The pyramidal structure of bureaucracy, where power was concentrated at the top, seemed perfect to "run a railroad." And undoubtedly for the routinized tasks of the nineteenth and early twentieth centuries, bureaucracy was and still is an eminently suitable social arrangement. However, rather than a placid and predictable environment, what predominates today is a dynamic and uncertain one in which there is a deepening interdependence among the economic and other facets of society.

5. Finally, the problem of *revitalization.* As Alfred North Whitehead says:

> The art of free society consists first in the maintenance of the symbolic code, and secondly, in the fearlessness of revision. . . . Those societies which cannot combine reverence to their symbols with freedom of revision must ultimately decay . . .

Growth and decay emerge as the penultimate conditions of contemporary society. Organizations, as well as societies, must be concerned with those social structures that engender bouyancy, resilience, and a "fearlessness of revision."

I introduce the term "revitalization" to embrace all the social mechanisms that stagnate and regenerate and with the process of this cycle. The elements of revitalization are:

- An ability to learn from experience and to codify, store, and retrieve the relevant knowledge.
- An ability to "learn how to learn," that is, to develop methodologies for improving the learning process.
- An ability to acquire and use feedback mechanisms on performance, to develop a "process orientation," in short, to be self-analytical.
- An ability to direct one's own destiny.

These qualities have a good deal in common with what John Gardner calls "self-renewal." For the organization, it means conscious attention to its own evolution. Without a planned methodology and explicit direction, the enterprise will not realize its potential.

Integration, Distribution of Power, Collaboration, Adaptation, and Revitalization are the major human problems of the next 25 years. How organizations cope with and manage these tasks will undoubtedly determine the viability and growth of the enterprise.

ORGANIZATIONS OF THE FUTURE[12]

Against this background I should like to set forth some of the conditions that will determine organizational life in the next two or three decades:

1. The Environment

Rapid technological change and diversification will lead to interpenetration of the government with business.

Partnerships between government and business will be typical. It will be a truly mixed economy. Because of the immensity and expense of the projects, there will be fewer identical units competing for the same buyers and sellers.

Organizations will become more interdependent.

The four main features of the environment are:

- Interdependence rather than competition.
- Turbulence and uncertainty rather than readiness and certainty.
- Large scale rather than small scale enterprises.
- Complex and multi-national rather than simple national enterprises.

2. Population Characteristics

The most distinctive characteristic of our society is, and will become even more so, education. Within 15 years, two-thirds of our population living in metropolitan areas will have attended college. Adult education is growing even faster, probably because of the rate of professional obsolescence. The Killian report showed that the average engineer required further education only 10 years after gaining his degree. It will become almost routine for the experienced physician, engineer, and executive to go back to school for advanced training every two or three years. Some 50 universities, in addition to a dozen large corporations, offer advanced management courses to successful men in the middle and upper ranks of business. Before World War II, only two such programs existed, both new, both struggling to get students.

All of this education is not just "nice," it is necessary. As Secretary of Labor Wirtz recently pointed out, computers can do the work of most high school graduates—cheaper and more effectively. Fifty years ago education was regarded as "nonwork" and intellectuals on the payroll were considered "overhead." Today the survival of the firm *depends* on the effective exploitation of brain power.

One other characteristic of the population which will aid our understanding of organizations of the future is increasing job mobility. The ease of transportation, coupled with the needs of a dynamic environment, change drastically the idea of "owning" a job—or "having roots." Already 20 percent of our population change their mailing address at least once a year.

3. Work Values

The increased level of education and mobility will change the values we hold about work. People will be more intellectually committed to their *professional* careers and will probably require more involvement, participation, and autonomy.

Also, people will be more "other-directed," taking cues for their norms and values from their immediate environment rather than tradition. We will tend to rely more heavily on temporary social arrangements.[13] We will tend to have relationships rather than relatives.

4. Tasks and Goals

The tasks of the organization will be more technical, complicated, and unprogrammed. They will rely on intellect instead of muscle. And they will be too complicated for one person to comprehend, to say nothing of control. Essentially, they will call for the collaboration of specialists in a project or a team-form of organization.

There will be a complication of goals. Business will increasingly concern itself with its adaptive or innovative-creative capacity. In addition, meta-goals will have to be articulated; that is, supragoals, which shape and provide the foundation for the goal structure. For example, one meta-goal might be a system for detecting new and changing goals; another could be a system for deciding priorities among goals.

Finally, more conflict and contradiction can be expected from diverse standards of organizational effectiveness. One reason for this is that professionals tend to identify more with the goals of their profession than with those of their immediate employer. University professors can be used as a case in point. Within the University, there may be a conflict between teaching and research. Often, more of a professor's income derives from outside sources, such as foundations and consultant work. They tend not to be good "company men" because they divide their loyalty between their professional values and organizational goals.

5. Organization

The social structure of organizations of the future will have some unique characteristics. The key word will be "temporary"; there will be adaptive, rapidly changing *temporary systems.* These will be "task forces" organized around problems-to-be-solved by groups of relative strangers who represent a diverse set of professional skills. The groups will be arranged on an organic rather than mechanical model; they will evolve in response to a problem rather than to programmed role expectations. The "executive" thus becomes a coordinator or "linking pin" between various task forces. He must be a man who can speak the diverse languages of research with skills to relay information and to mediate between groups. People will be evaluated not vertically according to rank and status, but flexibly and functionally according to skill and professional training. Organizational charts will consist of project groups rather than functional groups. This trend is already visible today in the aerospace and construction industries, as well as many professional and consulting firms.

Adaptive, problem-solving, temporary systems of diverse specialists, linked together by coordinating and task evaluating specialists in an organic flux—this is the organizational form that will gradually replace bureaucracy as we know it. As no catchy phrase comes to mind, I call this an organic-adaptive structure.

6. Motivation

The organic-adaptive structure should increase motivation, and thereby effectiveness, because it enhances satisfactions intrinsic to the task. There is a harmony between the educated individual's need for meaningful, satisfactory, and creative tasks and a flexible organizational structure.

There will, however, also be reduced commitment to work groups, for these groups, as I have already mentioned, will be transient structures. I would predict that in the organic-adaptive system, people will learn to develop quick and intense relationships on the job, and learn to bear the loss of more enduring work relationships. Because of the added ambiguity of roles, time will have to be spent on continual rediscovery of the appropriate organizational mix.

The American experience of frontier neighbors, after all, prepares us for this, so I don't view "temporary systems" as such a grand departure. These "brief encounters" need not be more superficial than long and chronic ones. I have seen too many people, some occupying adjacent offices for many years, who have never really experienced or encountered each other. They look at each other with the same vacant stares as people do on buses and subways, and perhaps they are passengers waiting for their exit.

Europeans typically find this aspect of American life frustrating. One German expatriate told me of his disenchantment with "friendly Americans." At his first party in this country, he met a particularly sympathetic fellow and the two of them fell into a warm conversation which went on for several hours.

Finally, they had to leave to return to their homes, but like soul-mates, they couldn't part. They went down into the city street and walked round and round on this cold winter night, teeth chattering and arms bound. Finally, both stiff with cold, the American hailed a cab and went off with a wave. The European was stunned. He didn't know his new "friend's" name. He never saw or heard from him again. "That's your American friendship," he told me.

That *is* American friendship: intense, spontaneous, total involvement, unpredictable in length, impossible to control. They are happenings, simultaneously "on" and transitory and then "off" and then new lights and new happenings.

A Swiss woman in Max Frisch's *I'm Not Stiller* sums it up this way: "Apparently all these frank and easy-going people did not expect anything else from a human relationship. There was no need for this friendly relationship to go on growing."[14]

TRAINING REQUIREMENTS FOR ORGANIZATIONS OF THE FUTURE

How can we best plan for the organizational developments I forecast? And how can training and development directors influence and direct this destiny? One thing is clear: There will be a dramatically new role for the manager of training and development. Let us look at some of the new requirements.

1. Training for Change

The remarkable aspect of our generation is its commitment to change, in thought and action. Can training and development managers develop an educational process which:

- Helps us to identify with the adaptive process without fear of losing our identity?
- Increases our tolerance for ambiguity without fear of losing intellectual mastery?
- Increases our ability to collaborate without fear of losing individuality?
- Develops a willingness to participate in our own social evolution while recognizing implacable forces?

Putting it differently, it seems to me that *we should be trained in an attitude toward inquiry and novelty rather than the particular content of a job;* training for change means developing "learning men."

2. Systems Counseling

It seems to me that management (and personnel departments) have failed to come to grips with the reality of *social systems.* It is embarrassing to state this after decades of research have been making the same point. We have proved that productivity can be modified by group norms, that training effects fade out and deteriorate if training goals are not compatible with the goals of the social system, that group cohesiveness is a powerful motivator, that intergroup conflict is a major problem facing modern organization, that individuals take many of their cues from their primary work group, that identification with the work group turns out to be the only stable predictor of productivity, and so on. Yet this evidence is so frequently ignored that I can only infer that there is something naturally preferable (almost an involuntary reflex) in locating the sources of all problems in the individual and diagnosing situations as functions of faulty individuals rather than as symptoms of malfunctioning social systems.

If this reflex is not arrested, it can have serious repercussions. In these new organizations, where roles will be constantly changing and certainly ambiguous, where changes in one sub-system will clearly affect other sub-systems, where diverse and multinational activities have to be coordinated and integrated, where individuals engage simultaneously in multiple roles and group memberships (and role conflict is endemic), a systems viewpoint must be developed. Just as it is no longer possible to make any enduring change in a "problem child" without treating the entire family, it will not be possible to influence individual behavior without working with his particular sub-system. This means that our training and development managers of the future must perform the functions of *systems counselors.*

3. Changing Motivation

The rate at which professional-technical-managerial types join organizations is higher than any other employment category. While it isn't fully clear what motivates them, two important factors emerge.

The first is a strong urge to "make it" professionally, to be respected by professional colleagues. Loyalty to an organization may increase if it encourages professional growth. Thus, the "good place to work" will resemble a super-graduate school, abounding with mature, senior colleagues, where the employee will work not only to satisfy organizational demands but, perhaps primarily, those of his profession.

The other factor involves the quest for self-realization, for personal growth which may not be task-related. That remark, I am well aware, questions four centuries of encrusted Protestant Ethic. And I feel uncertain as to how (or even *if*) these needs can be met by an organization. However, we must hope for social inventions to satisfy these new desires. Training needs to take more responsibility for attitudes about continuing education so that it is not considered a "retread" or a "repair factory" but a natural and inescapable aspect of work. The idea that education has a terminal point and that adults have somehow "finished" is old-fashioned. A "drop-out" should be redefined to mean anyone who *hasn't returned* to school.

However the problem of professional and personal growth is resolved, it is clear that many of our older forms of incentive, based on lower echelons of the need hierarchy, will have to be reconstituted.

4. Socialization for Adults

In addition to continuing education, we have to face the problem of continuing socialization, or the institutional influences which society provides to create good citizens. Put simply, it means training in values, attitudes, ethics, and morals. We allot these responsibilities typically to the family, to church, to schools. We incorrectly assume that socialization stops when the individual comes of age. Most certainly, we are afraid of socialization for adults, as if it implies the dangers of a delayed childhood disease, like whooping cough.

Or to be more precise, we frown not on socialization, but on conscious and responsible control of it. In fact, our organizations are magnificent, if undeliberate, vehicles of socialization. They teach values, inculcate ethics, create norms, dictate right and wrong, influence attitudes necessary for success and all the rest. The men who succeed tend to be well socialized and the men who don't, are not: "Yeah, Jones was a marvelous worker, but he never fit in around here." And most universities grant tenure where their norms and values are most accepted, although this is rarely stated.

Taking conscious responsibility for the socialization process will become imperative in tomorrow's organization. And finding men with the right technical capability will not be nearly as difficult as finding men with the right set of values and attitudes. Of course, consciously guiding this process is a trying business, alive with problems, not the least being the ethical one: Do we have the right to shape attitudes and values? We really do not have a choice. Can we avoid it? How bosses lead and train subordinates, how individuals are treated, what and who gets rewarded, the subtle cues transmitted and learned without seeming recognition, occur spontaneously. What we can choose are the mechanisms of socialization—how coercive we are, how much individual freedom we give, how we transmit values. What will be impermissible is a denial to recognize that we find some values more desirable and to accept responsibility for consciously and openly communicating them.

5. Developing Problem-Solving Teams

One of the most difficult and important challenges for the training and development manager will be the task of promoting conditions for effective collaboration or building synergetic teams. Synergy is where individuals actually contribute more and perform better as a result of a collaborative and supportive environment. They play "over their heads," so to speak. The challenge I am referring to is the building of synergetic teams.

Of course, the job isn't an easy one. An easy way out is to adopt the "zero synergy" strategy. This means that the organization attempts to hire the best individuals it can and then permits them to "cultivate their own gardens." This is a strategy of isolation that can be observed in almost every university organization.

[Until universities take a serious look at their strategy of zero synergy, there is little hope that they will solve their vexing problems. The Berkeley protests were symptomatic of at least four self-contained, uncommunicating social systems (students, faculty, administration, trustees) without the trust, empathy, interaction (to say nothing of a tradition) to develop meaningful collaboration. To make matters even more difficult, if possible, academic types may, by nature (and endorsed by tradition) see themselves as "loners" and divergent to the majority. They all want to be independent together, so to speak. Academic narcissism goes a long way on the lecture platform but may be positively disruptive for developing a community.]

Another approach has the same effect but appears different. It is the pseudo-democratic style, in which a phony harmony and conflict-avoidance persists.

In addition to our lack of background and experience in building synergy (and our strong cultural biases against group efforts), teams take time to develop. They are like other highly complicated organisms and, just as we wouldn't expect a newborn to talk, we shouldn't expect a new team to work effectively from the start. Teams require trust and commitment and these ingredients require a period of gestation.

Expensive and time-consuming as it is, building synergetic and collaborative frameworks will become essential. The problems that confront us are too complex and diversified for one man or one discipline. They require a blending of skills, slants, and disciplines for their solution and only effective problem-solving *teams* will be able to get on with the job.

6. Developing Supra-Organizational Goals and Commitments

The President of ABC (the fictitious name of a manufacturing company) was often quoted as saying: "The trouble with ABC is that nobody aside from me ever gives a damn about the overall goals of this place. They're all seeing the world through the lenses of their departmental biases. What we need around here are people who wear the ABC hat, not the engineering hat or the sales hat or the production hat."

After he was heard muttering this rather typical president's dirge, a small group of individuals, who thought they could wear the ABC hat, formed a group they called the ABC HATS. They came from *various* departments and hierarchical levels and represented a microcosm of the entire organization. The ABC HATS group has continued to meet over the past few years and has played a central role in influencing top policy.

It seems to me that training and development managers could affect the development of their organizations if they would encourage the formation of HATS groups. What worries me about the organization of the future, of specialized professionals and an international executive staff, is that their professional and regional outlook brings along with it only a relative truth and a distortion of reality. This type of organization is extremely vulnerable to the hardening of pseudo-species and a compartmentalized approach to problems.

Training and development can be helpful in a number of ways:

- They can identify and support those individuals who are "linking pins" individuals who have a facility for psychological and intellectual affinity with a number of diverse languages and cultures. These individuals will become the developers of problem-solving teams.
- They can perform the HATS function, which is another way of saying that training and development managers should be managers who keep over-all goals in mind and modulate the professional biases which are intrinsic to the specialists' work.
- They can work at the interfaces of the pseudo-species in order to create more inter-group understanding and interface articulation.

Today, we see each of the intellectual disciplines burrowing deeper into its own narrow sphere of interest. (Specialism, by definition, implies a peculiar slant, a segmented vision. A cloak and suit manufacturer went to Rome and managed to get an audience with His Holiness. Upon his return a friend asked him, "What did the Pope look like? The tailor answered, "A 41 Regular.") Yet, the most interesting problems turn up at the intersection between disciplines and it may take an outsider to identify these. Even more often, the separate disciplines go their crazy-quilt way and rely more and more on internal standards of evidence and competence. They dismiss the outsider as an amateur with a contemptuous shrug. The problem with intellectual effort today (and I include my own field of organization psychology) is that no one is developing the grand synthesis.

Organizations, too, require "philosophers," individuals who provide articulation between seemingly inimical interests, who break down the pseudo-species, and who transcend vested interests, regional ties, and professional biases in arriving at the solution to problems.

To summarize, I have suggested that the training and development director of the future has in store at least six new and different functions: (1) training for change, (2) systems counseling, (3) developing new incentives, (4) socializing adults, (5) building collaborative, problem-solving teams, and (6) developing supra-organizational goals and commitments. Undoubtedly there are others and some that cannot be anticipated. It is clear that they signify a fundamentally different role for personnel management from "putting out fires" and narrow maintenance functions. If training and development is to realize its true promise, its role and its image must change from maintenance to innovation.

I have seen this new role develop in a number of organizations, not easily or overnight, but pretty much in the way I have described it here. It might be useful to review briefly the conditions present in the cases I know about:

> The personnel manager or some subsystem within personnel (it might be called "employee relations" or "industrial relations" or "career development") took an *active, innovative* role with respect to organizational goals and forcibly took responsibility for organizational growth and development.
>
> Secondly, this group shifted its emphasis away from personnel functions *per se* (like compensation and selection) and toward organizational problems, like developing effective patterns of collaboration, or fostering an innovative atmosphere or reducing inter-group conflict, or organizational goal-setting and long-run planning.
>
> Thirdly, this group developed a close working relationship to various sub-systems in the organization, an organic, task-oriented relationship, not the frequently observed mechanical "line-staff" relationship.
>
> Fourthly, they were viewed as full-fledged members of the management team, instead of the "head-shrinkers" or the "headquarters group." This was the hardest to establish in all cases, but turned out to be the most important. In fact, in one case, the man responsible for spearheading the organizational development effort has recently taken an important line job. The reverse happens too. Line management participates in so-called personnel activities, almost as if they are an adjunct to staff. Distinctions between line and staff blur in this context and an organic linkage develops, often serving as a prototype of a collaborative, problem-solving team.

One single factor stands out in retrospect over all others. There was always the conviction and the ability to make the training and development department the leading edge, the catalyst for organizational change and adaptability. Rather than performing the more traditional role, these groups became centers for innovation and organizational revitalization, and their leaders emerged as change-agents, the new managers of tomorrow's organizations.

I should now add another point in conclusion. It emerges from the previous points. They describe a far more autonomous, organizationally influential, self-directed role than trainers have been given or have asked for in the past.

If the training group is to be concerned with adult socialization, for example, it would be myopically irresponsible if not worse for them to define socialization in terms of momentary needs of the organization. Rather, they must take at least some of the responsibility for enunciating the goals and conditions of the enterprise. In a way, their systems counseling function is "organizational socialization." If they take responsibility for socializing both the members as people and the organization as a human system, then they must have values and standards which are somehow prior and outside both.

In fact, the emerging role I outline implies that the roles of the top management and training director become more inter-changeable than ever before.

NOTES

1. "The Decline of Bureaucracy and Organizations of the Future." Invited address presented to the Division of Industrial and Business Psychology at the American Psychological Association meeting, Los Angeles, Calif., Sept. 5, 1964.

2. A. H. Rubenstein and C. Haberstroh, *Some Theories of Organization,* (Revised Edition). Irwin-Dorsey, Homewood, Ill., 1966.

3. Richard J. Barber, "American Business Goes Global." *The New Republic.* April 30, 1966, 14–18.

4. Victor R. Fuchs, "The First Service Economy." *The Public Interest.* Winter 1966, 7–17.

5. Chris Argyris, *Interpersonal Competence and Organizational Effectiveness.* Homewood, Ill.: Irwin-Dorsey, 1962.

6. *The Varieties of Religious Experience.* The Modern Library, Random House, N.Y., 1902, 475–476.
7. D. Ron Daniel, "Team at the Top." *Harvard Business Review,* March-April 1965, 74–82.
8. Robert R. Blake, Herbert A. Shepard and Jane S. Mouton, *Managing Intergroup Conflict in Industry,* Gulf Publishing, Houston, Texas, 1964.
9. Carl Rogers, "Dealing with Psychological Tensions." *Journal of Applied Behavioral Sciences,* Jan.-Feb.-March 1965, 6–24.
10. Personal communication, Jan. 1966.
11. Erik Erikson, "Ontogeny of Ritualization." Paper presented to the Royal Society in June 1965.
12. Adapted from my earlier paper, "Beyond Bureaucracy," *Trans-Action,* July-August 1965.
13. "On Temporary Systems." In M. B. Miles (ed.), *Innovation in Education,* Bureau of Publications, Teachers College, Columbia University, N.Y., 1964, 437–490.
14. Penguin Books, Harmondsworth Middlesex. 1961, p. 244.

32

Policy Analysts: A New Professional Role in Government Service

Yehezkel Dror

The main contemporary reform movement in the federal administration of the United States (and in some other countries as well) is based on an economic approach to public decision-making. The roots of this approach are in economic theory, especially micro-economics and welfare economics, and quantitative decision-theory; the main tools of this approach are operations research, cost-effectiveness and cost-benefit analysis, and program budgeting and systems analysis; and the new professionals of this approach are the systems analysts. Together, these elements constitute main components of the Planning-Programming-Budgeting System, as first developed in the Department of Defense and now being extended to most executive departments and establishments.

In essence, these reforms constitute an invasion of public decision-making by economics. Going far beyond the domain of economic policy-making, the economic approach to decision-making views every decision as an allocation of resources between alternatives, that is, as an economic problem. Application of suitable tools of economic analysis should therefore, in this opinion, contribute to the improvement of decision-making, whatever the subject matter of the decision may be. This is the main innovation of the Planning-Programming-Budgeting System, which is in essence a restatement of earlier budgeting theory combined with systems analysis and put into a coherent and integrated framework.[1]

The invasion of public decision-making by economics is both unavoidable and beneficial, but fraught with danger. It is unavoidable because economics provides the only highly developed the-

Source: From *Public Administration Review* 27 (September 1967), pp. 197–203.

oretical basis for improvement in highly critical decision-making processes. It is beneficial because the economic approach in the systems analysis and PPBS form can contribute to the improvement of public decision-making, if carefully utilized. It is fraught with dangers because of the inability to deal adequately with many critical elements of public policy-making and the possible distortion in decision-making resulting therefrom.

A main question is how to reap the full benefits of the economic approach and to improve public decision-making and policy-making while avoiding its pitfalls. This question becomes more and more acute with the present tendency to apply PPBS and systems analysis throughout governmental administration.

SYSTEMS ANALYSIS AND DECISION-MAKING

In considering the dangers of systems analysis (by itself and as a critical part of PPBS), we must keep in mind an important consideration: I accept as a fact that systems analysis has made very important, though limited contributions to better decision-making up to now, especially in the Department of Defense, but much of this contribution may have been due more to the wisdom, sophistication, and open-mindedness of the few outstanding practitioners of systems analysis and their readiness to fight organizational inertia and muddling-through tendencies than to their defined professional tools. Now systems analysis is to become a profession with defined job responsibilities throughout government, to be practiced by a larger group of specially trained staff officers. If this is so, we cannot rely any longer on the tacit qualities and multiple backgrounds (including, for instance, physics and engineering, in addition to economics) of the small number of highly gifted individuals who pioneered systems analysis. Instead, we must develop institutional arrangements, professional training, and job definitions which will provide the desired outputs with good and hopefully very good, but not necessarily outstanding, personnel.

When we look at the basic characteristics of systems analysis as a professional discipline (as distinguished from the personal wisdom of some of its pioneers), a number of weaknesses can be identified. These weaknesses are not transitory features of a new discipline, but seem to be endemic to the nature and origin of systems analysis and are introduced through it into PPBS.

Some of the important weaknesses of systems analysis from the point of view of public decision-making can be summed up as follows:[2]

1. Strong attachment to quantification and dependence upon it, including both need for quantitative models and for quantitative parameters for the variables appearing in the models.
2. Incapacity to deal with conflicting noncommensurate values (other than through neutralizing the issue when possible, by seeking out value-insensitive alternatives).
3. Requirement of clear-cut criteria of decision and well-defined missions.
4. Neglect of the problems of political feasibility and of the special characteristics of political resources (such as the power-producing effect of using political power).[3]
5. Lack of significant treatment of essential extra-rational decision elements, such as creativity, tacit knowledge, and judgment.

6. Inability to deal with large and complex systems other than through suboptimization, which destroys the overall *Gestalt* of the more difficult and involved issues.
7. Lack of instruments for taking into account individual motivations, irrational behavior, and human idiosyncrasy.

As a result of these weaknesses, systems analysis as such is of doubtful utility for dealing with political decisions, overall strategic planning, and public policy-making. This does not disparage the importance of systems analysis for operational planning and control[4] or the essential contributions of systems analysis as one of the bases of a broader professional discipline of policy analysis. But by itself, or as a part of PPBS, systems analysis cannot deal with issues and situations where the problem is to move on from one appreciative system[5] or multidimensional space to another, or to get from one curve to a different curve.

POSSIBLE BOOMERANG EFFECTS

Even so, a good prima facie argument can be made for taking systems analysis as it is and applying it to public decision-making. The principal claims in favor of this position are that systems analysis will at least permit some improvements in public decision-making. To paraphrase one of the founders of modern systems analysis, even in the situations where technology and objectives change very swiftly, good systems analysis will at least try to get on an entirely different curve and not look for a peak of a rather flat curve.[6] Furthermore, with the help of systems analysis and PPBS—so the argument may go—at the very least, we will begin to get out of the rote of inertia and incremental change onto the highway of doubting conventional wisdom and introducing desirable innovations.

These arguments would be valid if one condition is met, namely, that both the professional systems analysts and the senior staff and line of the agencies in which they serve are highly sophisticated in respect to the possibilities and limitations of systems analysis. But this is a completely unrealistic requirement. The successes of systems analysis in some domains in the Department of Defense, the brilliance of its main pioneers and first practitioners, and the exaggerated claims of some of its advocates and proponents combine to create an unrealistic level of expectation. Being evaluated in terms of such an unrealistic level of expectation, systems analysis and PPBS will often be judged as a failure. As a result, there is a great risk that the strong anti-innovation forces will be vindicated, will become stronger entrenched, and will be better able to oppose significant reforms in the future. Unsophisticated reliance on systems analysis in this way may also impair and indeed nullify the potential benefits of other important parts of PPBS, such as future-orientation and multiple-year programming.

FROM SYSTEMS ANALYSIS TO POLICY ANALYSIS

What is needed is a more advanced type of professional knowledge, which can be used with significant benefits for the improvement of public decision-making. This professional knowledge should do for public decision-making in various issue-areas what systems analysis did in some areas of defense decision-making. To fill this rather difficult order, the various orientations, ideas, and tools of systems analysis must be developed so as to be applicable to complex and nonquantifiable issues and systems. Furthermore—and this is more important and more difficult—politics and political phenomena must be put into the focus of analysis. The term "policy analysis" seems to be suitable for the proposed professional discipline, as it combines affinity with systems analysis with the concept of policy in the broad and political sense.[7]

In essense, what is required is an integration between revised disciplines of political science and public administration on the one hand and systems analysis, decision theory, and economic theory on the other hand. This combination should be in the form of a compound rather than a mix, so as to provide a more advanced form of knowledge, rather than an eclectic collection of unrelated items. Care must be taken to achieve a real synthesis, rather than an uncritical subordination of the political to economic models, in which the specific features of politics may be lost.

To clarify the idea, let me point out some main features of policy analysis, as compared with systems analysis.

1. Much attention would be paid to the political aspects of public decision-making and public policy-making (instead of ignoring or condescendingly regarding political aspects). This includes much attention to problems of political feasibility, recruitment of support, accommodations of contradicting goals, and recognition of diversity of values. Especially important are development of theories and construction of models which do full justice to the special characteristics of politics and political behavior and do not try to force them into a procrustean bed of economic terminology and theory.
2. A broad conception of decision-making and policy-making would be involved (instead of viewing all decision-making as mainly a resources allocation). Many types of critical decisions cannot be usefully approached from an economic resource allocation framework, e.g., determining the content of diplomatic notes or changing the selective draft to a randomized process. Here, qualitative exploration of new alternatives is necessary, beyond quantitative analysis and cost-benefit estimation.
3. A main emphasis would be on creativity and search for new policy alternatives, with explicit attention to encouragement of innovative thinking (instead of comparative analysis of available alternatives and synthesis of new alternatives as one of the elements of analysis). A good example is the problem of reducing smoking—where the problem is clearly one of inventing new promising alternatives, rather than cost-benefit analysis of different known alternatives, none of which is good. The requirement of creativity and innovation of alternatives has far-reaching implications, as there is reason to suspect incompatibility between the personality traits, training, and organizational arrangements optimal for analysis (in the strict meaning of the term) and those optimal for invention of alternatives. The latter requires more "creative" personalities, structural tools for search for new ideas (for instance, through knowledge-surveys), pro-innovating organizational arrangements (e.g., cross-fertilization and stimulation through brain trusts and interdisciplinary teams), imaginative and prorisk entrepreneurship atmosphere, and changes in overall organizational climate (e.g., raising organizational levels of aspiration). Combining systems analysis with budgeting, as in PPBS, may be good for quantitative analysis, but is not a way to encourage and stimulate new and risky and expensive-looking policy ideas.
4. There would be extensive reliance on tacit understanding, *Gestalt*-images,

qualitative models, and qualitative methods (instead of main emphasis on explicit knowledge and quantitative models and tools). This involves imaginative thinking, systematic integration of trained intuition into policy analysis (e.g., through the Delphi Method), development of qualitative tools (such as metaphor construction, scenarios, counterfactual thinking), and construction of broad qualitative models of complex issues in cooperation with social scientists and other professionals (instead of ignoring the latter, in effect, or regarding them as passive sources of quantitative data).

5. There would be much more emphasis on "futuristic"[8] thinking with long-range predictions, alternative states-of-the-future, and speculative thinking on the future (in most areas up to the year 2000) as essential background for current policy-making.
6. The approach would be looser and less rigid, but nevertheless systematic, one which would recognize the complexity of means-ends interdependence, the multiplicity of relevant criteria of decision, and the partial and tentative nature of every analysis (instead of striving for a clear-cut criterion and dominant solutions). In policy analysis, sequential decision-making and constant learning is dominant,[9] and clarification of issues, invention of new alternatives, more consideration of the future, and reduction of primary disagreements to secondary disagreements are main goals.

POLICY ANALYSTS AS GOVERNMENT STAFF OFFICERS

To introduce urgently needed improvements in public decision-making, while avoiding the possible boomerang effects of systems analysis, policy analysis must become an important new professional role in government service. Policy analysis staff positions should be established in all principal administrative agencies and establishments, near the senior policy-determining positions, operating, in general, formally as advisory staff to top executives and senior line positions and actually establishing with them a symbiotic cooperative relationship. Certainly, the professional staff of the federal Planning-Programming-Budgeting System units should be trained also in policy analysis.

Policy analysis does not presume to bring about a radical change in policy-making. It does not presume to create omniscient units, which exist outside any socio-political-organizational framework and operate by a "downward and disaggregative flow" of top policy and policy directions.[10] Good policy analysis can at best become an additional component in aggregative policy-making, contributing to that process some better analysis, some novel ideas, some futuristic orientation, and some systematic thought. Policy analysis are one of the bridges between science and politics,[11] but they do not transform the basic characteristics of "the political" and of organizational behavior.[12] In order to contribute to the improvement of policy-making, policy analysts should be dispersed throughout the higher echelons of government service (and, indeed, throughout the social guidance cluster) as part of the effort to improve aggregate policy-making through introducing into the clash and interaction between competing partisan interests[13] an additional element.[14] Such redundancy will increase the aggregate effect of policy analysis on policy-making, while also providing a safeguard against trained incapacities, one-sided value bias, and professional prejudices.

The main role of policy analysts in government—as parts of PPBS, in distinct high-level staff units, in separate independent advisory corporations, and in various other organizational locations—is to contribute to public decision-making a broad professional competence, based simultaneously on systems analysis and quantitative decision-theory and on a new outlook in political science and public administration. The aim of policy analysis is to permit improvements in decision-making and policy-making by permitting fuller consideration of a broader set of alternatives, within a wider context, with the help of more systematic tools. No metamorphosis of policy-making is aimed at, but improvements of, say, 10 to 15 percent in complex public decision-making and policy-making can be achieved through better integration of knowledge and policy-making with the help of policy analysis—and this is a lot. This, I think, is certainly much more than can be achieved by systems analysis, outside relatively simple issue-areas and sub-systems.

It is premature to try and set down in detail the characteristics of the new professional role of policy analysis in government. These must be evolved largely through a careful process of learning and sequential decision-making. Nevertheless, some suggestive features can be presented tentatively in the form of a comparison between systems analysis and policy analysis (*see Table 1*).

SOME IMPLICATIONS

The decision in 1965 to introduce PPBS in the federal administration and the preparation for including a social report in the State of the Union message[15] both provide in the United States an opportunity to introduce policy analysis as a new professional role in government service and create an urgent need to do so as expediently as possible. This involves a number of steps.

Immediately needed is a change in conception in respect to the introduction of PPBS, with explicit recognition of the necessity to move in the direction of policy analysis. As already pointed out, the main pioneers of systems analysis are highly sophisticated in their substantive work and often actually practice some policy analysis. This actual sophistication must be put into the formalized system and institutionalized directives. More important still, the schemes for training of staff for PPBS at the various special university programs must be changed, so as to move from nearly exclusive preoccupation with quantitative methods to full emphasis of qualitative and political analysis.[16] Later on, policy analysis units of different forms should be established at focal decision centers throughout the social guidance cluster.

The development of policy analysis depends on a number of transformations in the disciplines of political science and public administration. The one-sided invasion of public decision-making by economics was caused largely by the inability of modern political science and public administration to make significant contributions to governmental decision-making. Economics developed a highly advanced action-oriented theory and put it to the test of innovating economic policy-making. At the same time, the modern study of political science and public administration became sterilized by an escape from political issues into behavioral "value-free" research and theory, or exhausted itself in suggestions for insignificant incremental improvements on the technical level.

This trend must be revised. A new approach in political science and public administration, oriented towards the study and improvement of public policy-making, constitutes, in the longer run, a main avenue for the improvement of public decision-making.[17] A new interdiscipline of "policy science" may also be necessary to provide a sound theoretical and institutional basis for policy analysis knowledge and policy analysis professionals. In the meantime, serious boomerang effects and damage can and should be avoided and the foundations for such a study and profession can and should be laid by changing the present efforts to introduce systems analysis in government service in the direction of policy analysis.

NOTES

1. This is brought out both from the papers published in "Planning-Programming-Budgeting System: A Symposium," *Public Administration Review* (December 1966), pp. 243–310

TABLE 1 • A TENTATIVE COMPARISON OF SOME FEATURES OF SYSTEMS ANALYSIS AND POLICY ANALYSIS

Feature	Systems Analysis	Policy Analysis
Base discipline	Economics, operations research, quantitative decision sciences	As systems analysis, *plus* political science, public administration, parts of the social sciences and psychology (in the future, new interdiscipline of policy sciences)
Main emphasis	Quantitative analysis	Qualitative analysis and innovation of new alternatives
Main desired qualities of professionals	Bright, nonconventional, high analytical capacities	As systems analysis, *plus* maturity, explicit and tacit knowledge of political and administrative reality, imagination, and idealistic realism
Main decision criteria	Efficiency in allocation of resources	Multiple criteria, including social, economic, and political
Main methods	Economic analyses, quantitative model construction	As systems analysis, *plus* qualitative models and analyses, imaginative and futuristic thought, and integration of tacit knowledge
Main location	In PPBS—in Bureau of the Budget and agency budget units	Throughout the social guidance cluster in different forms
Main outputs when applied to public decision-making	Clearly better decisions with respect to limited issues; possible boomerang effect if applied to highly complex political issues	Somewhat better decisions on highly complex and political issues; educational impact on political argumentation and long-range improvements in operation of public policy-making system
Requisites for development of knowledge and preparation of professionals	Already operational; further develoment requires some changes in university curricula	Changes in orientation of political science and public administration as academic disciplines—establishment of new university curricula and of new policy science interdisciplines

(hereafter referred to as *Symposium*) and from the literature on program budgeting, e.g., David Novick, ed., *Program Budgeting* (Cambridge: Harvard University Press, 1965). The well-taken communication by Frederick C. Mosher in *Public Administration Review* (March 1967), pp. 67–71, mentions this important innovation of PPBS, but does not give it the emphasis which it deserves.

2. Many of the pioneers of systems analysis are aware of some of these weaknesses. A number of them have left systems analysis and devote themselves to development of broader tools, mainly in the area of strategy and conflict studies (e.g., Herman Kahn and Albert Wohlstetter). Others, at the Rand Corporation, continue to broaden systems analysis by developing non-quantitative tools, such as the Delphi Method and Operational Gaming. See, for instance, Olaf Helmer, *Social Technology* (New York: Basic Books, 1966). Recently, some important and able efforts have also been made to examine explicitly the relations between systems analysis and the political process, though without adequate attention to required and possible changes in the methods of systems analysis, so as to adjust them to broader political issues. See, for instance, James R. Schlesinger, *Systems Analysis and the Political Process* (Santa Monica: Rand Corp., June 1967, p. 3,464). These are important, though too timid, steps on the way from systems analysis to policy analysis. But "systems analysis" as usually presented and as it appears in PPBS does not share the benefits of these first-step new advances.

3. The overwhelming influence of economic ideas influences even highly sophisticated political scientists to view political power as similar to economic resources while ignoring the critical differences—such as the often immediate power-producing effect of using political resources in the form of favors or coercive moves (see *Symposium*, p. 309). The economic models of resources which, for instance, can either be consumed or invented with continuous, concave, production possibility frontier curves do not apply to political power.

4. For the distinction between strategic planning, management control, and operational control, see Robert N. Anthony, *Planning and Control Systems: A Framework for Analysis* (Boston: Graduate School of Business Administration, Harvard University, 1965).

5. For the concept of "appreciative system" and its importance in public decision-making, see Sir Geoffrey Vickers, *The Art of Judgment: A Study of Policy Making* (New York: Basic Books, 1965), Chapter 4.

6. See Albert Wohlstetter, "Analysis and Design of Conflict Systems," in Edward S. Quade, ed., *Analysis for Military Decisions* (Chicago: Rand McNally, 1964), p. 106.

7. One weakness of the term "analysis" is its calculative-logical connotation. In policy analysis a very important part of the job is to invent new alternatives and to engage in creative and imaginative thinking. Nevertheless, I prefer a concept which somewhat understates the role rather than too presumptuous, too "political," and too frightening a term, such as "policy advertiser" or "policy consultant."

8. E.g., see Dennis Gabor, *Inventing the Future* (New York: Alfred A. Knopf, 1964) and Bertrand de Jouvenel, *The Art of Conjecture* (New York: Basic Books, 1967; French original published in 1964). For an application to political science, see Benjamin Akzin, "On Conjecture in Political Science," *Political Studies* (February 1966), pp. 1–14.

9. These methods are sometimes mentioned in passing, but are not at present actually integrated into systems analysis and PPBS, e.g., see *Symposium*, p. 262.

10. *Symposium*, p. 258.

11. For the concept, see Don K. Price, *The Scientific Estate* (Cambridge: Belknap Press of Harvard University Press, 1965), esp. pp. 123–126.

12. The tendency in systems analysis and PPBS to ignore organizational behavior is illustrated by the intention to rely on planned outputs as a standard for appraising actual outputs (*Symposium*, p. 275). As is well known, both from organization theory and from bitter experience, the defensive tendencies of organizations will operate to put planned output in line with expected output, well below optimal or even preferred outputs. The DOD may have been in some respects an exception as a result of its special structure, the personality of the Secretary of Defense, Presidential backing, and—perhaps most important of all—the external pressure of acute competition with active adversaries. But in ordinary organizations, cooperation by the senior executives is essential for significant changes in the quality of outputs. Interestingly enough, none of the papers in the *Symposium* mentions this requisite.

13. Compare Charles E. Lindblom, *The Intelligence of Democracy* (New York: Free Press, 1965).
14. The dangers of a nonaggregative view of policy-making are illustrated by doubtful conclusions in respect to the effects of the establishment of the Council of Economic Advisors (*Symposium*, p. 254) and of unrestricted federal grants-in-aid (*Symposium*, p. 268). See Edward S. Flash, Jr., *Economic Advice and Presidential Leadership* (New York: Columbia University Press, 1965), esp. chapters VIII, IX, and Walter W. Heller, *New Dimensions of Political Economy* (Cambridge: Harvard University Press, 1966), chapter III.
15. See Bertram M. Gross, *The State of the Nation: Social Systems Accounting* (Tavistock Publications Ltd., 1966). An earlier version is "The State of the Nation: Social Systems Accounting," in Raymond A. Bauer, ed., *Social Indicators* (Cambridge: The M.I.T. Press, 1966), pp. 154–271. See also Bertram M. Gross, ed., "Social Goals and Indicators for American Society." *Annals of the American Academy of Political and Social Science*, May 1967. At present, Senate hearings have already started on S-843, which proposes establishment of a council of social advisers and an annual social report of the President.
16. Some possibilities for doing so are illustrated by a seven-month graduate course for systems- and policy-analysis staff officers organized by the Israeli government as part of an effort to improve decision-making and administrative planning. See Yehezkel Dror, "Improvement of Decision-Making and Administrative Planning in the Israel Government Administration," in *Public Administration in Israel and Abroad 1966* (Jerusalem, 1967), pp. 121–131.
17. For an effort in this direction, see my book, *Public Policy-Making Reexamined (San Francisco: Chandler, 1967, in press).*

33

The Life Cycle of Bureaus

Anthony Downs

HOW BUREAUS COME INTO BEING

Types of Bureau Genesis

Bureaus are generally created in one of four different ways. First, a bureau can be formed by what Max Weber called the routinization of charisma.[1] A group of men brought together by their personal devotion to a charismatic leader may transform itself into a bureaucratic structure in order to perpetuate his ideas. Second, a bureau may be deliberately created almost out of nothing by one or more groups in society in order to carry out a specific function for which they perceive a need. Many of the agencies in the federal government formed during the New Deal years are of this type. Third, a new bureau can split off from an existing bureau, as the Air Force did from the Army after World War II. Fourth, a bureau may be created through "entrepreneurship" if a group of men promoting a particular policy (such as communism) gains enough support to establish and operate a large nonmarket organization devoted to that policy.

All of these geneses have three things in common: the bureau is initially dominated either by advocates or zealots, it normally goes through an early phase of rapid growth, and it must immediately

Source: From Anthony Downs, *Inside Bureaucracy*, pp. 5–23, copyright © 1967, 1966 by the RAND Corporation. Reprinted by permission of the publisher, Little, Brown and Company, and the RAND Corporation.

begin seeking sources of external support in order to survive.

Dominance by Advocates or Zealots in New Bureaus

In a vast majority of cases, a bureau starts as the result of aggressive agitation and action by a small group of zealots who have a specific idea they want to put into practice on a large scale. This is true by definition of bureaus created through "spontaneous entrepreneurship." Charismatic leaders also qualify as zealots. They attract a small group of disciples who eventually need to support themselves. This need tends to modify the original group into some more formal organization. In many cases, it becomes a predominantly bureaucratic organization. Thus, the Franciscan Order can be considered a bureaucratic offshoot from the leadership of St. Francis.

Almost every bureau formed by splitting off from an existing bureau is initially generated by the zealotry of a few members of the existing bureau. Some zealots are found in all bureaus—indeed, in almost all human organizations. This is true because the personal characteristics necessary for zealotry occur spontaneously in a certain fraction of any society's population. This fraction is higher in modern societies than in tradition-oriented societies, since the former encourage innovation in general. Also, the proportion of zealots in a given bureau may differ sharply from that in society as a whole, because some bureaus tend to attract zealots and others to repel them. As a result, the proportion of zealots in different bureaus varies widely. Nevertheless, a certain number appear spontaneously in every bureau.

When a group of such zealots somehow conceive a new function they believe their bureau should undertake, they form a nucleus agitating for change. Enthused by their idea, they persuade their superiors to give them some resources and manpower to develop it. If their efforts prove successful, they gradually enlarge their operations. For these operations to generate a new bureau, they must be technically distinct from the other activities of the parent bureau. As the practitioners of the new specialty become more immersed in it, their terminology, interests, and even policy outlooks become more unlike those of the remainder of the parent bureau. Hence a growing conflict usually springs up between these two groups. The new specialists eventually become convinced that they cannot fully exploit the potentialities of their operations within the parent bureau. This marks a critical stage in the life of the new section. It can either be suppressed by the traditionalists, or be successful in breaking off into a new bureau. The key factor is the amount of support the new section generates outside of the parent bureau. If the new section's leaders can establish a strong clientele or power base beyond the control of their immediate superiors, then they have some leverage in agitating for relative autonomy. In some cases, they will establish autonomy very quickly; in others it will take years of struggle and a strong push from the external environment. But in all cases, it is purposeful agitation by men specifically interested in promoting a given program that generates the splitting off of new bureaus from existing ones (or new sections within a bureau from existing sections). Hence the new bureau (or section) is initially dominated by the zealots whose efforts have brought it into being.

Only in bureaus created out of nothing by external agents is there initially no "small band of warriors" whose agitation has founded the bureau. In this case, politicians, existing bureaucrats, or members of private firms or unions have discerned the need for a new organization designed to accomplish a specific purpose. They round up the legal authority to establish this organization, select someone to run it, and give him an initial set of resources. Examples of such creation are the Commodity Credit Corporation[2] and the new campuses of the University of California.

However, new bureaus thus formed out of nothing usually behave very much like those formed around a nucleus of zealots. The ideas upon which a new bureau is based have generally originated with some group of zealots. In many cases, the leading proponents of these ideas are immediately put in charge of the bureau. In any case, whoever is running a bureau entrusted with a new function soon finds that his recruiting efforts are most successful with men who have a proclivity toward that function—including the zealots who started the idea, or their disciples. Moreover, since the top administrator and his staff will normally be judged by their success in carrying out this function, they also tend to become strong advocates themselves.

The Struggle for Autonomy

No bureau can survive unless it is continually able to demonstrate that its services are worthwhile to some group with influence over sufficient resources to keep it alive. If it is supported by voluntary contributions, it must impress potential contributors with the desirability of sacrificing resources to obtain its services. If it is a government bureau, it must impress those politicians who control the budget that its functions generate political support or meet vital social needs.

Generation of such external support is particularly crucial for a new bureau. True, some "new" bureaus have already succeeded in gaining support, or else they would not have been able to split off from their parent agency. Similarly, an organization created by entrepreneurship can grow large enough to qualify as a bureau only if it has external support. Even bureaus formed by the routinization of charisma have attracted outside support because of the personal magnetism of their original leader. Thus only bureaus created almost out of nothing come into being without already having provided valuable services for "outsiders." Even they have some ready-made sources of external support, since their functions were being demanded by someone.

Yet the survival of new bureaus is often precarious. Their initial external sources of support are usually weak, scattered, and not accustomed to relations with the bureau. The latter must therefore rapidly organize so that its services become very valuable to the users. Only in this way can it motivate users to support it.

Once the users of the bureau's services have become convinced of their gains from it, and have developed routinized relations with it, the bureau can rely upon a certain amount of inertia to keep on generating the external support it needs. But in the initial stages of its life, it must concentrate on developing these "automatic" support generators. This critical drive for autonomy will determine whether or not it will survive in the long run.

This does not mean that members of the new bureau are interested solely in its survival. In fact, they are more interested in performing its social functions. This follows from the fact that the new bureau is initially dominated by advocates or zealots, who are not primarily motivated by self-interest.

In some cases, the social functions involved are inherently incapable of generating external support in the long run. For example, a bureau set up to plan a specific operation (such as the invasion of Normandy) eliminates its external support when it carries out its function. However, most bureaus have functions that cannot be adequately discharged in the long run if the bureaus do not continue to exist. Hence even pure altruism would lead their top officials to be vitally concerned about bureau survival.

To this motive must be added the motive of self-interest described by Peter Clark and James Wilson: "Few [organizations] disband willingly, as neither executives nor members are eager to end an activity that rewards them."[3] Thus officials in almost every new bureau place a high priority on creating conditions that will insure the bureau's survival.

As Clark and Wilson point out, bureau survival is closely related to the creation of relative autonomy by each bureau:

> The proliferation of associations and the division of labor in society has meant that there is almost no way for an organization to preserve itself by simply seeking ends for which there are no other advocates. Thus, the maintenance of organizational autonomy is a critical problem. By *autonomy* we refer to the extent to which an organization possesses a distinctive area of competence, a clearly demarcated clientele or membership, and undisputed jurisdiction over a function, service, goal, issue, or cause. Organizations seek to make their environment stable and certain and to remove threats to their identities. Autonomy gives an organization a reasonably stable claim to resources and thus places it in a more favorable position from which to compete for those resources. *Resources* include issues and causes as well as money, time, effort, and names.[4]

Rapid Growth of Young Bureaus

Few bureaus ever achieve such perfect autonomy that they are immune from threats to their survival. However, a bureau can attain a certain initial degree of security as noted above. This presupposes that it has become large enough to render useful services, and old enough to have established routinized relationships with its major clients. We will refer to these minimal size and age levels as the bureau's *initial survival threshold.*

There is always a certain time interval between the beginnings of a bureau and the attainment of the initial survival threshold. Sometimes this period occurs before its formal "birth" as a separate organization. In other cases, a bureau's fight to reach the threshold begins with its formal establishment.

As a general rule, a bureau arrives at this threshold after a period of rapid growth in both its size and the relative social significance of its functions. This usually occurs in response to external environmental conditions favorable to the expansion of the bureau's functions. For example, the Army Air Force grew extremely rapidly during World War II in response to the need for military air power. This experience convinced Congress (stimulated by members of the Army Air Force seeking autonomy) that it should establish a separate Air Force. The formal birth of the Air Force thus marked the end of its critical creation period, which began in the 1920s.

For bureaus that do not develop by splitting off from existing agencies, rapid growth normally occurs immediately after they have been formally born as separate agencies. The leaders of such a new bureau must quickly serve enough customers to reach an initial survival threshold before their original allocation of resources is exhausted, or its replenishment is blocked.

Bureaus created through entrepreneurship are generally not successful until the zeal of the nucleus group coincides with environmental conditions favorable to the function they are promoting. Then other agents in society bestow enough resources on this nucleus so it can rapidly expand to meet the need its members have long been advocating.

Bureaus formed through the routinization of charisma generally do not experience rapid expansion until after the attraction of the charismatic leader has been transformed into organizational machinery. In most religions, this has not occurred until after the original leader's death.

Whatever its origin, a fledgling bureau is most vulnerable to annihilation by its enemies immediately before it attains its initial survival threshold. Then it has not yet generated enough external support to resist severe attacks.

Since most organizations have both functional and allocational rivals, the possibility that a bureau will be destroyed by its enemies is a real one. Its *functional* rivals are other agencies whose social functions are competitive with those of the bureau itself. Private power companies are competitive in this way with the Rural Electrification Administration. Its *allocational* rivals are other agencies who compete with it for resources, regardless of their functional relationships with it. In government, all bureaus supported by the same fund-raising agency (such as Congress) are allocationally competitive. In the private sector, allocational competition is usually indirect. The community fund, for example, competes with all forms of private expenditure for consumers' dollars. Thus the general scarcity of resources makes almost everyone an enemy of a new bureau unless it can demonstrate its usefulness to him. A bureau's infancy therefore nearly always involves a fight to gain resources in spite of this latent hostility.

If the new bureau has strong functional rivals, or if it is designed to regulate or inhibit the activities of powerful social agents, then it will be severely opposed from the start. These antagonists often seek to capture the new bureau's functions themselves, or suppress them altogether. Hence they try to block it from establishing a strong external power base. The bureau may have to fight strongly during its infancy to avoid being disbanded or swallowed by some larger existing bureau.

Some bureaus never succeed in reaching their initial survival threshold but may exist for years in a state of continuous jeopardy. An example is the Civilian Defense Agency, which has recently been swallowed by the Army. Such agencies have been unable to establish firm autonomy largely because they have no strong clientele with power in the U.S. political system. Their functions do not endow them with a host of well-organized domestic beneficiaries, or a powerful set of suppliers with no alternative markets (such as the suppliers of the Department of Defense). Thus, the single most important determinant of whether a bureau can establish autonomy (and how fast it can do so) is the character of its power setting. If its suppliers or beneficiaries are strong and well organized in comparison with its rivals and sufferers, then it will probably quickly gain a clearly autonomous position.

THE DYNAMICS OF GROWTH

The Cumulative Effects of Growth or Decline

The major causes of both growth and decline in bureaus are rooted in exogenous factors in their environment. As society develops over time, certain social functions grow in prominence and others decline. Bureaus are inevitably affected more strongly by these external developments than by any purely internal changes. However, the interplay between external and internal developments tends to create certain cumulative effects of growth or decline. They occur because bureaus can experience significant changes in the character of their personnel in relatively short periods of time. In spite of the career nature of bureau employment, there is often a considerable turnover of personnel in specific bureaus. Also, growth that doubles or triples the size of a bureau in a short time can swiftly alter its whole structure and character.

1. *Dominance in Bureaus.* A shift in only a small proportion of the officials in a bureau can have a profound effect upon its operations. If most of the officials occupying key positions in a bureau are of one type (that is, conservers, climbers, and so on), then the bureau and its behavior will be *dominated* by the traits typical of that type. This relatively small group of key officials can exercise dominance even if a majority of bureau members are of other types.

The possibility of a few men dominating the activities and "spirit" of a whole bureau arises because its hierarchical structure tends to concentrate power disproportionately at the top. In some situations, however, it is difficult to tell whether a bureau really is dominated by one type, or is staffed by such a mixture of officials that no one type is dominant.

2. *The Growth Accelerator Effect.* Let us imagine a bureau in a state of "perfect equilibrium" with a zero growth rate over time. Suddenly its social function becomes much more important than it had been. As a result, the bureau's sovereign and other agents in its environment direct it to expand its activities and staff rapidly, giving it the resources to do so. An example is NASA's experience shortly after Sputnik I.

Any organization experiencing rapid overall growth provides many more opportunities for promotion in any given time period than a static one. New supervisory positions are created, thereby attracting new personnel who are interested in rapid promotion; that is, climbers. At the same time conservers will not be drawn to fast-growing bureaus, or may even be repelled by them, because rapid growth is normally accompanied by uncertainty, constant shuffling of organizational structure, and hard work.[5] As a result, fast-growing bureaus will experience a rising proportion of climbers and a declining proportion of conservers. Moreover, this proportional increase in climbers will be larger in high-level positions than in the bureau as a whole. Climbers will rise faster because they deliberately pursue promotion more than others. They are much more innovation-prone than conservers, and the bureau needs innovators in order to carry out its newly expanded functions. Hence objective "natural selection" within the bureau, as well as the subjective selection caused by differences in personal motivation, will cause climbers to be selected for promotion faster than conservers. This means that the prominence of climbers (and other innovation-prone officials such as zealots and advocates) will increase in a fast-growing bureau, even if that bureau is initially dominated by conservers.

The bureau becomes continuously more willing and able to innovate and to expand its assigned social functions by inventing new ones or "capturing" those now performed by other less dynamic organizations. Such further expansion tends to open up even more opportunities for promotion. This in turn attracts more climbers, who make the bureau still more willing and able to innovate and expand, and so on. Rapid growth of a bureau's social functions thus leads to a cumulative change in the character of its personnel which tends to accelerate its rate of growth still further.

3. *Brakes on Acceleration.* This growth acceleration soon runs into serious obstacles. First, even though the bureau's original social function expanded greatly in relative importance, that function must still compete allocationally with others for social attention and resources. Therefore, as the accelerating bureau grows larger, it encounters more and more resistance to further relative growth of this function at the expense of other activities in society. This has certainly happened to NASA.

Second, the ever-expanding bureau soon engenders hostility and antagonism from functionally competitive bureaus. Its attempt to grow by taking over their functions is a direct threat to their autonomy. Hence the total amount of bureaucratic opposition to the expansion of any one bureau rises the more it tries to take over the functions of existing bureaus.

Third, the bureau encounters the difficulty of continuing to produce impressive results as its organization grows larger and more unwieldy. The bureau cannot generate external support (except among its suppliers) without producing services beneficial to someone outside its own members. Therefore, a bureau must periodically come up with impressive results if it wishes to sustain its growth. NASA's staging of dramatic events at well-spaced intervals illustrates this concept. But as the bureau grows larger and takes on more functions, it often becomes increasingly difficult to produce such convincing results. Increased size and complexity cause greater difficulties of planning and coordination. Also, a higher proportion of the efforts of top-echelon officials will be devoted to coordination and planning. This means that the best talent in the bureau will be diverted away from action into administration.

As the bureau gets larger, the average level of talent therein is likely to decline. This level may initially rise as ambitious and promotion-oriented climbers flow into it during the first phase of its fast growth. This is especially likely because of a certain "critical mass" effect. It is hard for a bureau to recruit one well-known physicist when it has none; but once it has two or three, others are attracted by the chance to work with this distinguished team. Nevertheless, the tendency for average talent to rise with growth eventually reverses itself. Once the bureau has all the high-level talent it can command during its first stages of growth, it must satisfy itself with lesser talent as it grows even larger. True, if the bureau expands into entirely different fields, it can start all over again at the top of the talent list. Hence, this growth-braking effect is less serious if the bureau grows by taking on new or different functions than if it grows by performing one set of functions more intensively.

Fourth, conflicts among the climbers who flood into a fast-growing bureau provide an internal check. As the proportion of climbers rises, a higher proportion of their efforts is devoted to internal politics and rivalry rather than performance of their social functions. This also tends to reduce the bureau's ability to provide impressive demonstrations of its efficiency.

The declining ability to produce impressive results as the bureau grows larger may be offset for a time by increasing economies of scale. Such economies may enable the bureau to produce more outputs per unit of input, but they do not reduce the amount of external opposition generated by every attempt to expand the bureau's total inputs. Eventually these factors choke off accelerated (or perhaps all) growth. This prevents the bureau from expanding indefinitely once it has experienced an initial spurt of high-speed growth.

4. *The Decelerator Effort.* Whenever the relative growth rate of a bureau declines below the average for all bureaus, its personnel may change in ways almost exactly opposite to those that make up the growth accelerator. This *decelerator effect* is most likely to occur when the bureau is forced to reduce its total membership because of a sharp drop in the relative significance of its social function. Such a decline, stagnation, or just slower than average growth tends to reduce the opportunity for promotion within the bureau to a level below that prevailing in comparable organizations. This will usually serve notice for climbers to depart. However, not all climbers have skills that are easily transferable to other organizations. Such transferability is an important factor determining the climber's mobility from bureau to bureau. Still, in most cases, many climbers will respond to a sharp decline in the bureau's growth rate by jumping to other bureaus. Also, those who have reached high positions in the bureau will lose hope of climbing much higher, and will tend to become conservers instead of climbers. Such changes reduce the proportion of climbers in the bureau and increase the proportion of conservers in key positions. As a result, the entire bureau will shift toward greater conserver dominance, thereby reducing its ability to innovate and the desire to expand its functions. Then, whenever opportunities for innovation or function-expansion do present themselves, the bureau will be less able, or willing, to take advantage of them. It may even lose functions to other more aggressive and innovation-prone bureaus. Thus, once a bureau starts to shrink, or even just experiences an abnormally slow growth rate over an extensive period, it sets in motion forces that tend to make it shrink even faster, or grow even more slowly.

However, this decelerator effect is not entirely symmetrical with the growth accelerator for the following reasons. First, the climbers who are left in the bureau will still tend to rise faster than nonclimbers. Second, the number of top jobs (which are soon occupied by climbers) will go up faster during acceleration periods than it goes down during deceleration periods. Third, since all types of officials, including conservers, resist shrinkage in their importance of resources, the resistance aroused by reductions in bureau size tends to be stronger than the enthusiasm caused by growth. Accelerators and decelerators cause more of a ratchet movement in the life of a single bureau than a smooth up-and-down curve.

These factors function as checks on the tendency of the decelerator to reduce the size of a bureau once it has stopped growing. The fact that reduction of a bureau's services below some minimal level will create strong protests from its direct beneficiaries serves as another check.

5. *"Qualitative Growth" without expansion.*[6] A logical deduction from our accelerator and decelerator principles is that slow-growing or stable organizations of a certain type will generally be staffed by less talented personnel (in terms of innovation ability) than fast-growing organizations of the same type. However, this conclusion seems at variance with the experience of U.S. university faculties. In recent years, the fastest expansion in total faculty size has occurred at state-financed schools, yet

nearly all measures of faculty quality show that the best-rated private universities have managed to maintain a higher caliber than their faster-growing state rivals. The reason for this is that these private universities have experienced rapid qualitative growth without quantitative expansion.

What really attracts climbers is not promotion *per se,* but increased power, income, and prestige. Normally, bureaus offer their members these perquisites primarily through promotion. They can usually promote many people rapidly only if fast growth creates more high-level positions. However, if the organization in essence promotes everyone simultaneously by increasing the power, income, and prestige of nearly all its members without growing larger, it can achieve the same effects. This is precisely what top-level private universities have accomplished. They have continued to offer both new recruits and existing faculty members higher salaries, more freedom from bureaucratic interference, and greater time for research than their state-financed rivals. Moreover, the extremely high turnover in most university faculties has made it possible to offer low-level members relatively rapid increases in rank without either expanding, forcibly ejecting present high-ranking members, or drastically increasing the ratio of high-ranking to low-ranking positions.

An organization can maintain high-quality personnel (in terms of innovation ability) even if it does not experience relatively rapid growth in size, so long as it experiences such growth in the incentives it offers its members. But this implies that it receives ever more resources from its environment for performing tasks requiring no more man-hours of input. This can happen only if the value of the members' outputs per man-hour of input rises sharply. Normally, such increased productivity occurs only when there is a dramatic increase in the relative social value of the organization's function. Again, this is precisely what has been going on at top-level private universities. As the total number of students seeking higher education has shot upward, the demand for education at the best-rated schools has zoomed even faster. Moreover, an increased emphasis on basic research occurred at the same time, thanks to the impact of Sputnik I. Therefore, top-level private universities have been able both to raise their tuitions and to attract larger research grants. These added funds have made it possible for them to up-grade the incentives offered to their faculties without experiencing rapid growth in size.

6. *Some Effects of Rapid Growth in a Fragmentalized Bureaucracy Carrying Out a Single Function.* The above discussion of universities illustrates the operation of *fragmentalized systems of bureaus* all carrying out the same function. Some bureaus enjoy a relative monopoly of responsibility for social functions in a given area. Examples are the U.S. Post Office Department and the Soviet Army. Other bureaus are individual units in much larger fragmentalized systems of organizations serving a single major social function. Relatively pure examples are universities and churches. Less pure examples are elementary and high schools and local governments in metropolitan areas. They have a monopoly in a given area, but their clients can and do move in order to be within the jurisdiction of the particular bureau whose services they desire.

When there is a rapid growth in the relative social importance of the function served by such a system, the system as a whole normally expands to meet this increased demand. This can involve the addition of new bureaus to the system, the expansion of existing bureaus, or both. Under such conditions, the "laws" of acceleration and deceleration we have set forth above apply to the system as a whole rather than just to individual units therein. Thus, the great relative increase in demand for university faculty members has resulted in the attraction of many climbers into this field whose counterparts in former years went into business or other fields.

The "top" of the system to which climbers rise rapidly consists of positions that provide the highest levels of income, prestige, power, and other perquisites. It is at least conceivable that these top positions may be disproportionately concentrated within a few bureaus. This is particularly likely if the demand for the highest quality of service provided by the system has risen even faster than the demand for its service as a whole. In such a case, the particular bureaus providing the highest quality of service may be able to increase their incomes (by getting more appropriations, more donations, and higher prices) faster than the system as a whole. Then they can offer their members a more rapid upgrading of incentives than the rest of the system. As a result, the most ambitious climbers will gravitate to these top-ranking bureaus, even if they do not individually expand in size. In fact, by deliberately refusing to expand, these bureaus can avoid the dilution of these top-quality personnel with the less-talented people necessary to staff rapid quantitative growth. This will reinforce their reputations for high quality, and thereby attract even higher demand for their services.

This is approximately what has happened among universities. The situation is complicated by the fact that universities depend significantly upon voluntary quid pro quo transactions for their incomes, and are therefore only quasi-bureaucratic in terms of our definition. However, the foregoing analysis illustrates that the basic conclusions made here about bureaus apply to those in fragmentalized systems too, but must sometimes be considered applicable to the system as a whole rather than individual bureaus therein.

Why Bureaus Seek to Expand

C. Northcote Parkinson's famous first law states that, "Work expands so as to fill the time available for its completion."[7] Its major corollary further adds that, "In any public administrative department not actually at war, the staff increase . . . will invariably prove to be between 5.17 per cent and 6.56 per cent (per year), irrespective of any variation in the amount of work (if any) to be done."[8] These humorous views express a widely prevalent notion that bureaus have an inherent tendency to expand, regardless of whether or not there is any genuine need for more of their services. In fact, all organizations have inherent tendencies to expand. What sets bureaus apart is that they do not have as many restraints upon expansion, nor do their restraints function as automatically.

The major reasons why bureaus inherently seek to expand are as follows:

- An organization that is rapidly expanding can attract more capable personnel, and more easily retain its most capable existing personnel, than can one that is expanding very slowly, stagnating, or shrinking. This principle was examined in the preceding section.
- The expansion of any organization normally provides its leaders with increased power, income, and prestige; hence they encourage its growth. Conservers are the only exception, for they place little value on gaining more status for themselves.[9] This principle does not imply that larger organizations necessarily have more power or prestige than smaller ones. Rather, it

implies that the leaders of any given organization can normally increase their power, income, and prestige by causing their organization to grow larger.

- Growth tends to reduce internal conflicts in an organization by allowing some (or all) of its members to increase their personal status without lowering that of others. Therefore, organizational leaders encourage expansion to maximize morale and minimize internal conflicts. Every bureau's environment changes constantly, thereby shifting the relative importance of the social functions performed by its various parts, and the resources appropriate to each part. Such shifts will be resisted by the sections losing resources. But these dissensions can be reduced if some sections are given more resources without any losses being experienced by others.
- Increasing the size of an organization may also improve the quality of its performance (per unit of output) and its chances for survival. Hence both loyalty and self-interest can encourage officials to promote organizational growth. As William H. Starbuck has pointed out in his analysis of organizational growth, there may be significant operational advantages to being a very large organization.[10] Among these are the following:

  —The organization may achieve economies of scale through greater specialization, ability to use up excess capacities, and reduction of stochastic errors through increasing sample sizes.

  —Large organizations have a better chance of survival than small ones.

  —Large organizations are harder to change than small ones (because they embody greater sunk costs); so they tend to be more resistant to external pressures. They also spend more on research and development (both in total and per employee), hence they can better develop new techniques useful in augmenting their power.

  —Very large organizations can impose a certain degree of stability upon their external environment, whereas smaller ones cannot. Increased environmental stability reduces uncertainty and anxiety and solidifies the control of high-ranking officials.

- Finally because there is no inherent quid pro quo in bureau activity enabling officials to weigh the marginal return from further spending against its marginal cost, the incentive structure facing most officials provides much greater rewards for increasing expenditures than for reducing them. Hence officials are encouraged to expand their organization through greater spending. The basis for this asymmetry of incentives will be explained in Chapters III and IX. Unlike the other sources of growth-pressure described above, this one is not found in most market-oriented organizations.

The Effects of Age upon Bureaus

Bureaus, like men, change in predictable ways as they grow older. Following are the most important such changes, and their effects.

Bureaus learn to perform given tasks better with experience. Given the initial level of resources allocated to the bureau, this increased efficiency in effect allows the bureau to generate additional productive capacity just by growing older, without any added input of resources. The added capacity can be utilized by producing more of the same services, by absorbing the new capacity as organizational slack, or by devoting it to creating new functions or seeking to "capture" existing ones from other bureaus. Another possibility—cutting inputs—is unlikely, since all officials avoid reducing the resources under their control. It must be remembered that when a new process is undertaken, learning at first produces great economies, but the "learning curve" soon tends to flatten out.

As bureaus grow older, they tend to develop more formalized rule systems covering more and more of the possible situations they are likely to encounter. The passage of time exposes the bureau to a wide variety of situations, and it learns how to deal with most of them more effectively than it did in its youth. The desire for organizational memory of this experience causes the bureau's officials to develop more and more elaborate rules. These rules have three main effects. First, they markedly improve the performance of the bureau regarding situations previously encountered, and make the behavior of each of its parts both more stable and more predictable to its other parts. Second, they tend to divert the attention of officials from achieving the social functions of the bureau to conforming to its rules—the "goal displacement" described by sociologists. Third, they increase the bureau's structural complexity, which in turn strengthens its inertia because of greater sunk costs in current procedures. The resulting resistance to change further reduces the bureau's ability to adjust to new circumstances. Consequently, older bureaus tend to be more stable and less flexible than young ones.

As a bureau grows older, its officials tend to shift the emphasis of their goals from carrying out the bureau's social functions to insuring its survival and growth as an autonomous institution. When a bureau is first created, it is usually dominated by zealots or strong advocates who focus their attention upon accomplishing its social functions. As it grows older, its rules and administrative machinery become more complex and more extensive, demanding more attention from top officials. The conservers in the bureau tend to become more important because they are oriented toward preserving rules. Zealots become less important, because they are uninterested in administration and poor at allocating resources impartially.

As a bureau ages, its officials become more willing to modify the bureau's original formal goals in order to further the survival and growth of its administrative machinery.[11] This shift of emphasis is encouraged by the creation of career commitments among a bureau's more senior officials (in terms of service). The longer they have worked for the bureau, the more they wish to avoid the costs of finding a new job, losing rank and seniority, and fitting themselves into a new informal structure. Hence they would rather alter the bureau's formal goals than admit that their jobs should be abolished because the original goals have been attained or are no longer important.

As a bureau grows older, the number and proportion of administrative officials therein tends to rise. This tendency has been demonstrated by Starbuck in his analysis of the effects of longevity upon bureaus.[12] The main reasons why this shift to administration occurs as a function of age rather than size are as follows. First, administrators tend to have more job security and stability than production workers, partly because administrators are usually more senior in rank. Therefore, whenever attrition in personnel occurs, nonadministrative officials are normally discharged first. The longer a bureau has survived, the more likely it is to have lived through a number of such shrinkages in the past. Second, the older a bureau is, the more different types of functions it is likely to carry out. As a result, a higher proportion of the bureau's personnel must be engaged in coordination. Third, until recent developments in the technology of business machines, production jobs were historically subject to a greater mechanization than administrative jobs. The older a bureau is, the more time it has been exposed to these effects of technical change.

If a bureau experiences a period of relative stability in total size following a period of rapid growth, the average age of its members tends to rise as the bureau grows older. This tends to increase the influence of conservers in the bureau, for many officials of other types are likely to become conservers as they grow older. The next section of this chapter discusses this in detail.

These effects of age upon a bureau lead to the Law of Increasing Conservatism: *All organizations tend to become more conservative as they get older, unless they experience periods of very rapid growth or internal turnover.* This principle is especially applicable to bureaus because they are relatively insulated from competition.

From this Law and the other effects of age examined, we can draw the following additional conclusions:

- The older a bureau is, the less likely it is to die. This is true because its leaders become more willing to shift major purposes in order to keep the bureau alive.
- The best time to "kill" a bureau is as soon as possible after it comes into existence.
- In general, the older a bureau is, the broader the scope of the social functions it serves. If a bureau is relatively long-lived, it has usually survived sizable fluctuations in the importance of its various social functions. Its initial functions declined in relative importance, pressuring its leaders to take on new functions. However, it probably did not relinquish its original ones. Therefore, as time passes, bureaus, like private firms, tend to diversify to protect themselves from fluctuations in demand.

The "Age Lump" Phenomenon and Its Effects

One of the effects of increasing age upon a bureau is the tendency of the average age of the bureau's members to rise. Earlier, this chapter showed that almost every bureau goes through a period of rapid growth right before it reaches its initial survival threshold. During this period, it usually contains a high proportion of zealots (because they established it) and climbers (because they are attracted by fast growth). These people, moreover, tend to be relatively young, for youthful officials are more optimistic and full of initiative than older ones.

Soon after this initial spurt, the growth rate slows down, and the bureau is likely to enter a "growth plateau." This means that a high proportion of its total membership consists of the persons who joined it during the fast-growth period (unless it has a very high turnover). This group constitutes a "lump" of personnel, all about the same age. As they grow older, the average age of the bureau's members rises too, since they form such a large fraction of its total membership. This creates the following significant effects:

- There is a squeeze on the members of the age lump regarding promotions because so many of them attain the necessary qualifications all at once. Not all who are objectively suitable for promotion to the few high-level posts can be shifted upwards. Hence relatively low-level jobs continue to be occupied by very senior people.
- A high proportion of the bureau's membership tends to be changed into conservers because of increasing age and the frustration of ambitions for promotion. In any organization, officials tend to become conservers as they get older if they are not in the mainstream of promotion to the top. Hence the whole bureau tends to become more conserver-dominated as members of this lump become older.
- The squeeze on promotions tends to drive many climbers out of the organization into faster-growing organizations (if any alternatives are available). The proportion of conservers in the bureau tends to rise for this reason too. The most talented officials are the most likely to leave, since they

naturally have more opportunities elsewhere. The bureau, therefore, becomes ever more dominated by mediocrity, unless there are really no alternative organizations to join (for example, the Russian Communist Party has no competitors within Russia).

- Up to the period just before most members of the age lump retire, it will be very difficult to attract able young people into the bureau. Climbers will be discouraged from joining because they see that the road upward is already clogged. Zealots will be discouraged by the conserver-domination of the bureau. However, when the main portions of the age lump are about to retire, the prospects of so many top-level jobs being suddenly vacated may attract both climbers and zealots.
- The bureau will experience a crisis of continuity when the age lump arrives at the normal retirement age. Almost all of the upper echelons will suddenly be vacated by members of the group that will have dominated the bureau's policies for many years. As a result, the bureau will go through a time of troubles as its remaining members struggle for control over its policies and resources.
- Many of these rather unfavorable consequences of age lumps can be offset by the following events:

  —Additional spurts of rapid growth, which produce multiple age lumps within the bureau.

  —Speeded-up retirement of bureau members who are not promoted. The U.S. Armed Forces used some version of this up-or-out system to counteract the lumps in their age structures resulting from World War II.

  —Purges of upper-level officials.

  —Survival of the bureau over such a long period that the original age lump tends to be replaced by a more even age distribution.

- Because growth in many bureaus normally occurs in uneven spurts rather than at a steady pace, age lumps and their consequences are widespread phenomena.

The Death of Bureaus

The ability of bureaus to outlive their real usefulness is part of the mythology of bureaucracy. Our theory supplies several reasons why bureaus—particularly government bureaus—rarely disappear once they have passed their initial survival thresholds.

Normally, organizations die because they fail to perform social functions of enough importance to make their members or clientele willing to sacrifice the resources necessary to maintain those functions. Such an inability can occur for three reasons: the specific functions performed by the organization decline in relative importance; the functions remain important but the organization is unable to perform them efficiently; or the functions remain important but some other organization performs them better. When the demise of a bureau is caused by the first two of these conditions, the bureau tends to disappear altogether. However, when its death is caused by the capture of its functions by another organization, the bureau's members are sometimes transferred to the other organization. In such cases, the bureau is swallowed and continues to live after a fashion.

There are several reasons why bureaus are unlikely to die once they have become firmly established:

- Bureaus are often willing to shift functions in order to survive; hence the relative decline of their initial social functions will not kill them if they are agile enough to undertake new and more viable functions before it is too late.
- The nature of bureaus leads their clients to create pressure to maintain them after their usefulness no longer justifies their costs. A bureau's clients normally receive its services without making full (or any) direct payments for them. These clients, therefore, pressure the central allocation agency to continue the bureau's services,

even if they would be unwilling to pay for those services directly if they had to bear their full costs.

- A few of the clients or suppliers of nearly every bureau receive such large and irreplaceable net benefits from the bureau's services that they will continue to demand those services even if the marginal benefits thereof have declined below the marginal cost for most clients. Government bureaus are especially likely to have such zealous clients, since they usually perform services that cannot be duplicated by private agents acting alone. Defense contractors, for example, are unlikely to find any private buyers for missiles or space vehicles.
- The absence of any explicit quid pro quo relationship between bureau costs and benefits tends to conceal situations in which the costs of maintaining the bureau outweigh its benefits. This often allows the natural proclivity of any organization's members to keep the organization alive to function successfully even when the bureau really "ought" to die.
- Bureaus tend to be less willing to engage in all-out conflicts with each other than private profit-making firms; hence they are less likely to kill each other. Private firms are more willing to engage in struggles to the death than bureaus for two main reasons. First, in freely competitive markets containing a large number of small firms, intense competition is relatively impersonal and is a prerequisite to survival. In contrast, when one bureau "invades" the territory of another, this is a deliberate act aimed at a specific opponent. In essence, bureaus resemble large oligopolistic firms. Like such firms, they try to avoid all-out wars because they are too costly to all involved. Second, if two or more bureaus engage in a "war" concerning control over certain social functions, they inevitably attract the attention of the government's central allocation agencies (both executive and legislative). This is extremely hazardous because the bureau's opponents are sure to call attention to some of its major shortcomings. Moreover, top officials in every bureau fear any detailed investigation, since it is almost certain to uncover embarrassing actions.
- Experience shows that the "death rate" among both bureaus and large oligopolistic firms is extremely low. This demonstrates that the single most important reason why bureaus so rarely die is that they are large, and all large organizations have high survival rates. Large organizations can withstand greater absolute fluctuations in available resources than small ones, and they also enjoy certain other advantages set forth earlier in this chapter. Hence size, rather than type of function, is the number one determinant of survival. Since all bureaus are large by definition, and the vast majority of business firms are small, direct comparisons of the overall death rates among bureaus and private firms are bound to be misleading.
- Even if a bureau cannot muster sufficient external support to continue as an autonomous agency, it might survive by getting some other aggrandizing bureau to swallow it.
- Despite the low death rates of bureaus within their own cultures, very few bureaus—or organizations of any kind—have managed to survive for really long periods of time, that is, hundreds of years. Most government bureaus disappear when the particular government that created them is replaced as did Roman bureaus. Similarly, private bureaus do not usually outlive the cultures that spawn them. Churches and universities seem to be the hardiest species, as the Roman Catholic Church and Oxford University illustrate.

NOTES

1. Max Weber, *The Theory of Social and Economic Organization,* trans. A. M. Henderson and Talcott Parsons (New York: The Free Press of Glencoe, 1947), pp. 363 ff.
2. For an account of the origin of the Commodity Credit Corporation, see Arthur M. Schlesinger, Jr., *The Coming of the New Deal* (Boston: Houghton Mifflin, 1959), pp. 61–67.
3. Peter B. Clark and James Q. Wilson, "Incentive Systems: A Theory of Organizations,"

Administrative Science Quarterly (September 1961), p. 157.

4. *Ibid.*, p. 158.

5. Of course, if there is a great deal of unemployment, all types of officials who do not have jobs may be drawn to an expanding bureau.

6. I am indebted to Professor George Stigler of the University of Chicago for raising the problem of university faculties, and thereby stimulating the development of this section.

7. C. Northcote Parkinson, *Parkinson's Law and Other Studies in Administration* (Boston: Houghton Mifflin, 1962), p. 2.

8. *Ibid.*, p. 12.

9. This inherent cause of bureau growth is essentially identical to William J. Baumol's argument that the managers of profit-making corporations try to maximize sales within a minimum-profit constraint. See William J. Baumol, "On the Theory of Expansion of the Firm," *American Economic Review* 52 (December 1962), pp. 1,078–1,087.

10. William H. Starbuck, "Organizational Growth and Development," in *Handbook of Organizations*, ed. J. G. March (Chicago: Rand McNally, 1964).

11. *Ibid.*, p. 303.

12. *Ibid.*, p. 366–376.

34
Public Administration in a Time of Revolution

Dwight Waldo

I want to address myself to subjects such as these: *Are* we in a time of revolution? Assuming we are—as I shall argue—how is public administration responding? Ought public administration to respond more than it is? *How* should public administration respond? What course does an intelligent and judicious blend of self-interest and altruism, of realistic appraisal and idealistic commitment indicate that we follow? I shall be asking more questions than I answer, even in a summary way. I won't even claim to be entirely consistent in what I say.

CONTEMPORARY "REVOLUTIONS"

First, to the subject of whether we *are* in a time of revolutions. Let me concede to begin with that there is ample opportunity for illusion and self-delusion. There is a tendency, of course, for every generation to regard its own troubles as unique and unmanageable. One of the nice witticisms of recent years has Adam saying to Eve, "My dear, you must appreciate that we live in a time of unprecedented change and upheaval." But to sustain the position that one is talking about an unstable and threatening world and not merely reflecting his own disturbed psyche there would seem to be—unfortunately—"objective evidence" enough.

The question of whether we are in a time of revolutions has both a semantic and an empirical side. As to the semantic, a friend of mine thinks it leads to confusion to use the word

Source: From *Public Administration Review* 28 (July-August 1968), pp. 362–368. Some subheadings shortened.

"revolution" in any loose and metaphorical way, even if the changes referred to are highly significant. Now I *hope* I am not talking about revolution in the strict sense of overthrow of government by force. However, given certain developments, given a dialectic of violence and ever more rapid change, who knows what the future holds? That our system of government, always being changed by "natural selection," may be changed by "mutation" as well, I entertain as more than an idle speculation. That is, the forces in motion and forces that may be put in motion may well cause rapid and significant changes in the governmental system, whatever name is put to them.

Let me speak briefly to the empirical side. Let me pass briefly in review some of the phenomena, events, and currents which are often referred to as revolutions, or as revolutionary in their implications. This will be but a brief cataloguing, a "reminding," so to speak.

Item: A revolution in science and technology. According to data with which you may be familiar—indeed, fatigued—there is an exponential increase in the scientific-technological enterprise. Ninety per cent of the scientists who ever lived are now living; and the time lag between basic scientific discovery and technological and industrial application is constantly narrowing. Changes in the condition of man at least equal to those caused by the Industrial Revolution are implied, and indeed if those who study such matters are correct, the implications are really much greater. There are seers and prophets, so to speak, who think that science and technology are now in the saddle and riding us hard; that they are now uncontrolled, if not indeed uncontrollable.

Item: A growing reaction *against* science and technology. I refer to a mounting feeling that science and technology create a cold, artificial, impersonal, dehumanized, and even monstrous world. On one level it is a revolution against the machine and everything machinelike and machine-made. But it is much more, and at another level is a revolution against a "system" that sustains and promotes a machine technology. The revolution against science and technology is seen positively as a revolution on behalf of the individual and individualism, against the invasion of privacy and for individual rights. The IBM card is often a symbol of the enemy, and beards and bare feet are seen as the symbols of emancipation and rebellion.

Item: A revolutionary increase in the means of violence and a counterrevolutionary—or whatever it may be called—revolution against the use of violence. The past two or three generations, and especially the past generation, have seen quantum jumps in the increase of man's ability to inflict violence and death on other human beings. No need to spell this out. The result is something of a counter-revolution against the use of force and violence which takes many forms. It may be "Ban the Bomb." It may be complete pacifism. It may be "I'll pick my own war—the hell with the government." In some moods and expressions, the reaction against violence may be also reaction against patriotism, civil loyalty, and national identity. Indeed, that they often and perhaps increasingly *are* is both a revolutionary symptom and potential.

Item: A reaction against gradualism and a growing commitment to violence. The phenomena I refer to here are especially associated, of course, with the civil rights struggle, and with the effort on behalf of or by minority groups to get their fair share of what America is supposed to offer all its citizens; but they are associated also with opposition to foreign policy, one "movement" often blending into the other. There is often a sense of urgency or desperation that makes lawbreaking seem the "only answer." Paradoxically, a revulsion *against* violence and a commitment *to* violence often occur in the same person or movement; that is, I am against *that* violence but I am for *this* violence. There are some very violent, nonviolent people around. Incidentally—if you think I oversimplify, I confess I do; but I am also prepared to argue that a great deal of nonviolence is violent in motive and result.

Item: A crisis in race relations. This is, of course, closely related to the preceding item though it has other dimensions. Whatever resolution there may be of the forces that have been building up, the result will be revolutionary: assume the best resolution you can imagine from your point of view and call it "evolutionary" if you like, still from another point of view this resolution will be "revolutionary."

Item: A severe generational gap, or the revolt of the young. This is a theme as old as the pyramids, of course, but I think there is abundant evidence to substantiate the point of view that we now have an acute attack of a chronic disease. In this connection, and as a relevant "aside"—I quote a magazine editor:

> It's even worse than you imagine. The fifteen-year-olds don't understand the twenty-year-olds. The twenty-year-olds have a world separate from the twenty-five-year-olds. And the twenty-five-year-olds won't be caught dead at thirty. The only thing these young people have in common is their unanimous nonunderstanding of human life beyond thirty-five.

The revolt of youth takes many forms, some corrosive as to established institutions, some deleterious as to personal well-being. Optimists tell us of "pay-offs," present and potential. But even these can be disturbing.

Item: The urban revolution. The cities grow in size and in number. They both pile up and spread out. They grow where they should not and decay where they should grow. The larger ones increasingly are referred to as "ungovernable."

Item: Upward, and still upward, rates of crime and violence. At one end of this spectrum are increases in individual crimes that are crimes by the moral codes of any civilization. At the other end of the spectrum—which includes middle-class crimes of a respectable white-collar variety, and organized crime—is group violence (often beginning as and perhaps still asserted to be "nonviolence") justified in the name of a "higher good." The appeal to a "higher good" as against the established order, whether from Left or Right, is one of the surest signs and accompaniments of a revolutionary period.

Item: Revolutions in morals and values. This is very complex and this is not the time to explore it. Suffice it to say, it's related to the items already mentioned, and those following.

One could of course extend the list that I have just constructed. One could talk about revolutions in the arts and literature. He could talk about such things as the revolutionary potential of changing perceptions induced by exposure during formative years to new communications media—"the medium is the message." One could talk of the pervasive mood: it is one of disaffection, alienation, frustration, nastiness, anger, and violence.

The list could be a longer one. I make no brief, incidentally, for the way I have cut and divided the world. You can use your own classification system and your own terminology; but I would be surprised if your list were shorter or your general perspective much different from mine.

I am not *for* revolutions, you understand. The point is that I think that if you face one or are in one, you'd better be intelligent about it. The potential for revolutionary events strikes me as clear and indisputable. The "items" I listed are *there*. In many cases one flows into, colors, and reinforces another. The various revolutions are capable, I think, of reacting in a highly synergistic way one with the other. Events such as severe military setback, widespread rioting, or an international monetary collapse are capable of triggering the synergism. Repeat: I am not predicting a revolution by force resulting in a complete change of government. I *do* predict continuing and revolutionary *change*. And under certain circumstances the cumulative effect could be disturbances of established institutional arrangements far beyond any in our recent history.

PA'S RESPONSIBILITY FOR CONTEMPORARY REVOLUTIONS

Let me ask now: What is public administration's responsibility for contemporary revolutions? This question has two aspects, at least: (1) did public administration help cause them? (2) ought public administration do something about them? I'll postpone consideration of the second question. Let me focus on the first.

Did we help cause them? Of course we did—both by what we did do, and by what we did not do.

Ours is a nation or society which, in the perspective of history, is rich beyond the dreams of avarice. Without trying to factor out our own distinctive contribution, I suppose you would agree with me that we have made a contribution to this result by providing both stimulus and stability. If you agree to that, then you agree that public administration bears some of the responsibility for the revolutions: *this* because the revolutions can't be disassociated from the causes, consequences, and nature in general of our spectacular affluence.

Should our civilization fail and fall, there are paradoxes and ironies enough to engage whole generations of future historians.

The very causes of this affluence—at least in part—such as the big and efficient organizations and the new and improved technologies, have within them the source of their own opposition if not the seeds of their own destruction. A great deal in contemporary culture is an anti-organizational, antitechnological revolt. Since our civilization is so deeply organizational and technological, the revolt often seems and in a sense is against civilization itself.

Ours is one of the few societies in history wealthy enough to have peace and war at the same time. But our past has not prepared us for this situation of moral complexity. We have historically given sets of values, expectations, and procedures for war and peace *singly*; but these values, expectations, and procedures are *different* if not outright *opposites*. Small wonder that there is doubt, hesitation, bad conscience, frustration, anger, bitter charges of hypocrisy.

Ours is a society so rich that it seems to many of our citizens absurd and immoral for there to be poverty in our midst. This poverty, coupled with discrimination—particularly racial discrimination—seems to be a hypocritical denial of what we have claimed to be our national tradition. Raised in the midst of affluence, our children can afford altruism in a way that we couldn't—or thought we couldn't. Bitter irony: the "Square World" that they reject is what made it possible for them to reject the "Square World."

Perhaps we in public administration helped to create the present situation by our *failures* as well as by our *successes.* Perhaps we ought to have taken the initiative in moving sooner on a number of problems that are now in the center of the stage. So much admitted, let me say that in my opinion there is nothing to be gained by taking the time to ask and try to answer the questions: Where did we go wrong? What should we have done?

Instead, before passing along, I'll underscore the positive paradox: success, affluence create their own problems. *If* we have so much wealth, and *if* we have so much know-how—and we brag a lot about both, you know—why can't we create a livable environment, shackle violence, abolish poverty, and generally secure equal treatment and justice? To a new generation—and to a lot of the older generation who have never had to work at it—it all seems *so simple.*

HOW IS PA INVOLVED WITH CONTEMPORARY REVOLUTIONS?

Another question: How is public administration involved with the contemporary revolutions? When I first made an outline of my remarks, I worded this: How is public administration being affected by the contemporary revolutions? But it is a very complex pattern that one finds—and hence, to speak of "involved with" seemed more accurate or less vulnerable than "affected by." The point is that overall, there is a very complex pattern of action and interaction, cause and effect. In some cases public administration is obviously a revolutionary agent, though it may be so either in ignorance or simply through enforcement of the law. In other cases it is helping society to respond or adjust to revolutions caused elsewhere. In still other cases, revolutionary process or effects are an intimate part of the machinery and processes of administration.

Let me suggest some of these interactions. What I say will be familiar to you. What may be *un*familiar is the thought that familiar things are deeply involved in revolutions.

Item: Domestic "technical assistance" in agriculture goes back well over a century, and it would be hard to find a function of government more traditional. At the same time it would be hard to find one that has been more revolutionary in its consequences. When one traces out its effects in such things as urban migration and foreign policy, he finds that American agriculture (which is in large measure what it is because of government policies) is one of the great revolutionary forces of the twentieth century.

Item: State departments of motor vehicles and of highways are seldom thought of as agents for revolution, but plainly they are deeply involved in revolutionary activities. In all of history it would be hard to find a revolutionary device more revolutionary than the internal combustion engine mounted on four wheels. It is deeply implicated in at least half of the "revolutions" noted at the outset.

Item: Changing the focus to look at revolutionary technologies *in* public administration, what better example than the computer? The impulses and mechanisms that led to the development of the computer were centrally governmental, administrative. In less than one human generation we have had three computer generations, and we are told that this is only the beginning. The computer is now deeply involved in a wide range of governmental activities at every level of government activity.

Item: Some types of government agencies are in a fairly obvious sense reacting *to* or *against* one or more revolutionary developments, such as the scientific-technological, or the urban revolution. I have in mind here those government agencies engaged in campaigns against water and air pollution, or *for* the preservation of open space and other amenities; or those attempting, one way or another, to deal with the urgent problems of the central city.

Item: Sometimes government agencies are charged with the dual or simultaneous process of responding to revolutions and creating one. I have in mind here the agencies created to respond to the pressure for racial equality, and to help create that equality; and the agencies created to respond to the demand of the poor for a share of the good life, and to help *create* the conditions under which this can be true.

Item: Sometimes the revolutions of our day *invade* or affect public administration in another way. I have in mind here the two forces of *professionalization* and *unionization.* Increased specialization and professionalization are facts to American life. Increasingly they "invade" the public service. Likewise *unionization.* It is no news to you that unionization in the public service is a hot issue, presenting extremely difficult issues posed by employee militancy, the strike, and all that. How these dual forces of unionization and professionalization are going to interact in public administration is a momentous question. Will they conflict? Will they coalesce? Will one become dominant at the expense of the other? Whatever the answers, traditional personnel administration (for other reasons as well) is becoming increasingly irrelevant or obsolete. From recruitment to retirement it must be rethought and reshaped.

PA AND THE CONSCIOUS RESPONSE TO REVOLUTIONS

Let me now advance the discussion—I hope—by posing these questions. What is the necessary or proper response of the bureaucracy to, or in a time of, revolutions? Ought a bureaucracy to respond at the *self-conscious level* to revolutions—assuming that it *can* do so?

Let me suggest some of the classic stances or answers. One is a stereotype that is both *popular* and *literary.* It is very effectively stated in the novel *The Plague* by Albert Camus. This, you may recall, is a sort of fable for modern man: the plague strikes Oran, Algeria, and the story turns on, and the morals are pointed by, how people individually and collectively respond to catastrophe. In this situation the bureaucrat, or government official, is pictured as impersonal, rigid, unattractive, irrelevant. Instead of acting, he "sends for instructions." As the protagonist Tarrou remarks, "What they're short on is imagination. Officialdom can never cope with something really catastrophic." "In the very midst of catastrophe offices could go on functioning serenely and take initiatives of no immediate relevance, and often unknown to the highest authority, purely and simply because they had been created originally for this purpose."

The central historic interest of the sociologist in bureaucracy in a "genuine" revolution has something in common with this literary view. The question that has intrigued the sociologist is whether a bureaucracy in a time of revolution is a machine to be driven in any direction by any person or party that can get into the driver's seat. The questions are: *Will* a bureaucracy go in any direction in which it is driven? How much of it has to be *changed* in order to make it go in a different direction? *How* can it be changed to make it go in a different direction?

Now our view of *ourselves,* in turn, has something in common with both the literary and the sociological perspectives. What I mean is: traditionally, so to speak, we have had as theory or rationale for the bureaucracy—that is, the public service—that it has no business making policy or engaging in politics. One expression of this is the idea of civil service neutrality: a civil servant should be officially nonpartisan, a civil service ought to mind its own professional-governmental business and faithfully serve the party in power—assuming always, of course, that the party is legitimate and has made the law according to constitutional procedures. The duty of the civil servant is precisely to do his duty, and that is to follow instructions and (or) to carry out the law.

Now this theory or ideology is far from silly. It can be argued cogently that by and large it has served us well, that it still is full of vitality, and that to abandon it is to open the gate to grave evils. On the other hand, all sorts of questions can properly be asked about it: Has it been more a useful myth than description of reality? Assuming that it *has been* a useful myth, is it *now* a useful myth? Didn't we, as a profession or discipline, decide some time ago administration is perforce intimately involved in the political process? That is, that we *have* and *should have* some role in making laws and deciding upon policies, as well as simply in carrying them out in a mechanical fashion? That to conceive of ourselves as mere automata is demeaning and, under some circumstances, even irresponsible or immoral? If this is true, if this is what we believe, what are the implications for our behavior in a time of revolutions?

I'm going to take the position that we ought to respond more consciously, more *self-consciously,* to the revolutions of the day. But let me acknowledge that the case is far from being completely one-sided. The idea—fiction, ideology, call it what you will—of civil service neutrality has served its purposes, and real dangers *are* created by abandoning it. It can be argued with some persuasiveness that the proper role of a bureaucracy is to act as a stabilizing force in the midst of vertiginous change, and that this is what it is doing when it seems to be unresponsive and stupid. In this view it has a balance-wheel or gyroscopic function. In an idiom of the day—or what I *think* may still be an idiom of the day—in the heat of revolutions, the bureaucracy ought to keep its cool. Instead, by acting in its routinized, mechanical, ponderous way it helps society to keep its cool.

Having admitted that this point of view has some force and validity, let me say that on balance I reject it. For reasons I have already partly suggested, I think it's unrealistic and wrong, at least beyond a certain point. Any institution that doesn't adjust to the rapidly changing milieu of the contemporary revolutions will not be effective in terms of its purpose or assignment. Long range, it will not even survive. The public service, by intelligent and imaginative response to the revolutionary realities, may serve not only its own "immediate" interest, but help society change and adjust in ways that maximize the potentials for "goods" and minimize the potentials for "bads."

PROBLEMS, OPPORTUNITIES, AND STRATEGIES

Let me first ask the question: Is public administration responding at a high level of consciousness and self-consciousness to the fact that we are in a time of revolutions? Despite all I said above about our being deeply involved one way or another—as cause, effect, and process—my own response would be: No. My assignment as Editor-in-Chief of *Public Administration Review* offers me a good vantage point from which to look around. The manuscripts that I receive are on the whole continually better—sharper, deeper, more imaginative. Still, the level of response to what *I* think are genuine crisis situations is not very high.

Not to write us down too much, let me say that in some ways I do think we do very well. In the last generation, for example, we have come a long way in making bureaucracies rewarding and fulfilling places for the people who work in them. Certainly we have been aware of the *problem* of adjusting organizations to the people in them, and have worked toward solutions. We have tried not simply to squeeze the most out of people, but to make public organization internally fulfill the objectives of a democratic society. We hoped and presumed the two objectives of efficiency and humanity were congruent.

However, in my opinion, we have advanced very little in making public bureaucracies acceptable and efficient in working with many of the clienteles. I will return to this point in a bit.

In some ways, I think PPBS illustrates both our strengths and our weaknesses—our dilemma. It has been the greatest technical or professional advance of this decade. It has received a great deal of attention and caused much excitement. It's the center of much activity. I won't argue its strengths and advantages. I will simply admit that it has them. But I think it's a serious question whether it doesn't cause systematic blindnesses and inhibit creative responses to environmental change and challenge. Does it (despite sincere denial) attempt to solve political and ethical problems by turning them into technical problems—thereby creating bigger political and ethical problems? Does it, in its attempt to reach firm conclusions on hard data, cause an undue restriction of vision, lead to overnarrow parameters and oversimplification of premises? Are some of our difficulties in the central city and in Vietnam thus related? I don't know the answer—I am not making accusations—but I think the questions are worth serious reflection. It is possible that historians of the future will puzzle over our fascination with our "technology" while alarm bells were ringing in all directions.

There is one aspect of the current revolutionary scene that I think we should be well aware of as we try to find our way through. I refer to the development of the so-called New Left. The significance of this for us, as I see it, is that the New Left seems significantly antigovernmental, antiadministrative, antiorganization—indeed, in some respects, nihilistic, anarchistic. Now, generally speaking, during the past two or three generations most of the political spectrum in the United States anywhere left of center was *pro*-government action, *pro*-administrative solution, *pro*-organizational approach. (Attention: I am not saying that Big Government was simply a product of pressures from the Left—it's a much more complicated business—and in fact the pressures often came from Center or even Right.) There was a belief that what were perceived as ills were susceptible of governmental amelioration or solution. *To a very important degree that is not now true.* Among the ironies of the day is the fact that

New Left often joins Old Right in opposition to solution to problems through governmental means, in a praise of local solutions through personal action. We are simply purblind if we are not aware of this fact, and ardent in trying to find out what it means in terms of the actions we need to take. Or refrain from taking.

Let me go further and say that much of the quantity and quality, the tone and character, of public administration during the past two or three generations has been given by the "pressures," so to speak, from *both* Left and Right. By "Right" I mean in this context the pressure for efficiency and economy. This continues at the present time and is accentuated. With widespread disillusionment with government as an instrument of social change and progress, do we then lose counterbalancing force from the Liberal Left? Do we risk in this context an undue concentration upon the "efficiency and economy" aspects of our operation because this is the course of least resistance? If and as the public "field" in which we have our professional being becomes even more disturbed by multiple vectors of force, will we tend to retreat behind the shield of professional neutrality, and concentrate more and more on techniques?

Let it be repeated, on the other hand, that there are unknowns and imponderables, as well as clear dangers, in abandoning historic ideologies and stances of public administration. While there is a very good case that we should become more involved with policy-making than we are, and even become more political than we have been in recent decades, there are serious risks. And one must make distinctions. There are "politics" of different kinds. There seems to be general agreement that politics in a strictly partisan sense, and politics in the sense of business-as-usual-through-the-old-political-establishment is part of the "problem" in the antipoverty program. Anyhow, pursuing the road of political involvement, we eventually reach problems of overall political structure and constitutional arrangements which are beyond public administration in any ordinary sense.

Yet, I am certain the proper response to new and baffling problems is not simply to say: traditional organizations, traditional procedures, traditional theories, can't and won't be changed. I think that experimentation in new organizational styles is in order. Some of the new organizations and procedures won't fit any of the approved patterns and traditional textbooks.

This is "radical" speculation, you may think. But it is also "conservative," in this mixed-up era. Yesterday I received a copy of a speech by the executive vice president of the First National City Bank, calling for the invention and utilization of "self-liquidating bureaucracies" in solving urban problems. To a bureaucrat, you can't get any more radical than *that!*

To conclude: I wish I had answers to some of the problems I have posed. I haven't. Maybe, even, I haven't been addressing myself to reality. Maybe the dangers and problems *I* see are figments of a faulty and overheated imagination.

Maybe. But if you think so, I suggest the possibility of *another* "maybe." I'll put it in the form of that wonderful parody of Kipling's "If" poem: "If you can keep your head when all about you are losing theirs—maybe you don't know what the score is."

35 Rescuing Policy Analysis from PPBS

Aaron Wildavsky

Everyone knows that the nation needs better policy analysis. Each area one investigates shows how little is known compared to what is necessary in order to devise adequate policies. In some organizations there are no ways at all of determining the effectiveness of existing programs; organizational survival must be the sole criterion of merit. It is often not possible to determine whether the simplest objectives have been met. If there is a demand for information the cry goes out that what the organization does cannot be measured. Should anyone attempt to tie the organization down to any measure of productivity, the claim is made that there is no truth in numbers. Oftentimes this is another way of saying, "Mind your own business." Sometimes the line taken is that the work is so subtle that it resists any tests. On other occasions the point is made that only those learned in esoteric arts can properly understand what the organization does, and they can barely communicate to the uninitiated. There are men so convinced of the ultimate righteousness of their cause that they cannot imagine why anyone would wish to know how well they are doing in handling our common difficulties. Their activities are literally priceless; vulgar notions of cost and benefit do not apply to them.

Anyone who has weathered this routine comes to value policy analysis. The very idea that there should be some identifiable objectives and that attention should be paid to whether these are achieved seems a great step forward. Devising alternative ways of handling problems and considering the future costs of each solution appear creative in comparison to more haphazard approaches. Yet policy analysis with its emphasis upon originality, imagination, and foresight, cannot be simply described. It is equivalent to what Robert N. Anthony has called strategic planning: ". . . the process of deciding on objectives of the organization, on changes in these objectives, on the resources used to attain these objectives. . . . It connotes big plans, important plans, plans with major consequences."[1] While policy analysis is similar to a broadly conceived version of systems analysis,[2] Yehezkel Dror has pointed up the boundaries that separate a narrow study from one with larger policy concerns. In policy analysis,

> 1. Much attention would be paid to the political aspects of public decision-making and public policy-making (instead of ignoring or condescendingly regarding political aspects). . . .
> 2. A broad conception of decision-making and policy-making would be involved (instead of viewing all decision-making as mainly a resources allocation). . . .
> 3. A main emphasis would be on creativity and search for new policy alternatives, with explicit attention to encouragement of innovative thinking. . . .
> 4. There would be extensive reliance on . . . qualitative methods. . . .

Source: From *Public Administration Review,* 29 (March-April 1969), pp. 189–202.

> 5. There would be much more emphasis on futuristic thinking. . . .
>
> 6. The approach would be looser and less rigid, but nevertheless systematic, one which would recognize the complexity of means-ends interdependence, the multiplicity of relevant criteria of decision, and the partial and tentative nature of every analysis. . . .[3]

Policy analysis aims at providing information that contributes to making an agency politically and socially relevant. Policies are goals, objectives, and missions that guide the agency. Analysis evaluates and sifts alternative means and ends in the elusive pursuit of policy recommendations. By getting out of the firehouse environment of day-to-day administration, policy analysis seeks knowledge and opportunities for coping with an uncertain future. Because policy analysis is not concerned with projecting the status quo, but with tracing out the consequences of innovative ideas, it is a variant of planning. Complementing the agency's decision process, policy analysis is a tool of social change.

In view of its concern with creativity, it is not surprising that policy analysis is still largely an art form; there are no precise rules about how to do it. The policy analyst seeks to reduce obscurantism by being explicit about problems and solutions, resources and results. The purpose of policy analysis is not to eliminate advocacy but to raise the level of argument among contending interests. If poor people want greater benefits from the government, the answer to their problems may not lie initially in policy analysis but in political organization. Once they have organized themselves, they may want to undertake policy analysis in order to crystallize their own objectives or merely to compete with the analyses put forth by others. The end result, hopefully, would be a higher quality debate and perhaps eventually public choice among better known alternatives.

A belief in the desirability of policy analysis—the sustained application of intelligence and knowledge to social problems—is not enough to insure its success, no more than to want to do good is sufficient to accomplish noble purposes. If grandiose claims are made, if heavy burdens are placed on officials without adequate compensation, if the needs of agency heads are given scant consideration, they will not desire policy analysis. It is clear that those who introduced the PPB system into the federal government in one fell swoop did not undertake a policy analysis on how to introduce policy analysis into the federal government.

In a paper called "The Political Economy of Efficiency"[4] written just as PPBS was begun in national government, I argued that it would run up against serious difficulties. There is still no reason to change a single word of what I said then. Indeed, its difficulties have been so overwhelming that there is grave danger that policy analysis will be rejected along with its particular manifestation in PPBS. In this essay I shall assess the damage that the planning-programming-budgeting system has done to the prospects of encouraging policy analysis in American national government. Then I would like to suggest some ways of enabling policy analysis to thrive and prosper.

WHY DEFENSE WAS A BAD MODEL

A quick way of seeing what went wrong with PPBS is to examine the preconditions for the use of this approach in the Defense Department, from which it was exported throughout the federal government. The immediate origins of PPBS are to be found in The RAND

Corporation,[5] where, after the Second World War, a talented group of analysts devoted years of effort to understanding problems of defense policy. It took five years to come up with the first useful ideas. Thus the first requisite of program budgeting in Defense was a small group of talented people who had spent years developing insights into the special problems of defense strategy and logistics. The second requisite was a common terminology, an ad hoc collection of analytical approaches, and the beginnings of theoretical statements to guide policy analysis. When Secretary of Defense Robert McNamara came into office, he did not have to search for men of talent nor did he have to wait for a body of knowledge to be created. These requisites already existed in some degree. What was further necessary was his ability to understand and to use analytical studies. Thus the third requisite of program budgeting is top leadership that understands policy analysis and is determined to get it and make use of it.

The fourth requisite was the existence of planning and planners. Planning was well accepted at the various levels of the Defense Department with the variety of joint service plans, long-range requirement plans, logistical plans, and more. Military and civilians believed in planning, in coping with uncertainty and in specifying some consequences of policy decisions. The problem as the originators of PPBS saw it was to introduce cost considerations into planning; they wanted to stop bluesky planning and to integrate planning and budgeting. They wanted to use the program budget to bridge the gap between military planners, who cared about requirements but not about resources, and budget people, who were narrowly concerned with financial costs but not necessarily with effective policies.

Policy analysis is expensive in terms of time, talent, and money. It requires a high degree of creativity in order to imagine new policies and to test them out without requiring actual experience. Policy analysis calls for the creation of systems in which elements are linked to one another and to operational indicators so that costs and effectiveness of alternatives may be systematically compared. There is no way of knowing in advance whether the analysis will prove intellectually satisfying and politically feasible. Policy analysis is facilitated when: (a) goals are easily specified, (b) a large margin of error is allowable, and (c) the cost of the contemplated policy makes large expenditures on analysis worthwhile. That part of defense policy dealing with choices among alternative weapons systems was ideally suited for policy analysis. Since the cost of intercontinental missiles or other weapons systems ran into the billions of dollars, it was easy to justify spending millions on analysis.[6] The potential effectiveness of weapons like intercontinental missiles could be contemplated so long as one was willing to accept large margins of error. It is not unusual for analysts to assume extreme cases of damage and vulnerability in a context in which the desire for reducing risk is very great. Hence a goal like assuring sufficient destructive power such that no enemy strike could prevent devastation of one's country may be fuzzy without being unusable. If one accepts a procedure of imagining that possible enemies were to throw three times as much megatonnage as intelligence estimates suggest they have, he need not be overly troubled by doubts about the underlying theory. If one is willing to pay the cost of compensating against the worst, lack of knowledge will not matter so much. The point is not that this is an undesirable analytic procedure, quite the contrary, but the extreme cases were allowed to determine the outcomes.

Inertia

The introduction of new procedures that result in new policies is not easy. Inertia is always a problem. Members of the organization and its clientele groups have vested interests in the policies of the past. Efforts at persuasion must be huge and persistent. But there are conditions that facilitate change. One of these is a rising level of appropriations. If change means that things must be taken away from people in the organization without giving them anything in return, greater resistance may be expected. The ability to replace old rewards with larger new ones helps reduce resistance to change. The fact that defense appropriations were increasing at a fast rate made life much easier for Mr. McNamara. The expected objections of clientele groups, for example, were muted by the fact that defense contractors had lots of work, even if it was not exactly what they expected. Rapid organizational growth may also improve the possibilities for change. The sheer increase in organizational size means that many new people can be hired who are not tied to the old ways. And speedy promotion may help convince members that the recommended changes are desirable.

The deeper change goes into the bowels of the organization, the more difficult it is to achieve. The more change can be limited to central management, the greater the possibility for carrying it out. The changes introduced in the Defense Department did not, for the most part, require acceptance at the lower levels. Consider a proposed change in the organization of fighting units that would drastically reduce the traditional heavy support facilities for ground forces. Such a change is not easily manipulated from Washington. But the choice of one weapons system over another is much more amenable to central control. The kinds of problems for which program budgeting was most useful also turned out to be problems that could be dealt with largely at the top of the organization. The program budget group that McNamara established had to fight with generals in Washington but not with master sergeants in supply. Anyone who knows the Army knows what battle they would rather be engaged in fighting.

The ability of an organization to secure rapid change depends, of course, on the degree of its autonomy from the environment. I have argued elsewhere[7] that the President of the United States has much more control over America's foreign policy than over its domestic policy. In almost any area of domestic policy there is a well-entrenched structure of interests. In foreign and defense policy, excluding such essentially internal concerns as the National Guard, the territory within the American political system is not nearly so well defended; there are far fewer political fortifications, mines, and boobytraps.

Personnel

Experienced personnel may be a barrier to change. They know something about the consequences of what they are doing. They may have tried a variety of alternatives and can point to reasons why each one will not work. If I may recall my low-level Army experience (I entered as a private first class and was never once demoted), the usual reply to a question about the efficacy of present practice was, "Have you ever been in combat, son?" But the most dramatic changes introduced in the Pentagon had to do with questions of avoiding or limiting nuclear war, in which no one had a claim to experience and in which the basic purpose of analysis is to make certain that we do not have to learn from experience. If the system fails, the game is over. And since McNamara's men possessed a body of doctrines on defense policy, they had an enormous advantage over regular military who were for a long time unable to defend themselves properly in the new field.[8]

The new policy analysts did not accept the currency of military experience. In their view, naked judgment was not a satisfactory answer to why a policy should be adopted. The Army might know the fire-power of an infantry division, but the fire-power was not "effectiveness." Competition among the services for appropriations, however, was favorable to PPBS. There was a defense budget that covered virtually all of the Department's subject matter. There were defense missions in which trade-offs could be made between the services. Resources could actually be diverted if the analysis "proved" a particular service was right. Programs could easily be developed because of the facile identification of program with weapons systems and force units. Once the military learned the jargon, they were willing to play the game for an extra division or carrier. So long as dollar losses in one program were more than made up by gains in another, the pain of policy analysis was considerably eased.

The favorable conditions for the limited use of program budgeting in the Department of Defense do not exist in most domestic agencies. There are no large groups of talented policy analysts expert in agency problems outside of the federal government. These nonexistent men cannot, therefore, be made available to the agencies. (The time has passed when eighth-rate systems engineers in aerospace industries are expected to solve basic social problems overnight.) Most agencies had few planners and even less experience in planning. There is no body of knowledge waiting to be applied to policy areas such as welfare and crime. A basic reason for wanting more policy analysis is to help create knowledge where little now exists. There are only a few agencies in which top managers want systematic policy analysis and are able to understand quantitative studies. Goals are not easily specified for most domestic agencies. Nor do they usually have handy equivalents for programs like expensive weapons systems. What Thomas Schelling has so pungently observed about the Department of State—it does not control a large part of the budget devoted to foreign policy—is true for the domestic departments and their lack of coverage as well.[9]

Except for a few individual programs like the proposals for income supplements or assessing the desirability of a supersonic transport, the cost of most domestic policies does not rise into the billions of dollars. Congress and interested publics are not disposed to allow large margins of error. Instead of increasing, the availability of federal funds began declining soon after the introduction of program budgeting. A higher level of conflict was inevitable, especially since the acceptance of proposed changes required the acquiescence of all sorts of people and institutions in the far-flung reaches of the agencies. Social workers, city officials, police chiefs, welfare mothers, field officers, and numerous others were involved in the policies. Program budgeting on the domestic side takes place in a context in which there is both less autonomy from the environment and a great deal more first-hand experience by subordinates. On these grounds alone no one should have been surprised that program budgeting in the domestic agencies did not proceed as rapidly or with as much ostensible success as in the Defense Department.[10]

NO ONE CAN DO PPBS

In past writings I argued that program budgeting would run up against severe political difficulties. While most of these arguments have been conceded, I have been told that in a better world, without the vulgar intrusion of political factors (such as the consent of the governed), PPBS would perform its wonders as advertised. Now it is clear that for the narrow purpose of predicting why program budgeting would not work there was no need to mention political problems at all. It would have been sufficient to say that the wholesale introduction of PPBS presented insuperable difficulties of calculation. All the obstacles previously mentioned, such as lack of talent, theory, and data, may be summed up in a single statement: *no one knows how to do program budgeting.* Another way of putting it would be to say that many know what program budgeting should be like in general, but no one knows what it should be in any particular case. Program budgeting cannot be stated in operational terms. There is no agreement on what the words mean, let alone an ability to show another person what should be done. The reason for the difficulty is that telling an agency to adopt program budgeting means telling it to find better policies and there is no formula for doing that. One can (and should) talk about measuring effectiveness, estimating costs, and comparing alternatives, but that is a far cry from being able to take the creative leap of formulating a better policy.

Pattern of Events

On the basis of numerous discussions with would-be practitioners of program budgeting at the federal level, I think I can describe the usual pattern of events. The instructions come down from the Bureau of the Budget. You must have a program budget. Agency personnel hit the panic button. They just do not know how to do what they have been asked to do. They turn, if they can, to the pitifully small band of refugees from the Pentagon who have come to light the way. But these defense intellectuals do not know much about the policy area in which they are working. That takes time. Yet something must quickly come out of all this. So they produce a vast amount of inchoate information characterized by premature quantification of irrelevant items. Neither the agency head nor the examiners in the Bureau of the Budget can comprehend the material submitted to them. Its very bulk inhibits understanding. It is useless to the Director of the Budget in making his decisions. In an effort to be helpful, the program analysis unit at the Budget Bureau says something like, "Nice try, fellows; we appreciate all that effort. But you have not quite got the idea of program budgeting yet. Remember, you must clarify goals, define objectives, relate these to quantitative indicators, project costs into the future. Please send a new submission based on this understanding."

Another furious effort takes place. They do it in Defense, so it must be possible. Incredible amounts of overtime are put in. Ultimately, under severe time pressure, even more data is accumulated. No one will be able to say that agency personnel did not try hard. The new presentation makes a little more sense to some people and a little less to others. It just does not hang together as a presentation of agency policies. There are more encouraging words from the Budget Bureau and another sermon about specifying alternative ways of meeting agency objectives, though not, of course, taking the old objectives for granted. By this time agency personnel are desperate. "We would love to do it," they say, "but we cannot figure out the right way. You experts in the Budget Bureau should show us how to do it." Silence. The word from on high is that the Bureau of the Budget does not interfere with agency operations; it is the agency's task to set up its own budget. After a while, cynicism reigns supreme.

PPBS must be tremendously inefficient. It resembles nothing so much as a Rube Goldberg apparatus in which the operations performed bear little relation to the output achieved. The data inputs into PPBS are huge and its policy output is tiny. All over the federal government the story is the same: if you ask what good has PPBS done, those who have something favorable to say invariably cite the same one or two policy analyses. At one time I began to wonder if the oil shale study[11] in the Interior Department and the maternal and child health care program[12] in Health, Education, and Welfare were all that had ever come out of the programming effort.

The orders to expand PPBS did not say, "Let us do more policy analysis than we have in the past." What it said was, "Let us make believe we can do policy analysis on everything." Instead of focusing attention on areas of policy amenable to study, the PPBS apparatus requires information on *all* agency policies.

Program Structure

The fixation on program structure is the most pernicious aspect of PPBS. Once PPBS is adopted, it becomes necessary to have a program structure that provides a complete list of organization objectives and supplies information on the attainment of each one. In the absence of analytic studies for all or even a large part of an agency's operations, the structure turns out to be a sham that piles up meaningless data under vague categories.[13] It hides rather than clarifies. It suggests comparisons among categories for which there is no factual or analytical basis. Examination of a department's program structure convinces everyone acquainted with it that policy analysis is just another bad way of masquerading behind old confusions. A mere recitation of some program categories from the Department of Agriculture—Communities of Tomorrow, Science in the Service of Man, Expanding Dimensions for Living—makes the point better than any comment.

Even if the agency head does understand a data-reduction-summarization of the program budget, he still cannot use the structure to make decisions, because it is too hard to adjust the elaborate apparatus. Although the system dredges up information under numerous headings, it says next to nothing about the impact of one program on another. There is data but no causal analysis. Hence the agency head is at once over-supplied with masses of numbers and undersupplied with propositions about the impact of any action he might undertake. He cannot tell, because no one knows, what the marginal change he is considering would mean for the rest of his operation. Incremental changes at the Bureau of the Budget at the agency level are made in terms of the old budget categories. Since the program structure is meant to be part of the budget, however, it must be taken as a statement of current policy and it necessarily emerges as a product of organizational compromise. The program structure, therefore, does not embody a focus on central policy concerns. More likely, it is a haphazard arrangement that reflects the desire to manipulate external support and to pursue internal power aspirations. Being neither program nor budget, program structure is useless. It is the Potemkin Village of modern administration. The fact that generating bits of random data for the program structure takes valuable time away from more constructive concerns also harms policy analysis. The whole point of policy analysis is to show that what had been done intuitively in the past may be done better through sustained application of intelligence. The adoption of meaningless program structures, and their perversion into slogans for supporting existing policies, does not—to say the least—advance the cause of policy analysis.

Gorham Testimony

I do not mean to suggest that the introduction of PPBS has not led to some accomplishments. Before we consider the significance of these accomplishments, however, it is essential that we understand what PPBS has manifestly *not* done. One could hardly have a better witness on this subject than William Gorham, formerly Assistant Secretary (Program Coordination), Department of Health, Education, and Welfare, and now head of the Urban Institute, who is widely acknowledged to be an outstanding practitioner of program budgeting.

At the highest level of generality, it is clear that PPBS does not help in making choices between vast national goals such as health and defense, nor is PPBS useful in making trade-offs between more closely related areas of policy such as health, education, and welfare. In his testimony before the Joint Economic Committee, Gorham put the matter bluntly:

> Let me hasten to point out that we have not attempted any grandiose cost-benefit analysis designed to reveal whether the total benefits from an additional million dollars spent on health programs would be higher or lower than that from an additional million spent on education or welfare. If I was ever naïve enough to think this sort of analysis possible, I no longer am. The benefits of health, education, and welfare programs are diverse and often intangible. They affect different age groups and different regions of the population over different periods of time. No amount of analysis is going to tell us whether the Nation benefits more from sending a slum child to pre-school, providing medical care to an old man or enabling a disabled housewife to resume her normal activities. The "grand decisions"—how much health, how much education, how much welfare, and which groups in the population shall benefit—are questions of value judgments and politics. The analyst cannot make much contribution to their resolution.[14]

It turns out that it is extremely difficult to get consensus on goals within a single area of policy. As a result, the policy analysts attempt to find objectives that are more clearly operational and more widely acceptable. Gorham speaks with the voice of experience when he says:

> Let me give you an example. Education. What we want our kids to be as a result of going to school is the level of objective which is the proper and the broadest one. But we want our children to be different sorts of people. We want them to be capable of different sorts of things. We have, in other words, a plurality of opinions about what we want our schools to turn out. So you drop down a level and you talk about objectives in terms of educational attainment—years of school completed and certain objective measures of quality. Here you move in education from sort of fuzzy objectives, but very important, about what it is that you want the schools to be doing, to the more concrete, less controversial, more easily to get agreed upon objectives having to do with such things as educational attainment, percentage of children going to college, etc.
>
> I think the same thing is true in health and in social services, that at the very

> highest level objective, where in theory you would really like to say something, the difficulty of getting and finding a national consensus is so great that you drop down to something which is more easily and readily accepted as objectives.[15]

What can actually be done, according to Gorham, are analytic studies of narrowly defined areas of policy. "The less grand decisions," Gorham testified, "those among alternative programs with the same or similar objectives within health—can be substantially illuminated by good analysis. It is this type of analysis which we have undertaken at the Department of Health, Education, and Welfare."[16] Gorham gives as examples disease control programs and improvements in the health of children. If this type of project analysis is what can be done under PPBS, a serious question is raised: Why go through all the rigamarole in order to accomplish a few discrete studies of important problems?

A five-year budget conceived in the hodge-podge terms of the program structure serves no purpose.[17] Since actual budget decisions are made in terms of the old categories and policy analysis may take place outside of the program structure, there is no need to institutionalize empty labels. If a policy analysis has been completed, there is no reason why it cannot be submitted as part of the justification of estimates to the Bureau of the Budget and to Congress. For the few program memoranda that an agency might submit, changes could be detailed in terms of traditional budget categories. Problems of program structure would be turned over to the agency's policy analysts who would experiment with different ways of lending intellectual coherence to the agency's programs. There would be no need to foist the latest failure on a skeptical world. Nor would there be battles over the costs of altering a program structure that has achieved, if not a common framework, at least the virtue of familiarity. The difference is that stability of categories in the traditional budget has real value for control[18] while the embodiment of contradictions in the program structure violates its essential purpose.

INCENTIVES FOR POLICY ANALYSIS

PPBS discredits policy analysis. To collect vast amounts of random data is hardly a serious analysis of public policy. The conclusion is obvious. The shotgun marriage between policy analysis and budgeting should be annulled. Attempts to describe the total agency program in program memoranda should be abandoned. It is hard enough to do a good job of policy analysis, as most agency people now realize, without having to meet arbitrary and fixed deadlines imposed by the budget process.[19] There is no way of telling whether an analysis will be successful. There is, therefore, no point in insisting that half-baked analyses be submitted every year because of a misguided desire to cover the entire agency program. The Budget Bureau itself has recently recognized the difficulty by requiring agencies to present extensive memoranda only when major policy issues have been identified. It is easier and more honest just to take the program structure out of the budget.

The thrust of the argument thus far, however, forces us to confront a major difficulty. Policy analysis and budgeting were presumably connected in order to see that high quality analysis did not languish in limbo but was translated into action through the critical budget process. Removing policy analysis from the annual budget cycle might increase its intellectual content at the expense of its practical impact. While formal program structures should go—PPBS actually inhibits the prospects for obtaining good analysis that is worth translating into public policy—they should be replaced with a strong incentive to make policy analysis count in yearly budgetary decisions. I am therefore proposing a substitute for PPBS that maintains whatever incentive it provided for introducing the results of policy analysis into the real world without encouraging the debilitating effects.

The submission of program memoranda supported by policy analysis should be made a requirement for major dollar changes in an agency's budget. The Bureau of the Budget should insist that this requirement be met by every agency. Agency heads, therefore, would have to require it of subunits. The sequence could operate as follows:

1. Secretary of agency and top policy analysts review major issues and legislation and set up a study menu for several years. Additions and deletions are made periodically.
2. Policy analysts set up studies which take anywhere from six to 24 months.
3. As a study is completed for a major issue area, it is submitted to the Secretary of the agency for review and approval.
4. If approved, the implications of the study's recommendations are translated into budgetary terms for submission as a program memorandum in support of the agency's fiscal year budget.

No one imagines that a mechanical requirement would in and of itself compel serious consideration of policy matters. No procedure should be reified as if it had a life of its own apart from the people who must implement it. This conclusion is as true for my suggestion as for PPBS. We must therefore consider ways and means of increasing the demand for and supply of policy analysis.

Increasing Demand and Supply

The first requirement of effective policy analysis is that top management want it. No matter how trite this criterion sounds, it has often been violated, as Frederick C. Mosher's splendid study of program budgeting in foreign affairs reveals.[20] The inevitable difficulties of shaking loose information and breaking up old habits will prove to be insuperable obstacles without steady support from high agency officials. If they do not want it, the best thing to do is concentrate efforts in another agency. Placing the best people in a few agencies also makes it more likely that a critical mass of talent will be able to achieve a creative response to emerging policy problems.

Policy analysis should be geared to the direct requirements of top management. This means that analysis should be limited to a few major issues. Since there will only be a few studies every year, the Secretary should have time to consider and understand each one. The analytical staff should be flexible enough to work on his priority interests. Consequently, one of the arguments by which program budgeting has been oversold has to be abandoned. Policy analysis will not normally identify programs of low priority. Top management is not interested in them. They would receive no benefit from getting supporters of these programs angry at them. Instead, agency heads want to know how to deal with emergent problems. Practitioners of policy analysis understand these considerations quite well. Harry Shooshan, Deputy Undersecretary for Programs, Department of the Interior, presents a perceptive analysis:

> . . . We have tried to more heavily relate our PPB work and our analytical work to the new program thrusts, and major issues, not because it is easier to talk about new programs, but rather, there is a good question of judgment, on how much time one

> should spend on ongoing programs that are pretty well set. So you restate its mission and you put it in PPB wrapping and what have you really accomplished?
>
> There are going to be new program proposals, new thrusts of doing something in certain areas. Let's relate our analyses to that and get the alternatives documented as well as we can for the decision-makers. So it is a combination of on the one hand it being difficult to identify low priorities in a manner that really means something and on the other hand, it is the fact of what have we really accomplished by simply putting old programs in new wrappings when new programs really should get the emphasis right now in terms of what are the decisions now before, in my case, the Secretary of the Interior, in terms of what should he know before he makes decisions relative to where he is attempting to go. If I can relate PPB to the decision on his desk today and the near future, I can sell him and in turn, our own Department on the contribution that we can make.[21]

The implications of Shooshan's point go beyond making policy analysis more desirable by having it meet the needs of top management. The subjects for policy analysis ought to be chosen precisely for their critical-fluid-emergent character. These are the places where society is hurting. These are the areas in which there are opportunities for marginal gains. Indeed, a major role for top management is scanning the political horizon for targets of opportunity. Yet the characteristics of these new problems run counter to the criteria for selection that PPBS currently enforces, since they are identified by ambiguity concerning goals, lack of data upon which to project accurate estimates of costs and consequences, and pervasive uncertainty concerning the range of possible changes in program.

There would be a much larger demand for policy analysis if it were supplied in ways that would meet the needs of high level officials. Let us consider the example of the President of the United States. He can certainly use policy analysis to help make better decisions. Substantial policy studies would give him and his staff leverage against the bureaucracy. Knowledge is power. Indeed, command of a particular field would enable Presidents to exert greater control over the agenda for public decision and would give them advantages in competition with all sorts of rivals. Presidents could use perhaps a dozen major policy studies per year of their most immediate concerns. If even a few of these turn out well, the President may be motivated to make use of them. Contrast this with the present inundation of the Executive Office by endless streams of program "books," summaries, and memoranda that nobody ever looks at.

What is true of the President is also true for important executives in the agencies. Policy-oriented executives will want to get better analysis. Executives wishing to increase their resource base will be interested in independent sources of information and advice. Those who would exert power need objectives to fight for. It is neither fashionable nor efficient to appear to seek power for its own sake. In polite society the drive is masked and given a noble face when it can be attached to grand policy concerns that bring benefits to others as well as to power seekers. The way to gain the attention of leaders is not to flood them with trivia but to provide examples of the best kind of work that can be done. The last years of the Johnson Administration witnessed a proliferation of secret commissions to recommend new policies. The department secretary often became just another special pleader. If they have any interest in curbing this development, secretaries may find that producing their own policy analyses allow them to say that outside intervention is not the only or the best way to generate new policies.

Congressional Demand

If strategically located Congressmen demanded more policy analysis, there is little doubt that we would get it. What can be done to make them want more of it? The answer does not lie in surrounding them with large staffs so that they lose their manifestly political functions and become more like bureaucrats. Nor does the answer lie in telling Congressmen to keep away from small administrative questions in favor of larger policy concerns. For many Congressmen get into the larger questions only by feeling their way through the smaller details.[22] A threat to deprive Congressmen of the traditional line-item appropriations data through which they exert their control of agency affairs also does not appear to be a good way of making Congressmen desire policy analysis.

Policy analysis must be made relevant to what Congressmen want. Some legislators desire to sponsor new policies and they are one clientele for analysis. For other Congressmen, however, policy is a bargainable product that emerges from their interactions with their fellows. These members must be appealed to in a different way. They often have a sense of institutional loyalty and pride. They know that Congress is a rare institution in this world—a legislative body that actually has some control over public policy. They are aware that the development of new knowledge and new techniques may freeze them out of many of the more serious decisions. Policy analysis should be proposed to these men as an enhancement of the power of Congress as an institution. The purpose of analysis would be, in its simplest form, to enable Congressmen to ask good questions and to evaluate answers. Oftentimes it is hardest for a layman to recognize the significant questions implicit in an area of policy. Are there other and better questions to be asked, other and better policies to be pursued?

A Congress that takes seriously its policy role should be encouraged to contract for policy analysis that would stress different views of what the critical questions are in a particular area of policy. Each major committee or subcommittee should be encouraged to hire a man trained in policy analysis for a limited period, perhaps two years. His task would be to solicit policy studies, evaluate presentations made by government agencies, and keep Congressmen informed about what are considered the important questions. In the past, chairmen have not always paid attention to the quality of committee staffs. Following the lead of the Joint Economic Committee, seminars might be held for a couple of weeks before each session. At these seminars discussions would take place between agency personnel, committee staff, and the academics or other experts who have produced the latest policy analysis. If all went well, Congressmen would emerge with a better idea of the range of issues and of somewhat different ways of tackling the problems, and the policy analysts would emerge with a better grasp of the priorities of these legislators.

Suppliers of Policy Analysis

Thus far we have dealt solely with the incentive structure of the consumers who ought to want policy analysis—agency heads, Presidents, Congressmen. Little has been said about the incentive structure of the suppliers who ought to provide it—analysts, consultants, academics. Our premise has been that the supply of policy analysis would be a function of the demand. Now, the relationships between supply and demand have long been troublesome in economics because it is so difficult to sort out the mutual interactions. Upon being asked whether demand created supply or supply created demand, the great economist Marshall was reported to have said that it was like asking which blade of the scissors cuts the paper. There is no doubt, however, that changes in the conditions and quality of supply would have important effects on the demand for policy analysis.

Disengaging policy analysis from PPBS would help build the supply of policy analysis by:

1. Decreasing the rewards for mindless quantification for its own sake. There would be no requests from the Bureau of the Budget for such information and no premium for supplying it.
2. Increasing the rewards for analysts who might try the risky business of tackling a major policy problem that was obviously not going to be considered because everyone was too busy playing with the program structure. Gresham's Law operates here: programmed work drives out unprogrammed activity, make-work drives out analysis.

One way of increasing the supply of policy analysis would be to improve the training of people who work directly in the various areas of policy. Instead of taking people trained in policy analysis and having them learn about a particular policy area, the people in that area would be capable of doing policy analysis. Three-day or three-month courses will not do for that purpose. A year, and possibly two years, would be required. Since it is unlikely that the best people can be made available for so long a period, it is necessary to think in terms of education at an earlier period in their lives. There is a great need for schools of public policy in which technical training is combined with broader views of the social context of public policy. Although no one knows how to teach "creativity," it is possible to expose students to the range of subjects out of which a creative approach to public policy could come.

Another way of increasing the supply of policy analysis would be to locate it in an organizational context in which it has prestige and its practitioners are given time to do good work. Having the policy analysis unit report directly to the secretary or agency head would show that it is meant to be taken seriously.[23] But then it is bound to get involved in day-to-day concerns of the agency head, thus creating a classic dilemma.

Tactics

The effective use of a policy analysis unit cannot be specified in advance for all agencies. There are certain tensions in its functions that may be mitigated on a case-by-case basis but cannot be resolved once and for all. Serious policy analysis requires months, if not years, of effort. A unit that spends its time solely on substantial policy analysis would soon find itself isolated from the operational concerns of the agency. There would be inordinate temptations on the part of its members to go where the action is. Before long, the policy unit might become more immediately relevant at the expense of its long-term impact. The frantic nature of day-to-day emergencies drives out the necessary time and quiet for serious study and reflection. What can be done? One tactic is for the policy unit to consider itself an educational as well as an action group. Its task should be to encourage analysis on the part of other elements of the organization. It should undertake nothing it can get subunits to do. The role of the policy unit would then be one of advising subunits and evaluating their output.

A second tactic would be to contract out for studies that are expected to take the longest period of time. The third tactic is the most difficult, because it calls for a balancing act. Immediate usefulness to top management may be secured by working on problems with short lead times while attempting to retain perhaps half of the available time for genuine policy analysis. To the degree that serious policy analysis enters into the life of the organization and proves its worth, it will be easier to justify its requirements in terms of release from everyday concerns. Yet the demand for services of the analysts is certain to increase. Failures in policy analysis, on the other hand, are likely to give the personnel involved more time for reflection than they would prefer. Like headquarters-field relationships, line and staff responsibilities, and functional versus hierarchical command, the problems of the policy unit are inherent in its situation and can only be temporarily resolved.

These comments on incentives for increasing the supply and demand for policy analysis are plainly inadequate. They are meant merely to suggest that there is a problem and to indicate how one might go about resolving it. We do not really know how to make policy analysis fit in with the career requirements of Congressmen, nor can we contribute much beside proverbial wisdom to the structure and operation of policy analysis units. There are, however, opportunities for learning that have not yet been used. One of the benefits flowing from the experience with PPBS is that it has thrown up a small number of policy analyses that practitioners consider to be good. We need to know what makes some live in the world and others remain unused. Aside from an impressive manuscript by Clay Thomas Whitehead,[24] however, in which two recent policy analyses in defense are studied, there has been no effort to determine what this experience has to teach us. Despite the confident talk about policy analysis (here and elsewhere), a great deal of work remains to be done on what is considered "good" and why. The pioneering work by Charles E. Lindblom should not be wrongly interpreted as being anti-analysis, but as a seminal effort to understand what we do when we try to grapple with social problems.

Reexamination

Critical aspects of policy analysis need to be reexamined. The field cries out for a study of "coordination" as profound and subtle as Martin Landau's forthcoming essay on "Redundancy."[25] That most elemental problem of political theory—the proper role of the government versus that of the individual—should be subject to a radical critique.[26] The fact that cost-benefit analysis began with water resource projects in which the contribution to national income was the key question has guided thought away from other areas of policy for which this criterion would be inappropriate. There are policies for which the willingness of citizens to support the activity should help determine the outcome. There are other policies in which presently unquantifiable benefits, like pleasure in seeing others better off or reduction of anxiety following a visible decrease in social hostility, should be controlling. Although social invention is incredibly difficult, the way is open for new concepts of the role of government to liberate our thoughts and guide our actions.

In many ways the times are propitious for policy analysis. The New Deal era of legislation has ended and has not yet been replaced by a stable structure of issues. People do not know where they stand today in the same way they knew how they felt about Medicare or private versus public electric power. The old welfare state policies have disenchanted former supporters as well as further enraged their opponents. Men have worked for 20 years to get massive education bills through Congress only to discover that the results have not lived up to their expectations; it takes a lot more to improve education for the deprived than anyone had thought. There is now a receptivity to new ideas that did not exist a decade ago. There is a willingness to consider new policies and try new ways. Whether or not there is sufficient creativity in us to devise better policies remains to be seen. If we are serious about improving public policy, we will go beyond the fashionable pretense of PPBS to show others what the best policy analysis can achieve.

NOTES

1. Robert N. Anthony, *Planning and Control Systems: A Framework for Analysis,* (Boston: Harvard University Press, 1965), p. 16.
2. Aaron Wildavsky, "The Political Economy of Efficiency," *Public Administration Review* 26 (December 1966), pp. 298–302.
3. Yehezkel Dror, "Policy Analysts: A New Professional Role in Government Service," *Public Administration Review* 27 (September 1967), pp. 200–201. See also Dror's major work, *Public Policy-Making Reexamined* (San Francisco: Chandler, 1968).
4. Aaron Wildavsky, *op. cit.*
5. See David Novick, "Origin and History of Program Budgeting," The RAND Corporation, October 1966, p. 3,427.
6. I once tried to interest a graduate student who had experience with defense problems in doing research in the City of Oakland. He asked the size of Oakland's budget. "Fifty million dollars," I said. "Why, in the Air Force we used to round to that figure," was his reply.
7. Aaron Wildavsky, "The Two Presidencies," *Trans-action* 4 (December 1966), pp. 7–14.
8. For further argument along these lines see my article, "The Practical Consequences of the Theoretical Study of Defense Policy," *Public Administration Review* 25 (March 1965), pp. 90–103.
9. Thomas C. Schelling, "PPBS and Foreign Affairs," memorandum prepared at the request of the Subcommittee on National Security and International Operations of the Committee on Government Operations, U.S. Senate, 90th Congress, First Session, 1968.
10. Dr. Alain Enthoven, who played a leading role in introducing systems analysis to the Defense Department, has observed that: "The major changes in strategy, the step-up in production of Minutemen and Polaris and the build-up in our non-nuclear forces including the increase in the Army, the tactical air forces, and the air lift . . . were being phased in at the same time that PPBS was being phased in. . . . We speeded up the Polaris and Minuteman programs because we believed that it was terribly important to have an invulnerable retaliatory force. We built up the Army Land Forces because we believed it was necessary to have more land forces for limited non-nuclear wars. We speeded up the development of anti-guerrilla forces or special forces because we believed that was necessary for counter-insurgency. Those things would have happened with or without PPBS. PPBS does not make the strategy." Subcommittee on National Security and International Operations of the Committee on Government Operations, U.S. Senate, *Hearings, Planning-Programming-Budgeting,* 90th Congress, First Session, Part 2, Sept. 27 and Oct. 18, 1967, p. 141.
11. *Prospects For Oil Shale Development* (Washington, D.C.: Department of the Interior, May 1968).
12. The study is presented in *ibid.*, pp. 10–45.
13. Similar difficulties under similar conditions evidently occur in the business world. It is worth citing Anthony's comments: "Strategic planning [that is, policy analysis] is essentially *irregular.* Problems, opportunities, and 'bright ideas' do not arise according to some set timetable; they have to be dealt with whenever they happen to be perceived. . . . Failure to appreciate the distinction between regular and irregular processes can result in trouble of the following type. A company with a well-developed budgeting process decides to formalize its strategic planning. It prepares a set of forms and accompanying procedures, and has the operating units submit their long-range plans on these forms on one certain date each year. The plans are then supposed to be reviewed and approved in a meeting similar to a budget review meeting. Such a procedure does not work. . . . There simply is not time enough in an annual review meeting for a

careful consideration of a whole batch of strategic proposals. . . . It is important that next year's operating budget be examined and approved as an entity so as to ensure that the several pieces are consonant with one another. . . . Except for very general checklists of essential considerations, the strategic planning process follows no prescribed format or timetable. Each problem is sufficiently different from other problems so that each must be approached differently." *Planning and Control Systems, op. cit.*, pp. 38–39.

14. Joint Economic Committee, Congress of the United States, *Hearings, The Planning, Programming-Budgeting System: Progress and Potentials,* 90th Congress, First Session, September 1967, p. 5.

15. *Ibid.*, pp. 80–81. One might think that a way out of the dilemma could be had by adopting a number of goals for an area of policy. When Committee Chairman William Proxmire suggested that more goals should be specified, Gorham replied, "I would like to be the one to give the first goal. The first one in is always in the best shape. The more goals you have, essentially the less useful any one is, because the conflict among them becomes so sharp" (p. 83).

16. *Ibid.*, p. 6.

17. Anthony again supplies a useful comparison from private firms that makes a similar point: "An increasing number of businesses make profit and balance sheet projections for several years ahead, a process which has come to be known by the name 'long-range planning.' . . . A five-year plan usually is a projection of the costs and revenues that are anticipated under policies and programs *already approved,* rather than a device for consideration of, and decision on, new policies and programs. The five-year plan reflects strategic decisions already taken; it is not the essence of the process of making new decisions. . . . In some companies, the so-called five-year plan is nothing more than a mechanical extrapolation of current data, with no reflection of management decisions and judgment; such an exercise is virtually worthless" (*Planning and Control System, op. cit.*, pp. 57–58).

18. An excellent discussion of different purposes of budgeting and stages of budgetary development is found in Allen Schick, "The Road to PPB: The Stages of Budget Reform," *Public Administration Review* 26 (December 1966), pp. 243–258.

19. In another paper ("Toward A Radical Incrementalism," *op. cit.*) I have proposed that policy analysis would be facilitated by abolishing the annual budget cycle. One of the great weaknesses of governmental policy making is that policies are formulated a good two years before funds become available. Given the difficulties of devising policies in the first place, the time lag wreaks havoc with the best analysis. Since no one seems disposed to consider this alternative seriously, I mention it merely in passing as a change that would fit in with what has been suggested.

20. Frederick C. Mosher, "Program Budgeting in Foreign Affairs: Some Reflections," memorandum prepared at the request of the Subcommittee on National Security and International Operations of the Committee on Government Operations, U.S. Senate, 90th Congress, Second Session, 1968.

21. *Hearings, The Planning-Programming-Budgeting System: Progress and Potentials, op. cit.*, pp. 77–78.

22. "Toward A Radical Incrementalism," *op. cit.*, pp. 27–29.

23. When Charles Hitch was Controller of the Defense Department, the policy analysis unit reported directly to him, as did the budget unit. One reported result is that the policy unit was able to do its work without being drawn into the daily concerns of the budget men. When policy analysis (called systems analysis) was given separate status, with its own assistant secretary, there was apparently a much greater tendency for its members to insist upon control of immediate budgetary decisions. Hence the distinction between longer-run policy analysis and shorter-run budgeting tended to be obscured. It would be interesting to know whether the participants saw it in this way. Optimal placement of a policy analysis unit is bound to be a source of difficulty and a subject of controversy.

24. Clay Thomas Whitehead, "Uses and Abuses of Systems Analysis," The RAND Corporation, September 1967.

25. See Martin Landau, "Redundancy," *Public Administration Review,* scheduled for publication in Vol. 29 (July-August 1969).

26. For a fine example of original thought on this question, see Paul Feldman. "Benefits and the Role of Government in a Market Economy," Institute For Defense Analysis, Research Paper, February 1968, p. 477.

36
The Peter Principle
Laurence J. Peter & Raymond Hull

When I was a boy I was taught that the men upstairs knew what they were doing. I was told, "Peter, the more you know, the further you go." So I stayed in school until I graduated from college and then went forth into the world clutching firmly these ideas and my new teaching certificate. During the first year of teaching I was upset to find that a number of teachers, school principals, supervisors and superintendents appeared to be unaware of their professional responsibilities and incompetent in executing their duties. For example my principal's main concerns were that all window shades be at the same level, that classrooms should be quiet and that no one step on or near the rose beds. The superintendent's main concerns were that no minority group, no matter how fanatical, should ever be offended and that all official forms be submitted on time. The children's education appeared farthest from the administrator's mind.

At first I thought this was a special weakness of the school system in which I taught so I applied for certification in another province. I filled out the special forms, enclosed the required documents and complied willingly with all the red tape. Several weeks later, back came my application and all the documents!

No, there was nothing wrong with my credentials; the forms were correctly filled out; an official departmental stamp showed that they had been received in good order. But an accompanying letter said, "The new regulations require that such forms cannot be accepted by the Department of Education unless they have been registered at the Post Office to ensure safe delivery. Will you please remail the forms to the Department, making sure to register them this time?"

I began to suspect that the local school system did not have a monopoly on incompetence.

As I looked further afield, I saw that every organization contained a number of persons who could not do their jobs.

A UNIVERSAL PHENOMENON

Occupational incompetence is everywhere. Have you noticed it? Probably we all have noticed it.

We see indecisive politicians posing as resolute statesmen and the "authoritative source" who blames his misinformation on "situational imponderables." Limitless are the public servants who are indolent and insolent; military commanders whose behavioral timidity belies their dread-naught rhetoric, and governors whose innate servility prevents their actually governing. In our sophistication, we virtually shrug aside the immoral cleric, corrupt judge, incoherent attorney, author who cannot

Source: Reprinted by permission of William Morrow and Co., Inc. from THE PETER PRINCIPLE by Laurence J. Peter & Raymond Hull.

write and English teacher who cannot spell. At universities we see proclamations authored by administrators whose own office communications are hopelessly muddled; and droning lectures from inaudible or incomprehensible instructors.

Seeing incompetence at all levels of every hierarchy—political, legal, educational and industrial—I hypothesized that the cause was some inherent feature of the rules governing the placement of employees. Thus began my serious study of the ways in which employees move upward through a hierarchy, and of what happens to them after promotion.

For my scientific data hundreds of case histories were collected. Here are three typical examples.

Municipal Government File, Case No. 17

J. S. Minion *(Some names have been changed, in order to protect the guilty.)* was a maintenance foreman in the public works department of Excelsior City. He was a favorite of the senior officials at City Hall. They all praised his unfailing affability.

"I like Minion," said the superintendent of works. "He has good judgment and is always pleasant and agreeable."

This behavior was appropriate for Minion's position: he was not supposed to make policy, so he had no need to disagree with his superiors.

The superintendent of works retired and Minion succeeded him. Minion continued to agree with everyone. He passed to his foreman every suggestion that came from above. The resulting conflicts in policy, and the continual changing of plans, soon demoralized the department. Complaints poured in from the Mayor and other officials, from taxpayers and from the maintenance-workers' union.

Minion still says "Yes" to everyone, and carries messages briskly back and forth between his superiors and his subordinates. Nominally a superintendent, he actually does the work of a messenger. The maintenance department regularly exceeds its budget, yet fails to fulfill its program of work. In short, Minion, a competent foreman, became an incompetent superintendent.

Service Industries File, Case No. 3

E. Tinker was exceptionally zealous and intelligent as an apprentice at G. Reece Auto Repair Inc., and soon rose to journeyman mechanic. In this job he showed outstanding ability in diagnosing obscure faults, and endless patience in correcting them. He was promoted to foreman of the repair shop.

But here his love of things mechanical and his perfectionism become liabilities. He will undertake any job that he thinks looks interesting, no matter how busy the shop may be. "We'll work it in somehow," he says.

He will not let a job go until he is fully satisfied with it.

He meddles constantly. He is seldom to be found at his desk. He is usually up to his elbows in a dismantled motor and while the man who should be doing the work stands watching, other workmen sit around waiting to be assigned new tasks. As a result the shop is always overcrowded with work, always in a muddle, and delivery times are often missed.

Tinker cannot understand that the average customer cares little about perfection—he wants his car back on time! He cannot understand that most of his men are less interested in motors than in their pay checks. So Tinker cannot get on with his customers or with his subordinates. He was a competent mechanic, but is now an incompetent foreman.

Military File, Case No. 8

Consider the case of the late renowned General A. Goodwin. His hearty, informal manner, his racy style of speech, his scorn for petty regulations and his undoubted personal bravery made him the idol of his men. He led them to many well-deserved victories.

When Goodwin was promoted to field marshal he had to deal, not with ordinary soldiers, but with politicians and allied generalissimos.

He would not conform to the necessary protocol. He could not turn his tongue to the conventional courtesies and flatteries. He quarreled with all the dignitaries and took to lying for days at a time, drunk and sulking, in his trailer. The conduct of the war slipped out of his hands into those of his subordinates. He had been promoted to a position that he was incompetent to fill.

AN IMPORTANT CLUE!

In time I saw that all such cases had a common feature. The employee had been promoted from a position of competence to a position of incompetence. I saw that, sooner or later, this could happen to every employee in every hierarchy.

Hypothetical Case File, Case No. 1

Suppose you own a pill-rolling factory, Perfect Pill Incorporated. Your foreman pill roller dies of a perforated ulcer. You need a replacement. You naturally look among your rank-and-file pill rollers.

Miss Oval, Mrs. Cylinder, Mr. Ellipse and Mr. Cube all show various degrees of incompetence. They will naturally be ineligible for promotion. You will choose—other things being equal—your most competent pill roller, Mr. Sphere, and promote him to foreman.

Now suppose Mr. Sphere proves competent as foreman. Later, when your general foreman, Legree, moves up to Works Manager, Sphere will be eligible to take his place.

If, on the other hand, Sphere is an incompetent foreman, he will get no more promotion. He has reached what I call his "level of incompetence." He will stay there till the end of his career.

Some employees, like Ellipse and Cube, reach a level of incompetence in the lowest grade and are never promoted. Some, like Sphere (assuming he is not a satisfactory foreman), reach it after one promotion.

E. Tinker, the automobile repair-shop foreman, reached his level of incompetence on the third stage of the hierarchy. General Goodwin reached his level of incompetence at the very top of the hierarchy.

So my analysis of hundreds of cases of occupational incompetence led me on to formulate *The Peter Principle: "in a hierarchy, every employee tends to rise to his level of incompetence."*

A NEW SCIENCE!

Having formulated the Principle, I discovered that I had inadvertently founded a new science, hierarchiology, for the study of hierarchies.

The term "hierarcy" was originally used to describe the system of church government by priests graded into ranks. The contemporary meaning includes any organization whose members or employees are arranged in order of rank, grade or class.

Hierarchiology, although a relatively recent discipline, appears to have great applicability to the fields of public and private administration.

THIS MEANS YOU!

My Principle is the key to an understanding of all hierarchal systems, and therefore to an understanding of the whole structure of civilization. A few eccentrics try to avoid getting involved with hierarchies, but everyone in business, industry, trade-unionism, politics, government, the armed forces, religion and education is so involved. All of them are controlled by the Peter Principle.

Many of them, to be sure, may win a promotion or two, moving from one level of competence to a higher level of competence. But competence in that new position qualifies them for still another promotion. For each individual, for *you,* for *me,* the final promotion is from a level of competence to a level of incompetence. (The phenomena of "percussive sublimation" (commonly referred to as "being kicked upstairs") and of "the lateral arabesque" are not, as the casual observer might think, exceptions to the Principle. They are only pseudo-promotions, and will be dealt with in Chapter 3.)

So, given enough time—and assuming the existence of enough ranks in the hierarchy—each employee rises to, and remains at, his level of incompetence. Peter's Corollary states: *in time, every post tends to be occupied by an employee who is incompetent to carry out its duties.*

WHO TURNS THE WHEELS?

You will rarely find, of course, a system in which *every* employee has reached his level of incompetence. In most instances, something is being done to further the ostensible purposes for which the hierarchy exists.

Work is accomplished by those employees who have not yet reached their level of incompetence.

37

Administrative Decentralization and Political Power

Herbert Kaufman

Curious as it may seem today, bureaucrats in the '30's were regarded by many as heroes in the struggles for a better social order. As late as 1945, Paul Appleby, a prominent New Deal official, felt impelled to dedicate a book to "Bill Bureaucrat,"[1] and much of the literature of professional and academic public administration had a confident, approving, consensual tone.

By mid-'50's it was possible to discern emerging conflicts of doctrine and practice among those who previously applauded and defended bureaucrats. A major shift of outlook and values in governmental design seemed to be taking place.

It was not the first such shift to occur in our history. On the contrary, the administrative history of our governmental machinery can be construed as a succession of shifts of this kind, each brought about by a change in emphasis among three values:

Source: From *Public Administration Review,* 29 (January-February 1969), pp. 3–15. Some subheadings shortened.

representativeness, politically neutral competence, and executive leadership.[2] None of these values was ever totally neglected in any of our past modifications of governmental design, but each enjoyed greater emphasis than the others in different periods.

Thus, for example, our earliest political institutions at all levels can be interpreted as reactions against executive dominance in the colonial era. Later on, extreme reliance was placed on representative mechanisms, which made the post-Revolutionary years an interval of great power for legislatures and elective officials and of comparative weakness for executives in most jurisdictions. By the middle of the 19th century, however, legislative supremacy, the long ballot, and the spoils system resulted in widespread disillusionment with our political institutions, which in turn gave impetus to efforts to take administration out of politics by lodging it in independent boards and commissions and by introducing the merit system to break the hold of parties on the bureaucracies. But the fragmentation of government reduced both efficiency and representativeness, and the search for unification led to the popularly elected chief executives; the 20th century was marked by a rapid growth in their powers.

This is not to say the values are pursued abstractly, as ends in themselves, or that there is universal agreement on which should be emphasized at any given time. On the contrary, different segments of the population feel differentially disadvantaged by the governmental machinery in operation at any given moment, and agitate for structural changes to improve their position—i.e., to increase their influence—in the system. Discontent on the part of various groups is thus the dynamic force that motivates the quest for new forms. Some groups feel resentful because they consider themselves inadequately represented; some feel frustrated because, though they are influential in forming policy, the policy decisions seem to be dissipated by the political biases or the technical incompetence of the public bureaucracies; some feel thwarted by lack of leadership to weld the numerous parts of government into a coherent, unified team that can get things done. At different points in time, enough people (not necessarily a numerical majority) will be persuaded by one or another of these discontents to support remedial action—increased representatives, better and politically neutral bureaucracies, or stronger chief executives as the case may be. But emphasis on one remedy over a prolonged period merely accumulates the other discontents until new remedies gain enough support to be put into effect, and no totally stable solution has yet been devised. So the constant shift in emphasis goes on.

No matter how vigorous the pursuit of any one value at any given time, the other two are never obliterated. And no matter how determined the quest for any one value, it is never realized as fully as its most extreme advocates would like. Even after a century of efforts to strengthen neutral competence and executive leadership, partisan influence still retains great vitality and executive institutions at all levels of government are still remarkably fragmented. And after a century of denigration of "politics," politicians, and "special interests," representativeness is still a powerful force in American government. But in that century of building professional bureaucracies and executive capacities for leadership, the need for new modes of representation designed to keep pace with new economic, social, and political developments did not arouse equal concern. Partly for this reason, and partly because the burgeoning of large-scale organizations in every area of life contributes to the sensation of individual helplessness, recent years have witnessed an upsurge of a sense of alienation on the part of many people, to a feeling that they as individuals cannot effectively register their own preferences on the decisions emanating from the organs of government. These people have begun to demand redress of the balance among the three values, with special attention to the deficiencies in representativeness.

CURRENT DISSATISFACTION

America is not wanting in arrangements for representation. More than half a million public offices are still elective.[3] Legislatures and individual legislators retain immense powers, and do not hesitate to wield them liberally. Parties are still strong and attentive to the claims of many constituencies. Interest groups are numerous and press their demands through myriad channels. The mass media serve as watchdogs of governmental operations. Administrative agencies incorporate manifold procedures for representation into their decision-making processes, including quasi-judicial and quasi-legislative hearings, representative or bipartisan administrative boards, and advisory bodies.[4] Opportunities for participation in political decisions are plentiful. Why, then, is there dissatisfaction with these arrangements?

Fundamentally, because substantial (though minority) segments of the population apparently believe the political, economic, and social systems have not delivered to them fair—even minimally fair—shares of the system's benefits and rewards, and because they think they cannot win their appropriate shares in those benefits and rewards through the political institutions of the country as these are now constituted. These people are not mollified by assurances that the characteristics of the system thwarting them also thwart selfish and extremist interests; it appears to them that only the powerful get attention, and that the already powerful are helped by the system to deny influence to all who now lack it. Thus, the system itself, and not just evil men who abuse it, is discredited.

At least three characteristics of the system contribute heavily to this impression on the part of the deprived: first, existing representative organs are capable of giving only quite general mandates to administrative agencies, yet it is in the day-to-day decisions and actions of officials and employees in the lower levels that individual citizens perceive the policies. There are often gross discrepancies between the promise of the programs (as construed by the populace to be served) and performance—sometimes because the expectations of the populace are unrealistically optimistic, sometimes because programs are impeded by difficulties that could not be foreseen, and sometimes because bureaucracies are too bound by habit or timidity to alter their customary behavior in any but the most modest ways.[5]

Second, the pluralistic nature of the political system provides abundant opportunities for vetoes by opponents of change. Each proposed innovation must run a gamut of obstacles, and ends as a product of bargains and compromises. So change usually comes slowly, by small advances, in bits and pieces. Those who regard particular problems as requiring urgent, immediate action are prone to condemn a system that behaves so "sluggishly."

Third, the scale of organization in our society has grown so large that only through large-scale organization does it seem possible to have a significant impact. This impression alone is enough to make individual people feel helplessly overwhelmed by huge, impersonal machines indifferent to their uniqueness and their humanity. In addition, however, some interests—notably those of Negroes and of youth—have recently begun to develop the organizational skills to mobilize their political resources only to find that it takes time to build channels of access to political structures. Rather than wait for admission to these structures—where, incidentally, they are likely to encounter larger, more experienced, well-entrenched organizations opposed to them—these groups, while continuing to strive for recognition in the older institutions, have adopted a strategy of deriding those institutions and seeking to build new ones in which they can have greater, perhaps dominant, influence.

Thus, the plenitude of traditional modes of representation no longer suffices; the existing methods do not adequately accommodate many of the demands upon them. Just as the adaptation of governmental design during the past century has gravitated toward furnishing expertise and leadership, so it is now under pressure from several quarters to accord a greater role to representativeness.

MORE REPRESENTATIVE ADMINISTRATIVE AGENCIES

The quest for representativeness in this generation centers primarily on administrative agencies. Since administrative agencies have grown dramatically in size, function, and authority in the middle third of this century, this is hardly surprising. Chief executives, legislatures, and courts make more decisions of *sweeping* effect, but the agencies make a far greater number of decisions affecting individual citizens in *intimate* ways. In them lies the source of much present unrest; in them, therefore, the remedies are sought.

One type of proposal for making administrative agencies more representative is traditional in character; situating spokesmen for the interests affected in strategic positions within the organizations. Often, this means nothing more than filling vacancies on existing boards and commissions with appointees enjoying the confidence of, or perhaps even chosen by, those interests.[6] In the case of the controversial police review boards, it involves injecting into administrative structures new bodies, dominated by ethnic minority groups or their friends, to survey and constrain bureaucratic behavior. Architecturally, such plans do not require drastic modifications of existing organizations, and their objectives could probably be met by changes in personnel at high organizational levels.

More unorthodox, but swiftly gaining acceptance, is the concept of a centralized governmental complaint bureau, clothed with legal powers of investigation, to look into citizen complaints against administrative agencies and to correct inequities and abuses—the office of "ombudsman."[7] Once, it was chiefly through his representative in the appropriate legislative body, or through the local unit of his political party, that a citizen of modest status and means petitioned for a remedy of a grievance. But professionalization of administration and the insulation of bureaucrats from party politics have reduced the ability of the parties to be of real help, and the constituencies of legislators have grown so large that they rarely intervene in more than a *pro forma* fashion on behalf of most individual constituents. Today, some observers contend that only a specialized fulltime official, wise in the ways of bureaucracy, having a vested interest in correcting its errors, and supported by adequate staff and authority, can perform this function effectively; apparently, it takes a bureaucrat to control a bureaucrat. Advocates of this proposed new agency defend it on the grounds that it would constitute a channel of representation for people who now have no satisfactory alternative.

The most sweeping expression of the unrest over lack of representativeness is the growing demand for extreme administrative decentralization, frequently coupled with insistence on local clientele domination of the decentralized organizations. Dramatic manifestations of this movement occurred in the antipoverty program and in education.

In the antipoverty program the original legislation included a provision that community action be "developed, conducted, and administered with maximum feasible participation of residents of the areas and members of the groups served." Initially by interpretation of the Office of Economic Opportunity, and later by statute, the provision was construed to mean that community action boards should try to allot some of their chairs to the poor, so that the poor would have a voice in the highest policy councils of the community programs. Whatever the original intent of the drafters of the phrase (about which there is some disagreement), it has come to mean the program is to be run in substantial degree *by* the poor, not merely *for* the poor.[8]

In public education the new trend is exemplified by recent events in New York City. During 1967, demands for decentralization of the municipal school system gathered force swiftly: Leaders in the state legislature urged it. Three separate public reports recommended it in the strongest possible terms. The mayor endorsed the principle unequivocally. When concrete proposals were introduced into the legislature the following year, however, vehement opposition from the teachers' union, the school administrators' association, and the City Board of Education resulted in modification of many of the provisions the objectors found unacceptable. The measure ultimately enacted emerged weaker than the plans favored by the advocates of decentralization, but it was a major step in their direction; the thrust toward decentralization and neighborhood control of schools was slowed but not stopped, and resistance, however determined and forceful, seemed destined to give way over a broad front.

The outcry has not been limited to the war on poverty and to education. It was taken up in public housing when the Secretary of Housing and Urban Development unveiled a program to modernize low-rent projects that included an augmented role for tenants in their operation.[9] At a meeting of the American Institute of Planners, a dissenting group, calling itself Planners for Equal Opportunity, demanded a larger place for the poor in city planning, and exhorted its members to engage in "advocate planning," which is to say expert counsel for neighborhood associations unhappy with official plans for renewal in their areas. New York City recently began experimenting with a process of "affiliating" its public hospitals with voluntary hospitals that would be responsible for their administration, a plan that would presumably include lay boards representing the community served by each institution, and its Police Department is cooperating with experimental community security patrols of locally recruited young people. Similarly, a neighborhood council in Washington, D.C., "asked for more citizen control over police, either in the form of local police aides or resurrection of the auxiliary police force used here in World War II." The American Assembly, assessing the role of law in a changing society, called for development of "rapid procedures at the neighborhood level . . . to adjudicate disputes over simple transactions."[10] In response to the Poor People's Campaign in Washington, "Five agencies—Health, Education and Welfare, Agriculture, Labor, Housing and Urban Development and the Office of Economic Opportunity—said they would review their plans to involve poor people themselves in local decisions affecting welfare, food, employment, housing and other antipoverty programs."[11]

The movement is not confined to public agencies; it reaches into colleges and universities, where students, often by direct action, have been asserting a claim to participation in the policies of these institutions—one activist reportedly going so far as to predict that American universities will soon resemble Latin American institutions, in which students hire and fire professors and determine the curricula. A sociologist recently suggested establishment of closed-circuit television stations in which the neighborhood listeners might control programming.[12] In the Roman Catholic Archdiocese of New York, a committee of priests presented a petition to the archbishop-designate requesting, among other things, a voice in the selection of auxiliary bishops and other high officials, and establishment of a Pastoral Council of priests, nuns, and laymen to be consulted in advance on projected programs and budgets, a request to which he partially acceded on taking office. Later, priests formed a national organization, the National Federation of Priests Councils, to seek a stronger voice in church affairs. In Washington, D.C., classes at a high school were suspended in the face of a boycott by students demanding "a real say on what goes on inside the school."

But it is in the government sphere that the tendency has been winning widest endorsement. Indeed, some of our general forms of government, as well as specific agencies, have come under attack. The president of the American Political Science Association, for example, in his 1967 presidential address,[13] raised questions about the compatibility of large units of government—national, state, and urban—with the principles of democracy. Searching for a unit large enough to avoid triviality yet "small enough so that citizens can participate extensively," he suggested 50,000 to 200,000 as the optimum size range for democratic city governments. Moreover, he concluded that even in polities of this size, "participation is reduced for most people to nothing more than voting in elections," and he therefore commended experimentation to decentralize power and authority still further in order to discover viable "smaller units within which citizens can from time to time formulate and express their desires, consult with officials, and in some cases participate even more fully in decisions."

Similarly, the Advisory Commission on Intergovernmental Relations in Washington, at almost the same time, was recommending that "Neighborhood initiative and self-respect be fostered by authorizing counties and large cities to establish, and at their discretion to abolish, neighborhood subunits endowed with limited powers of taxation and local self-government."[14] At Ithaca, N.Y., the Office of Regional Resources and Development concluded that larger metropolitan centers should be decentralized because they have reached a point at which "it is almost impossible to deal with human problems on a human scale," and called for investigation of strategies for more effective use of cities with 50,000 to 500,000 residents—

proposals that won the editorial plaudits of *The Washington Post.*[15]

A meeting of Americans for Democratic Action was warned by Daniel P. Moynihan, an outspoken liberal, that "Liberals must divest themselves of the notion that the nation, especially the cities of the nation, can be run from agencies in Washington.[16] Senator Robert F. Kennedy, campaigning for the Democratic presidential nomination in Los Angeles, promised audiences a revolution in the distribution of political power that would, among other things, reduce the authority of the federal bureaucracy in Washington. "I want," he said, "the control over your destinies to be decided by the people in Watts, not by those of us who are in Washington."[17] Richard M. Nixon similarly urged the federal government to relinquish some of its powers to state and local governments, voluntary associations, and individuals, saying, "One reason people are shouting so loudly today is that it's far from where they are to where the power is," and that power should be brought closer to them rather than exercised from remote centers. In important respects, the Heller-Pechman plan rests partly on the premise that federal surpluses should be shared with states and cities in time of peace because they can be more effectively spent by the smaller units of government than by Washington directly.[18]

In short, "decentralization" of administration is in the air everywhere.[19] While it is sometimes defended on grounds of efficiency, it is more frequently justified in terms of effective popular participation in government. Reformers of earlier generations succeeded in raising the level of expertise and professionalism in the bureaucracies, and to a lesser extent, in improving capacity of chief executives to control the administrative arms of government. Now, people are once again turning their attention to representativeness, and are trying to elevate it to a more prominent place in the governmental scheme of things.

THE CONTINUING SEARCH FOR LEADERSHIP

Public bureaucracies are under fire not only from critics outside the machinery of government, but also from inside. Chief executives who once championed measures to insulate the bureaucracies from partisan politics as steps toward enlarging their own control over administrative agencies discovered that these measures did not make the agencies more responsive to executive direction; rather, they increased agency independence. This independence, in turn, makes it difficult for the executives to secure enthusiastic adoption of new approaches to social problems; money pumped into new programs administered by established agencies tends to be used more for intensification of traditional ways of operating than for inventive departures from familiar patterns. Furthermore, it results in massive problems of coordination of effort, and even in dissipation of energies in interbureau rivalries. Consequently, just as segments of the public are upset by the alleged unresponsiveness of administration to their demands, so chief executives have been increasingly concerned about the unresponsiveness of agencies to their leadership.

We may therefore look forward to new waves of administrative reorganization proposals. One principal thrust of the movement will, as in the past, be toward rationalizing, enlarging, and strengthening the executive-office staffs of the heads of governmental units at all levels, and toward building up the staffs of the administrators who report directly to the heads. More and more, chief executives will reach out for new devices to coordinate policy decisions, to work up fresh programs to deal with emergent problems, and to maintain the momentum of innovations adopted.[20] Executive offices will be redesigned; the U.S. Bureau of the Budget, for example, has only recently undergone a major reorganization.[21] New vigor will be applied to the exploration of "superdepartments," with the Department of Defense as a prototype; Mayor Lindsay, for instance, has expended much political capital on introducing this concept into the government of New York City. Programming-planning-budgeting systems, in many variants, will continue to spread.[22] There will be a new burst of literature calling attention to the relative powerlessness of our highest public executives.[23]

Another stream of recommendations will urge strengthening executive leadership through what its advocates will call "decentralization," but which, in fact, is better characterized as organization by area as opposed to the present almost exclusive organization by functional departments and bureaus.[24] The justification for it will be couched in terms of efficiency—the need to speed decisions in the field without referral to headquarters and without loss of coordination among field personnel in different bureaus. The consequences will extend further, however, because areal officers in the field would give top executives lines of communication and control alternative to existing functional channels, thus actually strengthening central authority. At the federal level, this will mean renewed attempts to set up much stronger regional representatives of the heads of cabinet departments than any we have had in the past. It will also mean intensified efforts to establish regional presidential representatives in the field.[25] Similarly, we may anticipate governors and their department heads will follow the same strategies with respect to regions within the states. At the local level, Mayor Lindsay has already sought—with very limited success—to win approval for "little city halls" throughout New York. Distinctively American versions of the European prefect may yet make an appearance.

In short, dissatisfaction with public bureaucracies will furnish ammunition for the defenders of executive leadership as well as for the proponents of increased representation of the consumers of public services. The bureaucracies will be pressed from both above and below.

CONFLICT AND COALITION

Sources of Conflict

It has long been recognized that much public policy is shaped largely by clusters of bureaus, their organized clienteles, and legislative committees and legislators specializing in each public function[26]—health, education, welfare, etc. The arguments for strengthening chief executives and their department heads *vis-à-vis* the clusters are based chiefly on the need to offset the resulting fragmentation of government by introducing sufficient central direction to unify the policies and administration of these separate centers of power. The arguments for new modes of participation by the public in these centers rest on the conviction that hitherto excluded and unorganized interests have little to say about decisions that affect them profoundly. But it is most unlikely that the arguments of either kind will be warmly received by those already in key positions in each decision center.

They will resist not simply out of abstract jealousy of their own power or stubborn unwillingness to share their influence with each other, though these motives will doubtless not be absent. They will oppose because, in addition, the proposed reforms threaten those values which present arrangements protect. Bureau chiefs and the organized bureaucracies perceive intervention by political executives as the intrusion of partisan politics into fields from which doctrine has for many years held that politics should be excluded; they see jeopardy for the competence nurtured so carefully and painfully against political distortion or extinction. Similarly, opening the system to lay members of local communities looks like a negation of the expertise built up by the specialist. Legislators regard strong regional officials responsive to chief executives and their cabinets as executive attempts to invade legislative districts and usurp the representative function of legislative bodies. In like fashion, local control of administrative programs could conceivably weaken the representative basis of legislative institutions, a development that men of goodwill may fear for quite public-spirited reasons.

So the champions of executive leadership and the evangelists of expanded representativeness have many obstacles to overcome before they have their respective ways. For example, Congress has been cautious about presidential recommendations of added funds and personnel for the heads of cabinet departments, and has always looked with suspicion on so relatively innocuous an innovation as field offices for the Bureau of the Budget.[27] The Office of Economic Opportunity in the Executive Office of the President always operated chiefly through established bureaus and engaged in independent administration only in limited ways; gradually, through delegation, it has been relinquishing its control over programs to the bureaus and the future of even those few programs it manages directly is uncertain. Moreover, its community-action program aroused resentment among both congressmen and local executives, to whom the action agencies appeared as springboards for political rivals; consequently, legislation in 1967 authorized greater control of the agencies by local governments. In New York City, the mayor's "little city halls," which he presented as a device for bringing the people and their government closer together, were soundly defeated by a City Council (dominated by the opposite party) denouncing the plan as a strategy for establishing political clubhouses throughout the city at public expense.[28] And, when the plan for school decentralization appeared, the largest teachers' union and the Board of Education—which not long before had been at each other's throats in labor disputes—each took a similar firm stand against it. In Board-sponsored experiments with community control of schools in Harlem and in Brooklyn, the community leaders and the head of the same teachers' union engaged in acrimonious battles with each other. The reformers are not having an easy time of it.

A Coalition of Executives

To advance their cause, troubled chief executives at all levels, all suffering similar frustrations, could conceivably make common cause with one another. Thus, the President may well find it strategically advantageous to build closer ties with governors and big-city mayors than was ever the case before. Congress would find it more uncomfortable to resist presidential demands for creation of strong field representatives with jurisdiction over bureau field personnel if state and local officials in their own home areas support the demands than if the President alone advances them. And these state and local officials may be receptive to such an association because the fragmentation of the system is as vexing to them as it is to the President himself.

Gubernatorial and big-city mayoral vexations spring from three sources. First, procedures in many intergovernmental programs are irritatingly slow; it often takes months—sometimes more than a year, in fact—to get decisions on projects and financing from federal agencies, partly because so much business is referred to Washington for approval.[29] To be sure, state and municipal executives have no wish to speed negative decisions on their requests, but hanging decisions are even worse; they can neither plan programs nor try to get the decisions reversed. They can only wait while dangerous pressures build up in their jurisdictions, and whole networks of interrelated programs are slowed or brought to a halt.

Second, procedures are often labyrinthine and uncoordinated,[30] so that it takes specialists to keep track of terminal dates, filing of applications for renewal of grants, compliance with accounting requirements, meshing of separate grants in individual projects, and explanations of variations in allowances (such as differences in relocation allowances for businesses and individual tenants moved for highway construction on the one hand and urban renewal on the other), that bewilder and annoy the public. These intricacies almost paralyze action at the grassroots, and divert needed manpower from substantive program operations to administrative routine.

Third, federal grants for very specific purposes encourage a tendency toward what the 1955 Commission on Intergovernmental Relations referred to as "a more or less independent government of their own" on the part of functional specialists at all levels of government who are only nominally under the control of their respective chief executives.[31] In point of fact, the chief executives are apparently reduced in many instances to virtually ceremonial ratification of the intergovernmental arrangements worked out by such specialists, and to the most superficial oversight of the administration of the arrangements.

So governors and big-city mayors have reason to applaud the introduction of federal regional officers with authority to rationalize the actions of federal field personnel in the bureaus. For reasons of their own, they may well find the "prefectoral" pattern of organization, which, as we have seen, will suggest itself ever more insistently to the President, coincides with their own preferences.

This congruence of presidential, gubernatorial, and mayoral interests is not entirely speculative; indications of it have already appeared. Late in 1966, for example, President Johnson sent to a number of his top officials a memorandum[32] directing that federal assistance programs "be worked out and planned in a cooperative spirit with those chief officials of State, county and local governments who are answerable to the citizens. To the fullest practical extent, I want you to take steps to afford representatives of the Chief Executives of State and local governments the opportunity to advise and consult in the development and execution of programs which directly affect the conduct of State and local affairs." A few months later, to implement the President's memorandum, the Bureau of the Budget issued a circular[33] spelling out procedures for consultation, and identifying as one of its central policies the requirement that "The central coordinating role of heads of State and local governments, including their role of initiating and developing State and local programs, will be supported and strengthened." Meanwhile, former Florida Governor Farris Bryant, director of the Office of Emergency Planning in the Executive Office of the President, was leading teams of federal officials to 40 state capitals for discussions with governors and other state administrators;[34] Vice President Humphrey was conducting a program of visits and discussions with mayors, county officers, and other local executives;[35] and the President was formulating and announcing a plan to assign each member of his cabinet responsibility for liaison with four or five states, "with instructions to maintain personal contact between the Governors and the White House."[36] And in early 1968, the Advisory Commission on Intergovernmental Relations recommended that:

> 1. Coordination of Federal grant programs being administered by a variety of Federal departments and agencies be strengthened through the Executive Office of the President;
> 2. The authority to review and approve plans developed as a condition of Federal formula-type grants to State and local governments be decentralized to Federal regional offices and wide variations in boundaries of Federal administrative regions be reduced.[37]

An alliance of public chief executives is already taking shape.

Confluence of Leadership and Representativeness

At the same time, groups clamoring for local control of administrative programs, confronted with the suspicion and resentment of bureaucracies and their legislative and interest-group allies, will probably discover that they get their most sympathetic hearings from chief executives, especially from big-city mayors. For such groups can provide the executive with the counterweights to the bureaucracies: they constitute an alternative channel of information about administrative performance, reducing executive dependence on the bureaucracies on the one hand and on the mass media (with their bias toward the sensational) on the other. The groups are a constituency that can be mobilized to help exert leverage on bureaucracies resistant to executive leadership. They furnish a direct conduit to localities from the executive mansions. They can serve as the nuclei of discrete, executive-oriented campaign organizations. Chief executives probably could not create the groups if they set out deliberately to do so, but it would be surprising if they did not eventually perceive the advantages of collaborating with them now that a variety of complaints has brought the groups spontaneously into being.

It will be an uneasy, mutually wary relationship. To neighborhood and community associations, the paradox of turning to remote chief executives in a quest for local control will be disturbing. To chief executives, the risk of opening a Pandora's box and releasing uncontrollable disintegrative forces will give pause. Yet each can gain so much from an alliance with the other that it is hard to avoid the feeling the attractions will overcome the anxieties. I do not mean to imply the alliance will be formal or structured. I mean only to suggest each side will turn to the other as appropriate occasions arise, and that the occasions will arise with increasing frequency in the years ahead. In this way, the new voices of representatives and the more familiar voices of executive leadership will be joined in a common challenge to those who speak for neutral competence and for older institutions of representation.

THE SUBSEQUENT PHASE OF THE CYCLE

So it seems reasonable to anticipate that "decentralization" of two types will indeed occur: concessions will be made to the demands for greater local influence on public programs, and there will be some headway toward establishing territorial officers with at least limited authority over field personnel of the functional bureaus.

It will not take long for the price of these changes to make itself felt. Decentralization will soon be followed by disparities in practice among the numerous small units, brought on by differences in human and financial resources, that will engender demands for central intervention to restore equality and balance and concerted action; the factors underlying the movement toward metropolitan units of government and toward conditional federal grants-in-aid will, in other words, reassert themselves. Decentralization will stand in the way of other goals, such as school integration (as did "states' rights" doctrines in other times). It will give rise to competition among the units that will be disastrous for many of them, which will find it more difficult to attract talent and money than others that start from a more advantageous position. In some units, strong factions may well succeed in reviving a new spoils system, thus lowering the quality of some vital services. Decentralization of public administration will not necessarily be accompanied by decentralization of the other institutions with which public units deal, such as unions of public employees, so that the local units may find themselves at a serious disadvantage in negotiations and unable to resist the pressures of special interests. Economies of scale, which are admittedly overstated very frequently, nevertheless do exist, and the multiplication of overhead costs in local units will divert some resources from substantive programs to administrative housekeeping. Initially, all these costs will be regarded by those concerned with representativeness as well worth paying, but the accumulation of such grievances over time will inspire a clamor for unification and consolidation.[38]

Similarly, area officials reporting directly to chief executives will soon develop autonomous bases of political power in the regions to which they are assigned. Rapid rotation from area to area will help to reduce their independence, but the rate of rotation will decline because each new assignment will necessitate a period of familiarization with the new territory during which actions and decisions are held in abeyance, and because of local interests, having established comparatively stable relationships with their regional officers, will protest and resist frequent transfers. As the regional officers get more and more involved in regional complexes, they will become more and more ambassadors from the regions to the chief executives instead of the executives' men in the regions.[39] Regional differences and competition will become sources of irritation and controversy. Moreover, regional posts may become convenient and effective springboards to elective office. At first these dangers will seem remote and therefore less important than the immediate gains, but time is likely to reverse the balance.

So the wave of reform after the one now in progress will rally under a banner of earlier days: Take administration out of politics and politics out of administration. Disappointed partisans of the current movement on behalf of representativeness, having won some of their points, will acquiesce in the efforts of a new generation of idealists to elevate the quality, the consistency, the impartiality, the morale, and the devotion to duty of bureaucrats by strengthening and broadening central control and supervision. Chief executives anxious to regain command of the administrative field forces in each of their regions will rediscover the virtues of strong central direction of those forces by functional administrative agencies whose chiefs identify with the executives,[40] and whose standards can be applied evenhandedly everywhere. From above and below, to escape the distortions of purpose inflicted by the vigorous factional politics of localities and regions (as they once sought to free themselves from the toils of self-seeking factions in state and congressional district politics), the apostles of good government will turn back to insulating the bureaucracies against such political heat. The neutrality and independence of the civil service will again be extolled.

It should not be inferred that the process is fruitless because the succession of values is repetitive. Wheels turning on their own axes do advance. Each time the balance among the values is redressed, only to require redress again, some new accommodation among the myriad interests in the society is reached.

Precisely what shape the subsequent resurgence of neutral competence will take in the years beyond, it is impossible to prophesy now. But if the hypothesized cycle of values is at all valid, then strange as it may seem to this generation of reformers, innovators of tomorrow will defend many of the very institutions (as transformed in the course of current controversies) under attack today. And many a forgotten tome and obscure article on public administration, long gathering dust on unpatronized shelves and in unopened files, will be resurrected and praised for its prescience, only to subside again into temporary limbo when another turn of the wheel ends its brief moment of revived relevance.

NOTES

1. Paul H. Appleby, *Big Democracy* (New York: Alfred A. Knopf, 1945). Actually, the dedication was "To John Citizen and Bill Bureaucrat."
2. Herbert Kaufman, "Emerging Conflicts in the Doctrines of Public Administration," *American Political Science Review* 50 4 (December 1956), p. 1,073.
3. U.S. Bureau of the Census, *1967 Census of Governments*, Volume 6, *Popularly Elected Officials of State and Local Governments*, pp. 1 ff.
4. Avery Leiserson, *Administrative Regulation: A Study in Representation of Group Interests* (Chicago: The University of Chicago Press, 1942).
5. See, for instance, the criticism of professional bureaucracy and the demand for "public participation" in resource management decisions by Yale Law School Professor Charles A. Reich in his *Bureaucracy and the Forests* (Santa Barbara, Calif.: Center for the Study of Democratic Institutions, 1962).
6. For example, *The New York Times* reported on November 29, 1967, that "A [New York City] citizen group demanded yesterday that a Negro and a Puerto Rican be named to the city's nine-man Community Mental Health Board." And a high-ranking city antipoverty administrator (suspended for failing to file tax returns) went on a hunger strike to dramatize his demand that Puerto Ricans be named to the Board of Education, the State Board of Regents, the citywide Model Cities Advisory Committee, the Civil Service Commission, and the City Housing Authority (*The New York Times*, June 29, 1968).
7. Walter Gellhorn, *When Americans Complain* (Cambridge, Mass.: Harvard University Press, 1966), and *Ombudsmen and Others* (Cambridge, Mass.: Harvard University Press, 1966); Stanley Anderson (ed.), *Ombudsmen for American Government* (Englewood Cliffs, N.J.: Prentice-Hall, 1968).
8. See the article by S. M. Miller this symposium.
9. *The New York Times*, November 18, 1967. John W. Gardner, former Secretary of Health, Education, and Welfare, and currently chairman of the Urban Coalition, went even further and urged a larger role for Negroes in helping solve the urban crisis generally (*The New York Times*, May 6, 1968).
10. *Report of the American Assembly on Law and the Changing Society* (Chicago: Center for

Continuing Education, University of Chicago, March 14–17, 1968).

11. *The New York Times*, June 30, 1968.

12. Seymour J. Mandelbaum, "Spatial and Temporal Perspectives in the U.S. City," mimeo., (University of Pennsylvania, 1968).

13. Robert A. Dahl, "The City in the Future of Democracy," *American Political Science Review* 61 (December 1967), pp. 967, 969.

14. Advisory Commission on Intergovernmental Relations, *Ninth Annual Report* (Washington, D.C.: the Commission, 1968), p. 21.

15. *The Washington Post*, October 10, 1967.

16. *The New York Times*, September 24, 1967. But he criticized school decentralization a short time later (*The New York Times*, June 5, 1968).

17. *The Washington Post*, March 26, 1968. See also the arguments of a former foreign service officer for "dismantling the present overgrown bureaucratic apparatus" in Washington, Gordon Tullock, *The Politics of Bureaucracy* (Washington, D.C.: Public Affairs Press, 1965), chapter 25. That liberals have thus adopted a position taken by conservatives in New Deal days is an irony to which attention has been drawn by James Q. Wilson, "The Bureaucracy Problem," *The Public Interest* (Winter 1967), pp. 3–4. Note the similarities between the new liberal language and the position of former Governor George C. Wallace of Alabama: "I would," he said, "bring all those briefcase-toting bureaucrats in the Department of Health, Education, and Welfare to Washington and throw their briefcases in the Potomac River. . . ." *The New York Times*, February 9, 1968. His attack on bureaucrats is, of course, based on their zeal in defense of civil rights; the liberals' indictment is constructed on a diametrically opposite appraisal. The impulse toward decentralization thus comes from both the political right and the political left for entirely different reasons—but with combined force.

18. "Revenue sharing expresses the traditional faith most of us have in pluralism and decentralization. . . ." Walter W. Heller and Joseph A. Pechman, *Questions and Answers in Revenue Sharing* (Washington, D.C.: Brookings Institution, 1967), p. 12.

19. Like all slogans, it means different things to different people, however. It is a much more complex and ambiguous concept than it seems; see note 24, below.

20. The Executive Office of the President was created in 1939, when the federal budget was under $9 billion. It has grown since, but not nearly as much as the budget, now 15 times larger and many hundreds of times more complex. Some reordering seems almost inevitable.

21. U.S. Bureau of the Budget, "Work of the Steering Group on Evaluation of the Bureau of the Budget: A Staff Study," July 1967. The reorganization took effect shortly afterwards.

22. The origins of PPBS are many and varied; see Allen Schick, "The Road to PPB," *Public Administration Review* 26 (December 1966), pp. 243–258. But it was the system's utility to the Secretary of Defense from 1961 on in gaining control of his own department that gave widespread currency to the idea and induced the president to make it government-wide in 1965; see U.S. Senate, 90th Congress, 1st Session (1967), Committee on Government Operations, Subcommittee on National Security and International Operations, *Program-Planning-Budgeting: Official Documents*, pp. 1–6, and *Program-Planning-Budgeting: Hearings, Part 1* (August 23, 1967). This new impetus will doubtless lead to adaptive imitation in other governments.

23. Arthur M. Schlesinger, Jr., *A Thousand Days* (Boston: Houghton Mifflin, 1965), pp. 679–680, reports, "he [President Kennedy] had to get the government moving. He came to the White House at a time when the ability of the President to do this had suffered steady constriction. The cliches about the "most powerful office on earth" had concealed the extent to which the mid-century Presidents had much less freedom of action than, say, Jackson or Lincoln or even Franklin Roosevelt. No doubt the mid-century Presidents could blow up the world, but at the same time they were increasingly hemmed in by the growing power of the bureaucracy and of Congress. The President understood this." Similarly, President Johnson's assistant for domestic programs, Joseph A. Califano, Jr., recently complained publicly of the limitations of presidential power, observing that the powers of the office have not kept pace with its growing responsibilities; *The Washington Post*, May 6, 1968.

24. James W. Fesler, *Area and Administration* (University, Ala.: University of Alabama Press, 1949), especially pp. 8–18, and "Approaches to the Understanding of Decentralization," *Journal of Politics* 27 (August 1965), pp. 557–561. See also the essay by John D. Millett, "Field Organization and Staff Supervision,"

in *New Horizons in Public Administration: A Symposium* (University, Ala.: University of Alabama Press, 1945), pp. 98–118.

25. Fesler, *op. cit.*, pp. 88–89. Fesler's writing on this subject anticipated long in advance the problems that were to engender a more general awareness when programs of the New Frontier and the Great Society overwhelmed the administrative machinery.

26. See J. Leiper Freeman, *The Political Process: Executive Bureau-Legislative Committee Relations* (New York: Random House, revised edition, 1965), and the works therein cited in chapter one.

27. Bureau of the Budget field offices were set up in mid-1943 but were eliminated in the early years of the Eisenhower Administration. Recent efforts to revive them, even on a limited basis, ran into stiff opposition; see U.S. Senate, 90th Congress, 1st Session, Subcommittee of the Committee on Appropriations, *Hearings on H.R. 7501: Treasury, Post Office and Executive Office Appropriations for Fiscal Year 1968* (Washington, D.C.: U.S. Government Printing Office, 1967), pp. 973–990. Note especially the comments of Senator Monroney at p. 981: "The reason the committee cut your request for additional personnel last year was because it did not wish to have field offices established. . . . My impression was that we were afraid they would grow into a 50-state bureaucracy with state and regional offices."

28. The mayor proposed 35 local mayor's offices soon after his inauguration; encountering opposition in the Board of Estimate, he tried to set up five by executive order, but the City Council refused to support him, and the comptroller refused to approve payment of their bills. The mayor tried again in May 1967, but was again rebuffed by the Council and the Board of Estimate. Eventually, four local offices were opened, but they were much weaker than was originally anticipated. For the time being, at least, the plan seems emasculated.

29. Stephen K. Bailey, "Co-ordinating the Great Society," *The Reporter* 34 (March 24, 1966), p. 39.

30. *Ibid.*

31. *The Final Report* of the Commission on Intergovernmental Relations (Washington, D.C.: U.S. Government Printing Office, 1955), p. 44. See also Coleman B. Ransone, Jr., *The Office of the Governor of the United States* (University, Ala.: The University of Alabama Press, 1956), p. 249.

32. "The President's Memorandum to Heads of Certain Federal Agencies. November 11, 1966. Subject: Advice and Consultation with State and local officials."

33. Bureau of the Budget Circular No. A-85, June 28, 1967.

34. Advisory Commission on Intergovernmental Relations, *Ninth Annual Report* (Washington, D.C.: the Commission, 1968), p. 12.

35. *Ibid.*, pp. 12–13.

36. The plan grew out of "Mr. Johnson's continuing determination to build domestic as well as foreign bridges by working to sort out the tangled Federal-state relations that have been increasingly complicated by the administration of the Great Society Programs." *The New York Times*, June 8, 1967. See also Terry Sanford, *Storm Over the States* (New York: McGraw-Hill, 1967), pp. 164–166; here a former governor calls on the White House to help state and local governments and quotes James Reston's comment that "He [the President] is reaching out of the governors and mayors of America for a new political, social, and economic partnership."

37. Advisory Commission on Intergovernmental Relations, *op. cit.*, p. 22.

38. Some anxieties about the costs of decentralization have already been voiced in Irving Kristol, "Decentralization for What?" *The Public Interest* 11 (Spring 1968), p. 17, and echoed by Daniel P. Moynihan as he assailed school decentralization as likely to lead to segregated bureaucracies, *The New York Times*, June 5, 1968. Note also the dissents by Governors Rhodes and Rockefeller from a hearty endorsement of neighborhood subunits with limited powers of taxation and local self-government, Advisory Commission on Intergovernmental Relations, *op. cit.*, p. 21.

39. Herbert Kaufman, *The Forest Ranger* (Baltimore: The Johns Hopkins Press, 1960), pp. 75–80.

40. A hint of what lies ahead is suggested by the experience with regional development commissions. Encouraged by the federal government, their establishment was hailed as a step toward decentralization. But their plans began to conflict and compete with each other, and with the work of other federal and state agencies; moreover, powerful political blocs began to aggregate around them. The President had to direct the Secretary of Commerce to coordinate them, giving strong powers of review over their proposals and the aid of a

council of assistant secretaries from ten federal agencies, a measure greeted as a partial re-centralization. *The Washington Post,* December 30, 1967. This dilemma was explicitly foreseen by James W. Fesler, *op. cit.*, especially pp. 100–102.

38
The End of Liberalism: The Indictment

Theodore J. Lowi

The corruption of modern democratic government began with the emergence of interest-group liberalism as the public philosophy. Its corrupting influence takes at least four important forms, four counts, therefore, of an indictment for which most of the foregoing chapters are mere documentation. Also to be indicted, on at least three counts, is the philosophic component of the ideology, pluralism.

SUMMATION I: FOUR COUNTS AGAINST THE IDEOLOGY

1. Interest-group liberalism as public philosophy corrupts democratic government because it deranges and confuses expectations about democratic institutions. Liberalism promotes popular decision-making but derogates from the decisions so made by misapplying the notion to the implementation as well as the formulation of policy. It derogates from the processes by treating all values in the process as equivalent interests. It derogates from democratic rights by allowing their exercise in foreign policy, and by assuming they are being exercised when access is provided. Liberal practices reveal a basic disrespect for democracy. Liberal leaders do not wield the authority of democratic government with the resoluteness of men certain of the legitimacy of their positions, the integrity of their institutions, or the justness of the programs they serve.

2. Interest-group liberalism renders government impotent. Liberal governments cannot plan. Liberals are copious in plans but irresolute in planning. Nineteenth-century liberalism was standards without plans. This was an anachronism in the modern state. But twentieth-century liberalism turned out to be plans without standards. As an anachronism it, too, ought to pass. But doctrines are not organisms. They die only in combat over the minds of men, and no doctrine yet exists capable of doing the job. All the popular alternatives are so very irrelevant, helping to explain the longevity of interest-group liberalism. Barry Goldwater most recently proved the irrelevance of one. The *embourgeoisement* of American unions suggests the irrelevance of others.

Source: Reprinted from *The End of Liberalism* by Theodore J. Lowi, by permission of W. W. Norton & Company, Inc.

The Departments of Agriculture, Commerce, and Labor provide illustrations, but hardly exhaust illustrations, of such impotence. Here clearly one sees how liberalism has become a doctrine whose means are its ends, whose combatants are its clientele, whose standards are not even those of the mob but worse, are those the bargainers can fashion to fit the bargain. Delegation of power has become alienation of public domain—the gift of sovereignty to private satrapies. The political barriers to withdrawal of delegation are high enough. But liberalism reinforces these through the rhetoric of justification and often even permanent legal reinforcement: Public corporations—justified, oddly, as efficient planning instruments—permanently alienate rights of central coordination to the directors and to those who own the corporation bonds. Or, as Walter Adams finds, the "most pervasive method . . . for alienating public domain is the certificate of convenience and necessity, or some variation thereof in the form of an exclusive franchise, license or permit. . . . [G]overnment has become increasingly careless and subservient in issuing them. The net result is a general legalization of private monopoly. . . ."[1] While the best examples still are probably the 10 self-governing systems of agriculture policy, these are obviously only a small proportion of all the barriers the interest-group liberal ideology has erected to democratic use of government.

3. Interest-group liberalism demoralizes government, because liberal governments cannot achieve justice. The question of justice has engaged the best minds for almost as long as there have been notions of state and politics, certainly ever since Plato defined the ideal as one in which republic and justice were synonymous. And since that time philosophers have been unable to agree on what justice is. But outside the ideal, in the realms of actual government and citizenship, the problem is much simpler. We do not have to define justice at all in order to weight and assess justice in government, because in the case of liberal policies we are prevented by what the law would call a "jurisdictional fact." In the famous jurisdictional case of *Marbury v. Madison* Chief Justice Marshall held that even if all the Justices hated President Jefferson for refusing to accept Marbury and the other "midnight judges" appointed by Adams, there was nothing they could do. They had no authority to judge President Jefferson's action one way or another because the Supreme Court did not possess such jurisdiction over the President. In much the same way, there is something about liberalism that prevents us from raising the question of justice at all, no matter what definition of justice is used.

Liberal governments cannot achieve justice because their policies lack the *sine qua non* of justice—that quality without which a consideration of justice cannot even be initiated. Considerations of the justice in or achieved by an action cannot be made unless a deliberate and conscious attempt was made by the actor to derive his action from a general rule or moral principle governing such a class of acts. One can speak personally of good rules and bad rules, but a homily or a sentiment like liberal legislation, is not a rule at all. The best rule is one which is relevant to the decision or action in question and is general in the sense that those involved with it have no direct control over its operation. A general rule is, hence, *a priori.* Any governing regime that makes a virtue of avoiding such rules puts itself totally outside the context of justice.

Take the homely example of the bull and the china shop. Suppose it was an op art shop and that we consider op worthy only of the junk pile. That being the case, the bull did us a great service, the more so because it was something we always dreamed of doing but were prevented by law from entering and breaking. But however much we may be pleased, we cannot judge the act. We can only like or dislike the consequences. The consequences are haphazard; the bull cannot have intended them. The act was a thoughtless, animal act which bears absolutely no relation to any aesthetic principle. We don't judge the bull. We only celebrate our good fortune. Without the general rule, the bull can reenact his scenes of creative destruction daily and still not be capable of achieving, in this case, aesthetic justice. The whole idea of justice is absurd.

The general rule ought to be a legislative rule because the United States espouses the ideal of representative democracy. However, that is merely an extrinsic feature of the rule.[2] All that counts is the character of the rule itself. Without the rule we can only like or dislike the consequences of the governmental action. In the question of whether justice is achieved, a government without good rules, and without acts carefully derived therefrom, is merely a big bull in an immense china shop.

4. Finally, interest-group liberalism corrupts deomcratic government in the degree to which it weakens the capacity of governments to live by democratic formalisms.[3] Liberalism weakens democratic institutions by opposing formal procedure with informal bargaining. Liberalism derogates from democracy by derogating from all formality in favor of informality. Formalism is constraining; playing it "by the book" is a role often unpopular in American war films and sports films precisely because it can dramatize personal rigidity and the plight of the individual in collective situations. Because of the impersonality of formal procedures, there is inevitably a separation in the real world between the forms and the realities, and this kind of separation gives rise to cynicism, for informality means that some will escape their collective fate better than others. There has as a consequence always been a certain amount of cynicism toward public objects in the United States, and this may be to the good, since a little cynicism is the father of healthy sophistication. However, when the informal is elevated to a positive virtue, and hard-won access becomes a share of official authority, cynicism becomes distrust. It ends in reluctance to submit one's fate to the governmental process under any condition, as is the case in the United States in the mid-1960's.

Public officials more and more frequently find their fates paradoxical and their treatment at the hands of the public fickle and unjust when in fact they are only reaping the results of their own behavior, including their direct and informal treatment of the public and the institutions through which they serve the public. The more government operates by the spreading of access, the more public order seems to suffer. The more public men pursue their constituencies, the more they seem to find their constituencies alienated. Liberalism has promoted concentration of democratic authority but deconcentration of democratic power. Liberalism has opposed privilege in policy formulation only to foster it, quite systematically, in the implementation of policy. Liberalism has consistently failed to recognize, in short, that in a democracy forms are important. In a medieval monarchy all formalisms were at court. Democracy proves, for better or worse, that the masses like that sort of thing too.

Another homely parable may help. In the good old days, everyone in the big city knew that traffic tickets could be fixed. Not everyone could get his ticket fixed, but nonetheless a man who honestly paid his ticket suffered in some degree a dual loss: his money, and his self-esteem for having so little access. Cynicism was widespread, violations were many, but perhaps it did not matter, for there were so few automobiles. Suppose, however, that as the automobile population increased a certain city faced a traffic crisis and the system of ticket fixing came into ill repute. Suppose a mayor, victorious on the Traffic Ticket, decided that, rather than eliminate fixing by universalizing enforcement, he would instead reform the system by universalizing the privileges of ticket fixing. One can imagine how the system would work. One can imagine that some sense of equality would prevail, because everyone could be made almost equally free to bargin with the ticket administrators. But one would find it difficult to imagine how this would make the total city government more legitimate. Meanwhile, the purpose of the ticket would soon have been destroyed.

Traffic regulation, fortunately, was not so reformed. But many other government activities were. The operative principles of interest-group liberalism possess the mentality of a world of universalized ticket fixing: Destroy privilege by universalizing it. Reduce conflict by yielding to it. Redistribute power by the maxim of each according to his claim. Reserve an official place for every major structure of power. Achieve order by worshiping the processes (as distinguished from the forms and the procedures) by which order is presumed to be established.

If these operative principles will achieve equilibrium—and such is far from proven—that is all they will achieve. Democracy will have disappeared, because all of these maxims are founded upon profound lack of confidence in democracy. Democracy fails when it lacks confidence in its own authority.

Democratic forms were supposed to precede and accompany the formulation of policies so that policies could be implemented authoritatively and firmly. Democracy is indeed a form of absolutism, but ours was fairly well contrived to be an absolutist government under the strong control of consent-building prior to taking authoritative action in law. Interest-group liberalism fights the absolutism of democracy but succeeds only in taking away its authoritativeness. Whether it is called "creative federalism" by President Johnson, "cooperation" by the farmers, "local autonomy" by the Republicans, or "participatory democracy" by the New Left, the interest-group liberal effort does not create democratic power but rather negates it.

NOTES

1. Walter S. Adams and Horace Gray, *Monopoly in America*, (N.Y.: Macmillan, 1955) pp. 47–48.
2. As argued in Chapter 5, there is a high probability that efforts to make rules will lead to the legislature. A general rule excites continuous efforts at reformulation, which tend to turn combatants toward the levels of highest legitimacy and last appeal. Contrary to the fears of pluralists, the statement of a good rule can produce more flexibility and more competition than the avoidance of the rule. These tendencies are still further developed under proposals for reform.
3. One aspect of this was dealt with at some length at the end of Chapter 3. Another was dealt with at the end of Chapter 6. Here, at the risk of some repetition, the various aspects of it are put together.

CHAPTER V

The 1970s

Just as the 1960s represented expansion and growth for public administration, the 1970s became a time of review and reversal. In the span of a decade some of public administration's most cherished ideas would be shaken badly in the aftermath of the perceived failure of many of the Great Society programs, the debacle of Watergate and the first resignation of a president, the fall of Vietnam, and the mounting fiscal crises that ravaged many state and local governments. To some critics, the 1970s were an era of "resource scarcity"[1] or "retrenchment" dominated by the tactics and strategies of what Charles Levine called "cutback management."[2] While the 1960s seemed a time of optimism and experimentation for public administration, the 1970s followed with pessimism and consolidation.

The decade began with a thorough examination of the profession both in terms of personnel and public service ideals. The concerns of public personnel administration, having been relegated to an intellectual backwater since the initial success of the reform movement, began to experience a renaissance in the 1960s. A variety of factors contributed to this: the explosive growth of public employee unions, the demand for equal employment opportunity, and the needs of managing and motivating a more sophisticated and professionalized workforce. David T. Stanley (1916–) of the Brookings Institution discusses in his 1970 *Public Personnel Review* article, "What Unions are Doing to Merit Systems," reprinted here, the impact of the public employee union movement on merit systems.[3] His analysis can accurately be described as prophetic when read today.

Stanley correctly regarded the initial relationship between public employee unionism and public service merit systems as "dynamic and immature." Drastic change would and did occur on both ends—by the end of the decade the Civil Service Reform Act of 1978 would restructure the U.S. Civil Service Commission into three new entities: the Office of Personnel Management, the Merit Systems Protection Board, and the Federal Labor Relations Authority. At all levels of government the ideal of a civil service commission as both protector of the merit system and of the rights of individual employees would give way to personnel directors responsible only to the jurisdiction's chief executive;[4] the interests of employees would henceforth be looked after by quasi-judicial merit systems review boards or the unions themselves. Change was experienced by the unions, too. As increasing numbers of state and local governments adopted collective bargaining, employee relations took on a whole new perspective, as Stanley predicted. Public sector strikes, even when illegal, would occur, dramatically challenging the traditional ideals embodied in the concept of public service. Stanley saw that public administration was beginning to learn how to live in a collective bargaining environment and that a long period of adjustment was in order. Public sector unions, he predicted, would certainly become more aggressive over time; but not necessarily any wiser than their management counterparts. Certainly the experience of the failed air traffic controller's strike[5] in 1981 bears this out. Overall, Stanley's framework for understanding the critical issues between merit systems and public unions is still appropriate today.

During the late 1960s and early 1970s serious questions were being raised concerning the state of the discipline and profession of public administration. Dwight Waldo, having noted that public administration was "in a time of revolution," called a conference of younger academics in public administration, through the auspices of his position as editor-in-chief of *Public Administration Review* and with some funds from the Maxwell School of Syracuse University. Held in 1968 at Syracuse University's Minnowbrook conference site, the papers that came out of it were edited by Frank Marini (1935–), then managing editor of *Public Administration Review,* and published in 1971 under the title *Toward a New Public Administration: The Minnowbrook Perspective.*[6] The goal of the meeting was to identify what was relevant about public administration and how the discipline had to change to meet the challenges of the 1970s. H. George Frederickson's (1934–) paper, "Toward a New Public Administration," which is reprinted here, called for social equity in the performance and delivery of public services.[7] In many ways, Frederickson's paper epitomized what was called the "new public administration" movement that called for what Frederickson termed *second generation behavioralism* in which administration would be more responsive to the public, more prescriptive, more client-oriented, and more normative; yet still be more scientific. Overall the new public administration called for a proactive administrator with a burning desire for social equity to replace the traditional impersonal, neutral gun-for-hire bureaucrat. Such a call was heeded by few, but discussed by many.

Frederickson and the other new public administration theorists placed a significant emphasis on organizational theory and behavior. During the 1970s organizations, especially their decentralized structures, came under special scrutiny. In the 1960s, Warren Bennis started writing about the temporary nature of organizational and societal arrangements brought about by the increasingly professional nature of the workforce (see Chapter IV). In 1968 Frederick C. Mosher (1913–)[8], of the University of Virginia, published his now classic *Democracy and the Public Service,*[9] an examination of the history and evolution of the American public service and the major impact of ever-increasing professionalism upon it. In his 1971 *Public Administration Review* article, "The Public Service in the Temporary Society," reprinted here, Mosher accepts Bennis' premise of the "temporary society" and returns to his earlier concern with the impact of professionalism on the modern public service.

Mosher sees professionalism as perhaps the most distinguishing feature of the modern public service era. The problem with professionalism is that specialization is deepening and narrowing professionals at a time when social problems were becoming more ambiguous and unbounded. Professionals were increasingly hard pressed to solve policy and program problems even in their own areas of expertise. As the various professions grow increasingly in need of each other to cope with multifaceted social, technical, and managerial problems, a "functional interdependence" among the professions continuously evolves. Overall, Mosher provides an assessment of the public policy and personnel management implications of the fact that "two-fifths of all professionals in this country will be employed directly or indirectly by governments." In the last section of his article, Mosher addresses the academic discipline of public administration which has experienced vast growth since the early 1960s—in terms of both the numbers of universities offering programs awarding degrees and the numbers of students in such programs.

By the beginning of the 1970s, it was generally conceded that many of the Great Society programs initiated during the Johnson administration were not working nearly as well as it was originally hoped. As these and other social programs came under increasing criticism, the field of program evaluation gained increasing prominence. Aaron Wildavsky, in his 1972 *Public Administration Review* article, "The Self Evaluating Organization," reprinted here, provided an insightful discussion about the difficulties of evaluating public programs in a dynamic political environment.

Wildavsky's arguments on evaluation followed a different though familiar tack from his work on budgeting. Wildavsky might well be given the title of public administration's greatest critic because, above all, his voice has constantly reminded the field of its inherent political nature and its limitations. The problem with evaluation, according to Wildavsky, was that no matter how compelling the case for change, change was precisely what evaluation emphasized most and organizations abhorred most. Most public managers, he argued, are hard pressed to cope with day-to-day operational demands; thus they strive for stability—not constant reorder and reformulation. The costs of change had to be born, too, and evaluation seldom considered this. Finally, since the most politically feasible organizational strategies would be ones that minimized disruption, managers would tend to resist or ignore evaluation.

Wildavsky's arguments notwithstanding, evaluation would not be denied. In 1967, Edward Suchman of Columbia University published the first major work on evaluation theory, *Evaluative Research.*[10] Suchman's work argued that evaluation was essentially a field of study; that evaluative research and practice can and must be studied in a general context outside of evaluation applications in the various fields of specialization—evaluation was generic. While the early 1970s produced other significant works on the various facets of evaluation,[11] Carol H. Weiss' *Evaluation Research: Methods for Assessing Program Effectiveness*[12] has best stood the test of time; it is simply the very best introduction to the subfield. Reprinted here is her second chapter on "The Purposes of Evaluation." Weiss, a professor of education at Harvard University, does more than simply outline evaluation methodologies; she also considers the political and administrative issues of evaluation. Her coverage includes many of the most critical and sensitive issues, including the perennial problems of evaluation design, questions of purpose and use, and the choices and trade-offs represented between inside and outside evaluations.

The General Accounting Office, under the leadership of Elmer Staats, also helped elevate the general quality and value of program evaluation by setting evaluation standards and working actively to professionalize program evaluation as part of the expanded scope of audit.[13] Many state governments would initiate legislative evaluation commissions based on the GAO idea. In 1976, Colorado would be the first state to enact a sunset law—in which certain agencies and programs are given fixed termination dates and a comprehensive evaluation is conducted before program or agency reenactment. But by the mid-1970s evaluation was a vital and integral part of public administration.[14]

Policy analysis also responded to the problems of failure in the 1960s. Jeffrey L. Pressman (1943–) and Aaron Wildavsky wrote their now classic case study of federal programs in the city of Oakland in which they made popular the term *implementation* as a new focus for public administration. The title of their work tells part of the story in itself: *Implementation: How Great Expectations in Washington Are Dashed in Oakland; Or, Why It's Amazing that Federal Programs Work at All; This Being a Saga of The Economic Development Administration As Told by Two Sympathetic Observers Who Seek to Build Morals on a Foundation of Ruined Hopes.* What Pressman and Wildavsky relate in their landmark book, the preface of which is reprinted here, seems almost simplistic—that policy planning and analysis weren't taking into account the difficulties of execution or "implementation." Their purpose in this work was to consider how a closer nexus between policy and implementation could be achieved. A direct result of their book would be a spate of works[15] reconsidering how policy analysis should accomplish this objective—an objective, it is fair to say, that has yet to be implemented.

"Watergate" refers to a hotel-office-apartment complex in Washington, D.C. When individuals associated with President Nixon's reelection campaign were caught breaking into the Democratic National Committee Headquarters (then located in the Watergate complex) in 1972, the resulting cover-up and national trauma was condensed into one word—Watergate. The aftermath of Watergate brought a major review of what was called the "administrative presidency."[16] Much of the focus of public administration's development since the 1930s had been to concentrate power and control in the executive branch. Now that it had been accomplished, Watergate provided a dramatic lesson in what could happen if such centralized power was abused. The public administration community responded with its own review of Watergate. In response to a request from the Senate Select Committee on Presidential Campaign Activities, a special panel of the National Academy of Public Administration chaired by Frederick C. Mosher, examined the situation and produced a report, *Watergate: Implications for Responsible Government,*[17] which provided a detailed indictment of the Nixon administration's abuses of executive and administrative authority and power. The report's "Overview" and its epilogue on "Ethics and Public Office" are reprinted here. Educational institutions were urged to "focus more attention on public sector ethics." Although codes of ethics have been around for years, the panel concluded that more sophisticated and effective codes of conduct and standards were needed. In a sense, the real significance of the report was the infusion back into public administration of a concern for ethics and the encouragement of a new generation of literature on the subject.

The next stage of budget reform was embodied in the form of zero-base budgeting. Peter A. Pyhrr (1942–) first developed it for Texas Instruments and then for the State of Georgia while Jimmy Carter was governor. In 1976, presidential candidate Carter made the installation of zero-base budgeting a campaign promise, and in 1977, as president, he ordered its adoption by the federal government. Phyrr's 1977 *Public Administration Review* article, reprinted here, explains the theory and methods of "The Zero-Base Approach to Government Budgeting." The initial reaction to ZBB paralleled the reaction to PPBS in the 1960s; only the downfall of ZBB was even more rapid.

In large part, ZBB failed because the conditions that prevailed for most of the previous budgeting systems reforms changed. In an era of acute resource scarcity ZBB had little utility because there was little real chance that funding could be provided for any levels of program growth. Even Wildavsky and Schick were agreed on the failure of this budgeting system. In fact, Schick even proclaimed it "decremental budgeting."[18] Other critics were even less kind—either assaulting it as a "fraud" or decrying it as a nonsystem of budgeting. ZBB's fate in the federal government was tied to the Carter presidency. After the inauguration of a new president in 1981, it was quietly rescinded. Still, numerous state and local governments use ZBB techniques or some adaptation of ZBB. Now that the hype has subsided, it remains an important part of public budgeting.

The changes of the 1960s and the reaction of the 1970s mask certain patterns in the development of American public administration. On the surface, the increase in budgetary expenditures have been extraordinary, increasing from 46.3 billion in 1960 to 92.5 billion in 1979 at the federal level. But when the expenditure figures are calculated as a percentage of the gross national product, the ratio is about the same (18.5 to 20.8 percent of GNP). Federal civilian employment increased from 2.4 million to 2.9 million over this twenty-year period, but in relation to the population federal employment in 1979 was at the 1950 level. Yet, state and local government employment over this same twenty-year period increased from 4.2 to 13.1 million. According to Frederick C. Mosher, these seemingly contradictory trends "are a consequence of fundamental shifts in the purposes, emphases, and methods of federal operations."[19]

Essentially, Mosher argues, the federal government has changed its pattern of involvement over the past two decades—from overt to covert. While the federal government has decreased the number and level of activities it performs directly, it has through income supports, contracts and grants, regulations, loans and loan guarantees, stimulated massive efforts by state and local governments, nonprofit organizations, and even private business. The result is a federal administrative posture that increasingly relies on indirect administrative coordination and funds transfers. Mosher complains that this massive change has yet to be reflected "in our research, our literature, our teaching."[20] While the focus of public administration has been on the federal government, the action has been inexorably shifting to other levels. This is a trend that would only increase under the Reagan administration.

NOTES

1. There was even a growing body of "scarcity" literature. See, for example: William Ophus, *Ecology and the Politics of Scarcity* (San Francisco: Freeman, 1977); Richard J. Barnet, *The Lean Years: Politics in the Age of Scarcity* (New York: Simon & Schuster, 1980).
2. Charles H. Levine, "Organizational Decline and Cutback Management," *Public Administration Review* 38 (July-August 1978).
3. For an expanded version of Stanley's analysis of public sector unionism, see his: *Managing Local Government Under Union Pressure* (Washington, D.C.: Brookings Institution, 1972).
4. For an account of this movement to abolish traditional civil service commissions, see: Jean J. Couturier, "The Quiet Revolution in Public Personnel Laws," *Public Personnel Management* 5 (May-June 1976).
5. For accounts of how 11,500 striking controllers were fired and their union destroyed, see: David B. Bowers, "What Would Make 11,500 People Quit Their Jobs?" *Organizational Dynamics* (Winter 1983); Herbert R. Northrup, "The Rise and Demise of PATCO." *Industrial and Labor Relations Review* (January 1984).
6. (Scranton, Pa.: Chandler Publishing Co., 1971).
7. Frederickson has continued to expand his thoughts on his new public administration. See his: "The lineage of the New PA," *Administration and Society* 8 (August 1977); *The New Public Administration* (University, Ala.: University of Alabama Press, 1980).
8. Frederick C. Mosher is the son of William E. Mosher (1877–1945), the first dean of the Maxwell School at Syracuse University, the first president of the American Society for Public Administration, and coauthor, with J. Donald Kingsley, of the first major text on public personnel administration. Frederick C. Mosher has proven to be that rare person who enters the profession in which his father was a giant and becomes a person of equal, if not greater, influence in his own right. Other works by Frederick C. Mosher include: *Governmental Reorganization: Cases and Commentary* (Indianapolis, Ind.: Bobbs-Merrill, 1967); *Programming Systems and Foreign Affairs Leadership* (New York: Oxford University Press, 1970); *American Public Administration: Past, Present, Future* (University, Alabama: University of Alabama Press, 1975); *Basic Documents of American Public Administration, 1776–1950* (New York: Holmes & Meier Publishers, 1976); *Basic Literature of American Public Administration, 1787–1950* (New York: Holmes & Meier Publishers, 1981.)
9. (New York: Oxford University Press, 1968; second edition, 1982).
10. (New York: Russell Sage Foundation, 1967).
11. Most notably, Alice Rivlin's *Systematic Thinking for Social Action* (Washington, D.C.: Brookings Institution, 1971) and Joseph S. Wholey's *Federal Evaluation Policy* (Washington, D.C.: The Urban Institute, 1970).
12. (Englewood Cliffs, N.J.: Prentice-Hall, 1972).
13. For the GAO's definition of the expanded scope of audit (which includes program evaluation), see: Comptroller General of the United States, *Standards For Audit of Governmental Organizations, Programs, Activities, and Functions* (Washington, D.C.: U.S. General Accounting Office, 1981).

14. For a state-of-the-art summary of program evaluation by the end of the decade, see: Albert C. Hyde and Jay M. Shafritz, eds., *Program Evaluation in the Public Sector* (New York: Praeger Publishers, 1979).
15. Examples include: Eugene Bardach, *The Implementation Game* (Cambridge, Mass.: MIT Press, 1977); Robert T. Nakamura and Frank Smallwood, *The Politics of Policy Implementation* (New York: St. Martin's Press, 1980); George C. Edwards III, *Implementing Public Policy* (Washington, D.C.: Congressional Quarterly Press, 1980); Walter Williams and Others, *Studying Implementation: Methodological and Administrative Issues* (Chatham, N.J.: Chatham House, 1982).
16. This is Richard Nathan's descriptive term for how Richard Nixon sought to use administrative tactics—reorganization, decentralization, and impoundment—to assert presidential authority over the federal bureaucracy. See Nathan's *The Plot That Failed: Nixon and the Administrative Presidency* (New York: John Wiley & Sons, 1975).
17. (New York: Basic Books, 1974).
18. For Schick's "obituary" of ZBB, see his "The Road from ZBB," *Public Administration Review* 38 (March-April 1978).
19. Frederick C. Mosher, "The Changing Responsibilities and Tactics of the Federal Government," *Public Administration Review* 40 (November-December 1980), p. 541.
20. Ibid., p. 547.

A CHRONOLOGY OF PUBLIC ADMINISTRATION: 1970–1979

1970 The National Civil Service League revises its Model Public Personnel Administration Law to call for the replacement of traditional civil service commissions with (1) personnel directors directly responsible to an elected political executive, and (2) a labor relations board.

The Intergovernmental Personnel Act allows for the temporary exchange of staff between the federal government and state, local, and nonprofit organizations.

The Bureau of the Budget is given more responsibility for managerial oversight and renamed the Office of Management and Budget.

Postal Reorganization Act creates the United States Postal Service as a public corporation within the executive branch and allows for collective bargaining over wages by postal employee unions.

David T. Stanley in "What Unions are Doing to Merit Systems" correctly predicts structural changes in both public sector personnel systems and public sector unions.

Hawaii becomes the first state to allow state and local government employees the right to strike.

The Occupational Safety and Health Act creates the Occupational Safety and Health Administration (OSHA).

The Environmental Protection Agency is established.

1971 The Supreme Court attacks restrictive credentialism when in *Griggs v. Duke Power Company* it rules that Title VII of the Civil Rights Act of 1964 "proscribes not only overt discrimination but also practices that are discriminatory in operation;" thus, if an employment practice operating to exclude minorities "cannot be shown to be related to job performance, the practice is prohibited."

PPBS formally is abandoned in the federal government by the Nixon administration.

Graham T. Allison's *Essence of Decision* demonstrates the inadequacies of the view that the decisions of a government are made by a "single calculating decisionmaker" who has control over the organizations and officials within his government.

1972 Equal Employment Opportunity Act amends Title VII of the Civil Rights Act to include prohibitions on discrimination by public sector employers.

Watergate scandal erupts when men associated with the Committee to Reelect the President are caught breaking into the campaign headquarters of the Democratic opposition located in the Watergate hotel-office-apartment complex.

Wildcat strike at General Motors' Lordstown, Ohio, automobile assembly plant calls national attention to the dysfunctions of dehumanized and monotonous work.

The Equal Rights Amendment is passed by Congress; it never becomes law because too few states will ratify it.

The Technology Assessment Act creates the Office of Technology Assessment to help Congress anticipate and plan for the consequences of the uses of technology.

Harlan Cleveland in *The Future Executive* asserts that decision making in the future will call for "continuous improvisation on a general sense of direction."

Charles Perrow's *Complex Organizations* is a major defense of bureaucratic forms of organization and an attack on those writers who think that bureaucracy can be easily, fairly, or inexpensively replaced.

H. George Frederickson's paper "Toward a New Public Administration" makes him the leading voice in the call for a more responsive, more prescriptive, and more normative public administration.

Frederick C. Mosher in "The Public Service in the Temporary Society" accepts Warren Bennis' premise of a "temporary society" and assesses its implications for public administration.

James H. Boren testifies before Congress on the merits of "policy thwartation" and "dynamic inactivism."

1972 Revenue sharing is introduced with the passage of the State and Local Fiscal Assistance Act.

Aaron Wildavsky's "The Self Evaluating Organization" analyses the problems of evaluating public programs in a dynamic political environment.

Carol H. Weiss' *Evaluation Research* considers the methodological, political, and administrative issues of program evaluation.

1973 Vice President Spiro Agnew resigns after pleading "no contest" to a charge of tax evasion stemming from illegal payments made to him by contractors when he was governor of Maryland; Gerald R. Ford becomes Vice President.

The Comprehensive Employment and Training Act creates a program of financial assistance to state and local governments to provide job training and employment opportunities for the economically disadvantaged, unemployed, and underemployed.

Pressman and Wildavsky publish *Implementation* and create a new subfield of public administration and policy analysis.

1974 Congressional Budget and Impoundment Control Act revises the congressional budget process and timetable; and creates the Congressional Budget Office.

The Supreme Court in *United States v. Nixon* denies President Nixon's claim of an absolute and unreviewable executive privilege, and Nixon is forced to resign in the face of certain impeachment because of Watergate.

Gerald R. Ford becomes president and grants former president Nixon a full pardon for all possible crimes.

At the request of the Congress a panel from the National Academy of Public Administration headed by Frederick C. Mosher examines the administrative abuses of Watergate: in their report, *Watergate: Implication for Responsible Government,* they urged educational institutions to "focus more attention on public service ethics."

Samuel Krislov's *Representative Bureaucracy* builds upon Kingsley's concepts and denies that the goal of government employment is efficiency; rather it is to minimize social conflict and gain the acquiescence of the governed.

An amendment to the Social Security Act provides for automatic cost-of-living adjustments in social security payments.

1975 The federal government adopts the factor evaluation system of position classification for nonsupervisory positions.

The Municipal Assistance Corporation (Big MAC) is created to lend money to New York City so that the city can avoid default.

1976 The Sharon Report finds extensive corruption in the U.S. Civil Service Commission.

Uniform Guidelines on Employee Selection Procedures issued by the four federal compliance agencies.

Colorado is the first state to enact "sunset laws" as a method of program review and evaluation.

1977 Zero-base budgeting is required of all federal agencies by Carter administration; Peter A. Phyrr becomes the guru of "The Zero-Base Approach to Government Budgeting."

Hugh Heclo's *A Government of Strangers* becomes the leading analysis of the relationships between political and career executives in the federal bureaucracy.

The Presidential Management Intern Program is established as a special means of bringing public administration masters' graduates into the federal bureaucracy.

The Government in the Sunshine Act requires all multiheaded federal agencies to have their business sessions open to the public.

Herbert Kaufman's *Red Tape* finds that "one person's 'red tape' may be another's treasured procedural safeguard."

The Department of Energy is created.

1978 The Civil Service Reform Act abolishes the U.S. Civil Service Commission and replaces it with (1) the Office of Personnel Management, (2) the Merit Systems Protection Board, and (3) the Federal Labor Relations Authority.

Ethics in Government Act seeks to deal with possible conflicts of interest by former federal employees by imposing postemployment restrictions on their activities.

Proposition 13 requiring reductions in local property taxes is voted into law in California.

The Supreme Court in *Regents of the University of California v. Bakke* ruled that a white male applicant denied admission to medical school in favor of minorities with lesser objective credentials was discriminated against and had to be admitted; but at the same time the Court held that race was a factor that could be taken into account in admissions decisions.

The Supreme Court in *City of Los Angeles, Department of Water and Power* v. *Manhart* rules that Title VII of the Civil Rights Act requires that male and female employees contribute equally to pension plans even though females as a group live longer.

The Pregnancy Discrimination Act amends Title VII of the Civil Rights Act to include prohibitions on discrimination on the basis of pregnancy, childbirth, or related medical conditions.

Charles H. Levine, in a *Public Administration Review* symposium on the issue, uses "cutback management" to describe the decline of public organizations in times of fiscal stress.

1979 The Department of Health, Education, and Welfare is divided into (1) the Department of Education and (2) the Department of Health and Human Services.

39
What Are Unions Doing to Merit Systems?

David T. Stanley

As unions of public employees grow in numbers and influence the question naturally arises, "What are unions doing to merit systems?" The question may have a tone of alarm for long-term practitioners, advocates, and beneficiaries of civil service systems. The gains of civil service systems, now nearing its century mark in this country, have been won and maintained with difficulty; alternatives are understandably dismaying. This question has been explored in the past by expert and interested persons in this journal and other publications.

We now have some preliminary results from a study of the impact of unions on public administration that throws further light on this question as it applies to local governments.[1] Our raw material comes from about ten days of interviewing and document-grabbing in each of fifteen cities and four urban counties. (Cities: Binghamton, New York; Boston, Massachusetts; Buffalo, New York; Cincinnati, Ohio; Dayton, Ohio; Detroit, Michigan; Hartford, Connecticut; Milwaukee, Wisconsin; New Orleans; Louisiana; New York, New York; Philadelphia, Pennsylvania; San Francisco, California; St. Louis, Missouri; Tacoma, Washington; and Wilmington, Delaware. Counties: Dade, Florida; Los Angeles, California; Multnomah, Oregon; and New Castle, Delaware.)

The localities studied all have merit systems, but differences in strength, competence, and age of these systems were very obvious. There is great variety also in the state laws governing the conditions under which public employees may unionize and bargain. All these variations make it hard to generalize from the experience of these nineteen governments, but we can present some of the patterns we found. We do not contend that these cities and counties are truly representative of all local governments, only that they show what is going on in a variety of places where unions have been active.

A mixed and moderate report results from the study. Civil service is not disappearing, nor is it fighting unions to a standstill, nor is there beautiful collaboration everywhere. In general, unions, bargaining, and contractual provisions are invading more and more precincts previously occupied only by civil service commissions of personnel offices. How good or how bad this is depends upon the value systems of the beholder.

What do we mean by merit systems? We should distinguish them from the merit principle under which public employees are recruited, selected, and

Source: From *Public Personnel Review* (April 1970). Reprinted by permission of the International Personnel Management Association, 1313 East 60th Street, Chicago, Illinois 60637. Some subheadings shortened.

advanced under conditions of political neutrality, equal opportunity, and competition on the basis of merit and competence. Public employee unions do not question this principle in general and have done little to weaken it, as yet. When we say merit systems, however, this has come to mean a broad program of personnel management activities. Some are essential to carrying out the merit principle: recruiting, selecting, policing of antipolitics and antidiscrimination rules, and administering related appeals provisions. Others are closely related and desirable: position classification, pay administration, employee benefits, and training. Unions are of course interested in both categories.

What unions are we talking about? We refer particularly to the American Federation of State, County, and Municipal Employees; the Service Employees International Union, the International Association of Firefighters, the various police associations, the nursing associations, the International Brotherhood of Teamsters, the unions of licensed practical nurses.

This article will speak rather generally of union attitudes and pressures. Some are expressed through the collective bargaining process, with the results embodied in a formal agreement; some are stated as representations to the boards of local government. Or the pressure may be more informally applied, as when a union delegation meets with a department head or a steward meets with the first-line or second-line supervisor.

THE IMPACT IN GENERAL

The major and most distinct effect of union activity is a weakening of what might be called management-by-itself. The era of unilateralism, of unquestioned sovereignty, is about over. The age of bilateralism—consultation, negotiation, and bargaining—is already here. The "independent" civil service commission, responsible over the years for rule-making, for protection of career employees from arbitrary personnel changes, for adjudication of appeals from employees, still exists but is losing functions. Civil service commissions may not go out of business, but more and more of their vital organs will be removed by the bargaining process until, whether officially in existence or not, they are husks of their former selves. This change is occurring not because employees are clearly dissatisfied with existing merit systems but because they feel that unions will get more for them—more pay, more benefits, more aggressive protection against possible arbitrary management actions.

At the same time management is becoming more careful, more responsible, and more responsive. The fact that management at all levels is prodded, observed, objected to, and reasoned with by union stewards and business agents means that management must watch its step. Another effect is that this change from unilateralism to bilateralism brings transitional difficulties. First-line and second-line supervisors in government are not used to dealing with unions, and the unions have many inexperienced stewards who are busy fumbling hot potatoes. The passage of time and the application of effort and good will should reduce these problems.

PATTERNS OF ORGANIZATION

Each of the governments we studied has had to provide organizationally for dealing with unions. In Hartford and Philadelphia, for example, the function has been clearly lodged within the city personnel office. This contrasts with Detroit and New York where a separate labor relations office operates in cooperation (and some competition) with a civil service commission. In other governments labor relations are handled by some different administrator: a fiscal executive in Buffalo; the assistant to the mayor in Binghamton; the chairman of the Board of County Commissioners in Multnomah County, and the county manager in Dade County.

These varied patterns of organization result from both tradition and personality. It is much too early to say that any one system works better than another, and indeed, our findings may reflect personalities rather than organization schemes. It seems natural to predict, however, that the longer labor relations functions are separated from personnel functions, the more trouble we are going to have in the future. The activities of "independent" civil service commissions intensify the diffusion of managerial authority and make union negotiations more difficult. Even more important, it is impossible for a personnel officer (or civil service executive secretary) to be both an impartial defender of employees' rights and an adversary of unions as a management negotiator. It is perfectly possible to foresee governments adopting the industrial pattern: a department of labor relations headed by a vice-mayor or assistant city manager for labor relations who will supervise not only bargaining and employee relations, but also selection and training activities.

HIRING

We have already noted that unions accept the merit principle, and our field research shows that they are inclined to accept most of the qualification requirements and examining methods that are customarily part of the civil service system. Here and there we found some union resistance to the lowering of qualification standards, such as height requirements for policemen, high school graduation for custodians, or college degrees for caseworkers. There are various motives for such resistance: the wish to work with well-qualified associates (or with people like themselves) and the wish to argue that higher qualifications deserve higher pay.

On the whole unions have shown little interest in examining methods except where they have taken up the cause of citizens whose educational experiences do not prepare them to excel on pencil-and-paper tests. In those cases unions would naturally prefer performance tests to examinations which involve verbal aptitude. The civil service office discussing this should be in a position to show that the tests used are valid for the intended purposes. Unions have also affected selection by pushing management to shorten probation periods. Such a change clearly limits management's freedom to discharge unsatisfactory employees.

When the government runs special recruitment and training programs for disadvantaged citizens of the cities, the unions are put in a somewhat difficult position. Union leaders support such programs both because of altruism and because they see the new recruits to city service as potential union members. On the other hand, union members do not want to see these less privileged citizens occupying a preferred position in selection and training in comparison to themselves. ("I had to take a civil service examination to get that job. Why doesn't he?" "We had to have high school diplomas before we could have such a job. Why don't they?") So acceptance depends on whether those recruited under the "new careers" and other comparable programs are regarded as allies or as threats to employees who are the real backbone of the union membership.

More important than all of these factors is the increased adoption of the union shop. Four of our localities (Hartford, Philadelphia, New Castle County, and Wilmington) provided this form of union security. The effect is that employment is limited to citizens willing to join unions—who may or may not be the best-qualified candidates. The effect is slightly less for the agency shop (Dayton, Detroit, and Boston) under which employees, if not willing to be union members, must pay fees in lieu of union dues because they presumably benefit from union services.

PROMOTIONS

The unions' naturally strong interest in promotions is expressed in support of measures that favor inside candidates for jobs and limit management's freedom of selection. When a job above the usual entrance level is to be filled, they strongly prefer that promotion lists be used ahead of open competitive lists and departmental promotion lists ahead of servicewide promotion lists. These policies are reflected anyway in many civil service laws and procedures perhaps to excess, so the union influence reinforces some preexisting rigidities. In some cities promotion lists are limited to the union bargaining unit. This provision may be another wave of the future.

Another point of emphasis, clearly consistent with the others, is insistence on "rule-of-one" certification. Even in some places where "rule-of-three" prevails, union pressures are directed toward selecting the top person certified unless there is some extremely compelling reason for not doing so. In effect, management has to show cause why the top eligible on the list should not be appointed.

In rating candidates for promotion, unions have rather consistently opposed the use of oral examinations and performance ratings, at least arguing for a reduced weighting to be given such factors, and for increased weight to be given to seniority. They would prefer promotion by strict seniority among those basically qualified for the higher job. Thus far, however, this last provision has been negotiated in only a few contracts. Where we did find it, the promotions were not to supervisory positions but to higher-rated nonsupervisory jobs (laborer to truck driver, truck driver to bulldozer operator) within the bargaining unit. In these respects unions are still supporting the merit principle but maintaining that senior employees have more merit.

TRANSFERS

There is little union interest in interdepartmental transfers except in cases where the union helps an employee move to another department because he is facing disciplinary action or is involved in a personality conflict in his present department.

The situation is different, however, with respect to transfers to new locations or to other shifts within a department. Unions would like to have assignments to preferred places or times made on a basis of seniority among those who request such assignments. We found this policy in a few contracts, but in general management has full freedom to assign employees where they are needed.

TRAINING

Unions have had two kinds of impact on employee training programs. First, they urge or even arrange training to help their members gain promotions, such as on-the-job training in operation of more complex equipment or group training to prepare for promotion examinations. In Detroit, for example, the Teamsters Union in cooperation with the civil service commission has arranged for drivers to learn heavy equipment operation. The Service Employees International Union in California is pressing for training of psychiatric technicians to meet new state licensure requirements. Second, management has had to train its supervisors in labor relations, sometimes with the aid of university professors. In general, however, training continues to occupy an unfortunately low position in the unions' scale of values, as in that of management.

GRIEVANCES AND APPEALS

One of the clearest patterns to emerge from our field research is the trend in grievance procedures. Most of the governments studied use negotiated procedures, usually going through four or five steps and ending in third-party arbitration, which is more often binding than advisory. This pattern replaces the usual grievance procedure which advances from lower to higher levels of management, ending with the civil service commission as the final "court of appeal." The arbitration provided in the new pattern may take various forms. A single arbitrator may be chosen from a list supplied by an impartial source. Or there may be a panel of arbitrators of whom the aggrieved employee (or his organization) appoints one member, management appoints a second, and the two agree upon a third, sometimes using nominations, again from an impartial source.

When we speak of grievances covered by these procedures, we are referring to grievances on supervisory relationships or working conditions. Work assignments and eligibility for premium pay are frequent subjects for such appeals. We are not referring to appeals of adverse personnel actions such as suspensions, demotions, or discharges. In most of the governments studied such adverse actions are still handled through civil service channels. A trend is beginning, however to administer them like other grievances, and it is only a matter of time before adverse actions will be subject to arbitration in unionized urban governments. Without this change unions will continue to maintain that civil service decisions are made by pro-management bodies.

CLASSIFICATION

The position classification process—sorting jobs by occupation and level—is still a management activity but it is under several kinds of pressure from employee groups. Unions may claim that some jobs are undervalued in relation to others and urge, sometimes successfully, that they be upgraded. Unions also press for new job levels (e.g., supervising building custodian, senior caseworker) which will provide promotion opportunities for their members. Such claims and pressures may be expressed in the bargaining process. In Detroit and New York, for example, union and management bargainers have agreed on joint recommendations to civil service authorities.

A related problem arises from the insistence by unions that employees be paid at the proper rate for out-of-classification work. Sometimes there are difficult management determinations as to whether the employee really did work out of the classification, and for how long. Unions contend that differences over such matters should be resolved through the grievance procedure. In one of the cities we studied, however, the civil service authorities went to court to insist that such cases be settled under management's classification authority, not through the grievance procedure. Civil service lost this one.

PAY

In all but a few of the localities studied, pay changes are made as a result of collective bargaining. In one of the remaining cities (New Orleans) only part of the local government is covered by collective bargaining procedures. In still others (San Francisco and St. Louis) the urges of employees to have fatter paychecks are expressed through group pressures on the civil service commission and more intensively on the legislative body. This form of pressure may be just as effective as bargaining. In all these bargaining-for-pay situations the end result is resolution of a complex group of factors: surveys of prevailing pay levels; the skill and influence of the chief executive; the political and economic power of the unions; the responsiveness of the city council to all sorts of pressures; the attitude of the state government, and many others.

It is terribly hard to say whether unions are getting more for employees through bargaining or other pressures than less organized employees might have obtained for themselves. Another study will undertake to demonstrate statistically the extent to which effective unionization correlates with salary increases. Our own data are not conclusive on this point. We know, of course, that both union and non-union pay have risen impressively. Looking at our nineteen governments as a whole (and it is very hard to generalize) pay rose seven to ten per cent on the average in each of the last two years, when the consumer price index was going up only four or five per cent a year. In a couple of these local governments where employees had not been given a raise for quite a time, they "caught up" with something like a 20 per cent increase. There are also the special case of underpaid groups like some laundry, food service, and custodial workers who have been compensated so poorly for so long that union pressure results in a significant jump in their incomes.

FRINGE BENEFITS

Fringe benefits too show great variation in local governments, depending upon charter provisions, management attitudes, and priorities of union objectives. The clearest trends are those toward increased leave allowances and more generous financing of health benefits.

LOOKING TO THE FUTURE

It is clear that unions are here to stay, to grow, to become involved in more and more public personnel activities. Their influence is exerted now in many different ways but will increasingly be felt through formalized collective bargaining ending in written agreements.

In general unions do not quarrel with the merit principle although their definition of merit may be a little different from that of management. They are inclined to question the ability of management to determine who is the best of a number of employees or candidates, particularly if there are rating differences of only a point or two. Unions will resist such fine distinctions and will favor seniority as a basis for assignment and promotion.

It is clear also that pressure from unions brings increases in pay and fringe benefits which will at least keep up with and may outrun the advances in the cost of living and perhaps in prevailing wages. The time will come, however, when unions will have won the major gains that are possible in this area, and at that point one can expect them to turn their attention more aggressively to the make-up of work crews, the conditions of assignment to shifts, and other aspects of work assignment and supervision.

Public personnel jurisdictions will have to give a great deal of thought to the way in which they are organized to meet the evergrowing strength of employee organizations. It is clear that the "independent" civil service commission is waning in power and influence and that personnel departments (whether or not subservient to a civil service commission) will also decline in influence unless they can take on the labor relations functions, as they have done very satisfactorily in some places.

I am inclined to predict that ultimately governments will establish strong labor relations departments, part of whose work will be the personnel function as we have known it in the past. With or without such a change in organization, public personnel systems need strong and experienced hands to conduct collective bargaining, to deal with grievances, and to be management's voice in matters which go to arbitration.

In general, the relationship between unions and merit systems is dynamic and immature. We are only beginning to learn the lesson that private commerce and industry learned more than a generation ago. Urban administrators would be well advised to ponder some of these lessons, notably those which concern management's freedom to organize the work and to select employees for promotion to supervisory positions. Finally, management people at all levels should somehow take the time and summon the energy to consult systematically with and listen sympathetically to union representatives.

NOTE

1. This is one of five studies on unions, collective bargaining, and public employment, sponsored by the Brookings Institution with the aid of the Ford Foundation. The other four concern: (1) the nature and types of unions; (2) laws governing labor-management relations; (3) structure of collective bargaining, including recognition, representation, and impasse resolution; and (4) effects of unions on the wages of unionized workers in the public service. All relate only to local government, and except for the fourth, exclude school systems. All five are to be published as Brookings books.

40

Toward a New Public Administration

H. George Frederickson

In full recognition of the risks, this is an essay on new Public Administration. Its first purpose is to present my interpretation and synthesis of new Public Administration as it emerged at the Minnowbrook Conference on New Public Administration. Its second purpose is to describe how this interpretation and synthesis of new Public Administration relates to the wider world

Source: "Toward a New Public Administration" by H. George Frederickson from *Toward a New Public Administration: The Minnowbrook Perspective* edited by Frank Marini.

of administrative thought and practice. And its third purpose is to interpret what new Public Administration means for organization theory and vice versa.

To affix the label "new" to anything is risky business. The risk is doubled when newness is attributed to ideas, thoughts, concepts, paradigms, theories. Those who claim new thinking tend to regard previous thought as old or jejune or both. In response, the authors of previous thought are defensive and inclined to suggest that, "aside from having packaged earlier thinking in a new vocabulary there is little that is really new in so-called new thinking." Accept, therefore, this caveat. Parts of new Public Administration would be recognized by Plato, Hobbes, Machiavelli, Hamilton, and Jefferson as well as many modern behavioral theorists. The newness is in the way the fabric is woven, not necessarily in the threads that are used, and in arguments as to the proper use of the fabric—however threadbare.

The threads of the Public Administration fabric are well known. Herbert Kaufman describes them simply as the pursuit of these basic values: representativeness, politically neutral competence, and executive leadership.[1] In different times, one or the other of these values receives the greatest emphasis. Representativeness was preeminent in the Jacksonian era. The eventual reaction was the reform movement emphasizing neutral competence and executive leadership. Now we are witnessing a revolt against these values accompanied by a search for new modes of representativeness.

Others have argued that changes in Public Administration resemble a zero-sum game between administrative efficiency and political responsiveness. Any increase in efficiency results *a priori* in a decrease in responsiveness. We are simply entering a period during which political responsiveness is to be purchased at a cost in administrative efficiency.

Both the dichotomous and trichotomous value models of Public Administration just described are correct as gross generalizations. But they suffer the weakness of gross generalizations: They fail to account for the wide, often rich, and sometimes subtle variation that rests within. Moreover, the generalization does not explain those parts of Public Administration that are beyond its sweep. Describing what new Public Administration means for organization theory is a process by which these generalizations can be given substance. But first it is necessary to briefly sketch what this student means by new Public Administration.

WHAT IS NEW PUBLIC ADMINISTRATION?

Educators have as their basic objective, and most convenient rationale, expanding and transmitting knowledge. The police are enforcing the law. Public-health agencies lengthen life by fighting disease. Then there are firemen, sanitation men, welfare workers, diplomats, the military, and so forth. All are employed by public agencies and each specialization or profession has its own substantive set of objectives and therefore its rationale.

What, then, is Public Administration?[2] What are its objectives and its rationale?

The classic answer has always been the efficient, economical, and coordinated management of the services listed above. The focus has been on top-level management (city management as an example) or the basic auxiliary staff services (budgeting, organization and management, systems analysis, planning, personnel, purchasing). The rationale for Public Administration is almost always better (more efficient or economical) management. New Public Administration adds *social equity* to the classic objectives and rationale. Conventional or classic Public Administration seeks to answer either of these questions: (1) How can we offer more or better services with available resources (efficiency)? or (2) How can we maintain our level of services while spending less money (economy)? New Public Administration adds this question: Does this service enhance social equity?

The phrase social equity is used here to summarize the following set of value premises. Pluralistic government systematically discriminates in favor of established stable bureaucracies and their specialized minority clientele (the Department of Agriculture and large farmers as an example) and against those minorities (farm laborers, both migrant and permanent, as an example) who lack political and economic resources. The continuation of widespread unemployment, poverty, disease, ignorance, and hopelessness in an era of unprecedented economic growth is the result. This condition is morally reprehensible and if left unchanged constitutes a fundamental, if long-range, threat to the viability of this or any political system. Continued deprivation amid plenty breeds widespread militancy. Militancy is followed by repression, which is followed by greater militancy, and so forth. A Public Administration which fails to work for changes which try to redress the deprivation of minorities will likely be eventually used to repress those minorities.

For a variety of reasons—probably the most important being committee legislatures, entrenched bureaucracies, nondemocratized political-party procedures, inequitable revenue-raising capacity in the lesser governments of the federal system—the procedures of representative democracy presently operate in a way that either fails or only very gradually attempts to reverse systematic discrimination against disadvantaged minorities. Social equity, then, includes activities designed to enhance the political power and economic well-being of these minorities.

A fundamental commitment to social equity means that new Public Administration attempts to come to grips with Dwight Waldo's contention that the field has never satisfactorily accommodated the theoretical implications of involvement in "politics" and policy-making.[3] The policy-administration dichotomy lacks an empirical warrant, for it is abundantly clear that administrators both execute and make policy. The policy-administration continuum is more accurate empirically but simply begs the theoretical question. New Public Administration attempts to answer it in this way: *Administrators are not neutral. They should be committed to both good management and social equity as values, things to be achieved, or rationales.*

A fundamental commitment to social equity means that new Public Administration is anxiously engaged in change. *Simply put, new Public Administration seeks to change those policies and structures that systematically inhibit social equity.* This is not seeking change for change's sake nor is it advocating alterations in the relative roles of administrators, executives, legislators, or the courts in our basic constitutional forms. Educators, agriculturists, police, and the like can work for changes which enhance their objectives and resist those that threaten those objectives, all within the framework of our governmental system. New Public Administration works in the same way to seek the changes which would enhance its objectives—good management, efficiency, economy, and social equity.

A commitment to social equity not only involves the pursuit of change but attempts to find organizational and political forms which exhibit a capacity for continued flexibility or routinized change. Traditional bureaucracy has a demonstrated capacity for stability, indeed, ultrastability.[4] New Public Administration, in its search for changeable structures, tends therefore to experiment with or advocate modified bureaucratic-organizational forms. Decentralization, devolution, projects, contracts, sensitivity training, organization development, responsibility expansion, confrontation, and client involvement are all essentially counterbureaucratic notions that characterize new Public Administration.[5] These concepts are designed to enhance both bureaucratic and policy change and thus to increase possibilities for social equity. Indeed, an important faculty member in one of the best-known and largest Master in Public Administration programs in the country described that degree program as "designed to produce change agents or specialists in organizational development."

Other organizational notions such as programming-planning-budgeting systems, executive inventories, and social indicators can be seen as enhancing change in the direction of social equity. They are almost always presented in terms of good management (witness McNamara and PPB) as a basic strategy, because it is unwise to frontally advocate change.[6] In point of fact, however, PPB can be used as a basic device for change (in McNamara's case to attempt to wrest control from the uniformed services, but in the name of efficiency and economy). The executive inventory can be used to alter the character of the top levels of a particular bureaucracy, thereby enhancing change possibilities. Social indicators are designed to show variation in socioeconomic circumstances in the hope that attempts will be made to improve the conditions of those who are shown to be disadvantaged.[7] All three of these notions have only a surface neutrality or good-management character. Under the surface they are devices by which administrators and executives try to bring about change. It is no wonder they are so widely favored in Public Administration circles. And it should not be surprising that economists and political scientists in the "pluralist" camp regard devices such as PPB as fundamentally threatening to their conception of democratic government.[8] Although they are more subtle in terms of change, PPB, executive inventories, and social indicators are of the same genre as more frontal change techniques such as sensitivity training, projects, contracts, decentralization, and the like. All enhance change, and *change is basic to new Public Administration.*

New Public Administration's commitment to social equity implies a strong administrative or executive government—what Hamilton called "energy in the executive." The policy-making powers of the administrative parts of government are increasingly recognized. In addition, a fundamentally new form of political access and representativeness is now occurring in the administration of government and it may be that this access and representativeness is as critical to major policy decisions as is legislative access or representativeness. *New Public Administration seeks not only to carry out legislative mandates as efficiently and economically as possible, but to both influence and execute policies which more generally improve the quality of life for all.* Forthright policy advocacy on the part of the public servant is essential if administrative agencies are basic policy battlefields. New Public Administrationists are likely to be forthright advocates for social equity and will doubtless seek a supporting clientele.

Classic Public Administration emphasizes developing and strengthening institutions which have been designed to deal with social problems. The Public Administration focus, however, has tended to drift from the problem to the institution.[9] New Public Administration attempts to refocus on the problem and to consider alternative possible institutional approaches to confronting problems. The intractable character of many public problems such as urban poverty, widespread narcotics use, high crime rates, and the like lead Public Administrators to seriously question the investment of ever more money and manpower in institutions which seem only to worsen the problems. They seek, therefore, either to modify these institutions or develop new and more easily changed ones designed to achieve more proximate solutions. *New Public Administration is concerned less with the Defense Department than with defense, less with civil-service commissions than with the manpower needs of administrative agencies on the one hand and the employment needs of the society on the other, less with building institutions and more with designing alternate means of solving public problems. These alternatives will no doubt have some recognizable organizational characteristics and they will need to be built and maintained, but will seek to avoid becoming entrenched, nonresponsible bureaucracies that become greater public problems than the social situations they were originally designed to improve.*

The movement from an emphasis on institution building and maintenance to an emphasis on social anomalies has an important analogue in the study of Public Administration. The last generation of students of Public Administration generally accept both Simon's logical positivism and his call for an empirically based organization theory. They focus on generic concepts such as decision, role, and group theory to develop a generalizable body of organization theory. The search is for commonalities of behavior in all organizational settings.[10] The organization and the people within it are the empirical referent. The product is usually description, not prescription, and if it is prescription it prescribes how to better manage the organization internally. The subject matter is first *organization* and second the type of organization—private, public, voluntary.[11] The two main bodies of theory emerging from this generation of work are decision theory and human-relation theory. Both are regarded as behavioral and positivist. Both are at least as heavily influenced by sociology, social psychology, and economics as they are by political science.

New Public Administration advocates what could be best described as "second-generation behavioralism." Unlike his progenitor, the second-generation behavioralist emphasizes the *public* part of Public Administration. He accepts the importance of understanding as scientifically as possible how and why organizations behave as they do but he tends to be rather more interested in the impact of that organization on its clientele and vice versa. He is not antipositivist nor antiscientific although he is probably less than sanguine about the applicability of the natural-science model to social phenomena. He is not likely to use his behavioralism as a rationale for simply trying to describe how public organizations behave.[12] Nor is he inclined to use his behavioralism as a facade for so-called neutrality, being more than a little skeptical of the objectivity of those who claim to be doing science. He attempts to use his scientific skills to aid his analysis, experimentation, and evaluation of alternative policies and administrative modes. *In sum, then, the second-generation behavioralist is less "generic" and more "public" than his forebear, less "descriptive" and more "prescriptive," less "institution oriented" and more "client-impact oriented," less "neutral" and more "normative," and, it is hoped, no less scientific.*

This has been a brief and admittedly surface description of new Public Administration from the perspective of one analyst. If the description is even partially accurate it is patently clear that there are fundamental changes occurring in Public Administration which have salient implications for both its study and practice as well as for the general conduct of government. The final purpose of this chapter is a consideration of the likely impact of new Public Administration on organization theory particularly and the study of administration generally. (The term "theory" is used here in its loose sense, as abstract thought.)

ORGANIZATION THEORY AND NEW PUBLIC ADMINISTRATION

Understanding of any phenomenon requires separating that phenomenon into parts and examining each part in detail. In understanding government this separation can reflect institutions such as the traditional "fields" in political science—Public Administration, legislative behavior, public law, and so forth. Or this separation can be primarily conceptual or theoretical such as systems theory, decision theory, role theory, group theory—all of which cut across institutions.

Public Administration has never had either an agreed upon or a satisfactory set of subfields. The "budgeting," personnel administration," "organization and management" categories are too limiting, too "inside-organization" oriented, and too theoretically vacant. The middle-range theories—decisions, roles, groups, and the like—are stronger theoretically and have yielded more empirically, but still tend to focus almost exclusively on the internal dynamics of public organizations. The new Public Administration calls for a different way of subdividing the phenomenon so as to better understand it. This analyst suggests that there are four basic processes at work in public organizations and further suggests that these processes are suitable for both understanding and improving Public Administration. The four suggested processes are: the distributive process; the integrative process; the boundary-exchange process; and the socioemotional process.

The Distributive Process

New Public Administration is vitally concerned with patterns of distribution. This concern has to do first with the *external* distribution of goods and services to particular categories of persons, in terms of the benefits that result from the operation of publicly administered programs.

Cost-utility, or cost-benefit, analysis is the chief technique for attempting to understand the results of the distributive process. This form of analysis presumes to measure the utility to individuals of particular public programs. Because it attempts to project the likely costs and benefits of alternative programs it is a very central part of new Public Administration. It is central primarily because it provides a scientific or quasi-scientific means for attempting to "get at" the question of equity. It also provides a convenient or classic Public Administration rationale for redistribution. Take, for example, McNamara's justifications for decisions based on cost-utility analysis in the Department of Defense. These justifications were generally urged on the basis of substantive military criteria.

Because of the emergence of "program-planning-budgeting systems" we are beginning to see, in the policy advocacy of the various bureaus and departments of government, their attempts to demonstrate their impact on society in terms of utility. Wildavsky and Lindblom have argued that rational or cost-utility analysis is difficult if not impossible to do. Further, they contend, rational decision making fundamentally alters or changes our political system by dealing with basic political questions within the arena of the administrator. To date they are essentially correct, empirically. Normatively they are apologists for pluralism. Cost-benefit analysis can be an effective means by which inequities can be demonstrated. It is a tool by which legislatures and entrenched bureaucracies can be caused to defend publicly their distributive decisions. The inference is that a public informed of glaring inequities will demand change.

Like the executive budget, rational or cost-benefit decision systems (PPB) enhance the power of executives and administrators and are, again, a part of new Public Administration. Because PPB is being widely adopted in cities and states, as well as the national government, it seems clear that new Public Administration will be highly visible simply by a look at the distributive processes of government over the next decade or two. The extent to which PPB will result in a redistribution which enhances social equity remains to be seen.

Benefit or utility analysis in its less prescriptive and more descriptive form, known in political science as "policy-outcomes analysis," attempts to determine the basic factors that influence or determine policy variation.[13] For example, "outcomes analysts" sketch the relationship between variations in public spending (quantity) and the quality of nonspending policy outcomes. The policy-outcomes analyst attempts to determine the relationship between the levels of spending in education and the IQ's, employability, college admissibility, and the like of the products of the educational process. This analysis is essentially after the fact, and indeed is commonly based on relatively out-of-date census data. It is, therefore, useful to new Public Administration, but only as a foundation or background.

A newer form of distributive analysis is emerging. This approach focuses on equity in the distribution of government services within a jurisdiction and asks questions such as: Does a school board distribute its funds equitably to schools and to the school children in its jurisdiction, and if not is inequity in the direction of the advantaged or disadvantaged? Are sanitation services distributed equitably to all neighborhoods in the city, and if not in what direction does inequity move and how is it justified? Is state and federal aid distributed equitably, and if not how are inequities justified?[14]

Patterns of internal-organization distribution are a traditional part of organization theory. The internal competition for money, manpower, status, space, and priorities is a staple in organization theory as any reading of the *Administrative Science Quarterly* indicates. We learn from this literature the extent to which many of the functions of government are in essence controlled by particular bodies of professionals—educators, physicians, attorneys, social workers, and the like. We learn how agencies age and become rigid and devote much of their energies to competing for survival purposes. We learn the extent to which distribution becomes what Wildavsky calls a triangulation between bureaus, legislatures (particularly legislative committees), and elected executives and their auxiliary staffs.[15] Finally, we have whole volumes of aggregated and disaggregated hypotheses which account for or attempt to explain the decision patterns involved in the internal distributive process.[16]

In new Public Administration the internal distributive process is likely to involve somewhat less readiness to make incremental compromises or "bargain" and somewhat more "administrative confrontation." If new Public Administrators are located in the staff agencies of the executive, which is highly likely, they will doubtless be considerably more tenacious than their predecessors. The spokesman for an established agency might have learned to pad his budget, to overstaff, to control public access to records, and to expand his space in preparation for the compromises he has learned to expect. He might now encounter a zealot armed with data which describe in detail padding, overstaffing, and supressed records. Therefore an organization theory based primarily on the traditional administrative bargaining process is likely to be woefully inadequate. There is a need to develop a theory which accounts for the presence of public administrators considerably less willing to bargain and more willing to take political and administrative risks.

It is difficult to predict the possible consequences of having generalist public administrators who are prepared to rationalize their positions and decisions on the basis of social equity. Administrative theory explains relatively well the results of the use of efficiency, economy, or good management as rationale. We know, for instance, that these arguments are especially persuasive in years in which legislatures and elected executives do not wish to raise taxes. But we also know that virtually anything can be justified under the rubric "good management." When public administrators leave the safe harbor of this rhetoric, what might occur? The best guess is a more open conflict on basic issues of goals or purposes. Some administrators will triumph, but the majority will not; for the system tends to work against the man seeking change and willing to take risks for it. The result is likely to be highly mobile and relatively unstable middle-level civil service. Still, actual withdrawal or removal from the system after a major setback is likely to be preferred by new public administrators to the psychic withdrawal which is now common among administrators.

One can imagine, for instance, a city personnel director prepared to confront the chief of police and the police bureaucracy on the question of eligibility standards for new patrolmen. He might argue, backed with considerable data, that patrolman height and weight regulations are unrealistic and systematically discriminate against deprived minorities. He might also argue that misdemeanor convictions by minors should not prohibit adults from becoming patrolmen. If this were an open conflict, it would likely array deprived minorities against the majority of the city council, possibly against the mayor, and certainly against the chief and his men (and no doubt the Police Benevolent Association). While the new public administrator might be perfectly willing to take the risks involved in such a confrontation, present theory does not accommodate well what this means for the political system generally.

The Integrative Process

Authority hierarchies are the primary means by which the work of persons in publicly administered organizations is coordinated. The formal hierarchy is the most obvious and easiest-to-identify part of the permanent and on-going organization. Administrators are seen as persons taking roles in the hierarchy and performing tasks that are integrated through the hierarchies to constitute a cohesive goal-seeking whole. The public administrator has customarily been regarded as the one who builds and maintains the organization through the hierarchy. He attempts to understand formal-informal relationships, status, politics, and power in authority hierarchies. The hierarchy is at once an ideal design and a hospitable environment for the person who wishes to manage, control, or direct the work of large numbers of people.

The counterproductive characteristics of hierarchies are well known.[17] New Public Administration is probably best understood as advocating modified hierarchic systems. Several means both in theory and practice are utilized to modify traditional hierarchies. The first and perhaps the best known is the project or matrix technique.[18] The project is, by definition, temporary. The project manager and his staff are a team which attempts to utilize the services of regularly established hierarchies in an ongoing organization. For the duration of the project, the manager must get his technical services from the technical hierarchy of the organization, his personnel services from the personnel agency, his budgeting services from the budget department, and so forth. Obviously the project technique would not be effective were it not for considerable top-level support for the project. When there are conflicts between the needs of the project and the survival needs of established hierarchies, top management must consistently decide in favor of the projects. The chief advantage of projects are of course their collapsible nature. While bureaucracies do not disestablish or self-destruct, projects do. The project concept is especially useful when associated with "one time" hardware or research and development, or capital improvement efforts. The concept is highly sophisticated in engineering circles and theoretically could be applied to a large number of less technical and more social problems.[19] The project technique is also useful as a device by which government contracts with industry can be monitored and coordinated.

Other procedures for modifying hierarchies are well known and include the group-decision-making model, the link-pin function, and the so-called dialectical organization.[20] And, of course, true decentralization is a fundamental modification hierarchy.[21]

Exploration and experimentation with these various techniques is a basic part of new Public Administration. The search for less structured, less formal, and less authoritative integrative techniques in publicly administered organizations is only beginning. The preference for these types of organizational modes implies first a relative tolerance for variation. This includes variations in administrative performance and variations in procedures and applications based upon differences in clients or client groups. It also implies great tolerance for the possibilities of inefficiency and diseconomy. In a very general sense this preference constitutes a willingness to trade increases in involvement and commitment to the organization for possible decreases in efficiency and economy, particularly in the short run. In the long run, less formal and less authoritative integrative techniques may prove to be more efficient and economical.

There are two serious problems with the advocacy by new Public Administration of less formal integrative processes. First, there may develop a lack of Public Administration specialists who are essentially program builders. The new Public Administration man who is trained as a change agent and an advocate of informal, decentralized, integrative processes may not be capable of building and maintaining large, permanent organizations. This problem may not be serious, however, because administrators in the several professions (education, law enforcement, welfare, and the like) are often capable organization builders, or at least protectors, so a Public Administration specialist can concentrate on the change or modification of hierarchies built by others.

The second problem is in the inherent conflict between higher- and lower-level administrators in less formal, integrative systems. While describing the distributive process in Public Administration it was quite clear that top-level public administrators were to be strong and assertive. In this description of the integrative process there is a marked preference for large degrees of autonomy at the base of the organization. The only way to theoretically accommodate this contradiction is through an organizational design in which top-level public administrators are regarded as policy advocates and general-policy reviewers. If they have a rather high tolerance for the variations in policy application then it can be presumed that intermediate and lower levels in the organization can apply wide interpretive license in program application. This accommodation is a feeble one, to be sure, but higher-lower-level administrative relations are a continuing problem in Public Administration, and the resolution of these problems in the past had tended to be in the direction of the interests of upper levels of the hierarchy in combination with subdivisions of the legislative body and potent interest groups. New Public Administration searches for a means by which lower levels of the organization and less potent minorities can be favored.

The Boundary-Exchange Process

The boundary-exchange process describes the general relationship between the publicly administered organization and its reference groups and clients. These include legislatures, elected executives, auxiliary staff organizations, clients (both organized and individual) and organized interest groups. The boundary-exchange process also accounts for the relationship between levels of government in a federal system. Because publicly administered organizations find themselves in a competitive political, social, and economic environment, they tend to seek support. This is done by first finding a clientele which can play a strong advocacy role with the legislature, then by developing a symbiotic relationship between the agency and key committees or members of the legislature, followed by building and maintaining as permanent an organization as possible.

The distributive and integrative processes which have just been described call for vastly altered concepts of how to conduct boundary exchange in new Public Administration.[22] Future organization theory will have to accommodate the following pattern of boundary exchange. First, a considerably higher client involvement is necessary on the part of those minorities who have not heretofore been involved. (It is unfair to assume that minorities are not already involved as clients: farmers, bankers, and heavy industries are minorities and they are highly involved clients. In this sense all public organizations are "client" oriented.) This change probably spells a different kind of involvement. A version of this kind of involvement is now being seen in some of our cities as a result of militancy and community-action programs, and on the campuses of some universities. A preferred form of deprived-minority-client involvement would be routinized patterns of communication with decentralized organizations capable of making distributive decisions that support the interests of deprived minorities, even if these decisions are difficult to justify in terms of either efficiency or economy.

In a very general way, this kind of decision making occurs in time of war with respect to military decision making. It also characterizes decision patterns in the Apollo program of the National Aeronautics and Space Administration. These two examples characterize crash programs designed to solve problems that are viewed as immediate and pressing. They involve a kind of backward budgeting in which large blocks of funds are made available for the project and wide latitude in expenditures is tolerated. The detailed accounting occurs after the spending, not before, hence backward budgeting. Under these conditions what to do and what materials are needed are decided at low levels of the organization. These decisions are made on the presumption that they will be supported and the necessary resources will be made available and accounted for by upper levels of the organization. This same logic could clearly be applied to the ghetto. A temporary project could be established in which the project manager and his staff work with the permanently established bureaucracies in a city in a crash program designed to solve the employment, housing, health, education, and transportation needs of the residents of that ghetto. The decisions and procedures of one project would likely vary widely from those of another, based on the differences in the circumstances of the clientele involved and the political-administrative environments encountered. The central project director would tolerate the variations both in decisions and patterns of expenditures in the same way that the Department of Defense and NASA cover their expenditures in time of crisis.

The danger will be in the tendency of decentralized projects to be taken over by local pluralist elites. The United States Selective Service is an example of this kind of take-over. High levels of disadvantaged-minority-client involvement are necessary to offset this tendency. Still, it will be difficult to prevent the new controlling minorities from systematic discrimination against the old controlling minorities.

From this description of a boundary-exchange relationship, it is probably safe to predict that administrative agencies, particularly those that are decentralized, will increasingly become the primary means by which particular minorities find their basic form of political representation. This situation exists now in the case of the highly advantaged minorities and may very well become the case with the disadvantaged.

The means by which high client involvement is to be secured is problematic. The maximum-feasible-participation notion, although given a very bad press, was probably more successful than most analysts are prepared to admit. Maximum feasible participation certainly did not enhance the efficiency or economy of OEO activities, but, and perhaps most important, it gave the residents of the ghetto at least the impression that they had the capacity to influence publicly made decisions that affected their well-being. High client involvement probably means, first, the employment of the disadvantaged where feasible; second, the use of client review boards or review agencies; and third, decentralized legislatures such as the kind sought by the Brownhill School District in the New York City Board of Education decentralization controversy.

The development of this pattern of boundary exchange spells the probable development of new forms of intergovernmental relations, particularly fiscal relations. Federal grants-in-aid to states and cities, and state grants-in-aid to cities will no doubt be expanded, and probably better equalized.[23] In addition, some form of tax sharing is probably called for. The fundamental weakness of the local governments' revenue capacity must be alleviated.

The use of the distributive and integrative processes described above probably also means the development of new means by which administrators relate to their legislatures. The elected official will probably always hold continuance in office as his number-one objective. This means that a Public Administration using less formal integrative processes must find means by which it can enhance the reelection probabilities of supporting incumbents. Established centralized bureaucracies do this in a variety of ways, the best known being building and maintaining of roads or other capital facilities in the legislators' district, establishing high-employment facilities, such as federal office buildings, county courthouses, police precincts, and the like, and distributing public-relations materials favorable to the incumbent legislator. The decentralized organization seems especially suited for the provision of this kind of service for legislators. As a consequence it is entirely possible to imagine legislators becoming strong spokesmen for less hierarchic and less authoritative bureaucracies.

The Socioemotional Process

The Public Administration described herein will require both individual and group characteristics that differ from those presently seen. The widespread use of sensitivity training, T techniques, or "organizational development" is compatible with new Public Administration.[24] These techniques include lowering an individual's reliance on hierarchy, enabling him to tolerate conflict and emotions, and indeed under certain circumstances to welcome them, and to prepare him to take greater risks. From the preceding discussion it is clear that sensitizing techniques are parallel to the distributive, integrative, and boundary-exchange processes just described.

Socioemotional-training techniques are fundamental devices for administrative change. These techniques have thus far been used primarily to strengthen or redirect on-going and established bureaucracies. In the future it is expected that the same techniques will be utilized to aid in the development of decentralized and possibly project-oriented organizational modes.

A recent assessment of the United States Department of State by Chris Argyris is highly illustrative of the possible impact of new Public Administration on organizational socioemotional processes.[25] Argyris concluded that "State" is a social system characterized by individual withdrawal from interpersonal difficulties and conflict; minimum interpersonal openness, leveling, and trust; a withdrawal from aggressiveness and fighting; the view that being emotional is being ineffective or irrational; leaders' domination of subordinates; an unawareness of leaders' personal impact on others; and very high levels of conformity coupled with low levels of risk taking or responsibility taking. To correct these organizational "pathologies" Argyris recommended that:

> 1. A long-range change program should be defined with the target being to change the living system of the State Department.
> 2. The first stage of the change program should focus on the behavior and leadership style of the most senior participants within the Department of State.
> 3. Simultaneously with the involvement of the top, similar change activities should

be initiated in any subpart which shows signs of being ready for change.
4. The processes of organizational change and development that are created should require the same behavior and attitudes as those we wish to inculcate into the system (take more initiative, enlarge responsibilities, take risks).
5. As the organizational development activities produce a higher level of leadership skills and begin to reduce the system's defenses in the area of interpersonal relations, the participants should be helped to begin to reexamine some of the formal policies and activities of the State Department that presently may act as inhibitors to organizational effectiveness (employee evaluations and ratings, promotion process, inspections). The reexamination should be conducted under the direction of line executives with the help of inside or outside consultants.
6. The similarities and interdependencies between administration and substance need to be made more explicit and more widely accepted.
7. The State Department's internal capacity in the new areas of behavioral-science-based knowledge should be increased immediately.
8. Long-range research programs should be developed, exploring the possible value of the behavioral disciplines to the conduct of diplomacy.

The characteristics of the State Department are, sad to say, common in publicly administered organizations. While Argyris' recommendations are particular to "State," they are relevant to all highly authoritative hierarchy-based organizations.

While new Public Administration is committed to wider social equity, the foregoing should make it clear that a more nearly equitable internal organization is also an objective.

CONCLUSIONS

The search for social equity provides Public Administration with a real normative base. Like many value premises, social equity has the ring of flag, country, mother, and apple pie. But surely the pursuit of social equity in Public Administration is no more a holy grail than the objectives of educators, medical doctors, and so forth. Still, it appears that new Public Administration is an alignment with good, or possibly God.

What are the likely results for a *practicing* public administration working from such a normative base? *First*, classic public administration on the basis of its expressed objectives commonly had the support of businessmen and the articulate and educated upper and upper-middle classes. The phenomenal success of the municipal-reform movement is testament to this. If new Public Administration attempts to justify or rationalize its stance on the basis of social equity, it might have to trade support from its traditional sources for support from the disadvantaged minorities. It might be possible for new Public Administration to continue to receive support from the educated and articulate if we assume that this social class is becoming increasingly committed to those public programs that are equity enhancing and less committed to those that are not. Nevertheless, it appears that new Public Administration should be prepared to take the risks involved in such a trade, if it is necessary to do so.

Second, new Public Administration, in its quest for social equity, might encounter the kinds of opposition that the Supreme Court has experienced in the last decade. That is to say, substantial opposition from elected officials for its fundamental involvement in shaping social policy. The Court, because of its independence, is less vulnerable than administration. We might expect, therefore, greater legislative controls over administrative agencies and particularly the distributive patterns of such agencies.

Third, new Public Administration might well foster a political system in which elected officials speak basically for the majority and for the privileged minorities while courts and the administrators are spokesmen for disadvantaged minorities. As administrators work in behalf of the equitable distribution of public and private goods, courts are increasingly interpreting the Constitution in the same direction. Legislative hostility to this action might be directed at administration simply because it is most vulnerable.

What of new Public Administration and academia? First, let us consider the theory, then the academy.

Organization theory will be influenced by new Public Administration in a variety of ways. The uniqueness of *public* organization will be stressed. Internal administrative behavior—the forte of the generic administration school and the foundation of much of what is now known as organization theory—will be a part of scholarly Public Administration, but will be less central. Its center position in Public Administration will be taken by a strong emphasis on the distributive and boundary-exchange processes described above.

Quantitatively inclined public-organization theorists are likely to drift toward or at least read widely in welfare economics. Indeed it is possible to imagine these theorists executing a model or paradigm of social equity fully as robust as the economist's market model. With social equity elevated to the supreme objective, in much the way profit is treated in economics, model building is relatively simple. We might, for example, develop theories of equity maximization, long- and short-range equity, equity elasticity, and so on. The theory and research being reported in the journal *Public Choice* provides a glimpse of this probable development. This work is presently being done primarily by economists who are, in the main, attempting to develop variations on the market model or notions of individual-utility maximization. Public organization theorists with social-equity commitments could contribute greatly by the creation of models less fixed on market environments or individual-utility maximization and more on the equitable distribution of and access to both public and private goods by different groups or categories of people. If a full-blown equity model were developed it might be possible to assess rather precisely the likely outcomes of alternative policies in terms of whether the alternative does or does not enhance equity. Schemes for guaranteed annual income, negative income tax, Head Start, Job Corps, and the like could be evaluated in terms of their potential for equity maximization.

The less quantitatively but still behaviorally inclined public-organization theorists are likely to move in the direction of Kirkhart's "consociated model." They would move in the direction of sociology, anthropology, and psychology, particularly in their existential versions, while the quantitatively inclined will likely move toward economics, as described above. And, of course, many public-organization theorists will stay with the middle-range theories—role, group, communications, decisions, and the like—and not step under the roof of the grand theories such as the consociated model, the social-equity model, or the so-called systems model.

What does new Public Administration mean for the academy? One thing is starkly clear: We now know the gigantic difference between "public administration" and "the public service." The former is made up of public-management generalists and some auxiliary staff people (systems analysis, budgeting, personnel, and so on) while the latter is made up of the professionals who man the schools, the police, the courts, the military, welfare agencies, and so forth. Progressive Public Administration programs in the academy will build firm and permanent bridges to the professional schools where most public servants are trained. In some schools the notion of Public Administration as the "second profession" for publicly employed attorneys, teachers, welfare workers will become a reality.

Some Public Administration programs will likely get considerably more philosophic and normative while others will move more to quantitative management techniques. Both are needed and both will contribute.

The return of policy analysis is certain in both kinds of schools. Good management for its own sake is less and less important to today's student. Policy analysis, both logically and analytically "hard-nosed," will be the order of the day.

Academic Public Administration programs have not commonly been regarded as especially exciting. New public administration has an opportunity to change that. Programs that openly seek to attract and produce "change agents" or "short-haired radicals" are light years away from the POSDCORB image. And many of us are grateful for that.

NOTES

1. Herbert Kaufman, "Administrative Decentralization and Political Power," *Public Administration Review* (January-February, 1969), pp. 3–15.
2. Frederick Mosher and John C. Honey wrestle with the question of the relative role of professional specialists as against the generalist administrator in public organizations. See Frederick Mosher, *Democracy and the Public Service* (New York: Oxford University Press, 1968), pp. 99–133. See also John C. Honey, "A Report: Higher Education for the Public Service," *Public Administration Review* (November, 1967).
3. Dwight Waldo, "Scope of the Theory of Public Administration," in James C. Charlesworth, ed., *Theory and Practice of Public Administration: Scope, Objectives and Methods* (Philadelphia: The American Academy of Political and Social Sciences, October, 1968), pp. 1–26.
4. Anthony Downs, *Inside Bureaucracy* (Boston: Little, Brown, 1967).
5. In a very general way most of these are characteristics of what Larry Kirkhart (see Chap. 5 above) calls the consociated model.
6. See especially Charles L. Schultze, *The Politics and Economics of Public Spending* (Washington, D.C.: Brookings Institution, 1969).
7. The general "social equity" concern expressed in the essays in Raymond A. Bauer, *Social Indicators* (Cambridge, Mass.: MIT Press, 1967) is clearly indicative of this.
8. Aaron Wildavsky, *The Politics of the Budgetary Process* (Boston: Little, Brown, 1964) and Charles Lindblom, *The Intelligence of Democracy* (New York: Glencoe Free Press, 1966).
9. See especially Orion White's essay in this volume (Chap. 3) on this point.
10. See especially James March and Herbert Simon, *Organizations* (New York: John Wiley & Sons, 1963).
11. See especially Amitai Etzioni, *A Comparative Analysis of Complex Organizations* (New York: Glencoe Free Press, 1961).
12. An exchange occurring at an informal rump session of the Minnowbrook Conference is especially illustrative of this. Several conferees were discussing errors in strategy and policy in the operations of the United States Office of Economic Opportunity. They were generalizing in an attempt to determine how organizations like OEO could be made more effective. Several plausible causal assertions were advanced and vigorously supported. Then a young but well-established political scientist commented that causal assertions could not be supported by only one case. True correlations of statistical significance required an "N" or "number of cases" of at least thirty. The reply was, "Has Public Administration nothing to suggest until we have had thirty O.E.O.'s? Can we afford thirty O.E.O.'s before we learn what went wrong with the first one? By ducking into our analytical and quantitative shelters aren't we abdicating our responsibilities to suggest ways to make the second O.E.O. or its equivalent an improvement on the first?"

13. For a good bibliographic essay on this subject see John H. Fenton and Donald W. Chamberlayne. "The Literature Dealing with the Relationships Between Political Process, Socioeconomic Conditions and Public Policies in the American States: A Bibliographic Essay," *Polity* (Spring, 1969), pp. 388–404. See also Chap. 9 above.
14. Equity is now a major question in the courts. Citizens are bringing suit against governments at all levels under the "equal protection of the laws" clause claiming inequities in distribution. Thus far the courts have taken a moderate equity stance in education and welfare. See John F. Coons, William H. Clune, and Stephen D. Sugerman, "Educational Opportunity: A Workable Constitutional Test for State Structures," *California Law Review* (April, 1969), pp. 305–421.
15. Aaron Wildavsky, *op. cit.*
16. March and Simon, *op. cit.*; Downs, *op. cit.*; and James L. Price, *Organizational Effectiveness* (Homewood, Ill.: Richard D. Irwin, 1968).
17. See Victor Thompson, *Modern Organization* (New York: Alfred A. Knopf, 1961); Robert V. Presthus, *The Organizational Society* (New York: Alfred A. Knopf, 1962); and Downs, *op. cit.*
18. David I. Cleland and William R. King, *Systems Analysis and Project Management* (New York: McGraw-Hill, 1968); David I. Cleland and William R. King, *Systems, Organizations, Analysis, Management: A Book of Readings* (New York: McGraw-Hill, 1969); George A. Steiner and William G. Ryan, *Industrial Project Management* (New York: Macmillan, 1968); John Stanley Baumgartner, *Project Management* (Homewood, Ill.: Richard D. Irwin, 1963).
19. H. George Frederickson and Henry J. Anna, "Bureaucracy and the Urban Poor," mimeographed.
20. See Rensis Likert, *New Patterns of Management* (New York: McGraw-Hill, 1961); and Orion White, "The Dialectical Organization: An Alternative to Bureaucracy," *Public Administration Review* (January-February, 1969), pp. 32–42.
21. Kaufman, *op. cit.*
22. James Thompson, *Organizations in Action* (New York: McGraw-Hill, 1967).
23. Deil S. Wright, *Federal Grants-in-Aid: Perspectives and Alternatives* (Washington, D.C.: American Enterprise Institute for Public Policy Research, 1968).
24. See especially the essays of Larry Kirkhart (Chap. 5) and Orion White (Chap. 3) above.
25. Chris Argyris, "Some Causes of Organizational Ineffectiveness Within the Department of State" (Washington, D.C.: U.S. Government Printing Office [Center for International Systems Research, Occasional Paper No. 2], November, 1966).

41

The Public Service in the Temporary Society

Frederick C. Mosher

This essay is addressed to two related questions:

1. With respect to the public administrative services in the United States, where are we going?
2. How can and should we prepare our public services to meet probable future demands in our systems of higher education and public service management?

But there is a question prior to these which requires attention. It concerns the changing nature and probable future directions of the society from which the public services are drawn, within which they operate, and which they are presumed to serve. This essay therefore begins with some observations about the society and its demands upon government, including some of the underlying

Source: From *Public Administration Review* 31 (January-February 1971), pp. 47–62. Some subheadings shortened.

dilemmas which seem to me most salient to the public service of the near future. Its second part is a discussion of the probable implications of these social directions and dilemmas for public administrative organizations, the public service, public personnel systems, and the universities.

I pretend no expertise in that increasingly popular field of study and speculation known as futuristics. No predictions are offered about the public services and the society of the United States in the year 2000. My ambition is more modest. It is to cull from our experience of the last few years—the decade of the '60's—some probabilities about the next few—the decade of the '70's; and to deduce from these what we (in public administration) should be doing about it. The didactic tenor of many of the sentences which follow, the frequent use of the unqualified verb "will," conveys falsely a sense of confidence and even omniscience on the part of the author. All should be qualified by the adverb "probably"; and I would hesitate to give a numerical value to the margins of error. The prognostications are tentative and hopefully provocative, not definitive.

THE TEMPORARY SOCIETY

"The Temporary Society" is an expression cribbed from the book of that title by Warren G. Bennis and Philip E. Slater[1] and is used here in two senses, only the second of which is theirs. In the first sense, the society is temporary in that it is widely known and appreciated that it is changing rapidly and will, in effect, be transformed into another society within a relatively short span of years, say 10 or 15. Societies of the past have of course changed, particularly in the West, but none with such speed and few with such awareness. Basic social changes of long ago can, by historians, be described in terms of eras; later, in terms of centuries; more recently in terms of generations. But the "social generation" of today is considerably shorter than the "human generation." The parent of the '70s is preparing his infant offspring for a society not the same as his own and not even once removed from his own. It is more nearly twice removed.

The second sense in which our society may be described as temporary concerns the institutions and organizations within it and the attachments, the moorings of those individuals who compose it. Bennis, in his chapters of the earlier-cited work, connotes the term with the allegedly changing nature of productive organizations and the evolving patterns of individual roles and associations within them.

> The social structure of organizations of the future will have some unique characteristics. The key word will be "temporary." There will be adaptive, rapidly changing *temporary* systems . . . of diverse specialists, linked together by coordinating and task-evaluating executive specialists in an organic flux—this is the organization form that will gradually replace bureaucracy as we know it.[2]

Although he acknowledges that "the future I describe is not necessarily a 'happy one,' "[3] Bennis is basically optimistic about the prospect as releasing the individual, encouraging his revitalization, and legitimizing fantasy, imagination, and creativity. Slater, in his discussion of the social consequences of temporary systems and particularly of the effects upon the family, is less reassuring.

In both of the senses here described, the term "temporary society" may exaggerate and overdramatize. As any student of anthropology or reader of Arnold

Toynbee knows, no society is permanent, although some manage to survive with little change for some centuries. And clearly there are still many stable organizations in the United States and a good many people who do have firm organizational and institutional mooring—probably a solid majority in fact. But in both senses the trend toward temporariness seems likely; and both have significance for the American public service of the future.

OTHER OBSERVATIONS AND ASSUMPTIONS

First among the other assumptions that seem to me most significant for purposes of this discussion is one that is negative, though, from my point of view at least, optimistic: that, in the next several years, there will be no nuclear holocaust, no civil war between races or other groups, no revolution which suddenly overthrows governments or other established institutions, or which reverses existing systems of values and beliefs. In other words, while social change and changes in institutions and behavior will continue with a rapidity at least equal to that of the present, steps in the future will be made from footprints marked today and in the recent past.

A second assumption has to do with the extent, the depth, and the application of human knowledge. The era since World War II has been variously labeled: the post-industrial revolution, the scientific revolution, the professional revolution, the information revolution, the cybernetic revolution, the knowledge explosion, the technological era. The emphases among these various pseudonyms have differed, but the central themes are compatible: that knowledge, particularly in the hard sciences and in technology, is growing at a rapid rate, and, as it is applied to the affairs of people, is bringing about rapid and tremendous changes in the nature of society and the capabilities, the values, and the behavior of human beings. Furthermore, in the words of Paul T. David, ". . . the oncoming world of the future, however described, will evidently be a world of increasing potential for human intervention and control both good and bad."[4] As a correlate, knowledge itself, its procreation and its application, have assumed greater and greater importance in the eyes of men, as have the institutions which develop, apply, and transmit it. Wealth, or income-producing ability, is increasingly perceived as knowledge, and its application, decreasingly as property. It is here assumed that this emphasis will continue.

A third assumption concerns the role of government in determining the strategies, the courses and means of action, for the future. Government has ceased to be merely the keeper of the peace, the arbiter of disputes, and the provider of common and mundane services. For better or worse, government has directly and indirectly become a principal innovator, a major determiner of social and economic priorities, the guide as well as the guardian of social values, the capitalist and entrepreneur or subsidizer and guarantor of most new enterprises of great scale. This development has added to American politics and public administration dimensions both of scope and range and of centrality and importance for which the only precedents occurred in the conduct of the World Wars and during the depth of the Great Depression of the '30's. On virtually every major problem and every major challenge and opportunity we turn to government—whether it be the cultivation of the ocean bottom, control of the weather, exploration of outer space, training the disadvantaged for jobs, providing day-care centers for working mothers, controlling population growth, eliminating discrimination on the basis of race or sex, juggling the interest rate, reducing the impact of schizophrenia, rescuing a bankrupt railroad, safeguarding children from dangerous toys, or cleaning the air. True, government can turn its back on problems, but if the problems continue to fester and grow, it will eventually have to confront them. True, too, government relies heavily upon organizations and individuals in the private sector to carry out many of its programs, but it cannot escape responsibility for guidance, regulation, often financial support, and results.

Finally the variety and range of governmental responsibilities, coupled with the continuing development of new knowledge and new techniques with which to deal with them, have added enormously to the reliance of the whole society upon the people who man governmental posts, who collectively make its decisions. This is true of officials in all three branches of government, but it is most conspicuous and probably also most significant of the elective and appointive officers in the executive agencies. As the range of public problems and programs broadens, and as knowledge relevant to each grows and deepens, it becomes less and less possible for politically elected representatives to get a handle on more than a few of the significant issues. Even on these, they must rely heavily upon the information, analysis, and judgment of the appointive public servants. This reliance upon administrative personnel will, I assume, continue to grow.

ANOMALIES

But there are other areas relevant to the public service of tomorrow where the signals are less clear, where we seem to be moving in two or more directions at once. One of these concerns *rationality* and *objectivity* in reaching public decisions. It is epitomized by the system known as planning-programming-budgeting (PPBS), which future historians may consider the most significant administrative innovation of the 1960's. PPBS in some form and to some degree is now installed in most federal agencies—all the large ones—in the majority of states, and in many of the largest cities and counties. It is doubtful that any definition would satisfy all students and practitioners of PPBS, but most would agree that a central feature is the objective analysis of the probable cost and effectiveness of alternative courses of action to achieve goals, independent of political considerations (in the narrow sense of "political"), bureaucratic considerations, and personal wishes or hunches. In the words of one federal official: "PPBS is simply a means to make public decision making more rational."

Yet, during this same decade of PPBS rationality, there were at least three waves of thought or practice which were distinctively "unrational," if not "antirational." The first was the realist school which argued that public decisions, particularly budgetary decisions, are incremental in nature, based on last year's experience, seldom responsive to overall, comprehensive analysis. Year-to-year changes are relatively small in amount and reflect estimates of what the political market will bear rather than optimization in allocation of resources. Outcomes are the products of bargaining within fairly narrow ranges of political feasibility. Finally, policy decisions should give at least as much weight to political as to economic costs and benefits.

A second nonrational school of thought of the '60's is that now widely known as organizational development, an outgrowth of the earlier human relations movement. Its focus is upon the affective rather than the cognitive or analytical aspects of organizational behavior, and its premise is that organizational effectiveness (or health) will be improved if each member understands himself as a personality, is sensitive of the feelings of his associates, and is given a significant discretionary role in the shaping and carrying out of organizational goals. Among its by-words are openness, sensitivity, confrontation, democratic leadership, participation, flat hierarchy (if any at all), organization by objective.

The third movement of the 1960's is more clearly antirational than these other two, at least in the sense that term is used here. It is the politics of confrontation, which must by this time be familiar to most Americans. Its premises are moral categorical imperatives. Certain conditions or actions or decisions are wrong, in the sense not of being incorrect but of being evil. Such wickedness—whether it be war or racial discrimination or police brutality or alleged repression or the college grading system—is immediately apparent and should be instantly corrected. There is neither need nor time to analyze costs and consequences before taking action against things that are, on their face, evil. It is understandable but paradoxical that the politics of confrontation was born on the campuses of universities which one might have expected would be the seats of rationality and tolerance. But clearly it is a phenomenon of our times which must be reckoned with in the public service. Already, it is being practiced within some governmental agencies and is supported by a growing literature including some writings in the field of public administration.

Though their premises are different, it appears entirely possible that the incremental approach to decision making and the approach of organizational development can be reconciled with the rationality approach of PPBS. In fact, some students and practitioners have argued that policy analysis can be used effectively to enrich, rather than undermine, the bargaining process behind public decisions. There has been less dialogue between the PPBS proponents and the disciples of organizational development. Yet, in one agency, the Department of State, the same group of officers endeavored to introduce both types of approaches at about the same time during the mid-'60's. Neither effort succeeded, but it was the conclusion of many participants that the systems approach failed because organizational development had begun too late. Reconciliation between the rationality emphasis and the politics of confrontation appears less likely because the two are so diametrically opposed in their central premises.

Emphases on Systems and Processes

A second area in which the crystal ball seems cloudy concerns the conflicting emphases upon *systems* and *processes.* The charge has been leveled by more than one critic that the study and the practice of government have overemphasized the processes through which decisions are reached and executed with too little consideration of the effects or outcomes of those decisions and actions.[5] They question—I think correctly—the assumption that if the democratic and administrative processes are legal and proper, the consequences will be optimal, or at least the best that is feasible in the American polity. They contest the line of thought growing from Bentley, that given appropriate access to decision channels, interest groups will conflict, balance each other out, and force proper decisions. Finally, they feel that too much faith has been lodged in the procedures governing nominations, elections, interest group access, the merit system, the budget system, and other related processes in the confidence that they will result in the best policies; in short, in a political/administrative "invisible hand" quite comparable to the market system so long relied upon by economists. Manifestly, the "invisible hand" has been less than optimally successful in both the political and economic realms. Yet, while the systems approach, which would analytically seek the best solutions to our public problems, is gaining in both administrative and academic circles, the emphasis upon process continues. In fact, the thrust of behavioralism in political and administrative sciences, with its undertones of determinism, tends to give it added support.

Participation

The current and increasing popularity of *participation* in decision making and in administration generally is a third source of confusion. It appears in at least three quite different forms. One is participation by those citizens most directly affected by given programs in decisions about those programs and their operations. Epitomized in the Economic Opportunity Act by the expression "maximum feasible participation," variations on the theme are found in a good many other federal programs, and some of them, like the draft, price control, and agricultural allotments, have a long history. It has been prominent at the local level in the drives to return the control of schools to local district boards and to govern the police through citizen review boards. A second manifestation of the participation drive has been the rapid growth of unionism, collective bargaining, and strikes of public servants. A third is the movement, mentioned earlier, toward organizational development, which includes among its central tenets participation, individually and in groups, in decision making.

Participation in decisions affecting public policy by any group of citizens (including employees) not politically representative of the whole or responsible to such political representation may, in theory and sometimes in practice, collide with that central premise of American governance which Redford has described as "overhead democracy."[6] The expression describes a polity resting ultimately on majority control through political representatives, wherein administrative officers are primarily responsible and loyal to their superiors for carrying out the directions of the elective representatives. Of course, legislatures may, and frequently have, delegated to citizen and employee participants policy areas over which they have discretion. But the proper and feasible limits of such delegation remain hazy.

All three types of participation mentioned here offer potential opposition to the ideal of rationality, and all three may lead—and sometimes have led—to the politics of confrontation. Participation by private citizens runs a collision course with the drive toward professionalization, which is discussed later.

Decentralization Trends

Associated and sometimes identified with the participation thesis is the recent push toward *decentralization* of governmental policy and action to lower levels—from Washington to regional offices or to states, cities, or school districts; from states to local jurisdictions; from cities and countries to community organizations and districts. The paradox is that the decade of the 1960's was one of the most vigorously centralizing eras in our history except in wartime. And there is no sign that the trend is slackening, despite the pleas for decentralization. Growth, technology, population mobility are forcing geographic interdependence; and interdependence forces centralization in public (as well as private) policy. The people of California have a stake in the educational standards of Mississippi, as do those of Buffalo in the waste disposal practices of Cleveland, those of New York in the economic and manpower situation in Puerto Rico, and all of us in the antipollution devices put on new cars in Detroit. The advantage of the federal government and some of the states in access to revenues encourages centralization, as does the failure of many states and local units to realize their own revenue potential in response to public needs.

Continuing centralization seems inevitable; yet decentralization is a plain necessity. Only a small share, in number if not in importance, of public decisions should or can be made in Washington. The federal structure is so functionally specialized as to make broad developmental decisions on a geographic basis extremely difficult—whether for a federal region, a state, a city, or a community. A challenge for administrators of the present and future is to devise, test, effect, and operate mechanisms whereby we can move in both directions at the same time.[7] That is: devices for communities to initiate and make community decisions within regional and/or state guidelines, standards, and policies, and within nationwide objectives and standards. Already there are experiments with such mechanisms, as in the poverty program, model cities, and education. The recent proposal by CED for a two-tier, federated system for metropolitan government with a powerful metropolitan unit and semiautonomous community units is a move in the same two directions.

Specialization and Professionalization

Another anomaly arises from the narrowing and deepening of *specialization* and *professionalization* among organizations, fields of knowledge, and individuals. This phenomenon, which has been remarked by a great many writers before this one, is particularly significant in governmental enterprises, partly because professionalism has become so prevalent in so many public fields; partly because so many important public organizations are dominated by a single professional elite. As the focus of specialisms has narrowed, the boundaries around social problems have broadened and fuzzed. A consequence is that few professions can now claim total competence to handle basic problems even within those functional areas in which they once were recognized as exclusive monopolists. This is a product of growing *functional interdependence*, which is entirely comparable to the growing geographic interdependence mentioned earlier, and of the external effects—both costs and benefits—of actions taken in one field upon others. It would probably be more accurate to say that the growth has been less in the actual interdependence of different fields and more in the recognition of such interdependence. Crime is no longer a problem for the police alone nor health for doctors alone nor highways for engineers alone nor justice for lawyers alone. Progressive practitioners and educators are articulating and deploring the limitations of their own fields with increasing shrillness. As will be discussed later, this dilemma is bringing about a rethinking of professional—and interprofessional—education and practice.

Growth

A final anomaly for our future public administration is the impending desanctification of *growth*, particularly economic growth, as the ultimate goal of society and its rate as the measure of social progress. The progress of defrocking has begun. Already it is clear: that overall population growth must ultimately be reduced to zero—and "ultimately" may not be very many decades away; that our largest, "greatest" cities are near-disaster areas for many of their inhabitants; that the biggest organizations are among the most dangerous threats to resources, environment, culture, and even people.

John Kenneth Galbraith, after emphasizing growth as a dominant and pervasive goal of the "technostructure," notes that it is supported by its consistency with the more general goal of economic growth. "No other social goal is more strongly avowed than economic growth. No other test of social success has such nearly unanimous acceptance as the annual increase in the Gross National Product."[8] But faith in GNP growth as an indicator of social betterment must soon decline in the face of its increasingly apparent clumsiness and flimsiness. Expenditures for war and defense are of course part of GNP, and indeed the surest way to increase it rapidly would be a major (non-nuclear) war. The social costs incident to productive enterprise and urbanization are nowhere deducted from GNP: despoliation of resources, pollution of all kinds, crime and other costs related to population density, and many others. Further, whatever dollar expenditures are made to counteract these real costs are *added into,* not *deducted from,* GNP.[9] The costs of producing and merchandising goods that are trivial, worthless, or actually damaging (like tobacco, liquor, guns, and DDT) are part of GNP. And GNP of course takes no account whatever of the distribution of income and wealth among the population.

Of course, much work has already been done toward the development of more sensitive and meaningful measures of social betterment than GNP. The harder and probably slower job will be to modify the underlying faith in growth for many decades: the faith that equates "more" with "better" and "growth" with "progress." Administrators cannot much longer rely upon crude measures of growth—whether or not economic—to provide their goals or to appraise their effectiveness. They must help to find, and must learn and apply subtler and more qualitative goals and indices; and they must play some part in communicating these to the public.

To recapitulate: The emerging public administration, the truly "new" public administration, will bear responsibilities of a range and an importance that are hardly suggested in any current textbook. It will have to anticipate and deal with changes in a society that is changing more rapidly than any in human history. It, too, will have to be rapidly changeable and flexible. It will have to press for greater rationality and develop and utilize ever more sophisticated tools for rational decisions, at the same time accommodating to forces that seem unrational. It must concern itself more than in the past with human goals—"life, liberty, and the pursuit of happiness"—but without damage to the processes which make democracy viable. And these goals must be more sophisticated than simple quantitative growth. It must recognize the functional and geographic interdependence of all sectors of the society without too much sacrifice to the values of professional specialism and local interest. It must develop collaborative workways whereby centralization and decentralization proceed simultaneously, and assure high competence at every level of government.

These are tall orders for public administration. Their implications are described more specifically in the balance of this article.

IMPLICATIONS FOR PUBLIC ORGANIZATIONS

The statements about public organizations which follow are not purely predictive. All have some basis in observations of current developments. And all are responsive to the societal trends and problems described earlier.

First are the increasing emphasis in and among organizations upon problems and problem solving, and the growing distrust of established and traditional routines which have failed to provide solutions.

There will be increasing dependence upon, and increasing acceptance of, analytical techniques in planning and evaluating public programs, centering upon specialized units near the top of agencies, but spreading downwards to lower and operating echelons seeking rationalized defense of their programs. One might anticipate, too, a broadened and more sophisticated approach to analytic techniques which takes into account elements beyond purely economic and quantitative considerations. But there will be increasing concern about long-term objectives, alternative measures for reaching such objectives, social—as distinguished from purely economic—indicators, and improved information systems concerning both costs and effects of programs. There will also be more efforts toward experimentation in undertakings whose prospects are untried and unproven.

As the interconnection and interdependence of social problems is increasingly perceived, there will be growing reliance upon ad hoc problem-solving machinery—task forces, commissions, special staffs to executives, interagency committees, and institutionalized though ad hoc mechanisms within agencies.

Both the second and third developments cited above will force increased attention on the inherently obstinate problems of translating new or changed program decisions into effective action through—or in spite of—existing and traditional agencies and operations. In fact, one of the weakest links in public administration today is that of giving operational meaning to planning decisions, however sophisticated may be the analysis behind the plans and however effective the collaboration in reaching agreement on the plans.

Political executives, under unrelenting pressure from elements in the society and dissatisfied with the answers available from the established bureaucracy, tend to develop and utilize machinery directly responsible to them for developing new programs and changing old ones. At the national level, this is manifest in the emergence of the National Security Council, the new Domestic Council, and a number of presidential program initiatives. Governors like Rockefeller and mayors like Lindsay have responded in substantially comparable ways. So have strong department heads, dissatisfied with recommendations, or lack thereof, from established line bureaus.

There will continue to be vigorous attacks against "entrenched" bureaucracies within departments and agencies. They may be expressed through reorganizing a bureau out of business or scattering its functions or taking over key activities as planning, personnel, and budget or politicizing its top positions.

Partly in self-defense, bureaus and comparable agencies will undertake to broaden their bases and broaden their capabilities through the engagement of people in relevant specializations but not typical of the elite profession of the bureau. They will also increasingly seek and welcome collaborative relationships with other bureaus and agencies and with other levels of government. And they, too, will become more problem oriented.

As these characteristics of problem orientation and collaboration develop at one level of government, particularly the federal, they will encourage and sometimes enforce comparable approaches at other levels with which it deals.

As local constituencies become more vociferous and more vigorous, and as the capabilities of personnel in federal regional offices, the states, and local governments are upgraded, there will be growing demand for decentralizing decision-making power. My guess is that this kind of decentralization will proceed but a little more slowly than the centralization process implied above.

Finally, there will be a growing premium on responsiveness to social problems and speed in planning and taking action on them. This will be forced, in part, by the politics of confrontation, mentioned earlier.

In short, administrative organizations will be more political, especially at the leadership levels, in the broader Aristotelian sense of politics. But not with any loss of brain power and specialized knowledge. The movements toward the latter and the need for them will continue to grow. Agencies, though continuing to reflect a heavy functional emphasis in their structure, will necessarily look beyond their specific functions to related functions and agencies. And they will be more flexible.

These developments will not occur equally in all public agencies any more than they have to date. Indeed, there are a good many public activities for which they will not occur at all. They will be most evident in those problem areas of articulate public concern and in connection with new or radically changed programs; that is, in controversial fields. There will be an abundance of President Truman's "kitchens" around Washington and in other capitals in the United States. One can foresee no diminution of intra and interorganizational conflict.

Partly as a result of the developments suggested above, there will probably be profound changes within administrative organizations in their patterns and behavioral styles. The old Weberian description of bureaucracy, with its emphasis upon formal structure, hierarchy, routinization, and efficiency in its narrow sense, is rapidly becoming obsolete in many organizations. It is inadequate particularly for "thought" organizations, agencies which operate within a particularly turbulent political environment, agencies facing increasing complexity in their programs, and agencies staffed heavily with highly professional or scientific personnel. Such organizations must, if they are to survive, be responsive, adaptive, flexible, creative, and innovative. This means, among other things, that they will increasingly be structured around projects or problems to be solved rather than as permanent, impervious hierarchies of offices, divisions, and sections. Permanent hierarchical structures will remain for a variety of administrative purposes and for the affixing of final responsibility. But work itself will be organized more collegially on a team basis. Generalist decisions will be reached through the pooling of the perspectives and techniques of a variety of specialists. Leadership will be increasingly stimulative and collaborative rather than directive.

This "new" style of bureaucracy is not wholly wishful nor simply the paraphrasing of the writings of social psychologists about what an organization ought to be. The movement toward it is evident in many public and private enterprises and dominant in a few, particularly those involved in research and development, such as units of NASA, NIH, and the scientific laboratories. It is more and more prevalent in the social fields as illustrated by their growing reliance upon intra and interagency task forces, work groups, and committees. It is reflected also in the nature and assignments of a large portion of the so-called "political" appointees who are not politicians and whose party regularity is incidental, if not, in some instances, totally irrelevant. Many of these appointments appear to be predicated upon professional competence in an appropriate field, ability to apply their skills to a variety of problems, and competence in working with and through (rather than over) others.

IMPLICATIONS FOR THE PUBLIC SERVICE

More than half of the products of the nation's universities and colleges, graduate and undergraduate, are educated in specializations that are intended to prepare them for one or another professional or scientific occupation. Not including housewives, the majority of the other college graduates will later return for professional graduate training or will enter upon some line of work, like the Foreign Service, wherein they will acquire the accoutrements of professionalism on the job. Ours is increasingly a professional society or, more accurately, a professionally led society.

And American governments are principal employers of professionals. Very probably within a few years as many as two-fifths of all professionals in this country will be employed directly or indirectly by governments. I perceive no signals that this trend toward professionalism in government will decline. The program now developing to help the underprivileged find satisfying careers in government and elsewhere may involve lowering educational requisites for some kinds of jobs. But the extent that such programs are successful will be measured by the numbers of their participants who rise to professional or at least paraprofessional levels. What is challenged is not professionalism but the orthodoxy of the traditional routes to attain it.

Books can and should be written about the impact of professionalism upon the public service. I would like to mention very briefly only a few implications that seem salient to this discussion.

- Professionals generally, though not universally, have an orientation to problems or cases; they are prepared to move from one problem to another, somewhat different, one, or to keep several balls in the air at the same time. This problem orientation described above in connection with public organizations is entirely in keeping with the professional way of life.
- All professions (with the possible exception of the ministry) view themselves as rational, but their ways of viewing and defining rationality vary widely. Rationality is no monopoly of administrators, economists, or lawyers. Probably the nearest approach to "pure rationality," with respect to any given problem, must be the product of a mix of differing professional perspectives on that problem.
- Professional study and practice has tended to foster increasing specialism and increasing depth, decreasing breadth of both student and practitioner, in the professions. This has been further encouraged by the explosion of knowledge in most fields. Until quite recently it has tended to crowd out the consideration of general social consequences of professional behavior and the philosophical consideration of social values from both education and practice. In most fields it has also minimized education or practice in politics, administration, or organization.
- Insofar as professionalism requires many years of training and experience (varying in different fields) in specialized subjects, it has an inhibiting effect upon movement from one occupation to another. But it encourages mobility from place to place and from organization to organization (or

self-employment), especially when the move promises new and greater challenges. This is probably truest among the best qualified, most innovative, and most problem-oriented individuals.

- Professional behavior tends to be conditioned more by the norms, standards, and workways of the profession than by those that may be imposed by an employing organization. Within those standards professionals seek a considerable degree of autonomy and discretion in the application of their particular skills. They resist working under close supervision of others, especially when the others are not members of the same profession.
- When professionals work on problems requiring a number of different occupational skills—and these include almost all problems in the social arena—they prefer to work with others on an equal or team basis, founded in mutual respect.
- Most of the professions are increasingly grounded in some branches of science. Science is in turn grounded in the search for truth and, for any given problem, the finding of the correct answer. Scientists—and many professionals—are intolerant of ambiguity, of politics, and all too often of other ways of looking at problems.

These alleged attributes of professionalism of course do not apply equally to all professions nor equally to all members of any given profession. Where and to the extent that they do apply, it may be noted that some of them are entirely congruent and encouraging to the kind of organizational behavior suggested in the preceding section. These include:

orientation to problems, projects, and cases;
mobility or willingness to move from place to place and from job to job;
collegial relationships in working with others on common problems.

But in certain other respects, the education and practice of typical professions is a good deal less than optimal for the public service of tomorrow. First, there is insufficient stress upon and concern about human and social values. All professions allege their dedication to the service of society, and most take for granted that activities their members perform within professional standards are useful and beneficial to the public. There has been rather little reexamination of these assumptions in the face of a rapidly changing society and rapidly expanding governmental responsibilities. And individual practitioners are provided little motivation or intellectual grounding to stimulate concern about general social values in relation to their day-to-day problems. This is only incidentally a matter of codes of ethics, most of which are essentially negative and very few of which even mention any special ethical problems arising from public service, even when substantial portions of the profession are employed by governments. The kind of need I perceive is more of the order, for example, that:

engineers who plan highways or airports or sewage plants take into consideration the secondary and tertiary effects of these undertakings on the quality of life in America and in the places for which they are planning;
lawyers look beyond due process, *stare decisis*, the adversary system, etc., to the roots of our social difficulties;
economists look beyond primary and quantitative costs and benefits, the market analogy, and the GNP growth rate to where we as a society and as individuals are going—both as a whole and in relation to individual economic decisions; etc.

Second and closely related to the values question is the need of a great many more professionals who have a sophisticated understanding of social, economic, and political elements and problems of our times, including an understanding of the relation of their own work to that setting.

Third is the need for humility and for tolerance of others, their ideas and perspectives, whether or not professionals; and an ability to communicate with others on shared problems.

Fourth is an ability to work in situations which are uncertain and on problems for which there is no correct solution—in short, a tolerance for ambiguity.

Fifth is an understanding of organizations and how they work, particularly in the context of American politics and government; skill in managing in the larger sense of getting things done with and through other people.

Sixth, there should be a greater incentive for—and much less discouragement of—creativity, experimentation, innovation, and initiative.

Seventh is the need for a much higher degree of mobility—within agencies, between agencies, between governments, and in and out of government. Despite the observation made earlier that professionalism encourages such mobility, public employment by and large has inhibited it, even for its professionals. One result is that the majority of those who rise to the near top have had effective experience in only one agency, often only one division of that agency. This is a disservice to the man—the absence of challenge and of different and broadening kinds of experiences. It is a misfortune for the government because it tends to solidify bureaucratic parochialism and, in some degree, discourages the problem approach which was stressed earlier. Ten years of experience in one job may be merely one year of experience repeated ten times. The idea of temporariness should extend much further than it has in the civil services of governments.

Finally, there should be greater opportunities for challenge and for rapid advancement for the able young, for the underprivileged, and for women. In government, this means opportunities for professionalizing the nonprofessionals and for rapid advancement through a variety of challenging assignments for those who prove effective.

IMPLICATIONS FOR PERSONNEL SYSTEMS

Obviously, the strengths and weaknesses of the public service can be attributed only partially to personnel systems—the systems whereby people are employed and deployed, advanced, and retired. And changes in the systems have only a partial and usually rather slow influence in changing the nature and calibre of the public service. Yet I doubt that there is any other manipulable element with as much potential impact. The system and its popular image condition the kinds and capabilities of people who seek entrance and their expectations. It also influences the expectations of those already on the job, their motivation, the rewards and penalties of differing kinds of behavior, their movement from job to job, and the way they work together.

Personnel administration has since World War II, but particularly in the decade of the 60's, been undergoing a radical transition in the national government and, in varying degrees, in the states and the cities. It has been marked by:

- decentralization and delegation from central civil service agencies in the direction of line managers;
- growing emphasis upon personnel as a management service rather than as a control or police activity;
- growth of employee and executive development programs, particularly through institutionalized training;
- growth and recognition of employee organizations and collective bargaining;

concern about and programs for equal opportunity for the handicapped, underprivileged, minority groups, and women;
relaxation of rules and requirements for standardized personnel actions, particularly as they apply to professionals;
"positive" recruitment in the educational institutions and elsewhere.

The extent and significance of these and other changes are not, I think, sufficiently appreciated. If one were to compare an annual report of the U.S. Civil Service Commission of a pre-War year such as 1939 or even of 1955 with *Blueprint for the Seventies*, its report for 1969, he could hardly believe that they were produced by the same agency. (Though a glance at the appendices might make the identity of the three more recognizable.) Most of these changes have been constant with the changing nature and needs of the society.

Yet there linger some tenets of civil service administration—and the image of them perceived by both bureaucrats and the general public—which seem inconsistent with the directions of the society and dysfunctional in terms of its demands upon the public service. I should like to focus upon two of them, both born of reform movements and both with a distinguished history of about half a century or longer. The first is here referred to as *careerism*. It is that feature built upon the expectation that individuals will be recruited soon after completion of their education; that they will spend the bulk of their working lives in the same organization; that they will be advanced periodically as they gain experience and seniority, such advancement made on the basis of competition with their peers; and that they will be protected in such advancement against competition with outsiders. The second is *position classification* or, more particularly, the thesis that the content of a given position or class of positions be the hub around which other personnel actions and indeed management generally should revolve.

Careerism has historically been associated with such commissioned corps systems as the Army, Navy, and Foreign Service, but it is now clear that it is equally or more virile in many of the well-established agencies under civil service in the federal and all other levels of government. Typically in the United States—and most other industrialized nations of the world—careers are associated with individual agencies—departments, bureaus, services, divisions—rather than with the government as a whole. And typically they are identified with a particular type of professional specialization, dominant or subordinate, within the given agency. Careerism may contribute to managerial flexibility in the provision of a corps of qualified people within the organization who are available for different kinds of assignments. At the same time, it inhibits overall elasticity in terms of quick changes in total manpower resources or the provision of persons with different kinds of skill and perspectives. It discourages lateral entry or the ingestion of new blood above the bottom or entering level, and some agencies have absolutely banned it. More often than not, careerism provides built-in, though usually unwritten, incentives for individuals to pursue orthodox careers within the agency and to avoid unusual assignments which might sidetrack or delay advancement. Overall, careerism probably is an important discourager of creativity, innovation, and risk taking because of the perceived or imagined dangers of stepping out of line. And insofar as it assures that the older officers within the system will hold the top positions of the agency, it assures continuity, stability, and conservatism in agency policy.[10] It is probably the principal ingredient of the cement which binds an agency into a strong, autonomous, and perhaps impervious entity against outsiders—whether above in the Executive Branch or outside in the legislature or the public.

It is apparent that many aspects of careerism run counter to effective government responsiveness to the needs of the temporary society. Among the items it discourages are: collaborative relationships with other agencies and specializations toward the solution of common problems; interchange of personnel among agencies, among jurisdictions of government, and between government and the private sector; ad hoc but temporary assignments that are unorthodox in terms of career advancement; responsiveness and rapid change to meet rapidly changing problems. Insofar as the gates of entry upon a government career are based upon orthodox educational credentials—and most of them are—it inhibits employment programs for aspiring potential professionals of minority groups. The bar against lateral entry effectively shuts out mature and qualified women after they have raised their families. And the whole image of government as life-long career systems in single agencies discourages some of the most alert, idealistic, and action-oriented of American youth.

Like careerism, position classification is not necessarily a dysfunctional process. Indeed, it is hard to imagine any sizable organization operating without at least a skeleton of a classification plan, even if it is unwritten. The problem arises from the centrality and dominance which positions and their classification came to assume in personnel administration, in management generally, and in the psychology of officers and employees. Thirty years ago classification had become the jumping-off point for most activities in the field of personnel: pay, recruitment and selection, placement, promotions, transfers, efficiency ratings, even training. It provided the blocks for what some have called the building-block theory of organization—an essentially static and mechanistic concept. It was the restraining leash around the necks of aggressive public managers, and the more successful of them were often the ones who could successfully slip or unfasten it. It has subtler though perhaps more important negative effects upon such matters of status, motivation, willingness to work with others on common problems, communications, flexibility, and adaptability: in short, pervasive impairment to what Agyris has labeled "organizational health."

The whole concept of position classification runs somewhat counter, or restraining, to the concept of organization as a fluid, adaptive, rapidly changing entity, oriented to problems and motivated by organizational objectives. To the extent that it is coercive and binding, detailed and specific, and difficult to change, classification has the effects of:

- retarding organizational change and adaptation;
- discouraging initiative and imagination beyond the definition of the position class;
- inhibiting special, ad hoc assignments or otherwise working "out of class";
- discouraging recognition of unusual contributions and competence through rapid advancement.

Bennis confidently predicted that: "People will be differentiated not vertically according to rank and role but flexibly according to skill and professional training."[11] His forecast is not totally reassuring, since "skill and professional training" sound suspiciously like credentialism, and differentiation by credentials can certainly be vertical. But it is clear that the dominance of classification in government has declined a great deal and nearly vanished in some sectors except as a convenience to management. In the federal government the flexibility of the management intern and FSEE programs at the lower rungs of the ladder and, to a slight degree, of the Executive Manpower System at the upper rungs are examples. But clearly in many federal agencies and state and local governments we need to go much further and faster.[12]

I have not intended in this section to suggest that governments cease assuring careers to prospective and incumbent employees, nor that position classification be abandoned. Both seem to me essential. But some of the unintended consequences of both could and should be alleviated in terms consonant with the trends of the society and its demands on government. What is really needed is a PPBS-type analysis of public personnel practices in terms of their long-range costs and benefits towards governmental objectives. My prediction is that such analyses would indicate that there should be:

a de-emphasis of careerism and tenurism;
more lateral entry, exit, and reentry;
more mobility and flexibility in assignment and reassignments;
rewards rather than implicit penalties for broadening experience in other agencies, other governments, and the private sector;
more emphasis in rank, status, and rewards upon the man and his performance, less upon his position description;
declining reliance upon examinations and rank-order lists in entrance and advancement, and more reliance upon performance and references;
more opportunities for reeducation and retraining, and for broadening education and training, especially for professional personnel;
more emphasis upon rewards and recognition for initiative and work well done, with less concern about discipline and penalties for nonconformity;
broadening of the subjects of negotiation in collective bargaining and, with some exceptions, recognition of the right to strike.

IMPLICATIONS FOR THE UNIVERSITIES

The proper mission and role of higher education in American society is today more in dispute than ever before. I acknowledge my bias in thinking that the universities and colleges do and should have a broad responsibility for preparing public leaders for their occupational roles. But this is not to be constructed, as it has been in many places and many fields in the past, as a narrowly vocational preparation. In the majority of professions it is increasingly recognized that most of the techniques and workways of day-to-day operations are best learned on the job. But the universities are uniquely qualified to provide a theoretical base and some methodological principles for such techniques. They are also equipped to open the students' minds to the broader value questions of the society and of their professions' roles in that society. As the procreators and warehouses of knowledge in vast ranges of fields, they can provide some comprehension of social and political complexity, and of the interconnection and interdependence of social problems with which they will deal.

The universities have not been as successful in these capacities as they might be. One reason, I think, lies in the history of professional education. The Morrill Act of more than a century ago and the land-grant colleges to which it gave rise were tremendously effective in revolutionizing the technology of agriculture and industry. But they provided what is today an unfortunate heritage that persons can qualify to operate as full-grade professionals with degrees as bachelors, masters, even doctors in their fields with virtually no education beyond that perceived as immediately relevant and necessary to the practice of their profession, plus some grounding in the sciences regarded as foundational to that practice. As some professional education developed in many other fields—education, business administration, forestry, journalism, etc.—a similar pattern was adopted. Later, advances in knowledge tended to drive out or inhibit the development of liberal arts courses in the preparation for some other professions such as medicine and the sciences, physical and social. A majority of our public and private leaders are products of such professional and scientific education, and a good many of them have little systematic study beyond the high school level about the society and culture in which they will live and practice their trades.

This deficiency has been recognized in some universities, in a growing number of professional schools, and in some of the professions themselves. They are seeking to build up offerings and requirements in the humanities and the social sciences. My own feeling is that our minimal target should be that all who go to college should have the equivalent of at least two years of liberal arts beyond the field of their major, and that all aspiring professionals have at least one course which relates their specific profession to the society and to the social problems to which it is relevant. This course should go well beyond the Boy Scout code level of traditional courses in professional ethics.

A second shortcoming of higher education is an outgrowth of the increasing depth and specialization of disciplines and subdisciplines which have been a consequence of the knowledge explosion. These have tended to inhibit interdisciplinary and interprofessional study and to deemphasize the connections and interdependencies which have been stressed earlier in this essay. Recognition of this difficulty is attested by the growth on many campuses of cross-disciplinary institutes which are focused on problem areas rather than the traditional disciplinary divisions. It has also given rise to a growing variety of cross-disciplinary educational programs such as comprehensive health planning, urbanology, city planning and public administration, engineering and medicine, economics and about every professional field, and many others. Such programs should be encouraged, as should the recognition by all college faculties that no discipline is equipped to handle adequately even its own problems by itself.

A third shortcoming of the universities lies in their almost systematic ignoring, if not derogation, of the possibilities of social invention, experimentation, innovation, and direction to resolve and correct public problems; and of the mechanisms whereby these actions can be carried out. This I think is true not alone of most professional schools but also of the humanities and the social and natural sciences, not excluding political science. The academic manifestations of the politics of confrontation are, in some part, a product of frustration; and the frustration is, in some part, a product of ignorance about the potentialities and the tactics of social change in a democratic polity. If the assumptions stated earlier in this article are near the mark, change and innovation are increasingly controllable by human beings, acting through political and administrative mechanisms of government; and they are heavily dependent upon the effectiveness of appointive public administrators who are, in major proportion, products of the universities. To the extent that these institutions fail to arouse interest in and awareness about the challenges, the obstacles, and the mechanics of government and, perhaps worse, to the extent they excite hostility toward politics and public administration, they may in fact be inhibiting the possibilities of real social reform. Recent evidence on many campuses of renewed interest of many professors and students in current problems and in politics may signal a turn in the pendulum: But clearly there is a long way to go.

A fourth area in which the institutions of higher education need accelerated development is continuing education, particularly for those in middle and upper levels of public service. With the rapid growth of knowledge and equally rapid changes in social problems, renewed education for persons already in professional practice has come to be regarded as essential in some fields. There has been some recognition and provision for it in some branches of the public service, but altogether too little. Continuing or mid-career education for public servants of five different types is needed:

1. Refresher or updating education in one's own professional field;
2. Broadening education about social problems and developments—both those directly relevant to the program of one's agency and those widely significant to the continuing understanding of a dynamic society;
3. Education about American politics and government and about public organization without previous study in these fields who are about to assume responsible administrative positions;
4. Education about newly developed techniques of analysis, data processing, etc., with particular emphasis upon their uses, potential, and limitations;
5. Training in sensitivity, in self-understanding, and in interpersonal communication, understanding, and adaptation.

For the many reasons cited earlier in this article, programs in all these categories are likely to become increasingly crucial in the years ahead.

A CLOSING NOTE: SCHOOLS OF PUBLIC AFFAIRS

During the '60's, there was a considerable growth of new schools in the public affairs area and a substantial redirection of the programs of some of the older ones. Most of these additions and changes have been responsive to the wave of popularity of PPBS and have focused upon techniques of rational analysis of public programs. Within limits, this is a desirable development. Public administration programs of the past were, like governments themselves, not conspicuously strong in hardheaded, sophisticated analysis. Administrators need to know the how's and why's of policy analysis as well as its uses and limitations. But analysis is a tool of decision reaching, not decision making itself; and a solid command of analytical techniques is no assurance of a good administrator. I think it at least as important today as in the heyday of scientific management that we not permit administration, in its response to major public issues, to be mistaken for sophisticated, academically aesthetic techniques.

Yet I feel strongly that schools of public affairs of the future may play a unique and a crucially important role in the improvement of governmental responses to rapidly changing public demands. They will not be a resurrection of the earlier efforts to create a profession built around POSDCORB, nor of current efforts to create a management science based either on sociological theory of organizations or on operations research and PPBS—although all of these will play a part. They will be grounded rather in an understanding of social values, social and governmental institutions, and the mechanisms of induced social and political change; in a sensitivity to the feelings and desires of others, both as groups and individuals and the capacity to reason and work with them in finding and effectuating solutions to problems. They will be motivated by an unremitting search for that elusive but holy ghost, the public interest. They will rely upon the study of problems and the application to those problems of varieties of research techniques, methodologies, and disciplinary and professional perspectives. And this will involve working through and around the multifold obstacles and roadblocks of other human beings generally and governmental institutions particularly.

All of these things obviously cannot be taught on a campus by a single school—or even by all schools and departments severally. The unique role of a school of public affairs is that it can provide a focus on a university campus for those students—both preservice and mid-career—who will spend a significant portion of their working lives in pursuit of public purpose. Many, even most of its resources will be formally or informally derived from the faculties of other professional schools and other disciplines. And the primary, or at least the initial, major field of the majority of its students will be in studies other than public affairs, broadly defined. It can, and hopefully will become the central link between governments and the many semiautonomous elements which collectively comprise the multiversity. Its primary and its unique feature is explicit in the first word of its title: *public.*

NOTES

1. Warren G. Bennis and Philip E. Slater, *The Temporary Society* (New York: Harper & Row, 1968).
2. *Ibid.*, pp. 73–74, 76.
3. *Ibid.*, p. 75.
4. Paul T. David, "The Study of the Future," *Public Administration Review* 28 (March-April 1968). p. 193.
5. Among the most forceful of these critics have been Theodore S. Lowi in his book, *The End of Liberalism: Ideology, Policy and the Crisis of Public Authority* (New York: W. W. Norton, 1969), and Allen Schick in his article, "Systems Politics and Systems Budgeting," *Public Administration Review* 39 (March-April 1969). pp. 137–151. Comparable points of view are implicit or explicit in much of the writing of those who are identified with the "new left" in the fields of political science, public administration, other social sciences, and indeed intellectuals in general.
6. Emmette Redford, *Democracy in the Administrative State* (Fairlawn, N.J.: Oxford University Press, 1969), p. 70.
7. John W. Gardner, whose experience as head of the Department of Health Education and Welfare and then of the Urban Coalition would seem to qualify him uniquely on this subject, recently stated the problem succinctly: "I do not believe that major institutional change will be initiated at the local level. Local groups can do a lot of important things—significant, useful things. . . . If you want effective social change, you've got to know what's bothering people and you've got to have leadership at the local level. But grass roots leadership without national links just becomes sentimental." Quoted by the Associated Press in *The Daily Progress*, Charlottesville, Virginia, August 2, 1970. p. 3–A.
8. John Kenneth Galbraith, *The New Industrial State* (Boston: Houghton Mifflin, 1967), p. 173.
9. For a devastating and frightening analysis along this line, see the work by an unusual economist, Ezra J. Mishan, *The Cost of Economic Growth* (New York: Praeger Publishers, 1967).
10. Some of the dysfunctional effects of careerism in the upper levels of the U.S. civil service provoked the recent proposal of the Bureau of Executive Manpower, U.S. Civil Service Commission, for changes in the management of super grades. Among many other things, it recommended that super-grade employees

be engaged on contracts of five-year duration. Upon completion of the contracts, they could be separated or returned to grade 15 levels or have their contracts renewed on a one-year basis.

11. Bennis and Slater, *op. cit.*, p. 74.

12. It is noteworthy that a congressional committee recently asked the U.S. Civil Service Commission to conduct a thorough two-year study, now under way, of federal classification and its effects.

42 The Self-Evaluating Organization

Aaron Wildavsky

Why don't organizations evaluate their own activities? Why do they not appear to manifest rudimentary self-awareness? How long can people work in organizations without discovering these objectives or determining the extent to which they have been carried out? I started out thinking it was bad for organizations not to evaluate and I ended up wondering why they ever do it. Evaluation and organization, it turns out, are to some extent contradictory terms. Failing to understand that evaluation is sometimes incompatible with organization, we are tempted to believe in absurdities much in the manner of mindless bureaucrats who never wonder whether they are doing useful work. If we asked more intelligent questions instead, we would neither look so foolish nor be so surprised.

Who will evaluate and who will administer? How will power be divided among these functionaries? Which ones will bear the costs of change? Can evaluators create sufficient stability to carry on their own work in the midst of a turbulent environment? Can authority be allocated to evaluators and blame apportioned among administrators? How to convince administrators to collect information that might help others but can only harm them? How can support be obtained on behalf of recommendations that anger sponsors? Would the political problem be solved by creating a special organization—Evaluation Incorporated—devoted wholly to performing the analytic function? Could it obtain necessary support without abandoning its analytic mission? Can knowledge and power be joined?

EVALUATION

The ideal organization would be self-evaluating. It would continuously monitor its own activities so as to determine whether it was meeting its goals or even whether these goals should continue to prevail. When evaluation suggested that a change in goals or programs to achieve them was desirable, these proposals would be taken seriously by top decision makers. They would institute the necessary changes; they would have no vested interest in continuation of current activities. Instead they would steadily pursue new alternatives to better serve the latest desired outcomes.

Source: From *Public Administration Review* 32 (September-October 1972), pp. 509–520.

The ideal member of the self-evaluating organization is best conceived as a person committed to certain modes of problem solving. He believes in clarifying goals, relating them to different mechanisms of achievement, creating models (sometimes quantitative) of the relationships between inputs and outputs, seeking the best available combination. His concern is not that the organization should survive or that any specific objective be enthroned or that any particular clientele be served. Evaluative man cares that interesting problems are selected and that maximum intelligence be applied toward their solution.

To evaluative man the organization doesn't matter unless it meets social needs. Procedures don't matter unless they facilitate the accomplishment of objectives encompassing these needs. Efficiency is beside the point if the objective being achieved at lowest cost is inappropriate. Getting political support doesn't mean that the programs devised to fulfill objectives are good; it just means they had more votes than the others. Both objectives and resources, says evaluative man, must be continuously modified to achieve the optimal response to social need.

Evaluation should not only lead to the discovery of better policy programs to accomplish existing objectives but to alteration of the objectives themselves. Analysis of the effectiveness of existing policies leads to consideration of alternatives that juxtapose means and ends embodied in alternative policies. The objectives as well as the means for attaining them may be deemed inappropriate. But men who have become socialized to accept certain objectives may be reluctant to change. Resistance to innovation then takes the form of preserving social objectives. The difficulties are magnified once we realize that objectives may be attached to the clientele—the poor, outdoor men, lumbermen—with whom organizational members identify. The objectives of the organization may have attracted them precisely because they see it as a means of service to people they value. They may view changes in objectives, therefore, as proposals for "selling out" the clients they wish to serve. In their eyes evaluation becomes an enemy of the people.

Evaluative man must learn to live with contradictions. He must reduce his commitments to the organizations in which he works, the programs he carries out, and the clientele he serves. Evaluators must become agents of change acting in favor of programs as yet unborn and clienteles that are unknown. Prepared to impose change on others, evaluators must have sufficient stability to carry out their own work. They must maintain their own organization while simultaneously preparing to abandon it. They must obtain the support of existing bureaucracies while pursuing antibureaucratic policies. They must combine political feasibility with analytical purity. Only a brave man would predict that these combinations of qualities can be found in one and the same person and organization.

Evaluation and organization may be contradictory terms. Organizational structure implies stability while the process of evaluation suggests change. Organization generates commitment while evaluation inculcates skepticism. Evaluation speaks to the relationship between action and objectives while organization relates its activities to programs and clientele. No one can say for certain that self-evaluating organizations can exist, let alone become the prevailing form of administration. We can learn a good deal about the production and use of evaluation in government, nonetheless, by considering the requirements of obtaining so extraordinary a state of affairs—a self-evaluating organization.

THE POLICY-ADMINISTRATION DICHOTOMY REVISITED

Organization requires the division of labor. Not everyone can do everything. Who, then, will carry out the evaluative activity and who will administer the programs for which the organization is responsible?

Practically every organization has a program staff, by whatever name called, that advises top officials about policy problems. They are small in numbers and conduct whatever formula evaluation goes on in the organization. They may exert considerable power in the organization through their persuasiveness and access to the top men, or they may be merely a benign growth that can be seen but has little effect on the body of the organization. Insofar as one is interested in furthering analytical activities, one must be concerned with strengthening them in regard to other elements. The idea of the self-evaluating organization, however, must mean more than this: a few men trying to force evaluation on an organization hundreds or thousands of times larger than they are. The spirit of the self-evaluating organization suggests that, in some meaningful way, the entire organization is infused with the evaluative ethic.

Immediately we are faced with the chain of command. How far down must the spirit of evaluation go in order to ensure the responsiveness of the organization as a whole? If all personnel are involved there would appear to be insuperable difficulties in finding messengers, mail clerks, and secretaries to meet the criteria. If we move up one step to those who deal with the public and carry out the more complex kind of activity, the numbers involved may still be staggering. These tens of thousands of people certainly do not have the qualifications necessary to conduct evaluative activities, and it would be idle to pretend that they would. The forest ranger and the national park officer may be splendid people, but they are not trained in evaluation and they are not likely to be. Yet evaluational activity appropriate to each level must be found if evaluation is to permeate the organization.

There has long been talk in the management circles of combining accountability with decentralization. Organizational subunits are given autonomy within circumscribed limits for which they are held strictly accountable to their hierarchical superiors. Central power is masked but it is still there. Dividing the task so that each subunit has genuine autonomy would mean giving them a share in central decisions affecting the entire organization. Decentralization is known to exist only to the extent that field units follow inconsistent and contradictory policies. One can expect the usual headquarters—field rivalries to develop—the one stressing appreciation of local problems and interests, the other fearing dissolution as the mere sum of its clashing units. Presumably the tension will be manifested in terms of rival analyses. The center should win out because of its greater expertise, but the local units will always be the specialists on their own problems. They will have to be put in their place. We are back, it seems, to hierarchy. How can the center get what it wants out of the periphery without over-formalizing their relationship?

One model, the internalized gyroscope, is recorded in Herbert Kaufman's classic on *The Forest Ranger.* By recruitment and training, the forest rangers are socialized into central values that they carry with them wherever they go and apply to specific circumstances. Central control is achieved without apparent effort or innumerable detailed instructions, because the rangers have internalized the major premises from which appropriate actions may generally be deduced. The problem of the self-evaluating organization is more difficult because it demands problem solving divorced from commitments to specific policies and organizational structures. The level of skill required is considerably higher and the locus of identification much more diffuse. The Israeli Army has had considerable success in inculcating problem-solving skills (rather than carrying out predetermined instructions) among its officers.[1] But their organizational identification is far more intense than can be expected elsewhere.

Suppose that most organizational personnel are too unskilled to permit them to engage in evaluation. Suppose it is too costly to move around hundreds of thousands of government officials who carry out most of the work of government. The next alternative is to make the entire central administration into an evaluative unit that directs the self-evaluating organization. Several real-world models are available. What used to be called the administration class in Great Britain illustrates one type of central direction. They move frequently among the great departments and seek (with the political ministers involved) to direct the activities of the vast bureaucracy around them. They are chosen for qualities of intellect that enable them to understand policy and for qualities of behavior that enable them to get along with their fellows. At the apex stands the Treasury, an organization with few operating commitments, whose task it is to monitor the activities of the bureaucracy and to introduce changes when necessary. Economic policy, which is the special preserve of the Treasury, is supposed to undergo rapid movement, and its personnel are used to changing tasks and objectives at short notice. Though divorced in a way from the organizations in which they share responsibility with the political ministers, top civil servants are also part of them by virtue of their direct administrative concerns. Complaints are increasingly heard that these men are too conservative in defense of departmental interests, too preoccupied with immediate matters, or too bound by organizational tradition to conduct serious evaluation. Hence, the Fulton Report claimed, they adapt too slowly, if at all, to changing circumstances. Tentative steps have been taken, therefore, to establish a Central Policy Review Staff to do policy analysis for the cabinet and to otherwise encourage evaluative activity.

Germany and Sweden have proceeded considerably further in the same direction. Departments in Sweden are relatively small groups of men concerned with policy questions, while administration is delegated to large public corporations set up for the purpose.[2] The state governments in Germany (the *Lander*) do over 90 percent of the administrative work, with the central government departments presumably engaged with larger questions of policy. The student of public administration in America will at once realize where he is at. The policy-administration dichotomy, so beloved of early American administrative theorists, which was thoroughly demolished, it seemed, in the decades of the '40s and '50s, has suddenly reappeared with new vitality.

The policy-administration dichotomy originated with Frank Goodnow and others in their effort to legitimate the rise of the civil service and with it the norm of neutral-competence in government. They sought to save good government from the evils of the spoils system by insulating it from partisan politics. Congress made policy, and the task of the administrative apparatus was to find the appropriate technical means to carry it out. Administrative actions were thought to be less general and more technical so that well-motivated administrators would be able to enact the will of the people as received from Congress or the president. Civil servants could then be chosen on the basis of their technical merits rather than their partisan or policy politics. An avalanche of criticism, begun in earnest by Paul Appleby's *Policy and Administration,* overwhelmed these arguments on every side. Observation of congressional statutes showed that they were often vague, ambiguous, and contradictory. There simply were not clear objectives to which the administrators could subordinate themselves. Observation of administrative behavior showed that conflicts over the policy to be adopted continued unabated in the bureaus and departments. Important decisions were made by administrators that vitally affected the lives of people. Choice abounded and administrators seized on it. Indeed, they were often themselves divided on how to interpret statutes or how generally to frame policies under them. Interest groups were observed to make strenuous efforts to get favorable administrative enactments. Moreover, sufficiently precise knowledge did not exist to determine the best way to carry out a general objective in many areas. Given the large areas of uncertainty and ignorance, the values and choices of administrators counted a great deal. Taken at this level there was not too much that could be said for maintaining the distinction between policy and administration. Nevertheless, nagging doubts remained.

Were politics and administration identical? If they were, then it was difficult to understand how we were able to talk about them separately. Or was politics simply a cover term for all the things that different organs of the government did? If politics and administration could be separated in some way, then a division of labor might be based on them. No doubt the legislative will, if there was one, could be undermined by a series of administrative enactments. But were not these administrative decisions of a smaller and less encompassing kind than those usually made by Congress? Were there not ways in which the enactments of Congress were (or could be) made more authoritative than the acts of administrators? Overwhelming administrative discretion did violence to democratic theory.

As the world moves into the 1970's, we will undoubtedly see significant efforts to rehabilitate the policy-administration dichotomy. The dissatisfactions of modern industrial life are being poured on the bureaucracy. It seems to grow larger daily while human satisfaction does not increase commensurately. It has become identified with red tape and resistance to change. Yet no one can quite imagine doing away with it in view of the ever-increasing demand for services. So politicians who feel that the bureaucracy has become a liability,[3] clientele who think they might be better served under other arrangements, taxpayers who resent the sheer costs, policy analysts who regard existing organizations as barriers to the application of intelligence, will join together in seeking ways to make bureaucracy more responsive. How better do this than by isolating its innovative functions from the mass of officialdom? Instead of preventing administration from being contaminated by politics, however, the purpose of the new dichotomy will be to insulate policy from the stultifying influences of the bureaucracy.

WHO WILL PAY THE COSTS OF CHANGE?

While most organizations evaluate some of their policies periodically, the self-evaluating organization would do so continuously. These evaluative activities would be inefficient, that is, they would cost more than they are worth, unless they led to change. Indeed the self-evaluating organization is purposefully set up to encourage change.

The self-evaluating organization will have to convince its own members to live with constant change. They may think they love constant upset when they first join the organization, but experience is likely to teach them otherwise. Man's appetite for rapid change is strictly limited. People cannot bear to have their cherished beliefs challenged or their lives altered on a continuing basis. The routines of yesterday are swept away, to be replaced by new ones. Anxiety is induced because they cannot get their bearings. They have trouble knowing exactly what they should be doing. The ensuing confusion may lead to inefficiencies in the form of hesitation or random behavior designed to cover as many bases as possible. Cynicism may grow as the wisdom of the day before yesterday gives way to new truth, which is in turn replaced by a still more radiant one. The leaders of the self-evaluating organization will have to counter this criticism.

Building support for policies within an organization requires internal selling. Leaders must convince the members of the organization that what they are doing is worthwhile. Within the self-evaluating organization the task may initially be more difficult than in more traditional bureaucracies Its personnel are accustomed to question policy proposals and to demand persuasive arguments in their support. Once the initial campaign is proven successful, however, enthusiasm can be expected to reach a high pitch after all existing policies have been evaluated, new alternatives have been analyzed, and evidence has been induced in favor of a particular alternative. The danger here is overselling. Convinced that "science" is in their favor, persuaded that their paper calculations are in tune with the world, the evaluators believe a little too much in their own ideas. They are set up for more disappointment from those who expect less. How much greater the difficulty, then, when continuous evaluation suggests the need for another change in policy. Now two internal campaigns are necessary: the first involves unselling the old policy and the second involves selling the new one. All virtues become unsuspected vices and last year's goods are now seen to be hopelessly shoddy. Perpetual change has its costs.

Maintenance of higher rates of change depend critically on the ability of those who produce it to make others pay the associated costs. If the change makers are themselves forced to bear the brunt of their actions, they will predictably seek to stabilize their environment. That is the burden of virtually the entire sociological literature on organizations from Weber to Crozier. The needs of the members displace the goals of the organization. The public purposes that the organization was supposed to serve give way to its private acts. Its own hidden agendas dominate the organization.

Rather than succumb to the diseases of bureaucracy, the self-evaluating organization will be tempted to pass them on to others. The self-evaluating organization can split itself off into "evaluating" and "administering" parts, thus making lower levels pay the costs of change, or it can seek to impose them on other organizations in its environment. We shall deal first with difficulties encountered in trying to stabilize the evaluative top of the organization while the bottom is in a continuous state of flux.

Let us suppose that an organization separates its evaluative head from its administrative body. The people at the top do not have operating functions. They are, in administrative jargon, all staff rather than line. Their task is to appraise the consequences of existing policies, work out better alternatives, and have the new policies they recommend carried out by the administrative unit.

Who would bear the cost of change? One can imagine evaluators running around merrily suggesting changes to and fro without having to implement them. The anxiety would be absorbed by the administrators. They would have to be the ones to change gears and to smooth out the difficulties. But they will not stand still for this. Their belief about what is administratively feasible and organizationally attainable must be part of the policy that is adopted. So the administrators will bargain with the evaluators.

Administrators have significant resources to bring to this struggle. They deal with the public. They collect the basic information that is sent upward in one form or another. They can drag their feet, mobilize clientele, hold back information, or otherwise make cooperation difficult. The evaluators have their own advantages. They have greater authority to issue rules and regulations. They are experts in manipulating data and models to justify existing policies or denigrate them.

Held responsible for policy but prohibited from administering it directly, the evaluators have an incentive to seek antibureaucratic delivery systems. They will, for example, prefer an income to a service strategy.[4] The evaluators can be pretty certain that clients will receive checks mailed from the central computer, whereas they cannot be sure that the services they envisage will be delivered by hordes of bureaucrats in the manner they would like. Providing people with income to buy better living quarters has the great advantage of not requiring a corps of officials to supervise public housing. Evaluators do not have the field personnel to supervise innumerable small undertakings; they, therefore, will prefer large investment projects over smaller ones. They can also make better use of their small number of people on projects that are expensive and justify devotion of large amounts of analytical time. Contrarywise, administrators will emphasize far-flung operations providing services requiring large numbers of people that only they can perform. In a house of many mansions they will be the masters.

There are circumstances, of course, in which administrators and evaluators will reverse their normal roles. If the evaluators feel that there is not enough government employment, for example, they may seek labor-intensive operations. Should the administrators feel they are already over-burdened, they may welcome policies that are easily centralized and directed by machines performing rote operations. The more likely tendency, however, is for administrators and evaluators to expand into each other's domain. Each one can reduce the bargaining powers of the other by taking unto himself some of his competitors' advantages. Thus the administrators may recruit their own policy analysts to compete with the evaluators who, in turn, will seek their own contacts within the administrative apparatus in order to ensure a steady and reliable flow of information. If this feuding goes far enough, the result will be two organizations acting in much the same way as the single one they replaced but with additional problems of coordination.

EVALUATION INCORPORATED

It is but a short step from separating evaluation from administration to the idea of rival teams of evaluators. A rough equivalent of a competitive market can be introduced by allowing teams of evaluators to compete for direction of policy in a given area. The competition would take place in terms of price (we can accomplish a specified objective at a lower cost), quality (better policies for the same money), quantity (we can produce more at the same cost), maintenance (we can fix things when they go wrong), experience (we have a proven record), values (our policies will embody your preferences) and talent (when it comes down to it, you are buying our cleverness and we are superior). The team that won the competition would be placed in charge until it left to go elsewhere or another team challenged it. The government might raise its price to keep a talented team or it might lower it to get rid of an incompetent one. The incentives for evaluation would be enormous, restrained, of course, by ability to perform lest the evaluators go bankrupt when they run out of funds or lose business to competitors.

The first task of the new enterprise would be to establish its own form of organization. What organizational arrangements are necessary to make competition among evaluators feasible?

Evaluators must either be assured of employment somewhere or engage in other dispensible occupations from which they can be recruited at short notice. A handful of evaluators could always be recruited by ad hoc methods from wherever they are found. But teams of evaluators sufficient to direct major areas of policy would be difficult to assemble at short notice. They would all be doing different things instead of working together, which is part of the experience they need to be successful. Nor can they form a team unless they can all promise to be on the job at a certain time if their bid is successful, yet at the same time have other jobs to fall back on if they are turned down.

In the previous model, where the evaluators generate new policies and the administrators carry them out, these bureaucrats carried the major burden of uncertainty. Under the new model this imbalance is redressed because the evaluators have to worry about security of employment. Few people like to shift jobs all the time; even fewer like the idea of periodic unemployment alternating with the anxiety of bidding to get jobs and performing to keep them. Mechanisms will be found, we can be certain, to reduce their level of uncertainty to tolerable dimensions.

Evaluators may choose to work within existing administrative organizations, accepting a lower status, learning to live with disappointment, in return for job stability. This is one pattern that already exists. Evaluators may go to private industry and universities on the understanding they will be able to make occasional forays into government as part of a tiny group of advisors to leading officials. This is also done now. Both alternatives do away with the idea of competition, they merely graft a small element of evaluation onto existing organizations on a catch-as-catch-can basis.

In order to preserve evaluators who are in a position to compete for the direction of policy, it will be necessary for them to form stable organizations of their own. Like the existing firms of management consultants they resemble, these evaluators would bid on numerous projects; the difference would be that they would do the actual policy work as part of the public apparatus rather than making recommendations and then disappearing. Evaluation, Incorporated, as we shall call it, would contain numerous possible teams, some of whom would be working and others who would be preparing to go to work. The firm would have to demand considerable overhead to provide services for the evaluators, to draw up proposals, and to compensate those of its members who are (hopefully) temporarily out of work. Keeping Evaluation, Incorporated, solvent by maintaining a high level of employment will become a major organizational goal.

Evaluation, Incorporated, is an organization. It has managers who are concerned with survival. It has members who must be induced to remain. It has clients who must be served. So it will constitute itself a lobby for evaluation. When the demand for its service is high, it will be able to insist on the evaluative ethic; it will take its services to those who are prepared to appreciate (by paying for) them. But when demands are low, Evaluation, Incorporated, must trim its sails. It has a payroll to meet. Rather than leave a job when nonanalytical criteria prevail, it may have to swallow its pride and stay on. Its managers can easily convince themselves that survival is not only good for them but for society, which will benefit from the good they will be able to do in better times.

If their defects stem from their insecurities, the remedy will be apparent; increase the stability of evaluators by guaranteeing them tenure of employment. Too close identification with party or policy proved, in any event, to be a mixed blessing. They feasted while they were in favor and famished when they were out. Apparently they require civil service status, a government corporation, say, devoted to evaluation.

Perhaps the General Accounting Office (GAO), which is beginning to do analytic studies, will provide a model of an independent governmental organization devoted to evaluation. Since it has a steady source of income from its auditing work, so to speak, it can afford to form, break up, and recreate teams of evaluators. Its independence from the Executive Branch (the Accountant General is responsible to Congress and serves a 15-year term) might facilitate objective analysis. But the independence of GAO has been maintained because it eschews involvement in controversial matters. If the new General Evaluation Office (GEO) were to issue reports that increased conflict, there would undoubtedly be a strong impulse to bring it under regular political control. The old auditing function might be compromised because objectivity is difficult to maintain about a program one has sponsored, or because public disputes lower confidence in its operations. Opponents of its policy positions might begin to question its impartiality in determining the legality of government expenditures. Yet protection would be difficult to arrange because the new GEO did not have a political client.

By attending to the problems of an organization that supplies evaluation to others, we hope to illuminate the dilemmas of any organization that wishes to seriously engage in continuous analyses of its own activities.

Evaluation, which criticizes certain programs and proposes to replace them with others, is manifestly a political activity. If evaluation is not political in the sense of party partisanship, it is political in the sense of policy advocacy. Without a steady source of political support, without that essential manifestation of affection from somebody out there in society, it will suffer the fate of abondoned children: the self-evaluating organization is unlikely to prosper in an orphanage.

ADJUSTING TO THE ENVIRONMENT

The self-evaluating organization is one that uses its own analysis of its own programs in order to alter or abolish them. Its ability to make changes when its analysis suggests they are desirable is an essential part of its capacity to make self-evaluation a living reality. Yet the ability of any single organization to make self-generated changes is limited by the necessity of receiving support from its environment.

The leaders of a self-evaluating organization cannot afford to leave the results of their labors up to the fates. If their "batting average" goes way down, they will be in trouble. Members of the organization will lose faith in evaluation because it does not lead to changes in actual policy. Those who are attracted to the organization by the prospect of being powerful as well as analytical will leave to join more promising ventures, or old clients will become dissatisfied without new ones to take their place. As the true believers depart, personnel who are least motivated by the evaluative ethic will move into higher positions. Revitalization of the organization via the promotion and recruitment of professing evaluators will become impossible.

In order to avoid the deadly cycle—failure, hopelessness, abandonment—leaders of the self-evaluating organization must seek some proportion of success. They must select the organization's activities, not only with an eye toward their analytical justification, but with a view toward receiving essential support from their environment. Hence they become selective evaluators. They must prohibit the massive use of organizational resources in areas where they see little chance of success. They must seek out problems that are easy to solve and changes that are easy to make because they do not involve radical departures from the past. They must be prepared to hold back the results of evaluation when they believe the times are not propitious; they must be ready to seize the time for change whether or not the evaluations are fully prepared or wholly justified. Little by little, it seems, the behavior of the leaders will become similar to those of other organization officials who also seek to adapt to their environment.

The growing conservatism of the self-evaluating organization is bound to cause internal strains. There are certain to be disagreements about whether the organization is being too cautious. No one can say for sure whether the leaders have correctly appraised the opportunities in a rapidly shifting environment. If they try to do too much, they risk failure in the political world. If they try to do too little, they risk abandoning their own beliefs and losing the support of their most dedicated members. Maintaining a balance between efficacy and commitment is not easy.

Now the self-evaluating organization need not be a passive bystander negotiating its environment. It can seek to mobilize interests in favor of the programs it wishes to adopt. It can attempt to neutralize opposition. It can try to persuade its present clientele that they will be better off, or instill a wish to be served on behalf of new beneficiaries. One fears that its reputation among clientele groups may not be the best, however, because, as a self-evaluating organization, it must be prepared to abandon (or drastically modify) programs and with them the clientele they serve. The clients will know that theirs is only a marriage of convenience, that the self-evaluating organization is eager to consider more advantageous alliances, and that they must always be careful to measure their affection according to the exact degree of services rendered. The self-evaluating organization cannot expect to receive more love than it gives. In fact, it must receive less.

Evaluation can never be fully rewarded. There must, in the nature of things, be other considerations that prevail over evaluation, even where the powers that be would like to follow its dictates. The policies preferred by the self-evaluating organization are never the only ones being contemplated by the government, there are always multitudes of policies in being or about to be born. Some of these are bound to be inconsistent with following the dictates of evaluation. Consider the impact of fiscal policy upon analysis. Suppose the time has come for financial stringency; the government has decided that expenditures must be reduced. Proposals for increases may not be allowed no matter how good the justification. Reductions may be made whether indicated by analysis or not. Conversely, a political decision may be made to increase expenditure. The substantive merits of various policies have clearly been subordinated to their immediate financial implications.

Evaluation may be wielded as a weapon in the political wars. It may be used by one faction or party versus another. Of particular concern to the self-evaluating organization is a one-sided approach to evaluation that creates internal problems. It is not unusual, as was recently the case in Great Britain when the Conservative Party returned to office, for a government to view evaluation as a means of putting down the bureaucracy. A two-step decision rule may be followed: the recommendations of evaluation may be accepted when they lead to reduction and rejected when they suggest increases in expenditure. Before long the members of the organization become reluctant to provide information that will only be used in a biased way. The evaluative enterprise depends on common recognition that the activity is being carried out somehow in order to secure better policies, whatever these may be, and not in support of a predetermined position. If this understanding is violated, people down the line will refuse to cooperate. They will withhold their contribution by hiding information or by simply not volunteering to find it. The morale of the self-evaluating organization will be threatened because its members are being asked to pervert the essence of their calling.

It's the same the whole world over: the analytically virtuous are not necessarily rewarded nor are the wicked (who do not evaluate) punished. The leaders of the self-evaluating organization, therefore, must redouble their effort to obtain political help.

JOINING KNOWLEDGE WITH POWER

To consider the requirements necessary for a self-evaluating organization is to understand why they are rarely met. The self-evaluating organization, it turns out, would be susceptible to much the same kinds of anti-evaluative tendencies as are existing organizations. It, too must stabilize its environment. It, too, must secure internal loyalty and outside support. Evaluation must, at best, remain but one element in administrative organizations. Yet no one can say today that it is overemphasized. Flights of fancy should not lead anyone to believe that inordinate attention to evaluation is an imminent possibility. We have simply come back to asking how a little more rather than a little less might become part of public organizations. How might analytic integrity be combined with political efficacy?

Evaluative man seeks knowledge, but he also seeks power. His desire to do good is joined with his will to act powerfully. One is no good without the other. A critical incentive for pursuing evaluation is that the results become governmental policy. There is little point in making prescriptions for public policy for one's own private amusement. Without knowledge it would be wrong to seek power. But without power it becomes more difficult to obtain knowledge. Why should anyone supply valuable information to someone who can neither help nor harm him? Access to information may be given only on condition programmatic goals are altered. Evaluative man is well when he can pyramid resources so that greater knowledge leads to enhanced power, which in turn increases his access to information. He is badly off when the pursuit of power leads to the sacrifice of evaluation. His own policy problem is how to do enough of both (and not too much of either) so that knowledge and power reinforce rather than undermine one another.

The political process generates a conflict of interest within the evaluative enterprise. The evaluators view analysis as a means of deciding on better policies and selling them to others. Clients (elected officials, group leaders, top administrators) view analysis as a means of better understanding the available choices so they can control them. Talk of "better policies," as if it did not matter who determined them, only clouds the issues.

The evaluative group within an organization would hope that it could show political men the worth of its activities. The politicians, in turn, hope to learn about the desirability of the programs that are being evaluated. But their idea of desirability manifestly includes the support which programs generate for them and the organizations of which they are a part. Hence evaluation must be geared to producing programs that connect the interests of political leaders to the outcomes of governmental actions, otherwise, they will reject evaluation and with it the men who do it.

A proposed policy is partly a determinant of its own success; the support it gathers or loses in clientele is fed back into its future prospects. By its impact on the future environment of the organization, the proposed policy affects the kinds of work the organization is able to do. Pure evaluative man, however single-minded his concentration on the intrinsic merits of programs, must also consider their interaction effects on his future ability to pursue his craft. Just as he would insist on including the impact of one element in a system on another in his policy analysis, so must he consider how his present recommendations affect future ones. A proper evaluation includes the impact of a policy on the organizations responsible for it.

Consider in this organizational context the much-discussed problem of diverse governmental programs that may contribute to the same ends without anyone being able to control them. There may be unnecessary redundancy, where some programs overlap, side by side with large areas of inattention to which no programs are directed. More services of one kind and less of another are provided than might be strictly warranted. Without evaluation no one can really say whether there are too many or two few programs or whether their contents are appropriate. But an evaluation that did all this would get nowhere unless it resulted in different institutional processes for handling the same set of problems.

Even on its own terms, then, evaluation should not remain apart from the organizations on which it is dependent for implementation. Organizational design and policy analysis are part of the same governmental process. If an organization wishes to reduce its identification with programs (and the clients who support them), for example, so that it can afford to examine different types of policy, it must adopt a political strategy geared to that end.

The self-evaluating organization would be well advised not to depend too much on a single type of clientele. Diversification is its strategy. The more diverse its services, the more varied its clientele, the less the self-evaluating organization has to depend on any of them, the more able it is to shift the basis of its support. Diversity creates political flexibility.

Any organization that produces a single product, so to speak, that engages in a limited range of activities is unlikely to abandon them willingly. Its survival, after all, is bound up in its program. If the program goes, the organization dies. One implication drawn from these considerations is that the traditional wisdom concerning governmental organization badly needs revision.[5] If the basic principle of organization is that similar programs should be grouped together, as is now believed to be the case, these organizations will refuse to change. On the contrary, agencies should be encouraged to differentiate their products and diversify their outputs. If they are not faced with declining demand for all their programs, they will be more willing to abandon or modify a single one. The more varied its programs, the less dependent the organization is on a single one, the greater its willingness to change.

No matter how good its internal analysis, or how persuasively an organization justifies its programs to itself, there is something unsatisfying about allowing it to judge its own case. The ability of organizations to please themselves must ultimately (at least in a democratic society) give way to judgment by outsiders. Critics of organizations must, therefore, recognize that their role is an essential one. Opposition is part and parcel of the evaluative process. The goal would be to secure a more intelligent and analytically sophisticated level of advocacy on all sides. Diverse analyses might become, as Harry Rowen has suggested, part of the mutual partisan adjustment through which creative use is made of conflicts among organized interests.

Competition, *per se*, however, need not lead to fundamental change. Organizations may go on the offensive by growing bigger instead of better, that is, by doing more of the same. The change in which they are interested is a change in magnitude. We are all familiar with the salesmanship involved in moving to new technologies or larger structures where internal dynamism and grandiose conceptions are mistaken for new ideas. Motion may be a protection against change.

Competition, if it is to lead to desirable consequences, must take place under appropriate rules specifying who can make what kind of transaction. No one would advocate unrestrained competition among economic units in the absence of a market that makes it socially advantageous for participants to pursue their private interests in expectation of mutual gain. Where parties are affected who are not directly represented in the market, for instance, the rules may be changed to accommodate a wider range of interests. Competition among rival policies and their proponents also takes place in an arena that specifies rules for exercising power in respect to particular decisions. Evaluators must, therefore, consider how their preferred criteria for decision will be affected by the rules for decision in political arenas within which they must operate.

We have, it appears, returned to politics. Unless building support for policies is an integral part of designing them, their proponents are setting themselves up for disappointment. To say that one will first think of a great idea and then worry about how it might be implemented is a formula for failure.[6] A good evaluation not only specifies desirable outcomes but suggests institutional mechanisms for achieving them.

If you don't know how to make an evaluation, it may be a problem for you but not for anyone else. If you do know how to evaluate, it becomes a problem for others. Evaluation is an organizational problem. While the occasional lone rider may be able to fire off an analysis now and then, he must eventually institutionalize his efforts if he is to produce a steady output. The overwhelming bulk of evaluation takes place within organizations. The rejection of evaluation is done largely by the organizations that ask for it. To create an organization that evaluates its own activities evidently requires an organizational response. If evaluation is not done at all, if it is done but not used, if used but twisted out of shape, the place to look first is not the technical apparatus but the organization.

Organization is first but not last. Always it is part of a larger society that conditions what it can do. Evaluation is also a social problem. So long as organizational opposition to evaluation is in the foreground, we are not likely to become aware of the social background. Should this initial resistance be overcome, and individual organizations get to like evaluation, however, it would still face multiple defenses thrown up by social forces.

EVALUATION AS TRUST

For the self-evaluating organization all knowledge must be contingent. Improvement is always possible, change for the better is always in view though not necessarily yet attained. It is the organization *par excellence* that seeks knowledge. The ways in which it seeks to obtain knowledge, therefore, uniquely defines its character.

The self-evaluating organization would be skeptical rather than committed. It would continuously be challenging its own assumptions. Not dogma but scientific doubt would be its distinguishing feature. It would seek new truth instead of defending old errors. Testing hypotheses would be its main work.

Like the model community of scholars, the self-evaluating organization would be open, truthful, and explicit. It would state its conclusions in public, show how they were determined, and give others the opportunity to refute them. The costs and benefits of alternative programs for various groups in society would be indicated as precisely as available knowledge would permit. Everything would be above board. Nothing would be hidden.

Are there ways of securing the required information? Can the necessary knowledge be created? Will the truth make men free? Attempting to answer these profound queries would take me far beyond the confines of this exploratory article. But I would like to suggest by illustration that the answers to each of them depend critically on the existence of trust among social groups and within organizations. The acceptance of evaluation requires a community of men who share values.

An advantage of formal analysis, in which the self-evaluating organization specializes, is that it does not depend entirely on learning from experience. That can be done by ordinary organizations. By creating models abstracting relationships from the areas of the universe they wish to control, evaluators seek to substitute manipulation of their models for events in the world. By rejecting alternatives their models tell them will work out badly (or not as well as others), these analysts save scarce resources and protect the public against less worthy actions. Ultimately, however, there must be an appeal to the world of experience. No one, not even the evaluators themselves, are willing to try their theoretical notions on large populations without more tangible reasons to believe that the recommended alternatives prove efficacious.[7]

Since the defect of ordinary organizations is that they do not learn well from experience, the self-evaluating organization seeks to order that experience so that knowledge will be gained from it. The proof that a policy is good is that it works when it is tried. But not everything can be tried everywhere. Hence experiments lie at the heart of evaluation. They are essential for connecting alleged causes with desired effects in the context of limited resources.

The ability of the self-evaluating organization to perform its functions depends critically upon a climate of opinion that favors experimentation. If resources are severely constrained, for example, leading to reluctance to try new ventures, the self-evaluating organization cannot function as advertised. Should there exist strong feeling that everyone must be treated alike, to choose another instance, experimentation would be ruled out. Take the case of the "More Effective Schools" movement in New York City. The idea was to run an experiment to determine whether putting more resources into schools would improve the performance of deprived children. In order to qualify as a proper experiment, More Effective Schools had to be established in some places but not in others, so that there would be control groups. The demand for equality of treatment was so intense, however, that mass picketing took place at the school sites. Favored treatment for these schools was taken as *prima facie* evidence of discrimination. It became apparent that More Effective Schools would have to be tried everywhere or nowhere. Clearly the social requisites of experimentation would have to exist for self-evaluating organizations to be effective. Unless groups trust each other, they will neither allow experiments to be conducted nor accept the results.

Although ways of learning without experimentation may be found, no evaluation is possible without adequate information. But how much is enough? Hierarchies in organizations exist in order to reduce information. If the men at the top were to consider all the bits of data available in the far-flung reaches of the organization, they would be overwhelmed.

As information is weeded and compressed on its way through the hierarchy, however, important bits may be eliminated or distorted. One of the most frequently voiced criticisms of organizations is that the men at the top do not know what is going on. Information is being withheld from them or is inaccurate so that they make decisions on the basis of mistaken impressions. The desire to pass on only good news results in the elimination of information that might place the conveyer in a bad light. Top officials may, therefore, resort to such devices as securing overlapping sources of information or planting agents at lower levels. There are limits to these efforts, however, because the men at the top have only time to digest what they have been told. So they vacillate between fear of information loss and being unable to struggle out from under masses of data.

How might the self-evaluating organization deal with information bias? Organization members would have to be rewarded for passing on bad news. Those who are responsible for the flow of information must, at the least, not be punished for telling the truth. If they are also the ones in charge of administering the policy, it will not be possible to remove them for bad performance because once that is done their successors will be motivated to suppress such information. The top men must themselves be willing to accept the blame though they may not feel this is their responsibility and though their standing may be compromised. The very idea of a hierarchy may have to give way to shifting roles in which superior and subordinate positions are exchanged so that each member knows he will soon be in the other's position. The self-evaluating organization clearly requires an extraordinary degree of mutual trust.

The spread of self-evaluating organizations could enhance social trust by widening the area of agreement concerning the consequences of existing policies and the likely effects of change. Calculations concerning who benefited and to what degree would presumably aid in political cost-benefit analyses. The legitimacy of public institutions would be enhanced because they resulted from a more self-consciously analytical process that was increasingly recognized as such. Evaluation would be informative, meliorative, and stabilizing in the midst of change. It sounds idyllic.

More information, *per se,* need not lead to greater agreement, however, if the society is wracked by fundamental cleavages. As technology makes information more widely available, the need for interpretation will grow. Deluged by data, distrustful of others, citizens may actually grow apart as group leaders collect more information about how badly off they are compared to what they ought to be. The more citizens trust group leaders rather than governmental officials, the greater the chance their differences will be magnified rather than reconciled. The clarification of objectives may make it easier to see the social conflicts implicit in the distribution of income or cultural preferences concerning the environment or the differing styles of life attached to opposing views of the ideal society. Evaluation need not create agreement; evaluation may presuppose agreement.

NOTES

Author's Note: Presented at the National Conference of the American Society for Public Administration, New York City, March 24, 1972, as part of the first chapter of a book by Jeanne Nienaber and Aaron Wildavsky, *Buying Recreation Budgeting and Evaluation in Federal Outdoor Recreation Policy* (New York: Basic Books, forthcoming), this article stems from reflections on what at first glance may appear to be an entirely different problem. I had begun the study of line-item and program budgeting as they coexisted uneasily in several agencies concerned with outdoor recreation. The traditional budget was sensitive to politics but did not produce fundamental reexamination of activities, the program budget was insensitive to politics and also did not result in serious evaluation of current activities. Instead of asking which form of budgeting was superior, therefore, I turned my attention to the more fundamental question of why organizations ordinarily do not evaluate their own activities.

1. Dan Horowitz, "Flexible Responsiveness and Military Strategy: The Case of the Israeli Army," *Policy Sciences* 1 (Summer 1970), pp. 191–205.

2. Hans Thorelli, "Overall Planning and Management in Sweden," *International Social Science Bulletin* (1956).

3. The most dramatic and visible change can be found in the American presidency. Presidents have increasingly bureaucratized their operations. Within the executive office there now exist sizeable subunits, characterized by specialization and the division of labor, for dealing with the media of information and communication, Congress, foreign and domestic policy, and more. At the same time, presidents seek the right to intervene at any level within the executive branch on a sporadic basis. The administrators are being prodded to change while the president stabilizes his environment. Thus we find President Nixon saying that he wants something done about that awful Bureau of Indian Affairs, as if it did not belong to him, or asking citizens to elect him again so he can save them from the compulsory busing fostered by his own bureaucracy. He wants to escape blame for bureaucratic errors but keep the credit for inspiring changes.
4. See Robert A. Levine, "Rethinking our Social Strategies," *The Public Interest* 10 (Winter 1968).
5. William A. Niskanen, *Bureaucracy and Representative Government* (Chicago: Aldine-Atherton, 1971).
6. For further discussion along these lines see Jeffrey L. Pressman and Aaron Wildavsky, *Implementation: The Economic Development Administration in Oakland* (Berkeley and Los Angeles: University of California Press, forthcoming).
7. An exception of a kind is found in the area of defense policy where the purpose of the analytical exercises is to avoid testing critical hypotheses. Once the hypotheses concerning a nuclear war are tested, the evaluators may not be around to revise their analyses. See Aaron Wildavsky, "Practical Consequences of the Theoretical Study of Defense Policy," *Public Administration Review* 25 (March 1965), pp. 90–103.

43

Purposes of Evaluation

Carol H. Weiss

OVERT AND COVERT PURPOSES

People decide to have a program evaluated for many different reasons, from the eminently rational to the patently political. Ideally, an administrator is seeking answers to pressing questions about the program's future: Should it be continued? Should it be expanded? Should changes be made in its operation? But there are occasions when he turns to evaluation for less legitimate reasons.

Postponement. The decision maker may be looking for ways to delay a decision. Instead of resorting to the usual ploy of appointing a committee and waiting for its report, he can commission an evaluation study, which takes even longer.

Ducking Responsibility. Sometimes one faction in the program organization is espousing one course of action and another faction is opposing it. The administrators look to evaluation to get them off the hook by producing dispassionate evidence that will make the decision for them. There are cases in which administrators know what the decision will be even before they call in the evaluators, but want to cloak it in the legitimate trappings of research.

Public Relations. Occasionally, evaluation is seen as a way of self-glorification. The administrator believes that

Source: Carol H. Weiss, *Evaluation Research: Methods of Assessing Program Effectiveness*, © 1972, pp. 11–22. Reprinted by permission of Prentice-Hall, Englewood Cliffs, New Jersey.

he has a highly successful program and looks for a way to make it visible. A good study will fill the bill. Copies of the report, favorable of course, can be sent to boards of trustees, members of legislative committees, executives of philanthropic foundations who give large sums to successful programs, and other influential people. Suchman[1] suggests two related purposes: eyewash and whitewash. In an eyewash evaluation, an attempt is made to justify a weak program by selecting for evaluation only those aspects that look good on the surface. A whitewash attempts to cover up program failure by avoiding any objective appraisal.

The program administrator's motives are not, of course, necessarily crooked or selfish. Often, there is a need to justify the program to the people who pay the bills, and he is seeking support for a concept and a project in which he believes. Generating support for existing programs is a common motive for embarking on evaluation.

Fulfilling Grant Requirements. Increasingly, the decision to evaluate stems from sources outside the program. Many federal grants for demonstration projects and innovative programs are tagged with an evaluation requirement; for example, all projects for disadvantaged pupils funded under Title I of the Elementary and Secondary Education Act are required to be evaluated.

From the point of view of the funders, who are taking a chance on an untried project, it is reasonable to require that there be some evidence on the extent to which the project is working. To the operators of a project, the demands of starting up and running the new program take priority. Plagued as they often are by immediate problems of staffing, budgets, logistics, community relations, and all the other trials of pioneers, they tend to neglect the evaluation. They see it mainly as a ritual designed to placate the funding bodies, without any real usefulness to them.

Evaluation, then, is a rational enterprise often undertaken for nonrational, or at least noninformational, reasons. We could continue the catalog of the varieties of covert purposes (justifying a program to Congress, "getting" the program director, increasing the prestige of the agency), but the important point is that such motives have consequences for the evaluation that can be serious and bleak.[2]

An evaluator who is asked to study a particular program usually assumes that he is there because people want answers about what the program is doing well and poorly. When this is not the case, he may in his naiveté become a pawn in intraorganizational power struggles, a means of delaying action, or the rallying point for one ideology or another. Some evaluators have found only after their study was done that they had unwittingly played a role in a larger political game. They found that nobody was particularly interested in applying their results to the decisions at hand, but only in using them (or any quotable piece of them) as ammunition to destroy or to justify.

Lesson No. 1 for the evaluator newly arrived on the scene is: Find out who initiated the idea of having an evaluation of the program and for what purposes. Were there other groups in the organization who questioned or objected to the evaluation? What were their motives? Is there real commitment among practitioners, administrators, and/or funders to using the results of the evaluation to improve future decision making? If the real purposes for the evaluation are not oriented to better decision making and there is little commitment to applying results, the project is probably a poor candidate for evaluation. The evaluator might well ponder whether he wishes to get involved in the situation or whether he can find more productive uses for his talents elsewhere.

INTENDED USES

Even when evaluation is undertaken for bona fide purposes (that is, to learn how well the program is reaching its goals), people can have widely differing expectations of the kinds of answers that will be produced. If the evaluator is not to be caught unawares, it behooves him to know from the outset what kinds of answers are expected from his study.[3]

Who Expects What?

Expectations for the evaluation generally vary with a person's position in the system.[4] Top policymakers need the kind of information that will help them address the broad issues: Should the program be continued or dropped, institutionalized throughout the system or limited to a pilot program, continued with the same procedures and techniques or modified? Should more money be allocated to this program or to others? They want information on the overall effectiveness of the program.

The directors of the program face other issues. They want to know not only how well their program is achieving the desired ends, but also which general strategies are more or less successful, which are achieving results most efficiently and economically, which features of the program are essential and which can be changed or dropped.

Direct-service staff deal with individuals and small groups. They have practical day-to-day concerns about techniques. Should they spend more time on developing good work habits and less time on teaching subject matter? Put more emphasis on group discussions or films or lectures? Should they accept more younger people (who are not already set in their ways) or more older people (who have greater responsibilities and more need)? Practitioners, who are accustomed to relying on their own experience and intuitive judgment, often challenge evaluation to come up with something practical on topics such as these.

Nor do these three sets of actors—policymakers, program directors, and practitioners—exhaust the list of those with a possible oar in the evaluation. The funders of evaluation research, particularly when they are outside the direct line of operations, may have an interest in adding to the pool of knowledge in the field. They may want answers less to operating questions than to questions of theory and method. Can social group work help improve the parental performance of young couples? Does increasing the available career opportunities for low-income youth result in less juvenile delinquency? If coordination among community health services is increased, will people receive better health care? Here is another purpose for evaluation—to test propositions about the utility of concepts or models of service. The public too has a stake, as taxpayers, as parents of schoolchildren, as contributors to voluntary organizations.[5] They are concerned that their money is wisely and efficiently spent.

Recently, another actor has entered the decision-making arena—the consumer of services. He may see a use for evaluation in asking "client-eye" questions about the program under study. Is the program serving the goals that the intended beneficiaries of service value?[6] Recently, there has been rising opposition, particularly in some black communities, to traditional formulations of program goals.[7] Activists are concerned not only with how well programs work to improve school achievement or health care, but also with their political legitimacy. They are interested in community participation or community control of programs and institutions. When such issues are paramount, evaluative questions derive from a radically different perspective.

Compatibility of Purposes

With all the possible uses for evaluation to serve, the evaluator has to make choices. The all-purpose evaluation is a myth. Although a number of different types of questions can be considered within the bounds of a single study, this takes meticulous planning and design. Inevitably not even the best-planned study will provide information on all the questions that people will think of. In fact, some purposes for evaluation are incompatible with others. Let us consider the evaluation of a particular educational program for slow learners.

The teaching staff wants to use the results to improve the presentations and teaching methods of the course, session by session, in order to maximize student learning. The state college of education wants to know whether the instructional program, based on a particular theory of learning, will improve pupil performance. In the first case, the evaluator will have to examine immediate short-term effects (learnings after the morning drill). He need not be concerned about generalizing the results to other populations, and needs neither control groups nor sophisticated statistics. He will want to maximize feedback of results to the teachers so that they can modify their techniques as they go along.

On the other hand, when evaluation is testing the proposition that a program developed from certain theories of learning will be successful with slow learners, it is concerned with long-range effects. It requires rigorous design so that observed results can be attributed to the stimulus of the program and not to extraneous events. The results have to be generalizable beyond the specific group of students. The instructional program should be insulated from alterations during its course in order to preserve the clarity of the program that led to the effects observed.

In theory, it is possible to achieve both an assessment of overall program effectiveness and a test of the effectiveness of component strategies. Textbooks on the design of experiments[8] present methods of factorial design that allow the experimenter to discover both total effect and the effects of each "experimental treatment." In practice, evaluation can seldom go about the business so systematically. The constraints of the field situation hobble the evaluation—too few clients, demand for quick feedback of information, inadequate funds, "contamination" of the special-treatment groups by receipt of other services, drop-outs from the program, lack of access to records and data, changes in program, and so on.

Some researchers say that to try to satisfy a multiplicity of demands and uses under usual field conditions invites frustration. The evaluator who identifies the key decision pending and gears his study to supplying information relevant to that issue is on firmer ground. Others believe that there are ways—not necessarily formal and elegant—to study a range of issues concurrently.[9] Some of these methods will be discussed in Chapters 3 and 4. Nevertheless, it remains important for the evaluator to know the priority among the purposes. If the crunch comes, he can jettison the extra baggage and fight for the essentials.

Formative and Summative Evaluation

We have identified several types of uses for evaluation. Evaluation can be asked to investigate the extent of program success so that decisions such as these can be made:

1. To continue or discontinue the program
2. To improve its practices and procedures
3. To add or drop specific program strategies and techniques
4. To institute similar programs elsewhere
5. To allocate resources among competing programs
6. To accept or reject a program approach or theory

A useful distinction has been introduced into the discussion of purpose by Scriven.[10] In discussing the evaluation of educational curriculums, he distinguishes between *formative* and *summative* evaluation. Formative evaluation produces information that is fed back during the development of a curriculum to help improve it. It serves the needs of developers. Summative evaluation is done after the curriculum is finished. It provides information about effectiveness to school decision makers who are considering adopting it.[11]

This distinction can be applied to other types of programs as well, with obvious advantages for the clarification of purpose. Many programs, however, are never "finished" in the sense that a curriculum is finished, and continued modification and adaptation will be necessary both at the original site and in other locations that use the program. The evaluator still has some hard thinking to do.

In practice, evaluation is most often called on to help with decisions about improving programs. Go/no-go, live-or-die decisions are relatively rare. Even when evaluation results show the program to be a failure, the usual reaction is to patch it up and try again. Rare, too, is the use of evaluation in theory-oriented tests of program approaches and models. These are more readily studied under controlled laboratory conditions. It is the search for improvements in strategies and techniques that supports much evaluation activity at present.

Even when decision makers start out with global questions (Is the program worth continuing?), they often end up receiving qualified results ("There are these good effects, but . . .") that lead them to look for ways to modify present practice. They become interested in the likelihood of improved results with different components, a different mix of services, different client groups, different staffing patterns, different organizational structure, different procedures and mechanics. One of the ironies of evaluation practice is that it has performed well at assessment of overall impact, suited to the uncommon go/no-go decision; it is relatively undeveloped in designs that produce information on the effectiveness of comparative strategies.

WHOSE USE SHALL BE SERVED?

Some possible users of the evaluation have been mentioned:

1. A funding organization (government, private, foundation)
2. A national agency (governmental, private)
3. A local agency
4. The directors of the specific project
5. Direct-service staff
6. Clients of the program
7. Scholars in the disciplines and professions

Which purposes shall the evaluation serve and for whom? In some cases, the question is academic. The evaluator is on the staff of some organization—national organization, pilot program—and he does the job assigned to him. But more often, the evaluator has a number of options open. If he is on the staff of an outside research organization that is being asked to undertake the evaluation, he may have the opportunity to negotiate the purpose and focus of the study. Even if he is more closely attached to the project, there is commonly such an amazing lack of clarity among the other parties that he has wide room to maneuver.

If he can help shape the basic focus of the study, the evaluator will consider a number of things. First is probably his own set of values. A summer program for ghetto youth can be evaluated for city officialdom to see if it cools out the kids and prevents riots and looting. The evaluator may want to view the program from the youths' perspective as well and see if it has improved their job prospects, work skills, and enjoyment. The data such a study produces can give a wider frame of reference to the decision of whether or not to continue the summer programs. It is important that the evaluator be able to live with the study, its uses, and his conscience at the same time.

Beyond this point, the paramount consideration in what use the study should be designed to serve is: What decision has to be made? The pending question may be one of extending a small pilot program in one hospital ward to other wards in the same hospital. It may be allocating money to one project or to another. There may have to be a decision on the adoption of one technique (reduced case loads, nonprofessional aides) throughout the system. Perhaps the upcoming decisions have to do with staffing, structure, or target populations. Once the evaluator finds out what key decisions are pending and when they will come up, he can gear his study to provide the maximum payoff.

Often there is no critical decision pending, at least that anyone can identify at the moment. There are, however, "users" who are interested in learning from the study and applying the results and others who are not. When the local program managers are conscientiously seeking better ways to serve their clients while the policy makers at higher levels are looking primarily for "program vindicators," the local managers' questions may deserve more attention. On the other hand, if the locals want a whitewash and the higher levels want to know where to put further appropriations, the evaluator should place more emphasis on comparative assessment of overall outcome.

The next task, then, is designing the evaluation to provide the answers that are needed. Finding out what answers are needed is not always an easy job. As we shall see in Chapter 3, it is the rare program that is articulate about goals, objectives, criteria, and bases for decision. Nevertheless, based on his best estimate of intended use, the evaluator has to make decisions on the measures to be used (see Chapter 3), sources of information (Chapter 3), and research design (Chapter 4). He will be abetted or hindered by the location of the evaluation within the organizational structure. It is to this issue that we now turn.

STRUCTURE OF THE EVALUATION

An evaluation study can be staffed and structured in different ways. A research unit or department within the program agency can do the evaluation, or special evaluators can be hired and attached to the program. (This is often the way federally funded demonstration projects handle their evaluation requirement.) Outsiders, usually university faculty members, are sometimes paid to serve as consultants, and either advise the evaluators on staff or carry out some of the evaluation tasks themselves in close cooperation with staff. These kinds of arrangements can be lumped together as "in-house."

Another approach is for the agency to contract with an outside research organization to do the study. The research organization, whether it is an academic group, a nonprofit organization, or a commercial firm, is responsible to the persons (and the level in the program agency) who commission it. Still another kind of arrangement is for a national agency (such as the U.S. Office of Education or the national YMCA) to employ a research organization to study a number of the local programs it supports or oversees.

Inside versus Outside Evaluation

There is a long tradition of controversy, mainly oral, about whether in-house or outside evaluations are preferable.[12] The answer seems to be that neither has a monopoly on the advantages. Some of the factors to be considered are administrative confidence, objectivity, understanding of the program, potential for utilization, and autonomy.

Administrative Confidence. Administrators must have confidence in the professional skills of the evaluation staff. Sometimes agency personnel are impressed only by the credentials and reputations of academic researchers and assume that the research people it has on staff or can hire are second-raters. Conversely, it may view outside evaluators as too remote from the realities, too ivory-tower and abstract, to produce information of practical value. Occasionally, it is important to ensure public confidence by engaging evaluators who have no stake in the program to be studied. Competence, of course, is a big factor in ensuring confidence and deserves priority consideration.

Objectivity. Objectivity requires that evaluators be insulated from any possibility of biasing their data or its interpretation by a desire to make things look good. Points usually go to outsiders on this score, although fine evaluation has been done by staff evaluators of scrupulous integrity. It even happens that an outside research firm will sweeten the interpretation of program results (by choice of respondents, by types of statistical tests applied) in order to ingratiate itself with a program and get further contracts. In any event, safeguarding the study against even unintentional bias is important.

Understanding of the Program. Knowledge of what is going on in the program is vital for an evaluation staff. They need to know both the real issues facing the agency and the real events that are taking place in the program if their evaluation is to be relevant. It is here that in-house staffs chalk up points, although outsiders too can find out about program processes if they make the effort and are given access to sources of information.

Potential for Utilization. Utilization of results often requires that evaluators take an active role in moving from research data to interpretation of the results in a policy context. In-house staff, who are willing to make recommendations on the basis of results and advocate them in agency meetings and conferences, may be better able to secure them a hearing. But sometimes it is outsiders, with their prestige and authority, who are able to induce the agency to pay attention to the evaluation.

Autonomy. Insiders generally take the program's basic assumptions and organizational arrangements as given and conduct their evaluation within the existing framework. The outsider may be able to exercise more autonomy and take a wider perspective. While respecting the formulation of issues set by the program, he may be able to introduce alternatives that are a marked departure from the status quo. The implications he draws from evaluation data may be oriented less to tinkering and more to fundamental restructuring of the program.[13] However, such a broader approach is neither common among outsiders nor unknown among insiders.

All these considerations have to be balanced against each other. There is no one "best site" for evaluation. The agency must weigh the factors afresh in each case and make an estimate of the way which the benefits pile up.

Level in the Structure

Whoever actually does the evaluation, the evaluation staff fits somewhere in the organizational bureaucracy. The evaluator reports to a person at some level of authority in the program organization or its supervisory or funding body, and he is responsible to that person and that position for the work he does. If the evaluator is an insider, he reports on a regular basis. The outsider researcher also receives his assignment and reports his results to (and may get intermediate advice from) the holder of a particular organizational position.

The important distinction in organizational location for our discussion is the difference between the policy maker and the program manager. To abridge our earlier catalog of users of evaluation and the decisions they have to make, the key points are these:

Use	Decision
Policymaker	Whether to expand, contract, or change the program
Program manager	Which methods, structures, techniques, or staff patterns to use

The evaluation should be placed within the organizational structure at a level consonant with its mission. If it is directed at answering the policy questions (How good is the program overall?), evaluators should report to policy makers. If the basic shape of the program is unquestioned and the evaluation issue centers on variations in specific features, the evaluator should probably be responsible to the program managers.[14]

Real problems arise when the evaluation is inappropriately located in the structure. An evaluation that is initiated by and responsible to program managers is under all kinds of pressure not to come up with findings that disparage the effectiveness of the whole program. If it does, the managers are likely to stall the report at the program level and it will never receive consideration in higher councils.[15] On the other hand, when top policy-makers initiate and oversee the evaluation, their questions are paramount, and questions about operations may get the short end of the budget. Nor do the evaluators have the easy, informal contact with program managers and practitioners that allows them to hear and understand the problems and options they face. It sometimes becomes difficult to study the effectiveness of different program components because staff see the evaluators as "inspectors" checking up on them and become wary of divulging information that might reflect poorly on their performance. Nor are they always cooperative in maintaining the conditions necessary for evaluation research, particularly if there is competition among program levels and the evaluation is viewed as an effort to assert the priorities of the higher level.

The problem of structural location becomes more complex when the evaluation is serving both masters. By and large, it appears best to report in at the higher level. In that way, the evaluator maintains greater autonomy. But then he has to make special efforts to learn enough about critical issues in day-to-day program operations to incorporate them into the study and to maintain the support of local program managers for appropriate research conditions.

NOTES

1. Edward A. Suchman, "Action for What? A Critique of Evaluative Research," in *The Organization, Management, and Tactics of Social Research,* ed. Richard O'Toole (Cambridge, Mass.: Schenkman Publishing Co., Inc., 1970).
2. See Sar Levitan, "Facts, Fancies, and Freeloaders in Evaluating Antipoverty Programs," *Poverty and Human Resources Abstracts* 4 (1969): 13–16; Richard H. Hall, "The Applied Sociologist and Organizational Sociology," in *Sociology in Action,* ed. Arthur B. Shostak (Homewood, Ill.: Dorsey Press, 1966), pp. 33–38; Joseph W. Eaton, "Symbolic and Substantive Evaluative Research," *Administrative Science Quarterly* 6 (1962): 421–42; Lewis A. Dexter, "Impressions About Utility and Wastefulness in Applied Social Science Studies," *American Behavioral Scientist* 9 (1966): 9–10.
3. Downs makes the point that the extent of applied research should be economically justified by the value of the information it produces for decision making. Evaluators, like other researchers, can become fascinated with the problem and do more research than the program needs. But he also stresses the point that clients frequently need redefinition of the problem and the suggestion of alternative approaches. Anthony Downs, "Some Thoughts on Giving People Economic Advice," *American Behavioral Scientist* 9 (1965): 30–32. Of course, far more common than spending too much money is trying to conduct evaluation with funds grossly inadequate for the extent and precision of the results expected.
4. A useful discussion appears in Louis Ferman, "Some Perspectives on Evaluating Social Welfare Programs," *Annals of the American Academy of Political and Social Science* 385 (September 1969): 143–56.
5. Edward Wynne, in "Evaluating Educational Programs: A Symposium," *Urban Review* 3 (1969): 19–20.
6. Philip H. Taylor, "The Role and Function of Educational Research," *Educational Research* 9 (1966): 11–15; Edmund deS. Brunner, "Evaluation Research in Adult Education," *International Review of Community Development* 17–18 (1967): 97–102.
7. David K. Cohen, "Politics and Research: Evaluation of Social Action Programs in Education," *Review of Educational Research* 40 (1970): 232.
8. A good example is B. J. Winer, *Statistical Principles in Experimental Design* (New York: McGraw-Hill, 1962). F. Stuart Chapin, W. G. Cochran and G. M. Cox, D. R. Cox, A. L. Edwards, R. A. Fisher, R. E. Kirk and E. F. Lindquist, among others, have also written useful texts on experimental design. Some of these are listed in the third section of the bibliography.
9. See Robert E. Stake, "Generalizability of Program Evaluation: The Need for Limits," and James L. Wardrop, "Generalizability of Program Evaluation: The Dangers of Limits," *Educational Product Report* 2 (1969): 38–40, 41–42.
10. Michael Scriven, "The Methodology of Evaluation," in *Perspectives of Curriculum Evaluation,* ed. Ralph W. Tyler, Robert M. Gagné, and Michael Scriven, AERA Monograph Series on Curriculum Evaluation, No. 1 (Chicago: Rand McNally, 1967), pp. 39–83.
11. See also Thomas J. Hastings, "Curriculum Evaluation: The Why of Outcomes," *Journal of Educational Measurement* 3 (1966): 27–32.
12. See Elmer Luchterhand, "Research and the Dilemmas in Developing Social Programs," in *The Uses of Sociology,* ed. P. F. Lazarsfeld, W. H. Sewell, and H. L. Wilensky (New York: Basic Books 1967), pp. 513–17; Rensis Likert and Ronald Lippitt, "The Utilization of Social Science," in *Research Methods in the Behavioral Sciences,* ed. Leon Festinger and Daniel Katz (New York: Holt, Rinehart & Winston, 1953), pp. 581–646; Martin Weinberger, "Evaluating Educational Programs: Observations by a Market Researcher," *Urban Review* 3 (1969): 23–26.
13. Robert K. Merton, "Role of the Intellectual in Public Bureaucracy," in *Social Theory and Social Structure* (New York: Free Press, 1964), pp. 207–24.
14. This rule of thumb applies whether the evaluation is performed by an in-house evaluation unit or by an outside research organization. Either one should report in at the level of

decision to which its work is addressed. The outsiders probably have greater latitude in going around the organizational chain of command and finding access to an appropriate ear, but even they will be circumscribed by improper location.

15. This point is discussed in Likert and Lippitt, *op. cit.*

44
Implementation
Jeffrey L. Pressman & Aaron Wildavsky

PREFACE

Late in 1968 our attention was drawn to the Economic Development Administration's employment effort in Oakland by the appearance of a book with the arresting title, *Oakland's Not for Burning.* Written by a major participant in the EDA's Oakland venture,[1] the book appeared to suggest that the city had recently been saved from riot and ruin by the infusion of $23 million in federal funds. Because it created minority employment—thus sending out a beacon light of hope to a troubled nation—the EDA program was touted as a model worthy of imitation. Since Oakland Project members were not aware that the city had been delivered from evil, we inquired into the status of the program and discovered that in 1969, three years after it began, approximately $3 million had actually been spent. At that rate, another twenty years would pass before this emergency operation would have spent the money to create the jobs to employ the people who would prevent (or at least not participate in) riots. Part of the $3 million had gone to the city for the Hegenberger overpass to the coliseum (which we somehow thought would have been built anyway), and the rest had been spent on architects' fees. We indulged briefly in mild fantasies depicting local architects about to overthrow the Oakland City Council in a suave coup d'etat, only to be bought off at the last minute by EDA funds. But further investigation suggested that there were no easy targets or evident villains. Implementation of the EDA's program was just more difficult than any of us had thought.

This book begins at the end: We will concentrate on that part of a public program following the initial setting of goals, securing of agreement, and commitment of funds. A new agency called the Economic Development Administration (EDA) is established by Congress. The EDA decides to go into cities for the purpose of providing permanent new jobs to minorities through economic development. Oakland is chosen as an experiment in showing how the provision of public works and building loans can provide incentives for employers to hire minorities. Congress appropriates the necessary funds, the approval of city officials and employers is obtained, and the program is announced to the public amidst the usual fanfare. Years later, construction has only been partially

Source: Jeffrey L. Pressman and Aaron Wildavsky, *Implementation,* 1st ed. (Berkeley, California: University of California Press, 1973), pp. xi–xvii.

completed, business loans have died entirely, and the results in terms of minority employment are meager and disappointing. Why?

Some programs are aborted because political agreement cannot be obtained. Others languish because funds cannot be secured. Still others die because the initial agreement of local officials or private concerns is not forthcoming. All these conditions were met in the EDA employment program in Oakland, but the program could not be implemented in time to secure the desired results.

In our study of implementation, we have deliberately chosen case material in which dramatic elements that are essentially self-explanatory are ruled out. There was no great conflict. Everyone agreed. There was only minimum publicity. The issue was not one of overriding political importance. Essential funds were on hand at the right time. The evils that afflicted the EDA program in Oakland were of a prosaic and everyday character. Agreements had to be maintained after they were reached. Numerous approvals and clearances had to be obtained from a variety of participants. Failure to recognize that these perfectly ordinary circumstances present serious obstacles to implementation inhibits learning. If one is always looking for unusual circumstances and dramatic events, he cannot appreciate how difficult it is to make the ordinary happen.

People now appear to think that implementation should be easy; they are, therefore, upset when expected events do not occur or turn out badly. We would consider our effort a success if more people began with the understanding that implementation, under the best of circumstances, is exceedingly difficult. They would, therefore, be pleasantly surprised when a few good things really happened.

Implementation in recent years has been much discussed but rarely studied. Presidents and their advisers, department secretaries and their subordinates, local officials and groups in their communities complain that good ideas are dissipated in the process of execution. Yet, except for an excellent book by Martha Derthick,[2] we have not been able to locate any thoroughgoing analysis of implementation.[3] Complaints about implementation do not constitute serious efforts to grapple with the problem.

No doubt a comparative approach to problems of implementation would ideally be preferable to the one we have adopted. But not enough is known about the subject to develop appropriate categories, and there is no previous literature on which to rely for guidance. We do not make any claim to have undertaken a comprehensive analysis of implementation. We are not certain we know what all the problems are, let alone provide solutions to them. But a start must be made somewhere and we hope this is it.

Implementation, to us, means just what Webster and Roget say it does: to carry out, accomplish, fulfill, produce, complete. But what is it that is being implemented? A policy, naturally. There must be something out there prior to implementation; otherwise there would be nothing to move toward in the process of implementation. A verb like "implement" must have an object like "policy." But policies normally contain both goals and the means for achieving them. How, then, do we distinguish between a policy and its implementation?

In everyday discourse we use policy (when referring to decisions) in several strikingly different ways. Sometimes policy means a statement of intention: Our policy is to increase employment among minorities. Policy here is treated as a broad statement of goals and objectives. Nothing is said about what might be done or whether anything has been or will be done to accomplish that purpose. Other times we speak of policy as if it were equivalent to actual behavior: Our policy is to hire minorities, meaning that we actually do hire them. Policy in this sense signifies the goal and its achievement. Both these meanings of policy rule out the possibility of studying implementation. When policy remains a disembodied objective, without specifying actors or the acts in which they must engage to achieve the desired result, there is no implementation to study. When the statement of the objective includes its attainment, implementation is unnecessary.

We can work neither with a definition of policy that excludes any implementation nor one that includes all implementation. There must be a starting point. If no action is begun, implementation cannot take place. There must also be an end point. Implementation cannot succeed or fail without a goal against which to judge it.

Let us agree to talk about policy as a hypothesis containing initial conditions and predicted consequences. If X is done at time t_1, then Y will result at time t_2. If the federal government, through the Economic Development Administration, provides \$23 million in loans and grants to enterprises in Oakland, and if these enterprises agree to hire minorities after spending the money, then facilities will be built leading to the creation of new jobs that will go to minorities. Implementation would here constitute the ability to achieve the predicted consequences after the initial conditions have been met.

Implementation does not refer to creating the initial conditions. Legislation has to be passed and funds committed before implementation takes place to secure the predicted outcome. Similarly, agreements with the local enterprises would have to be reached before attempts are made to carry them out. After all, the world is full of policy proposals that are aborted. You can't finish what you haven't started. Lack of implementation should not refer to failure to get going but to inability to follow through.

To emphasize the actual existence of initial conditions we must distinguish a program from a policy. A program consists of governmental action initiated in order to secure objectives whose attainment is problematical. A program exists when the initial conditions—the "if" stage of the policy hypothesis—have been met. The word "program" signifies the conversion of a hypothesis into governmental action. The initial premises of the hypothesis have been authorized. The degree to which the predicted consequences (the "then" stage) take place we will call implementation. Implementation may be viewed as a process of interaction between the setting of goals and actions geared to achieving them.

Considered as a whole, a program can be conceived of as a system in which each element is dependent on the other. Unless money is supplied, no facilities can be built, no new jobs can flow from them, and no minority personnel can be hired to fill them. A breakdown at one stage must be repaired, therefore, before it is possible to move on to the next. The stages are related, however, from back to front as well as from front to back. Failure to agree on procedures for hiring minorities may lead the government to withhold funds, thus halting the construction. Program implementation thus becomes a seamless web.

Policies imply theories. Whether stated explicitly or not, policies point to a chain of causation between initial conditions and future consequences. If X, then Y. Policies become programs when, by authoritative action, the initial conditions are created. X now exists. Programs make the theories operational by forging the first link in the causal chain connecting actions to objectives. Given X, we act to obtain Y. Implementation, then, is the ability to forge subsequent links in the causal chain so as to obtain the desired results. Once the funds are committed and the local agreements reached, the task is to build facilities to create new jobs so that minorities will be hired.

We oversimplify. Our working definition of implementation will do as a sketch of the earliest stages of the program, but the passage of time wreaks havoc with efforts to maintain tidy distinctions. As circumstances change, goals alter and initial conditions are subject to slippage. In the midst of action the distinction between the initial conditions and the subsequent chain of causality begins to erode. Once a program is underway implementers become responsible both for the initial conditions and for the objectives toward which they are supposed to lead.[4]

The longer the chain of causality, the more numerous the reciprocal relationships among the links and the more complex implementation becomes. The first four chapters illustrate the movement from simplicity to complexity. The reader interested in implementation should, therefore, be conscious of the steps required to accomplish each link in the chain. Who had to act to begin implementation? Whose consent was required to continue it? How many participants were involved? How long did they take to act? Each time an act of agreement has to be registered for the program to continue, we call a decision point. Each instance in which a separate participant is required to give his consent, we call a clearance. Adding the number of necessary clearances involved in decision points throughout the history of the program will give the reader an idea of the task involved in securing implementation. We will perform this chore for him in chapter 5.

When objectives are not realized, one explanation is the assertion of faulty implementation. The activities that were supposed to be carried out were not executed or were subject to inordinate delays. Another appropriate explanation may be that aspirations were set too high. Instead of asking why the process of implementation was faulty, we ask why too much was expected of it. Studying the process of implementation, therefore, includes the setting of goals (policy, according to its earlier meaning) toward which implementation is directed. By paying attention to the structural position of those who set targets—top federal officials who wish large accomplishments from small resources in a short time—and those who must implement them—career bureaucrats and local participants characterized by high needs and low cohesion—we seek in chapter 6 to uncover the causes of setting targets that are unlikely to be met.

The possibility of a mismatch between means and ends calls into question the adequacy of the original policy design. Perhaps implementation was good but the theory on which it was based was bad. Could a different set of initial conditions have achieved the predicted results? To explore this possibility, we end the book with an analysis of the economic theory underlying the EDA program in Oakland. Perhaps, we suggest in chapter 7, it might have been better to subsidize the wage bill of private firms directly in order to increase employment instead of the more roundabout method of providing grants and loans to construct facilities to create jobs for which minorities would then be hired.

The study of implementation requires understanding that apparently simple sequences of events depend on complex chains of reciprocal interaction. Hence, each part of the chain must be built with the others in view. The separation of policy design from implementation is fatal. It is no better than mindless implementation without a sense of direction. Though we can isolate policy and implementation for separate discussion, the purpose of our analysis is to bring them into closer correspondence with one another.

NOTES

1. Amory Bradford, *Oakland's Not for Burning* (New York: McKay, 1968).
2. Martha Derthick, *New Towns In-Town* (Washington, D.C.: Urban Institute, 1972).
3. The splendid account of the Elementary and Secondary Education Act by Stephen Bailey and Edith Mosher reveals acute sensitivity to problems of implementation. But it is not their purpose to analyze implementation as a distinct phenomenon. See their *ESEA: The Office of Education Administers a Law* (Syracuse: Syracuse University Press, 1968). Jerome T. Murphy, in the article "Title I of ESEA: The Politics of Implementing Federal Education Before," *Harvard Educational Review* 41 (1971): 35–63, does address himself directly to the question of implementation. Although this article does not contain as thoroughgoing an analysis of implementation as is found in the Derthick study, the author does provide a number of insights into the problem.
4. After numerous discussions, we have come to understand why no one else has apparently tried to distinguish policy from implementation. One person says that he likes to think of implementation as problems that arise when goals are set at high levels of organizational decision but are not realized because of resistance or distortion at lower levels or organization performance. We cannot force anyone to accept our choice of words or concepts, but we do think it makes more sense to conceive of *organization* in an extended sense so that it encompasses those whose cooperation is necessary for a program to be carried out. To us, it seems strange to talk of a program as being implemented merely because lower-level participants in the sponsoring organization attempted to carry it out though essential support from others was not forthcoming. Support for a program within an organization is but one stage of implementation as we understand it.

   Another person claims that policy and implementation are not distinguishable. Policy includes intended effects—i.e., policy includes implementation. Hence, a policy is not real until the intended changes have taken place. Again, we do not gainsay others the vocabulary with which they are comfortable. But we think that this choice of words confuses rather than clarifies. If policy includes its own implementation, then by definition alone it is not possible to carry out an investigation concerning the implementation of a policy. The important thing, we suppose, is that there are differences between deriving goals or objectives, working out a theory of how to achieve them, embodying that theory in governmental action, and executing it as intended. We think that Webster is on our side, but anyone else is welcome to translate his vocabulary into our concerns.

45
Watergate: Implications for Responsible Government

Frederick C. Mosher & Others

OVERVIEW

Practitioners and scholars in the field of public administration have an extraordinary interest in the quality of governmental institutions. They share with all citizens a concern that the competence and dependability of governments be achieved and secured. But, beyond this, those who have committed most of their lives to public service—advisers on public policy, practitioners sworn to faithful execution of the laws, and educators of present and future administrators—feel a special obligation to preserve the values that have so long contributed to an effective and progressive social order. They particularly appreciate the absolute necessity of integrity of the leaders in every branch of government—legislative, executive, and judicial. Without such integrity, government cannot gain and retain the confidence of the people it serves.

For these reasons, this Panel of the National Academy of Public Administration is gratified and challenged by the invitation of the leaders of the Senate Select Committee on Presidential Campaign Activities to present its views on issues emerging from the Committee's hearings. The revelations, immediately or remotely associated under the umbrella term "Watergate," have had a shattering impact upon American government at all levels. They have played a major role in causing the citizenry to develop, and to give voice to, growing disillusionment, cynicism, and even contempt for government and politics generally. But there is also a potentially favorable side. The very dimensions of the scandals so far revealed provide an opportunity for reexamination and reform, not of the electoral process alone, but also of other related practices and institutions.

Some of the seeds which grew to Watergate were undoubtedly planted many years and many administrations ago. But the development of these seeds into malpractices seriously injurious to our democratic form of government calls for sober reevaluation of our political and administrative systems and the application of appropriate remedies.

This report is not directed to the identification of individual misdeeds or culprits. Rather it is an effort to identify underlying sources and pitfalls, and to suggest changes in American government and administration which will help make future Watergates less likely, and which will improve the effectiveness and credibility of democratic government over the long range.

Source: Frederick C. Mosher and Others, *Watergate: Implications for Responsible Government* (New York: Basic Books, 1974), pp. 3–11, 123–126.

Aberration, Extension, or Culmination?

Are the various deviations from proper behavior that are popularly associated with Watergate to be regarded as one-time events, the product of a particular combination of circumstances and of people, mostly at high levels, in a political organization and in the administration? Were they unique in American history and unlikely to recur in the future?

Or was Watergate simply an extension of trends in American politics and government that have been underway for a long time and which could, unless deliberately checked or reversed, be expected to continue, and even worsen, in the future? More profoundly, is it a reflection of developments and deterioration in the very fabric of American society, social, economic, moral, and technological?

Or, finally, was Watergate a cataclysmic shock, a peaking of the trends and forces suggested above, from which society and government may not recover without severe surgery?

It appears to this panel that Watergate permits all three of these interpretations. Surely it was an aberration in the sense that it resulted from bringing into positions of enormous power a group of people who shared characteristics of personal and ideological loyalty and inexperience in social responsibilities. Surely it will not soon recur—not necessarily because such a collection of people may not again be assembled, but because of the disastrous consequences for many of those involved individually and for the administration generally. Surely it is not the first scandal which sullied American public life. We have had Credit Mobilier, Teapot Dome, political corruption of public relief programs in the 1930s, and Internal Revenue malfeasance in the early 1950s, although none of these had the pervasiveness and shattering impact of Watergate.

On the other hand, one may observe that most of the perpetrators and directors of Watergate misdeeds were reputedly honest and upright persons before they entered the political campaign and/or the administration. Few if any had any record of unethical or dishonest, let alone criminal, activity. This suggests that Watergate was a product of a *system* which shaped and guided the behavior of its participants. (System, as the word is used here, is primarily the product of trends and forces from the past.)

President Nixon, as well as others in his administration, has defended some of his and their actions on the grounds that the same things were done by predecessors in high office. Regardless of the validity of this contention as defensive argument, it is entirely true that many of the actions deplored in this report and elsewhere have precedents in previous administrations of both parties. Indeed, the evidence suggests that most of such practices were growing gradually or sporadically during past decades. They include, for example: (1) use of governmental powers and resources in behalf of friends, against opponents (enemies); (2) politicization of the career services; (3) political espionage on American citizens; (4) excessive secrecy, usually on grounds of national security, whether or not justifiable; (5) use of governmental personnel and resources for partisan purposes, including political campaigns; (6) solicitation of political contributions from private interests with implicit or explicit assurances of support or favor, or of absence of disfavor; and (7) "dirty tricks."

Some have argued that Watergate was a logical, if not inevitable, consequence of trends in the larger systems of our society. Thus one reads and hears that its forebears include, among many other things: the weakening of the family unit and with it the sense of responsibility to and for others; the decline of personal and, therefore, of social morality and of the influence of the churches; the growing interdependence of major elements of the society and of the economy, and of the government with both of these; the increasing power of the national government; the growing interrelationships of the national government with other governments in the world; the increasing prevalence in both public and private spheres of huge bureaucracies, in which the individual is submerged; and the growing dominance of technology.

It would be both inappropriate and impossible for this Panel to address these alleged negative trends in the space and time permitted. The Panel does, however, agree that forces such as these may have contributed to Watergate. But it also believes that government, particularly the national government, has been in the past, and should be in the future, strong, beneficent, and flexible enough to influence these forces toward the benefit of the American people. The ethical and effective conduct of government must provide the model and the leadership for American society.

Watergate is thus both an aberration and an extension of earlier trends. It may also be a culmination of some, if not all, of those trends. As suggested earlier, the revelations in the 12 months of 1973 should themselves deter possible future perpetrators from at least the most blatant of such misdeeds. Certainly, these revelations have alerted the American people and their elected representatives to the danger of future Watergates and initiated a search for legal and other means to thwart or minimize them. Many basic reforms of American government, including the framing of the Constitution itself, have been sparked by conspicuous failings, scandals, tragedies, or disasters.

The Watergate revelations have already stimulated a great deal of concern and discourse about means of political and governmental reform. And there is reason to believe that the Congress and the people whom it represents are more receptive to basic changes than they have been in a long time. The "horrors" which have been, and are still being, exposed have a potentially positive side. They offer an opportunity for corrective actions, many of which should have been taken long ago. If the opportunity is grasped, Watergate will be more than an extension of long-term trends; it will be truly a culmination and watershed.

The Watergate Climate

Some of the witnesses before the Select Committee spoke about the unique and, it would appear, altogether unpleasant "climate" which pervaded the top levels of the administration and the Committee to Reelect the President during and before the Watergate period. In the words of John Dean, Watergate was an "inevitable outgrowth of a climate of excessive concern over the political impact of demonstrations, excessive concern over leaks, and insatiable appetite for political intelligence all coupled with a do-it-yourself White House staff regardless of the law."

The Watergate climate, for convenience, may be treated from two perspectives, the political and the administrative, even though the close interrelationship of the two was one of its central and most sinister features. The prime motivating drive behind both political and administrative activities seems to have been Presidential *power,* its enlargement, its exploitation, and its continuation. Power was perhaps sought by some in the Presidential entourage for its own sake, but it seems fair to conclude that most sought to impose upon the government the ideological views of the President. Paradoxically, a part of that ideology as expounded was to limit the powers of the national government; to return more powers to the people and their elected representatives at state and local levels. The zest for power in the Presidential office is a perfectly expectable, normal, and proper behavior of Presidencies, particularly in the current century—but within limits and constraints, many of which are embedded in the Constitution, and always subject to accountability.

The political climate in the months and, to a lesser extent, for several years before the 1972 election was apparently characterized by an obsessive drive for reelection of the President. It seems to have colored, or sought to color, governmental plans, decisions, and behavior during that period, even in fields of activity intended and believed to be politically neutral—administration of the revenue laws, antitrust prosecutions, allocation of grants and contracts, clearance of career service appointments and promotions, and many others.

Synchronized by the White House and its immediate appendage, the Committee to Reelect the President, the program was directed primarily, if not almost exclusively, to the reelection of the President, not to the victory of his party or of other nominees of the same party in the same general election. It is evident that the imperative to reelect was so driving as to override many other considerations, including the public interest and normal ethical and legal constraints.

The President, in explaining the behavior of his subordinates, described them as "people whose zeal exceed their judgment, and who may have done wrong in a cause they deeply believed in to be right." But some of those whose behavior the President described so mildly readily admitted later that, in their minds and consciences, the demand to reelect was so overwhelming as to justify acts admittedly criminal. John Mitchell, in his testimony before the Select Committee, made it clear that he considered the reelection of President Nixon to be more important than his obligation to tell the President that people around him were involved in perjury and other crimes, even though he could find no Constitutional basis for such a conclusion.

The political environment, both before and following the campaign of 1972, was entirely consonant with that of the campaign itself. The Administration was in a state of siege from its critics, some of whom were seen as threats not only to it alone, but also to the security of the nation itself. Administration proposals were advanced, the potential costs of which so far exceeded their potential benefits, even in strictly political terms, as later to be construed as stupid, even absurd. The White House became a command post for conduct by the President's staff of near warfare against those whom it considered "enemies."

Following the "mandate" of the 1972 election, the Administration moved to cleanse itself of senior officials in many executive agencies who were considered to be hesitant or doubtful followers of the views and ideology of the President. In terms of top-level political appointees, the transition between the first and second Nixon terms was as extreme as most transitions from one party to the other. Many experienced Republicans in key posts were replaced by others, usually younger, in whom the Administration presumably had greater confidence of personal and ideological loyalty, and who were innocent of prior allegiances to the agency of their appointment or its associated clienteles. In this and other ways the Administration undertook to carry out and enforce its electoral "mandate," even before the inauguration in 1973.

The administrative climate was, to some extent, a product of the political climate: aggressive efforts were made to use administrative machinery to carry out political and policy ends, and growing frustration and exasperation developed over alleged bureaucratic impediments. In part, it was a further step in the evolution of a strong Presidency—a movement which had begun generations earlier and which students of American government have generally approved, at least since the report of the President's Committee on Administrative Management (the Brownlow Report) submitted in 1937.

Taken individually, the majority of changes that the Administration instituted or sought were consistent with sound administrative practices; indeed, a good many leaders in public administration had recommended some of them earlier and specifically endorsed them after they were proposed by the President. They included:

- formation of regions with common headquarters and boundaries to encompass many of the domestic field agencies and activities;
- establishment of regional councils to provide better coordination of federal activities in regions and areas;
- delegation of federal powers from Washington to the field;
- unconditional grants to state and local governments (called general revenue sharing);
- broader categories of, and fewer strings on, functional grants to state and local governments (called special revenue sharing);
- formation of a Domestic Council to parallel, in domestic affairs, the National Security Council in foreign affairs;
- strengthening of the managerial role of the Bureau of the Budget (which became the Office of Management and Budget), and vesting of all of its statutory powers in the President;
- consolidation of the activities of most of the domestic departments in four "superdepartments," rationally organized according to subject matter areas;
- formation of a "Federal Executive Service" to encompass all supergrade employees whose qualifications would be approved and whose assignments and salaries would be flexible according to managerial needs;
- encouraging the administrative practices associated with the term "management by objective";
- placing postal activities in a quasi-governmental corporation and removing the Postmaster General from the Cabinet; and
- interposing above the specialized, professionalized, "parochial" bureaucracies generalists with a broader perspective.

But these mostly constructive actions and proposals were accompanied by a number of others which students of government, even those with the strongest commitment to Presidential energy and influence, found questionable. These included:

- usurpation by the White House of powers over both policy and day-to-day operations heretofore carried on in the departments and other established agencies;
- enormous growth of the White House staff, accompanied by the establishment of a tight hierarchy within it;
- by-passing of departments and agencies in areas of their assigned responsibilities, first in international and defense matters through the staff director of the National Security Council, and later through the staff director of the Domestic Council;
- veiling of White House activities on grounds of national security or executive privilege;
- negating of substantial majorities of both houses of the Congress on policy and program matters through accelerating use of the veto power and impoundment of funds;
- interposition of White House aides between the President and the official heads of the executive agencies, such aides having been appointed without confirmation or even public knowledge; and

- the abortive attempt to interpose Presidential counselors in the White House with substantial control over established departments.

Considered singly or separately, few of the actions or proposals in the foregoing lists would be cause for great alarm. However, if all of them had been effectuated, the administrative weather could have become very stormy indeed. The American state then would have approached a monocracy, ruled from the top through a strictly disciplined hierarchical system. It would have become difficult to pin responsibility for decisions or actions upon anyone short of the top man, and he was, for the most part, inaccessible and unaccountable. As some of his appointees have pointed out, the only ultimate means of holding the President answerable following his election or reelection is impeachment.

The administrative and political aspects of the governmental climate were increasingly interlocked, at least until the spring of 1973. Together they constituted a critical threat to many of the values and protections Americans associate with a democratic system of government, including:

- the right to participate or be represented in decisions affecting citizens;
- the right to equal treatment;
- the right to know;
- free and honest elections;
- assurance of Constitutional protections such as those in the First and Fourth Amendments;
- a balance of countervailing powers to prevent usurpation by any single power—as among the branches of government, the political parties or sectors of parties, interest groups, and geographic sections; and
- ethical conduct of public officials in pursuit of the public interest.

This panel entertains no delusions that these precepts have not been violated or threatened before—well before—the first Nixon administration. It is possible that many of the revelations of the last two years were repetitions of earlier actions never revealed. Indeed, we owe our present knowledge to an obscure and lonely guard in the Watergate Apartments, to the fact that there was an unmarked police car nearby, to a couple of aggressive reporters, to the Senate Select Committee, to the Special Prosecutors, and to some unidentified leaks to the press. The problems we here address are not partisan problems. They are problems for all parties, for all citizens.

EPILOGUE
ETHICS AND PUBLIC OFFICE

Most of this report has concerned, directly or indirectly, the subject of ethics in the public service. So did most of the hearings before the Senate Select Committee. The investigative power of the Congress may well be a more effective instrument than the criminal procedures of the courts in exposing, and thereby protecting the public from, unethical behavior on the part of its officials.

> The only thing that could and can avail the body politic *in extremis* is the charter of the Select Committee, committing it to the investigation of unethical—not just illegal—conduct in the 1972 campaign. The unethical is not necessarily—not even often—the illegal, as Congress attested in separating the two. It was the unethical not the illegal, activities in 1972 that did this country down. . . .[1]

Many of the actions associated with Watergate, the burglary of offices, the forgery of a letter, the laundering of money through Mexico, and so on, were clearly criminal. But in their relation to the national interest each by itself was less than crucial. What was important were the attitudes of mind, the modes of conspiring, and the narrow goals of those behind them. Many of these kinds of matters lie beyond the range of criminal law.

Public officials are of course bound by the same criminal laws as apply to other citizens. But their obligations to the public as a whole entail an additional and more rigorous set of standards and constraints associated with the concept of public trust. Many practices which are permissible, even normal, in the private sector are, or should be, forbidden in government: acceptance of certain kinds of gifts, discussion of appointments under certain circumstances, promise or threat of governmental action under some circumstances, carrying and secreting of large amounts of cash, withholding of information to which the public should be alerted, and, conversely, leaking or other disclosure of other kinds of information which should be private.

One of the characteristics of many of those implicated in Watergate was their perception of the roles and responsibilities of government, a perception which was at best simplistic, and at worst venal and dangerous. A democratic government is not a family business, dominated by its patriarch; nor is it a military battalion, or a political campaign headquarters. It is a producing organization which belongs to its members, and it is the only such organization whose members include *all* the citizens within its jurisdiction. Those who work for and are paid by the government are ultimately servants of the whole citizenry, which owns and supports the government.

Complementary to the ingenuousness of the appreciation of the sense of the word "public" in these recent developments was the apparent lack of understanding of "service." In a society in which sovereignty presumably rests in the people, it is indispensable that its officials be regarded and regard themselves as servants, not masters, of the people. They must have and exercise powers, but their powers are delegated, usually for temporary periods.

A ten-point Code of Ethics for Government Service was adopted by Congress in a concurrent resolution in 1958, and its provisions were subsequently incorporated in the *Federal Personnel Manual.* In May 1961 President Kennedy issued Executive Order 10939 as a Guide on Ethical Standards to Government Officials; it was specifically pointed to those occupying positions of highest responsibility. Many federal agencies have issued their own minimal standards of conduct, applying to the specific business of the individual agencies, and most of them have some machinery for guidance and enforcement through legal counsel or inspectorates. Yet Watergate happened.

The Panel has considered a number of possible steps the government might take to strengthen ethical standards, particularly of noncareer officials, and suggests them for the consideration of the Select Committee. They include:

- *Improving and making more sophisticated the codes and guidances of ethics in public service;*
- *Incorporating in the oath of office, sworn to by all new officers and employees, the Code of Ethics, and requiring each at the time to read it and certify in writing that he or she has done so;*
- *Requiring that new political appointees attend briefing sessions on the ethics of public service; such briefings would cover ethical conduct, accountability, the nature of checks and balances in government, the importance of responsiveness to the public, and the relationships between career and noncareer services;*
- *Creating a Federal Service Ethics Board, comparable to similar boards that have been established in some state and local governments, to set forth general guidelines for all employees and to investigate particularly important and difficult ethical questions that are brought before it;*

- *Providing a governmentwide ombudsman or one in each major agency to consider complaints of ethical violations in the federal service.*

The effectiveness of codes and mechanisms for their enforcement depends first upon continuing scrutiny of the decisions and actions of public officials: by their fellows in administration, by the other branches of government, by their professional associates in and out of government, by the media, and by the general public. Such scrutiny in turn hinges on openness and accountability. For those who might be tempted to unethical behavior for want of understanding or conscience, the threat of future revelation and scrutiny can be a considerable deterrent.

But there is no "fail-safe" mechanism whereby appropriate ethics of public officers and the public interest may be assured, and whereby the ethics of public employees may be enforced. Ultimately, the assurance of high standards of ethical behavior depends upon the people who aspire to and gain public office, and more particularly upon the system of values they have internalized. The panel reiterates its urging, in the Introduction to this report, that the educational institutions around the nation, especially those professional schools which provide significant numbers of public officials, focus more attention on public service ethics. A guiding rule of such instruction and of subsequent official decisions should be that propounded many years ago by Thomas Jefferson:

> Whenever you are to do a thing, though it can never be known but to yourself, ask yourself how you would act were all the world looking at you, and act accordingly.[2]

NOTES

1. Milton Meyer, "From Deliquescence to Survival—Watergate and Beyond," *Center Report*, Center for the Study of Democratic Institutions (February 1974), p. 27.
2. In a letter to Peter Carr from Paris, France, August 19, 1785.

46

The Zero-Base Approach to Government Budgeting

Peter A. Pyhrr

Zero-base budgeting is an emerging process, which has been adopted by a variety of industrial organizations in many sectors of the economy, as well as state and local governments.

As it is generally practiced today zero-base budgeting was developed at Texas Instruments Inc. during 1969. The process was first adopted in government by Governor Jimmy Carter of Georgia for the preparation of the fiscal 1973 budget, and the process is still being used today in Georgia. It would appear at this point that zero-base budgeting will be

Source: From *Public Administration Review* 37 (January-February 1977), pp. 1–8

adopted in the federal government, sponsored by both the President and Congress. The Government Economy and Spending Reform Act of 1976 (S. 2925) was introduced by Senator Muskie, and co-sponsored by more than 50 per cent of the Senate when it was reported out of the Government Operations Committee. The bill required a congressional zero-base review and evaluation of every government authorization for programs and activities every five years, and requires the Director of OMB to develop a program for zero-base budgeting for all departments and agencies of the Executive Branch.

There are three key users of the zero-base analysis in government: legislative (Congress, state legislature, city council); executive (President/OMB, governors, mayor/city manager); and agency (agency director, program and department managers).

The focus of each user is obviously different, with the legislature requiring more summarization and focusing on public priorities and objectives, the agencies requiring more detailed information and focusing on program implementation and efficiency, and the executive straddling the needs of legislature and agency. However, regardless of specific information needs and focus, the legislature, executive, and agencies must all address themselves to two basic questions: Are the current activities efficient and effective? and Should current activities be eliminated or reduced to fund higher-priority new programs or to reduce the current budget? These two questions are the focus of the zero-base budgeting process.

THE ZERO-BASE APPROACH

On December 2, 1969, at the Plaza Hotel in New York City, Arthur F. Burns, then counselor to the President of the United States, addressed the annual dinner meeting of the Tax Foundation on the "Control of Government Expenditures." In this speech, Dr. Burns identified the basic need for zero-base budgeting; but he also expressed his concern that such a process would be difficult if not impossible to implement:

> Customarily, the officials in charge of an established program have to justify only the increase which they seek above last year's appropriation. In other words, what they are already spending is usually accepted as necessary without examination. Substantial savings could undoubtedly be realized if [it were required that] every agency . . . make a case for its entire appropriation request each year, just as if its program or programs were entirely new. Such budgeting procedure may be difficult to achieve, partly because it will add heavily to the burdens of budget-making, and partly also because it will be resisted by those who fear that their pet programs would be jeopardized by a system that subjects every . . . activity to annual scrutiny of its costs and results.

Dr. Burns was advocating that government agencies re-evaluate all programs and present their requests for appropriation in such a fashion that all funds can be allocated on the basis of cost/benefit or some similar kind of evaluative analysis.

The fears of Dr. Burns that a zero-base approach "will add heavily to the burdens of budget-making" are unwarranted, as I view the matter. None of the organizations that I am familiar with that have implemented the approach have added additional time onto their calendar for the preparation of a zero-based budget (other than design and training prior to the budget preparation process which is a normal start-up requirement of any new process). To be sure, zero-base budgeting usually involves more managers and takes more management time than the traditional budget procedures. However, it must be taken into account that the zero-base approach includes objective setting, program evaluation, and operational decision making, as well as budget making, whereas traditional budgeting procedures often separate these management aspects. In the worst case, the traditional budget process is merely a way to obtain an appropriation with the operational decision making and operating budgets determined after the total appropriation has been obtained. If we added the total time of these additional management elements to the time used by the traditional budgeting process, then the time requirements of zero-base budgeting do not add to management's burdens. In fact, after the initial year's implementation, the zero-base approach can actually reduce management's burden as the zero-base thought process and methodology become ingrained into management's normal way of problem solving and decision making.

ZERO-BASE BUDGETING PROCEDURES

The zero-base approach requires each organization to evaluate and review all programs and activities (current as well as new) systematically; to review activities on a basis of output or performance as well as cost; to emphasize managerial decision making first, number-oriented budgets second; and to increase analysis. However, I should stress that zero-base is an approach, not a fixed procedure or set of forms to be applied uniformly from one organization to the next. The mechanics and management approach has differed significantly among the organizations that have adopted zero-base, and the process must be adapted to fit the specific needs of each user. In governmental jurisdictions, for example, certain expenditures may be fixed by law.

Although the specifics differ among organizations, there are four basic steps to the zero-base approach that must be addressed by each organization: identify "decision units;" analyze each decision unit in a "decision package;" evaluate and rank all decision packages to develop the appropriations request; and prepare the detailed operating budgets reflecting those decision packages approved in the budget appropriation.

Defining Decision Units

Zero-base budgeting attempts to focus management's attention on evaluating activities and making decisions. Therefore, the "meaningful elements" of each organization must be defined so that they can be isolated for analysis and decision making. For the sake of terminology, we have termed these meaningful elements "decision units." The definition of decision units in most organizations is straightforward, and the decision units may correspond to those budget units defined by traditional budget procedures.

For those organizations with a detailed budget unit or cost center structure, the decision unit may correspond to that budget unit. In some cases, the budget unit manager may wish to identify separately different functions or operations within his budget unit if they are significant in size and require separate analysis. He may therefore identify several "decision units" for a budget unit. If an organization has a well-developed program structure, the decision unit may correspond to that lowest level of the program structure (program element, activity, function). Decision units may be defined at the sub-program level if there are separate organizational units within that program element. The resulting decision packages at the sub-program element level can then be grouped to evaluate the program element. In the same manner, decision packages for each program element (or sub-program element) can be grouped to evaluate each program.

The decision packages built around each decision unit are the building blocks of the budget and program analysis. These building blocks can be readily sorted either organizationally or programmatically. For those organizations without a detailed program structure, the information and analysis developed by zero-base provides a readily usable data base from which a program structure can be developed.

Decision units can also be defined as major capital projects, special work assignments, or major projects. Each organization must determine for itself "what is meaningful." In practice, top management usually defines the organization or program level at which decision units must be defined, leaving it to the discretion of each manager to identify additional decision units if appropriate.

The Decision Package Concept

The "decision package" is the building block of the zero-base concept. It is a document that identifies and describes each decision unit in such a manner that management can (a) evaluate it and rank it against other decision units competing for funding and (b) decide whether to approve it or disapprove it.

The content and format of the decision package must provide management with the information it needs to evaluate each decision unit. This information might include: purpose/objective, description of actions (What are we going to do, and how are we going to do it?), costs and benefits, workload and performance measures, alternative means of accomplishing objectives, and various levels of effort (What benefits do we get for various levels of funding?).

The key to developing decision packages is the formulation of meaningful alternatives. The steps that should be used in developing decision packages include:

1. Alternative methods of accomplishing the objective or performing the operation: Managers should identify and evaluate all meaningful alternatives and choose the alternative they consider best. If an alternative to the current method of doing business is chosen, the recommended way should be shown in the decision package with the current way shown as the alternative not recommended.
2. Different levels of effort of performing the operation: Once the best method of accomplishing the operation has been chosen from among the various alternative methods evaluated, a manager must identify alternative levels of effort and funding to perform that operation. Managers must establish a minimum level of effort, which must be below the current level of operation, and then identify additional levels or increments as separate decision packages. These incremental levels above the minimum might bring the operation up to its current level and to several multiples of the current level of effort.

The identification and evaluation of different levels of effort is probably the most difficult aspect of the zero-base analysis, yet it is one of the key elements of the process. If only one level of effort were analyzed (probably reflecting the funding level desired by each manager), top management would be forced to make a yes or no decision on the funding request, thus funding at the requested level, eliminating the program, making arbitrary reductions, or recycling the budget process if requests exceeded funding availability.

A decision package is defined as one incremental level in a decision unit. There may be several decision packages for each decision unit. It is these incremental levels that get ranked. By identifying a minimum level of effort, plus additional increments as separate decision packages, each manager thus presents several alternatives for top management decision making:

Elimination: Eliminate the operation if no decision packages are approved.

Reduced Level: Reduce the level of funding if only the minimum level decision package is approved.

Current Level: Maintain the same level of effort if the minimum level, plus the one or two incremental levels (bringing the operation from the minimum level to the current level of effort) are approved. (*Note*: The current level of effort refers only to the level of output or performance sometimes referred to as a "maintenance level." However, even at the current level of effort, managers may have changed their method of operation and made operating improvements, so that the current level of effort may be accomplished at a reduced cost.)

Increased Levels: Increased levels of funding and performance if one or more increments above the current level is approved.

The minimum level of effort is the most difficult level to identify, since there is no magic number (i.e., 75 percent of the current level) that would be meaningful to all operations. The minimum level must be identified by each manager for his/her operations. The minimum level must be below the current level of effort. The minimum level should attempt to identify "that critical level of effort, below which the operation would be discontinued because it loses its viability of effectiveness." There are several considerations which can aid managers in defining the minimum level of effort:

1. The minimum level may not completely achieve the total objective of the operation (even the additional levels of effort recommended may not completely achieve the objective because of realistic budget and/or achievement levels.)
2. The minimum level should address itself to the most critical population being served or attack the most serious problem areas.
3. The minimum level may merely reduce the amount of service (or number of services) provided.
4. The minimum level may reflect operating improvements, organizational changes, or improvements in efficiency that result in cost reductions.
5. Combinations of 1 through 4.

By identifying the minimum level, each manager is not necessarily recommending his operation be funded at the minimum level, but is merely identifying that alternative to top management. If a manager identifies several levels of effort, he is recommending that all levels be funded.

Example: Air Quality Laboratory. The following example of the Georgia Air Quality Laboratory (Air Quality Control) illustrates the type of analysis that each manager needs to make in order to prepare decision packages. The Air Quality Laboratory tests air samples collected by field engineers throughout Georgia. It identifies and evaluates pollutants by type and volume, then provides reports and analyses to the field engineers. The manager involved made the typical two-part analysis; first, identifying different ways of performing the function; and second, identifying the different levels of effort.

1. *Different ways of performing the same function:*

a) **Recommended decision package:** *Use a centralized laboratory in Atlanta to conduct all tests.* Cost—$246,000. This expenditure would allow 75,000 tests and would determine the air quality for 90 per cent of the population (leaving unsampled only rural areas with little or no population problem).

b) **Alternatives not recommended:**

1. *Contract testing to Georgia Tech.* Cost—$450,000. The $6 per test charged by the University exceeds the $246,000 cost for doing the same work in the Air Quality Laboratory, and the quality of the testing is equal.

2. *Conduct all testing at regional locations.* Cost—$590,000 the first year due to set-up cost and purchase of duplicate equipment, with a $425,000 running rate in subsequent years. Many labs would be staffed at a minimum level, with less than full utilization of people and equipment.

3. *Conduct tests in Central Laboratory for special pollutants only, which require special qualifications for people and equipment, and conduct routine tests in regional centers.* Cost—$400,000. This higher cost is created because regional centers have less than full workloads for people and equipment.

The recommended way of performing this laboratory function was chosen because the alternatives did not offer any additional advantages and were more expensive. The manager therefore recommended the level of 75,000 tests, at $246,000. Each manager has complete freedom to recommend either *new ways* or the current way of doing business.

Once the manager had defined the basic alternatives and selected the one he considered best, he completed his analysis by describing different levels of effort for his chosen alternative. For the recommended Central Laboratory in Atlanta, the Air Quality Laboratory manager described and evaluated decision packages that called for different levels of effort for air quality tests. In this case, the manager believed that he could reduce the level of testing to 37,300 samples and still satisfy the minimum requirements of the field engineers who used his services. Therefore, he completed his analysis by identifying the minimum level and additional levels of effort for his recommended way of performing the testing as follows:

2. *Different levels of effort of performing the function*:

a) Air Quality Laboratory (1 of 3), cost—$140,000. Minimum package: Test 37,300 samples, determining air quality for only five urban areas with the worse pollution (covering 70 per cent of the population).
b)Air Quality Laboratory (2 of 3), cost—$61,000 (Levels 1 + 2 = $201,000). Test 17,700 additional samples (totaling 55,000, which is the current level), determining air quality for five additional problem urban areas plus eight counties chosen on the basis of worst pollution (covering 80 per cent of the population).
c) Air Quality Laboratory (3 of 3), cost—$45,000 (Levels 1 + 2 + 3 = $246,000). Test 20,000 additional samples (totaling 75,000), determining air quality for 90 per cent of the population, and leaving only rural areas with little or no pollution problems unsampled.

The Air Quality Laboratory manager thus prepared three decision packages (levels 1 of 3, 2 of 3, and 3 of 3).

Development of different levels as separate decision packages indicates that the functional manager thinks all levels deserve serious consideration within realistic funding expectations. He identifies three possible levels and leaves it to higher management to make trade-offs among functions and level of effort within each function.

An Example from City Operations. The decision package analysis can be applied to any federal, state, or local operation or program. The questions raised by the decision package, and the analysis required, are similar even for extremely diverse programs and operations.

To demonstrate this point, I have taken an example of residential refuse collection from the City of Garland,

Texas. Garland was the first city to my knowledge to have successfully implemented zero-base budgeting throughout all city departments. The residential refuse example clearly illustrates the zero-base analysis, and identifies the alternatives and funding decisions faced by city managers.

"Residential Refuse Collection" is the city operation responsible for collecting and transporting all residential solid waste for disposal. The manager of this function made the typical two-part analysis: first, identifying alternative means for accomplishing this activity; and second, identifying different levels of effort.

1. *Different ways of performing the same function:*

> a)**Recommended means:** *City provides the collection service, requiring the use of plastic sacks for all refuse.* Plastic sacks are purchased by each resident. Refuse trains are used for heavily populated areas. Front loading refuse trucks are used to empty the refuse trains on the route to transport the refuse to the landfill. Other types of trucks are used for the less-populated areas and country runs. Cost—$790,300.
>
> b)**Alternatives not recommended:**
>
> 1. *Collection without the use of plastic sacks:* Additional man required on each crew if garbage cans are used in place of plastic sacks. Added cost of $96,000.
>
> 2. *Collection of all refuse by the trains.* Use of other types of equipment (shupacks and barrel trucks) are more efficient in less densely populated areas. Purchase of three additional refuse trains and two front loaders would be required, plus eight additional personnel, for an additional cost of $150,000.
>
> 3. *Contract city refuse collection to a private contractor*: Cost $1,108,800 for twice-a-week collection; $900,000 for once-a-week collection.

The recommended means was chosen because the alternatives did not offer any additional advantages and were more expensive.

The residential refuse collection manager completed his zero-base analysis by identifying different levels of effort for performing the function. In this case, the manager believed he could reduce the level of refuse collection from twice a week to once a week and still satisfy the minimum sanitary requirements. Therefore, he completed his analysis by identifying the minimum level and additional levels of effort for his recommended means of refuse collection as follows:

2. *Different levels of effort for performing the function:*

> a)Residential Refuse Collection (1 of 3): cost $607,000 minimum level. Collect residential refuse once per week; brush pick up on Thursday and Friday.
>
> b)Residential Refuse Collection (2 of 3): cost—$142,800 (Levels 1 + 2 = $750,300). Add one additional collection per week, so that refuse is collected twice per week.
>
> c)Residential Refuse Collection (3 of 3): cost—$40,500 (Levels 1 + 2 + 3 = $790,300). Collection of brush and white goods an additional two days per week, so that brush is collected every collection day (Mon., Tues., Thurs., and Fri.).

The manager thus prepared three decision packages.

It should be pointed out that there is no magic number of funding levels, but two to five levels are most common. It is also common in many cases to have a great deal of back-up information and analysis, which the decision package itself displays in summary form. In the residential refuse case, there was extensive information and analysis regarding different types of equipment, detailed city maps with an analysis of different route alternatives, and an evaluation of different types of equipment for different routes. The city manager in this case reviewed the detailed analysis, and there were several revisions before the recommendations were put into final form.

The Ranking Process

The ranking process provides management with a technique to allocate its limited resources by making management concentrate on these questions: "How much should we spend?" and "Where should we spend it?" Management constructs its answer to these questions by listing all the decision packages identified in order of decreasing benefit to the organization. It then identifies the benefits to be gained at each level of expenditure and studies the consequences of not approving additional decision packages ranked below that expenditure level.

The ranking process establishes priorities among the incremental levels of each decision unit (i.e., decision packages). The rankings therefore display a marginal analysis. If the manager of the Air Quality Program in Georgia developed decision packages for the Air Quality Laboratory, Reviews and Permits, Source Evaluation, Registration, and Research, his ranking might appear as shown in Table 1.

From a practical standpoint, the rankings of the minimum levels for Reviews and Permits, Source Evaluation, Air Quality Laboratory, and Registration may be requirements, so that the absolute ranking of those decision packages (ranked 1–4) are not meaningful. However, the priority of the packages with a lower ranking become significant since management will ultimately make a decision on which packages will be funded. If packages one through eight are funded, management would approve a budget for Air Quality Control of $246,000. Management would have funded all three levels of the Air Quality Laboratory, thus increasing that budget; funded only the minimum level of Registration, thus decreasing that budget; and not funded any Research, thus eliminating that function. Discretionary programs may have the minimum level ranked at the medium or low priority, while increased levels for other programs may be given a high priority. Therefore, the rankings can produce dramatic shifts in resource allocations.

The key to an effective review and ranking process lies in focusing top management's attention on key policy issues and discretionary expenditures. In a small organization such as the City of Garland, Texas, all decision packages were reviewed by the city manager. The city manager took the lower priority packages from each organization that he thought were somewhat discretionary

TABLE 1

Rank	Decision Package	Incremental Cost	Cumulative Program Cost
1	Reviews and Permits (1 of 2)	$116,000	$116,000
2	Source Evaluation (1 of 4)	103,000	219,000
3	Air Quality Laboratory (1 of 3)	140,000	359,000
4	Registration (1 of 3)	273,000	632,000
5	Source Evaluation (2 of 4)	53,000	685,000
6	Air Quality Laboratory (2 of 3)	61,000	746,000
7	Source Evaluation (3 of 4)	45,000	791,000
8	Air Quality Laboratory (3 of 3)	45,000	836,000
9	Reviews and Permits (2 of 2)	50,000	886,000
10	Research (1 of 2)	85,000	971,000

and concentrated his ranking efforts on developing a consolidated ranking across all city organizations for those discretionary decision packages.

In large organizations, top management may be forced to rely primarily on management summaries in lieu of concentrating on the decision packages. In the state of Georgia, decision packages are ranked to the program level in each agency. The Budget Office prepares executive summaries based on the decision packages and program rankings submitted by each agency for the governor's review.

It is also possible to prepare "activity decision packages" (an activity being the lowest element in the program structure). Activity decision packages would then be ranked for each program. "Program decision packages" could then be prepared based on the activity decision packages and the ranking at the program level. The program decision packages could have a format and content similar to the activity decision package, but provide a summary and program analysis for use by top agency management and the executive and legislative review process.

Regardless of organizational size and form of top management review, the decision packages and rankings form the backbone of analysis and decision making. The nature of each review process must be specifically designed to fit the size and personality of each organization.

Preparing the Detailed Operating Budget

The budget or appropriation requests prepared by each organization are usually subject to some form of legislative review and modification. If the legislative appropriation differs markedly from the budget request, many organizations that have used traditional budgeting techniques are forced to recycle their entire budgeting effort to determine where the reductions should be made. Under the zero-base budgeting approach, the decision packages and rankings determine specifically the actions required to achieve any budget reductions. If the legislature defines reductions in specific program areas, we can readily identify the corresponding decision packages and reduce the appropriate program and organizational budgets. If the legislature identifies an arbitrary reduction (e.g., reduce budget five per cent), each agency can use its rankings and eliminate those decision packages that it considers to be the lowest priority.

In the final analysis, each organization will have a number of approved decision packages which define the budget of each program and organizational unit. The decision packages also define the specific activities and performance anticipated from each program and organizational unit. This information can provide the basis for both budget and operational reviews during the year.

PRACTICES AND PROBLEMS

The term "zero-base" has many different connotations. To those who have merely heard the term, it tends to mean "the process of throwing everything out and starting all over again from scratch," or "reinventing the wheel." These connotations are incorrect and imply an effort of impractical magnitude and chaos.

In a more practical vein, "zero-base" means the evaluation of all programs. The evaluation of alternatives and program performance may occasionally lead us to completely rethink and redirect a program, in which case we do "throw everything out and start all over again." However, in the great majority of cases, programs will continue, incorporating modifications and improvement. For the majority of programs, we will concentrate our analysis on evaluating program efficiency and effectiveness and the evaluation and prioritization of different levels of effort.

This pragmatic approach offers us an extremely flexible tool. Managers can "reinvent the wheel"in those situations where preliminary investigation indicates the need and potential benefits of such an approach, and can concentrate their effort on improving programs that appear to be headed in the right direction.

The zero-base approach has led to major reallocation of resources. For example:

> The State of Georgia experienced a $57 million (5 per cent of general funds) revenue shortfall. Governor Jimmy Carter used the zero-base analysis to reduce budgets across 65 agencies, with reductions ranging from 1 per cent to 15 per cent. Program reductions within each agency ranged from no change to elimination.

In a political environment, the expectations for major shifts in resource allocations must be qualified. The major reallocations of resources will normally take place within major agencies such as shifting administrative and maintenance cost savings into direct program delivery. However, it is unrealistic to expect a 20 per cent decrease in the Department of Education to fund a 40 per cent increase in Mental Health. The political realities do not usually allow such shifts. It is also unrealistic to expect an automatic tax reduction due to zero-base budgeting. When costs reductions are achieved, the overriding political tendency is to plow the money back into increased services in other programs.

If we can't realistically expect major funding reallocations among major agencies, and if we can't expect a tax decrease, then why do zero-base budgeting? I believe that there are four overriding reasons that make the zero-base approach worthwhile:

1. Low priority programs can be eliminated or reduced. How the savings are used is a completely separate question.
2. Program effectiveness can be dramatically improved. Such improvements may or may not have a budgetary impact.
3. High impact programs can obtain increased funding by shifting resources within an agency, whereas the increased funding might not have been made available had the agency merely requested an increase in total funding.
4. Tax increases can be retarded. The first three benefits can significantly reduce the necessity for increased taxes by allowing agencies to do a more effective job with existing revenues. For the hard-nosed executive or legislature, budgets can be reduced with a minimum of reduced services.

The zero-base approach is not without its problems. The major problem is the threat that many bureaucrats feel towards a process which evaluates the effectiveness of their programs. The zero-base process also requires a great deal of effective administration, communications, and training of managers who will be involved in the analysis. Managers may also have problems in identifying appropriate decision units, developing adequate data to produce an effective analysis, determining the minimum level of effort, ranking dissimilar programs, and handling large volumes of packages. For many programs, workload and performance measures may be lacking or the cause/effect and program impact may not be well defined so that the analysis will be less than perfect. Therefore, zero-base budgeting should be looked upon as a long-term management development process rather than a one year cure-all.

If done properly, the zero-base approach is not subject to the gamesmanship one might anticipate. The traditional budget approach offers maximum opportunity for gamesmanship because current operations are seldom evaluated and many discreet decisions are never explicitly identified and get "buried in the numbers." However, the zero-base approach removes the umbrella covering current operations and requires managers to clearly identify operating decisions. In zero-base, most obvious forms of gamesmanship would be to avoid identifying reasonable alternatives, to include the pet projects within the minimum level package, and to rank high priority programs low in the ranking in order to obtain additional funding. If the decision packages are "formatted" adequately to display the alternatives considered, workload and performance data, descriptions of actions, and enough cost data so that discretionary items cannot be built into the cost estimate, it becomes very obvious when such gamesmanship is attempted. Also, because the entire ranking must be displayed, it is very easy to challenge a high priority item that received a low ranking or a low priority item which received a high ranking.

The problems in implementing zero-base budgeting are not to be minimized. The specific needs, problems, and capabilities of each organization must be considered in adapting the zero-base approach. Although most of the basic concepts of the zero-base approach have been maintained, the specifics of administration, formats, and procedures have been different for each organization that has adopted the approach. Zero-base can be applied on an intensive basis throughout all levels of an organization, applied only to selected programs, or applied only at major program levels rather than involving all operating managers. The strategy of implementing the zero-base approach must be developed for each organization, depending on its specific needs and capabilities. It should be considered a management and budgetary improvement effort that may require several years to reach full utilization and effectiveness.

CHAPTER VI

The 1980s

In many respects it is still too early to assess what is classic from the work of the 1980s. We are too close to the time to see what will endure. Yet, the 1980s, at least the first half, seem to represent a period of return to political and economic conservatism. New reforms were initiated after a series of tax cuts and expenditure reductions that were aimed at contracting out many government functions and privatizing much of the public sector. State and local governments, which had experienced perhaps the largest growth in employment, expenditures, and program efforts, were increasingly hard-pressed by fiscal crises caused both by federal program curtailments and taxpayers' revolts. The three excerpts selected from the early 1980s are actually the best restatements of themes that have their origins in earlier decades: public-private distinctions, representative bureaucracy, and intergovernmental relations.

It was Wallace S. Sayre (1905–1972) who first asserted that business administration and public administration were "fundamentally alike in all unimportant aspects." Graham Allison, Jr., (1940–)[1] of Harvard University's Kennedy School of Government turns Sayre's assertion into a question and tries to answer it. In "Public and Private Management: Are They Fundamentally Alike in All Unimportant Aspects?", a paper from a public management research conference cosponsored by four federal agencies,[2] he provides one of the most influential reviews of this proposition.

Allison recognizes that the gap between the private and public sector has narrowed and that interactions between public sector managers and private sector managers have increased. In fact, many high-level politically appointed government executives are basically top-level private sector managers. In his analysis, Allison examines the differing contexts and environments of public sector and private sector management. Then he compares the perspectives of top managers from both sectors. How are they different? How does the orientation of one sector affect a manager's effectiveness and style? Finally he assesses the implications of this for further research in public management.

In 1944, J. Donald Kingsley (1908–1972), coauthor of the first full-scale text on public personnel administration,[3] had published his historical analysis, *Representative Bureaucracy: An Interpretation of the British Civil Service.*[4] In 1967 Samuel Krislov (1929–), a constitutional law scholar,[5] expanded upon Kingsley's concept of a governing bureaucracy made up from representative elements of the population being ruled.[6] Krislov in *The Negro in Federal Employment*[7] examined the advantages of "representation in the sense of personification" and thereby gave a name to the goal for the movement for the fullest expression of civil rights in government employment—representative bureaucracy.

In a subsequent work in 1974, also entitled *Representative Bureaucracy*,[8] Krislov explored the issues of merit systems, personnel selection, and social equity. Krislov asked more directly, how could any bureaucracy have legitimacy and public credibility if it didn't represent all sectors of its society? So, thanks in large part to Krislov, the phrase "representative bureaucracy" grew to mean that all social groups have a right to participation in their governing institutions. In recent years the phrase has even developed a normative overlay—that all social groups should occupy bureaucratic positions in direct proportion to their number in the general population.

A decade later, Krislov, writing with David H. Rosenbloom (1943–), the leading authority on the constitutional aspects of public employment,[9] reconsidered the concept from a number of political and legal perspectives in their *Representative Bureaucracy and The American Political System.*[10] In an excerpt reprinted here they accept the importance of the objectives embodied in representative bureaucracy, but note that there are a number of alternatives for achieving that goal, and consider the limitations inherent in the goal itself. Their analysis considers the personnel, administrative organization, and citizen participation issues of representative bureaucracy and provides a context for understanding the goals of affirmative action and equal employment opportunity.

Lastly, there is intergovernmental relations—the fiscal and administrative processes by which higher units of government share revenues and other resources with lower units of government, generally accompanied by special conditions that the lower units must satisfy as prerequisites to receiving the assistance. During the last two decades Deil S. Wright (1930–) of the University of North Carolina at Chapel Hill has been one of the most significant voices in the analysis of intergovernmental trends. His highly influential text, *Understanding Intergovernmental Relations*[11] is especially useful because of its evaluation of the effectiveness of the intergovernmental system. Wright's article, "Intergovernmental Relations in the 1980s: A New Phase of IGR,"[12] is reprinted here because it is representative of Wright's scholarship over the years and a summary of his major themes.

Wright assesses the intergovernmental conditions of the 1960s and 1970s as an era of tension and conflict, characterized by what the former Governor of North Carolina, Terry Sanford, called "picket fence" federalism.[13] This concept implies that bureaucratic specialists at the various levels of government exercise (along with clientele groups) considerable power over the nature of intergovernmental programs; they represent the pickets in the picket fence. These bureaucrats communicate with each other in their daily work, belong to the same professional organizations, and have similar training. They are likely to be in conflict with the cross pieces of the fence: those general purpose government officials (mayors, governors, etc.) who attempt to coordinate the various vertical power structures or pickets. Wright finds that the 1960s and 1970s were characterized by intense competition between policy and program or "friction between the vertical functional allegiances of administrators to their specialized programs and the horizontal coordination intentions of the policy generalists." While it was Terry Sanford who gave "picket fence" federalism its name, Wright's analyses of its operations over the years have made the concept particularly his own.

Wright sees the 1980s as a "calculative" period in intergovernmental relations, a period which really began in 1975. "Calculative," as the reader will see, refers to a new phase of intergovernmental relations that is specifically concerned with strategies designed to cope with severe fiscal constraints, loss of public confidence, and declining federal support.

NOTES

1. Allison is best known for his study of policy-making, *Essence of Decision: Explaining the Cuban Missile Crisis* (Boston: Little, Brown, 1971), which demonstrated the inadequacies of the view that the decisions of a government are made by a "single calculating decisionmaker" who has control over the organizations and officials within his government.
2. The General Accounting Office, the General Services Administration, the Office of Management and Budget, and the Office of Personnel Management.
3. William E. Mosher and J. Donald Kingsley, *Public Personnel Administration* (New York: Harper & Bros., 1936).
4. (Yellow Springs, Ohio: Antioch Press, 1944).
5. For example, see his: *The Supreme Court and Political Freedom* (New York: Free Press, 1968); *The Judicial Process and Constitutional Law* (Boston: Little, Brown 1972).
6. Kingsley's analysis dealt extensively with the British civil service in India.
7. (Minneapolis: University of Minnesota Press, 1967).
8. (Englewood Cliffs, N.J.: Prentice-Hall, 1974).
9. For example, see his: *Federal Service and the Constitution* (Ithaca, N.Y.: Cornell University Press, 1971); *Federal Equal Employment Opportunity* (New York: Praeger Publishers, 1977); *Public Administration and Law: Bench v. Bureau in the United States* (New York: Marcel Dekker, 1983); *Personnel Management in Government: Politics and Process*, 3rd ed., with Jay M. Shafritz and Albert C. Hyde (New York: Marcel Dekker, 1986).
10. (New York: Praeger Publishers, 1981).
11. (Monterey, Calif.: Brooks/Cole Publishing, 1978; 2nd ed., 1982).
12. It is reprinted from: Richard H. Leach, ed., *Intergovernmental Relations in the 1980s* (New York: Marcel Dekker, 1983).
13. See his: *Storm Over the States* (New York: McGraw-Hill, 1967).

A CHRONOLOGY OF PUBLIC ADMINISTRATION: 1980–1985

1980 EEOC issues legally binding guidelines holding that sexual harassment is sex discrimination prohibited by Title VII of the Civil Rights Act and that employers have a responsibility to provide a place of work that is free of sexual harassment or intimidation.

The Supreme Court in *Branti v. Finkel* rules that the dismissal of nonpolicymaking, nonconfidential public employees for their partisan affiliation violates the First and/or the Fourteenth Amendments.

The Supreme Court in *Fullilove v. Klutznick* rules that Congress has the authority to use racial quotas to remedy past discrimination.

Graham T. Allison seeks to answer Wallace S. Sayre's question of whether public and private management are "fundamentally alike in all unimportant respects?"

1981 President Carter's zero-base budgeting requirements are rescinded by President Reagan.

David Stockman, Director of the Office of Management and Budget tells the *Atlantic Monthly* that "none of us really understand what's going on with all these numbers."

Professional Air Traffic Controllers (PATCO) strike and President Reagan fires 11,500 of them for striking in violation of federal law.

Krislov and Rosenbloom in *Representative Bureaucracy and the American Political System* analyze the personnel, administrative organization, and citizen participation aspects of the goal of a representative bureaucracy.

1982 Grace Commission, The President's Private Sector Survey on Cost Control, finds widespread inefficiencies in the federal government.

The Comprehensive Employment and Training Act is superseded by the Job Training Partnership Act.

1983 The birthday of Martin Luther King, Jr., is made a national holiday.

Deil S. Wright in "Intergovernmental Relations in the 1980s: A New Phase of IGR" sees intergovernmental relations entering a "calculative" period where the emphasis will be on strategies designed to cope with severe fiscal constraints.

The Supreme Court questions the constitutionality of the legislative veto in the case of *Immigration and Naturalization Service* v. *Chadha*.

1984 American Society for Public Administration adopts Code of Ethics.

The Supreme Court in *Fire Fighters Local Union No. 1784* v. *Stotts* rules that courts may not interfere with seniority systems to protect newly hired minority employees from layoff.

1985 The Gramm-Rudman-Hollings Act is signed into law; it seeks to balance the federal budget by mandating across-the-board cuts over a period of years.

47
Public and Private Management: Are They Fundamentally Alike in All Unimportant Respects?

Graham T. Allison

My subtitle puts Wallace Sayre's oft quoted "law" as a question. Sayre had spent some years in Ithaca helping plan Cornell's new School of Business and Public Administration. He left for Columbia with this aphorism: public and private management are fundamentally alike in all unimportant respects.

Sayre based his conclusion on years of personal observation of governments, a keen ear for what his colleagues at Cornell (and earlier at OPA) said about business, and a careful review of the literature and data comparing public and private management. Of the latter there was virtually none. Hence, Sayre's provocative "law" was actually an open invitation to research.

Unfortunately, in the 50 years since Sayre's pronouncement, the data base for systematic comparison of public and private management has improved little. Consequently, when Scotty Campbell called six weeks ago to inform me that I would make some remarks at this conference, we agreed that I would, in effect, take up Sayre's invitation to *speculate* about similarities and differences among public and private management in ways that suggest significant opportunities for systematic investigation.

To reiterate: this paper is not a report of a major research project of systematic study. Rather, it is a response to a request for a brief summary of reflections of a dean of a school of government who now spends his time doing a form of public management—managing what Jim March has labeled an "organized anarchy"—rather than thinking, much less writing.[1] Moreover, the speculation here will appear to reflect a characteristic Harvard presumption that Cambridge either is the world, or is an adequate sample of the world. I say "appear" since as a North Carolinean, I am self-conscious about this parochialism. Nevertheless, I have concluded that the purposes of this conference may be better served by providing a deliberately parochial perspective on these issues—and thereby presenting a clear target for others to shoot at. Finally, I must acknowledge that this paper plagiarizes freely from a continuing discussion among my colleagues at Harvard about the development of the field of public management, especially from Joe Bower, Hale Champion, Gordon Chase, Charles Christenson, Richard Darman, John Dunlop, Phil Heymann, Larry Lynn, Mark Moore, Dick Neustadt, Roger Porter, and Don Price. Since my colleagues have not had the benefit of commenting on this presentation, I suspect I have some points wrong, or out of context, or without

Source: Proceedings for the Public Management Research Conference, November 19–20, 1979 (Washington, D.C.: Office of Personnel Management, OPM Document 127-53-1, February 1980), pp. 27–38.

appropriate subtlety or amendment. Thus I assume full liability for the words that follow.

This paper is organized as follows:

- Section 1 frames the issue: What is public management?
- Section 2 focuses on similarities: How are public and private management basically alike?
- Section 3 concentrates on differences: How do public and private management differ?
- Section 4 poses the question more operationally: How are the jobs and responsibilities of two specific managers, one public and one private, alike and different?
- Section 5 attempts to derive from this discussion suggestions about promising research directions and then outlines one research agenda and strategy for developing knowledge of and instruction about public management.

Section 1
Framing the Issue: What is Public Management

What is the meaning of the term "management" as it appears in Office of *Management* and Budget, or Office of Personnel *Management?* Is "management" different from, broader or narrower than "administration"? Should we distinguish between management, leadership, entrepreneurship, administration, policymaking, and implementation?

Who are "public managers"? Mayors, governors, and presidents? City managers, secretaries, and commissioners? Bureau chiefs? Office directors? Legislators? Judges?

Recent studies of OPM and OMB shed some light on these questions. OPM's major study of the "Current Status of Public Management Research" completed in May 1978 by Selma Mushkin of Georgetown's Public Service Laboratory starts with this question. The Mushkin report notes the definition of "public management" employed by the Interagency Study Committee on Policy Management Assistance in its 1975 report to OMB. That study identified the following core elements:

(1)	*Policy Management*	The identification of needs, analysis of options, selection of programs, and allocation of resources on a jurisdiction-wide basis.
(2)	*Resource Management*	The establishment of basic administrative support systems, such as budgeting, financial management, procurement and supply, and personnel management.
(3)	*Program Management*	The implementation of policy or daily operation of agencies carrying out policy along functional lines (education, law enforcement, etc.).[2]

The Mushkin report rejects this definition in favor of an "alternative list of public management elements." These elements are:

- Personnel Management (other than work force planning and collective bargaining and labor management relations)
- Work Force Planning
- Collective Bargaining and Labor Management Relations
- Productivity and Performance Measurement
- Organization/Reorganization
- Financial Management (including the management of intergovernmental relations)
- Evaluation Research, and Program and Management Audit.[3]

Such terminological tangles seriously hamper the development of public management as a field of knowledge. In our efforts to discuss public management curriculum at Harvard, I have been struck by how differently people use these terms, how strongly many individuals feel about some distinction they believe is marked by a difference between one word and another, and consequently, how large a barrier terminology is to convergent discussion. These verbal obstacles virtually prohibit conversation that is both brief and constructive among individuals who have not developed a common language or a mutual understanding of each others' use of terms. (What this point may imply for this conference, I leave to the reader.)

This terminological thicket reflects a more fundamental conceptual confusion. There exists no over-arching framework that orders the domain. In an effort to get a grip on the phenomena—the buzzing, blooming confusion of people in jobs performing tasks that produce results—both practitioners and observers have strained to find distinctions that facilitate their work. The attempts in the early decades of this century to draw a sharp line between "policy" and "administration," like more recent efforts to make a similar divide between "policy-making" and "implementation," reflect a common search for a simplification that allows one to put the value-laden issues of politics to one side (who gets what, when, and how), and focus on the more limited issue of how to perform tasks more efficiently.[4] But can anyone really deny that the "how" substantially affects the "who," the "what," and the "when"? The basic categories now prevalent in discussions of public management—strategy, personnel management, financial management, and control—are mostly derived from a business context in which executives manage hierarchies. The fit of these concepts to the problems that confront public managers is not clear.

Finally, there exists no ready data on what public managers do. Instead, the academic literature, such as it is, mostly consists of speculation tied to bits and pieces of evidence about the tail or the trunk or other manifestation of the proverbial elephant.[5] In contrast to the literally thousands of cases describing problems faced by private managers and their practice in solving these problems, case research from the perspective of a public manager is just beginning.[6] Why the public administration field has generated so little data about public management, my fellow panelist Dwight Waldo will explain. But the paucity of data on the phenomena inhibits systematic empirical research on similarities and differences between public and private management, leaving the field to a mixture of reflection on personal experience and speculation.

For the purpose of this presentation, I will follow Webster and use the term management to mean the organization and direction of resources to achieve a desired result. I will focus on *general managers,* that is, individuals charged with managing a whole organization or multifunctional sub-unit. I will be interested in the general manager's full responsibilities, both *inside* his organization in integrating the diverse contributions of specialized sub-units of the organization to achieve results, and *outside* his organization in relating his organization and its product to external constituencies. I will begin with the simplifying assumption that managers of traditional government organizations are public managers, and managers of traditional private businesses, private managers. Lest the discussion fall victim to the fallacy of misplaced abstraction, I will take the Director of EPA and the Chief Executive Officer of American Motors as, respectively, public and private managers. Thus, our central question can be put concretely: in what ways are the jobs and responsibilities of Doug Costle as Director of

EPA similar to and different from those of Roy Chapin as Chief Executive Officer of American Motors?

Section 2
Similarities: How Are Public and Private Management Alike?

At one level of abstraction, it is possible to identify a set of general management functions. The most famous such list appeared in Gulick and Urwick's classic *Papers in the Science of Administration.*[7] Gulick summarized the work of the chief executive in the acronym POSDCORB. The letters stand for:

- Planning
- Organizing
- Staffing
- Directing
- Coordinating
- Reporting
- Budgeting

With various additions, amendments, and refinements, similar lists of general management functions can be found through the management literature from Barnard to Drucker.[8]

I shall resist here my natural academic instinct to join the intramural debate among proponents of various lists and distinctions. Instead, I simply offer one composite list (see Table 1) that attempts to incorporate the major functions that have been identified for general managers, whether public or private.

These common functions of management are not isolated and discrete, but rather integral components separated here for purposes of analysis. The character and relative significance of the various functions differ from one time to another in the history of any organization, and between one organization and another. But whether in a public or private setting, the challenge for the general manager is to integrate all these elements so as to achieve results.

Section 3
Differences: How Are Public and Private Management Different?

While there is a level of generality at which management is management, whether public or private, functions that bear identical labels take on rather different meaning in public and private settings. As Larry Lynn has pointed out, one powerful piece of evidence in the debate between those who emphasize "similarities" and those who underline "differences" is the nearly unanimous conclusion of individuals who have been general managers in both business and government. Consider the reflections of George Shultz (former director of OMB, Secretary of Labor, Secretary of the Treasury; now president of Bechtel), Donald Rumsfeld (former congressman, director of OEO, director of the Cost of Living Council, White House chief of staff, and Secretary of Defense; now president of GD Searle and Company), Michael Blumenthal (former chairman and chief executive officer of Bendix, Secretary of the Treasury, and now vice chairman of Burrows), Roy Ash (former president of Litton Industries, director of OMB; now president of Addressograph), Lyman Hamilton (former budget officer in BOB, high commissioner of Okinawa, division chief in the World Bank and president of ITT), and George Romney (former president of American Motors, governor of Michigan and Secretary of Housing and Urban Development).[9] All judge public management different from private management—and harder!

Three Orthogonal Lists of Differences. My review of these recollections, as well as the thoughts of academics, has identified three interesting, orthogonal lists that summarize the current state of the field: one by John Dunlop; one major *Public Administration Review* survey of the

TABLE 1 • FUNCTIONS OF GENERAL MANAGEMENT

Strategy

1. **Establishing Objectives and Priorities** for the organization (on the basis of forecasts of the external environment and the organization's capacities).
2. **Devising Operational Plans** to achieve these objectives.

Managing Internal Components

3. **Organizing and Staffing:** In organizing the manager establishes structure (units and positions with assigned authority and responsibilities) and procedures (for coordinating activity and taking action); in staffing he tries to fit the right persons in the key jobs.*
4. **Directing Personnel and the Personnel Management System:** The capacity of the organization is embodied primarily in its members and their skills and knowledge; the personnel management system recruits, selects, socializes, trains, rewards, punishes, and exits the organization's human capital, which constitutes the organization's capacity to act to achieve its goals and to respond to specific directions from management.
5. **Controlling Performance:** Various management information systems–including operating and capital budgets, accounts, reports and statistical systems, performance appraisals, and product evaluation—assist management in making decisions and in measuring progress towards objectives.

Managing External Constituencies

6. **Dealing with "External" Units** of the organization subject to some common authority: Most general managers must deal with general managers of other units within the larger organization—above, laterally, and below—to achieve their unit's objectives.
7. **Dealing with Independent Organizations:** Agencies from other branches or levels of government, interest groups, and private enterprises that can importantly affect the organization's ability to achieve its objectives.
8. **Dealing with the Press and Public** whose action or approval or acquiescence is required.

*Organization and staffing are frequently separated in such lists, but because of the interaction between the two, they are combined here. See Graham Allison and Peter Szanton, *Remaking Foreign Policy* (Basic Books, 1976), p. 14.

literature comparing public and private organizations by Hal Rainey, Robert Backoff and Charles Levine; and one by Richard E. Neustadt prepared for the National Academy of Public Administration's Panel on Presidential Management.

John T. Dunlop's "impressionistic comparison of government management and private business" yields the following contrasts.[10]

1. **Time perspective.** Government managers tend to have relatively short time horizons dictated by political necessities and the political calendar, while private managers appear to take a longer time perspective oriented toward market developments, technological innovation and investment, and organization building.
2. **Duration.** The length of service of politically appointed top government managers is relatively short, averaging no more than 18 months recently for assistant secretaries, while private managers have a longer tenure both in the same position and in the same enterprise. A recognized element of private business management is the responsibility to train a successor or

several possible candidates while the concept is largely alien to public management since fostering a successor is perceived to be dangerous.

3. **Measurement of performance.** There is little if any agreement on the standards and measurement of performance to appraise a government manager, while various tests of performance—financial return, market share, performance measures for executive compensation—are well established in private business and often made explicit for a particular managerial position during a specific period ahead.
4. **Personnel constraints.** In government there are two layers of managerial officials that are at times hostile to one another: the civil service (or now the executive system) and the political appointees. Unionization of government employees exists among relatively high-level personnel in the hierarchy and includes a number of supervisory personnel. Civil service, union contract provisions, and other regulations complicate the recruitment, hiring, transfer, and layoff or discharge of personnel to achieve managerial objectives or preferences. By comparison, private business managements have considerably greater latitude, even under collective bargaining, in the management of subordinates. They have much more authority to direct the employees of their organization. Government personnel policy and administration are more under the control of staff (including civil service staff outside an agency) compared to the private sector in which personnel are much more subject to line responsibility.
5. **Equity and efficiency.** In governmental management great emphasis tends to be placed on providing equity among different constituencies, while in private business management relatively greater stress is placed upon efficiency and competitive performance.
6. **Public processes versus private processes.** Governmental management tends to be exposed to public scrutiny and to be more open, while private business management is more private and its processes more internal and less exposed to public review.
7. **Role of press and media.** Governmental management must contend regularly with the press and media; its decisions are often anticipated by the press. Private decisions are less often reported in the press, and the press has a much smaller impact on the substance and timing of decisions.
8. **Persuasion and direction.** In government, managers often seek to mediate decisions in response to a wide variety of pressures and must often put together a coalition of inside and outside groups to survive. By contrast, private management proceeds much more by direction or the issuance of orders to subordinates by superior managers with little risk of contradiction. Governmental managers tend to regard themselves as responsive to many superiors while private managers look more to one higher authority.
9. **Legislative and judicial impact.** Governmental managers are often subject to close scrutiny by legislative oversight groups or even judicial orders in ways that are quite uncommon in private business management. Such scrutiny often materially constrains executive and administrative freedom to act.
10. **Bottom line.** Governmental managers rarely have a clear bottom line, while that of a private business manager is profit, market performance, and survival.

The Public Administration Review's major review article comparing public and private organizations, Rainey, Backoff and Levine, attempts to summarize the major points of consensus in the literature on similarities and differences among public and private organizations.[11] Table 2 presents that summary.

Third, Richard E. Neustadt, in a fashion close to Dunlop's, notes six major differences between Presidents of the United States and Chief Executive Officers of major corporations.[12]

1. **Time-horizon.** The private chief begins by looking forward a decade, or thereabouts, his likely span barring extraordinary troubles. The first-term President looks forward four years at most, with the fourth (and now even the third) year dominated by campaigning for reelection. (What second-termers look toward we scarcely know, having seen but one such term completed in the past quarter century.)
2. **Authority** over the enterprise. Subject to concurrence from the Board of Directors which appointed and can fire him, the private executive sets organization goals, shifts structures, procedure, and personnel to suit, monitors results, reviews key operational decisions, deals with key outsiders, and brings along his board. Save for the deep but narrow sphere of military movements, a President's authority in these respects is shared with well-placed members of Congress (or their staffs); case by case, they may have more explicit authority than he does (contrast authorizations and appropriations with the "take-care" clause). As for "bringing along the Board," neither the Congressmen with whom he shares power or the primary and general electorates which "hired" him have either a Board's duties or a broad view of the enterprise precisely matching his.
3. **Career-System.** The model corporation is a true career system, something like the Forest Service after initial entry. In normal times the chief himself is chosen from within, or he is chosen from another firm in the same industry. He draws department heads et al. from among those with whom he's worked, or whom he knows in comparable companies. He and his principal associates will be familiar with each other's roles—indeed he probably has had a number of them—and also usually with one another's operating styles, personalities, idiosyncracies. Contrast the President who rarely has had much experience "downtown," probably knows little of most roles there (much of what he knows will turn out wrong), and less of most associates whom he appoints there, willy-nilly, to fill places by inauguration day. Nor are they likely to know one another well, coming as they do from "everywhere" and headed as most are toward oblivion.
4. **Media Relations.** The private executive represents his firm and speaks for it publicly in exceptional circumstances; he and his associates judge the exceptions. Those aside, he neither sees the press nor gives its members access to internal operations, least of all in his own office, save to make a point deliberately for public-relations purposes. The President, by contrast, is routinely on display, continuously dealing with the White House press and with the wider circle of political reporters, commentators, columnists. He needs them in his business, day by day, nothing exceptional about it, and they need him in theirs: the TV Network News programs lead off with him some nights each week. They and the President are as mutually dependent as he and Congressmen (or more so). Comparatively speaking, these relations overshadow most administrative ones much of the time for him.
5. **Performance Measurement.** The private executive expects to be judged, and in turn to judge subordinates, by profitability, however the firm measures it (a major strategic choice). In practice, his Board may use more subjective measures; so may he, but at risk to morale and good order. The relative virtue of profit, of "the bottom line" is its legitimacy, its general acceptance in the business world by all concerned. Never mind its technical utility in given cases, its apparent "objectivity," hence "fairness," has enormous social usefulness; a myth that all can live by. For

TABLE 2 • PUBLIC ADMINISTRATION REVIEW RESEARCH DEVELOPMENTS

SUMMARY OF LITERATURE ON DIFFERENCES BETWEEN PUBLIC AND PRIVATE ORGANIZATIONS: MAIN POINTS OF CONSENSUS

The following table presents a summary of the points of consensus by stating them as propositions regarding the attributes of a public organization, relative to those of a private organization

Topic	Proposition
I. Environmental Factors	
I.1. Degree of market exposure (reliance on appropriations)	I.1.a. Less market exposure results in less incentive to cost reduction, operating efficiency, effective performance.
	I.1.b. Less market exposure results in lower allocational efficiency (reflection of consumer preferences, proportioning supply to demand, etc.)
	I.1.c. Less market exposure means lower availability of market indicators and information (prices, profits, etc.)
I.2. Legal, formal constraints (courts, legislature, hierarchy)	I.2.a. More constraints on procedures, spheres of operations (less autonomy of managers in making such choices)
	I.2.b. Greater tendency to proliferation of formal specifications and controls
	I.2.c. More external sources of formal influence, and greater fragmentation of those sources
I.3. Political influences	I.3.a. Greater diversity of intensity of external informal influences on decisions (bargaining, public opinion, interest group reactions)
	I.3.b. Greater need for support of "constituencies"—client groups, sympathetic formal authorities, etc.
II. Organization-Environment Transactions	
II.1. Coerciveness ("coercive," "monopolistic," unavoidable nature of many government activities)	II.1.a. More likely that participation in consumption and financing of services will be unavoidable or mandatory, (Government has unique sanctions and coercive powers.)
II.2. Breadth of impact	II.2.a. Broader impact, greater symbolic significance of actions of public administrators. (Wider scope of concern, such as "public interest.")
II.3. Public scrutiny	II.3.a. Greater public scrutiny of public officials and their actions.

TABLE 2 • *(continued)*

Topic	Proposition
II.4. Unique public expectations	II.4.a. Greater public expectations that public officials act with more fairness, responsiveness, accountability, and honesty.
III. Internal Structures and Processes	
III.1. Complexity of objectives, evaluation and decision criteria	III.1.a. Greater multiplicity and diversity of objectives and criteria
	III.1.b. Greater vagueness and intangibility of objectives and criteria
	III.1.c. Greater tendency of goals to be conflicting (more "tradeoffs")
III.2. Authority relations and the role of the administrator	III.2.a. Less decision-making autonomy and flexibility on the part of the public administrators
	III.2.b. Weaker, more fragmented authority over subordinates and lower levels. (1. Subordinates can bypass, appeal to alternative authorities. 2. Merit system constraints.)
	III.2.c. Greater reluctance to delegate, more levels of review, and greater use of formal regulations. (Due to difficulties in supervision and delegation, resulting from III.1.b.)
	III.2.d. More political, expository role for top managers.
III.3. Organizational performance	III.3.a. Greater cautiousness, rigidity. Less innovativeness.
	III.3.b. More frequent turnover of top leaders due to elections and political appointments results in greater disruption of implementation of plans.
III.4. Incentives and incentive structures	III.4.a. Greater difficulty in devising incentives for effective and efficient performance
	III.4.b. Lower valuation of pecuniary incentives by employees
III.5. Personal characteristics of employees	III.5.a. Variations in personality traits and needs, such as higher dominance and flexibility, higher need for achievement, on part of government managers.
	III.5.b. Lower work satisfaction and lower organization commitment.

(III.5.a. and III.5.b. represent results of individual empirical studies, rather than points of agreement among authors.)

Source: Public Administration Review (March-April, 1976), pp. 236–237.

a President there is no counterpart (expect ***in extremis*** the "smoking gun" to justify impeachment). The general public seems to judge a President, at least in part, by what its members think is happening to them, in their own lives; Congressmen, officials, interest groups appear to judge by what they guess, at given times, he can do for or to their causes. Members of the press interpret both of these and spread a simplified criterion affecting both, the legislative box-score, a standard of the press's own devising. The White House denigrates them all except when it does well.

6. **Implementation.** The corporate chief, supposedly, does more than choose a strategy and set a course of policy; he also is supposed to oversee what happens after, how in fact intentions turn into results, or if they don't to take corrective action, monitoring through his information system, acting, and if need be, through his personnel system. A President, by contrast, while himself responsible for budgetary proposals, too, in many spheres of policy, appears ill-placed and ill-equipped, to monitor what agencies of states, of cities, corporations, unions, foreign governments are up to or to change personnel in charge. Yet these are very often the executants of "his" programs. Apart from defense and diplomacy the federal government does two things in the main: it issues and applies regulations and it awards grants in aid. Where these are discretionary, choice usually is vested by statute in a Senate-confirmed official well outside the White House. Monitoring is his function, not the President's except at second-hand. And final action is the function of the subjects of the rules and funds; they mostly are not federal personnel at all. In defense, the arsenals and shipyards are gone; weaponry comes from the private sector. In foreign affairs it is the *other* governments whose actions we would influence. From implementors like these a President is far removed most of the time. He intervenes, if at all, on a crash basis, not through organizational incentives.

Underlying these lists' sharpest distinctions between public and private management is a fundamental *constitutional difference.* In business, the functions of general management are centralized in a single individual: the Chief Executive Officer. The goal is authority commensurate with responsibility. In contrast, in the U.S. government, the functions of general management are constitutionally spread among competing institutions: the executive, two houses of Congress, and the courts. The constitutional goal was "not to promote efficiency but to preclude the exercise of arbitrary power," as Justice Brandeis observed. Indeed, as *The Federalist Papers* make starkly clear, the aim was to create incentives to compete: "the great security against a gradual concentration of the several powers in the same branch, consists in giving those who administer each branch the constitutional means and personal motives to resist encroachment of the others. Ambition must be made to counteract ambition."[13] Thus, the general management functions concentrated in the CEO of a private business are, by constitutional design, spread in the public sector among a number of competing institutions and thus shared by a number of individuals whose ambitions are set against one another. For most areas of public policy today, these individuals include at the federal level the chief elected official, the chief appointed executive, the chief career official, and several congressional chieftains. Since most public services are actually delivered by state and local governments, with independent sources of authority, this means a further array of individuals at these levels.

Section 4
An Operational Perspective: How Are the Jobs and Responsibilities of Doug Costle, Director of EPA, and Roy Chapin, CEO of American Motors, Similar and Different?

If organizations could be separated neatly into two homogeneous piles, one public and one private, the task of identifying similarities and differences between managers of these enterprises would be relatively easy. In fact, as Dunlop has pointed out, "the real world of management is composed of distributions, rather than single undifferentiated forms, and there is an increasing variety of hybrids." Thus for each major attribute of organizations, specific entities can be located on a spectrum. On most dimensions, organizations classified as "predominantly public" and those "predominantly private" overlap.[14] Private business organizations vary enormously among themselves in size, in management structure and philosophy, and in the constraints under which they operate. For example, forms of ownership and types of managerial control may be somewhat unrelated. Compare a family-held enterprise, for instance, with a public utility and a decentralized conglomerate, a Bechtel with ATT and Textron. Similarly, there are vast differences in management of governmental organizations. Compare the Government Printing Office or TVA or the police department of a small town with the Department of Energy or the Department of Health and Human Services. These distributions and varieties should encourage penetrating comparisons within both business and governmental organizations, as well as contrasts and comparisons across these broad categories, a point to which we shall return in considering directions for research.

Absent a major research effort, it may nonetheless be worthwhile to examine the jobs and responsibilities of two specific managers, neither polar extremes, but one clearly public, the other private. For this purpose, and primarily because of the availability of cases that describe the problems and opportunities each confronted, consider Doug Costle, Administrator of EPA, and Roy Chapin, CEO of American Motors.[15]

Doug Costle, Administrator of EPA, January 1977. The mission of EPA is prescribed by laws creating the agency and authorizing its major programs. That mission is "to control and abate pollution in the areas of air, water, solid wastes, noise, radiation, and toxic substances. EPA's mandate is to mount an integrated, coordinated attack on environmental pollution in cooperation with state and local governments."[16]

EPA's organizational structure follows from its legislative mandates to control particular pollutants in specific environments: air and water, solid wastes, noise, radiation, pesticides and chemicals. As the new Administrator, Costle inherited the Ford Administration's proposed budget for EPA of $802 million for federal 1978 with a ceiling of 9,698 agency positions.

The setting into which Costle stepped is difficult to summarize briefly. As Costle characterized it:

- "Outside there is a confusion on the part of the public in terms of what this agency is all about: what it is doing, where it is going."
- "The most serious constraint on EPA is the inherent complexity in the state of our knowledge, which is constantly changing."
- "Too often, acting under extreme deadlines mandated by Congress, EPA has announced regulations, only to find out that they knew very little about the problem.

The central problem is the inherent complexity of the job that the agency has been asked to do and the fact that what it is asked to do changes from day to day."

- "There are very difficult internal management issues not amenable to a quick solution: the skills mix problem within the agency; a research program with laboratory facilities scattered all over the country and cemented in place, largely by political alliances on the Hill that would frustrate efforts to pull together a coherent research program."
- "In terms of EPA's original mandate in the bulk pollutants we may be hitting the asymptotic part of the curve in terms of incremental clean-up costs. You have clearly conflicting national goals: energy and environment, for example."

Costle judged his six major tasks at the outset to be:

- assembling a top management team (six assistant administrators and some 25 office heads);
- addressing EPA's legislative agenda (EPA's basic legislative charter—the Clean Air Act and the Clean Water Act—were being rewritten as he took office; the pesticides program was up for reauthorization also in 1977);
- establishing EPA's role in the Carter Administration (aware that the Administration would face hard tradeoffs between the environment and energy, energy regulations and the economy, EPA regulations of toxic substances and the regulations of FDA, CSPS, and OSHA, Costle identified the need to build relations with the other key players and to enhance EPA's standing);
- building ties to constituent groups (both because of their role in legislating the agency's mandate and in successful implementation of EPA's programs);
- making specific policy decisions (for example, whether to grant or deny a permit for the Seabrook Nuclear Generating Plant cooling system. Or how the Toxic Substance Control Act, enacted in October 1976, would be implemented: this act gave EPA new responsibilities for regulating the manufacture, distribution, and use of chemical substances so as to prevent unreasonable risks to health and the environment. Whether EPA would require chemical manufacturers to provide some minimum information on various substances, or require much stricter reporting requirements for the 1,000 chemical substances already known to be hazardous, or require companies to report all chemicals, and on what timetable, had to be decided and the regulations issued);
- rationalizing the internal organization of the agency (EPA's extreme decentralization to the regions and its limited technical expertise).

No easy job.

Roy Chapin and American Motors, January 1977. In January 1967, in an atmosphere of crisis, Roy Chapin was appointed Chairman and Chief Executive Officer of American Motors (and William Luneburg, President and Chief Operating Officer). In the four previous years, AMC unit sales had fallen 37 percent and market share from over six percent to under three percent. Dollar volume in 1967 was off 42 percent from the all-time high of 1963 and earnings showed a net loss of $76 million on sales of $656 million. Columnists began writing obituaries for AMC. *Newsweek* characterized AMC as "a flabby dispirited company, a product solid enough but styled with about as much flair as corrective shoes, and a public image that melted down to one unshakeable label: loser." Said Chapin: "We were driving with one foot on the accelerator and one foot on the brake. We didn't know where the hell we were."

Chapin announced to his stockholders at the outset that "we plan to direct ourselves most specifically to those areas of the market where we can be fully effective. We are not going to attempt to be all things to all people, but to concentrate on those areas of consumer needs we can meet better than anyone else." As he recalled: "There were problems early in 1967 which demanded immediate attention, and which accounted for much of our time for several months. Nevertheless, we began planning beyond them, establishing objectives, programs and timetables through 1972. Whatever happened in the short run, we had to prove ourselves in the marketplace in the long run."

Chapin's immediate problems were five:

- The company was virtually out of cash and an immediate supplemental bank loan of $20 million was essential.
- Car inventories—company owned and dealer owned—had reached unprecedented levels. The solution to this glut took five months and could be accomplished only by a series of plant shutdowns in January 1967.
- Sales of the Rambler American series had stagnated and inventories were accumulating; a dramatic merchandising move was concocted and implemented in February, dropping the price tag on the American to a position midway between the VW and competitive smaller U.S. compacts, by both cutting the price to dealers and trimming dealer discounts from 21 percent to 17 percent.
- Administrative and commercial expenses were judged too high and thus a vigorous cost reduction program was initiated that trimmed $15 million during the first year. Manufacturing and purchasing costs were also trimmed significantly to approach the most effective levels in the industry.
- The company's public image had deteriorated: the press was pessimistic and much of the financial community had written it off. To counteract this, numerous formal and informal meetings were held with bankers, investment firms, government officials, and the press.

As Chapin recalls "with the immediate fires put out, we could put in place the pieces of a corporate growth plan—a definition of a way of life in the auto industry for American Motors. We felt that our reason for being, which would enable us not just to survive but to grow, lay in bringing a different approach to the auto market—in picking our spots and then being innovative and aggressive." The new corporate growth plan included a dramatic change in the approach to the market to establish a "youthful image" for the company (by bringing out new sporty models like the Javelin and by entering the racing field), "changing the product line from one end to the other" by 1972, acquiring Kaiser Jeep (selling the company's non-transportation assets and concentrating on specialized transportation, including Jeep, a company that had lost money in each of the preceding five years, but that Chapin believed could be turned around by substantial cost reductions and economies of scale in manufacturing, purchasing, and administration).

Chapin succeeded: for the year ending September 30, 1971, AMC earned $10.2 million on sales of $1.2 billion.

Recalling the list of general management functions in Table 1, which similarities and differences appear salient and important?

Strategy. Both Chapin and Costle had to establish objectives and priorities and to devise operational plans. In business, "corporate strategy is the pattern of major objectives, purposes, or goals and essential policies and plans for achieving these goals, stated in such a way as to define what business the company is in or is to be in and the kind of company it is or is to be."[17] In reshaping the strategy of AMC and concentrating on particular segments of the transportation market, Chapin had to consult his Board and had to arrange financing. But the control was substantially his.

How much choice did Costle have at EPA as to the "business it is or is to be in" or the kind of agency "it is or is to be"? These major strategic choices emerged from the legislative process which mandated whether he should be in the business of controlling pesticides or toxic substances and if so on what timetable, and occasionally, even what level of particulate per million units he was required to control. The relative role of the President, other members of the administration (including White House staff, Congressional relations, and other agency heads), the EPA Administrator, Congressional committee chairmen, and external groups in establishing the broad strategy of the agency constitutes an interesting question.

Managing Internal Components. For both Costle and Chapin, staffing was key. As Donald Rumsfeld has observed "the single, most important task of the chief executive is to select the right people. I've seen terrible organization charts in both government and business that were made to work well by good people. I've seen beautifully charted organizations that didn't work very well because they had the wrong people."[18]

The leeway of the two executives in organizing and staffing were considerably different, however. Chapin closed down plants, moved key managers, hired and fired, virtually at will. As Michael Blumenthal has written about Treasury, "if you wish to make substantive changes, policy changes, and the Department's employees don't like what you're doing, they have ways of frustrating you or stopping you that do not exist in private industry. The main method they have is Congress. If I say I want to shut down a particular unit or transfer the function of one area to another, there are ways of going to Congress and in fact using friends in the Congress to block the move. They can also use the press to try to stop you. If I at Bendix wished to transfer a division from Ann Arbor to Detroit because I figured out that we could save money that way, as long as I could do it decently and carefully, it's of no lasting interest to the press. The press can't stop me. They may write about it in the local paper, but that's about it."[19]

For Costle, the basic structure of the agency was set by law. The labs, their location, and most of their personnel were fixed. Though he could recruit his key subordinates, again restrictions like the conflict of interest law and the prospect of a Senate confirmation fight led him to drop his first choice for the Assistant Administrator for Research and Development, since he had worked for a major chemical company. While Costle could resort to changes in the process for developing policy or regulations in order to circumvent key office directors whose views he did not share, for example, Eric Stork, the deputy assistant Administrator in charge of Mobile Source Air Program, such maneuvers took considerable time, provoked extensive infighting, and delayed significantly the development of Costle's program.

In the direction of personnel and management of the personnel system, Chapin exercised considerable authority. While the United Auto Workers limited his authority over workers, at the management level he assigned people and reassigned responsibility consistent with his general plan. While others may have felt that his decisions to close down particular plants or to drop a particular product were mistaken, they complied. As George Shultz has observed: "One of the first lessons I learned in moving from government to business is that in business you must be very careful when you tell someone who is working for you to do something because the probability is high that he or she will do it."[20]

Costle faced a civil service system designed to prevent spoils as much as to promote productivity. The Civil Service Commission exercised much of the responsibility for the personnel function in his agency. Civil service rules severely restricted his discretion, took long periods to exhaust, and often required complex maneuvering in a specific case to achieve any results. Equal opportunity rules and their administration provided yet another network of procedural and substantive inhibitions. In retrospect, Costle found the civil service system a much larger constraint on his actions and demand on his time than he had anticipated.

In controlling performance, Chapin was able to use measures like profit and market share, to decompose those objectives to sub-objectives for lower levels of the organization and to measure the performance of managers of particular models, areas, divisions. Cost accounting rules permitted him to compare plants within AMC and to compare AMC's purchases, production, and even administration with the best practice in the industry.

Managing External Constituencies. As Chief Executive Officer, Chapin had to deal only with the Board. For Costle, within the executive branch but beyond his agency lay many factors critical to the achievement of his agency's objectives: the President and the White House, Energy, Interior, the Council on Environmental Quality, OMB. Actions each could take, either independently or after a process of consultation in which they disagreed with him, could frustrate his agency's achievement of its assigned mission. Consequently, he spent considerable time building his agency's reputation and capital for interagency disputes.

Dealing with independent external organizations was a necessary and even larger part of Costle's job. Since his agency's mission, strategy, authorizations, and appropriations emerged from the process of legislation, attention to Congressional committees, and Congressmen, and Congressmen's staff, and people who affect Congressmen and Congressional staffers rose to the top of Costle's agenda. In the first year, top level EPA officials appeared over 140 times before some 60 different committees and subcommittees.

Chapin's ability to achieve AMC's objectives could also be affected by independent external organizations: competitors, government (the Clean Air Act that was passed in 1970), consumer groups (recall Ralph Nader), and even suppliers of oil. More than most private managers, Chapin had to deal with the press in attempting to change the image of AMC. Such occasions were primarily at Chapin's initiative, and around events that Chapin's public affairs office orchestrated, for example, the announcement of a new racing car. Chapin also managed a marketing effort to persuade consumers that their tastes could best be satisfied by AMC products.

Costle's work was suffused by the press: in the daily working of the organization, in the perception by key publics of the agency and thus the agency's influence with relevant parties, and even in the setting of the agenda of issues to which the agency had to respond.

For Chapin, the bottom line was profit, market share, and the long-term competitive position of AMC. For Costle, what are the equivalent performance measures? Blumenthal answers by exaggerating the difference between appearance and reality: "At Bendix, it was the reality of the situation that in the end determined whether we succeeded or not. In the crudest sense, this meant the bottom line. You can dress up profits only for so long—if you're not successful, it's going to be clear. In government there is no bottom line, and that is why you can be successful if you appear to be successful—though, of course, appearance is not the only ingredient of success."[21] Rumsfeld says: "In business, you're pretty much judged by results. I don't think the American people judge government officials this way . . . In government, too often you're measured by how much you seem to care, how hard you seem to try—things that do not necessarily improve the human condition . . . It's a lot easier for a President to get into something and end up with a few days of good public reaction than it is to follow through, to pursue policies to a point where they have a beneficial effect on human lives."[22] As George Shultz says: "In government and politics, recognition and therefore incentives go to those who formulate policy and maneuver legislative compromise. By sharp contrast, the kudos and incentives in business go to the persons who can get something done. It is execution that counts. Who can get the plant built, who can bring home the sales contract, who can carry out the financing, and so on."[23]

This casual comparison of one public and one private manager suggests what could be done—if the issue of comparisons were pursued systematically, horizontally across organizations and at various levels within organizations. While much can be learned by examining the chief executive officers of organizations, still more promising should be comparisons among the much larger numbers of middle managers. If one compared, for example, a regional administrator of EPA and an AMC division chief, or two comptrollers, or equivalent plant managers, some functions would appear more similar, and other differences would stand out. The major barrier to such comparisons is the lack of cases describing problems and practices of middle-level managers.[24] This should be a high priority in further research.

The differences noted in this comparison, for example, in the personnel area, have already changed with the Civil Service Reform Act of 1978 and the creation of the Senior Executive Service. Significant changes have also occurred in the automobile industry: under current circumstances, the CEO of Chrysler may seem much more like the Administrator of EPA. More precise comparison of different levels of management in both organizations, for example, accounting procedures used by Chapin to cut costs significantly as compared to equivalent procedures for judging the costs of EPA mandated pollution control devices, would be instructive.

Section 5
Implications for Research on Public Management

The debate between the assimilators and the differentiators, like the dispute between proponents of convergence and divergence between the U.S. and the Soviet Union reminds me of the old argument about whether the glass is half full or half empty. I conclude that public and private management are at least as different as they are similar, and that the differences are more important than the similarities. From this review of the "state of the art," such as it is, I draw a number of lessons for research on public management. I will try to state them in a way that is both succinct and provocative:

- First, the demand for performance from government and efficiency in government is both real and right. The perception that government's performance lags private business performance is also correct. But the notion that there is any significant body of private management practices and skills that can be transferred directly to public management tasks in a way that produces significant improvements is wrong.

- Second, performance in many public management positions can be improved substantially, perhaps by an order of magnitude. That improvement will come not, however, from massive borrowing of specific private management skills and understandings. Instead, it will come, as it did in the history of private management, from an articulation of the general management function and a self-consciousness about the general public management point of view. The single lesson of private management most instructive to public management is the prospect of substantial improvement through recognition of and consciousness about the public management function.

Alfred Chandler's prize winning study, *The Visible Hand: The Managerial Revolution in American Business,*[25] describes the emergence of professional management in business. Through the 19th century most American businesses were run by individuals who performed management functions but had no self-consciousness about their management responsibilities. With the articulation of the general management perspective and the refinement of general management practices, by the 1920s, American businesses had become competitive in the management function. Individuals capable at management and self-conscious about their management tasks—setting objectives, establishing priorities, and driving the organization to results—entered firms and industries previously run by family entrepreneurs or ordinary employees and brought about dramatic increases in product. Business schools emerged to document better and worse practice, largely through the case method, to suggest improvements, and to refine specific management instruments. Important advances were made in technique. But the great leaps forward in productivity stemmed from the articulation of the general management point of view and the self-consciousness of managers about their function. (Analogously, at a lower level, the articulation of the salesman's role and task, together with the skills and values of salesmanship made it possible for individuals with moderate talents at sales to increase their level of sales tenfold.)

The routes by which people reach general management positions in government do not assure that they will have consciousness or competence in management. As a wise observer of government managers has written, "One of the difficult problems of schools of public affairs is to overcome the old-fashioned belief—still held by many otherwise sophisticated people—that the skills of management are simply the application of 'common sense' by any intelligent and broadly educated person to the management problems which are presented to him. It is demonstrable that many intelligent and broadly educated people who are generally credited with a good deal of 'common sense' make very poor managers. The skills of effective management require a good deal of uncommon sense and uncommon knowledge."[26] I believe that the most significant aspect of the Civil Service Reform Act of 1978 is the creation of the Senior Executive Service; the explicit identification of general managers in government. The challenge now is to assist people who occupy general management positions in actually becoming general managers.

- Third, careful review of private management rules of thumb that can be adapted to public management contexts will pay off. The 80–20 rule—80 percent of the benefits of most production processes come from the first 20 percent of effort—does have wide application, for example, in EPA efforts to reduce bulk pollutants.
- Fourth, Chandler documents the proposition that the categories and criteria for identifying costs, or calculating present value, or measuring the value added to intermediate products are not "natural." They are invented: creations of intelligence harnessed to operational tasks. While there are some particular accounting categories and rules, for example, for costing intermediate products, that may be directly transferable to public sector problems, the larger lesson is that dedicated attention to specific management

functions can, as in the history of business, create for public sector managers accounting categories, and rules, and measures that cannot now be imagined.[27]

- Fifth, it is possible to learn from experience. What skills, attributes, and practices do competent managers exhibit and less successful managers lack? This is an empirical question that can be investigated in a straight-forward manner. As Yogi Berra noted: "You can observe a lot just by watching."
- Sixth, the effort to develop public management as a field of knowledge should start from problems faced by practicing public managers. The preferences of professors for theorizing reflects deep-seated incentives of the academy that can be overcome only by careful institutional design.

In the light of these lessons, I believe one strategy for the development of public management should include:

- *Developing a significant number of cases on public management problems and practices.* Cases should describe typical problems faced by public managers. Cases should attend not only to top-level managers but to middle and lower-level managers. The dearth of cases at this level makes this a high priority for development. Cases should examine both general functions of management and specific organizational tasks, for example, hiring and firing. Public management cases should concentrate on the job of the manager running his unit.
- *Analyzing cases to identify better and worse practice.* Scientists search for "critical experiments." Students of public management should seek to identify "critical experiences" that new public managers could live through vicariously and learn from. Because of the availability of information, academics tend to focus on failures. But teaching people what not to do is not necessarily the best way to help them learn to be *doers.* By analyzing relative successes, it will be possible to extract rules of thumb, crutches, and concepts, for example, Chase's "law": wherever the product of a public organization has not been monitored in a way that ties performance to reward, the introduction of an effective monitoring system will yield a 50 percent improvement in that product in the short run. GAO's handbooks on evaluation techniques and summaries suggest what can be done.
- *Promoting systematic comparative research:* management positions in a single agency over time; similar management positions among several public agencies; public management levels within a single agency; similar management functions, for example, budgeting or management information systems, among agencies; managers across public and private organizations; and even cross-nationally. The data for this comparative research would be produced by the case development effort and would complement the large-scale development of cases on private management that is ongoing.
- *Linking to the training of public managers.* Intellectual development of the field of public management should be tightly linked to the training of public managers, including individuals already in positions of significant responsibility. Successful practice will appear in government, not in the university. University-based documentation of better and worse practice, and refinement of that practice, should start from problems of managers on the line. The intellectual effort required to develop the field of public management and the resources required to support this level of effort are most likely to be assembled if research and training are vitally linked. The new Senior Executive Service presents a major opportunity to do this.

The strategy outlined here is certainly not the only strategy for research in public management. Given the needs for effective public management, I believe that a *major* research effort should be mounted and that it should pursue a number of complementary strategies.

Given where we start, I see no danger of overattention to, or overinvestment in the effort required in the immediate future.

Any resemblance between my preferred strategy and that of at least one school of government is not purely coincidental.

NOTES

1. In contrast to the management of structured hierarchies, for which the metaphor of a traditional football game in which each team attempts to amass the larger number of points is apt, an organized anarchy is better thought of as a soccer game played on a round field, ringed with goals; players enter and leave the field sporadically, and while there vigorously kick various balls of sundry sizes and shapes towards one or another of the goals, judging themselves and being judged by assorted, ambiguous scoring systems. See Michael Cohen and James March, *Leadership and Ambiguity* (McGraw-Hill, 1974).
2. Selma J. Mushkin, Frank H. Sandifer and Sally Familton, *Current Status of Public Management: Research Conducted by or Supported by Federal Agencies* (Public Services Laboratory, Georgetown University, 1978), p. 10.
3. *Ibid.*, p. 11.
4. Though frequently identified as the author who established the complete separation between "policy" and "administration," Woodrow Wilson has in fact been unjustly accused. "It is the object of administrative study to discover, first, what government can properly and successfully do, and, secondly, how it can do these proper things with the utmost possible efficiency. . ." (Wilson, "The Study of Public Administration," published as an essay in 1888 and reprinted in *Political Science Quarterly*, December 1941, p. 481.) For another statement of the same point, see Brooks Adams, *The Theory of Social Revolutions* (Macmillan, 1913), pp. 207–208.
5. See Dwight Waldo, "Organization Theory: Revisiting the Elephant," *PAR*, (November-December 1978). Reviewing the growing volume of books and articles on organization theory, Waldo notes that "growth in the volume of the literature is not to be equated with growth in knowledge."
6. See *Cases in Public Policy and Management*, Spring 1979 of the Intercollegiate Case Clearing House for a bibliography containing descriptions of 577 cases by 366 individuals from 79 institutions. Current casework builds on and expands earlier efforts of the Inter-University Case Program. See, for example, Harold Stein, ed., *Public Administration and Policy Development: A Case Book* (Harcourt, Brace, and Jovanovich, 1952), and Edwin A. Bock and Alan K. Campbell, eds., *Case Studies in American Government* (Prentice-Hall, 1962).
7. Luther Gulick and Al Urwick, eds., *Papers in the Science of Public Administration* (Institute of Public Administration, 1937).
8. See, for example, Chester I. Barnard, *The Functions of the Executive* (Howard University Press, 1938), and Peter F. Drucker, *Management: Tasks, Responsibilities, Practices* (Harper and Row, 1974). Barnard's recognition of human relations added an important dimension neglected in earlier lists.
9. See, for example, "A Businessman in a Political Jungle," *Fortune* (April 1964); "Candid Reflections of a Businessman in Washington," *Fortune* (January 29, 1979); "A Politician Turned Executive," *Fortune* (September 10, 1979); and "The Ambitions Interface," *Harvard Business Review* (November-December, 1979) for the views of Romney, Blumenthal, Rumsfeld, and Shultz, respectively.
10. John T. Dunlop, "Public Management," draft of an unpublished paper and proposal, Summer 1979.
11. Hal G. Rainey, Robert W. Backoff, and Charles N. Levine, "Comparing Public and Private Organizations," *Public Administration Review* (March-April, 1976).
12. Richard E. Neustadt, "American Presidents and Corporate Executives," a paper prepared for a meeting of the National Academy of Public Administration's Panel on Presidential Management, October 7–8, 1979.
13. *The Federalist Papers*, **No. 51.** The work "department" has been translated as "branch," which was its meaning in the original papers.
14. Failure to recognize the fact of distributions has led some observers to leap from one instance of similarity between public and private to general propositions about similarities between public and private institutions or management. See, for example, Michael Murray, "Comparing Public and Private Management: An Exploratory Essay," *Public Administration Review* (July-August, 1975).

15. These examples are taken from Bruce Scott, "American Motors Corporation" (Intercollegiate Case Clearing House #9-364-001); Charles B. Weigle with the collaboration of C. Roland Christensen, "American Motors Corporation II" (Intercollegiate Case Clearing House #6-372-350); Thomas R. Hitchner and Jacob Lew under the supervision of Philip B. Heymann and Stephen B. Hitchner, "Douglas Costle and the EPA (A)" (Kennedy School of Government Case #C94-78-216); and Jacob Lew and Stephen B. Hitchner, "Douglas Costle and the EPA (B)" (Kennedy School of Government Case #C96-78-217). For an earlier exploration of a similar comparison, see Joseph Bower, "Effective Public Management," *Harvard Business Review* (March-April, 1977).
16. U.S. Government Manual, 1978/1979, 507.
17. Kenneth R. Andrews, *The Concept of Corporate Strategy* (Dow Jones-Irwin, 1971), p. 28.
18. "A Politician-Turned-Executive," *Fortune* (September 10, 1979), p. 92.
19. "Candid Reflections of a Businessman in Washington," *Fortune* (January 29, 1979), p. 39.
20. "The Abrasive Interface," *Harvard Business Review* (November-December 1979), p. 95.
21. *Fortune* (January 29, 1979), p. 36.
22. *Fortune* (September 10, 1979), p. 90.
23. *Harvard Business Review* (November-December 1979), p. 95.
24. The cases developed by Boston University's Public Management Program offer a promising start in this direction.
25. Alfred Chandler, *The Visible Hand: the Managerial Revolution in American Business* (Belnap Press of Harvard University Press, 1977).
26. Rufus Miles, "The Search for Identity of Graduate Schools of Public Affairs," *Public Administration Review* (November 1967).
27. Chandler, *op. cit.*, pp. 277–279.

48

Representative Bureaucracy and the American Political System

Samuel Krislov & David H. Rosenbloom

REPRESENTATIVE BUREAUCRACY

Can a public bureaucracy be made into a representational institution despite such organizational features as hierarchy, specialization, and formalization? This question is at once immensely important and perplexing. At stake is the possibility of effectively integrating bureaucratic power into democratic government.

Although some democratic theorists stress the need for limited governmental involvement in the life of the society, the extent of governmental power is more generally treated as a secondary concern. From the perspective of predominant democratic theory, power is neither good nor bad in and of itself. Thus, the amassing of power in government

Source: From pp. 21–26, 189–193 of *Representative Bureaucracy and the American Political System* by Samuel Krislov and David H. Rosenbloom.

does not preclude it from being democratic. The critical question is whether governmental power is legitimate from the point of view of democratic values. Such legitimation is generally conveyed through governmental representation of the public (that is, government of the people) and by public participation in government (government by the people).

Consequently, if public bureaucracies could be constituted so as to provide political representation of the general public, their power could be made to comport substantially with democratic values. If, in addition, meaningful mechanisms by which the public might participate in bureaucratic policymaking were present, then bureaucracies might be successfully combined with democratic political systems. In short, it is not the power of public bureaucracies per se, but their unrepresentative power, that constitutes the greatest threat to democratic government. If this power cannot be constrained by legislatures and political executives, it can nevertheless be made to operate democratically by making it representative of the public.

The notion of a public bureaucracy acting as a representative political institution is controversial. Part of the controversy results from the difficulty inherent in understanding the concept of representation itself. It has been said, for example, that "in spite of many centuries of theoretical effort, we cannot say what representation is" (Eulau 1967, p. 54). According to Hannah Pitkin (1967, pp. 8–9), this is partly because "representation taken generally means the making present in some sense of something which is nevertheless not present literally or in fact. Now, to say that something is simultaneously both present and not present is to utter a paradox, and thus a fundamental dualism is built into the meaning of representation." Much of the discussion of representation since the nineteenth century has centered on the issue of whether representatives should be considered the instructed delegates of those whom they ostensibly represent, or simply conceived of as general trustees of the public's interests who can ultimately be held accountable in some fashion.

Another aspect of the controversy surrounding the concept of representative bureaucracy is whether representation is feasible in the absence of elections. Despite the overwhelming concern of politicians, the media, and political scientists, it is both nearly self-evident and well-documented that elections do not guarantee representation (Miller and Stokes 1963; Campbell 1979). Moreover, it is certainly possible for nonelected leaders to represent their followers, as in traditional patrimonial societies or families.

In principle, therefore, the concept of representative bureaucracy is not self-contradictory. Representation can take place within bureaucratic structures. Three related aspects of representative bureaucracy have been advanced.

Representation by Personnel

The notion that administrative power and democratic government can be integrated through the composition of a civil service has a long tradition. For instance, in the United States, President Thomas Jefferson developed a concept of partisan representation in the nation's fledgling administrative system. He reasoned that the partisan composition of the federal service should broadly reflect the partisan balance found in the electorate at large. In 1829, President Andrew Jackson expanded upon this concept of representation by seeking to make the federal service reflect the social composition of the nation. He sought to ensure that the "road to office" was "accessible alike to the rich and the poor, the farmer and the printer" (Rosenbloom 1977, p. 35). Although much had occurred in the intervening years, in 1970 the Civil Service Commission voiced a related commitment: "We believe that to the extent practicable organizations of the Federal Government should in their employment mix, broadly reflect, racially and otherwise, the varied characteristics of our population" (Rosenbloom 1977, p. 109). Other nations, such as India, have established formal mechanisms to ensure the representation of various social groups in their public bureaucracies.

Contemporary intellectual interest in the concept of representative bureaucracy can be fairly dated from 1944, when J. Donald Kingsley's book by that title appeared. Although by present standards, Kingsley's *Representative Bureaucracy* bearly scratched the surface of the issues involved, he did advance the thesis that, at least in the context of British administration,

> There are obviously points beyond which a man cannot go in carrying out the will of another; and the fact that those limits have seldom been approached in the conduct of the Civil Service since 1870 bears witness to the unity of the middle class State. The convention of impartiality can be maintained only when the members of the directing grades of the Service are thoroughly committed to the larger purposes the State is attempting to serve; when, in other words, their views are identical with those of the dominant class as a whole. (Kingsley 1944, p. 278)

Thus, the propositions have been advanced that public bureaucracies can be transformed into representative political institutions through the partisan, social, and attitudinal composition of their work forces. These propositions raise at least three additional issues. First, can public bureaucracies be socially representative despite their need for expertise and middle-class skills? Will they not inherently overrepresent middle-class elements? To date, the evidence gathered suggests that such overrepresentation is likely, especially in societies with relatively small middle classes (Subramaniam 1967). However, here it should be noted that the political importance of middle-class overrepresentation varies directly with the extent to which politics in a given society revolves around social class divisions.

Second, there is the issue of whether public bureaucrats will retain values and attitudes stemming from their social backgrounds. Certainly, bureaucratic recruitment patterns and socialization processes may go a long way toward destroying any connection between the bureaucrat's background and his or her current attitudes and values. As Frederick Mosher writes:

> The fact is that we know too little about the relationship between a man's background and pre-employment socialization on the one hand, and his orientation and behavior in office on the other. Undoubtedly, there are a good many other intervening variables: the length of time in the organization, or the time-distance from his background; the nature and strength of the socialization process within the organization; the nature of the position . . . ; the length and content of preparatory education; the strength of associations beyond the job and beyond the agency; etc. (Mosher, 1968, p. 13)

Similarly, Kenneth Meier maintains that "the assumption . . . that socio-economic characteristics determine values for upwardly mobile, adult bureaucrats is in need of revision . . ." (Meier 1975, p. 529). How much in need of revision, is an issue addressed in chapter 2.

To the extent that bureaucratic representation through bureaucratic personnel takes place, however, several benefits for democratic government can be achieved. As Harry Kranz has argued, a representative bureaucracy would do the following:

> Lead not only to more democratic decision-making but to better decisions

> because it would expand the number and diversity of the views brought to bear on policy-making (1976, p. 110)
>
> Improve bureaucratic operations and outputs . . . by ensuring that the decisions and services were more responsive to the needs of agency clientele and potential consumers, particularly members of minority groups (1976, p. 110)
>
> Promote a more efficient use of the country's human resources (1976, p. 112)
>
> Increase, both symbolically and actually, the legitimacy of . . . [governmental] institutions . . . (1976, p. 115)
>
> Elevate social equity and justice to prime political values at least as important as the prevailing paradigm of "economy and efficiency" and its fellow traveler "stability" (1976, p. 116).

Thus, there is potentially much to be gained through representative bureaucracy by personnel, but obtaining such representation can be problematic.

Representation by Administrative Organization

Public bureaucracies can also represent various interests found in the political community through their organizational structures and missions. Indeed, this is reflected in the names of governmental departments, agencies and bureaus. Thus, in any modern nation one is likely to find departments or ministries of agriculture, labor, education, health, and commerce. In addition, bureaucratic organizations may represent the interests of various social groups, such as minorities and women. A system of representation along these lines is well developed in the United States. A few of the groups given formal bureaucratic recognition are consumers, farmers (including the specific representation of those producing various crops), aliens, Indians, children, the aged, urban populations, rural populations, women, the handicapped, and refugees.

Inevitably, there will be gaps in bureaucratic representation by organizational structure and mission. Some interests will go unrepresented; some agencies will be poor spokesmen for the groups they are presumed to represent. Nevertheless, it may be possible to reach a level of pluralistic representation in public bureaucracies that cannot be matched elsewhere in government. For instance, with specific reference to the United States federal bureaucracy, Roger Davidson observes that "the conflict between Congress and the executive can best be understood as a test of the representational capacities of these two institutions," and that "in many respects, the civil service represents the American people more comprehensively than does Congress" (Davidson 1966, pp. 378–95). Norton Long is among those who would concur with Davidson: "The bureaucracy is recognized by all interested groups as a major channel of representation to such an extent that Congress rightly feels the competition of a rival" (Long 1965, pp. 17–18). He points out that, "The party system provides no enduring institutional representation for group interests at all comparable to that of the bureaus of the Department of Agriculture. Even the subject matter committees of Congress function in the shadow of agency permanency" (Long 1965, p. 17).

This form of representation is likely to be most pronounced for groups that are organized. In public bureaucracies such as the United States federal service, the group organization process is spurred by bureaucratic fragmentation. Long points out:

> It is clear that the American system of politics does not generate enough power at any focal point of leadership to provide the conditions for an even partially successful divorce of politics from administration. Subordinates cannot depend on the formal chain of command to deliver

> enough political power to permit them to do their jobs. Accordingly they must supplement the resources available through the hierarchy with those they can muster on their own, or accept the consequences in frustration—a course itself not without danger. Administrative rationality demands that objectives be determined and sights set in conformity with a realistic appraisal of power position and potential. (Long 1965, p. 16)

Consequently, bureaucratic agencies often turn to, or even create, organized interest groups to supplement their power in the legislature and elsewhere. In Long's words, "agencies and bureaus more or less perforce are in the business of building, maintaining, and increasing their political support. They lead and in large part are led by the diverse groups whose influence sustains them" (Long 1965, p. 18). Moreover, this form of representation "extends the principle of representation over into administration, since it is predicated on the assumption that law making bodies and conventional procedures cannot and ought not make law" (Lowi 1969, p. 96). In the most pronounced cases of this kind of representation, the government agency may organize the constituency, as in the case of the Department of Agriculture and the American Farm Bureau Federation, and/or the interest group may come so to dominate the agency that for all intents and purposes there is "the conquest of segments of formal state power by private groups and associations" (McConnell 1966, p. 162), as has commonly occurred with federal regulatory commissions.

Representation through Citizen Participation

Closely related to bureaucratic representation of organized interest groups is such representation through citizen participation. One major distinction between the two kinds of representation is that in the former, interest groups may not adequately reflect the perspectives of the segments of society for which they claim to speak or of whom they are considered legitimate representatives. Another is that in the latter form, the citizen may participate as an individual or as an individual representative of the larger community.

As William Morrow points out, in the United States, "generally speaking, citizen participation in administration has assumed three forms: the citizen committee as an advisory group; the citizen committee as a governing group in a specific policy area; and the idea of neighborhood government, where citizens have direct responsibilities in a number of policy areas" (Morrow 1975, p. 191). Examples of each of these forms can be found in national and subnational bureaucracies in various political settings. To the extent that such representation is effective, it forges a link between the public and the government in the form of bureaucratic agencies. As such, citizen participation can contribute much to the integration of democracy and bureaucracy.

* * *

In a world that no longer blindly accepts the power of the authorities, that does not believe in divine right of kings (or ministers, or presidents), appointment to office needs some buttressing when important matters are at stake. Other factors both call for new concepts and methods and make them possible. The fact that most modern governmental posts potentially have broad social leverage makes appointment for personalistic reasons inappropriate. The stability of regimes makes personal loyalty less significant; in only a few modern societies is retaining power a matter of life or death for political leaders. Removal power has always been a cumbersome method of control—ill-suited to control subtle resistance to policy (as opposed to defiance) or to deal with low-grade performance (as opposed to significant misdeeds).

Selection by merit thus enhances office in the modern world, and confers not only the sanction of authority but also a certificate of ability issued by sanctioned authority. The Scarecrow's quest for a brain was solved to everyone's satisfaction in *The Wizard of Oz* by the Wizard's "officially" granting a Ph.D. to him. "Brain" was inferred from presumed achievement. Under the merit system public officials are appointed under a presumption not merely that they have the right to office, but also that they are right for the office. This coupling of merit with authoritative selection restores some of the divine perfection of authority when "the powers that be . . . are ordained of God." Under the rule of merit, they exercise office by virtue of God-given talents. Even an atheist must accept such an ordering.

The sophisticated attack upon the merit standard has many strands. A mordant look at the actual performance of bureaucrats raises questions, and it is the conviction in the United States especially that the quality of such position holders is in decline. More imporant, the intellectual underpinnings of the testing approach have not proved fully convincing under examination for racial or social bias or for relevance to performance. The dissatisfaction with civil service did not begin with the civil rights movement; its essentially negative nature had long been noted. Not only was the merit standard unable to insure top-flight talent, but it often served to prevent recruitment of the best. It is complex and unwieldy, and is too often evaded by the top managers. All of these doubts about quality had already been registered when the racial issue emerged. While little of the claim of race-related bias has been established, neither has it been totally shaken.

With merit as a questioned basis, reliance upon the selection and removal power as a means of control and validation becomes much less impressive. An expanded bureaucracy means low-level selection and little awareness of performance; procedural elaboration makes removal more costly and less likely.

Thus, we are driven to the basic structure and nature of the relationship with the body politic and even with public opinion. The constraints—budget policy directives, performance review, discipline, transfer, and removal—are real, live, but only partially effective. Cumbersome government proliferates autonomic policy. The more transactions a government is engaged in, the more difficult coordination becomes. As Thomas Cronin (1975) points out, U.S. presidents invariably promise that cabinet officers will become more significant figures in their administrations, but eventually tame them well before the end of the first term. Presidents learn the bureaucracy is like the universe, ever expanding away from their center, away from their control. Having no choice, they create and expand coordinating mechanisms that gradually also move beyond presidential control at a slow, but definite pace.

The erosion of patronage exacerbates all of this by making the few thousand "plums" dumping grounds for White House obligations as much as posts for assignment of responsibility and mobilization of talent. White House legacies are often not judged by normal standards of the need for policy implementation. Their ability to help carry Idaho may be more precious than their willingness to implement Social Security reform. With a team of appointees having access to the White House, power squabbles among the managers often take precedence over the "taming of the natives."

The problem is seldom one of outright defiance. It is one of remoteness, different priorities, and a lack of enthusiasm. Particularly strong agencies like J. Edgar Hoover's FBI, or Admiral Hyman Rickover's atomic submarine project, try to learn as little as possible of the president's world, but seldom cross swords with the political units. Continuous monitoring of a dreary and usually (not invariably) unworthy sort is necessary for an executive to gain compliance from a subordinate who is sitting out the term, well aware of the time limits set by the Constitution. Here, as elsewhere, executives must choose their battles.

Court controls also operate, and can hamstring agencies. Courts have the same tenacity and sense of timelessness that often prevail in the bureaucracy. Cases may go on seemingly forever. In bureaucratic terms such proceedings usually are a detriment to effective action, though on occasion they may in fact represent quasivictories, no matter what the outcome. (Regulatory cases costing the challenger dearly may induce general compliance, regardless of a particular outcome based on narrow circumstances.) Courts, however, are poorly equipped for systematic follow-through, and are even less inclined than the executive or legislature to monitor broad policies.

Bureaucrats are hypersensitive to the official, prescribed restraints. They respond quickly, even abjectly and sycophantically, to calls from the other branches, especially their political masters. In the nature of things, those calls are increasingly less systematic, more arbitrary, and idiosyncratic rather than genuinely programmatic.

It is difficult to track bureaucratic behavior. Modern management techniques, such as the advent of the computer, aid a bit. But they are better at evaluating quantities than quality of performance or programmatic integrity. The civil service in the modern world is continuously upgraded into the realms of discretionary management that are most difficult to map and grade. Sampling or other methods of review, common elsewhere, are difficult to implement because legal challenges to subjective evaluation are easily mounted. We have less and less knowledge of how well (or even what) bureaucrats do as they do more and more to affect us.

The vector of all these forces is an uncertain and wavering one. The bureaucracy is buffeted by influences of varying types, of a system in transition. Writers like Theodore Lowi (1969) argue that we have completed a transition to "interest group liberalism" in which the building blocks of political and legal analysis are groups and their claims, rather than individual rights. Yet certainly in the judicial system we maintain the preeminence of individual claims and reluctant acceptance of group participation. Many presidents—including Jimmy Carter—have viewed interest politics with suspicion (though Carter consummated affairs-of-convenience with labor and the National Education Association).

And while specific administrative agencies have close relations of varying kinds with differing clientele groups, these are hardly of the systematic nature of European corporative societies. This active, built-in representation of interests effected in a regulated sector occurs through meaningful formal participation or, more frequently, through systematic consultation of those groups. Decisions are reached as much as possible through consensus, achieved after marathon iterative discussions. In contrast, American agencies build limited constituencies, and agencies are more likely to move in idiosyncratic paths, colliding with other agencies moving in their own limited orbits. Part of the problem is the sheer magnitude of American society, so that determining an appropriate and comprehensive list of spokesmen is a Herculean and politically dangerous task.

Nearest to that state of affairs are the "cozy triangle" arrangements or clientele-controlled agencies discussed in earlier chapters. Additionally, the major regulatory agencies hold open hearings at which a wide (sometimes wild) variety of individuals and groups appear to present their points of view. This is a far cry from active representation in many ways. The volunteer aspect resembles a congressional hearing, and the regulators may value the views expressed or ignore them. Testimony is taken. Nothing like consultation or bargaining takes place. Presentation, not representation, is involved. If the system is moving toward either corporatism or active participation, neither the extent of current participation nor the trend is readily apparent.

The proliferation of organized groups, as is apparent from any perusal of the Washington telephone directory, might appear to contradict this and suggests a trend. But this growth has the opposite effect. The emergence of small numbers of peak organizations dominating a sector promotes corporatism. The continuous emergence of autonomous specialized groups or clusters of formerly unrepresented clienteles makes minimizing, formal, and noncommital contact imperative. Since the AFL-CIO is the only "three-ring circus" in town, the secretary of labor has been (especially, but not only, in Democratic administrations) the White House ambassador or liaison officer to the head of organized labor. But in areas like environmental controls, where businesses of different types have different interests and governmental concerns are equally complex, it is asking for trouble even to deal with the total set of existing groups, since others are likely to emerge in short order. The larger the number of potential groups, the more likely the regulator is to adopt an adjudicative rather than a negotiating style of conflict resolution.

The pattern, then, is largely crazy quilt. Every agency tries to find sustaining forces and relations in its complex environment. Abrupt changes and inconsistencies abound, as does stalling for time until it is known which way the wind blows. While presidents complain about inability to achieve control, bureaucrats seldom feel they are captains of their souls. Excessive obedience to a president may be frowned upon by a subsequent administration. It may be criticized by Congress or some relevant section thereof (including influential subcommittee chairmen or oratorial senators), even in a Congress controlled by the president's party.

As suggested earlier, this formlessness is a product of evolution, of ideas that administration is an unimportant or secondary extension of some other process of government. When this is combined with disagreement over which branch the extension of power is to enhance, problems are inevitable. The expansion took place in fits and starts, and different designers implemented their blueprints for change. European models were used to suggest devices, but significant changes were made. As often as not, political compromises were made without great concern for how tinkering with the structure of an agency would really affect operations or constrain policy choices. Even in those few instances where the lines of battle were precisely over that issue—as on the problem of the relation of banks and bankers to making Federal Reserve policy—concern was limited largely to the question of the number of seats controlled by bankers compared with the "public," although scores of intricate relationships have proved to be sticking points quite as significant as this basic one.

What emerges is that Americans have decided on personal authority as the chief means for bureaucratic control, then have drastically curtailed it. Reflecting a business, control mode of thinking, we still see tidal waves of change coming with a new administration. Politicians have visions of jobs from the "plum" book, a list of major positions available for patronage, now published by the Government Printing Office with each new administration and, in the Washington area at least, a best-seller. In American business thinking, a new executive needs a new team. In fact, as we have noted, White House leadership and new agency leaders struggle over who will assign the plum. All too often the new agency executive gets only the pits.

Europeans have thought in different terms. They have emphasized internalized modes of control, supplemented by transfer of personnel, not waves of "new people." Dismissal or transfer is a black mark against the bureaucrat, and also a reflection on the managerial ability of the political chief.

Internalized controls, as Herbert Kaufman has shown, require considerable initial indoctrination and continued operational voice or comment. In most European systems the higher civil servants have moved in from higher social strata. All too often they have shared a common education and have similar social aspirations. Under this umbrella élan and enthusiasm can be fostered, and agreement—more or less as to what constitutes success or failure in life—is fostered. An adult version of the schoolboy's code dominates and contributes to ambition and drive and avoidance of improper behavior (including overstepping of authority). Those bureaucrats' self-image has some of the attributes of P. G. Wodehouse's Jeeves—a fictional butler who by cool astuteness saves his muddle-headed master from disaster. But Jeeves, and they, know that not only must the master's external power and authority never be compromised, but the master's self-esteem must not be diminished. The European civil servant thus has strong ideas about whom to serve, and the need to preserve certain facts and fictions of power. The American civil servant, faced with multiple claims and little guidance as to authority, follows one of the cardinal rules of bureaucratic life: "When in doubt, mumble."

NOTES

Campbell, Bruce. (1979). *The American Electorate.* New York: Holt, Rinehart & Winston.

Cronin, Thomas. (1975). *The State of the Presidency.* Boston: Little, Brown.

Davidson, Roger. (1966). Congress and the Executive: The Race for Representation. In A. DeGrazia, ed., *Congress: The First Branch,* (pp. 317–413). New York: Anchor.

Eulau, Heinz. (1967). Changing Views of Representation. In Ithiel de Sola Pool, ed., *Contemporary Political Science,* (pp. 53–85). New York: McGraw-Hill.

Kingsley, J. Donald. (1944). *Representative Bureaucracy.* Yellow Springs, Ohio: Antioch University Press.

Kranz, Harry. (1976). *The Participatory Bureaucracy: Women and Minorities in a More Representative Public Service.* Lexington, Mass.: Lexington Books.

Long, Norton. (1965). Power and Administration. In Francis Rourke, ed., *Bureaucratic Power in National Politics,* (pp. 14–23). Boston: Little, Brown.

Lowi, Theodore. (1969). *The End of Liberalism.* New York: W. W. Norton.

McConnell, Grant. (1966). *Private Power and American Democracy.* New York: Alfred A. Knopf.

Meier, Kenneth. (1975). Representative Bureaucracy: An Empirical Analysis. *American Political Science Review*, 69, 526–42.

Miller, Warren, and Donald Stokes. (1963). Constituency Influence in Congress. *American Political Science Review*, 57, 45–56.

Morrow, William. (1975). *Public Administration.* New York: Random House.

Mosher, Frederick. (1968). *Democracy and the Public Service.* New York: Oxford University Press.

Pitkin, Hannah. (1967). *The Concept of Representation.* Berkeley: University of California Press.

Rosenbloom, David H. (1971). *Federal Service and the Constitution.* Ithaca: Cornell University Press.

Rosenbloom, David H. (1977). *Federal Equal Employment Opportunity.* New York: Praeger Publishers.

Subramaniam, V. (1967). Representative Bureaucracy: A Reassessment. *American Political Science Review*, 61, 1,010–19.

49

Intergovernmental Relations in the 1980s: A New Phase of IGR

Deil S. Wright

It is an accepted fact that since 1900 the U.S. political system has experienced significant changes that border on major but evolutionary upheavals. One approach to systematizing and understanding the events and shifts of nearly a century-long period of national-state-local relationships is to think of phases of IGR (intergovernmental relations). This approach has been elaborated elsewhere.[1] The aim here is to identify and explore only the most recent and current phase of IGR—the calculative phase. A short sketch of the five previous phases will provide a basis for exploring the current calculative phase.

The six phases of IGR and their approximate periods of prominence are:

Conflict:	pre-1930s
Cooperative:	1930s to 1950s
Concentrated:	1940s to 1960s
Creative:	1950s to 1960s
Competitive:	1960s to 1970s
Calculative:	1970s to 1980s

A condensed chart of the distinctive features of each phase is provided in Table 1.

For each phase of IGR three substantive components are identified. (See the second through fourth columns of Table 1.) First, what policy issues dominated the public agenda during each phase? Second, what dominant perceptions did the chief participants seem to have? What orientations or mind-sets guided their behavior in each phase? Third, what mechanisms and techniques were used to implement intergovernmental actions and objectives during each period? The fifth column of the table lists a metaphorical characterization of each phase. The metaphors

Source: Richard H. Leach, ed., *Intergovernmental Relations in the 1980s* (New York: Marcel Dekker, Inc., 1983), pp. 15–32.

TABLE 1 • PHASES OF INTERGOVERNMENTAL RELATIONS (IGR)

Phase Descriptor	Main Problems	Participants Perceptions	IGR Mechanisms	Federalism Metaphor	Approximate Climax Period
Conflict	Defining boundaries Proper spheres	Antagonistic Adversary Exclusivity	Statutes Courts Regulations	Layer-cake federalism	19th Century–1930s
Cooperative	Economic distress International threat	Collaboration Complimentary Mutuality Supportive	National planning Formula grants Tax credits	Marble-cake federalism	1930s–1950s
Concentrated	Service needs Physical development	Professionalism Objectivity Neutrality Functionalism	Categorical grants Service standards	Water taps (focused or channeled)	1940s–1960s
Creative	Urban-metropolitan Disadvantaged clients	National goals Great Society Grantsmanship	Program planning Project grants Participation	Flowering (proliferated and fused)	1950s–1960s
Competitive	Coordination Program effectiveness Delivery systems Citizen access	Disagreement Tension Rivalry	Grant consolidation Revenue sharing Reorganization	Picket fence (fragmented)	1960s–1970s
Calculative	Accountability Bankruptcy Constraints Dependency Federal Role Public confidence	Gamesmanship Fungibility Overload	General aid-entitlements Bypassing Loans Crosscutting regulations	Facade (confrontational)	1970s–1980s

Source: Wright, 1982, p. 45.

most commonly used are forms of federalism.

The dates for each period are approximate at best. Indeed, the phases actually overlap. Therefore, the idea of climax period is important—not only because it conveys a time of peak prominence but because it does not preclude the continuation of a phase beyond the dates given. For example, although the conflict phase climaxed before and during the 1930s, conflict patterns did not end then. They regularly recur today as subsidiary events during the current dominant calculative phase.

Thus, like successive, somewhat porous strata that have been superimposed on each other (by the interactions and perspectives of public officials), no phase ends at an exact point—nor does it in fact disappear. Each phase is continuously present in greater or lesser measure, bearing the weight, so to speak, of the overlying strata (subsequent phases) and producing carry-over effects much wider than the climax periods indicated in Table 1. Indeed, the present state of IGR results from multiple overlays of each of the six phases. The task of an IGR analyst is like that of a geologist: to drill or probe the several strata and from the samples make inferences about the substructure of the terrain.

Short sketches of the first five phases serve as backdrops for the more extended analysis of the sixth phase. The conflict, cooperative, concentrated, creative, and competitive phases are reviewed below.

CONFLICT PHASE

Until the 1930s the relationships between the national, state, and local governments were known largely for the conflicts they generated. Courts, legislative bodies, and elected executives seemed to be propelled by concerns over who had the "right" to act (or not act) on a problem, such as regulating child labor, promoting public health, or assuring a minimum standard of welfare. Various governmental bodies made an effort to define clearly the boundaries and "proper" spheres of action of local, state, and national governments. Scholars have correctly noted that submerged below the prominent conflicts were elements of cooperation.[2] Nevertheless, it was common to use a culinary metaphor in describing IGR prior to and into the 1930s—layer-cake federalism.

COOPERATIVE PHASE

The economic distress of the 1930s and the international demands and tensions of the 1940s brought public officials together in a spirit of cooperation. Collaboration between the national government and the states in the welfare field was a noteworthy result of the Depression. All governments and officials, of course, supported the war effort of 1941 to 1945. One perceptive observer[3] noted that:

> cooperative government by federal-state-local authorities has become a byword in the prodigious effort to administer civilian defense, rationing, and other war-time programs. Intergovernmental administration, while it is a part of all levels of government, is turning into something quite distinct from them all.

The degree of cooperation between national, state, and local officials in administrative affairs did not stop at the end of World War II. The continuing intertwining of IGR contacts gave rise to a new metaphor—marble-cake federalism.

CONCENTRATED PHASE

IGR became increasingly concentrated around a rising number of specific federal grant-in-aid programs. Over 20 major functional, highly focused grant programs were established in a 15-year postwar period, including programs for airports, defense education, libraries, sewage treatment, and urban renewal. The number, focus, fiscal size, and specificity of these grant programs produced an incremental but distinct policy shift in national-state and national-local relations.

The contacts now involved or were even dominated by exchanges between specialists and professionals in particular fields, such as airport engineering, library science, and health. Administrators, who were also program professionals, entered the scene as important participants. This rising professionalism was reflected in the entire public service and is the reason this phase is labeled "*concentrated.*" Mosher has referred to the 1950s as the "triumph of the professional state."[4]

In addition, between 1953 and 1955 a temporary presidential commission devoted considerable attention to policy and administrative questions involving IGR. Continuing attention to IGR has been assured since 1959, when the Congress created the permanent Advisory Commission on Intergovernmental Relations (ACIR). The ACIR is a representative body that conducts studies and makes recommendations to improve the functioning of the federal system. It is composed of 26 members: 3 private citizens, 9 national officials (3 each from the executive branch, House, and Senate), and 14 representatives of state and local governments.

CREATIVE PHASE

The cooperative and concentrated phases constituted the pilings if not the full foundation on which the creative phase of IGR was erected. The word for this phase comes from President Johnson's Great Society era, when he called for numerous program and policy initiatives under the banner of "Creative Federalism." The impact of the Johnson initiatives on IGR was stupendous. Over a hundred major new categorical grant programs were enacted (nearly 300 specific legislative authorizations). More significant from an administrative point of view was that the bulk of the new grant authorizations were *project* grants. Historically, most grants had formula provisions that apportioned the grant monies among the states (or occasionally among cities). But project grant funds for programs such as Model Cities and Urban Mass Transit were available for open competition, so to speak. Large numbers of cities could (and did) apply with specific and detailed project proposals, which were required to fit guidelines and regulations. Not only did federal program administrators write the regulations, but they also made most (if not all) of the decisions on which cities' projects were approved and funded. State and local administrators were similarly thrust into the policy-making limelight, in part because of the additional resources available to them and the clientele-building tasks needed to sustain new programs.

The revolution in IGR during the 1960s can be noted in financial terms. Federal aid to state and local governments more than tripled from $7 billion in 1960 to about $24 billion in 1970. A similar increase also characterized state aid to local units—from almost $10 billion in 1960 to almost $29 billion in 1970. Detailed breakdowns on the intergovernmental flows of funds are important but are too numerous for specific comment. Overall, the amounts show the magnitude of the links in 1970 between national, state and local governments. The creative phase of IGR produced a highly interdependent, tightly bonded set of regulations. The IGR links were sometimes referred to as "*fused federalism,*" and it was said that "when national policy makers sneeze, the state and local ones catch pneumonia."

COMPETITIVE PHASE

The apparent tight links of the creative phase of IGR overstated reality. Even before the creative phase peaked (in dollar terms) at the end of the 1960s, there were signs of tension, disagreement, and dissatisfaction among many IGR participants, especially those at the state and local levels. Senator Edmund Muskie perceptively pinpointed the nature of the tension. He had been a governor, and as a senator he chaired the Subcommittee on Intergovernmental Relations. As early as 1966 the senator observed, "The picture, then, is one of too much tension and conflict rather than coordination and cooperation all along the lines of administration—from top federal policymakers and administrators to the state and local professional administrators and elected officials" [1; p. 62]. One example might be the case of a state health department head supporting provisions in national health legislation that differ from the policy position taken by his/her state's governor.

The tension and conflict to which Muskie referred between the "line of administration" and "professional administrators" laid bare a new type of fracture in IGR. This was the split between policy-making generalists, whether elected or appointed, and the professional program specialists. Figure 1 displays what ex-governor Terry Sanford (of North Carolina) called picket-fence federalism.[5] The metaphor illuminates the friction between the vertical functional allegiances of administrators to their specialized programs and the horizontal coordination intentions of the policy generalists—represented by the position-based associations of the "big seven" groups in Figure 1.

The "picket-fence" metaphor is an oversimplification in several respects.[6] Nevertheless, it conveys some sense of the concerns and tensions present in IGR during the 1960s and early 1970s. Selective empirical research has shown the strong presence of specialized, functional attitudes among program administration officials.[7]

The tolerance and support of the officials in the seven public interest groups had worn thin on behalf of categorical grant programs of both formula and project varieties. References were made to the "vertical functional autocracies," "balkanized bureaucracies," and the "management morass" that seemed associated with categorical forms of federal aid. The public interest groups shifted toward new policy stances, including support of general revenue sharing (enacted in 1972), broad-based block grants (several were passed), grant consolidations, and other similar proposals. A concise statement about the autonomous and fragmenting impacts of federal aid in the competitive IGR phase of the late 1960s and the 1970s came from a local official (in 1969) who observed that "our city is a battleground among warring Federal cabinet agencies."[8] He was referring to the fact that various federal departments were funding, operating, and controlling "their" semiautonomous programs within the city.

CALCULATIVE PHASE

Previous discussion has pointed out that the time periods tied to each phase are imprecise and approximate. That point holds for the climax span of the current

FIGURE 1 • PICKET-FENCE FEDERALISM; A SCHEMATIC REPRESENTATION

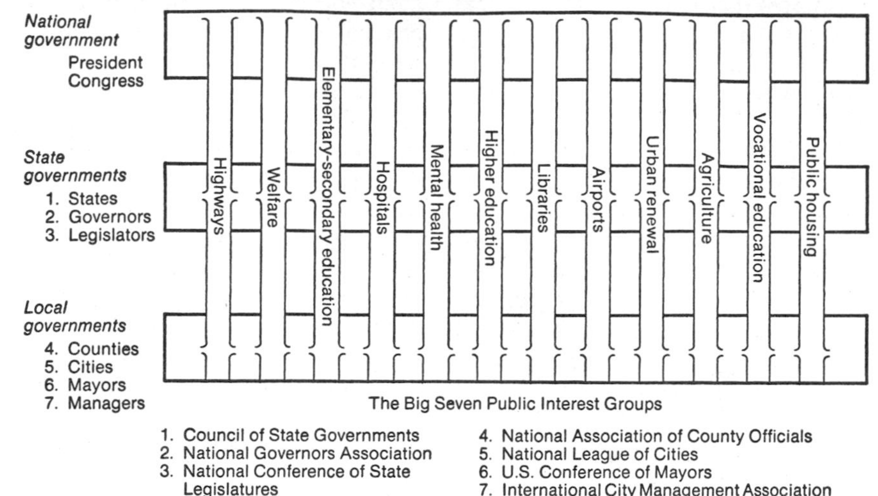

Source: Deil S. Wright © Jan. 17, 1977.

IGR phase—the calculative period. If forced to identify a precise date and event that signaled the rise of this phase, however, I would select 1975 and the event would be the near-bankruptcy of New York City. Telescoped into that episode, and into the continuing fiscal/social/economic plight of that city, were several issues that reflected some of the core problems of our society and our political system. Those problems range from accountability, bankruptcy, and constraints, to dependency, the federal role, and the loss of public confidence (see Table 1).

Main Problems

For years it had been difficult for New York City's citizens to identify and hold accountable those officials who were making major and costly public decisions.[9] For example, bond monies, ostensibly for capital construction, were used for equipment and even operating expenses. It finally took the private banking community, which was not without its share of blame for the malaise, to call a halt and push the city to the brink of bankruptcy. Constraints and severe cutback management were clamped on the city largely by national requirements connected with a temporary federal loan. The city also found itself attempting to cope with other externally mandated and less yielding constraints—the three E's of economy (especially stagflation), energy, and environment.

New York City's route into, and thus far its provisional route through, the crisis is illustrative of another common current problem in IGR—dependency. And dependency is intimately attached to a larger problem: What is the appropriate role of the federal government? (As we shall see shortly, this issue has reasserted itself in a manner and with a force that is reminiscent of the conflict phase.)

What are the boundaries and appropriate spheres within which the national government should (or should not) act? Finally, the problems of citizen confidence or public trust in government(s) can likewise be discerned in the New York City crisis.

New York City is a microcosm, albeit a large one, of an array of problems confronting our political system and its IGR dimensions. Fortunately, most other jurisdictions have not suffered, and hopefully, will not experience, the convergence of such a problem-set. The significance and the dispersion of the six problems mentioned above (see p. 21) across the nation are sufficient, however, to demand attention and precautionary or preventive actions. Perhaps the worst outlook or approach to adopt is to conclude that New York City's plight is completely irrelevant to the difficulties, issues, and operations of other governments—national, state, and local. Other entities and officials should avoid the complacent attitude expressed in the famous (or infamous) phrase: "It can't happen here!"

Participants' Perceptions and Behavior

What happened in IGR during the 1970s? What can be projected to extend well into the 1980s? What are the current prominent perceptions of the main participants in IGR processes? Three chief perceptions are suggested as dominating the calculative phase. (There may well be others.) The three are fungibility, gamesmanship, and overload. All three are tied directly to the characterization of this phase as calculative.

The word *calculative* is used in at least three senses. First, it means to think in advance of taking action, deliberating and weighing one or more avenues of action. A second meaning is to forecast or predict the consequences of anticipated actions; it implies the adoption of a rather sophisticated, quasi-scientific mode of thinking, perhaps best expressed in the form of the hypothetical statement: "If . . ., then . . ." Third, calculative means to count, to figure, or to compute—in a numerical sense. In other words, quantitative forecasting, usually measured in dollar units, is a prominent (but not universal) part of the term's meaning. There are several types of behavior identifiable in contemporary IGR that are calculative in character, and these behavior patterns are expected to prevail in the near future.

One current calculative feature is the increased tendency to estimate the "costs" as well as the benefits of getting a federal grant. Two illustrations will suffice.

In 1976 the coordinator of state-federal relations for New York State reported that New York refused to pursue over $2 million in funds available to New York under the Developmental Disabilities Act. He notes that: "It would have cost us more than the two million we would receive to do the things that were required as a condition for receipt of the funds; my recommendation was not to take it and that was a hard one to make."[10] Similarly at the local level, the city manager of a town with a population of 30,000 indicated (to the author) that unless a federal grant exceeded $40,000 he declined to inquire about or pursue it. Only a grant in excess of that "break-even" amount was sufficient to make it worth seeking. The calculation-based comment was made in 1973; subsequent inflation and increased federal regulations may have doubled that earlier threshold-seeking amount. It is clear from these illustrations that state and local administrators had become more cautious and calculative about their IGR fiscal efforts.

A second type of calculation involves the *formula game.* The formula game is the strategic process of attempting to change, in a favorable direction, one or more formulas by which federal funds are allocated among state and local governments. Increased attention to grant formulas has occurred since 1975 for two reasons. One is the widely heralded conflict between the snow belt and sun belt regions of the country. A second is that despite enactment of a large number of project grant programs, new as well as older formula grant programs account for nearly 80 percent of the $96 billion in estimated federal aid distributed in 1981.

An example of calculational strategy on a formula-grant occurred with the extension of the Community Development Block Grant (CDBG) Program in 1977. The factors used in allocating $3.4 billion in 1978 CDBG funds were changed chiefly by substituting for "housing overcrowding" the "age of housing" (built prior to 1940) in a city. This formula revision heavily favored older industrial cities in the northeast and north central states at the expense of newer, younger, and smaller cities in southern and western states.[11]

The stakes involved in calculative IGR can be huge. In any given year several formula grant programs totaling billions of dollars expire and must be reauthorized. It is easy to understand why experts, statistics, and computers have become commonplace in the present phase of IGR. A close observer of contemporary IGR captured the calculative propensities of this phase when he noted: "Public interest groups come into Washington with computer printouts with the [formula] weighting and what will happen if a certain weighting is approved."[12]

Calculative behavior in three other areas of activity can be described in general terms. One involves coping with constraints and developing skills in cutback management. The International City Management Association, for example, has developed a program seminar with the title: "Managing with Declining Resources." The purpose of the sessions is to perfect operational techniques, quantitative and analytical, wherever possible, for making deliberate decisions on program reductions. Extensive attention has been devoted in the past few years to cutback management and coping with fiscal stress.[13]

A second example of calculation involves profits of $300 to $400 million that will accrue to several states from making federally subsidized loans to students attending colleges and technical schools. These profits, accumulating between 1980 to 1985, will be realized by the 18 states issuing student loan bonds plus the 10 other states that may do so for the first time in 1980.[14]

This situation occurs as a result of high interest rates, recent national tax and education legislation, and the active entry of several states, and even some local governments, into the student loan field. The profits will accrue to state (or local) governments in a manner that is best explained by two paragraphs from a Congressional Budget Office report. The report formally identified and calculated the estimated costs to the national government—and profit for the states.

> Student loan bonds are issued to provide students better access to loans. For a number of years, the federal government has induced commercial lenders to make student loans voluntarily, by offering them interest subsidies (a "special allowance") and insurance against student default. Even with these inducements, however, commercial lenders have been unwilling to lend to all student applicants because of the high cost of servicing student loans. As a result, some students have had trouble finding banks willing to lend to them, and an increasing number of states

responded by issuing student loan bonds and then relending the proceeds to students.

States and localities raise money by issuing bonds at low, tax-exempt interest rates and use the proceeds to buy or make federally guaranteed student loans at significantly higher interest rates, paid in large part by the federal government. Although the interest costs of nearly all student loan bond authorities were under 7 percent in 1979, for example, the yield they received on student loans fluctuated between 11 and 16 percent. The profits accruing to the bond issuers is the difference between the yield on student loans and the level of associated expenses—interest on the bonds and administrative costs. Lenders receive 7 percent interest paid by the federal government until students leave school and by students thereafter. In addition, lenders receive special allowance payments from the federal government. The special allowance rate is recalculated each quarter and averaged 6.5 percent in 1979.[15]

A final illustration of calculative behavior might best be summarized as the *risk* of noncompliance. This feature derives directly from the rising regulatory dimensions of IGR. A recent Office of Management and Budget (OMB) study identified 59 crosscutting or general national policy requirements.[16] These requirements are called *crosscutting* because they apply to the national assistance programs of more than one agency or department. In some cases they apply to *all* assistance programs in *every* department or agency, for example, nondiscrimination because of race, color, national origin, or handicapped status.

The significance and relevance of these requirements to the calculative phase of IGR are straightforward and twofold. One is the cost of compliance with the regulations by the recipients of federal assistance. Estimated costs of compliance with the equal access provisions for handicapped persons[17] in the public transportation field alone are estimated at $3 to $4 *billion*.

Recently a systematic study of local government compliance costs was conducted by Muller and Fix of the Urban Institute.[18] The researchers examined the incremental costs of complying with six major regulations in seven communities. The local units were Alexandria (Va.), Burlington (Vt.), Cincinnati, Dallas, Fairfax Co. (Va.), Newark, and Seattle. Among the regulations were bilingual education and transit accessibility for the handicapped. The study encompassed both capital and operating costs. The locally funded incremental costs varied from $6 per capita in Burlington to $52 per capita in Newark. The average across the seven units was $25 per capita. The authors set these compliance costs within the larger federal aid framework with the following observation: "One statistic can put the figures . . . into sharp perspective: the aid that the seven jurisdictions received under federal revenue sharing averaged about $25 per capita a year—essentially the same as what it cost them, on average, to comply with these regulatory programs."[19]

Another type of "cost" associated with these crosscutting requirements is one of noncompliance or, more accurately, incomplete compliance. It is hard to imagine any recipient of federal assistance that can fully comply with all the applicable policy requirements. The calculations laid on assistance recipients are ones that require tradeoffs or choices between these mandates, *provided* that the recipient is even aware of the applicability of a particular requirement. The OMB study described the forced choices and costs of the policy mandates and also allowed for the possibility that recipients might not know of some requirements because no one in the national government has been charged with knowing what they are.

> Individually, each crosscutting requirement may be sound. But cumulatively the

conditions may be extraordinarily burdensome on federal agencies and recipients. They can distort the allocation of resources, as the conditions are frequently imposed with minimal judgement as to relative costs and benefits in any given transaction. Frequently, the recipients must absorb substantial portions of the costs. While the recipients may feel the full impact of these multiple requirements, there has been no one place in the federal government charged even with the task of knowing what all the crosscutting requirements are.[20]

The 1970s as the starting period for the calculative phase of IGR is supported in part by temporal data on the 59 crosscutting requirements. About two-thirds of the socioeconomic policy requirements are a product of the 1970s. Over half of the administrative/fiscal requirements were placed in effect during the 1970s. Continuation of the calculative phase through the 1980s seems assured based on the likely permanence of this regulatory dimension of national assistance programs.

The remaining aspects of the calculative phase of IGR (see Table 1) deserve mention and brief exposition. The perceptions of participants are summarized with three terms—gamesmanship, fungibility, and overload. The first refers to the way in which participants in IGR processes engage in strategic behavior. They play various "games." Grantsmanship, for example, is one well-established game which, while identified with the creative phase, has been perfected through the competitive phase to the point that it is possible to specify some of the rules by which the grantsmanship game is played.[21]

Fungible means interchangeable or substitutive. In intergovernmental terms fungibility means the ability to shift or exchange resources received for one purpose and accomplish another purpose. Several state governments will receive federal monies to subsidize student education loans. Those funds, once received by the states, are fungible after entering a state government's treasury and may be used for any purpose. General revenue sharing and block grant funds are noteworthy for their fungible or displacement effects. The receipt of such funds may permit the recipient unit to reduce the amount of its own resources devoted to the federally assisted program. The funds that are released from this substitution process can be allocated to other purposes or the process can result in a tax decrease.

An illustration of fungibility in connection with CETA funds in North Carolina is contained in Figure 2, "Fungible Funds from Federal Grants." CETA funds were used in 1975 to hire several hundred temporary employees by the Division of Highways. It was difficult to determine, however, how many of the federally funded positions were new jobs and how many were persons who were simply replacements in jobs that were previously state-funded. The average of state-paid jobs in 1974 was 1821 but dropped to 1532 in 1975. Peak state-paid employment in 1974 was about 2400; in 1975 it was below 2000.

Overload is a third dimension of participants' perspectives. The term gained considerable currency in the late 1970s, and it fits well the tone and temper of the calculative phase. A broader phrase, *political overload,* was used by James Douglas in 1976 to mean that "modern democratic governments [are] overwhelmed by the load of responsibilities they are called upon—or believe they are called upon—to shoulder."[22] Applied to the United States as a term criticizing governmental performance, the phrase has been interpreted to stand for excessive cost, ineffectiveness, and overregulation.[23] These themes, when combined with the prior discussion of

FIGURE 2 • FUNGIBLE FUNDS FROM FEDERAL GRANTS

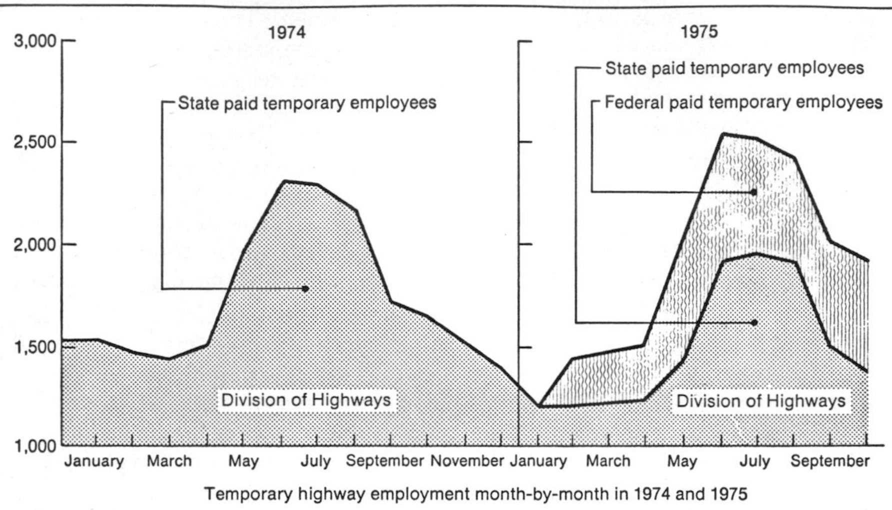

Source: From *The News and Observer*, Raleigh, N.C., Sunday, Dec. 7, 1975.

the crosscutting requirements, should adequately amplify the concept of overload.

A "weighty" example of overload recently surfaced at a New Jersey meeting attended by a staff member of the U.S. Regulatory Council (an interagency group that attempts to coordinate the 90 federal agencies issuing 2000 or more rules annually). Among the attendees was a mayor who had collected and weighed (literally) all the regulations and directives his city had received over the prior 18 months from different national and state agencies. The physical mass exceeded 2000 pounds![24]

IGR Mechanisms and Metaphors

Several mechanisms are used to implement IGR activities in the calculative phase. One, as implied previously, is discretionary aid—general aid and block grants. These funds are dispensed on a formula basis. The legal term used in connection with the disbursements is indicative of a shift in participants' mindset about aid funds. The funds obtained by recipients are called *entitlements*. Jurisdictions are legally entitled to receive funding. This not only specifies the self-interest stake of the recipients; it escalates the possessive and proprietary *rights* of recipients. One consequence of these altered perspectives has been the rise of a new body of case law. One part of the large OMB study for *Managing Federal Assistance in the 1980s* identified nearly 500 court cases dealing with grants, and this was a "quick-and-dirty" effort to inventory the area.[25] A special conference held by the ACIR in late 1979 focused exclusively on the current status of grant law.[26] Explaining the sudden rise in grant-related cases (over three-fourths of the cases have originated since 1975), one conference participant observed that "the financial strains on state and local governments and the resultant paring down of available funds have brought about numerous lawsuits challenging the denial of grants or regulations which limit eligibility for grants."[27] Shortly thereafter, the District of Columbia Bar sponsored a conference on "Federal Grant

Litigation," with the candid subtitle: "Suing the Hand That Feeds You."[28]

Associated with the mechanism of general aid is the technique of bypassing. Bypassing is the process of allocating federal monies directly to local governments without the funds passing through state government coffers. In 1960 only 8 percent of $7.2 billion, or $570 million, bypassed the states. This was an increase from $100 million in 1950. By 1970 about 16 percent of federal aid, or $3.5 *billion*, bypassed state governments. In 1980 about one-third of all federal aid went directly to local governments—approximately $30 billion.

Loans constitute a third implementing mechanism for IGR in the calculative phase. Many examples of loans in the IGR processes could be provided, two of which have been mentioned—to New York City and to students. The latter involved combined state and national financing participation with several states reaping handsome profits. Profit, however, was far from the mind of New York City officials during and after the bleak days of 1975.

The temporary federal loan in 1975 attached conditions which put the U.S. Secretary of the Treasury in the unique position of overseer of the city's financial operations and fiscal obligations. In statements and admonitions to city officials then Secretary William Simon called for reductions in expenditures, program cuts, management improvements, and so forth. But the Secretary also had several Simon-says mandates, for example, phasing out rent control and promptly implementing accounting and financial control systems. New York City's fiscal status remained in a near-crisis state for the remainder of the 1970s. It remained solvent only through the subsequent infusion of federal loans and grants. Yet the anomaly of a national cabinet official sitting in continuous oversight of the governance of New York City, or any other city, is no longer novel. It seems to be accepted as a normal state of affairs.

Regulation is the fourth and final implementing mechanism identified with the calculative phase. References to the *Federal Register,* crosscutting requirements, and grant law convey the prominence and significance of this subject. Perhaps the connecting point should be made with the participants perceptions column. Without the *Federal Register* and the *Catalog of Federal Domestic Assistance,* it is difficult to become involved in IGR gamesmanship and grantsmanship. Furthermore, it is hazardous to engage in fungibility without an intimate knowledge of the assistance-related regulations associated with these and other documents. It is, however, difficult to cope with these mountainous materials without political and administrative overload. Therein lies the crux and the paradox of the calculative phase of IGR.

It is a phase that still contains many of the surface trappings of federalism. Local and state governments have the appearance of making significant policy choices. A few such choices may still remain, but they seem to be few and elusive. The chief choice that most nonnational participants have is deciding whether to participate in federal assistance programs. Once that choice is made, a large array of more limited choices appears open to those who have entered the federal assistance arena. A great deal of bargaining and negotiation takes place within that arena. But these are constrained chiefly, if not exclusively, by nationally specified rules of the game. That is why *facade federalism* is selected as the metaphor characterizing the calculative phase of IGR.

The term "facade" is used in both of its two usual meanings. First, it means the front or forward part of anything (usually a building). In this sense, the leading or frontal parts of governmental units' laws, structures, and officials are involved in the IGR exchanges. In other words, executives, legislative bodies, and courts are active and prominent participants. Associated with such involvement is the tendency toward confrontations, that is, face-to-face exchanges (such as court proceedings) that may or may not be amicably resolved.

Facade also means an artificial or false front. Dual aspects of this meaning are pertinent to the calculative phase of IGR. First, the false front put forth by some participants in intergovernmental exchanges may be contrived or artificial to bluff the other participants. Some IGR "games" played in the calculative phase may be like poker, a goof bluff may win a "pot."

The other possible meaning of facade federalism is the absence or falseness of federalism. In other words, it could be argued that in some contemporary circumstances power has gravitated so heavily toward national officials that federalism, in its historical and legal sense, is nonexistent.

Whatever meaning is attached to facade federalism, it is clear that the 1980s will be a time in which the character and content of national-state-local relationships will continue to be debated and contested, refined and perhaps redefined. The nature and significance of the contests of refinements can be probed and understood, by student and practitioner alike, in minute events such as the making of student loans or in the passage of multibillion dollar aid programs, for example, the renewal of General Revenue Sharing.

CONCLUSION

One approach to understanding the contemporary character of intergovernmental relations is to see the present scene as the accretion of past patterns and relationships which fit a series of phases. These phases are analogous to layers of sedimentary rock in which the most evident is the current or surface layer. This present phase is called calculative, in part because of the emphasis on strategic or game-type behavior. This behavior has been encouraged, if not induced, by a startling array of events, problems, and difficulties that have confronted IGR participants and organizations.

Several elements of the calculative phase seem likely to persist through the 1980s. Indeed, the attitudes, actions, accomplishments, and proposals pursuant to the New Federalism of the Reagan administration seem destined to intensify calculative behavior among IGR participants. President Reagan's New Federalism is the fourth instance or variety of twentieth century policy initiatives designed to produce *new* departures in the arena of federalism and intergovernmental relations.[29] It may not be the last. But its four prominent thrusts of deconcentration, devolution, decrementalism, and deregulation appear likely to accentuate over the short run several of the patterns and perceptions of the calculative phase. To the extent that the current New Federalism is implemented, however, over the longer run it may produce a significant shift in intergovernmental patterns and result in yet another phase of IGR.

NOTES

1. Wright, Deil S. (1982). *Understanding Intergovernmental Relations.* Brooks/Cole, Monterey, California.
2. Elazar, Daniel J. (1962). *The American Partnership: Intergovernmental Cooperation in the Nineteenth Century,* University of Chicago Press, Chicago.
   Grodzins, Morton (1966). *The American System: A New View of Governments in the United*

States, (Daniel J. Elazar ed.)., Rand McNally, Chicago.

3. Bromage, Arthur W. (1943). Federal-state-local relations. *American Political Science Review 37:35.*
4. Mosher, Frederick (1968). *Democracy and the Public Service,* Oxford University Press, New York. See especially Ch. 4, "The Professional State."
5. Sanford, Terry (1967). *Storm Over the States,* McGraw-Hill, New York.
6. Hale, George E., and Marian Lief Palley (1979). Federal grants to the states: who governs? *Administration and Society 11* (May):3–26.

   Wright, Deil S. (1982). *Understanding Intergovernmental Relations,* Monterey, Calif.: Brooks/Cole.
7. Light, Alfred R. (1976). *Intergovernmental Relations and Program Innovation: The Institutionalized Perspectives of State Administrators,* Ph.D. Dissertation, University of North Carolina at Chapel Hill.
8. Sundquist, James, with David W. Davis (1969). *Making Federalism Work: A Study of Program Coordination at the Community Level,* Brookings Institution, Washington, D.C.
9. Sayre, Wallace, and Herbert Kaufman (1965). *Governing New York City,* Russell Sage Foundation, New York.

   Caro, Robert A. (1974). *The Power Broker: Robert Moses and the Fall of New York,* Alfred A. Knopf, New York.

   Auletta, Ken (1979). *The Streets Were Paved with Gold,* Random House, New York.
10. Greenblatt, Robert (1976). A comment on federal-state relations. In *Intergovernmental Administration: 1976- Eleven Academic and Practitioner Perspectives,* James D. Carroll and Richard W. Campbell, (eds.). Maxwell School of Citizenship and Public Affairs, Syracuse University, Syracuse, New York, pp. 143–171.
11. Adams, Jerome R., Thad L. Beyle, and Patricia J. Dusenbury (1979). The new "dual formula" for community development funds. *Popular Government 44:*33–37.
12. Walker, David B. (1979). Is there federalism in our future? *Public Management 61:*11.

    Stanfield, Rochelle L. (1978). Playing computer politics with local aid formulas. *National Journal* (December 9):1977–1981.
13. Levine, Charles H. (1978). Organizational decline and cutback management. *Public Administration Review 38:*315–325.

    Levine, Charles H. (1980). *Managing Fiscal Stress: The Crisis in the Public Sector,* Chatham House Publishers, Inc., Chatham, New Jersey.
14. Congressional Budget Office (1980). *State Profits on Tax-Exempt Student Loan Bonds: Analysis of Options,* CBO Background Paper, Washington, D.C.
15. Ibid., p. ix.
16. Office of Management and Budget (1980). *Managing Federal Assistance in the 1980's.* Government Printing Office, Washington, D.C.
17. Sec. 504, Rehabilitation Act of 1973, P.L.93–112.
18. Muller, Thomas, and Michael Fix (1980). Federal solicitude and local costs: the impact of federal regulation on municipal finances. *Regulation 4:*29–36.
19. Ibid., p. 31.
20. Office of Management and Budget (1980). *Managing Federal Assistance in the 1980's.* (Washington, D.C.: Government Printing Office), p. 20.
21. Wright, Deil S. (1980). Intergovernmental games: an approach to understanding intergovernmental relations. *Southern Review of Public Administration 3:*383–403.
22. Beer, Samuel H. (1977). Political overload and federalism. *Polity 10:*5–7, p. 5.
23. Heclo, Hugh (1977). A question of priorities. *The Humanist 37:*21–24.
24. Petkas, Peter J. (1981). The U.S. regulatory system: partnership or maze? *National Civic Review 70:*297–301.
25. Office of Management and Budget (1979). *Managing Federal Assistance in the 1980's: Working Papers—(A-7),* Survey of Case Law Relating to Federal Grant Programs, Executive Office of the President, Washington, D.C.
26. Advisory Commission on Intergovernmental Relations (ACIR) (1980). *Awakening the Slumbering Giant: Intergovernmental Relations and Federal Grant Law,* Government Printing Office, Washington, D.C.
27. *Public Administration Times* (1980). Aid Program Growth Spurs Rise of Grant Law, *3:*1.
28. Peters, Charles (1980). A way to control spending: FDR and Kennedy, and the games bureaucrats play. *The Washington Post,* April 25:F5.
29. Wright, Deil S. (1983). New federalism: recent varieties of an older species. *American Review of Public Administration* (forthcoming).

About the Authors

Jay M. Shafritz is a professor in the Graduate School of Public Affairs at the University of Colorado in Denver. Previously he has taught at the University of Houston in Clear Lake City, the State University of New York in Albany, and Rensselaer Polytechnic Institute. He is the author, coauthor, and editor of more than two dozen books on public administration and related fields, including *The Facts on File Dictionary of Public Administration* and *The Facts on File Dictionary of Personnel Management and Labor Relations.* Dr. Shafritz received his M.P.A. from the Baruch College of the City University of New York and his Ph.D. in political science from Temple University.

Albert C. Hyde is the Director of the Public Administration Program at San Francisco State University. Previously he has taught at the University of Houston in Clear Lake City, the University of Colorado in Denver, and Indiana University/Purdue University in Indianapolis. He has been a Foreign Service Officer in the U.S. Department of State and a senior associate with the New York State Legislative Commission on Expenditure Review. Dr. Hyde is the author of numerous books and articles, including *Personnel Management in Government: Politics and Process* (with Shafritz and Rosenbloom), Third Edition. Dr. Hyde received both his M.P.A. and Ph.D. degrees from the State University of New York in Albany.

A Note on the Type

Goudy Old Style is one of American Frederick W. Goudy's earlier type designs, and the printing industry has made use of it in both books and advertising since the late teens of this century. Like many of Mr. Goudy's types, his Old Style is a classic typeface and the capitals were modeled on renaissance lettering. The text of this book was adapted from Goudy's original design for the Penta 202 System.

Composed by Carlisle Graphics, Dubuque, Iowa.

Printed and bound by Kingsport Press, Kingsport, Tennessee.